www.wadsworth.com

www.wadsworth.com is the World Wide Web
site for Wadsworth and is your direct source to
dozens of online resources.

At *www.wadsworth.com* you can find out about
supplements, demonstration software, and
student resources. You can also send email
to many of our authors and preview new
publications and exciting new technologies.

www.wadsworth.com
Changing the way the world learns®

To all who teach, so that all might learn

Reading Assessment for Diagnostic-Prescriptive Teaching

Second Edition

ANTHONY V. MANZO
California State University, Fullerton

ULA C. MANZO
California State University, Fullerton

JULIE JACKSON ALBEE
Northwest Missouri State University

THOMSON
WADSWORTH

Australia • Canada • Mexico • Singapore • Spain • United Kingdom • United States

THOMSON

WADSWORTH

Publisher: Vicki Knight
Education Editor: Dan Alpert
Development Editor: Tangelique Williams
Editorial Assistant: Heather Kazakoff
Technology Project Manager: Barry Connolly
Marketing Manager: Dory Schaeffer
Marketing Assistant: Alanna Kelly
Advertising Project Manager: Shemika Britt
Project Manager, Editorial Production: Trudy Brown
Print/Media Buyer: Kris Waller
Permissions Editor: Sommy Ko

Production Service: Hockett Editorial Service
Copy Editor: Marianne Rogoff
Illustrator: Lotus Art
  Page 434: © 2003 Viacom International, Inc. All rights reserved. Nickelodeon, SpongeBob SquarePants, and all related titles, logos, and characters are trademarks of Viacom International, Inc. "SpongeBob SquarePants" created by Stephen Hillenburg.
Cover Designer: Laurie Anderson
Cover Image: © Dave Cutler/SIS
Compositor: TBH Typecast, Inc.
Text and Cover Printer: Transcontinental Printing/Louiseville

Printed in Canada

1   2   3   4   5   6   7   07   06   05   04   03

For more information about our products,
contact us at:
Thomson Learning Academic Resource Center
1-800-423-0563
For permission to use material from this text,
contact us by:
Phone: 1-800-730-2214
Fax: 1-800-730-2215
Web: http://www.thomsonrights.com

Library of Congress Control Number: 2003104791

ISBN 0-534-50829-4

Wadsworth/Thomson Learning
10 Davis Drive
Belmont, CA 94002-3098
USA

Asia
Thomson Learning
5 Shenton Way #01-01
UIC Building
Singapore 068808

Australia/New Zealand
Thomson Learning
102 Dodds Street
Southbank, Victoria 3006
Australia

Canada
Nelson
1120 Birchmount Road
Toronto, Ontario M1K 5G4
Canada

Europe/Middle East/Africa
Thomson Learning
High Holborn House
50/51 Bedford Row
London WC1R 4LR
United Kingdom

Latin America
Thomson Learning
Seneca, 53
Colonia Polanco
11560 Mexico D.F.
Mexico

Spain/Portugal
Paraninfo
Calle/Magallanes, 25
28015 Madrid, Spain

CONTENTS

4

ASSESSMENT OF LANGUAGE ARTS—SPELLING, WRITING, ORAL LANGUAGE—AND STUDY SKILLS   123

5

IN-DEPTH ASSESSMENT OF COLLATERAL FACTORS IN LITERACY DEVELOPMENT   147

6

FRAMEWORKS AND PRINCIPLES
FOR CORRECTIVE AND REMEDIAL INTERVENTION   192

8

PRECISION TEACHING OF COMPREHENSION   291

9

VOCABULARY: PRESCRIPTION FOR CONCEPT, CONTENT, AND COGNITIVE DEVELOPMENT   328

10

IMPROVING CONTENT AREA READING AND STUDY STRATEGIES 362

11

REMEDIES FOR READING-RELATED MOTIVATIONAL, PSYCHOLOGICAL, GENDER, AND MEDICAL ISSUES   408

PREFACE

This text is intended to help teachers identify, characterize, and provide assistance to struggling readers. If you appreciate the meaning in the Chinese proverb, "May you live in interesting times," you will delight in the material ahead. It is the complex and unfolding story of a field that has been much maligned in the popular press as being unable to address illiteracy in the nation, and yet has developed the most sophisticated knowledge base in professional education. For example, the overly optimistic idea of developing programs with total prevention of reading problems, and no provision for remediation, now has been rebalanced against the more realistic fact that there likely will always be some children in need of a little extra assistance, and some who will need a great deal. Today's classroom teachers are increasingly being expected to monitor, correct, and provide evidence of each student's progress in reading and language arts.

As the field continues to advance in understanding of the reading process, it seems to be rediscovering the diagnostic-prescriptive model that was one of the cornerstones of reading as an academic discipline, and to develop related assessment tools and techniques. Today's version of this "legacy" model includes assessment of strategies used by readers to accurately construct, interpret, and apply meaning from print, and attention to a wide range of "reading-related" factors that could be hindering optimal progress. It acknowledges the student's own self-evaluations, and actively invites readers to participate in identifying and correcting reading needs. Step aboard now and discover some remarkably effective ways to assess, teach, and monitor the improvement of reading, writing, thinking, and study habits of students of all levels—primary, intermediate, secondary, and adult. You are part of the first generation to have full access to this collection of knowledge, awareness, and growing wisdom—to which you undoubtedly will add.

OVERVIEW OF THE TEXT

This text outlines a diagnostic-prescriptive model for classroom and individual assessment. The text and Web site provide a wide range of practical instruments and techniques for use by teachers and reading specialists in *diagnosis:* evaluating student's acquisition of effective strategies for reading, writing, and thinking, and identifying specific areas of need. To facilitate *prescription,* the text offers research-supported methods for modeling and guiding students' acquisition of strategies for actively constructing meaning from print. These range from the earliest concepts about print and phonics, to development of fluency and competence in reading and responding to text, and include strategies for vocabulary and thinking development, as well as study strategies for learning from informational text in the content areas.

- *Chapter 1* outlines the basic information and concepts of literacy assessment, centered around a working definition of *reading* as an active meaning-making process.
- *Chapter 2* addresses individual diagnosis from the perspective of a student's story guided by principles of inquiry, and with aids such as practical "intake" inventories and procedures for conducting case studies and preparing formal case reports.
- *Chapter 3*, along with the Informal Reading-Thinking Inventory, provides 80% of the assessment tools and techniques a reading teacher or specialist might ever need, from emergent literacy to adult levels. Chapters 4 and 5 add many of the remaining 20% of the assessment materials that might be needed when evaluating reading-related factors.
- *Chapter 4* adds resources for evaluating reading-related language arts and study strategy evaluation.
- *Chapter 5* takes up more complex issues in determining the possible influences of physiological, neurological, cognitive, and affective factors.
- *Chapter 6* sets out a framework for systematic and direct instruction to meet corrective and remedial needs in classrooms and/or remedial or clinical settings.
- *Chapter 7* is a resource for developing precision instruction for children who have not yet "cracked the code," with teaching approaches and methods for readers at emergent literacy and beginning reading levels.
- *Chapter 8* begins with a more in-depth look at comprehension, followed by principles to guide precision teaching of comprehension including specific methods for providing instruction in fluency, schema activation, metacognitive monitoring and (self-guided) comprehension fix-up, and postreading reflection and schema-building.
- *Chapter 9* focuses on vocabulary acquisition as the basis for concept, content, and even cognitive development, with teaching methods designed not just to teach word meanings, but to raise *word consciousness* and impart self-instructional strategies, or habits of mind, for embracing and learning thought-enriching words.
- *Chapter 10* extends comprehension and vocabulary instruction with additional methods for teaching the three-phase reading process

(pre-, during, post-) with informational text in the content areas, and self-help methods for independent study.

- *Chapter 11* ventures into the least well understood areas of potential difficulty in reading, providing possible prescriptions for emotional, attitudinal, and motivational issues, environmental and cultural differences, and physiological factors.
- *Chapter 12* details some of the dilemmas, misunderstandings, and social-political issues surrounding diagnosis and remediation of students whose primary "needs" may simply be related to the fact that they are English Language Learners (ELL) and/or from a minority American linguistic and cultural tradition. Very specific methods are offered for both assessing and meeting such needs.
- *Chapter 13* is primarily for reading specialists, upper middle and high school teachers, and community college instructors. The material is important to the elementary teacher's broader understanding of the field since it extends diagnosis and remediation to adolescent and adult learners with functional literacy problems, and it provides a basis for unexpected career path changes. Appropriate adaptations to the basic case-based approach and instructional recommendations are outlined, with several additional teaching methods uniquely suited to the needs of these learners.

SPECIAL FEATURES

- The Informal Reading-Thinking Inventory, packaged with the textbook, is the reading teacher and specialist's first and primary tool for gathering basic information and generating hypotheses for further assessment in a case-based diagnostic-prescriptive approach.
- A *Content and Concept Organizer* and a detailed *Outline* at the beginning of each chapter help the reader to focus and read purposefully.
- Marginal *Heuristic/Pivotal Statements* interspersed throughout each chapter help the reader maintain concentration and engagement.
- The *Review* at the end of each chapter summarizes key concepts and directs anticipation toward the next chapter.
- The text Web site provides a variety of resources to instructors and students, including discussion and test questions, downloadable inventories, checklists, and reporting formats for use in conducting a case study, and additional aids to basic and extended comprehension of the contents and concepts in the text.

ACKNOWLEDGMENTS

The progress of a book from a set of ideas and possibilities into refinement, production, and distribution is a complex, collaborative, and supported process involving many people whose names and contributions under current conventions do not, but probably should, appear on the cover.

We had one of the best acquisitions editors in the business, Dan Alpert, a man of remarkable intelligence, considerable integrity, and nearly unparalleled sensitivity to the fragility of writers. He was supported, as were we, for over a two-year period by others at Wadsworth, including but not limited to Heather Kasakoff, Trudy Brown, Tangelique Williams, Neena Chandra, Shemika Britt, and Dory Schaeffer. Rachel Youngman of Hockett Editorial Service managed the day-to-day editing and production of the book.

Professional reviewers offered insightful perspectives and candid analyses of the life and learning type that can never be fully compensated. These, our respected colleagues, include:

- Marta J. Abele, University of Dubuque
- Rebecca S. Anderson, The University of Memphis
- Cynthia Fontaine, Purdue University, North Central
- Diana K. Garver, Ohio Northern University
- Deborah Ann Jensen, Hunter College-CUNY
- Judy C. Lambert, University of Wisconsin, Oshkosh
- Alden J. Moe, Lehigh University
- M. Priscilla Myers, Santa Clara University
- Barbara C. Palmer, Florida State University
- Nina L. Rynberg, Lake Superior State University
- Judith Shabaya, Park University
- Joy L. Stone, Monclair State University

We also thank Margaret Drew and Joyce Piveral of Northwest Missouri State University, who read and made suggestions on many of the chapters. Our children, mates, and friends got less of us than they deserve. They include Ula and Tony's son, Byron; Julie's husband, Mark; and her children, Tim, Christina, and Ben.

We extend a very special debt of appreciation to the generations of scholars, past and present, whose work we were permitted to draw upon with little more than a citation, and to those few who may not have received even this small gratitude as a result of inescapable human error.

CONCEPTUAL FOUNDATIONS OF LITERACY ASSESSMENT

When the mind is ready, the right teacher appears. – NATIVE-AMERICAN PROVERB

CONTENT AND CONCEPT ORGANIZER

This chapter provides an historical, conceptual, and pragmatic overview of the re-emergence of traditional diagnostic–remedial instruction as "diagnostic–prescriptive teaching," a more varied way to assess and precisely prevent and correct reading disorders.

OUTLINE

INTRODUCTION TO READING ASSESSMENT

As the Native-American proverb selected to open this chapter suggests, learning is a personal and developmental process, and instruction is most effective when it begins at the point when the "mind is ready." To find this point in reading instruction, there is a great deal to know about how literacy is acquired, how the natural developmental process may be inhibited or enhanced, and how to gather and interpret information about children's progress.

Experienced teachers build their "clinical wisdom" in literacy assessment by observing one struggling student at a time, closely—compiling information, observations, and speculations over time and through various intervention approaches—to learn about the nature of the child's learning behaviors and attitudes. These observations and speculations are sharpened by research-based knowledge of literacy acquisition and factors that influence (or do not influence) progress. Each such "case" becomes a rough category to guide the teacher's observation and informal assessment of other children. The human mind functions primarily by analogy: When it encounters something new or unexpected, its first response is to ask, "What's that like?" The teacher who has acquired a mental library of case categories is able to respond, "Oh, she's a bit like Jamie. I know just what to try first." Teachers prepared in this way to conduct informed intervention are prepared to teach children, rather than simply to present a curriculum.

The human mind functions primarily by analogy.

It should be noted here that the term "clinical" simply means "involving or depending on direct observation of human behavior." However, the term has acquired connotations, and even an abstract definition of something "analytical, detached, or coolly dispassionate." In our understanding, and what we hope will become yours, the process of clinical reading diagnosis and remediation may be analytical, but it is anything but detached or dispassionate. The teacher's "clinic" is the active, interactive classroom filled with unique individuals, each engaged (as often as possible) in "just the right task." The reading specialist's clinic, wherever its actual location, is the setting for equally inviting, personally tailored tutorials where students find that, as if by magic, the right teacher appears. One reading specialist who held an after-school reading clinic reported her surprising discovery that children who were not registered for the sessions had been "sneaking in" (Hurley & Ryan, 2002).

STATE STANDARDS

Each state believes it necessary to create its own sets of standards and guidelines for most every subject and skill, and how each should be assessed and addressed. This book is sufficiently comprehensive to exceed most any set of state standards for assessment and instruction. To ground the text in current school concerns and modes, however, the book is largely mapped into the Reading/Language Arts Framework for California Public Schools, the most populous state in the country. These standards are organized conveniently around three fundamental concepts of assessment:

- Entry-level assessment: Have students acquired the crucial prerequisite skills and knowledge appropriate to their grade level? Or, how much of the material to be taught do they already know?
- Monitoring of progress: Are students progressing toward achieving goals at a reasonable rate? Do they need better pre-teaching, re-teaching, or alternate teaching? Is an emphasis on some specific instructional components needed in the next series of lessons?
- Summative assessment: Have students actually achieved the goals defined by a given standard or group of standards?

Such standards presumably provide a map to classroom-based places to start, direct, and, as necessary, reroute instruction until its destination has been reached. The California Standards further stress some rudimentary ideas about assessment that are more fully addressed throughout the text. These include the following:

- Different types of assessment tools often must be used for different purposes.
- Assessment often needs to take a different tone and level of intensity at different grade levels.
- Assessment results are not always directly translatable into corrective measures—ability to name letters is correlated highly with successful early reading, but merely focusing on teaching the letter names will not ensure early reading success.

Although most state standards are very sensible, at other times they have been quirky or incomplete. For example, in Idaho there is a requirement for teachers to take a course in "psycholinguisitics," a term with many possible definitions and one associated with a considerable amount of controversial meaning in terms of how teaching should be undertaken. In a related vein, although the California Department of Education is very

Although most state standards are sensible, they also can be quirky.

succinct about how many things must be assessed, school districts are left to decide for themselves how to meet state-mandated standards for assessing each genre of writing and speaking at each grade level. On a state-by-state basis, there also are innumerable factors that might not be specifically targeted nor assessed that could and should be. Ideally, as practicing professionals, you will become instrumental in fostering the most comprehensive list of objectives and forms of assessment in your current state, or in one of the others where you may eventually come to live and work. In any case, you will become equipped with national, traditional, and emerging standards and practices.

OVERVIEW OF READING ACQUISITION: BACKDROP FOR READING ASSESSMENT

> Assessment begins by mentally placing an individual in a backdrop of where she or he "should" be, and then finding his or her individual "zone of proximal development."

"Grade levels" are the North American educational system's way of roughly attempting to provide instruction at the point where the "mind is ready." They are the 100-year-old system for approximating the learner's "zone of proximal development" (Vygotsky, 1978). Thus, assessment of any one individual should begin by mentally placing the individual against the backdrop of where she or he "should" be, according to grade in school. The following "slide show" attempts to evoke the "look and feel" of these grade-level stages in schools today.

Birth–Preschool and Kindergarten: Emergent Literacy

Children learn to talk and to understand spoken language without a curriculum design or formal instruction, although parents and siblings "teach" with each word, gesture, and touch. A small number of children learn to read in much the same unstructured, natural way before entering kindergarten. Most children, however, enter formal schooling with their own unique profiles of knowledge about print. The kindergarten curriculum is designed to formalize, through direct and incidental teaching and reinforcement, these emerging early learnings. These include: knowledge of the alphabet and awareness that letters represent sounds; awareness of sounds within words (phonemic awareness), and the ability to segment, blend, and substitute sounds; concepts about print, such as directionality of print and word boundaries; awareness that print carries the meaning in books; a few "known" words (sight words), usually beginning with the child's own name; and sometimes the ability to "pretend read" a favorite book or two.

The kindergarten teacher evaluates each child's entering profile of strengths and needs in these concepts and abilities to provide direct and incidental instruction that begins where young learners "are." Because children enter kindergarten with such differing backgrounds of experience with written language, the core of kindergarten teaching is a rich classroom library and frequent read-alouds, often from "big books" so that those who can may read along, and those who cannot can begin to recognize letters and words. Stories and poems of all varieties are first read aloud and then reviewed to build concepts about print and story, and to practice letter naming and sound identification and associations. Children's own dictated stories written in large print on chart paper are used in the same way (the Language Experience Approach). Children are encouraged to use their developing reading strategies and sight words outside the classroom. Possible activities include incorporating "environmental print" (such as cereal box labels and familiar store name signs) and activities that simulate real-life uses of reading and writing (such as mailbox centers for exchanging messages, and restaurant centers for writing and reading recipes and menus). Children are encouraged to "pretend read" a favorite book or two: when children engage in this pretend reading of easy, predictable books they have memorized, they independently gather the repeated exposures to words that are needed to acquire them as sight words. In daily "free writing," children make written meaning at their own developmental pace, beginning with pictures, then moving on to scribble writing, then to a mix of pictures and random letters, and eventually to early phonetic "invented" spelling, such as *n i t* for *night*. In the latter stage, the children's struggle to produce the letters that might represent the word they have in mind serves as a powerful reinforcement to the letter–sound associations and sight word vocabulary they are building through reading instruction.

Grades 1–2: Beginning Reading

In first and second grade, children build phonetic word attack strategies, expand their sight word vocabularies, and develop the ability to make personal connections with the characters and events in stories. First- and second-grade teachers continue to read aloud often, modeling oral reading fluency, comprehension strategies, and response to story content. However, increasing emphasis is placed on children reading on their own, from shared Language Experience stories and vocabulary-controlled materials constructed primarily from words that are likely to be in beginning readers' sight word vocabularies. Extensive reading of these "decodable texts" provides the repeated exposures to these words in print that are necessary for instant, automatic recognition (referred to as "automaticity"). Through direct instruction in the use of phonetic elements of words in reading and spelling, and the conventions of print (such as sentence and paragraph construction, punctuation, and usage), children build confidence in themselves as readers and writers and a growing awareness of print as an essential life tool. Children's increasing knowledge of social studies, science, and social interactions is accompanied by direct instruction in the concept vocabulary of these domains. Direct teaching of just a very few concept-content words—such as "community" and "vacuum"—can greatly raise children's awareness of environmental and media occurrence of these words and related concepts.

Grades 3–8: Intermediate Reading

By the beginning of third grade, most children have acquired a basic sight word vocabulary, effective word attack strategies, and read grade-level material fluently. These newly acquired abilities are reinforced in activities such as "Paired Reading," in which the class is formed into student pairs, with each pair taking turns reading aloud from a given reading selection and working together to complete a follow-up assignment. In these intermediate grades, direct word study continues, with attention now focused on identifying and learning new *meaning* vocabulary words (as distinct from sight word vocabulary words) and recognizing and using the structural features of words—such as meaningful prefixes, suffixes, and roots—as aids to predicting meaning. Children are able to apply surveying strategies, use background knowledge and experience to make predictions, and set reading purposes as they begin to read fiction or nonfiction. They are able to monitor their comprehension as they read, and use "fix-up strategies"— such as rereading, restating, or reading ahead a little bit—if comprehension begins to falter. They are able to organize information and ideas from reading into various graphic organizer forms as an aid to basic comprehension and recall. They are increasingly able to select independent reading materials, and respond accurately and thoughtfully to the content of stories and informational text. They can organize ideas and use conventions of print to write for varying purposes and audiences, and make the transition to conventional spelling.

Teachers in the early intermediate grades have an important opportunity to identify and assist children who are not making grade-level progress in reading, before they move on to middle school where time with each teacher is more limited. Classroom observation techniques are used to monitor children's development, and teachers work with the literacy specialist to obtain in-depth assessment and remediation as needed.

As children move on to middle school, the use of active reading strategies is supported in content area classrooms such as social studies, science, and mathematics. Content area teachers continue to model strategies for study reading and vocabulary concept development in the increasingly difficult subject area textbooks. They guide students in more sophisticated forms of researching and report writing, and continue to encourage independent reading. Increasingly, children develop their own personal reading interests, which are broadened and enriched by teacher recommendations for reading in both fictional genres and in subject areas that students might not have self-selected.

Grades 9–12: Pre-Adult Reading

Reading is essential to success in high school and all future learning. In most states, high school teachers of any subject are required to complete at least one course in "content area reading" to equip them with methods and techniques for supporting students' continued development in independent content knowledge acquisition, studying, reading, vocabulary concept development, and writing. Content area teachers also help to identify students who are struggling with reading and may need more assistance— sometimes more than can be provided in the regular classroom. Students who reach high school and still have reading difficulties typically have complex related difficulties resulting from years of unsuccessful experiences with reading. They have spent far less time reading than their peers and lack background information and familiarity with the academic language used in textbooks at their grade level. They avoid reading and become adept at "hiding" their reading problems. A high school teacher's referral to a reading specialist may be these students' last opportunity to receive needed assistance.

THE ART AND SCIENCE OF READING ASSESSMENT AND INSTRUCTION

An extraordinary amount of public attention has been paid over the years to controversies about how reading is or isn't being taught or ought to be taught. In truth, some of the basic concepts defining the testing and teaching of reading have changed relatively little since the evolution of basal readers in the 1930s. The term "basal," derived from "base," was a way of referring to where the learner "is" in reading—the grade level at which the learner should be taught. Published basal reader programs provided the opportunity for teachers to use books at varying levels within the same classroom to better match instruction to each child's developmental level. In one of the earliest reading education textbooks, Emmett Betts (1936) outlined a simple technique for using the graded basal reading books to evaluate children's reading levels. This technique, which he called an "Informal Reading Inventory," was conducted as follows:

- Select one short passage that a child has not yet read from the grade-level basal reader.
- Select one short passage each from the basal reader a few grades below and a few grades above the child's grade level.
- Write several comprehension questions on each passage (or select from those in the teacher's manuals).
- Have the child read the grade-level passage aloud and then answer the questions.
- If the child does well in oral reading accuracy and postreading comprehension (guidelines for determining this are given below), continue to give higher-grade passages until the material is clearly too difficult (these guidelines also given below).
- If the child does poorly on the first passage, give the next lower grade passage, and continue to give a lower passage until the child can easily read and answer the questions.

Betts used the term **Instructional** level to refer to where the child "is"— the grade-level passage where oral reading is 95 percent or better and comprehension is 75 percent or better. The child's **Independent** level is the grade level passage where oral reading is 99 percent or better and comprehension is 90 percent or better. **Frustration** level is the grade-level passage where oral reading falls below 90 percent *or* comprehension is below 50 percent (see Figure 1.1).

This formula has been applied in many commercial Informal Reading Inventories (IRIs), with a variety of fine-tuning options, such as those you will find in the IR(T)I—the T is for Thinking—provided with this textbook. The basic format, which grew out of experience and good intuition, still stands as the single best way to estimate where a learner "is," and what specific strengths and needs to address.

In the same education textbook, Betts outlined an approach to teaching which he called the "Directed Reading Activity." The approach called for the teacher to:

- Lead a prereading discussion about children's existing knowledge and background of experiences related to the story to be read, and introduce any new vocabulary words that might hinder comprehension.

FIGURE **1.1**

LEVELS OF READING

	Word Recognition (% of words read correctly during oral reading of a graded reading passage)		**Comprehension** (% of questions answered correctly after reading a graded reading passage)
Independent Level	99%	and	90%
Instructional Level	95%	and	75%
Frustration Level	90%	or	50%

- Have children pause at given points during reading to check and clarify comprehension by asking questions at literal, interpretive, and applied levels.
- Lead a postreading discussion using the same levels of questions.
- Guide follow-up application activities based on story content, including word recognition and comprehension skills instruction at appropriate levels.

This instructional approach is also among the most sound designs known for guiding reading progress. It shows up repeatedly on lists of the top 10 methods of reading specialists.

Betts articulated sound approaches for testing and teaching based on good intuition and observation of successful teachers: this is called "art." In the more than sixty years of research that have followed, much has been learned about why these approaches work and how to fine-tune and add to them, and some features that should be avoided: this is called "science."

WORKING DEFINITIONS OF READING AND LEARNING TO READ

A great deal has been learned since Betts's time about the nature of the reading process and how children learn to read, but much is yet to be clearly determined. However, it is one's understandings of (or assumptions about) these processes that guide the way one introduces children to reading, evaluates students' progress in reading, and teaches developing and struggling learners. Therefore, our "working definitions" are offered below, with further explanation of the basic and recently evolved concepts and terms explained immediately after in this section.

Reading is fluently recognizing words in print while applying strategies for schema activation, metacognition, and "fix-up" of comprehension or word identification, as needed, to make supportable reconstructions of a writer's stated and implied meanings, with sufficient reference to prior knowledge and experience to construct relevant internally or externally suggested evaluations and applications.

Learning to read involves acquiring and applying strategies for phonetic decoding for building a growing store of sight words, and for reconstructive and constructive comprehension of text.

> Learning to read involves acquiring and applying thinking strategies that become automatic.

Explanation of Terms Used to Define Reading

Terms are explained in the order in which they appear in the definitions above.

- **"fluency"** = oral reading that is as smooth and naturally phrased as spoken language, with intonation and expression that appropriately represents the meaning of the text.
- **recognizing words, or "word recognition"** = the instant connection made between a word in print and its spoken equivalent. At a reader's Independent level, virtually all the words are sight words (99%).
- **strategies** = cognitive actions used to direct thought while reading and/or learning, usually driven by "inner speech" phrases, often in question form, such as: "This reminds me of . . ."; "Does that last part make sense?" Examples include predicting, summarizing, rephrasing in one's own words, categorizing, identifying appropriate sources for needed information, clarifying cause and effect relationships, and so on, as well as schema activation, metacognition, word identification, and comprehension "fix-up," as explained next.
- **schema activation** = the reader's active, intentional calling to mind of information, experiences, and attitudes related to the reading task at hand. Schema activation strategies might include: "Stop and think about the title"; "Does this look like easy reading or study reading?"; "What is this probably about?"; "What is my purpose for reading this?"
- **metacognition** = awareness of when one is understanding what one is reading and when one is not. Metacognition strategies might include: "What was that paragraph mostly about?"; "Does that mean. . . ?"
- **fix-up strategies** = inner speech phrases used when the reader becomes aware that she or he is not comprehending fully what is being read. These include phrases such as: "Let me re-read that part";

prior knowledge

"Maybe I'll just read ahead a little bit"; "What word is causing a problem here?"; "What point is the author trying to make here?"

- **word identification** = the application of phonics, context, or structural analysis strategies to decode an unfamiliar word into its spoken equivalent. Word identification strategies might include: "Are there spelling patterns in this word that I know?"; "Are there meaningful parts in this word?"; "Does the context suggest a word that I know?"

- **reconstruction of stated and implied meanings** = the accurate understanding of what the writer has directly stated and additional inferences that can be directly supported by the text. These two reconstructive processes have been referred to as "reading the lines" and "reading between the lines"—simple inference is really quite literal.

- **constructing relevant evaluations, interpretations and applications** = drawing conclusions of all types, such as the perceived accuracy of the information, its importance, interest, stylistic and aesthetic quality, humor, or logic. This constructive process has been referred to as "reading beyond the lines."

- The qualification, **internally or externally suggested**, refers to the fact that in some instances readers move to the constructive level of their own accord, and in other instances they do so in response to a question or other assignment asked or given by another.

- **phonetic decoding** = using symbol-sound associations to identify the spoken equivalent of a written word.

Assessment of reading development is framed by our assumptions about what reading "is." Keep the above definition of reading in mind as you read about how one third-grader perceived it.

Reading instruction also must be aimed at teaching students to become literate and reflective.

Take Sammy, for Example

A few years ago, a student in one of our university classes (we'll call her Sara) was meeting for the first time with the third-grader (we'll call him Sammy) she had been assigned to work with during the semester. The two were sitting at a round table in the elementary school library, with the university professor sitting at another table nearby. Sara asked Sammy the first question from an inventory called "Myself as a Reader": Do you think you are a good reader? Sammy's reply went something like this:

> Well, in kindergarten, I was an OK reader, I think. I was in Miss Casey's class. We used to come here [to the library] and check out these little "I Can Read" books . . . from that shelf over there. We could take them home, and I would read them with my mom. Now, those books are . . .

really easy to read. In Miss Casey's class we had a story chart on, like, big paper, that we wrote class stories on and then learned words from. I used to like to read this one book about Curious George getting in trouble for calling the fire department and I could read it out loud like, like a grownup would read it even though I was just in kindergarten. I still like that book. In first grade, I could read as good as, I guess, most of the kids in my class. We had Reading–Writing Connection every day in class, and my teacher, Mrs. Matthews, taught us on the overhead how words go together, or word parts make words. She taught us these "helper words" too, and then she put them up on the wall to use to figure out hard words. I used to try to do what Mrs. Matthews said and s—t—r—e—t—c—h out a word if I didn't know it, or I would try to find a part of the word that I know, but I couldn't always figure out some words and I used to get mad then. Then in second grade, I didn't like reading very much but I liked math a lot. I was in Ms. Arnold's class in second grade. We had phonics pages every day and it was pretty boring but I did OK. Maybe it was good for me though, because I'm a pretty good reader now. I'm in Mrs. Carole's class now. Well, you saw my class. I like to read "Magic Tree House" books because those kids get to do interesting stuff, and see interesting things and learn facts, and all these magic things happen. The girl in those stories reminds me of my sister—she's always nagging but she has good ideas. It feels like I'm on adventures with them when I read about them. In my class now, we do reading circles and we get to pick, in our groups, what we want to read. Sometimes we pick a "Magic Tree House" book and then we talk about the parts we liked when our group meets in class. The other kids in my group are pretty good readers.

Sara and the eavesdropping professor sat stunned for several long moments, and then Sara went on with her inventory questions while the professor scrambled to try to reconstruct Sammy's amazing response in writing. Clearly, Sammy had thought about this before and drawn some conclusions. He had told us, in one "stream of consciousness," just about everything we needed to know about "himself as a reader." Listening to (or reading) Sammy's response, you realize that his perception of "himself as a reader" is firmly bound to mental images of each of his classrooms and teachers—their trips to the library, class stories, lessons with the overhead, words on the wall, and reading circles. These images also include recollections of reading outside the classroom and of how he has judged his progress against the standards of what he knows about adult reading and that of his classmates.

Of course, it isn't always this easy. This book is about how to inform instruction by discovering children's stories of "themselves as readers"— realizing that few children are as self-aware as Sammy, and remembering to ask—often—the simple question, "How do *you* think you're doing?"

Sammy's story reveals a bit of the fascination inherent in the struggle to better understand "reading" and more accurately evaluate and facilitate children's progress—a fascination that has led hundreds of educators to devote their professional lives to this pursuit. In recent years, however, research and development in the branch of this field of study known as Diagnosis and Remediation has been hindered by several popular but perhaps misguided political and education movements that only quite recently are being set aside, permitting the field to catch up in terms of practice.

A History of the Evolving Field of Diagnosis and Remediation

On entering any field of study it is important to acquire some level of knowledge of its history. History—the record of what has been thought, done, and tested—is what makes progress possible. It helps us avoid blind alleys and spot erroneous assumptions. Following is a brief history of some of the trends and schools of thought that have shaped the field of Diagnosis and Remediation.

History—the record of what has been thought, and done, and tested—is what makes progress possible.

    Early basal reading programs tended to be curriculum driven. Specific skills thought to be essential to reading and writing acquisition were identified and sequenced, to form the base for lessons designed to teach these skills. Assessment was based on the assumption that students should be tested periodically on the identified skills, re-taught in the regular classroom if possible, or, depending on the degree of shortfall, taken out of the regular classroom for a period of time each day, or several days each week, for small group or individual remediation. "Remediation" generally meant re-teaching the skills sequence. This assessment model, sometimes referred to as a "medical model," has been criticized on a number of points, with one frequent criticism being the obvious negative effects of "pull-out" and labeling of "remedial readers." Several competing schools of thought about understanding, evaluating, and remediating reading problems have gained popularity over the half-century in which basal reader approaches have been the "standard," but most are merging toward common ground. See Figure 1.2 (page 14) for a summary of the most widely recognized of these alternative efforts.

    In fact, there is a good deal of research to suggest that conventional remedial reading was effective. The evolution of remedial reading was slowed, however, by Learning Disabilities (LD) legislation of the late 1970s, and all but eliminated by the Whole Language movement of the late 1980s.

    The LD legislation of the '70s defined a learning disability as a specific disorder *not* related to psychological, sociological, or intelligence (IQ) factors. The legislation was well funded and politically correct for the times. A reading problem could be classified as a learning disability as long as it was

FIGURE **1.2**

A SUMMARY OF "SCHOOLS OF THOUGHT" IN DIAGNOSIS AND REMEDIATION

Traditional Diagnosis and Remediation	Frequent classroom testing to identify specific skills weaknesses; in-depth diagnosis when needed	Pull-out & re-teach skills in small group remedial or individual clinical settings
Early Content Area Reading Movement	Beyond elementary school, testing is not needed: reading problems are easily identified through observation, and it is too late to re-teach all the needed skills	Teach compensation techniques and provide alternative access to information (e.g., books on tape)
Cognitive Processing	Traditional skills testing is overdone [invalid]—diagnosis should focus on testing "thinking skills"	Teach broad thinking skills and reading skills will fall into place
Psycho-Educational Approach	Formal testing for both academic and psychological factors	Treat personal problems and academics will fall into place
Learning Disabilities Movement	Eliminate cases where reading difficulty is related to psychological, socioeconomic, or IQ factors; then formal testing to identify the cause of the disability	Mainstreaming guided by Individual Education Plans (IEPs)
Whole Language Philosophy	No need for formal testing—observe in natural settings (kid watching)	No concept of "remediation"—children develop at their own pace and are hindered by labels
Informed Intervention Approach	Assess all relevant reading-specific factors and any relevant reading-related factors	Use assessment information to develop a remedial plan to build specific knowledge and strategies

in no way psychological, socioeconomic, or simply the result of a low IQ. Teacher education programs began to respond to the feeling and funding of the times by downplaying and eventually simply ignoring their psychological roots and branches. LD legislation further mandated remediation in the "least restrictive" setting (that is, in the regular classroom whenever possible). Then teacher education programs began to minimize and feel guilty about their basic approach of categorizing children's reading progress as remedial (more than two grade levels below expected level, based on grade in school and IQ), corrective (one to two grade levels below), developmental (within one grade of expected level), or advanced (more than a grade above expected level). The programs began to qualify their assertion that children reading at remedial levels needed more direct and more specialized assistance than a teacher could provide in the classroom, and that the children should receive that assistance individually or in a small group with a trained reading specialist. Elementary school teachers tended to envy the remedial reading teacher's lighter student load and flexible schedule. Public attention was being called to the greater number of minorities in remedial reading classes, resulting in the concern that remedial reading groups seemed to be another case of de facto segregation. Public opinion culminating from all these elements was that remedial reading does not work (although it clearly does).

In many cases, admittedly, Diagnosis and Remediation (D&R) courses and practices needed to be re-examined and better aligned with research findings. For many years, the broader field of reading had fallen under the spell of basal reader publishers whose interpretation of reading theory tended to result in massive scope and sequence charts of sub-skills with accompanying workbooks and ditto masters. Once a child fell behind in these rigid programs and was placed in a "low group" in the classroom or a pull-out remedial reading class, it was difficult to catch up. Remedial reading programs are only as good as the remedial reading teacher. There is no single simple formula for success because many children reading at remedial levels tend to have more and deeper problems than the reading problem. They require an extraordinary level of teacher expertise in informed practice, problem solving, flexibility, and a healthy measure of old-fashioned friendliness.

The already shrinking D&R courses were all but wiped out by the bandwagon phenomenon of Whole Language philosophy, with its seemingly common sense assertion that if children are immersed in a language-rich environment, they will acquire formal reading and writing as naturally as they learn to listen and speak. Following from this premise was the outright rejection of testing in general, test-based labeling (remedial, corrective, developmental, advanced) in particular, and most especially, remediation of any form. From a Whole Language perspective, diagnosis need only be "kid watching" in naturalistic settings, and remediation is a misnomer because children will progress in their own ways in their own time given appropriately rich climates in which to act and interact. The traditional content of still-mandated D&R courses all but disappeared. Professors were themselves uncertain as to what to write or look for in a D&R textbook.

> We can identify and help troubled children, but not if we continue to say "it's not our job."

Twenty years later, this seems to be changing. Our definition of reading has evolved from an emphasis on "skills" acquisition to a new, research-based emphasis on strategic thinking processes. D&R is regaining confidence: diagnostic testing *facilitates* kidwatching—it always did—and now we have even better ways to do it. Remediation through individualized direct instruction often is the only way, in an imperfect world, to provide some children with the essential knowledge and strategy base for reading development. When schools eliminated remedial reading, private "learning centers" sprang up and flourished. Now schools are beginning to re-institute remedial reading programs. Literacy D&R still has not found its way back to a strong connection with its psychological roots. School administrators and state legislators continue to insist that teaching/learning can be separated from psychological development. But this too may be changing, with the rise of public concern for safe schools that is accompanying the national epidemic of adolescent (and preteen) violence and suicide. We can identify and help troubled children, but not if we continue to say "it's not our job."

Traditional D&R doesn't need to be dropped. It needs to be combed through, as has been done with practices in other branches of literacy, to "save the best, and add the rest." What needs to be saved is most of the traditional assessment technology and many of the traditional remediation methods. Some things that need to be added include:

The goal of modern D&R is to "save the best, and add the rest."

- enhancement of traditional assessment with naturalistic observation techniques;
- emphasis on inclusion approaches and methods for identifying and correcting problems in the regular classroom;
- techniques for tapping into children's innate capacity to be self-instructing;
- the new concept of identifying and correcting problems in higher-order literacy—an exciting new dimension of the field.

The bottom line is the point with which this chapter opened: classroom teachers need to know a great deal about how to assess and facilitate their students' progress in language, literacy, and thinking. They need the support of reading specialists, as found in exemplary reading programs (Bean, Swan, Knaub, 2003), who can conduct in-depth diagnosis and assist with the more severe cases of reading disability. We can't deny or ignore the psychological problems that often accompany learning disabilities, and we shouldn't shy away from providing remedial reading to children with serious literacy disorders because their IQ seems to be low. It seems that the field, the schools, and the public are at, or are on the verge of, this realization.

FOUNDATIONS OF THE DIAGNOSTIC-PRESCRIPTIVE MODEL OF READING INSTRUCTION

Definition and Knowledge Base

The **diagnostic-prescriptive model** of reading instruction is based on informed observation and informal and formal assessment as needed, for the purpose of **precision teaching** that targets individual learners' specific strengths and needs. Categories of knowledge necessary to this process include:

- the classroom literacy curriculum across the grades, including when and how direct instruction in reading-specific factors is best provided
- how to determine when a student may need more or different instruction than can be provided in the regular classroom
- how reading-*related* factors (such as vocabulary, language development, background of information, and so on) can influence developmental progress
- classroom-based assessment of reading-specific and reading-related factors
- structured informal and formal assessment standards, techniques, and tests of reading-specific and reading-related factors
- approaches and methods for classroom instruction in each reading-specific area, and for providing more intensive remediation in each factor when needed

The "regular" classroom reading curriculum was sketched out at the beginning of this chapter. The chart in Figure 1.3 (page 18), and the definitions that follow, outline this curriculum more precisely. Against this backdrop, the next important instructional decision, noted above, is, *how to determine when a student may need more or different instruction than can be provided in the regular classroom*. This decision is guided by the concept of Levels of Intervention.

Levels of Intervention:
Developmental, Corrective, Remedial, Clinical

The regular classroom curriculum is referred to as **Developmental Level** instruction. It is expected that most students will acquire the concepts and strategies targeted and taught at their grade level. At one time or another, many children will fall slightly behind in one reading-specific factor or another. Regular classroom instruction is designed to reinforce concepts and strategies slightly below those targeted in the developmental curriculum. This classroom reinforcement is referred to as **Corrective Level** instruction. It is the classroom teacher's responsibility to monitor, through ongoing assessment, when children need this extra assistance.

When a student falls so far behind the developmental curriculum in one or more reading-specific factors that the classroom teacher cannot reasonably be expected to provide the needed direct instruction and practice, it is necessary to provide additional instructional assistance in **Remedial Level** instruction in addition to regular classroom instruction that directly

The still-emerging diagnostic-prescriptive model of reading instruction is based on informed observation, followed by informal and formal assessment as needed, for achieving precision teaching.

FIGURE 1.3

FORMULA FOR READING INTERVENTION

Comprehension at Grade Level: No less than 75%*

Evaluate & teach active thinking strategies for "making sense" of print:
- Predicting
- Questioning
- Translating
- Summarizing
- Monitoring comprehension
- Switching perspectives
- Interpreting
- Noting incongruities
- Applying
- Making personal connections
- Responding
- Schema restructuring

Reading-Specific Factors in Developmental Reading Curriculum

Grade	Concepts About Print	Phonemic Awareness	Sight Words (basic)	Phonetic Word Attack	Sight Words (advanced)	Word Study/ Syntax	Fluency at Independent Level	Study Reading
12	Clincial	Clinical	Clinical	Clinical	Clinical	Clinical	Remedial	Remedial
11	Clincial	Clinical	Clinical	Clinical	Clinical	Remedial	Remedial	Corrective
10	Clincial	Clinical	Clinical	Clinical	Clinical	Remedial	Remedial	Corrective
9	Clincial	Clinical	Clinical	Clinical	Clinical	Remedial	Corrective	Developmental
8	Clincial	Clinical	Clinical	Clinical	Clinical	Remedial	Corrective	Developmental
7	Clincial	Clinical	Clinical	Clinical	Remedial	Corrective	Developmental	Developmental
6	Clincial	Clinical	Clinical	Clinical	Remedial	Corrective	Developmental	Developmental
5	Clincial	Clinical	Clinical	Remedial	Corrective	Developmental	Developmental	Developmental
4	Clincial	Clinical	Clinical	Remedial	Corrective	Developmental	Developmental	Introductory
3	Clincial	Clinical	Remedial	Corrective	Developmental	Developmental	Introductory	Advanced
2	Clincial	Remedial	Corrective	Developmental	Developmental	Introductory	Advanced	Advanced
1	Remedial	Corrective	Developmental	Developmental	Introductory	Advanced	Advanced	Advanced
K	Corrective	Developmental	Developmental	Introductory	Advanced	Advanced	Advanced	Advanced
Pre-K	Developmental	Developmental	Introductory	Advanced	Advanced	Advanced	Advanced	Advanced

*IRI Criterion for Instructional Level Comprehension is 75% on IRI-type questions (main idea, details, inference, vocabulary, sequence)

Corrective Level Comprehension = Comprehension Instructional Level 1 grade below grade in school
Remedial Level Comprehension = Comprehension Instructional Level 2 grades below grade in school
Severe Level Comprehension = Comprehension Instructional Level 3 or more grades below grade in school

addresses identified areas of need. Note that in the Formula for Reading Intervention provided in Figure 1.3, the first criterion at every grade is comprehension no less than 75 percent at grade level. Comprehension development is the only valid purpose of any type of reading assessment or instruction. Instruction in any aspect of reading should begin and end with comprehension: In any reading-based interaction, we are either teaching that "reading is always for meaning," or we are teaching that "reading doesn't always have to be for meaning." Clearly, we should be teaching the former. When a child's comprehension is one to two grades below grade in school, more in-depth diagnosis may be necessary to determine reading-specific areas of need and possible influencing factors that might be addressed in remedial or clinical level instruction. Note that the terms *developmental, corrective, remedial,* and *clinical* refer to categories of instruction, not categories of children.

In far fewer instances, a child's reading difficulties are serious and persistent, and can correctly be called a reading disorder that requires **Clinical Level** intervention. This level is generally defined as reading comprehension two or more grades below grade in school, and/or several reading-specific factors within Clinical Level ranges.

Levels of Intervention and "Expectancy" Estimations

Traditional diagnosis and remediation defined levels of intervention not simply in terms of the difference between achievement and grade placement, but in terms of the difference between "expectancy" level and grade placement. **Expectancy** is the level at which the student "should" be achieving, based on a measure of IQ. Thus, using a simple reading expectancy formula, a third-grade child with an IQ of 110 would be expected to be reading at a higher level than a third-grade child with an IQ of 90. Determination of whether either of these children should receive remedial assistance outside the classroom would be made on the basis of whether their reading was significantly below their *expected* levels, rather than whether it was below their actual grade level. To illustrate this concept, several techniques for estimating reading expectancy are detailed in Figure 1.4 (page 20).

The levels of intervention as described and detailed above are based on the introductory statement, "It is expected that most students will acquire the concepts and strategies targeted and taught at their grade level." While the concept of expectancy level has logical appeal in the abstract, it is difficult to apply in practical situations for three reasons:

1. It assumes that the test used to obtain an IQ estimate was a valid measure of that construct, was not culturally biased to any large degree, and was administered and scored accurately.

2. It would tend to exclude one category of children from access to remedial-level instruction (that is, children with below-average IQ scores, reading below grade level but still at "expectancy" level).

3. For practical purposes, the determination of when a child might need to receive remedial instruction outside the regular classroom is more reasonably based on the *nature of the additional assistance* the child needs, rather than on an abstract scale of "reading level." A third grader who needs additional assistance in phonics can be assisted reasonably at a corrective level by the third-grade teacher, but a fourth grader still needing this assistance should, more reasonably, be provided this assistance in a remedial setting—regardless of either child's IQ score, and even if the score is valid. Reading is not a single continuum. It is, at kindergarten and first-grade levels, an emphasis on concepts about print, phonemic awareness, and basic sight words; at second- and third-grade levels it emphasizes sound–symbol correspondence and decoding strategies; at fourth- through fifth-grade levels it is more advanced word and language study, fluency, and increased emphasis on reading to learn. For this reason, the chart in Figure 1.3 is a better guide to reading intervention than a formula that assumes linear development.

Nevertheless, the concept of IQ-based Reading Expectancy may have relevance in some cases and particularly in clinical settings. Several classic formulas are detailed in Figure 1.4.

Expectancy formulas are very carefully derived numerical estimations of the fuzziest of all human characteristics—what someone is capable of.

FIGURE **1.4**

READING EXPECTANCY FORMULAS

Background: The Concept of "Mental Age"

The first *Reading Expectancy* formula below uses the type of intelligence score often used in early intelligence tests. This "Mental Age" score can be easily calculated from the familiar "Intelligence Quotient," or IQ, score as follows:

$$MA = \frac{IQ \times CA}{100}$$

By this formula, an 8-year-old child with an IQ of 120 would be translated into a "Mental Age" of 9.6: the child's raw score was equal to the score of the average child of 9.6 years of age. On the other hand, an 8-year-old child with an IQ of 80 would be translated into a "Mental Age" of 6.4. It should be noted that most intelligence test producers have abandoned the use of "Mental Age" as a construct because it tends to give the misimpression that "Mental Age" somehow equals maturity level, when in fact it merely is an index of cognitive functioning.

Harris's Reading Expectancy Formula.

Albert Harris (1961) seems to have been the first to apply the idea of reading expectancy. A child's Mental Age score could be interpreted as his or her "Reading Expectancy Age." Simply by subtracting 5 (the number of years before entering school) from a child's Mental Age score, translates Mental Age into a grade level "Reading Expectancy":

$$\text{Reading Expectancy} = MA - 5$$

By this formula, an 8-year-old third grader with an IQ of 120, which translates into an MA of 9.6, would have a Reading Expectancy of 4.6, or 1.6 years above grade placement. An 8-year-old third grader with an IQ score of 80 would have a Mental Age score of 6.4, and a Reading Expectancy of 1.4, which is 1.9 years below grade placement. This second third grader, reading barely above first-grade level, would be considered to be reading up to expectancy, and not in need of remedial assistance.

Conceptually, this is somewhat problematic; if the high-IQ children above were reading on grade level, they would be in need of remedial assistance because they "should" be reading at close to a fifth grade level; the low-IQ children, even if reading on a first-grade level, would be considered to be reading up to expectancy and not in need of remedial assistance.

Harris and Sipay's Reading Expectancy Age

Harris and Sipay (1985) later adjusted the formula somewhat, to yield Reading Expectancy Age scores that would be slightly lower than Mental Age scores:

$$\text{REA (Reading Expectancy Age)} = \frac{2MA + CA}{3}$$

By this formula, an 8-year-old third grader with an IQ of 120 and Mental Age of 9.6 would have a Reading Expectancy Age of 9.1. An 8-year-old third grader with an IQ of 80 and Mental Age of 6.4 would have a Reading Expectancy Age of 5.6.

Harris has suggested that the differences between Reading Achievement (RA = a grade equivalent score on a reading achievement test) and Reading Expectancy Age (REA) should be considered of more significance at earlier grades and less significance at higher grades, according to the following guidelines:

Grade 1–3:   REA exceeds RA by 6 mo. (0.5 yr)
Grade 4–5:   REA exceeds RA by 9 mo. (0.7 yr)
Grade 6+:   REA exceeds RA by 1 year or more

The 8-year-old third grader with an IQ of 80 and a Reading Expectancy Age of 5.6 would need to have a Reading Achievement lower than age 5.1 (below first grade level) to be considered a significant problem.

Bond & Tinker's Formula

Bond & Tinker (1973) offered a formula for calculating reading expectancy (RE) directly from an IQ score without reference to mental age, and actual number of years in school (not counting kindergarten) rather than assuming that age minus 5 years is an accurate estimate of this figure.

$$RE = \frac{(\text{Years in School} \times IQ) + 1}{100}$$

The significant discrepancies suggested by Bond and Tinker are:

Grade 1:   RE exceeds RA by .50
Grade 2:   RE exceeds RA by .66
Grade 3:   RE exceeds RA by .75
Grade 4:   RE exceeds RA by 1.00
Grade 5:   RE exceeds RA by 1.50
Grade 6+:   RE exceeds RA by 2.00

By this formula, a third grader (who had been in school for three years) with an IQ of 80 would have a Reading Expectancy of 3.4

$$RE = (3 \times 80 / 100) + 1$$

and would be considered to have a significant problem if reading below grade 2.6; that is, if reading achievement fell 0.75 below this student's reading expectancy of 2.6:

$$3.4 - .75 = 2.6$$

Reading-Specific Factors

The chart in Figure 1.3 (page 18) lays out a general grade-level curriculum for reading according to current understandings about literacy acquisition. At every level the reading curriculum begins and ends with comprehension: strategies for making sense of print. The reading-specific factors woven into this instruction are described next.

Concepts about print are the fundamental understandings that children form from their earliest encounters with books and print. These understandings include:

- **directionality** of print in English, such as starting at the beginning of a book; turning pages left-to-right; following words in sentences left-to-right; following words top to bottom; and using a return sweep at the end of a line
- **word/letter concepts,** such as the concept of letter; the concept of word; first/last letter in a word; upper case/lower case letters; letter names; aware that letters are associated with sounds
- **recognizes punctuation, such as period, comma, question mark, and quotation marks**
- **reading concepts**, such as print (rather than pictures) carries the meaning; that what can be said can be written and what is written can be read; beginning, middle, and end of "story"; fact as distinct from fiction; and that story events and characters can be compared with personal experience

In many cases, children acquire these concepts naturally through observation and interactions with parents, siblings, and caretakers. For children who have had limited experiences with books before entering school, these concepts need to be taught directly during teacher read-alouds and informally throughout the school day.

Phonemic awareness is the learned ability to distinguish among and manipulate the sounds in spoken language. Because children often acquire this ability on their own, even before beginning school, and because it is not as readily "observable" as concepts about print, phonemic awareness is sometimes overlooked as a necessary early instructional stage. Acquisition of phonemic awareness has, in numerous studies, been shown to be among the strongest predictors of success in beginning reading. Aspects of phonemic awareness include:

- identifying individual words in a spoken phrase
- identifying individual syllables in a spoken word
- recognizing the beginning sound of a spoken word (referred to as "onset")
- recognizing the ending sound of a spoken word (referred to as "rime")
- recognizing the middle sound of a spoken one-syllable word
- blending two or more given sounds to form a single spoken word
- identifying the separate sounds in a single spoken word (phonemic segmentation)

Sight words are the words one can identify instantly, in context or in isolation, without the need to apply any word attack strategies. Typically, the first sight words children acquire are those most often seen, such as "stop" and "exit" and their own names. Each person's sight word vocabulary is unique, but by the end of third grade children's sight word vocabularies should include, at a minimum, the most frequently occurring words in the language. Contrary to popular belief, about 80 percent of the words in the English language are phonetically regular; however, about 80 percent of the *most frequently occurring* words are irregular. Therefore, it is doubly important for these irregular, often-encountered words to be acquired as sight words, and this is best done through direct instruction, using words plucked from meaningful print material for drill and practice routines.

Phonetic word attack is the application of learned strategies to decode an unfamiliar word. In the past, there has been a good deal of controversy over whether the teaching of reading should begin with teaching sight words or phonics, and just what "kind" of phonics instruction is best. With respect to the first question, most educators now agree that sight words and *phonemic awareness* should be reinforced and encouraged from the earliest stages, followed by continued direct instruction in sight words and phonics. Just about all words eventually need to become sight words, and any new word needs to be decoded before it becomes a sight word. Because many words *can* be phonetically decoded, phonetic word attack strategies are an important tool in building a sight word vocabulary. Essentially, phonetic word attack strategies are not useful as reading strategies but as fix-up strategies. If we have to use word attack strategies with more than a few words on a page, we begin to lose comprehension due to redirection of attention and are no longer reading; however, if we don't have word attack fix-up strategies for even those few words, we also lose comprehension because of missing word meanings.

As to what "kind" of phonics instruction should be used, the controversy continues. The synthetic phonics approach begins by teaching a phonics "rule," such as the "silent e" rule, and then providing practice in applying the rule to decode words. This has been referred to as a "deductive" approach: If this is the rule, you can deduce that the word must be this. The analytic phonics approach begins by teaching children several sight words that follow a given phonics rule, and then guiding them toward "discovering" the rule for themselves. This has been referred to as an "inductive" approach: If these words are all pronounced this way, then the rule must be this. The problem with the inductive approach is that it tends to delay direct instruction in phonics for too long. The question is, which way does the brain tend to work: deductively, inductively, or does it vary from person to person? The most recent research in literacy acquisition, summarized by Marilyn Adams (1990), suggests that the brain works in a different way entirely, and led to the creation of a teaching approach that has been labeled "analogic phonics" or "phonics by analogy":

> In essence, because of their vast experience in looking at English words, skillful readers do not recognize the letters of a word independently of one another. Instead, within their memories, the units responsible for recognizing individual letters have become linked to one another by an intermediating set of association units. The strengths of the associations between these units reflect the frequency with which the corresponding letters have been seen together in particular order and combination. (Marilyn Jager Adams, *Beginning to Read: Thinking and Learning About Print,* a research report on phonics instruction commissioned by the nationally funded Center for the Study of Reading, 108).

Cunningham's interpretation of Adams' research summary is that "the brain is a pattern detector, not a rule applier," meaning that when we encounter an unfamiliar word, we do not try to think of the rule that applies to the particular letter combinations; rather, we try to think of other words we know that contain those combinations. Upon encountering the (non)word "bimersion," we might quickly "test out" our pronunciation attempt of "by mer' zhun" against words such as bicycle, summer, and version. On the basis of this understanding of the reading process, the analogic phonics approach to beginning reading is to teach, as sight words, a set of words that contain the most frequently occurring letter clusters, and strategies for using those known words when they encounter unknown words, such as: "I know bicycle, summer, and version, so this would be "by" and this would be "mer" and this would be "zhun," so this would be "by mer' zhun."

One common way of testing children's ability to use phonetic word attack strategies is to ask them to read nonsense words because, in any given set of real words, there is no way to know which may be sight words for the person being tested: If the word is a sight word, you are not testing phonetic word attack. Some have argued that asking children to read nonsense words is too far removed from "real" reading, but this argument is irrelevant because the context is assessment and not instruction: Reading nonsense words is no less "real" than reading isolated words from a list. Patricia Cunningham offered a unique solution to this objection with The Names Test, a list of proper names that contain the most frequently occurring phonetic features (Cunningham, 1990).

Specific elements of phonetic word attack strength include ability to correctly pronounce:

- frequently occurring onsets such as initial single letters, initial consonant blends (such as *st, pl, br, str, and spl*) and digraphs (such as *ch, sh,* and *wh*)
- frequently occurring rimes (ending letter clusters such as *ight, ain,* and *tion*)
- long vowel sounds
- short vowel sounds

Word study/syntax. Word study includes study of the structural elements of words, and grade-level vocabulary study across the curriculum, including:

- *morphology*—the study of the meaningful parts within words, such as prefixes, suffixes, roots, and inflectional endings such as *ed*, *s*, and *ing*
- *etymology*—the study of word origins

Syntax is the aspect of "grammar" that governs the relationships among and sequencing of words in sentences. The ability to apply knowledge of word and sentence structure, like phonetic word attack, is important in comprehension fix-up.

Fluency is the ability to read aloud with the same phrasings and intonations used in speaking. Good readers, especially when reading difficult materials, use the comprehension strategy of attempting to "hear" the words they read in the same fluent way they might if someone were speaking them. Children who have acquired the impression that the important thing in reading is accuracy often read in a choppy monotone, referred to as "word calling," that hinders comprehension.

Study reading is the cluster of strategies that students use when reading to learn independently from text. It involves self-initiated use of the strategies presented above in the definition of reading for: prediction, metacognition, comprehension fix-up, reconstruction of stated and implied meanings, construction of relevant evaluations, and applications that are both internally and externally suggested. It includes study habits and techniques, attitudes toward school and learning, and confidence in oneself as a reader. Ideally, development of study reading strategies is a lifelong process.

In a section titled "Reaching the Broader Objectives" of his 1940 textbook *Improvement of Basic Reading Abilities*, Donald Durrell, one of the founders of the field of reading education, wrote, "The development of permanent habits in the use of reading depends largely on the methods of teaching employed in the content subjects. It is in subjects such as science, art, music, practical arts, physical education, history, and geography that reading may be employed for its highest practical value, that of getting the child closer to life through giving the background for appreciative observation, intelligent planning, and well-directed action. In these subjects, properly taught, the child will learn to turn to reading as one source of help in solving numerous practical problems."

Reading-Related Factors

When children look down at a page of print, a host of unseen factors and forces sit down with them (Figure 1.5). There are the influences of family, friends, and acquaintances. There are the children's own priorities and immediate interests. There are the voices of the children's prior successes and failures: not merely with reading but with school and life in general. There are even the voices of ancestors as embodied in inherited characteristics. Together, these influences determine how much children are willing and able to bring to the printed page—and, therefore, how much is likely to be derived from it.

Reading-*related* factors can be categorized as:

- environmental (such as language and sociocultural differences)
- psychological (such as cognitive, attitudinal, and emotional functions)
- physiological (such as vision, hearing, and neurological functions)

> When children look down at a page of print, a host of unseen factors and forces sit down alongside them.

FIGURE **1.5**

READING SUMS US UP

With so many factors and forces influencing the "simple" act of reading, it is little wonder that difficulties arise. Reading problems are not always traceable to a single cause, or even an undisputable *set* of causes. However, attempting to treat *only* the "symptom" of reading-specific educational gaps is like encouraging someone to exercise a broken arm. Good teachers, specialists, and clinicians see the child behind the student and often can help children surmount enormous educational deficits by "speaking to" the source of the problem.

Tools for Diagnostic-Prescriptive Teaching

In many ways, diagnostic-prescriptive teaching defies description. It may be as simple as changing the classroom seating arrangement, but it can be as complex as carefully selecting a book or article that addresses an emotionally sensitive issue in the student's life. Six professional tools typically are used to structure diagnostic-prescriptive teaching. These are known by a variety of different names, but tend to include the following terms and concepts: 1) Individual/Intensive Diagnosis; 2) Formal Testing; 3) Structured Informal Assessment; 4) Diagnostic-Teaching; 5) Trial Teaching; and 6) Improvisational Assessment.

> Six professional tools typically are used to structure diagnostic-prescriptive teaching.

Individual, or Intensive, Diagnosis is a process undertaken when routine data collection fails to identify the nature and/or source of some ongoing problem. The student typically is referred to a specialist or to a teacher team who compile information from cumulative records, parent and teacher interviews, tests, and interactions with the student to identify specific areas of need and make recommendations for precision teaching: in the classroom if the problem is determined to be corrective level, or in a small group or individual remedial setting if the problem is more severe. Typically, individual diagnosis begins with administration of an Informal Reading Inventory to estimate the student's Independent, Instructional, and Frustration levels, and to analyze oral reading accuracy and fluency, oral and/or silent reading comprehension, and other aspects of the reading process. Results of the Informal Reading Inventory are used to determine the types of follow-up assessment that reasonably should be done to identify specific strengths and needs, and factors that may be influencing reading progress. Follow-up assessment is guided by the search for patterns of strength and need, and may include formal standardized tests, structured informal assessment, as well as trial teaching, and improvisational assessment.

Although classroom teachers seldom conduct a complete individual diagnosis with a formal case report, experience with this type of assessment enhances the teacher's ability to interpret classroom observations and formal and informal assessment results. The "case-based reasoning" involved in individual diagnosis is a state of mind in which quick, intuitive guesses are followed by careful hypothesis formation and then alternating efforts to qualify and disqualify the hypotheses. Many rules can be written to guide this "back and forth," "up and down and all around" process, but these, like phonics rules, are best learned as the mind actually engages in this complex endeavor. No two cases are identical, but patterns are detectable, and lessons are learned much as they are from human experience—one "story" at a time.

Case-based reasoning is a state of mind.

Formal Testing is the use of standardized tests to evaluate a student's achievement or aptitude. Norm-referenced tests evaluate the student's performance by comparison with a "norm group" of students at the same age or grade. Criterion-referenced tests evaluate the student's performance by comparison with a predetermined standard. The results of formal, group-administered reading tests can be a useful starting point for a teacher or reading specialist; however, they are more useful for overall program evaluation than for evaluation of individual students. More information on formal testing is provided in Chapter 6.

Structured Informal Assessment is the use of flexible inventories, checklists, and techniques for collecting information on a variety of reading-specific and reading-related factors. These tools provide reminders of the knowledge base related to the factor being evaluated. A structured informal assessment of emergent literacy, for example, provides reminders of the various concepts about print that a child may or may not yet have acquired; an Informal Reading Inventory is a structured informal assessment that provides not just the reading selections and questions, but reminders of many aspects of reading that might need to be considered.

Diagnostic-Teaching is intentional evaluation of a wide range of reading-specific and reading-related factors while teaching a student something that has been problematic, and ideally, something that he or she seems to learn well. It relies on highly interactive teaching methods that provide a rich sampling of student thinking and talking or writing while attempting to learn. When assessment becomes an integral part of instruction, many subtle values are gained in efficiency and precision. These elements are especially valuable when working with second-language learners who need to pass through several rather predictable stages in progress toward being able to read and learn in the new language (Garcia, 1998). Diagnostic teaching is not a substitute for other forms of assessment; however, it accomplishes several important goals:

1. Because it is based on everyday classroom activities, it provides a window onto many aspects of learning, thinking, and doing.
2. It does not take away from instructional time as does conventional testing.

3. It takes the learning context into account.
4. It reflects and reveals individual students' inner-speech processes, with immediate opportunity to correct possible "malfunctions" or mis-understandings.
5. It establishes a more helping than testing relationship between the teacher and students.
6. Because it takes many factors into account, it can result in rapid progress toward learning goals.
7. It addresses broad educational goals, such as increasing *self-teaching* and reducing fear of *social consequences* of being perceived as a poor reader.

Several methods discussed in the chapters ahead exemplify the diagnostic-teaching paradigm (see especially: the ReQuest procedure; KWL-Plus; Question-Only; and Discovery Phonics).

Trial Teaching is an *informal* process of determining which of several possible methods may be the most efficient one for remedying a diagnosed need. It is often used as a follow-up to the IRI in individual diagnosis. In general, it is best to select from published teaching methods, as opposed to improvised activities; however, because it is informal, it can be altered "midstream." See Figure 1.6 as a brief example of Trial Teaching with a student who had difficulty in learning sight words.

The rationale for trial teaching was well stated by Feuerstein (1979) in reference to his research on intellectual assessment:

> The potential *for being modified by learning* should be the object of focus in psychometric assessment. This potential can be measured only by an active, involved, and involving process, and can never be revealed by a static enumeration of existing abilities. Indeed, one wonders why it has

FIGURE **1.6**

TRIAL TEACHING: SIGHT WORDS

Omar, a fifth-grade boy, had grade-level performance in phonetically decoding words. However, he had ongoing difficulty in learning sight words. It was concluded that he might be one of a small minority (about 10 percent) of readers who have this problem despite otherwise good progress in word attack and comprehension. This problem sometimes is misdiagnosed as a problem with fluency.

Omar was tested for speed of recognition on twenty-one fifth-grade-level "sight words." These were divided, then, into three sets of seven words each. He was taught each set with three variations on the Omnibus Paradigm for Teaching Sight Words (described in Chapter 8). He was retested on all twenty-one words one week later, and it was concluded that he learned best with the combination that included the greatest number of repetitions and uses of aural-oral support. This was true whether the words were regular or irregular in terms of phoneme-grapheme correspondence.

taken us so long to realize that the only way to assess potential for change is to attempt to modify the examinee in some way, while measuring the extent of the change and the means by which this was attained" (as cited in Carney & Cioffi, 1990, 49).

When trial teaching is used as part of an individual diagnosis, it is essential to describe the method(s) used in enough detail for the reader of the report to be able to make independent judgments about what occurred. Guidelines for reporting trial teaching are provided in the next chapter on developing the Case Report.

Improvisational (Peak Performance) Assessment, a seldom-used but potentially powerful tool, is the use of standardized tests in nonstandard ways to discover "peak" abilities. This is done by determining the extent to which the test's standard format may itself be an obstacle to accurate evaluation of a student's achievement or ability. For example, re-administering selected items from a "timed" test in untimed fashion would reveal the extent to which factors such as anxiety or English-language proficiency might be affecting a student's performance. Requiring a student to wait for two to three seconds before answering each question can indicate a tendency to answer too quickly and impulsively, without respect to actual comprehension. The teacher may sit down with a student to informally review a previously administered standardized test to try to discover just what may have caused a certain pattern of errors. The teacher may reword questions or ask the student why she selected a particular answer. The teacher may compare the original score on a portion of the test with the student's score when questions and answers are read to her. Such improvisations, or prompts, of course, invalidate the standardized "score," and results of such improvisations should not be interpreted using the norm-referenced tables that assume standard test administration conditions. However, the results can help the teacher to fill in missing pieces of information that could not be collected in either a standardized test format or by routine observation. This technique has a long history in testing and teaching (Barr, Sadow, & Blackowizc, 1990; Cioffi & Carney, 1983, 1990; Clay, 1985; Durrell, 1955; Hamilton, 1983; Johnston, 1987; Paratore & Indrisano, 1987). The increased proportions of second-language learners in today's classrooms are giving this tactic renewed currency. As with trial teaching, it is very important in reporting results of improvisational assessment to be specific about the types of prompts and assistance provided.

There is room—more, *need*—for improvisation and assessment.

John Carney & Grant Cioffi (1990) offer an example of improvisational assessment with the Stanford Achievement Test, reproduced in Figure 1.7. These master diagnosticians also offer some operational guidelines, or alternative ways, by which a skilled teacher can assess several other reading skills with alternate tasks (see Figure 1.8, page 32).

FIGURE 1.7

EXAMPLE OF IMPROVISATIONAL ASSESSMENT WITH THE STANFORD ACHIEVEMENT TEST

In this example, Carney and Cioffi illustrate how to better understand the nature of a poor reader's pattern of errors, in this case on a standardized test, by seeing just what kind of teaching must be done to overcome specific word analysis and recognition problems. The process is based on progressively "slicing" or simplifying component parts of the task until the student can handle it.

Gary, whose total reading score on the Stanford Achievement Test is at the twelfth percentile, begins by reading preprimer and primer lists with no errors. On the grade 2 list, Gary makes one error, reading the word "scarecrow" as "scarcrow." When the examiner presents the word structurally (scare crow), Gary responds correctly. At grade 3, Gary corrects two errors made on the initial flash presentation when the words are placed in context. The third word (though) is taught using several strategies, but Gary does not respond appropriately. The examiner then tells Gary what the word is. At both levels 4 and 5, Gary makes five initial errors on the ten word samples. He corrects all five errors at the grade 4 level as a result of dynamic intervention and four of five errors at grade 5. One instructional episode will illustrate the dynamic procedure. Gary reads the word "rough" as "rush," then "ranch." He does, however, recognize the word "tough" in context; the examiner then uses initial consonant substitution to move Gary from "tough" to "rough."

An analysis of Gary's performance under the two conditions—static, as measured by the initial response to the word, and dynamic—provides two very different profiles, particularly as Gary approaches his present grade/age placement. At the grade 4 and 5 levels, Gary's initial responses are incorrect in half the cases. Yet his performance with the instructional support provided in the dynamic assessment reaches levels that are age and grade appropriate (10/10 in grade 4; 9/10 in grade 5). In addition to these quantitative results, the analysis of the instructional episodes that constitute the dynamic assessment provides a pattern of behaviors that are a rich source of information for remedial intervention. In Gary's case, for example, it was found that most of his incorrect responses were graphically similar to the target word. In all cases the examiner was able to elicit an appropriate phonic generalization, either by presenting a similar word or by dividing the stimulus word into syllables or morphemes. This suggests that Gary has appropriate phonic skills to identify words at grade level but that he does not use phonic generalizations spontaneously. When cued to do so, Gary responds appropriately.

Carney & Cioffi, *Reading Psychology,* 1990, 182–183.

Many standardized test manuals now incorporate suggestions for how to undertake improvisational assessment. See Figure 1.9 (page 33) for an example of how Walter H. and Ruth K. MacGinitie invite use of the Gates-MacGinitie Reading Tests to discover when a student may be over-relying on "prior knowledge" to answer comprehension questions. The manual also provides helpful hints for addressing each particular problem.

These six assessment tools and techniques provide teachers and reading specialists with a variety of means for understanding and guiding students' progress. Ideally, these would be implemented collaboratively by teachers and reading specialists in various roles.

Roles of the Reading Specialist

One recurring problem with traditional pull-out remedial reading program designs was a lack of communication between the classroom teacher and

FIGURE **1.8**

GUIDELINES FOR IMPROVISATIONAL ASSESSMENT

Assessment Content (Anticipated Response)	Alternative Instructional Episodes
I. Word Recognition in Isolation (Rapid and Correct Identification)	display word for analysis present word in context (contextual analysis) divide word into syllables (phonic analysis) divide word into morphemes (structural analysis) compare word with a similar but easier item (initial phoneme substitution) identify word for student (direct instruction)
II. Word Recognition in Context	pre-teach low-frequency vocabulary (unrehearsed fluent reading) provide opportunity for rehearsal model passage for student
III. Comprehension—Oral and Silent Reading (Correct Response to Comprehension Questions)	*Prereading Activities* pre-teach low-frequency vocabulary activate appropriate prior knowledge pre-teach difficult concepts provide direction for reading identify organizing principles *Postreading Activities* provide forced-choice response ask student to find answers direct student to key section of the text

Carney & Cioffi, *Reading Psychology*, 1990, 188–189.

the special reading teacher about the instructional plans they were implementing with students, and about their perceptions of students' progress. A more recent means of providing extra assistance in remedial and learning disability programs has been referred to as "push-in" (Reynolds, Wang, & Walbert, 1987) designs: Instead of children leaving the classroom for small-group or individual assistance, the special area teacher comes into the regular classroom at planned times to assist identified children. In LD programs communication between teacher(s) and specialist(s) is formalized in a written IEP for each child; even in this design, however, important day-to-day communication still tends to depend on the compatibility of individual teachers' personalities and educational approaches. The need for better communication is complicated by the fact that today, many children receive assistance in reading-related areas from teachers in the "allied professions," such as learning disabilities, special education, psychology, counseling, library science, speech and language, and English as a Second Language.

FIGURE **1.9**

DYNAMIC USE OF STANDARDIZED TEST INFORMATION (TO DETERMINE PEAK PERFORMANCE)

Look at the student's wrong answers for the Comprehension Test. Many of the wrong answer choices are intended to be answers that a student might choose if answering on the basis of prior knowledge rather than from what the passage says.

The first answer (A) to question 7 in the Level 4, Form K Comprehension Test is such an answer. The passage and question are

> One day when Eliza's mother was out in the garden and Eliza's father was *taking* a shower, the baby started to cry. Eliza sat still and listened. The baby kept on crying. Eliza tiptoed into his room and peeked into the crib.
> "Andrew," she whispered.
> The baby stopped crying.

In this story the word "taking" means

- having
- *stealing*
- winning
- choosing

Did the student choose several such wrong answers? If the student did, it may be helpful to discuss with the student the *questions* that were answered incorrectly (provided, of course, that the student will not be tested again with those questions). Try to find out on what basis the student chose the answers. Ask the student to read the passage that the question is about, then read the question and choose an answer. Ask "How did you decide that one is right?" Even if the student does not choose again the "prior-knowledge" answer, you will be likely to learn something about how the student tries to make sense of what he or she reads.

One possibility that you will need to check is that the student who chose many "prior-knowledge" wrong answers was not reading the passages at all, but simply choosing plausible answers. When this proves to be the case, you will need to find out whether the student adopted this strategy because he or she had difficulty reading the passages or because he or she has developed a habit of jumping ahead to answer questions without reading the text.

Walter H. & Ruth K. MacGinitie, 1989, 38–39.

One way to increase communication is to better understand each other's roles and responsibilities. Although reading programs, and job titles and descriptions, vary greatly by region, state, and district, following are some generalizations about titles, roles, and responsibilities in reading education, as identified in surveys of exemplary reading programs (such as that of Bean, Swan, & Knaub, 2003).

A **reading specialist** is a certified teacher who has a graduate degree in reading, and usually is state certified in reading K–adult. Reading specialists may serve as reading teachers, reading resource teachers, reading coordinators, or clinicians. These roles may overlap, as when a reading teacher job description includes a partial teaching load, with some additional responsibilities of a reading resource teacher or reading coordinator; however, the distinctions made below should help to clarify these combinations and possibilities.

A **reading teacher** provides remedial and sometimes clinical-level assistance to individual and/or small groups of children outside the regular classroom setting (or in a "push-in" program) in public and private elementary, middle, and senior high schools, or teaches reading and study strategies classes and/or workshops in adult education, commercial schools and learning assistance centers, and in junior college or university programs. In public and private K–12 settings, reading teachers may assist classroom teachers in identifying students in need of remedial assistance by administering informal reading inventories or other assessments at the beginning of the school year, by doing observational assessment in the classroom, and by analyzing standardized test scores and other assessment information. Once students have been identified for remedial assistance, the reading teacher conducts follow-up assessment as needed, to design individual instructional plans for each student. The reading teacher should develop procedures for regular—at least weekly—exchanges of information with the classroom teacher(s) about what is being taught, and how the student is progressing. Reading teachers usually are based at a single school, but may sometimes serve a cluster of schools.

In elementary through high school levels, reading specialists may serve as **reading resource teachers**. Specialists in this role do not work directly with children, but work closely with teachers. They visit teachers' classrooms and offer in-service sessions to keep teachers current on teaching methodology and materials. They may work with teachers to create instructional units, locate supplementary materials and resources, and provide classroom demonstrations. Reading resource teachers may serve a single school, a cluster of schools, or an entire district. Often, several resource teachers are based in a district central office, and work together to develop plans and procedures for serving teachers across the district.

Reading coordinators also do not have teaching assignments, but are responsible for overall program development, implementation, and evaluation, including teacher training, curriculum development, and materials selection. Reading coordinators' roles may be designated as elementary, middle, or high school level only, but the more preferable arrangement is to assign K–12 responsibility, to ensure curricular and instructional articulation from level to level. Reading coordinators often oversee and coordinate the work of reading resource teachers and school-based reading teachers.

A **reading clinician** has specialized training and experience in diagnosing and working with individuals with severe reading disorders. A reading clinic may be affiliated with a school district, a university, a hospital, or other social service agency. The diagnostic process typically involves assessment of a variety of reading-specific and reading-related functions through observation, formal and informal testing, interviews, trial teaching, and referral to allied professionals for other specific evaluations. The in-depth diagnostic results, interpretations, conclusions and instructional recommendations are compiled in a formal Case Report, as described in the next chapter.

Synthesis

Insightful diagnostic-prescriptive teaching is one of a few qualities that separate great teachers from good teachers. It requires a great deal of technical knowledge, reflective experience, and the ability to contextualize a child's progress within the larger picture of the role of reading in the life of a literate person. One approach to this contextualization is to develop a thorough understanding of the stages of literacy acquisition, and to make comprehension the first objective in all reading instruction: All other objectives should be categorized as "necessary but not sufficient." Another approach is to interweave self-assessment questions into daily activities to see, as with Sammy, what they perceive reading to "be" and how they see "themselves as readers." Contextualizing a child's progress also serves as a constant and awesome reminder that without accurate assessment and direct, informed intervention, struggling readers will very soon fall below a level where they can reasonably receive the assistance they need from the classroom teacher in the developmental sequence. A first grader who has not yet developed phonemic awareness will not go far in phonics instruction until this shortfall is remedied. A third grader who has learned to "read" quickly and accurately with no effort to comprehend will begin to fall behind more slowly but just as surely. Finally, contextualizing a child's progress involves combining what you know and can infer about where the child has been, with what you observe and can discover about where the child is now, to make a prediction (or prognosis) about where the child is likely to go from here under various circumstances. In essence, the diagnostic-prescriptive approach is about thinking strategically about teaching. It is a habit of mind that guides daily evaluation and teaching of individual students. The reward for learning to implement it naturally and well is the greater ease and effectiveness with which you will be able to teach—in classrooms, remedial, and/or clinical settings.

The Diagnostics-Prescriptive approach is about thinking strategically about teaching.

Review

Preventive measures are sensible, but "prevention" is a myth. No matter how solid the initial instructional program, it is most likely that each year there will be children at every grade level who will underperform. There is no program that fits all and qualifies as a panacea. Some students, in any system, will require informal to intensive diagnostic assessment, and generic to precise and customized prescriptive instruction. Further, this will need to be done on a trial teaching, or provisional, basis.

PREVIEW

The next chapter begins to more fully address Individual Diagnosis and Case Reporting. These are the particulars facing field-based and case study courses. Such study is designed to open windows on many more issues and complexities than can fully be learned in a single course, or even program of study. It is more like the beginning of a new way of thinking diagnostically.

INDIVIDUAL DIAGNOSIS AND CASE REPORTING

Your music and lyrics lack lament. – IRVING BERLIN, TO A YOUNG COLE PORTER

CONTENT AND CONCEPT ORGANIZER

Diagnostic-Prescriptive Teaching is the top floor in complex problem solving, and this is true in every field from medicine to engineering. It has guidelines and patterns, but few hard and fast rules. It is not so much about collecting data and impressions, but parsing them for connections, meanings, and implications. This chapter lays out the historical and conceptual basis and issues surrounding the Diagnostic-Prescriptive Process, Philosophy, and Practices. Each of these principles of diagnosis and matched intervention is fleshed-out in later chapters as they are now being applied in both inclusionary classrooms and in clinical-tutorial settings.

CHAPTER OUTLINE

SLIGHTLY BACK TO THE FUTURE
The Way We Were
Re-Basing
Fine Tuning
It Started (and Continues) with Ordinary Teachers
　Doing Extraordinary Things

OVERVIEW OF INDIVIDUAL DIAGNOSIS
AND THE FORMAL CASE REPORT
Definitions
Diagnostic Process
The 6-D Model for Guiding Diagnostic
　Problem-Solving
Write It in Pencil!

PRINCIPLES OF DIAGNOSIS

DIAGNOSIS IS A *STORY WITH A POINT*

COLLECTING INTAKE INFORMATION
Teacher Referral
Planning and Conducting Intake Interviews

Different Linguistic and Cultural Backgrounds
Intake Observation

DEVELOPING THE CASE STUDY
A Problem-Solving Process for Case Study
　Development
The Purpose and Audience of the Case Report
Details on Writing Sections of the Case Report
Polishing the Case Report
Common Case Study Patterns

THE EXIT CONFERENCE

EXTENDED SAMPLE CASE REPORT

REVIEW

PREVIEW

SLIGHTLY BACK TO THE FUTURE

A great deal of external regulation by legislative and policy boards governs the workings of teachers and teaching. Occasionally stifling, a few of these requirements are enjoying more collaborative support. One consensus is a growing movement to expect teachers, especially reading specialists, to be more educated in conducting complex and nuanced assessment, matched by precise instructional interventions, one case at a time. A resurgence of Diagnostic-Prescriptive Teaching (DPT) could bestow prestige on the field of Literacy Education, and contribute to more *informed* as well as more "balanced" reading instruction. Diagnostic-Prescriptive Teaching serves a variety of individual learning needs at remedial, corrective, and developmental levels, for children from diverse linguistic and cultural backgrounds.

The case-based approach to Diagnostic-Prescriptive Teaching can be traced to the founders of the field of reading education. Many of these early–twentieth-century educators were psychologists, drawn to the study of reading by the realization that the complex "act" of reading draws from and sometimes sheds light on the reader's perceptions, attitudes, and feelings. There are a number of other ways in which the field seems to be moving forward with an increasing awareness of its past.

The Way We Were

Change is in the wind. A recent study of "exemplary schools" found the reading specialist to be playing the role of "collaborative consultant" (Bean, Swan, & Knaub, 2003). This is reminiscent of the period between 1955 and 1975, when most reading teachers were called "reading consultants" even when they operated out of only one school. The profession attracted some of the nation's leading minds. The historical record is evident in living memories and in primary resources. One such record is found in the *Webster's Third International Dictionary* (1971). Under the term *diagnose* the dictionary uses the following example to define this abstract level of problem-solving: "The teacher *diagnosed* and corrected the boy's reading difficulty." Under the related term *diagnostic* it offers this definition and example: "1. Adapted to or used for the furthering of diagnosis: employing or marked by the methods of diagnosis: concerned with diagnosis [as in] "diagnostic reading tests."

Consider now the term *remedial*. Of all the examples that could have been offered, that same unabridged dictionary makes the following notation: "2. concerned with the correction of faulty study habits, the improvement of skills imperfectly learned, and the raising of a pupil's general competence [as in] (remedial reading) (remedial instruction)."

There is a growing movement to expect teachers and reading specialists to be educated in conducting complex and nuanced assessment.

Between 1955 and 1975 most reading teachers were called "reading consultants" and the profession attracted some of the nation's leading minds.

Diagnosis and remediation, formerly this profession's stock-in-trade, has been in the closet in recent years. Microsoft Word 2000, the most widely used word processing system, does not even recognize the word *remediation*. So why does this "old world" model of assessing and teaching persist? What could have happened between the 1960s and the present to account for its decline and apparent rebirth?

Re-Basing

A recap of some of the points made in the historical overview in Chapter 1 sheds light on this question as well. A number of factors led to its decline. The most notable of these:

- Wrong Place, Wrong Time—Diagnostic-Prescriptive Teaching was employed during a time when the field was facing an onslaught of social, economic, and cultural challenges, for example, education for formerly disenfranchised populations, such as African Americans and new waves of immigrants, especially from Mexico and South America.
- Realizations about De Facto Segregation—There were concerns about an appearance of "de facto" segregation, as in remedial reading classes that had large proportions of African-American and Latino children.
- "Critical Literacy/Pedagogy"—This enlightened liberationist philosophy has quietly objected to Diagnostic-Prescriptive Teaching since it sometimes appeared to be more interested in testing, sorting, and tracking students, than in sorting out their needs and integrating them back into the mainstream.
- Whole Language—This once-reigning philosophy did not ascribe to intensive diagnosis. It offered essentially one prescription: read, read, and read some more.
- Reading Authorities' Doubts—Some otherwise savvy reading specialists have expressed doubts about Diagnosis and Remediation. Johnston and Allington (1991) did so implicitly in the *Reading Research Handbook II.* Klenk and Kibby (2000) were more explicit in *Reading Research Handbook III,* where they declare a *Requiem for Remedial Reading* despite an almost reluctant admission that it just won't go away, noting in fact that it seems to produce results, often at twice the rate of prior progress. (Klenk and Kibby also suggested that it be called "mediation" rather than "remediation.")
- Spurious Reasoning—Some seemingly innocent but invalidly reasoned ideas came into vogue and then doubled back on their own good intentions. One was the LD movement that became a protected part of federal law with the Americans with Disabilities Act. This provided

Some otherwise savvy reading specialists have expressed serious doubts about Diagnosis and Remediation.

incentives for students to have "Learning Disabled" designations rather than the stigmatizing designation "reading disabled"—even though 80 percent of LD students have reading problems.

- The "Matthew Effect"—This notion was intended to bring attention and resources to those who had fallen into what had previously been known as a "cumulative deficit." Instead, the rich were accused of getting richer at the expense of the poor getting poorer. In absolute terms this may not be true, and it tends to perpetuate every issue being reduced to one of race, gender, or class, more so than one of responsibility. This applies personally to students, and equally so on the parts of the school and individual teachers (Manzo, 2003).

- UnBalanced Reading—The field of reading has sometimes shown a weakness, despite extraordinary successes, for being unable to "balance," self-regulate, or immunize itself against a tendency toward excess, *over-prescriptions* of "this or that."

While these swings may be a symptom of progress, they have destabilized the field, and can be a public relations disaster. The most unsettling aspect may be the tendency to make teachers feel like dinosaurs as each new set of philosophies and strategies takes its (overreached) place. This is demoralizing to the profession and deserves careful review. Here is a place where the Diagnostic-Prescriptive tradition may be of value.

Fine Tuning

History and anecdotal accounts support the power of precision diagnosis and prescription. Once Cole Porter reluctantly asked Irving Berlin what his music lacked. What did Berlin have that resulted in Berlin composing so many classical lyrics and melodies, such as "Mammy," "America the Beautiful," and "White Christmas"? Berlin must have given his art and, by inference, Porter's shortcomings, considerable inner-address *before* this question was posed, because his answer changed the history of music. He said, "Cole, your music lacks 'lament.' That is the ingredient of my Yiddish heritage [*Yes, a Jewish man wrote the most popular Christmas carol of all times*], and my empathy and closeness to the 'Negro' experience and rhythms." Set on a course of self-correction, Porter produced a barrel of "soulful" American classics of his own.

What Berlin offered to Porter was precision diagnosis and prescription. It is neither medical nor scientific. It is that quality of thinking that excites penetrating, self-generating, synergistic solutions. It is the "source code" and resonator for science, art, medicine, and empathy—the most distinctive of human traits.

It Started (and Continues) with Ordinary Teachers Doing Extraordinary Things

The diagnosis and differential treatment of reading and learning disabilities started and continues with ordinary teachers doing extraordinary things. Teachers wisely realized that kids had different learning needs; when those needs could be reasonably met, students who might have languished began to thrive. This process of differentiation was "strategized" into the *diagnostic-prescriptive teaching model.* In this formal model, a savvy classroom teacher or reading specialist conducts an "assessment" to determine skill weaknesses. She then plans a series of steps, as simple as sitting "Charlie" closer to her, or lessons as un-extraordinary as teaching some high-frequency letter clusters like *ike* in *bike, Mike, like* so that "Charlie" and others struggling to learn phonics get a "rule-in-operation" rather than just a *rule.* We detect patterns more easily than we learn rules. So this simple lesson sets the stage for discovering and stating the pattern-based "rule": *The long sound for a vowel often is signaled by being followed by a consonant and a silent e.* Taking the next step, the teacher, now becoming a *diagnostic-prescriptive specialist,* pretests "Charlie" and friends on other high-frequency letter clusters, like *ing,* and *am,* and *eck.* She checks her "worksheets" to find some that suit the child's need for mastering letter clusters to make reading easier. Then she stops by their desks to make her presence felt, encourages attention to the page more than one another, and extends quick help, before frustration might set in. Finally, she may give "Charlie" a note for his parent, with an explanation to him, saying, "See if you can find two other words with the *eck* sound by tomorrow. Ask anyone at home for help." There it is: diagnosis, prescription, instruction, scaffolding, practice, and homework that extends learning/ thinking beyond the classroom.

Diagnosis started with ordinary teachers.

OVERVIEW OF INDIVIDUAL DIAGNOSIS AND THE FORMAL CASE REPORT

Definitions

Individual, or Intensive, diagnosis and formal reporting have a long tradition in the field of reading. A **Case Study** is a problem-solving process of analyzing an individual student's progress in reading, based on thoughtfully collected data, for the purpose of identifying the most beneficial set of instructional recommendations, based on precise identification of the student's current and predicted strengths and needs. The collected data may include any reasonable combination of objective observations; formal and informal assessment results; and background information from parents, teachers, and school records. Subjective interpretations of observations also have a place in the Case Study, but should be carefully worded to distinguish between inference from facts, and *pure conjecture*, which is acceptable as an intuitive possibility, but requires critical review and must be supported with evidence and sound logic. Typically, an Informal Reading Inventory is given early in the Case Study process, to evaluate word recognition and comprehension in comparison with the student's grade in school. The results of the reading test provide the basis for deciding what types of follow-up assessments need to be done. **Follow-up assessment** is the "second round" of information gathering. It is designed to clarify hypotheses generated by analysis of the individual reading test, and may address any relevant combination of reading-specific and reading-related factors. The **Case Report** is formal documentation of the Case Study process. A sample format for a basic Case Report is provided and explained later in this chapter, along with a sample case report.

Diagnostic Process

From the Greek, the origin of the word *diagnosis* reveals its meaning: "to know thoroughly."

Individual diagnosis, according to Angela Jaggar (1985), is high-level problem solving that requires the teacher to engage in profound and resourceful thinking. The origin of the word *diagnosis* itself reveals that it is from the Greek, meaning "to know thoroughly." In its original form, it implies taking something apart, or "looking through" an object to see its inner workings (Liddell & Scott, 1940). It is a kind of de-construction before re-construction. In short, diagnosis amounts to investigative research to uncover the nature of a specific student's reading problem, so that this bit of knowledge can add to the teacher's knowledge base for solving similar problems when working with other students. This process requires a great deal of knowledge, experience, sensitivity, adroitness, wisdom, objectivity, and even *prognosis*—looking into the future—to predict long-term effects. Importantly, this can be more positive than the over-extrapolation of the reading problem alone which can make a child's future look quite grim. This is why a quality diagnosis will also include noting a student's strengths.

Some secondary purposes of individual diagnosis are:

1. to acquire and interpret evidence needed to improve all learning and teaching;
2. to obtain process information to be added to the usual final (or product-oriented) exam;
3. to obtain a quality-control measure to determine whether each step of the instructional process has been working or needs to be changed; and

4. to get objective information to offset a possibly subjective or misleading impression gained from a classroom teacher. (Teachers are on target a great deal, but we all have made some "bad calls.")

Teachers, while often on target, occasionally make some "bad calls."

The 6-D Model for Guiding Diagnostic Problem-Solving

The creation of useful categories is always a landmark development in any area of knowledge, particularly in one requiring the collection, organization, and interpretation of large amounts of data. Categories are the building blocks of specialized schemata, or the "slots" used to receive and process information.

Weiner and Cromer (1967) have provided educators with such a set of categories. The intent of the Weiner-Cromer model was to point out that previous diagnostic models (such as those based on a scope and sequence of skills) essentially were "deficit models." The assumption was that if a student was behind in reading, the solution was to identify where in the skills sequence the student had broken down, and re-teach the sequence from that point on. The Weiner-Cromer "4-D" Model added three categories for more strategic consideration: differences, disruptions, and defects. The 4-D Diagnostic Model is a useful mental rubric: a reminder to consider all four categories of factors that may influence reading development, and to acquire the techniques and skills needed to guide informed observation, structured informal assessment, and prescriptive guidance in these four major areas of possible human dysfunction. We have found it useful to add two additional Ds. Together, the 6-D Model looks like this:

Deficits: educational factors: gaps in developmental learning, such as phonemic awareness, comprehension strategies, vocabulary knowledge, or general fund of information

Differences: environmental/cultural factors that may place the learner at a disadvantage in educational settings

Disruptions: emotional or attitudinal factors such as dependency, lack of motivation, intrusive thoughts (such as hostility, or feelings of being "put-upon") that interfere with clear thinking and hence educational progress

Defects: physiological, or inborn, factors such as vision, hearing, developmental disabilities, general health, or neurological organization that can inhibit "normal" educational progress

De-limitations: a reminder to consider problems that may have been created by "schooling," and by some of the poor choices educational institutions may have made in curriculum and instruction; we must take responsibility for a generation of youngsters who did not receive adequate education in phonetic analysis and computational skills, in writing and book-length reading.

Defaults: a reminder that students often have real strengths even though they may overly fall back on them when a weakness is challenged—as when a student overuses context to guess at how to pronounce a word rather than using word analysis strategies; while this clearly is overcompensation, and needs to be addressed with close instruction in attention to individual letters and words, it also can reveal a wonderful capacity for verbal banter and imagination, two admirable qualities that can serve one well in other aspects of the curriculum and in life. (Overall, whatever we "default" to when challenged is an area that can also be called a strength. For example, quick wit may get one in occasional trouble in an academic lesson, but it can make one a good companion as we face the uncertainties of each day.)

One of our Masters students, Ilona Takakura, has suggested a 7th that overlaps somewhat with De-Limitations, but may deserve separate attention. It is Discontinuities. These would include external disruptions to a learner's life circumstances, such as: prolonged illness, drugs/alcohol/violence in the home, or joint and unsettling custody arrangements. In general, these "models" become a system for seeking and sorting out relevant information. The categories are used to organize much of this text. They are repeated and extended in chapters ahead. Look especially for further examples of the *default* category, since it is a rather new diagnostic path in reading analysis. It is already showing up in the literature in the field as is evident in a recent Case Report from Dewitz and Dewitz (2003) that reads as follows: "When Mark could not make the necessary inferences, he *defaulted* to excessive elaboration, relying on prior knowledge, experience, and invented ideas to answer the questions" (428).

Write It in Pencil!

Regarding diagnosis: All conclusions should be considered provisional, or subject to modification, since:

- The reading process is filled with unknowns.
- We can never completely know someone else.

- Each person is in a state of change even while we are studying him or her. (This is especially true of children for whom each day is an experiment with different ways to feel, to think, and to be.)
- Any slight new piece of information can cause all other information to be re-aligned to form an entirely different picture than the one suggested on first analysis.
- There is infinitely more richness and complexity in nature than one can imagine.

Diagnosis is not easily mastered, although there are masters from whom much can be learned. Several have left us a legacy of their learnings and insights in their teachings, articles, books, and assessment instruments and protocols. The citations in this text were selected to provide a vicarious apprenticeship with these masters-of-the-craft. In addition, we suggest that educators cultivate the following mindsets and habits:

> Diagnosis is not easily mastered, although there are masters.

- Be attentive to the experiences that are shared with and channeled to you by your course instructor.
- Seek a variety of classroom teaching experiences at different levels and in different settings.
- Develop a special attentiveness to students with special needs.
- Stay abreast of the literature of the field throughout your career.
- Take advantage of opportunities to conduct and be part of diagnostic case studies.
- Reflect and compare notes on cases with peers and veteran diagnosticians.
- Make a commitment to be a lifelong student of the craft, even if you do not expect to practice it regularly.

Each case shared and experienced strengthens knowledge and skill in case-based reasoning. Eventually, knowledge of individual cases synergizes, and wisdom as well as knowledge begins to thrive.

PRINCIPLES OF DIAGNOSIS

Unlike rules, principles are flexible concepts derived from knowledge and human experience. Presented here are eight *principles* of diagnosis that have been deduced from a multitude of clinical cases, research reports, and human experience. Think of these as "talking points" for a professional seminar.

1. *Intensive diagnosis should always be undertaken for the purpose of instructional change.* Diagnosis is undertaken when a formal screening process or referral indicates that a student is not making optimal

> Diagnosis is undertaken to inform instructional change.

progress. The purpose of diagnosis is to alter the student's environment in ways that will enable him or her to make better progress. Diagnosis should not be undertaken unless there is a willingness to alter the instructional environment. There are two ways to ensure this: If at all possible, observe the student in the regular class setting. And remind yourself that the word "therefore" should implicitly follow each reported test finding.

Diagnosis is guided by subjective experience, but conducted objectively.

2. *Diagnosis should be guided by subjective experience, but conducted objectively.* Every little bit of human experience can become a voice from the past to help you find your way through a diagnostic work-up, but you must make every effort not to let that voice drown out the voice of the student before you.

In other words, it can be all right to say to yourself at some point, "Why, this child is just like my brother—he just doesn't do his homework, and he is reckless and irresponsible!" With this gut-level response, you have found a point of reference for the child before you. However, the professional diagnostician must dig deeper and raise questions like "How is he different from my brother?" and "Was my brother really irresponsible, or did he only appear that way to me—perhaps because I was too serious, and being the big brother/sister?" When this introspective set of questions is completed, some stronger hypothesis is formed. This should be checked wherever possible against a second opinion from someone who is different in nature from the first diagnostician or teacher. When the process is completed, the diagnostician should know the child better, the brother better, and him/herself better. In this way, the diagnostician's "subjective" inner voice has been made more objective, and every similar case encountered will benefit from the diagnostician's enriched understanding and intuition. This is also known as "secondary sense learning," as the learning theorist D. O. Hebb (1949) more properly referred to the remarkable human capacity to gather, abstract, generalize, store, and apply experiences and insights to new problems and situations.

3. *Diagnosis should be cross-referenced.* Diagnostic conclusions should never be drawn from single measures. Indications from any one test or observation should be cross-referenced with the student's performance on other same and similar tests and with reported observations of the student's behavior in the classroom, in peer settings, and/or at home. A good way to guide your conclusions is to imagine that the things you will say will be checked by an editor and a research staff before they will go public. This principle should not inhibit you from making guesses and exploring possibilities: Simply be certain to express them as guesses in need of verification.

4. *Diagnosis should be parsimonious.* Parsimony is the simplest and most relevant explanation of the "presenting problem." Don't overanalyze. Parsimony implies the need to include assessment of all factors pertinent to a student's problem, but avoid tests of irrelevant factors. With regard to this, the diagnosis should rule out all measures of factors that do not contribute to the individual student's problem. A useful way to remember this principle is provided by the maxim: When you hear hoofbeats, think horses, not zebras! (Unless you happen to be in the Serengeti.)

Parsimony requires the simplest explanation of the "presenting problem."

5. *Diagnosis should be continuous.* A Case Study is a snapshot in time, undertaken only in cases where it seems warranted, and should be considered part of the routine and ongoing assessment process for all students. The Case Study recommendations should be implemented, and the results periodically evaluated, before the next round of instructional decisions.

6. *Diagnosis should determine the seriousness and long-term effect of the problem.* The diagnostician is expected to make two important determinations: How acute or severe is the problem, and how chronic or long-standing, therefore resistant to change is it? Looking ahead to life after school can be a valuable means of understanding what needs to be done for the child. School puts everyone under pressure. Grading systems are inherently harsh, and tend to call up defensive postures and biochemical responses that are narrowing and self-destructive. Some individuals respond by compulsively completing every assignment and striving to "ace" every test. Others respond by missing assignments, and eventually succumbing, in stages that resemble near-death experiences, to the "fact" that they are failures. Our sense is that during the prolonged school experience, more than 60 percent of the school-age population eventually comes to feel terribly inadequate. For 50 percent this is simply because they attend schools obsessed with having everyone on grade level, even those children born with an IQ of 100 or less, who can be said to be doing "just fine" if their best efforts are yielding slightly "below average" grades.

School puts everyone under pressure.

The wise diagnostician will try to see the future, or formulate a "prognosis." This can be frightening sometimes, as when you see a child whose anger and frustration are monumental and building. For the most part, however, it should permit you to say things that are comforting to both parents and children, since most of us go on to lead successful and productive lives despite what happens to us in school.

Diagnosis is enriched by efforts at prognosis.

7. *Diagnosis should include student self-evaluation.* Diagnosis should not be "done to" students; it should be "done with" them. To make this shift, it is necessary to learn to engage in "diagnostic dialogs." That is, to converse with students by encouraging them to reflect on their learning behaviors, as well as participate in the selection and development of appropriate remedial strategies.

Diagnosis is the search for strengths as well as weaknesses.

8. *Diagnosis should search for strengths as well as weaknesses.* This principle is a reminder to consider the "whole child" in the evaluation process, rather than simply seeking out problem areas. The Default category above should help in making such projections. The message here is that overall human development is the primary goal of schooling, and that reading is merely our focus area, or touch-point, of responsibility.

DIAGNOSIS IS A STORY WITH A POINT

Diagnosis is about story.

At a metaphoric level, diagnosis is about *story,* specifically, *biography.* If it is approached in this way, the *steps* and *rules* become fairly evident. The goals of writing biographies for struggling readers are to help them to find their voices, to guide them in telling their stories in ways that evoke empathy more than sympathy, and to help set the next chapters of their lives onto a different path. Some stories will not be about academic achievement, but they should all be about lives well lived. To do this it is necessary to collect enough of the present picture and "backstory" to reasonably predict how the story will unfold with and without "intervention." Ideally, it becomes evident that this is an unfinished personal pilgrimage; the subject should be involved in co-writing it so that it becomes an *autobiography.* The Elements of the story are the Elements of Diagnosis: Characters (protagonists, antagonists, and tangential); Plot line (conflicts and achievements leading to today); Point of view (Whose voice tells the story or gives us the crucial information? Is there one "omniscient" narrator or multiple views? What would happen if other points of view were validated?). As the stories continue, try *storyboarding* the future with and without different prescriptions and levels of collaboration from the student, parents, and school. Stories contain structural and character elements that are familiar to most of us as "signposts" to help students think about themes in their own life plays that contain plausible or implausible actions. This is the heart of the therapeutic dialog with each student: What are the options? Which are best for this individual?

Notice that when we talk of diagnosis as *story,* questions about whether we should be investigating reading-related "psychological-social-physiological-familial" issues are answered in the affirmative. Everyone knows of lives, including our own, whose school days were defined, if not dominated, by seemingly remote matters: feeling shunned by peers; over-

or under-talkativeness; "looks"; vision/hearing problems; growing more or less than our peers; a teacher who moved you, or failed to; allergy headaches, and so on. Life and learning are complex, but familiar and more manageable and memorable as *story*. The human mind is constructed to function in a manner called *episodic,* or experience-based story recording and rehearsal, often in the form of "daydreaming" and lots of self-talk. Our natural human orientation and ongoing inner speech prompt us to make the individual child's *story* a more conscious part of diagnosis and prescription.

COLLECTING INTAKE INFORMATION

Teacher Referral

In most cases it is the classroom teacher who refers a student to the reading specialist, usually after consulting or meeting with the parent(s). In the sample referral form provided in Figure 2.1, note that the form includes a reminder to the teacher to inform the parent(s) that the specialist will likely be contacting them for additional background information.

An intake interview can be so productive that it may be in order even for youngsters you think you know well.

Planning and Conducting Intake Interviews

Interviews with parents, the child, and other teachers are an efficient means of learning about all aspects of a student's difficulties in learning. An intake interview can be so productive that it may be in order even for students you may think that you know well. Get ready for the interview by thinking of yourself as preparing to write a student's biography.

An interview is access to a student's ongoing life story with you as the biographer. When possible, interview the student, both parents (or guardians), and acquire anecdotal reports from teachers and childcare providers. When properly conducted, the interview can lead to insights for both the interviewer and the person interviewed. In this sense, it can be therapeutic in itself since it is a formal beginning to accepting and dealing with a problem.

The student interview often is conducted during your first meeting: It is an important opportunity to establish a working "rapport" with the student. **Rapport** is an easy, comfortable relationship that can be achieved when the teacher/interviewer is prepared to put the student at ease and enlist cooperation. Rapport is essential to a productive interview and to subsequent assessment sessions. If students are apprehensive or otherwise uncertain, they may not perform in a way that best represents their ability.

FIGURE **2.1**

SAMPLE REFERRAL FORM

School:_____   Student: _____

Teacher:_____   Grade: _____

Room #: _____   Birthdate:_____

Date of Referral:_____   Age: _____

Reason for Referral:

Describe the student's typical classroom work habits and behavior:

___ yes ___ no   The student's parent(s) have been informed of the referral (please explain briefly below).

___ yes ___ no   The student's parent(s) have been informed that the reading specialist will contact them for additional background information related to the evaluation.

Following are some additional guidelines for conducting effective student and parent interviews:

1. Enter the interview with a genuine interest in the student (the protagonist in the story that you are assembling).
2. Be sure the person interviewed (particularly if this is the student) understands who you are and what is being undertaken.
3. Follow an interview form, but don't ignore potentially useful information that might emerge, merely to get through each item on an interview form.
4. Familiarize yourself ahead of time with the interview form, and reword items as needed in language most comfortable for you.
5. Ask for permission to record the interview as well as to take notes.
6. Keep a neutral attitude by avoiding approving or rejecting remarks, or even by intermittently taking notes (try to write the same amount throughout the interview).
7. Ask occasionally if there is anything else that the child or parent might wish to add, even to simple biographical questions, then remember to *pause* for a response.

8. Ask intermittently "why" they think something is as they report (for example, "*Why* is it, do you think, that you don't like math?")
9. Remember to ask some open-ended questions: "Tell me about your reading"; "Do you think her reading problem is affecting other aspects of her school or personal life?"
10. Avoid unnecessary technical terms in asking questions ("Is the child an *introvert?*")
11. Be on guard against the tendency to become overly occupied with yourself in an interview. Self-consciousness and insecurity can cause subconscious ego defense on your part, such as talking too much, speaking in an affected manner, being overly apologetic, or simply appearing nervous.
12. Listen not only to what youngsters and parents say, but to what they might mean.

In general, keep in mind that "people operate from an internal dialog, one that reflects their own values and desires" (Heron, 2003, 569). Figures 2.2 and 2.3 offer sample interview forms: one for use with students, and one for parents. Figure 2.2 offers an interview schedule that is better directed at parents or guardians. First, however, consider the careful wording offered by Indrisano (1982) as a means of initiating an empathetic diagnostic conversation:

> Today we'll try to discover more about you and the ways you learn. We'll need two kinds of experts, one expert on learning and one expert on you. I've studied about learning. You've been making discoveries about yourself all of your life while you've been living there inside you. If we work together, we will have the information we need to help you. I'll begin by asking a few questions."

"Today we'll try to discover more about you. . . . We'll need two kinds of experts, one expert on learning and one expert on you." (Lee Indrisano)

The sample interview forms that follow include five areas that Indrisano pursues: what the youngster does well; does not do well; what coping strategies he or she is using; which coping or learning strategies he or she is not using; and what he or she would most like parents and teachers to know about him or her so they can help him or her to achieve.

Different Linguistic and Cultural Backgrounds

It is especially important to ask the above questions and prompt further responses from students with different linguistic and cultural backgrounds, since the context of their lives may have been quite different from most North American routines, experiences, and expectations. One way to uncover and better understand students from different cultural backgrounds is to adopt a strategy for teaching visual literacy to young children developed by Janet Richards and Nancy Anderson (2003). Essentially,

FIGURE **2.2**

SAMPLE STUDENT INTERVIEW FORM

Interviewer Information

Interviewer's Name: _____ Interview Date: _____

Student Information

Student's Name: _____ Birthdate: _____

Grade: _____ Teacher's Name: _____ Age (years/months): _____

1. Tell me what you usually do when you get home from school: _____

   _____

2. Do you have any brothers or sisters (names/ages)? _____

   _____

3. Tell me about your friends: Who are they? What are they like?_____

   _____

4. Whom do you get along best with at home? Whom don't you get along with? _____

   _____

5. Do you have pets? Do you help feed and take care of them? _____

   _____

6. Do you have regular chores at home? What are they? Do you tend to do them as you should? _____

   _____

7. What is your favorite television program? What do you like about it? _____

   _____

8. What is the name of your school? _____

9. How do you get along with your teacher and classmates?_____

10. What are your favorite and least favorite subjects in school? Why? _____

    _____

11. How do you feel when you are in school (hot/cold; healthy/sickly; comfortable/restless)?

    _____

12. What would you most like teachers to change about school? _____

    _____

13. What would you most like your parents to change about your home life? _____

    _____

14. What would you most like to change about yourself? _____

_____

15. If you had 3 wishes, what would they be? _____

_____

16. What would you like to do for a living when you grow up? _____

_____

Myself as a Reader

17. Tell me about your reading. Do you ever have trouble reading? _____

_____

18. Who has helped you learn to read? _____

19. What kinds of things do you like to read? _____

20. What kinds of things do you not like to read? _____

21. Do you often read at home? _____

22. What do you think makes a person a good reader? _____

23. Who is the best reader you know? _____

24. Is everyone in your family a good reader? _____

25. Do you think reading is important? _____

26. Which is better: reading or watching TV? _____

STW, as it is called (for "show," "think," "wonder"), involves showing a variety of pictures and having the student indicate: What do I see? What do I think? What do I wonder?

Intake Observation

Observing the student in the classroom is another means of obtaining rich diagnostic information. Even a brief observation can yield insights into the student's attitudes, interactions with peers, and behavior during instruction. Socio-historical theories of *agency*—a person's power to influence his or her situation—are useful in understanding classroom dynamics, since they allow for interpreting an individual's actions and the context that may be influencing those actions (Bakhtin, 1986; Heron, 2003). Figure 2.4 (page 57) provides a sample format for structuring an intake observation.

FIGURE **2.3**

SAMPLE PARENT INTERVIEW FORM

Interviewer's Name: _____   Interview Date: _____

Student's Name: _____   Birthdate: _____   Age: _____

Home Address: _____   Telephone: _____

School: _____   Grade: _____   Male/Female: _____

Person Being Interviewed: _____

(address and phone, if different): _____

I. Home Background

Father's Name: _____   Occupation: _____

Mother's Name: _____   Occupation: _____

Siblings: *Name*   *Sex*   *Age*   *Grade*

_____   _____   _____   _____

_____   _____   _____   _____

_____   _____   _____   _____

_____   _____   _____   _____

Other persons living in the home: _____

Marital status of parents: _____

With whom does child live? _____

Child's relationships with other family members (close to; at odds with): _____

Language spoken in the home: _____

Examples of reading material in the home: _____

Parent's attitude toward reading difficulties: _____

II. Physical Status

General health (poor, good, excellent): _____

Date of last complete physical examination: _____

Doctor's name and address: _____

Major chronic illnesses, operations, accidents, and allergies: _____

_____

Physical handicaps: _____

Present height: _____   Present weight: _____

Vision: _____   Hearing: _____   Speech: _____

Motor coordination: _____   Preferred hand: _____

Rest and sleep habits: _____

Energy and strength levels: _____

Eating habits; appetite: _____

Tensions: _____

Outdoor activities: _____Other: _____
_____

III. Emotional Factors

Indicate behavior patterns observed on a scale of 1 (low) to 5 (high)

_____ aggressive	_____ hyperactive	_____ overly dependent
_____ anxious	_____ hypoactive	_____ poor self-control
_____ apathetic	_____ immature	_____ sense of humor
_____ curious	_____ impulsive	_____ sensitivity
_____ daydreamer	_____ infantile behavior	_____ social success
_____ defensive	_____ inferiority complex	_____ talkative
_____ fearful	_____ nail biting	_____ thumb sucking
_____ hostile	_____ obsessive	_____ withdrawn

Comments on personal-social adjustment: _____
_____
_____

IV. School History

Day care/preschool experiences: _____

Kindergarten experience: _____

Age at entrance to first grade: _____

Schools attended: _____

Has attendance been regular? _____   Grades skipped or repeated: _____

Approximate report card grades or yearly grade level achievement (disregard if cumulative record is attached):

Grade: 1   2   3   4   5   6   7   8   9   10   11   12

Reading _____

Language Arts _____

Handwriting _____

Spelling _____

Mathematics _____

Social Studies _____

Science _____

Other _____
_____

Favorite subject: _____ Least favorite subject: _____

Special abilities: _____

Comments on schooling: _____

V. Reading Progress

Type of initial reading instruction: _____

Child's attitude toward reading: _____

Reading interests: _____

When were reading difficulties first noticed?_____

Type of difficulties noted: _____

Remedial effort of any type to date: _____

Present status in reading: _____

Are there any other factors in the child's reading or academic history that you think might help
to explain present difficulties in reading and learning?_____
_____

Observations/Notes:

_____

_____

_____

_____

_____

FIGURE **2.4**

SAMPLE INTAKE OBSERVATION FORM

Observer Information

Observer's Name: _____   Date of Observation: _____

Student Information

Student's Name: _____   Grade: _____   Teacher's Name: _____

Use the letter-coded list below to record the type of activity at each time interval. Observations should be recorded at approximately 10-minute intervals.

Activities: **A** Teacher-directed instruction   **B** Small group work   **C** Independent seatwork
            D Class discussion   **E** Other

Time	Activity	Observations

Interpretations: Use a scale of 1 (low) to 5 (high) to evaluate the student on each trait below:

_____ aggressive	_____ hyperactive	_____ overly dependent
_____ anxious	_____ hypoactive	_____ poor self-control
_____ apathetic	_____ immature	_____ sense of humor
_____ curious	_____ impulsive	_____ sensitivity
_____ daydreamer	_____ infantile behavior	_____ social success
_____ defensive	_____ withdrawn	_____ talkative
_____ fearful	_____ hostile	_____ obsessive

Conclusions: (Continue on back if needed.) _____

_____

DEVELOPING THE CASE STUDY

A Problem-Solving Process for Case Study Development

In preparing to develop a Case Report, a teacher should be guided by the same problem-solving process used to guide observation and testing. At this point, the process should look something like this:

State the problem:
Why is the student being
evaluated?

1. *State the "problem."* Based on referral information, a rough statement of the "problem" to be answered by the diagnostic problem-solving process is developed: Why is the student being evaluated?

2. *Gather the facts.* Appropriate rapport is established through informal conversation and initial observational assessment sessions. Initial data are gathered and recorded from some combination of: observations of the child during instruction (either in the classroom or in activities you have planned for your individual sessions); interviews or surveys of primary caregivers and teachers; information from school records. A starting point for assessment is identified, and formal assessment is begun. Usually a phonemic awareness assessment is given (if the student is judged to be reading below second-grade level) or an individual reading test (if the student is judged to be reading at or above second-grade level).

3. *Form a hypothesis.* Based on initial assessment results, a hypothesis about the child's reading progress is developed. The hypothesis should begin with the most relevant "presenting characteristic." Depending upon the child's "observed level," the diagnostic hypothesis should address *each* of the *relevant* dimensions of literacy development, as detailed for each level below.

> *Emergent literacy:* Address concepts about print, phonemic awareness, basic and higher-order listening comprehension, and sight word vocabulary.
>
> *Beginning reading:* Address phonemic awareness, sight word vocabulary, phonetic word attack strategies, oral reading fluency, basic and higher comprehension for oral reading, silent reading, and listening.
>
> *Intermediate to pre-adult reading:* Address sight word vocabulary, phonetic word attack strategies, oral reading fluency, basic and higher comprehension for oral reading, silent reading, and listening.

In addition to these basic dimensions of literacy, the hypothesis includes identification of literacy-related factors that have most strongly influenced and/or are influencing the child's progress. If the child is not making appropriate developmental progress, the hypothesis should "widen the net," to consider possible influence of physical, cognitive, affective, and attitudinal factors.

4. *Test the hypothesis.* Follow-up assessments, often including one or more trial-teaching sessions, are conducted to test the hypothesis.

5. *State the conclusions.* When the diagnostic process is completed, all data are analyzed to form and state the conclusions. Was the hypothesis confirmed by follow-up testing, or does it need to be revised in part or entirely? If it was confirmed, the conclusion will be a restatement of your hypothesis, with each component supported by specific test results and observations. If your hypothesis was not confirmed, it should be restated to align with the assessment results and each component supported, as above, with specific test results and observations. Next, this conclusion is translated into specific "strengths" and "needs." The final step in stating your conclusions is translating these strengths and needs into specific instructional recommendations.

Now you are prepared to document your diagnostic assessment by writing a Case Report. In the Case Report, you will formally present your initial *Observations,* your *Hypothesis,* a *List of Tests and Assessments* you have conducted, the *Results* of each test and assessment conducted, and your conclusions in the form of a *Summary* of results, providing specific support for each component of your initial or revised hypothesis, a list of specific *Strengths and Needs,* and a listing of specific *Instructional Recommendations.* See Figure 2.5 for a Sample Case Report Format.

FIGURE **2.5**

SAMPLE CASE REPORT FORMAT

Report of Reading Evaluation

Child's Name: _____

Grade: _____   Age (years, months): _____

School: _____

Birthdate: _____   Dates Tested: _____

Gender: _____   Evaluated by: _____

Reason for Referral: a brief statement indicating the reason for the evaluation. This may be a statement indicating that the child was evaluated by you as part of a course in reading diagnosis and remediation

Background Information: a summary in paragraph form of the findings from any pre-testing observations, parent or teacher interviews, or background information forms that may have been collected

Tests Administered: a *numbered list* of the titles of the "tests" given, including inventories and informal procedures such as a writing sample

Observations: a description of the child's physical characteristics and general behavior during the sessions, the setting in which the sessions took place, and any other relevant observations

Test Results: for each test listed above (and in the same order): a) name the test and give a brief description of what it measures and how; b) wherever reasonable, list the results of the test in *table form;* and c) write a paragraph stating what was learned from the results of this "test." This section should present results only, not interpretations or recommendations. A sample format for reporting IR-TI results is provided below.

Informal Reading-Thinking Inventory: This individually administered test provides an estimate of the student's Independent, Instructional, and Frustration levels, and can be used to compare silent with oral reading comprehension. It may also be used to evaluate higher-order comprehension at selected grade levels. The student's oral reading is analyzed to evaluate sight word acquisition, word attack strategies, and fluency. The student's responses to questions are analyzed to evaluate comprehension processes and products.

Results: Use a chart such as the one below to record scores for all sections of the test that were administered.

Level/ Form	Oral Reading Word Recog.	Basic Comprehension	Silent Rdg Comprehension	Listening Comprehension	Higher-Order Comprehension
___ ___	___ %	___ %	___ %	___ %	___ %
___ ___	___ %	___ %	___ %	___ %	___ %
___ ___	___ %	___ %	___ %	___ %	___ %

The following reading levels were established:

Independent = _____   Instructional = _____   Frustration = _____   Listening = _____

In paragraph form, compare the student's Instructional level to grade in school. State findings related to sight word recognition and word attack: Is there a pattern to the types of miscues (omissions, substitutions, etc.)? What level of cues does the child seem to be using (orthographic, syntactic, semantic)? If there are word attack problems, what *patterns* are revealed through structural analysis?

State findings related to reading comprehension. Summarize what you learned about the relationships between comprehension and prior knowledge, enjoyment, and metacognition, and the degree to which the student's responses were congruent with the questions. Discuss any patterns that were revealed in the analysis of question types. Compare oral to silent reading comprehension, and basic to higher-order comprehension. Indicate what you learned about listening comprehension.

Results of Trial Teaching: This section should be included if trial teaching was undertaken. Each trial-teaching session should be given a descriptive label, such as "Language Experience Approach, emphasizing sight-word practice and initial consonant blends." For each trial-teaching session, state the type of lesson conducted, the reason why that particular type of lesson was undertaken, and a brief narrative summary of the *results* of the session.

Interpretations: a discussion of your *interpretations* of the findings from all tests, observations, and trial-teaching sessions. In your judgment, what do these objective and subjective observations *mean? Begin with a general statement about the child's current reading progress* (is s/he reading on, below, or above grade level?) according to the IRI, and refer to assessment findings and observa-

tions that support or contradict this generalization. Then discuss all relevant factors in order of importance.

Summary of Strengths and Needs: a two-column list of brief statements of strengths in the first column, and brief statements of *needs* in the second column

Recommendations: a *numbered list,* in order of importance, of practical things a teacher or caregiver could do to support the child's strengths and provide guidance and practice in meeting needs. This list may include general suggestions, such as helping the student to find reading materials at an appropriate independent reading level, but must also include specific instructional strategies or techniques (where specific teaching methods are recommended *briefly* describe). Note that the Recommendations section may also include recommendations for further testing.

The Purpose and Audience of the Case Report

A Case Report requires professional technical writing. It is written for other educators, and possibly parents, both immediately and in future re-evaluations of progress. It must be free of errors in grammar and spelling, and consistent in use of present or past tense within sections, as appropriate. The style should be crisp and straightforward, with a minimum of "jargon." Inferences should be supported by factual observation. Like "predictable books" for children, the format for the Case Report is an aid to the reader. Many readers will scan quickly through the list of tests given, then turn directly to the "Strengths and Needs" and "Recommendations" sections, and, lastly, look back more carefully at the test results and summary to validate the writer's conclusions. Clear headings and formatting help the reader with this type of "study-reading" of the report.

Details on Writing Sections of the Case Report

Reason for Referral, Background Information, Tests Administered, and Observations.   These introductory sections should be brief and to the point, as outlined in the sample format in Figure 2.5. They should be clearly formatted so that information can be located quickly and easily. The list of "Tests Administered" may be sequenced differently from the order in which the tests were given: Often the Informal Reading Inventory is listed first, even if a rapport-building inventory and/or a writing activity were conducted first. If testing was done in several sessions, the "Observations" should reflect this, noting relevant differences in testing conditions from session to session.

Test Results.   Test results in this section should be presented in the same order as listed in the introductory list of "Tests Administered." The introductory list of tests gives the reader a quick overview of what was done. A copy of each of the completed record forms, score sheets, or completed inventories should be attached as appendices to the Case Report. In this "Results" section, the following information should be provided:

1. Name of the test/procedure. For published tests, simply list the title. For less widely-available tests, inventories, or personally-created writing prompts or other variations, it is helpful to attach a copy in an appendix to the report.

2. Purpose of test/procedure. This is a brief statement of the purpose of the test or procedure (what it is intended to measure).

3. Results of the test. Wherever possible and reasonable, results should be provided in numerical form, in a table, with raw scores translated into percent-correct. Reporting a raw score of 12, for example, is meaningless if the reader does not know whether the total possible was 15 or 50. Translating the raw score of 12 out of a possible 15, and reporting the result as 80%, is a logical help to the reader. All available "subtest" scores should also be reported. For example, if a graded vocabulary test was given, rather than reporting simply that a child scored at the sixth-grade level, the results would be more meaningful to the reader if reported as shown in the following example:

grade	% correct
4	95
5	100
6	90
7	70

In deciding how to report test results, it is important to consider the purpose of the test. For example, a sight word test is given to determine, first, whether the child has acquired a solid sight word vocabulary and, if not, what specific sight words need to be taught. In other words, it is a "criterion-referenced" measure, rather than a "norm-referenced" one. If testing confirms that a child has acquired sight words appropriate for grade in school, it would be reasonable simply to report the percent-correct at each level given, in a table similar to the example shown above for reporting results for a graded vocabulary test. However, if a child has not acquired sight words appropriate to his or her grade level, it would be reasonable to present the table along with a list of specific words missed on the highest word list given: These are the specific words that the child needs to acquire as sight words next.

For some tests or procedures, results may be reported as subjective judgments of the evaluator. Evaluation of a writing sample, for example, may be reported in a table listing various characteristics of written samples, with the evaluator's subjective judgment, on a scale of 1 to 5 (for example) on each.

4. Narrative summary test results. The narrative summary should briefly state the relevance of the findings. For example:

"On this vocabulary test, Marie scored one year above her grade in school."

"On this sight word list, Carol was able to read most words on the primer and first grade lists, but struggled with many words on the second-grade list, which is a year below her grade in school."

Results of Trial Teaching.   Many evaluations undertaken from a diagnostic-prescriptive perspective will include one or more trial-teaching sessions, designed to test a tentative hypothesis. Each such session should be labeled to indicate the type of lesson conducted. For each session, include: a) the type of lesson taught; b) the reason why that type of lesson was selected; and c) a narrative summary of the result. A more complete reporting of the trial-teaching session may be included in the appendix to the Case Report, with other test record forms.

Interpretations.   This section is written after you have sorted through, weighed, and cross-referenced all available information about the child, including background information, observations, and results of all test results and trial-teaching sessions. It is not simply a re*statement* or re-*listing* of the test results, but your analysis of the child's reading progress, as supported by your information. In most cases, it should begin with a statement of whether the child is reading on, above, or below grade level. It should be organized according to reading-specific factors, and factors that appear to be influencing this particular child's literacy development. This narrative "heart" of the Case Report should present a logical and clear explanation for the identification of the "strengths" and "needs" listed in the following section.

Summary of Strengths and Needs.   This is a simple but *specific* two-column listing of the strengths and needs explained in the "Interpretation of Test Results" section above. Strengths and needs should be stated as specifically as possible: The more specifically they are presented, the more easily they can be translated into recommendations. They should be sequenced in order of importance. See Figure 2.6 for examples of factors stated first too generally, and then more specifically.

When considering possible strengths and needs, consider both affective as well as cognitive factors, and reading-related as well as reading-specific factors.

Recommendations.   Recommendations should be specific, concise, and directly related to the lists of strengths and needs. They should be sequenced in order of importance. This section may be divided into "Recommendations for Further Assessment," and "Recommendations for Instruction." Recommendations for instruction should be made even in cases where the student is judged to be making excellent progress.

Recommendations for instruction should *not* be general, such as "work on sight words." Rather, each recommendation should specify a method or technique to be used, such as:

- Make word cards for first-grade sight words. Build on interest in science to create Language Experience stories about science-related pictures, and use a number of the word-card sight words. Use a variety of

Diagnostic-prescriptive perspective evaluations typically include some trial teaching.

FIGURE **2.6**

EXAMPLES OF STRENGTH/NEED SUMMARY STATEMENTS

Statements Presented Too Generally	Statements Presented More Specifically
Strengths	
Sight words	Sight words at instructional level, in isolation and in context
Vocabulary	Ability to define words used in instructional level material
Fluency	Fluency in oral reading of instructional level material
Phonetic word attack	Use of context and phonetic word attack strategies to decode unfamiliar words
Comprehension	Good basic and higher-order comprehension One grade above placement
Needs	
Sight words	Sight words at first-grade level
Vocabulary	Strategies for predicting word meaning from context, and connecting new word meanings to current knowledge and personal experience
Fluency	Phrasing, intonation, and attention to punctuation in oral reading of materials at first-grade level
Phonetic word attack	Attention to medial vowels in unfamiliar words, and strategies for decoding multisyllabic words
Comprehension	Metacognitive monitoring and fix-up strategies; making inferences based on facts

activities to practice the sight word cards, and put them on a "word ring" for independent practice. Make sentence strips from the Language Experience stories to arrange for additional practice. Have the student copy and illustrate favorite Language Experience stories.

- Use two, large, foamcore boards to create a portable "Word Wall" for use in decoding unfamiliar words. Add three to four words per session to the wall, following the steps in that method. Model and encourage analogic decoding strategies when the student encounters unfamiliar words in print.

- Build on interest in ice skating and strength in basic reading comprehension at grade 5 by finding and copying articles on the subject for use in developing vocabulary strategies. Have the student use a highlighter to mark all unfamiliar words in an article. After discussing the article, discuss possible meanings of the highlighted words. Use the Subjective Approach to Vocabulary and Motor

Imaging alternately to build strategies for learning new word meanings.

- Build on self-confidence, humor, and social adeptness to discourage "word calling," and focus attention on meaning. Locate a series of short, high-interest, news-type pieces, and have the student write short responses to each in a humorous vein. Use a tape recorder for "Radio Reading" practice, having the student re-read and re-record the pieces and the personal responses until they are of "radio quality." Play the finished recordings for a friend or parent.

Polishing the Case Report

Following are a few points to check as you review your Case Report:

1. Be sure all basic facts are current and accurate (age, grade, gender, and so on).
2. State the full name of every test employed, and what the test is designed to measure.
3. Use simple declarative sentences. Keep verb tense parallel within sections of the report.
4. Avoid unnecessarily technical language, but don't shy from appropriate professional language if the context supports it and makes its meaning clear to an intelligent lay reader.
5. Write to your "audience"—usually other teachers and/or parents.
6. We live in a litigious society; write as if your audience could become: a newspaper, a court, a child, an antagonist.
7. Use phrases and words that indicate when you are reporting interpretations, rather than facts (for example, "it seems," "it appears," "in all probability," and so on).
8. For the sake of brevity, describe and explain the full nature of tests or testing protocols only as it may be necessary to understand the significance of a certain finding.
9. Use standard English, avoiding colloquialisms, contractions, and other unnecessary informality.
10. Avoid value-laden comments.
11. When reporting test results, report scores with interpretative value, such as scaled scores, percentiles, or age or grade equivalents; do not report raw scores.
12. Do not try to paint either a rosy or a dark picture; let the facts speak for themselves.
13. Be sure to carefully edit, spell-check, and revise your report before going public with it.

Common Case Study Patterns

Acquiring diagnostic skill
is a process of parsing
and categorizing many
Case Studies.

Like most new areas of learning, conducting a Case Study and developing a Case Report is hardest the first time. Acquiring diagnostic skill essentially is a process of parsing and categorizing Case Studies: Once you have worked through a number of in-depth Case Studies, you will find that they begin to "chunk" together into categories of similar cases, such as:

- Students who read accurately and quickly, but with poor comprehension. Listening comprehension usually is no higher than oral or silent reading comprehension.
- Students who read haltingly, and with frequent repetition, but with good comprehension, both at basic and higher-order levels. Listening comprehension often is markedly higher than oral or silent reading.
- Students whose oral reading is characterized by many substitutions of words that change the meaning, and even "non-words," and whose comprehension is marginal to poor. Listening comprehension usually is no higher than oral or silent reading comprehension.
- Students whose oral reading is adequate, except when they encounter unfamiliar words: They have few phonetic word attack strategies, and tend to wait for the teacher to pronounce the word for them. Oral reading comprehension is adequate, but silent reading comprehension is lower (they tend to simply skip over unknown words). Listening comprehension often is higher than oral or silent reading comprehension.
- Use of the IR-TI is revealing a fair proportion of students whose basic comprehension is on or above grade level, but whose higher-order comprehension is well below grade level. Listening comprehension usually is no higher than basic comprehension.

Using a clinical reading population as their base, Malicky and Norman (1988) factor-analyzed miscues, re-tellings, and reading level variables to reveal six potentially significant "processing factors" that might come to be used to classify remedial readers.

Their results suggest that remedial (and perhaps other) readers can be categorized into six possible styles of reading based on how they decoded words and recalled what they read.

1. Those who use "integrative processing *during* reading" as their chief mode of reading. That is, they use word clues along with background information to decode words and get meaning. The miscues of this group tend to be consistent with author meaning. This process group did not correlate with reading level (poorer readers were as likely to use this process as were better readers).

2. Those who use "integrative processing *after* reading" as their chief mode of reading. That is, they use the text and background knowledge to infer text-implied meanings. This process group did correlate with reading level (poorer readers were less likely to do this than good readers).

3. Those who use "print-based processing" as their chief mode of reading. That is, they tended to over-rely on graphic cues, without moving beyond print to meaning. Like those in category #2, this process group also correlated with reading level (poorer readers were more likely to over-rely on graphic cues than were better readers).

4. Those who use "text-based processing" as their chief mode of reading. That is, they tended to rely on the text for meaning, without associating new information with appropriate prior knowledge (most poor readers would do this, but also some good readers).

5. Those who use "monitoring" as their chief mode of reading. That is, they tended to rely on self-correction of errors. Malicky and Norman found this category difficult to interpret due to the way the data was collected, and concluded that further study was required before anything more could be said about it.

6. Those who use "knowledge-based processing" as their chief mode of reading. That is, they would use background knowledge and experience to elaborate on recalls from the text, even to the extent of displacing exact recalls from the text.

Further research is needed before these modes of operating as readers are fully understood. There is little doubt, however, that this is a much more sophisticated system of classification, with more implications for instruction than anything else now available.

THE EXIT CONFERENCE

An **exit conference** is an assessment "debriefing" that attempts to pull together all that has been learned from referral, observation, interviewing, and testing. It involves the child, parents, and other professionals who may have participated in the diagnosis. Typically, the report is addressed to the parents, but much of the conference can and should be addressed to the student. Students usually find themselves flattered by the attention and tend to behave quite maturely. Parents typically are touched by the interest and concern shown for the child. A conference can serve an important healing role for a youngster who may be feeling a bit overexamined and overscrutinized. Every debriefing is a little bit different, but all are an education for all concerned.

In a team-based assessment, it is best to have each team member report on areas relevant to his or her expertise, or at least on the tests and the roles they play. The team leader should keep the discussion going, and ensure that each team member's presentation is concise and to the point. The best way to begin a conference is by addressing a question to the student who was diagnosed: "Can you tell us your idea of why you were here to be tested today?" Questions such as this can set the stage for easy and straightforward reporting of results. On occasion it also will open up a line of discussion and revelations that you could not have anticipated. These insights may even cause all previous information to be seen in a different light.

This and related questions and test results lead to some remarkably instructive interactions. In such situations, we have seen things like:

- a remedial level child who was surprisingly masterful at manipulating his parents
- parents whose excessive concern about the child's "reading problem" came to be recognized as a substitute for a more serious problem that they seemed on the brink of disclosing but never quite disclosed (we recommended family counseling)
- parents who wished to use the conferencing period as an opportunity to punish the child for failures, or as a vehicle for seeking help with their own interpersonal problems
- comments that revealed a family history of reading problems similar to those the child was displaying

In general, conferences tend to serve as an effective form of "reality therapy." They tend to confirm what everyone has been thinking and feeling, to establish more realistic expectations, and to raise hope, since the child's problems now are being labeled and addressed. (Einstein once noted that the best way to advance something is to label it.)

It is wise to begin to collect verbal phrases and sentences for talking with students and parents. When you have collected and tried a few repeatedly, you might hold a workshop for other teachers on how they have handled parent-teacher conferences and how you do so. Here are some examples of specific findings and the phrasing that generally is most appropriate for posttest conferencing situations.

Finding: Charles scored in the 37th percentile on a standardized reading test.

Phrasing: In reading, Charles' scores indicate that he reads as well as or better than about 37 children out of 100 children in his age and grade.

Finding: Thomas has an IQ score of 97.

Phrasing: Thomas's general intelligence is within the range classified as "average." With some effort and help, he should be able to improve his reading to near grade level.

Finding: David selected "dog" as his favorite animal on the MBI (renamed ahead in the text as the Cognitive-Affective Filter Inventory).

Phrasing: Testing suggests that David's reading will likely improve with individual or small-group tutoring. He feels most comfortable in these situations, and probably would be most responsive to this friendly, personal touch.

Finding: Brenda selected "hog" and "alligator" as her favorite animals on the MBI.

Phrasing: Our tests and observations support what you and her teachers report: Brenda seems to have a poor self-image and probably is more angry and difficult to deal with than she really wants to be. She does not need to be taught *what* to answer as much as *how* to answer. She needs guided practice in responding in ways that improve her confidence in herself, and everyone else's confidence in her as well.

Finding: Mark's score on a standardized vocabulary test is in the 20th percentile.

Phrasing: "Mark, what do you think of your vocabulary?" (Wait for response.)
"Well, you're right. It could be a lot better. Do you have any ideas about how to help make it better?"
(In a case such as this one, it sometimes is best to immediately begin to focus attention on the chief area of weakness, rather than dwelling on the entire array of low scores. The conferencing session then can become a briefing session on how to improve vocabulary. When the parents are present, they are likely to express interest in helping with this need. You might then make these suggestions: 1) use a more upscaled vocabulary at home; 2) watch at least a half hour a day of informational television; and 3) subscribe to some magazines that they and the child might be interested in.)

Finding: Mike, a seventh grader, has an IQ of 117, but is reading almost two years below grade level.

Phrasing: Mike's general intelligence score is within the range classified as "High Average." We believe his actual intelligence level may be even higher than the test score indicates. As you suspected, his reading and academic work are considerably beneath grade level. To investigate the possible causes for the difference between Mike's achievement and ability level, we asked him to complete several different types of learning tasks. Our observations suggested two possibilities. (Turning to address Mike and his parents:) Tell us what you think of these:

1. Mike has a tough time accepting corrections or criticisms; as soon as he hears criticism coming, he tightens up and doesn't hear much of anything afterward.
2. Mike is susceptible to distraction. When reading silently, his attention to words and meanings seems to be interrupted by his own thoughts, which appear to drift pretty far from the task at hand.

Does this sound accurate, Mike? (This can be followed with: How else do these two problems trouble you in school; among your friends; with your family?)

Conferencing has a way of putting reading problems into a larger perspective. In so doing, it often manages to lend assistance to parents, teachers, and children in a more far-reaching way than does a report itemizing the mere particulars of a child's reading deficiencies.

EXTENDED SAMPLE CASE REPORT

Sometimes directions, and even formats, sound like someone telling you how to make a bow in your shoelaces from the other side of a wall. Where complex twists and turns are concerned, it is helpful to see how some acceptable end products might look. One such student-prepared end product is offered here; another is offered online at our Web site. Names and other indicators of identity have been changed. The teacher-clinician in Figure 2.7 had over thirty hours of contact with the student, as compared with ten hours for the teacher-clinician found online. Typically, three to five measures would characterize a reading assessment. More are used here to provide additional examples of the varying types of assessment tools that might be included in a case report.

FIGURE **2.7**

SAMPLE CASE REPORT (PREPARED BY A MASTERS LEVEL STUDENT)

Report of Testing

Child's Name: Araba

Age: 8

Birth Date: 4-22-93

Gender: Male

Grade: 3

School: Southgate Elementary

Dates Tested: Oct/Nov, 2001

Evaluated by: Martha Hayes
(student's classroom teacher)

Reason for Referral:

This case study was conducted in partial fulfillment for a degree requirement at (name of institution) and supervised by (name instructor), the professor of record. Araba was referred for the evaluation based on concerns about his reading comprehension by his teacher and his parents.

Background Information:

Araba is of Pakistani-Indian descent; however, English is his primary "home" language. Both parents are well educated and concerned about their child's difficulties with reading comprehension. Araba demonstrates a high aptitude for mathematics, a trait he has in common with his father and older brother. At a recent parent-teacher conference, the mother shared that her son is in good health and has not suffered any traumatic illness or injury. She also stated that since first grade she and her husband have noted a lack of progress in Araba's reading comprehension skills, despite the fact that he appeared to be a fluent oral reader. Araba's elder brother (by two years) has no difficulty with reading comprehension.

Observations:

The student's cumulative record file revealed that Araba was in job share classrooms (two teachers who, on a part-time basis, share a single contract for the same class) in both first and second grade. This may have negatively impacted comprehension development.

Araba was assessed in both whole-class and one-on-one settings by the evaluator. He appeared most comfortable with groups. He was the least comfortable with

the individual assessments, though he demonstrated a positive, cooperative attitude in completing them. Araba and the evaluator (the child's third grade teacher) had excellent rapport throughout the evaluation process. It should be noted that assessments were delayed for two weeks while Araba recovered from a serious winter cold. Araba was on medication for the remaining sessions, which may have affected his ability to concentrate.

Tests Administered:

1) Manzo, Manzo, & McKenna Informal Reading-Thinking Inventory
2) Harcourt Brace Silent Reading Comprehension Test (Grade 3)
3) McLeod Assessment of Reading Comprehension (Elementary Level)
4) Burke Reading Inventory
5) Interest Inventory
6) Words Their Way Elementary Spelling Inventory (Forms 1 and 2)
7) Peabody Picture Vocabulary Test (Form IIIA)
8) Incomplete Sentence Inventory
9) Informal Vocabulary Inventory
10) Proverbs Test
11) Paragraph Writing Sample
12) CORE (Placentia Unified's Objectives for Reading Excellence) Test

Reciprocal Questioning Procedure

Test Results:

1) Informal Reading-Thinking Inventory: This individually administered test yields estimates of a student's Independent, Instructional, and Frustration levels in word recognition (in both isolation and oral reading context) and on several dimensions of comprehension: literal (reading the lines), interpretive (reading between the lines), and applied (reading beyond the lines). This test also provides optional estimates of such factors as: a congruency ratio (the proportion of responses made that are relevant to the question asked); metacognitive development (self-awareness of quality and accuracy of thinking in response to questions asked); and listening comprehension (capacity to answer questions about passage when listening replaces reading the material).

Graded Word List:
Independent: Level 2
Instructional: Level 4
Frustration: Level 5

Oral Reading Passages (Forms A and B):

Level/ Form	Oral Reading Word Recog.	Basic Comprehension	Silent Rdg Comprehension	Listening Comprehension	Higher-Order Comprehension
A1	98%	78%	___%	___%	75%
B1	___%	___%	66%	___%	50%
A2	96%	43%	___%	___%	67%
B2	___%	___%	33%	___%	75%
A3				75%	
A4				71%	

Estimated Levels
Independent: below Grade 1
Instructional: Grade 1
Frustration: Grade 2
Listening: Grade 3

Araba's Instructional level of Grade 1 is two years below his grade in school. His oral reading of the passages at Grades 1 and 2 was fluent, with one omission on the Grade 1 passage and one omission and one substitution on the Grade 2 passage. None of the miscues changed the meaning of the passages. In oral reading of words in isolation, Aruba's Instructional level was Grade 4—one year above his grade in school.

Araba's Prior Knowledge was scored 67% on three of the passages, and 100% on the fourth. He gave brief responses to these prereading questions, and did not elaborate. His Congruency Ratio was high: His incorrect answers corresponded to the questions, or he simply stated "I don't know," even when encouraged to guess. His Enjoyment/ Metacognition ratings were flat, with 3 and 4 ratings for each of these questions. An analysis of question types showed the following: Fact questions: 75% correct, Inference: 67%, Vocabulary: 25% correct. At Grades 1 and 2, oral reading comprehension was higher than silent reading comprehension. Listening comprehension was on grade level—two grades higher than current Instructional level.

2) Harcourt Brace Silent Reading Comprehension Test (Grade 3): This test assesses silent reading comprehension skills for: literal detail, vocabulary, main idea, and inference making.

Comprehension Skill	Score
Literal Detail (9 items)	67%
Vocabulary (4 items)	100%
Main Idea (3 items)	67%
Inference (8 items)	50%
Total:	67%

Placement Level: Below Grade Level

3) McLeod Assessment of Reading Comprehension (Elementary Level): This modified Cloze-type test with available choices (also called a "maze" test) assesses reading comprehension based on student ability to recognize and use both familiar word orders (syntax) and semantic (word/context/meaning) clues to demonstrate comprehension.

Total Score: 19/56 = 34%

Placement Level: Below Grade Level

4) Burke Reading Inventory: This individually conducted interview assesses the student's knowledge of reading and writing strategies.

The results of this interview show that Araba has an internalized set of rules to decode unknown words that includes the use of phonics and context clues. He is also familiar with the basic rules of writing in complete sentences. Araba would benefit from direct instruction of structural analysis, including roots and affixes. However, it appears that Araba has not internalized any reading comprehension strategies and would benefit from direct instruction at the literal, inferential, and evaluative levels.

5) Interest Inventory: This individually conducted interview assesses the student's interests, both in and out of school.

The results of this interview lead me to believe that Araba has a positive view of himself and his family. From his answers, it appears that Araba enjoys learning. He is aware of his difficulties with reading comprehension and would like to improve his skills.

6) Words Their Way Elementary Spelling Inventory (Forms 1 and 2): This test assesses a student's knowledge of orthography—the letter symbols used to represent speech sounds in spelling patterns.

The results of this assessment show Araba to be in the middle of "Within Word Pattern" stage, needing further instruction in vowel patterns, as well as grade-level-appropriate instruction in syllables, affixes, and derivational relations.

7) Peabody Picture Vocabulary Test (Form IIIA): This individually administered test assesses the student's receptive vocabulary knowledge by requiring the student to point to a picture that best defines a word that is orally presented.

Chronological Age	Standard Score	Age Equivalent
8.8	89	7.6

The results of this test would seem to indicate that Araba is in the low-average range of general intelligence.

8) Incomplete Sentence Inventory: This individually administered sentence completion inventory is a projective test assessing a student's levels of emotional response to a variety of home, life, and school situations. The results of this assessment demonstrate that Araba has a "healthy" overall level of emotional adjustment, exhibiting a positive view of himself and his family.

9) Informal Vocabulary Inventory: This individually administered oral test assesses a student's knowledge of "word meaning" vocabulary at grade level without the support of context clues.

Correct Responses: 13/25 = 52%

The results of this test indicate that Araba has knowledge of about half of the words at his grade level. This is relatively low, even for a student of low-average aptitude.

10) Proverbs Test: This individually administered informal inventory assesses ability to generalize the meaning of proverbs at an appropriately abstract level. This format is widely used to assess "abstract verbal reasoning."

There are no norms, as such, but approximate levels of difficulty have been determined based on estimates of readability, language difficulty, maturity of content, and prior usage.

The results of this assessment indicate that Araba has little trouble "reading" and re-telling, but that his comprehension is at a quite concrete, literal level.

11) Paragraph W8riting Sample: This test assesses the student's ability to write a grade-level-appropriate paragraph inclusive of a topic sentence, three to five detail sentences, and a closing sentence.

The results of this assessment reveal that Araba understands the rules for writing complete sentences and a paragraph. He correctly executed requirements for identifying a topic, details, and a closing sentence. However, his style of writing was very concrete and literal.

12) Placentia Unified's CORE Test (Fall): This district-wide test is normed on all students (2–12) in the Placentia Unified School District. It provides benchmarks of district students' knowledge of reading, language, and math.

Reading	Language	Math
52 percentile	62 percentile	88 percentile

The results of these tests indicate that Araba is within the district's identified "average" range in reading and language, and in a superior range on mathematics.

Trial/Diagnostic-Teaching: Using the Reciprocal Questioning Procedure (ReQuest):

This procedure engages the teacher and student in a reciprocal, instructional dialog in which effective thinking, via questioning and answering, is modeled and taught. This procedure focuses on the development of independent reading, comprehending, and metacognition strategies that promote learning. The ReQuest method is also a holistic diagnostic-teaching tool that incorporates and reflects student language, thinking, and social-personal skills in teaching-learning situations.

Observations:
The ReQuest Trial/Diagnostic-Teaching method was initially administered in a one-on-one setting. Araba did not respond well, exhibiting agitation and disinterest. In part this may have been the result of his cold medication, but more likely the evaluator's approach. The method was tried again with Araba in a small-group setting with two peers. This seemed to put Araba at ease, providing him with a more familiar setting. He responded better to

questions based on single sentences rather than paragraph passages, and was able to answer both literal and inferential questions. However, he only asked literal questions in return.

Results:

A five-day endeavor revealed that Araba lacks most self-guiding comprehension strategies, but appears capable of learning them. He responded well to modeling and guidance, particularly with literal information. He was able to answer inferential questions successfully, and with continued instruction, seems to have the potential to formulate such questions in the future. He seemed to benefit most from interacting with peers who provided him with models that he could easily copy and emulate.

Interpretations:

This third grade student's reading is Instructional level at Grade 1, with Frustration level at Grade 3, and Independent level at some point below Grade 1: He is best characterized as a Corrective Reader. Word recognition does not appear to be the primary concern in this case: Word recognition was Instructional level at Grades 1 and 2 (99% and 96% respectively). Recognition of words in isolation on the IR-TI Graded Word Lists was above grade level, at Grade 4. Araba read the Grade 1 and 2 passages fluently and with expression. However, silent reading was lower than oral reading at both Grades 1 and 2, indicating that fluency in silent reading needs further development.

In Araba's case, the primary concern is basic and interpretive comprehension, including meaning vocabulary and strategies for constructing meaning from text. In addition to an Instructional Level at Grade 1 on the IR-TI, he scored 67% on the Harcourt Brace Silent Reading Comprehension Test for Grade 3, which is considered below grade level; the McLeod Assessment of Reading Comprehension score was 34%, also considered below grade level, and the district CORE test placed him in the 52 percentile for Reading, and the 62 percentile for Language. In contrast, his score for Math on this test was at the 88 percentile.

The Peabody Picture Vocabulary score suggests that the comprehension lag may be due to aptitude: The score placed Araba's mental age more than a full year below chronological age. However, this test is a "screening" test that estimates IQ based on listening vocabulary level (point to the picture that best defines a word spoken orally). Other measures of Araba's vocabulary were mixed: He scored 100% on the vocabulary subtest of the

Harcourt Brace Silent Reading Comprehension Test for Grade 3, but this score was based on only four items. On the Informal Vocabulary Inventory for Grade 3, he scored 52% on the 25 items. On the IR-TI, he missed three of the four Vocabulary questions (25% correct). It is possible that although English is the primary language spoken in the home, since it is the parent's second language, Araba may not have been exposed to vocabulary at the level of children in typical English-speaking homes. His scores for Prior Knowledge on the IR-TI indicated gaps in this area, with 100% on one passage, but 67% on each of the other three passages. In working with Araba, I noticed large gaps in his schema as well. These factors would support the proposition that vocabulary knowledge is not an appropriate means of predicting cognitive aptitude in Araba's case. This proposition is supported by the low score on the McLeod Assessment of Reading Comprehension, a cloze-type test (words are deleted, with three choices from which to select the correct word) that predicts comprehension, but actually measures the student's familiarity with subtle language patterns in written English. (It is less a measure of vocabulary, because many of the deleted words are very simple words like "over" or "every.") Araba's score of 34% on this test would confirm that his overall language is weaker than would be expected in a third grader from a traditional English-speaking home. The low cloze score could be due to low aptitude as well, but Araba's score of 88 percentile in Math on the district CORE test suggests a higher overall aptitude than the PPVT prediction. The low PPVT score, in summary, is more likely due to vocabulary and familiarity with language patterns in written English than to aptitude.

Araba's comprehension lag does not appear to be related to emotional or social factors. His responses on the Interest Inventory and the Incomplete Sentence Inventory indicate that he is emotionally well adjusted, with a healthy self-concept, and a positive attitude toward learning and reading. The Proverbs test multiple-choice items each include one choice that would indicate "emotionality," but Araba's choices included only a very few of these. He appeared to be quite comfortable in group-assessment settings—even more than in individual settings. His parents are supportive of his progress in school.

Araba's parents report that he demonstrated fluent oral reading since first grade, but test results and observations in this evaluation indicate that he has not gained in comprehension at a typical developmental rate. There is a possibility that the developmental lag may be related, in some measure, to his placement in first and second grade in "job share" classrooms—a fairly novel arrangement which may not be in some students' best educational interests.

It is this evaluator's opinion that, for whatever reason, Araba has failed to acquire familiarity with language patterns and vocabulary meanings in English, and strategies for constructing meaning from print. His likely aptitude to do so is indicated by his early acquisition of decoding strategies and a strong sight word vocabulary, along with fluent oral reading in first grade (in first grade materials), supported by a current math score at the 88 percentile. In addition, Araba's Listening Comprehension score was Grade 3, indicating capacity to read and comprehend at grade level. He has demonstrated the ability to internalize and apply complex rules, as exhibited in mathematics and decoding. In classroom settings, I have observed that Araba responds well to prereading instruction enhanced by visual aids such as pictures and graphic organizers. It is most probable that he can be taught higher-level comprehension skills in the regular classroom setting, perhaps better than in a tutorial. Araba's aptitude to respond to instruction was evidenced in the ReQuest trial-teaching sessions, particularly those in which other students were included. Although his reluctance to participate in the first session supported the indication that he lacks self-questioning strategies for comprehension, he quickly began to participate, although limiting his questions to the literal level.

Of additional interest, in three of the four passages of the IR-TI which were given, Araba's higher-order comprehension was higher than his basic comprehension. This is curious in view of his literal level questioning in the ReQuest sessions. Perhaps he is personally inclined to think beyond the lines, but is not yet convinced that he is supposed to do so in school.

Summary of Strengths and Needs:

Strengths
- Basic decoding strategies
- Sight words
- Fluency at Instructional level
- Higher-order comprehension
- Emotional adjustment and self-concept
- Attitude toward learning and reading
- Writing structures (sentences; paragraph format and style)

Needs
- Vocabulary/concept development
- Background knowledge
- Self-questioning to build comprehension strategies: schema activation, metacognitive monitoring, and fix-up strategies
- Familiarity with language patterns in written English
- Critical/creative response to text
- Fluency at grade level
- Abstract generalizations
- Content and style in written compositions

Recommendations:
Araba's Corrective reading instruction should be provided in the regular classroom. Emphasis should be placed on the following types of instruction:
- Select materials with an eye toward developing background knowledge and vocabulary.
- Provide direct instruction in strategies of self-questioning for pre-reading schema activation, metacognitive monitoring, and comprehension fix-up, and post-reading critical and creative responses to text. Suggested methods include ReQuest, Question-Only, About-Point, and Graphic Organizers.
- Provide direct instruction in strategies for vocabulary building, using methods such as the Subjective Approach to Vocabulary and Motor Imaging to introduce difficult vocabulary during prereading instruction.
- Provide instruction in locating and learning meanings of unfamiliar words in passages using methods such as Vocabulary Self-Selection.
- Provide additional word study activities, emphasizing structural analysis as a tool for vocabulary building.
- Support strong personal and social adjustment with frequent cooperative structure components within and in addition to the above methods.
- Provide opportunity for frequent oral re-reading in grade level materials to build meaning vocabulary and fluency at grade level.
- Provide cloze-type activities to build familiarity with written language forms and styles, preferably to be completed in cooperative group activities.
- Provide writing process instruction, emphasizing prewriting activities and writing for real audiences.

Martha Hayes, Clinician and Teacher
November, 2001

REVIEW

Diagnosis essentially is about helping students in such a way that all concerned can contribute to and gain further insight into helping students continue to help themselves. It is not unlike the "writing process" where an interested person reads someone's current draft of his or her academic progress to date and suggests ways that he or she might rewrite the next draft; that is, his or her future.

PREVIEW

Now that you have a clear idea what diagnosis is, and what a case study looks like, it is time to learn how to construct one in the particular. The primary tool for doing so, as you may already know, is the format known as the Informal Reading Inventory. The name is deceptive since the format, though not rigid, has become quite structured by time and experience. The chapter ahead also covers a number of important concepts of tests and measurements.

STANDARDIZED AND STRUCTURED INFORMAL ASSESSMENT OF READING

The examiner pipes and the teacher must dance—
and the examiner sticks to the old tune. – H. G. WELLS, 1892

CONTENT AND CONCEPT ORGANIZER

All assessment is based on layering. It places one observation, or data point, over another in ways that have proven value in cross-verifying one another. It is the "scientific method" expressed through assessment of reading and learning. This chapter reviews the basics of standardized and structured informal assessment—the classroom teacher's and reading specialist's stock-in-trade. Underlying this, and all related chapters, is the proposition that we learn to administer many tests and inventories of many different types, so that we may become more able to administer just a few, and to extract the most information from these.

CHAPTER OUTLINE

DO WE TEST TOO MUCH?

This simple question is the one most frequently asked by teachers who must conduct testing, and are obliged to stand by as children suffer through this sometimes grim process. Ilona Takakura, a classroom teacher and M.S. in Reading Education candidate at Cal-State University—Fullerton, has undertaken a heroic attempt to answer this question with some finality in her Masters thesis. We reference this good teacher's efforts not because they are startling, but because they convey the complexity of the issues. Her early findings tell much about why we cannot yet answer this question clearly one way or the other based upon statistical analyses. What Ilona is finding thus far confirms many other studies that say that tests given in the early grades are the least reliable from one year to the next, becoming much more reliable beyond the sixth grade, and quite reliable by the eleventh grade. This would seem to suggest the need for more frequent and longer tests in the earlier grades since this would result in more reliable findings. However, testing takes up a considerable amount of time that could better be spent in teaching, and it is very costly. Further, the information gained from formal testing is very predictable from classroom-level assessment. It is argued, however, that it is through formal testing that we are able to confirm informal assessment, and it is through informal assessment that we are able to cross-validate results from formal testing.

Yes, we probably test too much.

All things taken together, the conclusion that seems most sensible at this time is that we tend to do too much testing at some times (like now) and too little at others (as in the prior twenty years). It also seems sensible, and more humane, to conclude that students who have scored in the very lowest ranges (below the 20th percentile), need to be pre-assessed in less formal ways. This would determine if they have made sufficient progress to justify having them sit through hours of formal testing to tell us what we already know. But teachers are not in charge of testing.

POWER OF THE EXAMINER

The power of the examiner is a long-standing and deeply rooted issue in education. In fact, the influence of testing may be greater now than at any time in our prior history. There are a variety of assessment movements with puzzling titles throughout the nation. In the past ten years, most states have first instituted and then dropped or redirected assessment procedures with names like *basic competencies, mastery learning, criterion-referenced* testing, and more recently, *holistic, authentic, outcomes-based,* and *performance-based* assessment. One measure, however, remains a constant since federal law mandates it.

National Assessment of Educational Progress (NAEP)

The NAEP is the nation's major benchmark of literacy. It was mandated by the Congress in 1969, and carried out on a mixed-subject schedule every two to three years. Students at grades 4, 8, and 12 receive fifty minutes to read graded passages and answer questions, both multiple-choice and written. There are four possible levels of competency that one can achieve: *below basic; basic; proficient;* and *advanced.* Three sets of data are relevant: 1992, 1994, and 1998. The 1994 data were the most shocking to the national conscience.

In that year, about 60 percent of adolescents, according to NAEP performance indicators, were able to read only at a basic level. They could gather details, identify a main idea, and recognize connections among textually explicit ideas. Fewer than 5 percent of youngsters surveyed, however, were able to perform at *advanced* levels where they were required to examine, extend, and elaborate meanings from representative fiction and nonfiction materials (Campbell et al., 1996). Results of the NAEP *writing* assessment (Applebee et al., 1994) revealed that *most all* students in grades 4, 8, and 12 had difficulty with writing tasks that required higher levels of coherent thinking and the important capacity to provide details to support points made. Some have called this a national crisis (Vacca & Alvermann, 1998). We tend to see it more as a part of an evolutionary challenge, and as a positive index of our elevated sense of concern for all children, regardless of background. The findings appear onerous due to the statistical inclusion of more Limited English Language–Proficient (LEP) kids who were not counted in the past.

There also is a collective raised sense of concern for the importance of a sound education to future earning power and global stability. However, there are some things about literacy in America about which to be distressed.

The '98 NAEP results have been heralded as showing "significant" progress over 1994. Actual scores, however, were not up in any meaningful way. For example, scores that are reported on a 500-point scale are up at fourth-grade level to 217 in '98, but that is only a 3-point gain. Similarly, the mean score of 264 for eighth graders is only a 4-point gain, and the 291 for seniors, another 4-point gain. The good news is that this is the first across-the-board gain at all levels tested in thirty years. The not-so-good news is that these gains, which come on the heels of huge expenditures and political focus, largely are rebounds from 1994, but about the same as 1992; (with the exception of eighth grade where some new highs are being seen). The fourth-grade results are the ones being most watched since they should reflect changes instituted at first-grade level. Those results, while encouraging, are not much to cheer about, since 38% of youngsters are *below basic;* 33% *basic;* 25% *proficient;* and only about 4% *advanced*. If we used a "normal curve" as a benchmark, there should be about the same proportion of pupils in the lowest category as in the highest, but there are nearly ten times as many in the lowest than the highest. Let us reflect now on some reasons for these anemic gains, and shed light on some possible solutions that are in the reach of most classroom teachers.

"FUNCTIONAL LITERACY" LEVELS DO NOT CONFIRM CRISIS

Initial results of the related 1992 National Adult Literacy Survey confirmed the bad news in the NAEP findings. As a result, it was widely broadcast that nearly half (47%) of Americans had scored in the lower two levels of a five-category rubric assessing *functional literacy*. And, more chillingly, 21%, or more than one in five, effectively were *functionally illiterate*. The 26,000 participants were asked to do a variety of "real-world" tasks, such as locating specific information on a pay stub, estimating the price per pound of peanut butter, and completing a Social Security card.

A recent re-analysis of this data, however, suggests that functional illiteracy is far less than first estimated (see Chapter 13 on Adolescent and Adult Literacy). This is raising serious doubts about the validity of "criterion-referenced" ("high-stakes") tests. A recent summary of progress in reading states that: *"It is an irrefutable fact that children in grades K–12 today read as well or better than children at any other time in the history of the United States"* (Klenk & Kibby, 2000, 667). This same summative report further notes this often-overlooked fact: *". . . American children score more than a full standard deviation above the scores of children in 1932 on individually administered IQ tests"* (667).

POSSIBLE "CAMBRIAN PERIOD" OF PROGRESS

Evidence suggests that for about 75 years now reading education has been a major player in leading education into a *Cambrian Period*—the wonderfully warming, magical period in the Paleozoic Era that gave way to multiple life forms on a previously lifeless planet (Manzo, 2003). Clearly, there has been more progress in pedagogic science and social consciousness in the last fifty to seventy-five years than in the previous 500. Classrooms are beginning to look different and teaching practices are increasingly marked by a confluence of activities. These include more reflective balances of direct instruction, strategy instruction, and reciprocal modeling; theme study and student-centered project work; collaborative and cooperative grouping; and levels of inclusion and heterogeneity not seen since the mythical one-room schoolhouse (where in point of fact all may have been present but only a few were educated). Now we are moving toward 24/7 wrapped-around support for learning through wired classrooms that have more outreach, information availability, and community-building capability than could ever before have been imagined. The very tests that have seemed to damn professional education may soon be cited in its praise. But we will all have to learn and know more about these complex instruments to break the current cycle of fear and misrepresentation.

PRIMER ON STANDARDIZED TESTS

Testing is a lot like fishing: You often have to try several different kinds of lures to discover what lies beneath the waters. Standardized tests are among the most widely used of the many kinds of tests that have been developed. The term **standardized** means that each student receives the same questions, which are administered under the same conditions (usually including time allotment), and scored according to the same criteria. Two types of standardized tests have evolved for different purposes: norm-referenced and criterion-referenced tests.

Norm-Referenced Tests

In norm-referenced test construction, some large and presumably representative sample group of students is given the test to establish reference points for the percent of correct answers students could be expected to make at different age or grade levels. These percentages then become benchmarks for interpreting the raw scores of others who are given the test.

Norm-referenced test scores typically are expressed as grade equivalents, percentiles, or stanines. A grade-equivalent score indicates that a student's raw score is the same as the average score of the sample students in a certain grade. It is reported in a whole number and a tenth to represent some portion of the year. Thus, 5.5 is equivalent to fifth grade, fifth month of school. There has been strong objection by some to the use of grade-equivalent scores since these might imply that there is a fixed level of performance that should be expected at each age and grade level. Exercise appropriate cautions and qualifications in referring to these.

Standardized tests tend to measure the easy things.

     A percentile score is another way of indicating how a student's raw score relates to that of the sample population. A raw score, for example, may be checked against a table that might show that score to be in the 57th percentile. This is another way of saying that the score is better than 57 percent of those in the sample group, and not as good as 43 percent. Sometimes, special norms are calculated to determine how that same raw score compares with the average score of students from similar regional, socioeconomic, or ethnic backgrounds. Finally, there is the stanine (or standard nine) score. This system was devised to get a sense of the band that a student is operating in. This is done by taking a raw score and checking it against a statistical table. Should that score be equivalent to the fourth stanine, this means that the student's performance on that test is in the fourth of nine possible segments, or one stanine below the fifth stanine, which is the standardized average score for stanine rankings.

     There are limitations to norm-referenced testing, despite their generally high levels of validity (assurance that they measure what they say they measure), and reliability (dependability that the score made will not vary greatly from one test situation to the next). Ironically, the limitations of this type of testing most frequently cited are not necessarily corrected by other types of testing. Therefore, think of the limitations stated below as precautions in interpreting all forms of testing:

    1. Tests tend to measure the easy things, which usually can be inferred from classwork and simple observation (such as level of comprehension, IQ, or achievement).

    2. The validity and reliability of an individual student's score cannot always be trusted, since tests usually are based on group norms that can misrepresent an individual's performance, and also can vary widely when individuals are retested with alternate forms of the same instrument.

    3. Most norm-referenced tests tend to provide a measure of a student's highest level of performance, or frustration level, rather than of instructional or independent levels. (To determine a student's instructional reading level from a norm-referenced test score, subtract one year from the score; to establish independent level, subtract one and a half to two years.)

4. High and low scores on tests can be especially misleading for the fact that scores rarely are on an equal-interval basis, and only relatively few items tend to distinguish performance at upper and lower ranges (the difference between the 75th and the 95th percentiles may be just two or three items, and similarly so for between the 10th and the 30th percentiles).

5. Most tests are not of much help in offering insights into how and why someone responded the way he or she did. Thus, while they offer huge amounts of quantitative information, there is little that is qualitative, and therefore useful in instructional planning.

Limitations such as these only serve to explain further why it is necessary for teachers and reading specialists to be well versed in testing and to be able to use a variety of testing methods and devices to cross-verify initial findings. It is largely as a result of this ongoing need that the criterion-referenced tests were evolved.

We learn about many tests so that we may learn from a few.

Criterion-Referenced Tests

In contrast to norm-referenced tests, this type of test does not compare students to one another, but to some defined objective. "Mastery tests," for example, are a form of criterion-referenced testing. Such tests are widely used by various states to ascertain whether a student has achieved "minimum competencies" in basic skills and operations. They are also used by state departments to convey a clear message about what government, business, and society expect schools to accomplish. Unlike norm-referenced tests, whose items are carefully guarded, most criterion-referenced tests are constructed by converting curriculum guides and objectives into test items.

The credibility of "teaching to the test" is maintained by the fact that most criterion-referenced tests represent essential minimum competencies, and that they are implicitly "normed" by years of trial-and-error learning about age-appropriate curriculum. Actual criteria are established from samples of students whose scores provide the state test makers with some benchmarks of the age and grade levels at which mastery should reasonably be expected. Even where this type of "norming" is not followed, the mastery criteria should approximate it by drawing from general knowledge of what children should know and be able to do at certain age and grade levels.

In short, unlike standardized tests that attempt to measure generalized states of knowledge, criterion-referenced tests tend to assess basic and often pragmatic skills, such as reading driver's manuals and following directions. Structured Informal Assessment, the next consideration, also could be considered criterion-based but tends to have a different purpose and orientation.

Limitations of standardized testing are not necessarily corrected by either criterion-referenced or informal testing.

STRUCTURED INFORMAL ASSESSMENT IN INDIVIDUAL DIAGNOSIS: WHERE TO BEGIN

Individual assessment is undertaken when classroom observation and standardized assessments reveal that further information about a student's literacy development is needed in order to provide appropriate instruction. The best approach, at this initial assessment level, generally is some form of structured informal assessment of reading-specific factors, as described below.

A **Structured Informal Assessment** technique is a nonstandardized, though experience- and tradition-governed, set of guidelines for eliciting and evaluating a given set of behaviors according to some pre-established standards. For children reading at about second-grade level and above, the usual technique of choice for initial individual assessment is an Informal Reading Inventory (IRI). For children whose reading development is estimated to be approximately first-grade level (that is, good concepts about print, and some sight words), it is best to begin with a structured informal assessment of phonetic word attack strategies and sight word vocabulary. Children below this level should be evaluated with techniques for assessing concepts about print and phonemic awareness. It often is necessary to "switch gears" early-on in initial individual assessment and move to a more appropriate technique upon learning more about the student's functioning level. Several examples of structured informal assessment are provided in this chapter, including the IRI, a Structured Observation of Concepts about Print, an Inventory of Phonemic Awareness, Sight Word Lists, and a Phonetic Word Attack Test.

Reading-specific factors, such as comprehension strategies, sight word vocabulary, and word attack strategies, should be evaluated first (refer to the formula for intervention in Figure 1.3 in Chapter 1). This is true even in cases where it appears evident from observation that the child's literacy development has been inhibited by one or several **reading-related influences,** such as overall language development, environmental factors, personality and social characteristics, or an earlier physical or educational problem or deficit. Each of these possible reading-related factors (also referred to as "correlates of reading difficulty") is discussed more fully in Chapter 4 on in-depth diagnosis. The important point here is that the first concern, in most cases, should be to discover the *effect upon literacy development* of these factors, because it is still the reading-specific factors that need to be taught. Determining the severity of the specific reading problem will clarify the extent to which further follow-up assessment of influencing factors needs to be undertaken.

Structured Informal Assessment provides standards for evaluating behaviors.

Consider, for example, a fourth-grade student for whom English is a partially acquired second language, and who is reading at the second-grade level. It should not be simply concluded that the student's below-level reading is the result of still-developing familiarity with English, and that reading will improve along with language development. The diagnostic question *still* should be "What has been the effect upon development of reading-specific factors?" The student's language level may have inhibited *ESL* acquisition of reading-specific factors, but reading-specific factors still need to be taught—along with language.

INFORMAL READING INVENTORIES

An IRI provides a good estimation of a child's Independent, Instructional, and Frustration levels, based on both word recognition and comprehension. It provides information about the child's decoding and thinking processes, as the child reads aloud and responds to various types of questions about the reading passages. In its most basic form, it provides a structure for recording the child's oral reading and responses to questions, so that these may be analyzed and interpreted in terms of the child's likely reading-specific strengths and needs. It also offers a number of optional "add-on" techniques, for use as the teacher judges appropriate.

Most teacher education programs, and many state certification standards, require that all elementary teachers learn to administer, score, analyze, and interpret an IRI. This is not because teachers will often administer full IRIs to their students, but because once they have learned to do so, they can informally use IRI techniques and criteria in their classroom interactions with children. The ability to administer, record, analyze, and interpret a structured IRI is an essential foundation for all other forms of literacy assessment. For example, many teachers do make time to administer an IRI-type administration of a single grade-level passage to each student at the beginning, middle, and end of the year, to include in the child's cumulative folder and to use in parent conferences. This only takes about ten minutes per child.

IRIs were originally intended to be constructed by teachers, from available basal materials. However, this takes a great deal of teacher time and technical knowledge. Researchers noted additional potential problems with teacher-constructed assessments, as follows.

1. Readability levels of the excerpts from basal readers were found to be unreliable (Bradley & Ames, 1977).

Teacher-constructed IRIs take a great deal of time and technical knowledge.

2. Questions often were shown not to be passage dependent; that is, they could be correctly answered without reading the passage (Schell, 1991).
3. When a school changed basals, the predictive or matching value of the IRIs fell off too sharply (Baumann, 1988a, b).

For these reasons commercial IRIs provide more reliable information. Several commercial IRIs are available, and published reading programs often produce IRI-type assessments to accompany the grade-level teacher support materials.

IRI Structure

A commercial IRI typically is a spiral-bound publication, with the following sections:

- A manual of directions for administering and scoring the test, and interpreting students' performance, often including reproducible worksheets for analyzing the child's responses in word recognition and comprehension
- A summary sheet to be reproduced for each testing and used to record the child's test results
- A section containing **teacher record forms,** which are to be reproduced for use when giving the test—the teacher writes student responses on the reproduced record form. Record forms are included for each graded word list, and for each graded reading passage. The teacher record form for each graded passage includes: a) a copy of the reading selection the child will be reading, so that the teacher can follow along and make notes while the child is reading aloud; b) comprehension questions for the passage, with correct answers noted, and space to write the child's responses; c) guidelines for calculating whether the child's performance on word recognition and comprehension on that particular passage falls into the range of Independent, Instructional, or Frustration level.
- The graded word lists, typically with the easiest level list in large type as is familiar to younger readers
- At least two sets of graded passages, again, in type sizes to correspond to the difficulty level

The Informal Reading–Thinking Inventory

The Informal Reading–Thinking Inventory that comes with this text is the first commercial IRI to include a variety of qualitative assessments of comprehension process *strategies,* such as level of interest or schema activation, active engagement with meaning-making, and metacognition, in addition to assessment of various forms of comprehension *outcomes* in response to direct questions. It also is the first to include options for assessment of higher-order comprehension in addition to literal and simple inferential comprehension, and a measure of *congruent,* or relevant, responding even though an answer may not be dead accurate (a sensitive measure of attentive listening). Basic administration procedures for the IR-TI are similar to other published versions. These are summarized below, with more specific instructions included in the IR-TI manual.

Basic IR-TI Administration Procedures

Establish Rapport As with any individual testing, the first step is to establish a comfortable atmosphere and congenial rapport with the student before proceeding with the inventory. Give the student an idea of why he or she is taking the test. For example, "This test will help me know what books you can read best." Also tell the child that you will write things down so you can remember how well s/he did. Some people have the student write his or her name on the test booklet. Your name and the date should also be placed on the booklet.

> The first step in all assessment is to establish a comfortable atmosphere and rapport with the student.

Graded Word Lists Most commercial IRIs provide a set of **graded word lists**—each list at a given grade-level difficulty. The word lists are the first step in testing, for the purpose of *estimating* the child's Independent level, which is the grade-level passage used to begin the next stage in the testing. Giving the child an easy passage to read first, and moving to more difficult passages is preferable to beginning with a passage that is difficult, and discouraging the child at the beginning of the testing; on the other hand, beginning at a level that is too low results in reading unnecessary passages. The Graded Word Lists also can be used alone, as a quick means of *estimating* a student's Independent, Instructional, and Frustration levels. The IR-TI Graded Word Lists are included in the IR-TI.

Graded Passages: Oral Reading Having estimated the child's Independent level with the word lists, the test administrator then turns to the IRI test booklet's series of **graded passages** (short reading selections of identified grade level difficulty), with comprehension questions of specific types, and locates the passage at that grade level. The child is asked to read the passage aloud, and then answer the questions (without looking back at the passage). As the child reads orally, the teacher marks any **"unexpected response"**—that is, anything other than precisely what is on the printed page. The purpose of recording the oral reading is to reproduce exactly what the child said, so that it can be analyzed for patterns at a later time. Unexpected responses may include: omission (leaving out a word); substitution (saying a word that is different from the word on the page); insertion (adding a word); teacher pronunciation (a word given by the teacher when the child pauses and, even with encouragement, waits to be told the word); self-correction (the child makes any of the above unexpected responses, but corrects it without being prompted); repetition (a word or phrase repeated); and hesitation (a pause of more than about a second). Self-corrections, repetitions, and hesitations are not counted as "errors" when tallying total percent-correct for word recognition in oral reading. The test administrator should make additional notes about the child's oral reading fluency, and any related behaviors, such as voluntarily asking questions or commenting about the contents of the passage.

Graded Passages: Comprehension Questions   When the child finishes reading the passage, the student booklet should be closed and the teacher should ask the comprehension questions from the teacher record form. Questions may be rephrased as long as the new wording does not provide additional clues. All responses should be recorded. If a student's response is the same as the suggested answer (provided in brackets), the printed answer may be underlined to indicate this equivalence. Any different wording should be written just above or just below the suggested answer. Responses may be studied later to check the accuracy of the original scoring, or to analyze the reasoning used by the student.

A question should be repeated if the student does not give an answer related to the question (for example, you may say, "Listen to the question again. . ."). Record a Q to indicate that the question had been repeated and write down the new response. When scoring questions, use [+] for correct, and [0] for incorrect responses. If a question indicates that a multiple response is required, such as "name two ways . . . ," full credit can be given only if the specified number of correct responses are provided. On such questions, partial credit may be awarded for partial responses (half credit for only one correct response). The question may be repeated if the student names just one.

If the child's performance on the first passage meets the criterion for Independent level (at least 99% correct word recognition in oral reading, *and* at least 90% correct comprehension in question answering), the administrator proceeds to the next higher passage, following the same procedures. The child is asked to read and answer questions at each progressively higher passage until Frustration level is reached (either below 90% word recognition or below 50% comprehension). Administration of the basic IR-TI can take from 25 minutes to an hour and a half, depending upon the number of passages that need to be included. Testing often is done over several sessions, particularly when optional techniques, as described next, are added.

IRI Administration Options

The techniques and structural elements of the IRI are sound and fairly constant though flexible, which is probably why it has stood the test of time. The *quantitative* criteria for estimating Independent, Instructional, and Frustration levels (that is, 95%+ word recognition *and* 75%+ comprehension for Instructional level) have remained the same since these were published by Betts in 1936 (with only slight variations from one published version to another). Many *qualitative* aspects, however, have kept pace with evolving and clearer understandings of the reading process. For example, when a child reads a passage orally in an IRI administration, the tester marks any words or phrases that are repeated, and any significant pauses. Early IRI scoring standards reflected the emphasis at the time on oral reading accuracy: each repetition and pause was counted as an error, and included a calculation of total percent-correct for word recognition. Most IRIs today are based on a view of reading that interprets repetitions and pauses as fix-up strategies that should be considered a reading *strength*, and these are not counted as errors in the scoring standards. During another period when silent reading was considered to be more important than oral reading (to the point where some reading educators felt that there should be no oral reading in the classroom, ever), diagnosticians simply added passages for silent reading to the IRI.

Current published IRIs offer many options in addition to basic administration. Some options, from the original techniques and newer additions, include: assessment of precise retellings without questions; listening comprehension; comparison of oral and silent comprehension; and assessment of reading rate. The IR-TI adds options for assessment of: schema activation, engagement, metacognition, higher-order comprehension, and writing in response to reading.

Assessment of Listening Comprehension   Listening comprehension

is an estimate of how well the student should be expected to understand if word recognition and fluency were perfect, and thus, it is a good predictor of the student's likely capacity for reading with comprehension, if decoding and/or fluency were improved (Durrell, 1969; Carroll, 1977; Sinatra, 1990). Listening capacity has a high correlation with verbal intelligence. A measure of listening comprehension is simple to obtain with an IRI. Once the student has reached frustration level, the next higher passage is read aloud *to* the student, and comprehension questions are asked. If comprehension is 75% or higher, the next higher passage and questions are used—continuing

Listening comprehension is a solid measure of intellectual capacity because it is what we do 99 percent of the time, and it is not subject to distortion by reading problems.

until comprehension falls below 75%. Note that the term "listening comprehension" is sometimes *misinterpreted* as a measure of "listening" as in "paying attention." This would imply that a child who scores lower than expected on this measure needs to be taught to listen better, which is not necessarily the case. The child is asked to listen to a passage and answer questions in order to learn more about the child's reading; a lower than expected score most likely calls for instruction in some aspect of processing print into meaning.

> A number of comprehension questions on conventional IRIs are unintentionally passage independent; the IR-TI intentionally includes and utilizes these.

In view of current understandings of Instructional level reading, Listening Comprehension probably is closer to an estimate of the child's potential Independent level than potential Instructional level. This is because listening to a passage is, by definition, a linear process—the words are read in order, straight through from beginning to end, which can be done, by definition, when reading at one's Independent level. Instructional level reading, however, is not a linear process—the reader engages in a variety of fix-up strategies, such as skipping ahead to get the gist of the passage, pausing to translate and reflect, and occasionally rereading words or sections. Thus, it is much more difficult to comprehend at the 75% level when listening than when reading on our own. The more current interpretation, therefore, is that listening comprehension estimates the child's *potential* Independent level. Sinatra (1990) has noted that "the processing of lengthy, connected text may require processing strategies that are qualitatively different from the strategies used in the processing of aural discourse" (126). Miller and Smith (1990) found the relationships of oral reading, silent reading, and listening to vary among low, average, and superior readers. Listening comprehension was equal to oral reading in lower readers, though both were superior to silent reading. Among average readers, listening comprehension was equal to silent reading, and both were superior to oral reading. For high-achieving readers, oral comprehension was equal to silent, and both were superior to listening comprehension: Scores for this latter group would suggest that these high-achieving readers were using meaning-making strategies when reading silently or aloud that they were not able to use when listening to material at an equal level of difficulty.

> When listening comprehension is well above oral and/or silent reading level, the student is a good candidate for short-term remedial/corrective instruction.

If the child's listening comprehension level is well above his or her Frustration level, it is a good indication that he or she has sufficient familiarity with the background information, vocabulary, and language patterns at this level, so that improvement in word recognition strategies and/or fluency should quickly improve the oral and silent reading Independent level up to the level of listening comprehension. Instructional level also may be significantly raised with improvement in word recognition and/or fluency; however, this depends on the degree to which the child has acquired active study reading strategies not measured by listening comprehension.

In many cases, the child will score below 75% on the first listening comprehension passage attempted, indicating that listening comprehension is at or below the child's Frustration level. In this scenario, the teacher may use the second set of graded passages to go down one level at a time in administering the listening comprehension test to determine just how low it is—keeping in mind that this is the level at which familiarity with background information, vocabulary, and language patterns should permit Independent level reading. If listening comprehension is below oral or silent Instructional reading level, but neither word recognition nor fluency is poor, it is likely that improvement is needed in active meaning-making strategies needed for Instructional level study-type reading.

Comparison of Oral and Silent Comprehension   In many cases it is useful to compare the child's oral and silent reading comprehension. If IRI testing is undertaken with this intention, the graded reading passages from Form A and Form B typically are given to the student in alternating order for oral and then silent reading. For example, if testing was begun at grade 2, the student would be given Form A, grade 2, to read orally, then answer questions; then Form B, grade 2, to read silently, then answer questions. When the criterion for Frustration level is met on either oral reading in Form A, or silent reading in Form B, testing for that form is stopped, but may continue in the other form if Frustration level has not yet been reached. The student may reach Frustration level in oral reading in Form A, grade 2, for example, but not reach Frustration level in silent reading comprehension of Form B passages until grade 4.

In other cases, rather than administering all grade levels both orally and silently, it may be preferable to complete the IRI administration using oral reading passages only, identify the student's Instructional level, and then have the student read the Form B passage at Instructional level silently, to compare oral with silent reading comprehension at one level only. If silent reading is significantly higher at that level, the next higher passage(s) from Form B may be used until the criteria for Instructional level are no longer met.

As a general rule, students reading at first- and second-grade levels comprehend better when reading orally. By third-grade level, students begin to make the transition to greater comprehension when reading silently. For students reading at higher levels, silent reading comprehension generally is stronger.

Assessment of Reading Rate   Rate of reading tends to be undervalued as a diagnostic indicator; however, it can be a good indicator of progress, and a surprisingly good bet as an ingredient in a program to stimulate gains

FIGURE **3.1**

ORAL AND SILENT READING RATES

Oral Reading Rate[a]		Silent Reading Rate[b]	
Grade Level	Words per minute	Grade	Words per minute
1.8	30–54	2	86
2.8	66–104	3	116
3.8	86–124	4	155
4.8	95–130	5	177
5.8	108–140	6	206
6.8	112	7	215
7.8	122–155	8	237
8.8	136–167	9	252
		12	251

[a]After Table 3, Manual of Directions, Gilmore Oral Reading Test, Copyright, 1968 by Harcourt Brace Jovanovich, Inc.
[b]Harris & Sipay, 1975, 549.

in overall reading fluency and comprehension (Erickson & Krajenta, 1991). Reading rate tends to grow in rather predictable increments through the grades. Figure 3.1 shows average oral reading rate gains from grade level 1.8 to 8.8, and silent reading rates from grades 2 to 12.

Reading rate typically should be calculated using a passage that is between a student's Instructional and Independent reading level. It is best to sample the rate twice on two different passages of about 50 to 75 words each, and calculate the average of the two. Rate is determined by using an accurate stopwatch to determine the number of seconds it takes for the student to read the given number of words. Rate is then calculated by dividing the number of words by the number of seconds. This yields words per second, which then must be recalculated into words per minute (WPM) by multiplying by 60.

Example:

	# words	time
Oral Passage #1	55	80 seconds
Oral Passage #2	59	90 seconds

seconds = 170
words = 114
114 words / 170 seconds = .67 words per second
.67 words per second × 60 seconds = 40 words per minute

Silent reading rate can be tested in a group setting. Students are given a passage to read silently and simply told to circle the word they are up to when you say "MARK" after precisely 1 minute of reading. The teacher, or student, then counts the number of words read in a minute, to determine rate in words per minute. Again, an average of two samples will yield a more reliable estimate of rate.

Flexibility   Flexibility is the silent reading equivalent of oral reading *fluency* (more on this ahead in the chapter). It is largely a function of rate. Silent reading rate, as can be seen in Figure 3.1, tends to level off at about 250 words per minute by the end of middle school. This does not increase through the high school years even though most students are capable of reading with equally high comprehension at rates between 300 and 400 words per minute (Carver, 1982). Thus, most students can benefit from instruction in reading rate. The broad goal of any focused instruction in reading rate, however, should be to improve reading *flexibility,* as much as reading *speed*. Flexibility refers to altering rate according to the *purpose* for reading and the *difficulty* level of the material. It is measured as the difference between words per minute in simple and difficult materials (Moe & Nania, 1959).

Instruction in reading rate and flexibility is particularly justified when other aspects of reading, such as vocabulary or comprehension, have shown improvement, but rate remains unchanged. Under these conditions, reading rate usually can be quickly improved through focused practice, since the lagging rate probably represents a lingering habit more than a deficiency. A chart of progress, showing reading rate and comprehension on a sequence of reading passages of comparable type and difficulty, can provide incentive for focused practice in reading rate.

Additional IR-TI Options

The IR-TI provides several additional options for testing. Some are built into the general administration procedures and can be used or omitted; others can be used for all, some, or none of the passages. 1) Each reading passage is introduced with a question or two related to its topic or relevant information. A student's response to this prereading questioning provides a means of evaluating prior knowledge while activating prereading **schema.** 2) When recording the student's answers to comprehension questions, a space is available for recording whether the answer is relevant to the question, or "congruent." This provides a means of evaluating the level of the student's **engagement.** 3) After the student has answered the basic comprehension questions, and again after the (optional) higher-order comprehension questions described next, the option is provided to ask students how well, on a scale of 1 to 5, they think they answered the questions, as a measure of **metacognition.** 4) For each reading selection, basic comprehension questions are provided for determining reading levels that will be comparable with other Informal Reading Inventories. Following the basic questions, optional **higher-order comprehension** questions require the student to think beyond the lines for a response. The higher-order questions may be given for each passage during initial test administration, or after the basic IRI format has been completed, and the student's reading levels established. If given later, the student should be asked to reread the passage silently or orally before being asked the additional questions. 5) Finally, at the end of the set of higher-order questions for each passage, there is a question that lends itself to a **reflective writing response,** as an additional option for gathering assessment data.

> It is okay to mark a question congruent when the answer is incorrect, but relevant.

Miscue Analysis

Kenneth Goodman (1973) developed a system he called "miscue analysis" as a way to better understand and interpret the types of problems children encounter in reading. In point of fact, this concept was an integral part of reading assessment for many prior decades. Miscue analysis is based on the psycholinguistic model of reading, which proposes that reading is a complex process of making predictions based on minimal clues and continuously checking the "sense" of these predictions. Traditional procedures for recording and scoring IRIs call for recording every deviation the reader makes from an exact and fluent reading, including repetitions of words or phrases, self-corrections, and lengthy pauses. Goodman proposed that these types of "errors" were not of equal importance. "Errors" such as repetitions, self-corrections, and pauses, in fact, often are indications that the reader is trying to create meaning, rather than simply decoding. Goodman proposed that, at the very least, all errors should be thought of as not as "errors," but as "miscues"—erroneous attempts to make use of available clues to meaning. He suggests that those miscues that do not tend to distort meaning (such as repetitions, self-corrections, and pauses) should not be counted in the total word recognition score. Further, miscues could be analyzed to learn more about the degree to which the reader is functioning as a meaning-maker, rather than just as a word decoder. Miscue analysis is described in more detail ahead, and procedures are included in the IR-TI, since the system is still widely used. Recently, however, it has been challenged on the basis of strong research evidence that word recognition accuracy and fluency are much more essential to comprehension than was proposed in psycholinguistic theory (Adams, 1990).

Miscue analysis is based on the premise that readers use different and increasingly sophisticated types of cues as they progress from beginning reading to mature reading. In order of sophistication, these include:

Orthographic cues. At this level, the reader is using individual letters and letter clusters to predict words. Beginning readers have to rely almost exclusively on these cues, making their reading slow and painstaking.

Syntactic cues. As readers acquire a vocabulary of words that can be recognized on sight, they are able to use elements of syntax, or sentence structure, to make predictions while reading.

Semantic cues. At the highest level readers use semantics, or meaning, as their primary guide while reading.

To emphasize the importance of interpreting oral reading "errors" as indications of the reader's ability to use increasingly sophisticated sets of cues, Goodman jokingly has called reading a "psycholinguistic guessing game." Figure 3.2 illustrates the process of evaluating miscues in terms of these cue systems, as opposed to interpretation based on simple error count.

Yetta Goodman and Carolyn Burke attempted to simplify miscue analysis, in an instrument called the Reading Miscue Inventory (1972). The Reading Miscue Inventory is based on having a student orally read an extended passage, while the examiner carefully records miscues. When interpreting the miscues, the examiner poses nine qualitative questions of each miscue, such as:

> Is there a dialect variation in the miscue?
> How much alike are the word and the miscue in appearance?
> Does the miscue change the meaning?

The reader's comprehension is then compared with the ability to maintain meaning in the miscues.

Several challenges inhibit the practicability of miscue analysis. Hood (1975–76) questioned the reliability of the scoring procedure. Groff (1980) has argued that the scoring is too subjective. Leslie & Osol (1978), Williamson & Young (1974), and Wixson (1979) have shown that the *types* of miscues students make change dramatically at the Instructional as compared to the Frustration levels of reading. The most practical objection has been voiced by Hittleman (1978) and Weaver (1988): the unwieldy two hours needed to administer, score, and interpret the inventory.

Despite these objections, the concept of miscue analysis has had an enduring impact on IRI testing. Most commercially published IRIs are designed to evaluate children's word recognition skills through a *qualitative* analysis of their oral reading, rather than a sum of "errors." Even without extensive miscue analysis, the concept of interpreting oral reading "errors" in the context of the degree to which the student is attempting to make

FIGURE **3.2**

USING MISCUE ANALYSIS VS. SIMPLE ERROR COUNT TO INTERPRET ORAL READING PERFORMANCE

Student A

walsps   *many*
The wasps buzzed around my head, as mad as could be, but they

there   *string*
couldn t get through to sting me.

Student B

                                                                                    s.c.
            fell   *hand*   *cold*
The wasps buzzed around my head, as mad as could be, but they

wouldn't   *in*   *steal*
couldn t get through to sting me.

Student C

        flew
The wasps buzzed around my head, as mad as could be, but they

could not   *in*   *hurt*
couldn t get through to sting me.

Student A made 4 miscues, not counting repetitions and pauses (including these would make a count of 6 "errors"). The student seems to be using orthographic cues alone to predict unknown words: for each of the 4 miscalled words, the student substituted a word that begins with the same letter, and 2 of the 4 substitutions had the same ending letter. None of the substitutions preserved meaning, and only one was a syntactically appropriate substitution.

Student B made 5 miscues, not counting repetitions, pauses, and self-corrections (including these would make a count of 8 "errors"). The student seems to be using primarily semantic cues: only 2 of the 5 miscalled words began with the same letter as the word in the text, and only one had the same ending letter. Only one of the substitutions preserved meaning, and all were syntactically appropriate substitutions (verbs for verbs, nouns for nouns, and so on).

Student C made 6 miscues, not counting pauses (including these would make a count of 7 errors). The 2 omissions did not alter the meaning, nor did any of the 4 substitutions. The substitutions were syntactically and semantically appropriate substitutions.

Counting "errors" alone, Student C would be judged the poorest reader, and Student A the best. Using miscue analysis, the evaluation is reversed.

meaning from print can guide and inform the diagnostician's judgment. Several simplified forms of miscue analysis also have been developed. Among the more notable are inventories by Bean (1979), Cunningham (1984), Siegel (1979), Tortelli (1976), Christie (1979), and Pflaum (1979). Perhaps the most interesting use of miscues is in Retrospective Miscue Analysis (RMA) where readers are invited to discuss the possible underlying logic of their miscues. One case study of an extended use of this simple technique reports a life-changing experience for one third grader in an urban school (Moore and Brantingham, 2003).

Cautions in the Use of IRIs

Several researchers have been tireless workers in analyzing the assumptions of Informal Reading Inventories. Here, in brief form, are some of the findings and recommendations of Frederick Duffelmeyer and associates, and Robert E. Leibert.

- Nearly 50 percent of graded passages on IRIs studied did not have explicitly stated main ideas (Duffelmeyer & Duffelmeyer, 1989).
- The vast majority of vocabulary questions on IRIs do not function properly: "They had an unacceptable level of passage independence; that is, the meaning of the target words used in the selections tended to be familiar to students" (Duffelmeyer, Robinson, & Squier, 1989, 147).
- An inordinate number of comprehension questions on IRIs are unintentionally passage independent; that is, they are better answered from prior knowledge than from textual clues (Duffelmeyer, 1980b; Duffelmeyer, Long, & Kruse, 1987). To combat such weaknesses in IRI testing, Robert E. Leibert (1981) recommends trial lessons that link findings to instruction. For example, if word power is identified initially as the instructional need, the introduction of new words should produce better accuracy during oral reading. Conversely, "a pupil whose needs stem from contextual reading rather than word power should not profit from the previous lesson" (1985, 114).

One additional shortcoming of IRIs is the lack of a measure of meaning vocabulary. For example, in a recent article on refining comprehension development with an IRI it reads: "Vocabulary problems only came to light when Mark asked what a word meant, which rarely happened . . ." (Dewitz and Dewitz, 2003, 427). To correct for this oversight see Appendix A, for a Vocabulary Estimator, grades 3–16.

Oddly, IRIs do not assess meaning vocabulary.

Widely Used Commercial Informal Reading Inventories

There are several excellent commercial IRIs, which are frequently revised and improved. Some of the more popular ones include: the Analytical Reading Inventory, the Basic Reading Inventory, the Classroom Reading Inventory, the Diagnostic Reading Inventory, the Diagnostic Reading Scales, the Edwards Reading Test, the Ekwall Reading Inventory, the Flynt-Cooter Reading Inventory for the Classroom, the Informal Reading

Reflection

To get a better grasp of some of the subtle and unusual possibilities that exist in interpreting diagnostic data, it is useful to ask three or four people, preferably representing different backgrounds and gender, some questions about their own reading habits and behaviors. Here are two questions that often elicit information that is particularly helpful in interpreting IRI results: Do you find that your oral and silent reading fluency are about the same, or is one considerably better than the other? How about comprehension when reading orally or silently? (Answer these questions first as you think others will answer them. Then get ready to revise your thinking.)

Assessment, the McCarthy Individualized Diagnostic Reading Inventory—Revised, the Standard Reading Inventory, the Sucher-Allred Reading Placement Inventory, and the Qualitative Reading Inventory.

STRUCTURED INFORMAL ASSESSMENT AT EMERGENT LITERACY LEVELS

Diagnostic concern at the kindergarten level is likely to be related to limited experiences with print and/or oral language. Two types of short one-to-one interactions with a child can be structured to gather information on the key aspects of literacy development at this level: "Evaluating Concepts about Print" (Figure 3.3) and the "Phonemic Awareness Inventory" (Figure 3.4).

STRUCTURED INFORMAL ASSESSMENT OF BEGINNING READING

In grades 1 and 2, it may become evident from observation that in-depth assessment needs to begin at the kindergarten level, using the tools described above. Or a teacher may be concerned that a child does not

FIGURE **3.3**

EVALUATING CONCEPTS ABOUT PRINT

· ·

Directions

Review the items on the checklist below, and mark each item as it is observed. Use an "S" to mark items that the child spontaneously demonstrates. Use a "Q" to mark items the child correctly demonstrates when questioned. Use an "O" to mark items the child is unable to demonstrate when questioned. Some of the word attack items under Strategies for Constructing Meaning may be marked "NA," for Not Applicable, for children who are not yet using word attack strategies. All items should be marked with one of the above notations.

Show the child a selection of 8 to 10 short "read-aloud" and "beginning reading" books. Tell the child that you would like to read with her, and talk about reading. Ask the child to choose a book, and ask whether she would like to read to you, or for you to read to her.

If the child chooses for you to read the story:

1. You may ask about some of the items as you read, but do no overly interrupt the flow of the story. You may start, for example, by asking the child, "Show me where the story begins."
2. Record whether the child makes spontaneous ("S") comments at this prereading stage, to connect the book with prior experiences. If not, ask prereading questions, and record whether the child responds appropriately ("Q" or "O").
3. Mark each item the child spontaneously demonstrates ("S") as you read and talk about the story.
4. As you read, pause to give the child opportunity to make comments or ask questions. Make comments and ask questions yourself as you read, to invite the child to do likewise.
5. After you have read, ask about any of the Book Concepts, Words/Letters, and Punctuation items not already checked.
6. Ask the child to reread the story to you. If the child says that he can't read, assure him that "it's okay to *tell* the story to me." Diagnosis can begin at the kindergarten level with an Emergent Literacy Checklist.
7. Record any Directionality and Strategies for Constructing Meaning items demonstrated as the child rereads.

8. Ask about any of the Directionality and Strategies for Constructing Meaning items not spontaneously demonstrated as the child reread (or told) the story.

If the child chooses to read the story herself:

1. Record whether the child makes comments at the prereading stage, to connect the book with prior experiences. If not, ask prereading questions, and record whether the child responds appropriately ("Q" or "O").
2. Record Directionality and Reading Concepts items the child spontaneously demonstrates while reading.
3. After the child has read, ask about any of the Book Concepts, Words/Letters, and Punctuation items not already checked.
4. Ask about any of the Strategies for Constructing Meaning items not spontaneously demonstrated as the child read the story. The items regarding "using memory" and "using pictures" to retell the story should be marked "NA."

Interpretation

- The child should be considered an *Emergent Reader* if she chose for the teacher to read the story initially, there are few "S" notations (particularly under Directionality), and many "Os" for Words/Letters (unable to answer when asked).
- The child should be considered a *Transitional Reader* if there are mostly "S" or "Q" notations under Directionality, Words/Letters, Punctuation, Reading Concepts, and Book Concepts. The child may be a Transitional Reader if she chose to read the story initially, and did so by using the pictures rather than the words to construct meaning.
- The child should be considered a *Beginning Reader* if he was able to use print to read the story (on initial reading or rereading after the teacher has read), and if there are mostly "S" or "Q" notations under Directionality, Words/Letters, Punctuation, Reading Concepts, and Book Concepts. The child should be considered a Beginning Reader rather than a Transitional Reader primarily based on observations recorded for the *word attack* strategies under Strategies for Constructing Meaning.

Concepts about Print

Child's Name: _____   Child's Age: _____

Teacher's Name: _____   Date: _____

Directionality

_____ Turns pages left-to-right

_____ Points to (or reads) words in sentences left-to-right

_____ Uses correct return sweep

_____ Follows words top to bottom

_____ Starts at the beginning of book

_____ Finishes at end of book

Words/Letters

_____ Identifies an individual word

_____ Identifies an individual letter

_____ Identifies the first letter in a word

_____ Identifies the last letter in a word

_____ Identifies a capital letter

_____ Identifies a small case letter

_____ Names some of the letters

_____ Identifies key words in isolation

Reading Concepts

_____ Demonstrates or explains that print carries the meaning

_____ Demonstrates or explains word boundaries

Punctuation

_____ Identifies a question mark

_____ Identifies a period

_____ Identifies a comma

_____ Identifies quotation marks

Book Concepts

_____ Identifies book cover

_____ Identifies book title

_____ Identifies title page

Strategies for Constructing Meaning

_____ Uses background experience to build connections to the story meanings

_____ Distinguishes between fact and fiction

_____ Asks questions to clarify understanding

_____ Uses memory for retelling the story

_____ Uses pictures for retelling the story

_____ Uses pictures to help with *word attack* when rereading or reading

_____ Uses language patterns to help with *word attack* when reading

_____ Uses story pattern to help with *word attack* when reading

_____ Uses word structure knowledge to help with *word attack* when reading

_____ Uses beginning letter sounds to help with *word attack* when reading

_____ Uses ending and medial sounds to help with *word attack* when reading

_____ Uses background experience to connect story

Type of book selected (read-aloud/beginning reading):

_____

Title of book: _____

Initial teacher read/child read: _____

_____

Qualifying observations (continue on the back if needed):

_____

_____

_____

_____

_____

_____

FIGURE **3.4**

MANZO, MANZO, ALBEE PHONEMIC AWARENESS INVENTORY

I'm going to ask you about some of the words and sounds in a song you probably know. Do you know "Itsy Bitsy Spider"? You can sing it with me if you like:

> "The itsy bitsy spider went up the water spout/Down came the rain and washed the spider out/ Out came the sun and dried up all the rain/And the itsy bitsy spider went up the spout again."

Hearing Words in Speech

How many words are there in this part of the song: "down came the rain"?   (4)
How many words are in "up the spout"?   (3)
How many words are in "out came the sun"?   (4)
How many words in "water spout"?   (2)

Hearing Syllables in Words

Now, hold up one finger if the word I say has one syllable, or main sound, and hold up two fingers if it has two main sounds.

drain   spout   itsy   down   spider   washed   sun   again

Beginning Sounds

I'm going to say two words. Give me a "thumbs up" if the words have the same beginning sound. Give me a "thumbs down" if the words have different beginning sounds.

down/drain   rain/came   spout/spider   rain/ran   washed/out

Final Sounds

Now, give me a "thumbs up" if the very last sound of the word is the same, or a "thumbs down" if the ending sounds are different. (Example: Do these words have the same very last sound: car/jar?)

down/sun   spout/flat   spider/sun   water/rain   up/help

Recognizing Rhymes

Some of the words in the "itsy bitsy spider" song *rhyme*. *Out* rhymes with *spout, rain* rhymes with *drain*. It's fun to try to think of words that rhyme! See if you can think of a word that rhymes with these words. What's a word that rhymes with:

sun   up   came   down   song

Blending

Now let's think about how sounds can be put together to make words. For example, we blend together the sounds—*(pause briefly between each sound)* s u n—to make the word "sun." See if you can blend the sounds I say to make a word *(pause briefly between each sound in the words below).*

f u n   r ai n   sh oe   t a ke   dr ie d

Phoneme Segmentation

Here's another way to listen to the sounds in words. I'll say a word and you hold up the right number of fingers for the number of sounds in the word. For example, the word "fun" has these sounds: *f u n (hold up 3 fingers)*— three sounds, right? How about *u p*? *(hold up two fingers)*. How about:

sun	dry	all	this	he
(3)	(3)	(2)	(3)	(2)
go	top	ride	icy	green
(2)	(3)	(3)	(3)	(3)

appear to be acquiring a beginning sight word vocabulary, making letter-sound associations, understanding the basic meaning of what is read, and/or making personal connections with print materials read independently or read aloud to the child. Assessment tests and techniques for structured informal assessment at these levels include: sight word vocabulary, phonetic word attack strategies, and story retelling.

Sight Word Acquisition

"Sight words" are the words one can identify instantly, in context or in isolation, without the need to apply word attack strategies. Typically, the first sight words children acquire are those most often seen, such as "stop" and "exit" and their own name. Each person's sight word vocabulary is unique, but by the end of second grade should include, at a minimum, the most frequently occurring words in the language. Contrary to popular belief, about 80 percent of the words in the English language are phonetically regular; however, about 80 percent of the *most frequently occurring* words are irregular. Therefore it is doubly important for these irregular, often-encountered words to be acquired as sight words, and this is best done through direct instruction using engaging drill and practice routines.

"Sight words" must be identified instantly, in context or in isolation.

Several commonly used sight word lists are useful for both assessment and instruction. The most traditional list was compiled by Edward Dolch (1951), and is found in Figure 3.5. Two more recent sight word lists, by Edward Fry (1980) and Marilyn Eeds (1985), are found in Figures 3.6 and 3.7. Fry's list is based on the frequency of occurrence of words in more recent school texts and trade books. Eeds' list is shorter, containing 227 words, also in order of frequency of occurrence, but in 400 storybooks for beginning readers, and therefore is more suitable for a "literature-based" reading program. There are also lists that are carefully mapped to a series, such as the Johnson-Moe Lexicon for the Ginn Basal Reading Series. There is no standardized routine for using a sight word list for assessment. The following tips, however, may be useful for this purpose.

FIGURE **3.5**

DOLCH BASIC SIGHT WORDS

Preprimer	Primer	First Grade	Second Grade	Third Grade
1. a	1. all	1. after	1. always	1. about
2. and	2. am	2. again	2. around	2. better
3. away	3. are	3. an	3. because	3. bring
4. big	4. at	4. any	4. been	4. carry

Preprimer	Primer	First Grade	Second Grade	Third Grade
5. blue	5. ate	5. as	5. before	5. clean
6. can	6. be	6. ask	6. best	6. cut
7. come	7. black	7. by	7. both	7. done
8. down	8. brown	8. could	8. buy	8. draw
9. find	9. but	9. every	9. call	9. drink
10. for	10. came	10. fly	10. cold	10. eight
11. funny	11. did	11. from	11. does	11. fall
12. go	12. do	12. give	12. don't	12. far
13. help	13. eat	13. going	13. fast	13. full
14. here	14. four	14. had	14. first	14. got
15. I	15. get	15. has	15. five	15. grow
16. in	16. good	16. her	16. found	16. hold
17. is	17. have	17. him	17. have	17. not
18. it	18. he	18. his	18. goes	18. hurt
19. jump	19. into	19. how	19. green	19. if
20. little	20. like	20. just	20. it's	20. keep
21. look	21. must	21. know	21. made	21. kind
22. make	22. new	22. let	22. many	22. laugh
23. me	23. no	23. live	23. off	23. light
24. my	24. now	24. may	24. or	24. long
25. not	25. on	25. of	25. pull	25. much
26. one	26. our	26. old	26. read	26. myself
27. play	27. out	27. once	27. right	27. never
28. red	28. please	28. open	28. sing	28. only
29. run	29. pretty	29. over	29. sleep	29. own
30. said	30. ran	30. put	30. tell	30. pick
31. see	31. ride	31. round	31. their	31. seven
32. the	32. saw	32. some	32. these	32. shall
33. three	33. say	33. stop	33. these	33. show
34. to	34. she	34. take	34. those	34. six
35. two	35. so	35. thank	35. upon	35. small
36. up	36. soon	36. them	36. us	36. start
37. we	37. that	37. then	37. use	37. ten
38. where	38. there	38. think	38. very	38. today
39. yellow	39. they	39. walk	39. wash	39. together
40. you	40. this	40. were	40. which	40. try
	41. too	41. when	41. why	41. warm
	42. under		42. wish	
	43. want		43. work	
	44. was		44. would	
	45. well		45. write	
	46. went		46. your	
	47. what			
	48. white			
	49. will			
	50. with			
	51. yes			

Betts, 1936, 456–460.

FIGURE **3.6**

FRY'S "THE NEW INSTANT WORD LIST"

First Hundred

First 25 Group 1a	Second 25 Group 1b	Third 25 Group 1c	Fourth 25 Group 1d
the	or	will	number
of	one	up	no
and	had	other	way
a	by	about	could
to	word	out	people
in	but	many	my
is	not	then	than
you	what	them	first
that	all	these	water
it	were	so	been
he	we	some	call
was	when	her	who
for	your	would	oil
on	can	make	now
are	said	like	find
as	there	him	long
with	use	into	down
his	an	time	day
they	each	has	did
I	which	look	get
at	she	two	come
be	do	more	made
this	how	write	may
have	their	go	part
from	if	see	over

Second Hundred

First 25 Group 2a	Second 25 Group 2b	Third 25 Group 2c	Fourth 25 Group 2d
new	great	put	kind
sound	where	end	hand
take	help	does	picture
only	through	another	again
little	much	well	change
work	before	large	off
know	line	must	play
place	right	big	spell
year	too	even	air
live	mean	such	away
me	old	because	animal
back	any	turn	house
give	same	here	pint
most	tell	why	page

very	boy	ask	letter
after	follow	went	mother
thing	came	men	answer
our	want	read	found
just	show	need	study
name	also	land	still
good	around	different	learn
sentence	form	home	should
man	three	us	America
think	small	move	world
say	set	try	high

Third Hundred

First 25 Group 3a	Second 25 Group 3b	Third 25 Group 3c	Fourth 25 Group 3d
every	left	until	idea
near	don't	children	enough
add	few	side	eat
food	while	feet	face
between	along	car	watch
own	might	mile	far
below	close	night	Indian
country	something	walk	real
plant	seem	white	almost
last	next	sea	let
school	hard	began	above
father	open	grow	girl
keep	example	took	sometimes
tree	begin	river	mountain
never	life	four	cut
start	always	carry	young
city	those	state	talk
earth	both	once	soon
eye	paper	book	list
light	together	hear	song
thought	got	stop	leave
head	group	without	family
under	often	second	body
story	run	late	music
saw	important	miss	color

Fry, 1990, *The Reading Teacher*, 286–287.

- *Preparation.* Type the words on separate sheets in large type, one column of words to a page, with a maximum of ten words to a column (or type two columns to a page, and fold the paper lengthwise when showing it to the child, so that only one column of words is shown at a time). Sight word lists are always sequenced from easiest to most difficult, so prepare and use your lists in that order. Use the smaller type version of the list for recording the child's responses.

FIGURE 3.7

HIGH-FREQUENCY WORDS FROM CHILDREN'S LITERATURE

Final Core 227 Word List Based on 400 Storybooks for Beginning Readers

word	count	word	count	word	count	word	count	word	count
the	1314	not	115	play	59	why	37	hard	26
and	985	like	112	let	59	who	36	push	26
a	831	then	108	long	58	saw	36	our	26
I	757	get	103	here	58	mom	35	their	26
to	746	when	101	how	57	kid	35	watch	26
said	688	thing	100	make	57	give	35	because	25
you	638	do	99	big	56	around	34	door	25
he	488	too	91	from	55	by	34	us	25
it	345	want	91	put	55	Mrs.	34	should	25
in	311	did	91	read	55	off	33	room	25
for	235	could	90	them	55	sister	33	pull	25
she	250	good	90	as	54	find	32	great	24
was	294	this	90	Miss	53	fun	32	gave	24
that	232	don't	89	any	52	more	32	does	24
is	230	little	89	right	52	while	32	car	24
his	226	if	87	nice	50	tell	32	ball	24
but	224	just	87	other	50	sleep	32	sat	24
they	218	baby	86	well	48	made	31	stay	24
my	214	way	85	old	48	first	31	each	23
of	204	there	83	night	48	say	31	ever	23
on	192	every	83	may	48	took	31	until	23
me	187	had	79	about	47	dad	30	shout	23
all	179	father	80	think	47	found	30	mama	22
be	176	went	82	new	46	lady	30	use	22
go	171	see	79	know	46	soon	30	turn	22
can	162	dog	78	help	46	ran	30	thought	22
with	158	home	77	grand	46	dear	29	papa	22
one	157	down	76	boy	46	man	29	lot	21
her	156	got	73	take	45	better	29	blue	21
what	152	would	73	cat	44	through	29	bath	21
we	151	time	71	body	43	stop	29	mean	21
him	144	love	70	school	43	still	29	sit	21
no	143	walk	70	yes	41	fast	28	together	21
so	141	came	69	morning	42	next	28	best	20
out	140	were	68	house	42	only	28	brother	20
up	137	ask	67	after	41	am	27	feel	20
are	133	back	67	never	41	began	27	floor	20
will	127	now	66	or	40	head	27	wait	20
look	126	friend	65	self	40	keep	27	tomorrow	20
some	123	cry	64	try	40	teacher	27	surprise	20
day	123	oh	64	has	38	sure	27	shop	20
at	122	Mr.	63	always	38	says	27	run	20
have	121	bed	63	over	38	ride	27	own	20
your	121	an	62	again	37	hand	26		
mother	119	very	62	side	37	hurry	26		
come	118	where	60	thank	37	pet	26		

Eeds, 1985, *The Reading Teacher*, 286–287.

- *Administration*. Tell the child that you would like to see what words s/he can read. Point to the first word. Encourage the child to "guess" if he or she doesn't think he or she knows the word. Use your judgment to determine when to stop. Permitting the child to continue too long when missing many words can be discouraging and frustrating; quitting too soon may underestimate the child's knowledge. A good "rule of thumb" (to apply flexibly) is when the child misses three out of four of any four words in a row, ask him or her to look down the list and tell you any of the other words he or she knows. Then stop with that list.
- *Interpretation*. Sight word testing is criterion-referenced: It is done to determine which specific words on a sight word list are not yet part of the child's personal sight word list, so that instruction can begin with those particular words.

Phonetic Word Attack Strategies

Tests of word attack strategies and knowledge of phonic elements of words can begin by asking the child to decode what is often known as pseudo or "nonsense words" such as "crail." These probably should be called "con-

Some teachers will cringe, but knowledge of phonic elements can best be estimated by asking a student to decode a "nonsense word" such as "crail."

FIGURE **3.8**

PHONIC ELEMENTS WORD ATTACK TEST
(adapted from several earlier scales)

· ·

Part 1—Nonsense Words

Here are some nonsense words. Tell me how you would read them.
(If student mispronounces examples, say them for him/her.)

Examples: bire   tolar .... *Now read these nonsense words for me.*

| clide | stainite | tresting | chated | grellon |
| brock | spicktion | shayter | chailer | trillent |

Criterion: 8/10   Score: _____

Part 2—Vowel Sounds

Here are some more nonsense words. How would you say each word if the vowel had its short sound?
(If student mispronounces examples, say them for him/her.)

Examples: rop   sen .... *Now read these nonsense words for me.*

| gat | dut | ret | tot | nit |

How would you say each word if the vowel had its long *sound?*
(If student mispronounces examples, say them for him/her.)

Examples: rop   sen .... *Now read these words, using the long vowel sound.*

| gat | dut | ret | tot | nit |

Part 3—Word Parts

Here are some parts of words. Read each word part for me.

ail	op	ell	tion	eep	ter	en
se	all	ow	in	est	ate	er
ay	ite	con	it	ain	ing	ed
and	ake	ill	di	ile	al	
ight	ent	ide	ock	ick	on	

Criterion: 26/33   Score: _____

Part 4—Initial Consonants

This word is "dark"; however, if the first letter were "b" it would be "bark." The next word is "bake"; however, if the first letter were "c" what would it be?

Examples: dark (b) bake (c)

What is this word? . . . If the first letter were _____ , what would it be?

ball (f)	last (f)	dear (h)	took (c)	hole (p)
man (c)	gate (l)	cent (w)	fine (m)	met (l)

Criterion: 8/10   Score: _____

Part 5—Consonant Blends & Digraphs

Here are some parts of words. Say each word part for me.

cl	tr	ch	br	sh
gr	sp	st	pr	th
wh	pl	dr	ck	fl

Criterion: 12/15   Score: _____

Part 6—Letter Sounds and Names

Here are some letters. Tell me the sound each letter makes. .... Now tell me the name of each letter.

s	q	n	l	j	d	c
f	h	b	k	m	p	g
r	t	y	w	z	x	v

(sounds) Criterion: 17/21   Score: _____

(names) Criterion: 17/21   Score: _____

trived words" since they are not random letters but collections designed to assess specific phonemes and corresponding graphemes. It is difficult to use "real" words because there is no way to know whether and which test words might be in a particular child's sight word vocabulary: If the word is a sight word, no word attack strategies are used or tested. If a child has difficulty decoding such nonsense words, it is then useful to know what the child knows about a number of phonic elements of words, such as: short and long vowel sounds, single and double letter onsets, consonant substitution, common rhymes, and recognition of upper- and lower-case letters. The (Manzo, Manzo, Albee) Phonic Elements Word Attack Test in Figure 3.8 is one such test. When using the Phonic Elements Test, it is advisable to reproduce the words, letter clusters, and letters in each of the six test "Parts" in a fairly large font for the student to read from.

Story Retelling

An alternative to questioning, for comprehension assessment, is "retelling"—simply asking the reader to recall all he or she can about the passage. Ringler and Weber (1984) suggest the following retelling prompts:

"Retelling" is a popular, though not necessarily better, alternative to questioning for assessment of comprehension.

- Tell me what you have read, using your own words.
- What is the text about?
- Tell me as much information as you can about what you have just read.

Retellings can be evaluated in a number of ways. Clark (1982) suggested this simple system:

- Break the passage into pausal units, placing a slash wherever a good reader would normally pause during oral reading. These boundaries typically fall at punctuation marks and at connectives such as *and, but,* and *because*. During the student's retelling, check each pausal unit recalled. Give the student credit for responses that capture the gist of the unit. A percent score can then be obtained from number of total units compared to number of units recalled.
- Rate the level of importance for each pausal unit by assigning 1 to the most important units, 2 to the next most important units, and 3 to the least important units. This can be simplified by reading through the passage first to identify the *most* important units (1s), and then again to identify the *least* important units. The remaining units are assigned as 2s. To score this aspect of retelling, add the value of each of the pausal units recalled by the student, and divide by the number of units recalled, to obtain the average importance level of units recalled.
- Record the order in which the pausal units are recalled by numbering them in the order in which they are retold. Sequence of retelling is evaluated subjectively, on a scale of 1 to 5, with 1 being low and 5 high.

Studies have indicated that the initial recall in acceptable retellings averages from 33 to 50%—much lower than the 75 to 90% criterion required by the IRI questioning protocol (Clark, 1982). After initial retelling has been recorded, general prompts can be given, to determine whether the student has offered all that he or she remembers. These prompts should not be directed to specific information in the passage, but simply encourage the student to tell more, if he or she can. Lipson and Wixson (1991) suggest these questions for prompting recall:

- Tell me more about what you have read.
- Tell me more about what happened.
- Tell me more about the people you just read about.
- Tell me more about where this happened.

Figure 3.9 provides a sample retelling recording/scoring form following Clark's format.

As useful as retellings can be, the task does introduce some problems of its own. It can be influenced, for example, by the reader's learning style: "sequential" (linear) learners have an obvious advantage over "simultaneous" processors. It can be influenced, too, by common shyness. And it is very much influenced by prior training: students who have only been exposed to conventional question-answer strategies will have less expectation for what is meant by "retelling" than those exposed to other experiences of this type.

The Durrell Analysis of Reading Difficulty (circa 1957) is an instrument with a rich tradition of using retellings in assessment. The student is told to recall as much as possible. For scoring purposes, the selection is reproduced in segments down a page for marking purposes. This permits the examiner to note a number of possible aspects of the retelling: its accuracy under unprompted and prompted conditions, its sequence, the relative importance of various points recalled, and other more elaborate post-retelling analyses. These include, whether the retelling contained the features of a story grammar (cf, Nancy Marshall, 1983) and other such aspects of effective communication and involvement.

Beth Davey and associates (1989) have provided these additional points of information from their considerable research on formats and factors involved in comprehension assessment:

Vocabulary level correlates best with every other factor in language learning.

- timed testing tends to bias outcomes against less skilled readers (Davey, 1988a)
- poor readers and deaf readers tend to perform comparably to good readers on multiple-choice tests but far worse on free response items (Davey & LaSasso, 1984)
- being able to look back during question answering tends to enhance scores on the free-response items but not on multiple-choice tests (Davey, 1989)
- good readers tend to profit more from lookbacks than poor readers (Davey, 1987, 1988b; Davey & LaSasso, 1984)

Davey (1989) speculates that the latter two findings suggest that poor readers do not have good test-taking strategies—often preferring to leave

FIGURE **3.9**

STORY RETELLING

To prepare

Select a story at the student's *Instructional* grade level. List the thought units in the story on the lines provided.

To administer

1. Have the child read the story either aloud or silently; remove the text and ask the child to retell the story.
2. As the child tells the story, record *numbers* in the "Retelling Sequence" column, to show the sequence of the child's retelling (write a "1" beside the first thought unit the child mentions, a "2" beside the next, and so on).
3. After the child has finished the retelling, ask questions to see if he/she recalls additional information. In the "Prompted Retelling" column, place a check beside any thought units the student *adds* after your questioning.

Story Title: _____   **Grade Level Difficulty:** _____

Thought Units (write these on the lines below)	First Retelling: Sequence	Prompted Retelling: (check)
_____	_____	_____
_____	_____	_____
_____	_____	_____
_____	_____	_____
_____	_____	_____
_____	_____	_____
_____	_____	_____
_____	_____	_____
_____	_____	_____
_____	_____	_____
_____	_____	_____
_____	_____	_____
_____	_____	_____
_____	_____	_____
_____	_____	_____
_____	_____	_____
_____	_____	_____

Percent of thought units included in first retelling	_____ %
Percent of thought units included in first retelling *plus* prompted retelling	_____ %

an item blank rather than going to their own heads when the answer is not explicitly stated.

STRUCTURED INFORMAL ASSESSMENT OF INTERMEDIATE AND UPPER READING LEVELS

When evaluating the reading of intermediate-grade and older students, a variety of additional factors may need to be considered. Several additional reading-specific factors include fluency, meaning vocabulary, and comprehension strategies.

Fluency in Oral Reading

Analysis of a student's oral reading on the Informal Reading Inventory usually provides a sufficient indication of fluency at his or her Instructional level. Most IRI record forms provide a reminder to subjectively evaluate oral reading, including: attending to punctuation, using voice inflections as appropriate to meaning, minimal pauses and repetitions, and rate approximating the rate of oral language. In generating follow-up hypotheses, it is important to consider the possible influence of nonfluent oral reading on comprehension. For nonfluent readers, it is useful to compare comprehension on oral reading with comprehension on silent reading at Instructional level. Curiously, boys who are thought of as being a bit more outgoing tend to be most self-conscious about reading orally. Therefore, it is best to take care to compare their oral reading and silent reading comprehension before determining whether they are sufficiently fluent.

> Nonfluent oral reading clearly influences comprehension; however, lack of oral fluency sometimes has little or no impact on silent reading comprehension.

Meaning Vocabulary

A reader's general vocabulary knowledge is considered to be the best single predictor of how well that reader can understand text (Anderson & Freebody, 1981). This is because meaning vocabulary *correlates* more highly with reading comprehension than any other single factor. Of course, this correlation is not one-directional: We tend to understand better when we know the meanings of all words read, but we also tend to learn the meanings of more words when we read well and widely. The vocabulary list by grade level in Appendix A can be used to generate individual vocabulary tests of any length, such as the (Manzo, Manzo, Albee) Quick-Screening test (grades 3–10) in Figure 3.10.

FIGURE **3.10**

VOCABULARY QUICK TEST

- Make a copy of the word list, without grade-level designations, and place the student copy of the words in front of the child.
- Begin with the list that is at the student's *independent reading level.*
- Say to the student: *I am going to show you some words, and ask you to tell me what they mean.*
- Then point to the first word, *say the word for the student,* and ask what it means. (You can also use the phrases, *what does [insert word] mean,* or *what is a/n [insert word]?*)
- Count the item correct if the child explains the meaning or gives a correct example.
- Do not go *above* the list where the student makes 2 or more errors.
- If the student makes 2 or more errors on the first list attempted, give the next list *down* until he or she makes fewer than 2 errors on a list.
- USE THIS PAGE AS THE RECORD FORM: MARK CORRECT ITEMS WITH +; INCORRECT ITEMS WITH 0. *WRITE IN* THE CHILD'S RESPONSES TO ITEMS MISSED.

BE SURE THE CHILD IS ABLE TO *SEE* THE WORDS, BUT IS NOT ASKED TO *READ* THEM

GRADE 3

accuse—*to blame*
adventure—*exciting happening*
discuss—*talk over*
harbor—*where ships load/unload*
hobby—*favorite free time activity*

GRADE 4

banquet—*big formal meal*
concert—*musical program*
desert—*very dry land*
industrious—*hard-working*
manufacture—*make things*

GRADE 5

abolish—*get rid of*
furious—*very angry*
generous—*unselfish*
horrify—*make afraid*
inventive—*creative*

GRADE 6

camouflage—*disguise*
eliminate—*get rid of*
generation—*people about the same age*
hospitable—*friendly to guests*
society—*group of people*

GRADE 7

manual—*book of instructions*
mockery—*making fun of*
regretfully—*sadly*
sociology—*study of society*
solar—*of the sun*

GRADE 8

astound—*surprise greatly*
flourish—*thrive*
legislator—*a lawmaker*
persuasive—*convincing*
pessimistic—*gloomy*

GRADE 9

descendants—*children/grandchildren*
emissary—*agent or messenger*
fortification—*a defense building*
habitual—*regular*
mandatory—*required*

GRADE 10

carnivorous—*meat-eating*
fiscal—*about money*
heartfelt—*sincere*
lore—*traditions and legends*
matchmaker—*finds marriage partners*

Strategy Acquisition

Metacomprehension Strategy Index   The act of monitoring one's own thinking, or metacognition, is based upon self-knowledge, task knowledge, and self-monitoring. In other words, it is about keeping track of when you are understanding, what you are understanding, when you are not

FIGURE **3.11**

METACOMPREHENSION STRATEGY INDEX (MSI)

I. In each set of four, choose the one statement which tells a good thing to do to help you understand a story better *before* you read it.

1. Before I begin reading, it's a good idea to:
   A. See how many pages are in the story.
   B. Look up all of the big words in the dictionary.
   C. Make some guesses about what I think will happen in the story.
   D. Think about what has happened so far in the story.

2. Before I begin reading, it's a good idea to:
   A. Look at the pictures to see what the story is about.
   B. Decide how long it will take me to read the story.
   C. Sound out the words I don't know.
   D. Check to see if the story is making sense.

3. Before I begin reading, it's a good idea to:
   A. Ask someone to read the story to me.
   B. Read the title to see what the story is about.
   C. Check to see if most of the words have long or short vowels in them.
   D. Check to see if the pictures are in order and make sense.

4. Before I begin reading, it's a good idea to:
   A. Check to see that no pages are missing.
   B. Make a list of the words I'm not sure about.
   C. Use the title and pictures to help me make guesses about what will happen in the story.
   D. Read the last sentence so I will know how the story ends.

5. Before I begin reading, it's a good idea to:
   A. Decide on why I am going to read the story.
   B. Use the difficult words to help me make guesses about what will happen in the story.
   C. Reread some parts to see if I can figure out what is happening if things aren't making sense.
   D. Ask for help with the difficult words.

6. Before I begin reading, it's a good idea to:
   A. Retell all of the main points that have happened so far.
   B. Ask myself questions that I would like to have answered in the story.
   C. Think about the meanings of the words which have more than one meaning.
   D. Look through the story to find all of the words with three or more syllables.

7. Before I begin reading, it's a good idea to:
   A. Check to see if I have read this story before.

B. Use my questions and guesses as a reason for reading the story.
   C. Make sure I can pronounce all of the words before I start.
   D. Think of a better title for the story.

8. Before I begin reading, it's a good idea to:
   A. Think of what I already know about the pictures.
   B. See how many pages are in the story.
   C. Choose the best part of the story to read again.
   D. Read the story aloud to someone.

9. Before I begin reading, it's a good idea to:
   A. Practice reading the story aloud.
   B. Retell all of the main points to make sure I can remember the story.
   C. Think of what the people in the story might be like.
   D. Decide if I have enough time to read the story.

10. Before I begin reading, it's a good idea to:
    A. Check to see if I am understanding the story so far.
    B. Check to see if the words have more than one meaning.
    C. Think about where the story might be taking place.
    D. List all of the important details.

II. In each set of four, choose the one statement which tells a good thing to do to help you understand a story better *while* you are reading it.

11. While I'm reading, it's a good idea to:
    A. Read the story very slowly so that I will not miss any important parts.
    B. Read the title to see what the story is about.
    C. Check to see if the pictures have anything missing.
    D. Check to see if the story is making sense by seeing if I can tell what's happened so far.

12. While I'm reading, it's a good idea to:
    A. Stop to retell the main points to see if I am understanding what has happened so far.
    B. Read the story quickly so that I can find out what happened.
    C. Read only the beginning and the end of the story to find out what it is about.
    D. Skip the parts that are too difficult for me.

13. While I'm reading, it's a good idea to:
    A. Look all of the big words up in the dictionary.
    B. Put the book away and find another one if things aren't making sense.

C. Keep thinking about the title and the pictures to help me decide what is going to happen next.
D. Keep track of how many pages I have left to read.

14. While I'm reading, it's a good idea to:
A. Keep track of how long it is taking me to read the story.
B. Check to see if I can answer any of the questions I asked before I started reading.
C. Read the title to see what the story is going to be about.
D. Add the missing details to the pictures.

15. While I'm reading, it's a good idea to:
A. Have someone read the story aloud to me.
B. Keep track of how many pages I have read.
C. List the story's main character.
D. Check to see if my guesses are right or wrong.

16. While I'm reading, it's a good idea to:
A. Check to see that the characters are real.
B. Make a lot of guesses about what is going to happen next.
C. Not look at the pictures because they might confuse me.
D. Read the story aloud to someone.

17. While I'm reading, it's a good idea to:
A. Try to answer the questions I asked myself.
B. Try not to confuse what I already know with what I'm reading about.
C. Read the story silently.
D. Check to see if I am saying the new vocabulary words correctly.

18. While I'm reading, it's a good idea to:
A. Try to see if my guesses are going to be right or wrong.
B. Reread to be sure I haven't missed any of the words.
C. Decide on why I am reading the story.
D. List what happened first, second, third, and so on.

19. While I'm reading, it's a good idea to:
A. See if I can recognize the new vocabulary words.
B. Be careful not to skip any parts of the story.
C. Check to see how many of the words I already know.
D. Keep thinking of what I already know about the things and ideas in the story to help me decide what is going to happen.

20. While I'm reading, it's a good idea to:
A. Reread some parts or read ahead to see if I can figure out what is happening if things aren't making sense.

B. Take my time reading so that I can be sure I understand what is happening.
C. Change the ending so that it makes sense.
D. Check to see if there are enough pictures to help make the story ideas clear.

III. In each set of four, choose the one statement which tells a good thing to do to help you understand a story better *after* you have read it.

21. After I've read a story it's a good idea to:
A. Count how many pages I read with no mistakes.
B. Check to see if there were enough pictures to go with the story to make it interesting.
C. Check to see if I met my purpose for reading the story.
D. Underline the causes and effects.

22. After I've read a story it's a good idea to:
A. Underline the main idea.
B. Retell the main points of the whole story so I can check to see if I understood it.
C. Read the story again to be sure I said all of the words right.
D. Practice reading the story aloud.

23. After I've read a story it's a good idea to:
A. Read the title and look over the story to see what it is about.
B. Check to see if I skipped any of the vocabulary words.
C. Think about what made me make good or bad predictions.
D. Make a guess about what will happen next in the story.

24. After I've read a story it's a good idea to:
A. Look up all of the big words in the dictionary.
B. Read the best parts aloud.
C. Have someone read the story aloud to me.
D. Think about how the story was like things I already knew about before I started reading.

25. After I've read a story it's a good idea to:
A. Think about how I would have acted if I were the main character in the story.
B. Practice reading the story silently for practice of good reading.
C. Look over the story title and pictures to see what will happen.
D. Make a list of the things I understood the most.

---

*Underlined responses indicate metacomprehension strategy awareness.

Schmitt, 1990, *The Reading Teacher,* 459–461.

understanding, and knowing what needs to be done to improve comprehension, rate, recall, or some other aspect of faltering learning (Brown, Campione, & Day, 1981; Manzo & Manzo, 1990a; Sanacore, 1984; Wagoner, 1983). Logically, it is also a solid indicator of personal responsibility and social-emotional adjustment.

Since metacognition is a strand of self-examination that can and should run through all aspects of living and learning, it is potentially visible and therefore measurable in a variety of ways. However, student metacognitive functioning, like miscues in oral reading, appear to vary with the difficulty level of the material, and therefore require thoughtful interpretation.

The assessment of metacognition took a significant step forward with Maribeth Cassidy Schmitt's (1990) development of the Metacomprehension Strategy Index (see Figure 3.11). The MSI was found to correlate well with other indices and measures of metacognitive awareness and comprehension: .48 with the Index of Reading Awareness (Paris, Cross, & Lipson, 1984); .50 with an error detection task (for example, finding irrelevant or contradictory elements in a passage); and .49 with a cloze task (Schmitt, 1988). Lonberger (1988) reported a very respectable internal reliability of .87 for the MSI.

Prior to taking the test, students are told: "Think about what kinds of things you can do to help yourself understand a story better before, during, and after you read it. Read each of the lists of four statements and decide which one of them would help you the most. There are no right answers. It is just what you think would help the most." Ironically, there is only one choice in each item that indicates appropriate metacomprehension strategy awareness, and it yields a score of 1 point.

Metacognition is knowing *when* you know, knowing *what* you know, knowing what you *need to know,* and *knowing what needs to be learned.*

The MSI can be administered orally or silently. It is designed to measure strategies specific to narrative, more so than expository, comprehension. However, items can be adapted to use with content textbooks. The inventory assesses behaviors that fit within six broad categories:

   a) predicting and verifying (item nos. 1, 13, 14, 15, 16, 18, 23)
   b) previewing (item nos. 2, 3)
   c) purpose setting (item nos. 5, 7, 21)
   d) self-questioning (item nos. 6, 14, 17)
   e) drawing from background knowledge (item nos. 8, 9, 10, 19, 24, 25)
   f) summarizing and applying fix-up strategies (item nos. 11, 12, 20, 22)

See Figure 3.12 for Schmitt's suggestions for how to use and interpret the MSI.

Think-Aloud Assessment   "Think-alouds," where a student attempts to externalize his or her thought processes, offer another way to listen in, diagnostically, on a student's inner-speech, or metacognitive processing.

FIGURE **3.12**

USE AND INTERPRETATION OF THE **MSI**

Interpreting the MSI

The results of the MSI can be used to help teachers design programs of reading comprehension instruction for individual students. Following is an MSI class record for a hypothetical fourth-grade class. Included are the students' scores for each of the six clusters of items, total MSI score, and percentile rank for the comprehension subtest of a standardized achievement test. MSI results can be interpreted both quantitatively and qualitatively. Following are descriptions of the decision-making processes for Linda and Emily in this fourth-grade class.

Class Record for Fourth Graders

	MSI Data							Comprehension Percentile	Teacher Observations
	P/V (7)	Pre (2)	Pur (3)	Que (3)	B/K (6)	S/FU (4)	Total (25)		
Linda A.	6	2	2	3	5	4	22	89	A strong, competent reader performing at a higher level on all reading comprehension tasks
Emily B.	2	0	1	1	1	1	6	12	Struggles with most reading tasks; tends to over-rely on the graphophonic cue system
Dwayne B.	6	2	2	2	4	3	19	17	A capable student and a good decoder, but he has difficulty in many comprehension tasks; does not always seem to apply skills well
Constance C.	3	0	1	2	1	2	9	67	A good reader with no apparent problems in reading comprehension

Key:
P/V = Predicting and Verifying   Que = Self-Questioning
Pre = Previewing   B/K = Drawing from Background Knowledge
Pur = Purpose Setting   S/FU = Summarizing and Applying Fix-Up Strategies
The number of items within each metacomprehension category is indicated by parentheses.

Linda A. Linda performed at a high level on the MSI, selecting 22 out of 25 responses that are indicative of metacomprehension awareness. Further, her standardized test score suggests that she is a skilled comprehender, and her teacher's opinion of Linda's abilities was consistent with both of these findings. Thus, the MSI served to affirm the teacher's belief that Linda was a competent, strategic reader.

Emily B. Emily's performance on the MSI suggests low strategy awareness, and her performance on the standardized test suggests a low general performance in reading comprehension. Emily's teacher sees her struggling with reading comprehension and also notes that Emily tends to focus on accurate word pronunciation during reading rather than reading for meaning. As a result, Emily's miscues tend to be semantically unacceptable though they are good phonic representations of the words she attempts to pronounce. Consistent with this finding is Emily's tendency to select responses on the MSI that were related to word identification (for example, she chose "Sound out words I don't know," "Check to see if the words have long or short vowels in them").

In addition, Emily tended to select responses that were inappropriate with the phase of reading. For example, for item 6, which probed for a before-reading behavior, Emily selected "Retell all of the main points that have happened so far," a during- or after-reading behavior. This suggests that she is unaware of when to select specific strategies for use. Emily's teacher concludes that she would benefit from a program of instruction that involves explicit teaching of metacomprehension strategies and when to apply those strategies; the program of instruction should also enable Emily to achieve a balance in drawing from graphophonic and meaning cues.

Schmitt, 1990, *The Reading Teacher*, 455–457.

Cloze passage exercises are a useful way to elicit think-alouds. Here is a recommended procedure for using cloze in this way:

1. Identify three to five passages of varying difficulty.
2. Make *two* short (nonstandard) cloze type tests from *each* passage: one with every fifth word deleted and one with every ninth word deleted, with up to 25 deletions. Be sure that the first sentence is left intact.
3. Read the passage to the student who has the ninth-word deletions and that is closest to that student's independent level. Ask the student to orally suggest replacement words. Record responses and periodically, about five times throughout the oral examination, ask the student questions such as:
   - Do you think that you are understanding this story so far?
   - Do you think that you came up with the correct word here?
   - What made you guess that word?
   - How are you trying to figure out which word to say? What is helping you?
4. Administer the *same passage,* but with fifth-word deletions in a silent reading mode. Ask the student to give an estimation of their correctness by marking above each word they replace whether that word is probably correct (+), or incorrect (–). Do not use "uncertain" with cloze. It is too easy to say "uncertain" for items on this test.
5. Score by: a) accepting reasonable synonyms; b) comparing a student's estimation of correctness on each item with actual correctness.

Another, even more informal approach to think-alouds is simply to have a student read a short segment of text (a few sentences will do) and then tell what he or she was thinking as he or she read (Afflerbach & Johnston, 1986; Davey, 1983; Ericsson & Simon, 1980). To gain further insights into student self-monitoring and thought processes, students can be asked to perform certain conventional reading operations and to comment aloud on their thinking about these. Operations such as summarizing, predicting, verifying, relating information to prior knowledge, and evaluating the material to determine if they like it are all good means of eliciting clues to internal processing.

This same process can be done in a silent reading and writing mode. Simply mark off and number certain sections of text—words, phrases, sentences, or paragraphs, and have students stop at these points and write out "anything and everything that you are thinking at this point" (Baumann, 1988).

Suzanne Wade (1990) developed a specific procedure for administering and scoring a comprehension think-aloud. During the process of using the procedure with second- through ninth-grade students referred for tutoring

Inner speech is an ongoing function of the conscious mind . . . it has enormous implications for whether a student is engaged in self-teaching/learning.

in reading by their teachers, five categories of readers evolved. This seems to be an important step toward more precise diagnostic-prescriptive teaching, even while she did not report particular inteventions. The name of each category, a description, and possible causes that would place a child in this category are listed below:

1. The good comprehender—interactive reader, constructs meaning and monitors comprehension, uses extensive background knowledge, makes reasonable inferences, recognizes when more information is needed, and leaves original idea when the text information suggests a different focus.

2. The non-risk taker—bottom-up processor, passive reader, doesn't go beyond the text to make hypotheses, cannot retell what the story is about or repeats exact words and phrases from the text, looks to the teacher for clues, won't risk being inaccurate.

Possible causes—lack of background knowledge, overreliance on decoding and text, difficulty in activating appropriate schema.

3. The non-integrator—develops new hypotheses for every part of the text based on text clues and prior knowledge, fails to connect new hypotheses with previous ones or new information with previous information, doesn't go beyond the text to integrate knowledge.

Possible causes—decoding problems may consume all of their attention, may have trouble understanding or remembering the relationship between ideas.

4. The schema imposer—holds on to an initial hypothesis and disregards incoming information that conflicts with the schema, not aware of alternative hypotheses, understands that reading is a meaning-based process.

Possible causes—overreliance on top-down processing, may have decoding difficulties so guesses at general meaning, lacks strategies for comprehension monitoring.

5. The storyteller—draws heavily on prior knowledge or experience and not on information in the text, strongly identifies with the character, makes causal inferences based on own preferences.

Possible causes—decoding difficulties, lack of strategies for comprehension monitoring.

(Summarized from Wade, *The Reading Teacher*, 1990, 444–449.)

Analyzing a child's think-aloud and then aligning the information learned with one of the five categories may provide direction for future instruction. Another way to encourage strategic reading is through strategic reasoning.

The meaning and significance of certain skills and abilities vary considerably by age-grade level . . . it's important to know these differences.

Strategic reasoning, or strategic self-talk, is a small aspect of the larger function of inner-speech that we have referred to previously as an ongoing condition of the conscious mind. Strategic reasoning is defined by Herrmann (1992) as "the complex thinking processes used before, during, and after reading to construct meaningful interpretations of text and to create meaningful texts" (428). This provides another window into a child's metacognitive processing. According to Herrmann (1992), the main difference between think-alouds and strategic reasoning is an emphasis on thinking processes, not just the end result of thinking. It is critical for the teacher to model strategic reasoning examples before asking the students to share them. Then prompts such as, "Clearly describe the kind of thinking you are using to construct meaning," "What comprehension difficulties/blockages are you experiencing?" and "How do you attempt to resolve comprehension difficulties/blockages?" are used to encourage strategic reasoning after a student has read a passage (Herrmann, 1992). This information may be shared orally or written in a student journal. Read the following fifth-grade student's journal excerpt containing a description of a comprehension blockage and how the student removed it:

> "Yesterday I was reading *The Wizard of Oz* and I had trouble with some of the words they used to describe the people in that strange country. The words were *shepherdesses* and *bodices* and *breeches* and *ermine* robes. I thought about what I had already read about the country and different types of clothing, then I tried to picture what those people must have looked like" (Herrmann, 1992, 432).

Strategic reasoning assists students and teachers in thinking about and verbalizing their own thinking processes as they read. Another instructional technique that helps students' metacognitive development focuses on different types of questions and the source of their answers.

Question-Answer Relationships   Teaching the Question-Answer Relationships (QAR) (Raphael, 1984) technique encourages children to cognitively monitor the type of information contained in the text and the information that is "in their heads." Struggling readers frequently say, "I can't find the answer to this question" when it is an open-ended or inferential question that requires a response based on the child's background knowledge. To help children understand that different types of questions rely on information from different sources (text, yourself, and a combination of both), Taffy Raphael (1984) developed four questioning strategies. First, a teacher models each of the four questioning strategies separately, providing guided practice for one before moving on to the next. Then students read a short passage and begin to identify each type of question that the teacher models. The four question types are:

In the Book QARs:

1. **Right There**—literal thinking or reading the lines

   The answer to a "Right There" question is in the text information and is usually easy to find. The words used to make up the question and words used to answer the question are "Right There" in the same sentence.

2. **Think and Search**—literal thinking or reading the lines

   The answer to a "Think and Search" question is in the story, but the reader needs to put together different sections of information to find it. Words for the question and words for the answer are not found in the same sentence, but they come from different parts of the text.

In My Head QARs:

3. **Author and Me**—interpretive thinking or reading between the lines

   The answer to an "Author and Me" question is not directly found in the text. The author provides information in the text that has to be combined with what the reader already knows (prior knowledge, previous chapters, and so on) to answer the question.

4. **On My Own**—applied thinking or reading beyond the lines

   The answer to an "On My Own" question is related to information in the text, but the answer is based primarily on the student's prior knowledge.

Elementary through high school age students (especially those with average and low abilities) who are trained to use the QAR technique consistently show significant improvement in their ability to answer questions about their thinking in a variety of subject areas (McInstosh & Draper, 1995; Helfeldt & Henk, 1990; Raphael, 1986, 1984). Assessing a child's knowledge of the sources of answers for different types of questions and identifying the reader category can assist in instructional planning. The method has one drawback. It can tend to become a conversation about comprehension, more than about the text. This is easily fixed; do not permit the discussion of where a response is coming from to overly exceed attention to the response.

Strategy Pictograms.   An interesting technique begins with a teacher-guided discussion of reading strategies: "What are some things you do to make sense of what you read?" "What is the very first thing you do when you start to read something for school? . . . What do you do next?" Following this open-ended discussion, students are asked to draw a series of pictograms, or simple drawings, to represent what they do when they read challenging material. This technique can be used to initiate a beneficial diagnostic-prescriptive session with a student. Several teachers have devised variations on this method. The one that younger children seem to enjoy most begins with a cut out of a palm tree to which fronds are added with labels for each new reading strategy learned. The act of seeking to understand and use various strategies seems to be advanced by the hands-on additions of colorful fronds.

REVIEW

This chapter covered the fundamentals of standardized and field-based assessment of typical deficits in reading, and specific areas, including metacognition. These factors are the most frequently measured on most classroom and conventional achievement tests. You now know several ways to cross-verify and challenge such findings in contrast to one another.

PREVIEW

The next chapter addresses assessment of several language arts factors often referenced in definitions of reading progress, but sporadically assessed. You probably will be called upon to assess these. They include: schema (general knowledge), spelling, language development, and study skills.

ASSESSMENT OF LANGUAGE ARTS—SPELLING, WRITING, ORAL LANGUAGE—AND STUDY SKILLS

Little by little does the trick. – AESOP (CIRCA 600 BC)

CONTENT AND CONCEPT ORGANIZER

Relatively separate skill sets travel together under the label "Reading and Language Arts." Some are related on a logical level, like spelling to reading, but not by numerical correlation. Others are highly related to reading logically and by correlation, such as prior knowledge (schema). This chapter addresses assessment, sorting-out, and implications to diagnosis and instruction of each of these, including elements of writing, normal language development, and the sometimes overlooked acquisition of study habits. These are further considerations under the "Deficit" category of the "6D" model that provides much of the organizing principle of this book.

CHAPTER OUTLINE

DEFICITS IN DEVELOPMENT OF READING-
    RELATED LANGUAGE ARTS

ASSESSING READING-RELATED "DEFICITS"
    Schema Assessment
    Quick Spelling Assessment
    The "Spelling Assessment System"
    Language-Thinking Functions
    Language–Learning Disabled (LLD)
    Pattern Recognition and Language Development
    Cloze Passage Testing

WRITING: CRAFT AND CONTENT
    "Universal Assessment System"
    Informal Writing Inventory

STUDY SKILLS AND HABITS OF MIND
    Study Skills
    Informal Textbook Inventory
    Rogers' Study–Reading Skills Checklist

REVIEW

PREVIEW

DEFICITS IN DEVELOPMENT OF READING-RELATED LANGUAGE ARTS

The "Deficit" category is the one most closely and frequently assessed.

The Deficit, or skill set, category of the 6D model is the most closely and frequently monitored and assessed. Beyond reading per se this category includes schema (prior knowledge/dispositions), spelling, aspects of language development, writing, and study skills. This category also includes intangibles that are easily overlooked in typical and standardized ("high stakes") assessment, even though no one would argue that they are anything but highly influential and integral to verbal reasoning and social-emotional adjustment. These can be referred to as Trace Elements of progress toward reading, language, thinking, and social-emotional maturity. These factors parallel the mineral trace elements in the human body such as zinc and potassium that are so essential to normal brain functioning, and include:

- inclination and skill in thinking abstractly
- ability to critique and be critiqued (or give and take *constructive* review)
- emotional intelligence
- inclination and ability to read between and beyond the lines
- inclination and ability to deal with ambiguities
- inclination to think about and refine understandings of the world about oneself (schema and world view building)
- tendency toward self-examination, particularly metacognitive functions in reading and learning (as covered in the previous chapter)

There are slight, but significant Trace Elements in reading just as there are slight, but significant mineral trace elements in the functioning of the human body and brain.

It is difficult to assign quantitative values to Trace Elements; nonetheless, they ought to be considered when conducting in-depth diagnostic assessment. In a manner of speaking, these may be the ultimate purpose of schooling, a reminder of education's larger goals as we detail quantitative assessment of Language Arts Deficits.

ASSESSING READING-RELATED "DEFICITS"

Schema Assessment

Schema is the personal organization of information and experiences related to a topic. There is much discussion of the role of schema in reading and learning, but little familiarity with how simple it is to assess and interpret. Schema is best assessed by looking at a student's grades and grade point average: These are almost pure measures of one's general knowledge of literature, content, and word-based concepts. Schema theory is based on the assumption that print itself conveys no meaning (Adam & Collins, 1977), but rather provides the reader with stimuli for reconstructing the author's meaning, extending meaning and thought, and building new schemata—additional factual and idea structures for catching and screening the worthwhile information that passes by us in and out of the classroom. *Schema* is also a reference to the "subtext" of understandings that authors assume readers have available when they read. Without assumptions, communication would be like a conversation with a toddler. To use another metaphor, it has been suggested that words in text are like the buttons on a push-button telephone: They connect us with the information, concepts, and functions that we need to follow and build upon an author's message (Rude & Oehlkers, 1984).

To do this for the wide variety of things we read and think about, the reader must "call-up" a variety of schemata to give meaning to, and build meaning on, even a simple message. A message such as: "A stitch in time saves nine" requires:

"Schema" is simply assessed by knowing a student's grades.

- prior knowledge (when in history or in personal experience that failure to act in a timely way resulted in problems and more effort and work)
- cultural orientation (the adage is very "Western" and assertive)
- ability to form abstractions and follow metaphors (how a "stitch" represents decisiveness and action)
- vocabulary knowledge (the definition of "stitch")
- understanding of figurative language ("in time," meaning in a timely way)
- healthy emotional outlook (avoiding undue anxieties or distortions of the intended meaning)
- an understanding of the world (as a place where timeliness often is important)

If the six words in the above proverb were thought of as a phone number, "assessing schema" means dialing-up all the factors and subworking systems mentioned above. Fortunately, from the standpoint of assessment, several of these factors tend to be highly correlated, and can be inferred from one another.

The easiest way to assess general schema, beyond grade point average, is to take an almost random measure of one's fund of general or topical knowledge, as it compares with others in that age-grade category. Most standardized tests and criterion-referenced tests offer such measures in each content or subject domain. Several other indices may be brought together to get a solid index of general schema. These include the following measures (discussed in the chapters ahead and in related appendices):

- Information, Comprehension, and Vocabulary subtests of the Weschler IQ Test (see Appendix B)
- Peabody Picture Vocabulary Test
- Proverbs Comprehension and Abstract Thinking Tests (see Appendix C)
- Cognitive and Affective Filter Inventory (Chapter 5)
- recognition-question tests of topical (content) knowledge
- interviews for personal topical (content) knowledge

Curiously, Sheila W. Valencia et al. (1990) did not find the latter two to be highly correlated. The researchers concluded nonetheless that recognition test questions are adequate for assessing a specific body of information; the interview format opens a broader window on a student's knowledge (that is, to the schemata), though it requires more subjective interpretation. "Old-fashioned" multiple-choice tests generally have much higher validity and reliability than informal interviews and subjective observations. Their shortfall is in what they do not measure, not in the accuracy and thoroughness of what they do measure.

Almost every aspect of living and learning interacts with our schemata and worldview, and can be tapped to gain insight into the breadth, depth, and content of this basic function. Equal educational opportunity is rooted in acquiring common branches of learning, or core curriculum (Camperell, 1984). Spelling, one of the most visible dressings of being learned, is not a very meaningful predictor of what we know. Nonetheless, no child should leave school shabbily dressed.

Quick Spelling Assessment

Gentry and Gillett (1993) developed a way to estimate spelling ability related to a stage theory of spelling development, and to identify specific needs. Simply dictate the ten words below for students to spell on paper. They are not expected to spell all words correctly. Use their attempts to determine their stage in spelling development by checking performance against the stages noted in language suggested by a teacher (see Figure 4.1). This same guide can be used as a rubric to determine progress in writing.

1. monster	6. human
2. united	7. eagle
3. dress	8. closed
4. bottom	9. bumped
5. hiked	10. type

FIGURE **4.1**

STAGES OF SPELLING DEVELOPMENT

Precommunicative Stage:

Spelling at this stage contains scribbles, circles, and lines with a few letters thrown in at random. These letters are usually just there and any connection between these letters and the words they are thinking is pure coincidence.

Semiphonetic Stage:

The second stage can be seen when words begin to be represented by a letter or two. The word *monster* may be written with just the *m* or an *mr* or a *mtr*. *Type* might be spelled with just a *t* or *tp*. This stage indicates that the child is beginning to understand letter-sound relationships and knows the consonant letters that represent some sounds.

Phonetic Stage:

In the third stage, vowels appear—not always the right vowels but vowels are used and most sounds are represented by at least one letter. Phonetic spellings of *mon-*

ster might include *munstr* and *mostr*. *Type* will probably be spelled *tip*. You can usually tell when a child is in the phonetic stage because you can read most of what children in this stage will write.

Transitional Stage:

In this stage all sounds are represented and the spelling is usually a possible English spelling, just not the correct spelling. *Monster* in this stage might be spelled *monstir* or *monstur*. *Type* is probably spelled *tipe*.

Conventional Stage:

Finally, the child reaches the stage of conventional spelling in which most words that children at that grade level could be expected to spell correctly are in fact spelled correctly.

The "Spelling Assessment System"

Gable, Hendrickson, and Meeks (1988) have assembled a dynamic five-step system of collecting, analyzing, and remedying spelling errors that is based on the Gentry model. It can be used along with other reading and language arts activities or as a separate, intensive training program. It can be used as a whole-class activity or in small-group or individual tutoring settings. The five-step system is largely based on the work of Anderson (1985), Henderson (1985), and other advocates of "invented spelling"—where students experiment with language while writing, as well as Gentry's (1982) stage model of progression that builds on the relationship of language skills to spelling. Gentry's self-defining stages, as shown in Figure 4.1, can be further reduced for reference and explanation in case reports as follows:

- precommunicative (little resemblance to the target word)
- semiphonetic (partially resembling the target word, usually accurate in the initial sounds)
- phonetic (having accurate sound representations despite incorrect spelling)
- transitional (marked by good phonetic and configurational representation but still contains inaccuracies)
- correct (accurate spelling)

Spelling is external dress, and no child should leave school shabbily dressed.

First-graders typically approach spelling strictly letter-by-letter, left-to-right. By the end of first grade, children begin to recognize patterns such as the final silent letter in single-syllable words. Later, they begin to recognize patterns in multisyllabic words, and the connections between (seeming) irregular spellings and word meanings.

The Spelling Assessment System is designed to help identify a student's spelling stage *and* to assist the student in advancing to the next stage. See Figure 4.2.

It is not widely appreciated, but it is possible to unobtrusively assess several specific aspects of language-thinking functions. If you are inclined to do so, you will be interested in this brief critique of these forming topics.

Language-Thinking Functions

Language can be defined as a complex and dynamic system of conventional symbols used in various modes of thought and communication (abbreviated from the American Speech-Language-Hearing Association, 1983). Where reading and learning are concerned, five aspects are frequently referenced:

- Phonology—the acoustic and phonetic features of words
- Semantics—governs the meanings of words and word combinations
- Morphology—inflections and auxiliary forms of words that change and convey tense
- Syntax—how words are combined into larger meaningful units of phrases, clauses, and sentences (also sometimes known as *prosody*—or the metrical nature of language patterns)
- Pragmatics—refers to the contextual and purposeful use of language, such as declaring, greeting, requesting, and answering (abstracted from Catts & Kamhi, 1999)

Katherine Maria (1990) reminds us that the chief purpose of all speaking and writing is communication. Within this main purpose, M. A. Halliday (1975) has delineated several categories of the Pragmatic aspects of language functioning. See Figure 4.3 (page 131). We have added Private (but audible) and Inner (silent) Speech to Halliday's categories, since it is essential to self-teaching and mediation, or self-guidance in problem-solving. Several approaches to assessment of Private and Inner speech categories were provided in Chapter 3.

Halliday's categories of language functions can be used to derive a fairly sophisticated profile of a student's oral and written language proficiency and overall thinking (see Figure 4.3). It is best to use this subjective scaling

FIGURE **4.2**

SPELLING ASSESSMENT SYSTEM

Steps in the Spelling Assessment System

Step 1. Sample and Identify

a) Obtain a sample of student spellings of approximately 50 words in any reasonable way, as by dictating a conventional word list or by dictating a paragraph roughly at a student's independent reading level. This can be done either way because students' spelling errors on paragraphs are quite consistent with those on word lists (DeMaster, Crossland, & Hasselbring, 1986).

b) Use the words missed to replenish a 5- to 10-word flow list of test-teach-test items, where a word is moved off the list and replaced when it is spelled correctly five consecutive times.

Step 2. Interview Students

Talk to students about their spelling to establish instructional priorities. Ask: "Are there any words you hate to spell? What confuses you about spelling that word? Tell me another word you tend to have trouble spelling." Also ask: "What part of this word (pointing to several, one at a time) do you tend to have trouble spelling?" Finally, ask: "What difficult words can you spell correctly? How did you learn these words? How do you remember these words?" This introspective approach can have a very generative payoff if it leads remedial students to realize and correct a serious strategy flaw that permeates their spelling and reading: They tend to invert the most productive order for decoding and spelling words, using a visual, whole-word approach to *reading* words, and a phonetic approach to *spelling* them (Clark, 1988).

Step 3. Analyze and Classify Errors

Errors, or invented spellings, can be analyzed in several possible ways. The letters-in-place method is recommended. With this method, strengths as well as patterns of errors become apparent; for example, the word is "bucket," the student writes "b-a-c-c-e-t." Errors-in-place reveals only two errors in this strange word (b a c c e t). Errors can be further categorized according to words that are regular, predictable, or irregular:

Word type	*Description*	*Examples*
Regular	Word contains exact phoneme-grapheme correspondence	pig, nap, set, see
Predictable	Word contains orthographic patterns or generalizations without strict phoneme-grapheme correspondence; spelled by applying rules to sound-letter correspondence	receive, may, day, sweet, soap
Irregular	Word does not conform to sound-letter or orthographic regularities; several graphemic clues exist	melon, through, might, laughing

Teacher's Analysis Chart for a Student's Spelling Errors

Student _____ Date _____

Material/level _____

Word source: Word list ( ) Paragraph ( ) Other _____

Type of analysis/scoring: Word ( ) Syllables ( ) Clusters ( ) Letters ( )

	Word Types			
	Regular	*Predictable*	*Irregular*	*Instructional Priority*
Error type	_____	_____	_____	_____
Rules/patterns	_____	_____	_____	_____
Consonants	_____	_____	_____	_____
Vowels	_____	_____	_____	_____
Error tendency				
Order	_____	_____	_____	_____
Substitution	_____	_____	_____	_____
Insertion	_____	_____	_____	_____
Omission	_____	_____	_____	_____

Beginning time _____   Ending time _____   Number of minutes _____

Correct _____   Errors _____

Step 4. Select a Corrective Strategy

Ten basic teaching strategies for spelling instruction have been grouped into three major diagnostic categories as shown below:

Corrective Spelling Strategies

For *regular* words
- Stress letter-sound correspondence
- Stress application rather than memorization

For *predictable* words
- Emphasize spelling rules
- Use mnemonic devices
- Teach rhyming words
- Teach word families

For *irregular* words
- Use flash cards
- Use look-cover-copy-compare
- Use multisensory VAKT approaches (detailed in Chapter 12)
- Use visual memory experiences (see ahead)

Note: For single errors associated with carelessness or inattention, simple corrective feedback is advised. For repeated mistakes, strategies such as modeling correct spellings or discriminating correct from incorrect spellings (verbal or written) are recommended.

Step 5. Evaluate the Program

To evaluate the effectiveness of the spelling program, collect sample student tests over a period of time. The traditional criterion for a set of words is 80%.

To arrive at some valid standards for remedial and exceptional children, collect scores of proficient and low-achieving students and establish a band within which reasonable levels of success can be expected.

Adapted from Hendrickson, Gable, & Hasselbring,1988; Gable, Hendrickson, & Meeks, 1988; DeMaster, Crossland, & Hasselbring,1986; Hasselbring & Owens, 1982 system over several samples. The samples are especially useful in keeping anecdotal records and in reporting. Awareness of these functions also serves as a reminder to the teacher to elicit each type of language, thereby providing students with appropriate practice in thinking and articulating effectively in each function area noted.

Reading and writing are said to be profoundly related, but in assessments they are not.

To provide an additional index of proficiency with language, administer either an oral or written Cloze Passage Test at the student's instructional level (McKenna & Robinson, 1980). A score higher or lower than that established on an IRI measure of word recognition and silent reading comprehension would indicate average, above, or below level of familiarity with language patterns (prosody) and related aspects of syntax. Guidelines for constructing, administering, scoring, and interpreting a Standard Cloze Passage Test are provided in Figure 4.4.

Language–Learning Disabled (LLD)

There is a growing sense among some researchers that there should be a category called Language–Learning Disabled (LLD) (Catts, Frey, & Tomblin, 1997). This category would allow educators to distinguish, identify,

FIGURE **4.3**

RATING SCALE FOR PRAGMATIC ASPECTS OF LANGUAGE FUNCTIONS

Rating	Function Areas of Language and Thought
____	1. Instrumental language—used to get things and for satisfying needs
____	2. Regulatory language—used to control and direct others
____	3. Interactional language—used for establishing and maintaining relationships with others
____	4. Personal language—used to express aspects of temperament, personality, or individuality
____	5. Imaginative language—used to create and describe one's own perspective or world view
____	6. Informative language—used to convey information, including how one is experiencing the world
____	7. Heuristic language—used to find things out, wonder, question, and hypothesize
____	8. Private and Inner-speech—used to mediate one's own thinking
____	9. Overall language—skillful and appropriate use of the other functions

A category called Language–Learning Disabled (LLD) could solve the problem of special instruction being limited to those with IQs higher than their reading performance.

and treat students who have weak (language) comprehension, and therefore low scores on IQ tests, in the same way that we do dyslexics who generally have poor phonological reading, but higher IQ scores. The treatment, they argue, would be aimed at comprehension, more so than word recognition and analysis, and could result in considerable progress in overall academic performance. While this dialog could bring together reading, LD, and speech and hearing specialists at some time in the future, for the present, language development in reading remains fairly bound to elements of word decoding and vocabulary knowledge, and recognition of "language patterns" in prose. Knowledge of how to diagnose and precisely address possible problems in pattern recognition is known, and could become a valuable bridging mechanism between these now disparate fields.

Pattern Recognition and Language Development

The ability to recognize and complete phrases is a key indicator of language development.

The ability to recognize and hence anticipate and complete phrases is part of a larger ability to recognize redundant patterns in prose. This prosody-type skill is best measured by Cloze Passage testing. It also is a powerful index of overall familiarity with second-language acquisition. Several aspects of second-language and related issues in culture acquisition are addressed more fully in Chapter 12, which is devoted to this growing need and concern.

Cloze Passage Testing

The term *cloze* has come to refer to any activities in which students are asked to fill in missing words in passages. The term was coined by Wilson Taylor (1953), who was using this fill-in-the-blanks activity to try to measure the psychological trait of "closure": the tendency to complete missing elements of an incomplete pattern and recognize it as a meaningful whole. Taylor's cloze test was not a good measure of *closure,* but he did find that it had a strong correlation with reading comprehension. As a result, the Standard Cloze Passage Test, developed later by Bormuth (1965), can be used to obtain a quick estimate of a student's ability to comprehend material at a given difficulty level. It yields a score indicating that the material used for the test is at the student's Independent, Instructional, or Frustration level. The cloze format effectively taps into the student's familiarity with the subtle language redundancy patterns within a passage (Weaver & Kingston, 1963). There are many variations on the cloze format, and many effective instructional uses. For purposes of diagnostic screening, however, the most reliable and valid results will be obtained when using the Standard Cloze Passage Test in the manner described in Figure 4.4. Adaptations of the format, such as varying the length, using alternative procedures for deleting words, or accepting synonyms, tend to be more friendly to students but invalidate the scoring system.

The issue of accepting or not accepting synonyms has been the subject of a good deal of controversy and research. For informal evaluation of a student's Cloze test responses, there is value in analyzing the extent to which "reasonable guesses," including synonyms, were used, as compared with word choices that totally failed to indicate comprehension of the test passage. Several early studies did, in fact, show somewhat greater validity and internal consistency when synonyms were accepted in scoring (McKenna, 1976; Porter, 1978; Schoelles, 1971). For formal uses of the Cloze test, where the object is to obtain standardized measures, it should be kept in mind that the results of synonym scoring have proven to be unreliable across raters. William Henk and Mary L. Selders (1984), who did a definitive study of this issue, concluded that "there does not seem to be any overt reason to credit synonyms on a Cloze test" (1984, 286).

The most telling reasons to believe that Cloze is more a measure of familiarity with language patterns than it is of comprehension are based on two findings. One is a study by Culver, Godfrey, and Manzo (1972) that revealed that scores on Cloze tests did not significantly improve when students were allowed to first read the Cloze test passage without deletions; in other words, knowledge of the content and context did not influence the "comprehension" score; therefore, Cloze cannot be measuring comprehension. Relatedly, one of the most widely used standardized tests

> Although the Standard Cloze Test can be frustrating for some students, it is a valid and reliable tool.

FIGURE **4.4**

STANDARD CLOZE PASSAGE TEST

Preparation of the Test

Select a passage of about 300 words from a selection of known difficulty level. Copy the first sentence with no deletions. Then select a word at random in the second sentence. Delete this word and every fifth word thereafter until 50 words have been deleted. Finish the sentence containing the fiftieth blank, and copy the next sentence with no deletions. The blanks should be typed lines, five spaces long, and numbered from 1 to 50. Students record their responses on numbered answer sheets.

Administration of the Test

When ready to give the test, inform students that the task will be difficult, but that 60% accuracy is a good score. Demonstrate the task of filling in the blanks.

Scoring the Test

Count the number of actual words filled in correctly. Do not count synonyms. Multiply this number by 2 (since there are 50 items) to get the percent correct.

Interpreting the Results

A score above 60% indicates that the material is within the child's Independent reading level. Scores between 40% and 60% indicate that the material is within the child's Instructional reading level. Scores below 40% tend to indicate that the material is in the child's Frustration level. It is best to allow a plus or minus 5 percentage point spread for error of measurement on each of these bands of scores.

of comprehension (the Gates-McGinitie Reading Tests) relies on a task that looks like Cloze, but that offers choices of words to complete the deletions. This test, which apparently does cause one to pay closer attention to contextual meaning more than syntax—or, language pattern recognition—correlates very highly with all other conventional measures of comprehension, and therefore changes the task to one primarily measuring comprehension.

There are some drawbacks to Standard Cloze passage testing. This task is much more difficult than the ones that students are familiar with: A score of 50% is respectable. Therefore, students can become quite frustrated. It is important to forewarn students of this fact, along with the fact that the Cloze assessment will be of value to you in providing appropriate instruction and materials for them. A student's score on a Cloze test constructed from a passage in a book is a very solid indicator of a student's likely level of comfort in reading *that* book.

Writing is another language function that develops alongside reading. For beginning readers, writing involves experimenting with and practicing the letter-sound associations that are essential to reading at this level; for older students, writing develops familiarity with written language forms, which raises familiarity with these forms encountered when reading. Writing builds thinking power as well, clearly the foundation for reading comprehension. Several means of assessing writing are provided in the next section.

WRITING: CRAFT AND CONTENT

Writing builds thinking power, the foundation for reading comprehension.

The recent literature on reading and language arts emphasizes the fact that reading and writing are closely connected. Nonetheless, the two are not so predictably related that performance in one can be reliably inferred from knowing the other. In other words, knowing a child reads well does not guarantee that he will write well. Nor does knowing that a child writes well predict that she will read with solid and inferentially accurate comprehension. Obviously, children who read well tend to write better, though not necessarily more imaginatively, than children of average reading ability. In general, children who read poorly do tend to compose and to write poorly, though again, not necessarily. When writing is clearly superior to reading, it is appropriate to suspect that there this could be at worst a "soft sign" indication of minimal brain dysfunction. But it also could be traced to a complex emotional source and, on rare occasions, it can be an unusual, but normal, function of a specific aptitude to encode (write and/or speak) well despite poor decoding and even listening comprehension.

Difficulty in establishing a clear quantitative relationship between reading and writing stems from several factors. Historically, there have been many talented and influential writers who were seriously convoluted thinkers (Hitler) and/or highly self-indulgent (the 19th century Romantics); whereas, there also have been enormously influential minds who never wrote a word, but whose teachings have instructed us in how to be civilized (for example, Confucius, Mohammed, Zarathustra, and Jesus Christ). But there are other reasons to approach and carefully sort-out evaluations of writing more cautiously, in the realm of tests and measurements. These include the following:

The mind boggles at how the brain can function and misfunction.

1. There is no commonly agreed-upon way to assess writing.
2. Most methods of writing assessment are not properly weighted to take into account factors that are *not* of equal importance (such as content and grammar).
3. Most methods of assessment contain a great deal of subjectivity.
4. Assessment is not based upon a consensual agreement on a set of norms or criteria.
5. Assessment does not tend to include separate appraisal of what are called the 5 stages of the writing process (planning, drafting, revising, editing, and publishing).
6. There is no assessment system that provides for the various stages or levels of development of students at different ages and grade levels.

There have been many attempts to assess writing by easy algorithms or quantifiable equations. These are not totally ineffective, but they tend to leave too much unaccounted for. For example, Hunt (1965) determined that the length of each clause, or T-unit as he called them, was a good indication of syntactical maturity and overall writing ability. Lundsteen (1979) countered with the point that would be clear to any observer: "It is not how long you make them, but how you make them long."

There is a simple, subjective way to assess writing that also can serve as a "Universal Assessment System" for many other fuzzy factors.

"Universal Assessment System"

At this time, writing is best assessed informally, holistically, and subjectively. Basically, this is done by looking at a piece of writing and estimating, from your knowledge and experience, whether it is *emerging, below average, average, above average,* or *advanced* for the student's age and grade level. Teachers have a remarkable ability to do this five-level type categorizing very effectively; so effectively, in fact, that we recommend the use of this simple, serendipitously discovered scheme for evaluating most anything and everything observable by teachers. Think of it as a "Universal Assessment System."

Informal Writing Inventory

To sharpen your ability to make these judgments, we recommend that you compare and discuss your appraisals with the judgments of others, and use some of the other means suggested below. These are detailed under the title Informal Writing Inventory, though we do not mean to suggest by this terminology that this system has the history and tradition of an IRI. It does, however, offer a fair means of estimating current level of writing and specific areas of possible instruction.

Informal Writing Inventories assess some of the key features of the writing process (planning, drafting, revising, editing, and publishing) as well as certain expectations at different age/grade levels. Collect samples of writing about every 30 days to chart progress. Offer students the opportunity to keep their best work in a portfolio.

At a more structured level, there is the Informal Writing Inventory.

Figure 4.5 provides an IWI for children from kindergarten through fourth grade levels. An IWI for fifth grade through high school is provided in Figure 4.6 (page 140).

FIGURE **4.5**

INFORMAL WRITING INVENTORY: PRIMER TO FOURTH GRADE
(also for upper grade students with more limited skills)

1. Have the student write his or her name and address (if able). Rank for:

	emerging	below average	average	above average	advanced
A. accuracy	1	2	3	4	5
B. legibility	1	2	3	4	5
C. spelling	1	2	3	4	5
D. placement on page (top left or center of page is best)	1	2	3	4	5

E. comments _____

2. Have the student speak or write a description of something that is pictured (see illustration). Record and rank for:

	emerging	below average	average	above average	advanced
A. accuracy (details)	1	2	3	4	5
B. reasonable sequence	1	2	3	4	5
C. cogency (lack of irrelevancies)	1	2	3	4	5
D. English usage	1	2	3	4	5

E. comments _____

Example

Name: Lana   Grade: 5

Directions: Describe the drawing below in about 25 words. Make up a title for this descriptive essay.

Description:

One day it was a gril name Jan
She was latte for school She got up
and took a qick bath Slipt her cothes on
and took her book to her friend doght [gave]
her a cookie Jan Said Tankeyou. She was
at scool and her theacher claect the home
work. The End (collected)

Title: Home work for school

IWI Profile:

A. accuracy (details)   2

B. reasonable sequence   3

C. cogency (lack of irrelevancies)   3

D. English usage   2

E. comments: Lana reacted to the picture, rather than *describing* it. Her story was coherent and sequential otherwise, though strictly speaking, not cogent, since the entire piece is irrelevant. Directions, spelling, and punctuation need some attention.

3. Invite the student to complete several sentences (see examples). Record and rank for:

	emerging	below average	average	above average	advanced
A. relevancy	1	2	3	4	5
B. English usage	1	2	3	4	5

C. comments _____

Examples

1. Cats make me . . .

student response	relevancy	English usage
(a) sneeze and choke	5	4
(b) run	4	4

2. I wish I could . . .

student response	relevancy	English usage
(a) go with my sister	4	3
(b) eat al thats I wanted	4	2

---

4. Have the student try to fill in a missing word from five sentences read to him or her. Record and rank for:

	emerging	below average	average	above average	advanced
A. accuracy (allow the student to change his mind)	1	2	3	4	5
B. syntax compatibility	1	2	3	4	5
C. semantics	1	2	3	4	5
D. prior knowledge	1	2	3	4	5

E. comments _____

Examples

The cat and the _____ were chased off by the store owner.

Incorrect student answers and evaluations:

	"mouse"	"street"
accuracy	2	1
syntax compatibility	5	1
semantics	4	2
prior knowledge	4	2

5. Dictate two to five sentences, repeating each three times. Rate the student's transcription of the sentences for:

	emerging	below average	average	above average	advanced
A. accuracy	1	2	3	4	5
B. spelling and punctuation	1	2	3	4	5
C. penmanship	1	2	3	4	5
D. comments					

6. Have a student tell you a story for 2 minutes. Offer the student three topic choices, and provide a minimum of 10 minutes for the student to prepare what he or she wishes to say. Record the story told, and rate for:

	emerging	below average	average	above average	advanced
A. imagination	1	2	3	4	5
B. sequence	1	2	3	4	5
C. story form (beginning, middle, end)	1	2	3	4	5
D. internal logic (coherence)	1	2	3	4	5
E. overall quality	1	2	3	4	5
F. comments					

7. Read or play back the story to the child, and ask what, if anything, he or she might like to revise. Limit the revision period to 10 minutes. Make suggested revisions without unnecessary comments, and rate the revised story for:

	emerging	below average	average	above average	advanced
A. inclination to correct	1	2	3	4	5
B. quality of corrections	1	2	3	4	5
C. comments					

STUDY SKILLS AND HABITS OF MIND

Study Skills

Study skills is a generic name given to a host of means and methods for acquiring inner speech strategies for operating more efficiently when reading and studying independently. With practice, these strategies become "habits of mind" that are automatically initiated at the prereading stage, and are used flexibly and effectively to construct meaning during reading and to improve retention following reading. Study skills are most observable, and therefore most measurable, in situations that require note-taking, long-term recall, evidence of efficient use of time, and through measures of deep, or study-type, reading.

If good spelling overcomes a look of shabbiness, studied learning adds a top hat and tails.

There are four popular means for assessing study skills: standardized tests, informal inventories, observational systems, and self-report

FIGURE **4.6**

INFORMAL WRITING INVENTORY: FIFTH GRADE THROUGH HIGH SCHOOL

1. Have students write a simple description (word translation) of a picture. Rate for:

	emerging	below average	average	above average	advanced
A. accuracy (details)	1	2	3	4	5
B. organization	1	2	3	4	5
C. usage/spelling/punctuation	1	2	3	4	5
D. overall	1	2	3	4	5
E. comments _____					

2. Have students make up a discussion of at least four to eight sentences between a youth and a mother as the youth is about to leave the house. Rate for:

	emerging	below average	average	above average	advanced
A. imagination	1	2	3	4	5
B. sequence	1	2	3	4	5
C. usage/spelling/punctuation	1	2	3	4	5
D. overall	1	2	3	4	5
E. comments _____					

3. Have students write a summary of a passage (250 to 500 words) at the students' Independent to Instructional reading level. Rate for:

	emerging	below average	average	above average	advanced
A. accuracy	1	2	3	4	5
B. sequence	1	2	3	4	5
C. absence of irrelevancies	1	2	3	4	5
D. usage/spelling/punctuation	1	2	3	4	5
E. overall	1	2	3	4	5
F. comments _____					

4. Have the student write a critical-evaluative piece on a topic such as "What I think of vegetarians" or a reaction piece to a statement such as "There surely is life on neighboring planets." Rate for:

	emerging	below average	average	above average	advanced
A. maturity of judgment	1	2	3	4	5
B. accuracy of facts	1	2	3	4	5
C. usage/spelling/punctuation	1	2	3	4	5
D. overall	1	2	3	4	5
E. comments _____					

Example

Name: Cindy   Grade: 7

Directions: Indicate whether you "totally disagree," "disagree," "partially agree," "agree," or "totally agree" with the statement that follows. Then explain why you feel as you do.

"There surely is life on neighboring planets."

> I totally disagree with this because if there were (x) I think we would know about it by now. Also the(re)cant possibly be any(x) because the planet in front of ours is too hot & the one behind ours is too cold.

Ratings:

A. maturity of judgment   4

B. accuracy of facts   2

C. usage/spelling/punctuation   2

D. overall   3

E. comments: Cindy shows some immature but basically sound scientific thinking.
Punctuation needs some work.

---

5. Have student offer a constructive resolution to a problem, such as: "What can be done about the enormous amount of waste that the society generates?" or "What can you do if someone decides to give you the silent treatment for no good reason?" Rate for:

	emerging	below average	average	above average	advanced
A. maturity	1	2	3	4	5
B. inventiveness	1	2	3	4	5
C. accuracy and relevance of facts	1	2	3	4	5
D. usage/spelling/punctuation	1	2	3	4	5
E. overall	1	2	3	4	5
F. comments _____					

Study Skills are self-selected strategies that become efficient habits of mind.

inventories. Many schools have at least one standardized measure of study skills available on students in the form of the "Work-Study Skills" subtest of the Iowa Test of Basic Skills (Hieronymus, Hoover, & Lindquist, 1986). This test, and similar ones by other major standardized test makers, generally offer measures of a student's ability to: 1) read and interpret maps, charts, graphs, and tables; 2) use various parts of a book; and, 3) use standard reference materials such as dictionaries, encyclopedias, and almanacs. This potentially vital information can usually be found in a student's cumulative record file.

Informal Textbook Inventory

The Informal Textbook Inventory—an open book test customized to the class text—defines "diagnostic-teaching."

Informal textbook inventories are most suitable to secondary and community college use. You may find published informal instruments, such as McWilliams and Rakes' "Content Inventories: English, Social Studies, and Science" (1979). There is also an Informal Textbook Inventory format for teachers to make their own study skills inventory using a class text. The procedure by which this is constructed and administered provides an excellent example of Diagnostic-Prescriptive Teaching, since it is administered as an open book test that then becomes a series of lessons on how to use a text and related references efficiently and effectively. This approach to simultaneous testing and teaching is especially suitable for secondary and postsecondary students and environment. Figure 4.7 details the construction and use of this valuable assessment tool.

Rogers' Study–Reading Skills Checklist

A sound way to assess these is the Rogers' Study–Reading Skills Checklist.

Observational systems, the other "study" assessment approach, typically are built upon a checklist that also is intended to guide teachers in observing and appraising student abilities to do things previously mentioned, such as: use a book effectively, employ appropriate retention strategies (underlining, note-taking, memorizing), and use maps, charts, and graphs to aid comprehension. Douglas B. Rogers' (1984) Study–Reading Skills Checklist is one of the better-known, criterion-referenced observational systems (see Figure 4.8).

Finally, there are several self-report scales, such as the Study Habits Checklist by Preston and Botel (1981). One of the oldest of these, the SSHA, or Survey of Study Habits and Attitudes (Brown & Holtzman, 1967) has been standardized on seventh to twelfth graders and, after 45 years of use, still is available from the publisher, Psychological Corporation.

FIGURE **4.7**

CONSTRUCTING, ADMINISTERING, AND INTERPRETING THE INFORMAL TEXTBOOK INVENTORY

Constructing the ITI

I. Organization and Structure of the Text

   A. Understanding the Textbook Organization
   Develop three to five straightforward questions about how the text is structured and how to use the comprehension aids provided within the text.

   B. Using the Text Organization Effectively
   Develop three to five questions that students can answer by referring to the index, table of contents, glossary, appendices, or other text sections and/or aids.

II. Basic Comprehension

   Select a short portion of the text that contains an important concept with supporting details and at least one graph, chart, or picture. (The same selection can be used in the following section on applied comprehension.)

   A. Comprehending the Main Idea
   Develop one or two fill-in or multiple-choice questions that direct students to state or select the main idea of the material read.

   B. Noting Supporting Details
   Develop three or more fill-in, multiple-choice, or matching questions about specific facts or ideas in the selection.

   C. Understanding Vocabulary in Context
   Develop three or more fill-in, multiple-choice, or matching questions that direct students to state or select a definition for key terms used in the selection.

   D. Understanding Information Presented in Graphic or Pictorial Form
   Develop one or more questions requiring students to state or select an interpretation of a graph, chart, or picture that adds information not explicitly stated in the selection.

III. Applied Comprehension

   Questions in these sections can be based on the same text selection used in Part II.

   A. Drawing Conclusions and Critical Thinking
   Develop one or more questions that require students to draw valid conclusions based on the information presented.

   B. Evaluating and Judging
   Develop one or more questions that require students to evaluate and apply information from the text in terms of their own experiences, values, and existing knowledge base.

IV. Specialized Options

   A. Assess special requirements of the discipline. This could mean understanding geographical directions in social studies, a section on understanding style or mood in literature, or a section on applying symbols in mathematical formulas.

   B. Assess student abilities to deal with the linguistic features of the text with a Standard Cloze Passage test (described earlier in this chapter).

Administering the ITI

Before distributing the ITI to students, explain some of its features and purposes. It is not a "test" in the usual sense of the word; every text differs slightly from every other, and this is a way to find out how well they will be able to use this particular text. Also point out that answers will be discussed as a group. Encourage students to attempt to complete the worksheets as thoroughly and accurately as possible in order to yield a quality assessment of the appropriateness and value of the text. Provide adequate time for all students to complete the inventory. It may take two or more class periods, and students who finish early should be provided with an alternate activity.

Interpreting the ITI

When students have completed the ITI, collect and score the tests. A "total score" need not be recorded on the students' papers, since the purpose of the test is to identify strengths and needs in the various subsections. For diagnostic purposes, any error is taken as a sign of need in that category. Guide a class discussion of the items in each section. This discussion can take from one-half to three full class periods, depending on student abilities and the difficulty of the text.

FIGURE **4.8**

ROGERS' STUDY–READING SKILLS CHECKLIST

Degrees of skill	Absent	Low	High
I. Special study–reading comprehension skills			
A. Ability to interpret graphic aids			
Can the student interpret these graphic aids?			
1. maps	____	____	____
2. globes	____	____	____
3. graphs	____	____	____
4. charts	____	____	____
5. tables	____	____	____
6. cartoons	____	____	____
7. pictures	____	____	____
8. diagrams	____	____	____
9. other organizing or iconic aids	____	____	____
B. Ability to follow directions			
Can the student follow. . .			
1. simple directions?	____	____	____
2. a more complex set of directions?	____	____	____
II. Information location skills			
A. Ability to vary rate of reading			
Can the student do the following?			
1. scan	____	____	____
2. skim	____	____	____
3. read at slow rate for difficult materials	____	____	____
4. read at average rate for reading level	____	____	____
B. Ability to locate information by use of book parts			
Can the student use book parts			
to identify the following information?			
1. title	____	____	____
2. author or editor	____	____	____
3. publisher	____	____	____
4. city of publication	____	____	____
5. name of series	____	____	____
6. edition	____	____	____
7. copyright date	____	____	____
8. date of publication	____	____	____
Can the student quickly locate and understand the function of the following parts of a book?			
1. preface	____	____	____
2. foreword	____	____	____
3. introduction	____	____	____
4. table of contents	____	____	____
5. list of figures	____	____	____
6 chapter headings	____	____	____
7. subtitles	____	____	____
8. footnotes	____	____	____
9. bibliography	____	____	____

Degrees of skill	Absent	Low	High
10. glossary	_____	_____	_____
11. index	_____	_____	_____
12. appendix	_____	_____	_____

C. Ability to locate information in reference works
   Can the student do the following?

	Absent	Low	High
1. locate information in a dictionary			
a. using the guide words	_____	_____	_____
b. using a thumb index	_____	_____	_____
c. locating root word	_____	_____	_____
d. locating derivations of root word	_____	_____	_____
e. using the pronunciation key	_____	_____	_____
f. selecting word meaning appropriate			
to passage under study	_____	_____	_____
g. noting word origin	_____	_____	_____
2. locate information in an encyclopedia			
a. using information on spine			
to locate appropriate volume	_____	_____	_____
b. using guide words to locate section	_____	_____	_____
c. using index volume	_____	_____	_____
3. use other reference works such as:			
a. telephone directory	_____	_____	_____
b. newspapers	_____	_____	_____
c. magazines	_____	_____	_____
d. atlases	_____	_____	_____
e. television listings	_____	_____	_____
f. schedules	_____	_____	_____
g. various periodical literature indices	_____	_____	_____
h. others (_____)	_____	_____	_____

D. Ability to locate information in the library
   Can the student do the following?

	Absent	Low	High
1. locate material by using computer cataloguing			
a. by subject	_____	_____	_____
b. by author	_____	_____	_____
c. by title	_____	_____	_____
2. find the materials organized in the library			
a. fiction section	_____	_____	_____
b. reference section	_____	_____	_____
c. periodical section	_____	_____	_____
d. vertical file	_____	_____	_____
e. others (_____)	_____	_____	_____

III. Study and retention strategies

A. Ability to study information and remember it
   Can the student do the following?

	Absent	Low	High
1. highlight important information	_____	_____	_____
2. underline important information	_____	_____	_____
3. use oral repetition to increase retention	_____	_____	_____
4. ask and answer questions to increase retention	_____	_____	_____
5. employ a systematic study procedure (such as SQ3R)	_____	_____	_____

Degrees of skill	Absent	Low	High
6. demonstrate effective study habits			
a. set a regular study time	_____	_____	_____
b. leave adequate time for test or project preparation	_____	_____	_____
c. recognize importance of self-motivation in learning	_____	_____	_____
B. Ability to organize information			
Can the student do the following?			
1. take notes	_____	_____	_____
2. note source of information	_____	_____	_____
3. write a summary for a paragraph	_____	_____	_____
4. write a summary for a short selection	_____	_____	_____
5. write a summary integrating information from more than one source	_____	_____	_____
6. write a summary for a longer selection	_____	_____	_____
7. make graphic aids to summarize information	_____	_____	_____
8. write an outline of a paragraph	_____	_____	_____
9. write an outline for a short selection	_____	_____	_____
10. write an outline for longer selections	_____	_____	_____
11. write an outline integrating information from more than one source	_____	_____	_____
12. use the outline to write a report or to make an oral report	_____	_____	_____

Rogers, 1984, *Journal of Reading*, 346–354.

REVIEW

This chapter covered the fundamentals of field-based assessment of typical reading-related deficits of schema, spelling, language development, writing, and study habits. These factors are the most frequently measured on most classroom and conventional achievement tests. You now know better how to sort, cross-verify, and consider the relative significance of such findings in contrast to one another, and to the larger purposes of schooling.

PREVIEW

The next chapter addresses assessment of several *collateral* factors often referenced in definitions of reading progress, but infrequently to never assessed. You will not necessarily be called upon to assess these outside of this academic setting; nonetheless they are an important part of your education in assessment. You will be better prepared to make professional referrals with this knowledge, and positioned to address them in your classroom.

IN-DEPTH ASSESSMENT OF COLLATERAL FACTORS IN LITERACY DEVELOPMENT

A smooth sea never made a skillful mariner. – ENGLISH PROVERB

CONTENT AND CONCEPT ORGANIZER

This chapter reviews information and techniques for assessing physical factors (called Defects, for lack of a better term), psychological factors (called Disruptions,) and socio-cultural factors (called Differences). These are three of the categories in the book's system for content and concept organization. Look particularly to be informed about aspects of VISION and HEARING—two of the continuing areas of serious misinformation about reading disorders.

CHAPTER OUTLINE

COLLATERAL FACTORS INFLUENCING LITERACY ACQUISITION AND DEVELOPMENT

Reading assessment typically begins with assessment of reading-specific factors, as outlined in Chapter 3, and often involves assessment of relevant additional reading-related factors outlined in Chapter 4. The assessment considerations in this chapter sometimes are referred to as collateral factors. **Collateral factors** are innate or acquired attributes that may contribute to reading difficulty.

> **Many factors and combinations of factors can influence reading progress.**

In the context of assessing reading-resistant learning problems we might be well guided by the wisdom of a proverb: "There's many a slip between the cup and the lip." There are so many who learn to read almost effortlessly that it is difficult sometimes to even think of it as more difficult than lifting a cup to a lip that already has considerable experience with language and intentional action. But this only leaves us perplexed, and needing to think deeply about why and how others do not learn easily. Curiously, when we think deeply about this (seemingly) simple act of coding and decoding speech, we move to the other end of the spectrum of thought, and wonder how anyone learns to read at all. Reading is indeed a complex cognitive, affective, and social-cultural process that draws upon the individual's prior knowledge and experience, understanding of the reading process itself, motivation, self-perceptions, value systems, language development, sensory soundness (acuity), emotional organization, and subtle community and environmental forces.

UNIQUE PROPORTIONALITY

There seldom is one single cause of reading difficulty. In most cases it is a mixture of causes combining for each student in *uniquely proportional* ways that make each case different from another. At this level of individualized, in-depth analysis it becomes necessary to include collateral factors, including physical and physiological factors, such as vision, hearing, and neurological functions; psychological factors, such as cognitive, attitudinal, and emotional functions; and social-environmental factors, such as socio-cultural differences. Applying the concept of *unique proportionality,* a visual acuity (seeing) problem may be of absolutely no consequence to one child's reading progress. But it may be of considerable consequence to another, who is struggling with words at far point on a board 15 feet away, and at near point with a coded page 9 to 14 inches away.

The fifth "D," Delimitations, or school-based errors such as inappropriate choice of curricula and instructional methods, are threads that run throughout the text. The most frequent error in this category is typically one of omission—not attending to something—more than commission—doing something wrong.

ASSESSMENT OF POTENTIAL READING-RELATED DEFECTS

The Defect category refers to innate or constitutional factors: various aspects of mental aptitude and physical-physiological functioning, such as hearing, vision, neurological organization, chemistry, or any handicapping condition that might impede reading-learning progress in a given individual. This category is a reminder to check general medical information for frequently overlooked conditions such as anemia (a blood condition causing general weakness) or frequent headaches and allergies. The negative effect of these conditions on reading and learning is often overlooked when studies of their impact are based on larger numbers of people, or remain hidden as questions that are never asked. Conditions such as allergies (or "hay fever"), for example, are treated as unimportant. They are not asked about because they are "common," even though this one condition probably accounts for more seasonal erratic brain activity than all other neurological problems combined. As you consider factors within the Defect category, keep these guiding questions in mind:

Despite similarities, uniquely proportional balances make each case different.

- In what way might this factor be influencing individual reading progress?
- How serious does a problem have to be before reading is influenced?
- Since the problem is a physical one, how might it be physically corrected or accommodated?
- Even though the factor is largely physical, to what extent can it be, or has it been, influenced by environmental and psychological dynamics?

PHYSICAL-PHYSIOLOGICAL FACTORS

Vision

"Defects" has a sharp connotative sound, but is an important concept in assessment.

Vision is the physical ability of the eyes to see clearly and accurately. The term "acuity" is used to refer to the clarity of the physical reception of stimuli, without regard for mental interpretive processes. The ability to see things at a distance is called "far-point acuity." Far-point acuity typically is tested with the Snellen Eye Chart—the familiar poster showing rows of letters that get smaller and smaller as you read downward. The measurement of far-point acuity is expressed in terms of one's relative ability to read the letters on the Snellen chart from 20 feet away. Thus, the expression "20/20" vision means that one can read all of the letters from 20 feet away. A person with 20/80 vision sees the letters on the chart as if it were 80 feet away, or four times as far. Many children have far-point acuity in the 20/200 range, and some as great as 20/400 or more. These children see the chalkboard as if it were at the other end of a very long and dimly lit hallway.

The greatest period of deterioration of far-point vision takes place during the school years, between the ages of 6 and 18. Near-point vision, or the ability to see close-up, typically is not a serious problem until adulthood. Children with poor far-point vision need to be checked at least once a year if they are to remain in visual contact with the chalkboard and maintain attention in class. We have spoken to adults who claim to have "lost" up to three years of schooling because uncorrected acuity problems put them so out of touch with classroom activities that they developed the habit of daydreaming to cope with the long hours. The road back from such visual isolation can be difficult. It often requires some form of behavioral reconditioning to reverse habits of "daydreaming," and to catch up on the knowledge and skills that have been missed or are underdeveloped.

Effect of Vision Problems on Reading

Intensive reading work-ups have traditionally included a complete visual screening.

Intensive reading work-ups have traditionally included a complete visual screening. Oddly, over 50 years of research have failed to show that there is any visual problem that is causatively linked to reading disorders in any predictable way. Only one—weak binocular fusion—comes close. Weak binocular fusion is the inability of both eyes to comfortably bring and hold together an image on a printed page. Children with this problem often experience visual fatigue (asthaenopia). It is suspected that this side effect of reading may cause these children to avoid sustained reading. However, some time ago it was discovered that a severe fusion problem usually results in such sharp discomfort that the brain automatically corrects the problem by suppressing vision in one eye and subconsciously turning visual tasks such as reading over to the other (see the related problem of amblyopia in Figure 5.1 on Visual Impediments).

Optometrists have experimented with several forms of visual training for children with weak binocular fusion, including means of either strengthening the weak eye, forcing its suppression, or improving binocular fusion. There is no scientific evidence that these methods influence reading in any positive way, although they do result in improvements in certain visual tracking and fusion tasks, and there are many clinical and anecdotal reports of the uplifting effects of such training on morale, self-esteem, and grades. A new development in the area of visual training for reading is capturing national interest. This development, called Scotopic Sensitivity Training, also has been shown to have absolutely no relationship to reading as we now understand it.

Vision Testing

Instruments most frequently used for visual screening in reading diagnoses are the Bausch and Lomb School Vision Tester and the Keystone Telebinocular Test. The manuals for these and other visual testing systems give precise details about screening for a variety of visual impairments (see Figure 5.1 for a descriptive summary of major visual impairments). Where screening test results indicate the possibility of a significant vision problem, the child should be referred for professional testing. In diagnostic reporting and conferencing, keep in mind that these *screening* instruments, by definition, are not as reliable as specialized tests. They can detect the possibility of a problem, but results tend to vary from one testing situation to another. This is partly because children with poor vision have difficulty interpreting and expressing what they are seeing as they go through the items on a vision test. Children with vision problems also will tend to have lower test results if the test immediately follows a visually taxing activity. For this reason, where vision problems are suspected, it can be worthwhile to test before and following a visually taxing task. When a visual problem is suspected, referred, and professionally corroborated, it still is wise to check again at intermittent periods (about every 3 months) for signs of improvement or further deterioration.

The dilemma regarding just how much time and energy to put into vision testing in reading diagnosis is not easy to resolve. Some researchers have concluded that vision appears to have a significant influence on reading. Ekwall and Shanker (1988), for example, report that 4 years of records at a university reading clinic revealed that about 50 percent of their disabled readers had visual problems that had not been previously detected.

While *no* visual problem is causatively linked to reading disorders, one comes close, weak binocular fusion, and should be checked.

FIGURE **5.1**

VISUAL IMPAIRMENTS

Refractive, or light focusing, problems
1. **Hyperopia or farsightedness.** The ability to see at far-point but poor near-point vision (the 14-inch typical reading distance from the eye).
2. **Myopia or nearsightedness.** The ability to see things at near-point but not at far-point.
3. **Astigmatism or blurred vision.** Usually found with hyperopia or myopia, astigmatism is a defect in the eye's ability to focus on both a vertical and horizontal axis. It can aggravate fusion problems.

Fusion, or binocular, focusing problems
4. **Aniseikonia.** The images seen in each eye appear unequal in size.
5. **Strabismus.** The eyes do not fuse well due to a tendency of the eyes to turn inward (estropia, or cross-eyedness), or outward (exotropia), or where one turns higher than the other (hypertropia), or lower (hypotropia).
6. **Suppression.** One eye's message is not transmitted, or not accepted, by the brain.
7. **Amblyopia or lazy eye.** This is a form of mild to severe atrophy and loss of acuity that tends to occur in a suppressed eye.

On the other hand, Miles Tinker, one of the leading researchers on the relationship between vision and reading, came to a different conclusion. At 80 years of age, while addressing a plenary session of the National Reading Conference in 1968, Dr. Tinker said, "After 50 years of interest and personal research in the connection between reading and vision, I find *none*."

Hearing

A severe hearing loss can have a devastating effect on reading and intellectual development.

With over 95 percent of human learning occurring through, or in cooperation with listening, it should come as no surprise to learn that a severe hearing loss can have a devastating effect on reading and intellectual development. Fortunately, less than 1 in 1000 youngsters is deaf. However, approximately 45 in every 1000 have mild hearing loss (Davis & Silverman, 1970). Thus, an average-sized elementary school, with 500 students, is likely to have about 26 youngsters with hearing problems, and most high schools, with two or three times the total number of students, will have two or three times that number of students with hearing problems.

Two aspects of hearing are traditionally evaluated: *auditory acuity*— the ability to hear clearly and accurately, and *auditory discrimination*— the ability to distinguish similarities and differences in sounds of letters and words. It is arguable whether auditory discrimination should be evaluated as a hearing problem since it is an auditory perceptual (mental) task that is influenced by learning more than hearing. The two do become intertwined, however, since hearing losses in certain frequency ranges will result in poor auditory discrimination and even production of certain distinct speech sounds. It also is notable that most hearing losses can be traced back to birth difficulties or early illness, and therefore may be taken, in combination with other supporting evidence, as a possible "soft sign" of neurological impairment.

Effect of Hearing Problems on Reading

Contrary to popular misbeliefs, hearing has a much greater impact on reading acquisition than vision. Even a mild disorder (inability to hear sounds within certain volume and/or pitch ranges) prevents the child from making the sound-symbol associations that are essential to beginning levels of phonetic word attack. Depending upon the age at which the hearing disorder was detected and corrected (and the completeness of the correction) it will limit many other factors known to influence reading development, including:

- delayed oral language development
- poor phonemic awareness and potentially phonics skill acquisition
- weak fund of general information
- strained participation in class discussions of textual material
- poor listening, hence, poor speaking, reading, and writing vocabularies

An experience with a youngster in our own neighborhood provided dramatic evidence of the need for regular screening tests for hearing acuity than any research we have read. This neighbor boy had trouble getting along with the other children. He began to "put off," if not frighten off, people in the neighborhood by standing too close and staring at them while they spoke. His own speech was oddly loud and booming. As he grew older, he developed a fascination with magic tricks, and complicated Houdini-like escapes. After a poor showing in school for many years, he dropped out and tried to join the Navy. It was at that time, when the boy was seventeen years old, that it was discovered that he had severe hearing deficiencies in certain frequency ranges. Most extraordinary, however, was the fact that his mother was a school nurse. The simple conclusion to be drawn from this case is that hearing problems can be masked, and present themselves with masquerading symptoms; therefore, hearing needs to be checked on a routine basis.

Astute diagnosticians watch for Masquerading Symptoms.

Hearing Testing

There are several informal means of detecting auditory acuity problems, and even certain auditory perceptual deficits. The first means is simple observation. A comprehensive list of symptoms of hearing loss has been known and recommended to teachers for many years (Ekwall & Shanker, 1988). These include observing a child:

1. cupping a hand behind an ear to amplify sound
2. complaining of ringing or buzzing in the ear
3. staring and inattentive
4. drainage or discharge from ears and sinus cavities
5. tilting head while listening
6. listening with mouth open
7. frequent head colds and earaches
8. failing to respond to oral directions
9. speaking in unnatural voice tones
10. unusual enunciation of familiar words

Another informal means of assessing hearing loss is with the so-called "Whisper Test," a simple technique conducted in this way:

1. Construct five sentences of easy directions, find a quiet corner, and have the student listen and do what you then say.
2. Sit immediately behind the student and read these in the following order and with decreasing volume.
   a. To the right ear in a normal speaking voice say: "Raise the left hand on the other side of your body."
   b. To both ears in a lower voice say: "Raise the same hand you just raised."
   c. To the left ear in a lower voice say: "Raise the hand on this side of your body."
   d. In a whisper to the right ear say: "Raise the hand on this side of your body."
   e. In a lower whisper to both ears say: "This time raise both hands above your head."

The Whisper Test can be made somewhat more precise by using a tape recorder with numbered units on the volume control. After each directional sentence, lower the volume to a predesignated setting. It also can be done in quicker fashion. Simply state a phrase in a medium- low voice from a distance of about 15 feet and continue to repeat it at the same volume while moving closer about 2 feet at a time until the student can repeat it. The more legitimate alternative to informal assessment is to use specially calibrated instruments for evaluation of hearing.

Devices called **audiometers** are scientifically constructed and calibrated to make sounds at different pitches or frequencies, and at different decibel levels, delivered through earphones. These devices have specific

FIGURE **5.2**

MAICO AUDIOGRAM RECORD SHEET

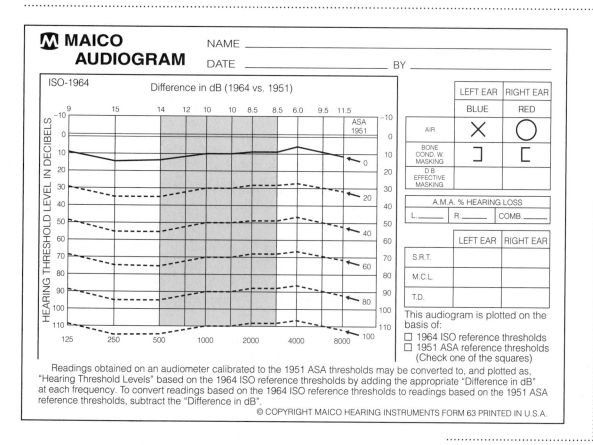

instructions and scoring forms to guide auditory evaluation. See the record form shown in Figure 5.2. Notice that the critical speech area is from about 500 to 3000 cycles per second, though most people can hear sounds between 125 and 8000 cycles per second. It is notable that youngsters with hearing losses in the 500 and higher frequency ranges are more likely to have problems in the early days of schooling since this higher range is more typical of the female voice, which typically is heard most from birth through the next six years of schooling. In general, a hearing loss under 15 decibels is not considered serious, and can be accommodated merely with better seating.

Hearing testing devices available for school and clinical use are very sensitive to fluctuations in temperature and humidity, and generally need to

A mild hearing loss in the higher frequency range of a woman's voice can be troublesome to speech, phonemic awareness, and cognitive development.

be recalibrated about every 6 months. Children suspected of having hearing loss should be retested by a physician or at a speech and hearing clinic.

Auditory ***discrimination*** testing is based on the ability to distinguish differences and likenesses (which usually is more difficult to do) between sets of sounds or words:

/gr/	&	/br/
/say/	&	/hay/
/lie/	&	/lie/

The most widely used tests of auditory discrimination include:

Wepman's Auditory Discrimination Test
Goldman-Fristoe-Woodcock Test of Auditory Discrimination
Kimmell-Wahl Screening Test of Auditory Perception

While these tests have been used for many years in reading evaluations, several studies have shown that:

- They do not correlate well with early reading success (Dykstra, 1966).
- They do not correlate well with one another (Koenke, 1978).
- Testing can be complicated by a variety of factors, such as dialect, prior knowledge and experience, vocabulary, and examiner bias (Geissal & Knafle, 1977).

We continue to qualitatively recommend the use of a quick test of auditory discrimination nonetheless, for these counterbalancing reasons:

- The test can be used as an indirect evaluation of possible hearing losses in various sounds in the speech range.
- Auditory discrimination is an aspect of phonemic awareness, which has a proven connection to reading progress.
- The testing protocol gives the examiner another look at the child engaged in a different task.
- Where need suggests, the information gained can be combined with the results of the Digit Span subtest of the WISC IQ test (see Appendix B for descriptions of the subtests of the WISC-R), and patterns of errors on IRIs and word lists to yield indices of auditory discrimination, auditory memory, auditory segmentation, auditory blending, and overall auditory perception.

Auditory perception, like visual perception, is a brain function. We now consider how perceptual processes are used as a basis for inferring neurological organization and possible neurological damage. (A much more sensitive and reading-related measure of "auditory perception"—the Manzo-Manzo-Albee Phonemic Awareness Inventory—was detailed in Chapter 3, Figure 3.4.)

Speech

It has been long recognized that there is a potentially important relationship between speech defects and severe reading disabilities. Several studies point to the fact that over 20 percent of severely disabled readers also have speech impediments. Oddly, those who stutter are few, although, as might be expected, most are male (Klasen, 1972). Quite possibly, both reading and speech impediments go back to a common origin, and are different aspects of one basic disorder.

There are two classes of speech impediments, one related to delayed speech and another to the production of odd-sounding speech. In general, when speech sounds are odd, it is wise to follow up with a careful hearing test. The child may well be reproducing the sounds he hears.

More commonly, however, unusual speaking is a form of delayed speech. In such cases, a student's speech production will tend to include sounds such as labial "r's" as in "wabbit" for "rabbit," and add-on's such as "th's", as in "li*th*ening" for "listening." In such cases, it is more efficient (parsimonious) to think that the problem is extended "baby-talk," and probably more emotionally driven, than related to serious speech, hearing, or neurological deficits. "Baby-talk" usually is related to delayed physical maturation, or ambivalence about growing up, and therefore can be a sign of emotional dependency—a frequent correlate of deficient reading. The literature of the field is sparse on diagnosing, interpreting, and treating the co-symptoms of speech impediment and reading disability. Better working relationships obviously need to be developed between speech and reading people at all levels.

Co-symptoms of speech and reading problems are not well understood.

There also is no means that we are aware of for routinely assessing the compositional side of speech, such as its relevance and coherence. This is done, however, in writing, as discussed above in the previous chapter.

NEUROLOGICAL CONSIDERATIONS

Neurological defects can be caused by hereditary factors, physiological (anatomy and chemistry) factors, or trauma from physical injury, and particularly from some viral diseases that may result in blood-starved brain tissue, and permanent lesions, or nonfunctional scar tissue. None of these causal factors is easily determined, although medical science has made a good deal of progress in recording and studying images of brain functions. We now know where many functions typically can be found on a map of the brain; unfortunately for this seemingly neat package, near-identical functions, with the same levels of proficiency, can also be found in a variety of

Brain functions neatly mapped to the same locations 100 times can be just as neatly mapped somewhere else the 101st time . . . supporting the need for case-by-case study.

other places in a given individual . . . supporting the need for case-by-case study.

Soft Signs: MBD

Determinations about brain functioning traditionally have been *inferred* by educators and psychologists, essentially from visual-perceptual and fine motor tasks. More recently, the evaluation of verbal fluency has been shown to provide highly reliable evidence of brain dysfunction (see the discussion of the Naming Test in the chapter on severe reading disabilities). Again, visual-perceptual functioning, a brain task, should not be confused with sight, a visual-anatomical task.

In visual-perceptual screening, children generally are shown a form or figure and are asked to reproduce it. The assumption is that the reproduction will be fairly accurate and properly oriented on the page if the child is neurologically, developmentally, and emotionally sound, and that the reproduction will be distorted, misplaced, or rotated if there are constitutional problems in any of these realms.

Figure 5.3 shows a typical set of patterns that a child might be asked to duplicate and illustrates some distortions that would signal potential difficulty.

Soft Signs Are Ambiguous

The problem with these inferential systems is that they do not distinguish easily among neurological, developmental, and emotional dysfunctions. In practice, these tests are sometimes treated as if they are sure "soft signs" of Minimal Brain Dysfunction (MBD) or simply some form of unusual neurological organization, or possibly disorganization. Examination of test manuals indicates that they routinely state that precautions should be exercised in forming conclusions about neurological or reading disorders from the test protocols. The fact that the relationship between visual-perceptual deficits and reading disability is inconclusive is drawn from research showing that programs designed to improve visual-perceptual "tracking," eye-hand-motor coordination, and visual-perceptual discrimination generally have no short- or long-term effects on reading (Leibert & Sherk, 1970).

"Soft signs" can be misleading, but should be read, nonetheless.

In general, visual-perceptual screening still appears to be worthwhile, since it does reveal dysfunction, even if it is uncertain as to whether the problem revealed is neurological, emotional, or both. Since neither of these problems, nor the reading problem, is improved by a program of visual-perceptual *training*, it seems wise to exercise great caution in recommending or conducting such training without some other compelling reason to do so.

FIGURE **5.3**

VISUAL-PERCEPTUAL COPY TASKS USED
TO INFER NEUROLOGICAL ORGANIZATION

Model	Student's Version	Interpretation
		Too small; poor reproduction
		Over-size; poor reproduction
		35 degree rotation; error in reproduction (upsweep on opposite side)

Several tests of visual-perceptual functioning are marketed as part of visual-perceptual training programs. The two most widely known and used tests in reading and learning diagnosis that are not part of a training program are:

1. Bender Visual Motor Gestalt Test (Bender, 1946), using the Koppitz scoring system
2. Minnesota Percepto-Diagnostic Test (Fuller, 1969)

The latter test is based on the student's ability to reproduce a drawn figure fairly accurately and without rotation on the page. We have found that some apparent rotations can be explained by the way the student turns the paper when drawing. When administering visual-perceptual tests, be sure that the student, the paper, and the test protocol are all properly oriented before and during the task. In a related vein, it has been experimentally shown that another common indicator of neurological dysfunction, namely reversals in children's writing, largely disappears if a line is drawn down the center of the page and the child is asked to reproduce the words, letters, or figures being reversed on the side of the page that causes the

There are many "signs" we know about but do not yet fully understand.

child to cross his or her body midline (Zaslow, 1966). Zaslow showed this to be true even with children who were known to be seriously brain damaged. This is another example of things that we *know about,* but do not really understand.

Suspicion of neurological dysfunction may be further inferred or refuted from a variety of other tests, subtests, and observational schedules. The House-Tree-Person test (Buck & Jolles, 1966), for example, asks the child to draw a picture of a house, a tree, and a person and then uses these protocols to infer a great many things about the child's intelligence, developmental history, emotional well-being, and neurological organization. There are several books and manuals offering years of clinical trials and observations on the H-T-P. Figure 5.4 offers an example of how an individual's drawing of a person is analyzed for "soft signs" of organicity, or brain dysfunction. The Wechsler IQ test described in the chapter also permits inferences of neurological dysfunction, usually from significant discrepancies between the child's overall verbal and performance (or nonverbal) aptitudes, and/or from erratic performance on selected subtests.

FIGURE **5.4**

INDICES OF NEUROLOGICAL DISORDERS

1. much erasing
2. little improvement in quality of picture
3. usually a side-view; simple and concrete figure
4. frequently broken, sketchy, and irregular lines
5. unclosed or incomplete parts

Rogers (1984)

Hints of possible neurological dysfunction or odd neurological organization may even be reasonably inferred from IRI protocols, such as when a child shows a great disparity between comprehension and word recognition, or between whole word recognition and phonic word attack skills, or a vast difference between reading and spelling. Three ways to further verify a supposition of neurological dysfunction are to: 1) ask the child to tell about his reading problem from his perspective: what can and can't you seem to do?; 2) engage the child in a "think-aloud" that may reveal divergent thinking patterns; and 3) carefully recheck the child's cumulative school records and information from interviews for signs of illness, trauma, or abnormal developmental patterns or unusual abilities as well as disabilities.

Let's look now at the assessment of intelligence, an aspect of brain functioning that can further help in distinguishing between attitude deficiencies and possible neurological and/or psychological disorders.

IRIs, and three other teacher-friendly methods, can reveal/verify "soft signs."

IQ TESTING AND OUR DIFFERENT MINDS

IQ Testing as Social Evolution

Many slings and arrows have been tossed at IQ testing. It often is viewed as the culprit in social stratification. In point of fact, the Stanford-Binet Intelligence Scale (1973), the historical predecessor of most all IQ testing, was first developed in the early 1900s by Simon Binet with a grant from the French government to better determine which (street) children would profit most from additional schooling. It was preceded by a similar test authorized by Wilhelm Bismark, the Prussian general who unified Germany in the mid-late 19th century, and ironically, may be the father of current civil service systems and programs, including pensions for these otherwise unsung people who keep government working. His idea was to use such tests to establish a "merit" system that would identify those best suited to government service rather than those of "noble birth" who typically were granted such sinecures—lifetime incomes for doing slight jobs. The IQ-type test may someday, when tensions have settled, be remembered as an important bit of social evolution away from family connections and towards a system of merit based on hard-won knowledge and innate capacity. As you will see ahead, it is not without problems, and the need remains for evolution to continue in modern, pluralistic societies.

There are three basic formats to IQ tests: verbal, performance (manipulative), and visual perceptual . . . they are not of equal predictive value.

Defining IQ: Rate and Capacity

An important consideration in a reading-learning diagnosis is the rate at which a student is likely to reach mastery of the varied tasks involved in

IQ testing often is viewed as the culprit in society, but that can be short-sighted.

decoding, comprehending, remembering, restating, and transferring. Rate of learning is essentially what is determined by an IQ test. However, it also measures depth, or "capacity"—one's "Zone of Proximal *Limitation*," where things no longer compute. This feeling is most real for many otherwise bright people when they meet calculus, a subject whose definition alone can sound forbidding: "A branch of mathematics that deals with limits and the differentiation and integration of functions of one or more variables" (*American Heritage Dictionary,* 3rd edition, 1992). Theoretically, there should not be such a zone of confusion and non-learning. Practically speaking, it is assumed to be the level at which one "bogs down" under typical instructional conditions, or where it becomes fairly obvious that the effort and time needed to teach exceed by far the likely benefits in such learning.

Interpreting IQ Scores

Intelligence Quotient scores, or *estimates* of rate of learning and intellectual capacity, are derived by translating raw scores into standard scores with an average of 100. By definition then, almost half of the population is expected to be above 100, and almost half below. It is important to note that scoring is relative and generally rising: Children today tend to score significantly higher than kids did in the 1930s (Klenk & Kibby, 2000). In general, scores between 80 and 119 are considered to be within the statistically "normal" range, since two-thirds of the population has scores within this range. Approximately 17 percent of scores fall above that range and 17 percent below. Because a certain degree of error in testing is unavoidable, and because IQ scores tend to be viewed with a certain degree of awe, a student's IQ score should be reported as falling within a certain "band," rather than as a numerical score. The descriptive "bands" recommended by the widely used Wechsler IQ tests are:

69 and below	Mentally Deficient
70–79	Borderline Deficient
80–89	Low Average
90–109	Average
110–119	High Average
120–129	Superior
130–145	Very Superior

In attempting to understand why some of us learn faster than others, researchers have defined many subfactors of cognitive learning. J. P. Guilford (1967), for example, defined 120 separate cognitive factors in his

"Structure of Intellect" model. Recent neurolinguistic research on what has come to be called the "discrete zones" hypothesis is verifying the high level of specificity of most brain functions; although it is puzzling that a particular skill or function is not always found in the same location from one brain to another. (This suggests that there probably are different "cognitive styles" of functioning, or ways that brains can "compute"—even though these have not fully translated into different "learning styles," or ways by which to teach those different minds.)

"Cognitive style" is not quite the same as "learning style."

Limitations of IQ Tests

Commonly used IQ tests are still quite limited in scope. Noticeably absent from these tests are assessments of intellectual factors such as: originality, creativity, artistic ability, social intelligence, and even common sense. Emerald Dechant, a salty, now deceased, professor of reading education, made this additional point about such testing: "IQ tests do not discriminate between ignorance and stupidity" (1968, 10). In other words, there is an important difference between not having been taught and having been taught but having failed to learn. Stated another way, capacity to learn is not equal to capacity to think.

While many of the factors that are *not* measured by IQ tests have a clear relationship to success in the real world, it is *rate of learning* that looms largest in schooling, where the struggle is to get everyone going in about the same direction at about the same pace. This also explains why most IQ tests are timed. When time constraints are removed from an IQ test, scores tend to bunch up, becoming much less discriminating, and much more homogeneous.

Certain other basic things can be said about most IQ tests:

1. About 70 percent of what they measure seems to be genetically determined.
2. Measures of intellectual prowess vary in fairly predictable ways across ethnic and socioeconomic groups.
3. About 30 percent of IQ test performance can be profoundly influenced by nurture, environment, and training.
4. Measures of IQ do not assess many valued intellectual functions, such as the ability to think fairly, objectively, creatively, and with good common sense.

IQ tests do not assess many of our most valued intellectual functions.

The most obvious use of the IQ test is to determine "mental age" (MA). From this we infer the rate of a student's learning by the age-grade equivalent the student might be *expected* to achieve. As shown previously in the section on expectancy formulas, this is a matter of multiplying IQ by chronological age and dividing by 100.

Mental age is basic and convenient, but it can be misleading.

$$MA = \frac{IQ \times CA}{100}$$

Example:

$$MA = \frac{110 \times 10}{100} = 11 \text{ years}$$

As the example illustrates, a child of 10 years old (and in the fifth grade), with an IQ of 110 would have a mental age of an 11-year-old, and would be expected to read closer to the performance level of sixth graders who are 11 years old. There are obvious limitations to the concept of mental age: A 10-year-old with an MA of 18 cannot reasonably be as intellectually mature as an 18-year-old. In general, as mental age increases, the difference between successive years decreases, making the concept of little value for older children and adults.

Ways of Assessing IQ

There are three popular ways of estimating IQ. One is based on verbal aptitude, another on performance (manipulation) tasks, and a third on visual-perceptual tasks. The latter two are sometimes taken together as a nonverbal group. In general, verbal scores tend to be better predictors of reading and school learning.

IQ tests can be used in complex ways, such as to examine for evidence of scatter, or variability among various subtests. Such analyses are done in an effort to pinpoint areas of specific cognitive weakness and strength.

Finally, subtest scores can be grouped in certain ways to look more closely at cognitive aptitudes that are represented by a certain logical or factor-analytically-created cluster. Some of these possibilities are sparingly described next along with the type of IQ tests that are most often used in making such analyses.

Verbal aptitude approach to IQ assessment is based largely on richness of vocabulary. The most popular and easily administered of these is the Peabody Picture Vocabulary Test (PPVT) (Dunn, 1970 and revisions). The PPVT is one of the only untimed IQ tests, yet it only takes about 15 minutes to administer. It is applicable from 3 years old to adulthood. Subjects are asked to identify one of four pictures on a card in response to an examiner's directions. The IQ scores yielded tend to be a bit higher than on other full-range IQ tests. The items with human content have also been found to be more difficult than those with nonhuman content, especially for children with known personal-social adjustment problems (Shipe, Cromwell, & Dunn, 1964, as cited in Dunn, 1965). This suggests that a certain amount of emotionality can be disruptive to thinking, even with fairly innocuous stimuli.

People pictures tend to conjure higher levels of emotionally disruptive thinking.

Some clinicians have reported that the test has some cultural biases, but these are not so serious as to negate its predictive value. Contrary to most expectations, minority group children, in our experience, tend to do better on the PPVT than on other types of IQ measures. Of course, such tests tend to underestimate ability in second-language learners. Ideally, the test should be administered to these students by someone fluent in the student's native language who could ask and recognize equivalent terms in the primary language of the pupil.

Make provisions for second-language learners.

Another form of IQ testing also is largely based on verbal aptitude but its questions probe areas of arithmetic and, at lower levels, even eye-hand-motor coordination. The most notable of these is the Slosson IQ test (1974, 1982), which contains items for subjects aged 2½ years to adulthood. The Slosson is a quick test, constructed to parallel the verbal portion of the more comprehensive Stanford-Binet IQ test described ahead. It takes only 30 minutes to administer and is highly correlated with the Stanford-Binet. It contains items such as the following:

- Which of these three circles is smaller?
- How is a pig different from a dog?
- Say: "Jump down!" Good. Now listen carefully and say exactly what I say: "Mary shouted to Tim, 'Quick, father is coming, jump down!'"
- What is meant by "infectious disease"?

Listening comprehension, as indicated in a previous chapter, is the act of orally reading graded passages *to* students, then checking their comprehension of those passages. It is widely accepted as a measure of **reading capacity,** or the level at which one can be expected to read. Such measures are not necessarily the best predictors of whether a student will actually make gains from instruction (Gauthier, 1988), but they are widely recognized as benchmarks, and should be used for this purpose, especially in conjunction with a cross-verifying vocabulary measure. See Chapter 4 for details on how to use the IRI to measure listening capacity and, by inference, how to derive an estimate of IQ as well.

Listening comprehension is nearly synonymous with IQ.

Visual-perceptual approach to IQ assessment is supposed to be the most culturally fair since there is no apparent need for language. Subjects study patterns and make determinations such as which of several possible figures best completes a pattern, or which figure in a pattern is different from the others shown (Figure 5.5).

IQ tests do not discriminate between ignorance and stupidity.

FIGURE **5.5**

PERCEPTUAL QUOTIENT TEST

Directions: Look at the first row and decide which picture is different from the others. Mark the letter on the answer sheet.

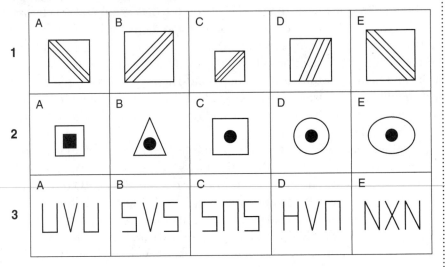

Nonverbal IQ tests can require high-level verbal functioning.

This format is used as a part of a variety of IQ tests. However, the Standard Progressive Matrices (Raven, 1938) and the Columbia Mental Maturity test (Baurgimeister, Blum, & Lorge, 1972) are based entirely on perceptual tasks. Raven's is a group-administered test that is best used with subjects in the upper-intermediate grades to college level, whereas the Columbia is individually administered and is ideal for young children.

Perceptually-based IQ tests have certain drawbacks. They have a generally lower correlation with full-scale IQ tests than do verbal tests. They tend to underestimate students who are impulsive and those who are overly perfectionistic. Young black minority children have been known to struggle to even understand the task (Jensen, 1980, 652). Asians, on the other hand, tend to do quite well with this task (Weiss, 1980). Those who work with patterns, such as seamstresses and engineers, do especially well with this approach to IQ testing. The task also is responsive to "training effects." Subjects' scores tend to rise significantly with any level of exposure to or training in the task. Notable too, in our experience, students with high perceptual skills seem to have remarkable "gaming" skills, even in verbal games where their measured abilities in verbal tasks may be relatively weak. They seem to be able to think in more multidimensional ways that might be the cognitive basis of "cunning."

In general, it is misleading to think of these nonverbal tests as culturally fair. The testing task assumes a certain type of cultural orientation and familiarity with a certain set of language-based patterns that guide thinking and problem solving. Efforts to improve visual-perceptual functioning generally are successful but do not seem to transfer to reading. Jensen (1980) argued that these tests are the best available measure of "pure" intelligence. On the other hand, an analysis of over twenty studies led one researcher to conclude that these tests are better referred to as measures of "Perceptual Quotient" (PQ) (Burke, 1958). J. C. Raven, the British psychologist, seemed to agree with this conclusion in an early manual accompanying his perceptual IQ test called the Standard Progressive Matrices test (Raven, 1960). This fact is especially worth noting since several states with high rates of foreign-born students, such as California and Texas, are increasingly using such tests. This is not necessarily a bad idea, but only where other facts and factors are taken into account.

> PQ may be the cognitive basis of cleverness.

Verbal and Performance (Perceptual)-Based IQ Assessment

IQ tests of this type are designed for individual administration. They often require a good deal of training, and regular practice in administration. There are too many judgments to be made and things to be manipulated to administer these tests validly without training, practice, and routine usage.

The Stanford-Binet Intelligence Scale (1973) is the historical predecessor of most all of these tests. As previously noted, it was first developed in the early 1900s by Simon Binet to help the French government to determine which children would profit most by additional schooling. It is standardized on subjects from 2½ years old to adulthood. However, it used to yield only one overall IQ score. Now it has added subscores.

The Wechsler Intelligence Scales for Children—Revised (WISC-R, 1974) contains the same type of items but groups them into 12 subtests in two categories of 6 subtests each. Scores yielded include a Verbal IQ, Performance IQ, and a combined Full-Scale IQ, in addition to the 12 subtest scores. These subscores make discrepancy and pattern analysis possible, and are largely responsible for the overwhelming popularity of the test. There are separate WISC tests available for very young children and adults; respectively, they are called the Wechsler Preschool and Primary Scale of Intelligence (WPPSI) and the Wechsler Adult Intelligence Scale (WAIS). A brief description follows of the Subtests of the WISC-R and Interpretations can be found in Appendix B: WISC-R and Interpretations. In truth, the WISC-R does not yield a subtest pattern that is dependably predictive of reading disability.

Value of the WISC and Challengers

The WISC-R is a legacy test with history on its side.

It might seem odd that a test continues to be used in individual reading diagnosis when it does not yield a predictable subtest pattern. There are four reasons for this; two are historical, and two logical.

The historical reasons stem from the fact that the WISC was one of the first IQ tests of its type. Secondly, it was developed by a psychologist, not an educator. Wechsler developed it for use in a psychiatric ward at Bellview Hospital in New York City. It originally was called the Wechsler-Bellview IQ test. This may explain why the test contains so many tasks related to social adjustment and emotional maturity such as Social Comprehension, Picture Arrangement, and Object Assembly. It also may explain why it does not measure more things specific to reading and learning. Several test makers have tried to challenge the WISC's supremacy with more educationally-oriented tests. Despite the special relevance of most of these, none has yet to win wide acceptance. The chief challengers are used largely in the field of Learning Disabilities, and include the following:

Woodcock-Johnson Psychoeducational Battery—Cognitive Abilities (WJPEB-CA)
Kaufman Assessment Battery for Children (K-ABC)
McCarthy Scales of Children's Abilities (MSCA)

The third reason for the continued popularity of the WISC, despite its uncertain predictiveness of reading disability, also may explain why the other tests continue to have difficulty in challenging it. It is the fact that there is a rich literature and clinical lore of experience associated with the WISC. That lore, or culture, is passed down in classes, clinics, and apprenticeships and has become invaluable in trying, not so much to find a pattern of reading disability, but to understand a given reading-disabled student. The WISC provides a familiar and common frame of reference for comparing clinical notes on how reading-disabled children differ from one another, rather than in how they are the same. Most clinicians agree that it is wise to encourage the development and use of other instruments that might better reflect the needs and concerns of classroom-based educators, but it also is agreed that it would be unwise to sever a 50-year-old connection and common frame of reference.

There may not be a clear pattern of reading learning disability to detect.

Finally, the reason that the WISC-R may not be predictive of a reading disability may be nested in that now several times repeated fact that brains are different, if not quirky. There are very few clear patterns of proficient brain functioning, so why should we expect to find a clear pattern for dysfunction? Clearly, brain function is the pioneering edge of educational research. It has already moved past "brain-mapping" of regions, however, and is moving toward the architecture of individual cells (microbiology).

Apparently a good deal of teaching and human experience becomes transformed into "learning" at the cellular level.

DISRUPTIONS: IDENTIFYING DISTORTING EMOTIONAL FILTERS

Disruptions are interruptions to learning that occur in the affective, or feeling, domain. This category is used by Weiner and Cromer to refer to *internal-emotional* factors that can cause disruptions to attention and, therefore, thinking and reading. Disruptions may result from a distressing family condition, unruly school situations, or extended exposure to emotionally unstable individuals (siblings, teachers, ministers, parents, peers, neighbors, and so on). Disruptions affect mental health in much the same way that a pebble in the shoe comes to affect even the will to walk. Proponents of a strictly Reading Deficit model would argue that whatever the cause, the effect has been a lack of learning of specific skills. The 6D advocates would counter that learning will continue to be inhibited unless the disruption is addressed. Most parents, most teachers, and most children know that personal-social adjustment is at least as important as academic success, and is a worthy goal of schooling and child rearing.

> Disruptive thinking can arise from a variety of conditions.

Emotional Characteristics Associated with Reading Disorders

Several emotionally charged behaviors have been linked to reading and learning disorders. The checklist described in Figure 5.6 is compiled from the work of: Albert Harris and Edward Sipay (1980), Edward Poostay and Ira Aaron (1982), Anthony Manzo (1987), Helen M. Robinson's classic study "Why Children Fail in Reading" (1946), and from our own recent interest and research in those who "read too much"—or who have **hyperlexia.** (See number 16 in Figure 5.6.)

> Yes, there is such a thing as excessive reading!

Professional Schema Building: Instruments for Gaining Psychological Insight

Various psychological instruments can be used to understand a student. Each is based in some way on the theory of projection, a concept that research has shown to be operative in reading and listening comprehension in a variety of ways (Lipson, 1982, 1983; Pichert & Anderson, 1977; Waern, 1977 a,b). Therefore, understanding projection is an integral part of assessing modernist aspects of schema and constructivist reading, or meaning making.

> Specific psychological problems can affect reading, but more importantly, reading is a means to advance mental heath and well-being.

FIGURE **5.6**

CHECKLIST OF EMOTIONAL CHARACTERISTICS ASSOCIATED WITH READING DISORDERS

____ 1. open hostility and refusal to learn

____ 2. disinclination to accept popular societal values, often accompanied by identification with "maverick" adults or peers

____ 3. hypersensitivity to anything that may be interpreted as criticism

____ 4. displaced hostility with school and teacher transferred from conflicted relationships with siblings, parents, or peers

____ 5. resistance to the ambitions of parents

____ 6. subconscious desire to remain dependent (reading is a natural road to knowledge and independence)

____ 7. lack of self-confidence and self-respect resulting in easy discouragement

____ 8. subconscious fear that success will breed resentment from underachieving parents and friends

____ 9. extreme distractibility or restlessness

____ 10. preoccupation with private inner world

____ 11. gender confusion when accompanied by fear, denial, and need to counterindicate

____ 12. sexual abuse, accompanied by hopelessness from need for help but fear of consequences of disclosure

____ 13. overcontrolling nature

____ 14. obsessive-compulsive tendencies and behaviors

____ 15. social isolation

____ 16. **hyperlexia** (two forms): one, organistic/genetic, as in William's Syndrome where otherwise low-functioning children love to read but have little capacity to comprehend what they are reading, and the other, a more psychological condition where excessive reading is used to support denial and frequent escape, more so than reprieve and comfort

Projection means that someone will reflect and project deep inner feelings when asked to respond to most any open-ended question or stimuli. In the widely known Rorschach test, for example, inkblots are shown and subjects are encouraged to say what they "see." Whatever they say is taken as an expression of what occupies, if not preoccupies, their minds. Interpretation of inkblots is very difficult, since it generally takes a great deal of knowledge and experience as a psychologist to make sense out of such free-association responding. In contrast, other tests narrow the range and reduce the difficulty of interpretation. They do this in a number of ways, telling the child what to draw, for example, as in the House-Tree-Person test (Buck & Jolles, 1966), or showing them pictures of people where the mood is ambiguous and the subject decides if the person is happy or sad, or whatever. The most widely known of this type is the Thematic Apperception Test, originally developed by Morgan and Murray (1935), and updated by John McClelland, et al. (1976). To get a mental image of the task, picture the enigmatic look of the Mona Lisa, then ask "What is she thinking?" or "What happened just prior to this picture?". Whatever comes to mind as you begin to answer these questions will reflect more of what is on your mind than is in the picture. Of course, it still is no simple matter to determine the meanings of these projective associations.

The real challenge is in distinguishing a student's *influenced pressured state,* from *uninfluenced steady state*. This can be the teacher's advantage over psychologists who don't see the day-to-day student. Other instruments are more accessible and useful to educators, and tend to take a more direct, less ambiguous tack. The California Psychological Inventory (CPI) (Gough, 1975), for example, is based on the widely used, adult, Minnesota Multiphasic Personality Inventory (Hathaway & McKinley, 1967) and uses a very direct approach. The cited version of the CPI consists of 480 statements to which true-or-false responses are made. Items then are analyzed and yield scores on eighteen different psychological factors. These include factors such as Dominance, Sociability, Sense of Well-Being, and even the very factor being discussed here: Psychological-Mindedness—the degree to which one is given to understanding human psychology, or inner needs, and motivation.

The Mona Lisa can be a projective test.

Psychological-Mindedness is itself a psychological characteristic.

Most of these instruments were developed or normed primarily with adults in mind, or they tend to contain scales on factors that are difficult for non-psychologists to understand or interpret. Some forms of emotional testing, however, are more accessible and easily interpretable by any professional who works with people and wishes to develop greater psychological insight. These include the Incomplete Sentences, the Adjective Checklist, and the Cognitive-Affective Filter Inventory, or CAFI (formerly the Manzo Bestiary Inventory). Each of these is described in a form that should permit you to explore them for yourself. Whether you use them or not in diagnostic assessment, they will serve as a useful stimulus for grasping and talking about patterns of behavior that you may be observing, but lack the language or schema to address.

"Incomplete Sentences": Psychological Link to Language Experience Activity

Sentence completion procedures were used as early as the 1800s, but it is Julian Rotter who has provided a simple, though relatively subjective,

Teachers are better able than psychologists to identify a student's uninfluenced steady state from the attitude du jour.

means of assessing general emotional adjustment. The best part of the Incomplete Sentence approach is that it is recorded in the student's own words, and then can be used as "language prompts" for dictating or writing a "language experience story." This provides a concrete way to show another professional, and/or a parent, what a student seems to be thinking/feeling. The same lines can even be played back to the student in a follow-up story using many of the same words, though in another character's mouth or mind, and then asking the student for an impression of the character using those words. This type of "improvisational" follow-up is the crux of cross-verification.

Informal Assessment of Affect with Quantitative Scoring

Instability and irrationality are fairly easy to assess.

At an informal level, one needs only to create a series of incomplete sentences (or use our version ahead). Ask students to complete them (in written or oral form), then judge each item on a 0 to 6 scale. Each response will strike you as healthy (0 to 2), neutral (3 to 4), or unhealthy (5 to 6) (Graham & Lilly, 1984). You can use as few as 7 items or as many as the 50 shown in Figure 5.8. The items also can be administered in two or three settings to correct for possible situational factors that may create an optimistic or pessimistic frame of mind.

Veteran teachers typically have internalized a great deal about what constitutes *normal* and *unusual* and potentially *abnormal* responses, from their wealth of experience in adult life and with students. Interpretation rests largely on listening, then cross-verifying with follow-up questions and related items. See Figure 5.7 for examples of such responses. Higher scores are suggestive of high levels of *emotionality* (instability and irrationality), and therefore a greater tendency to distort information in reading and listening. *Emotionality* is the extent to which one is distracted, disturbed, and conflicted by otherwise normal circumstances, and therefore, likely to become extremely agitated and misdirected by even the hint of more serious matters. In everyday wisdom and parlance it is being "wound too tight," "edgy," "overly sullen, melancholy, or touchy." Some of us seem to be born with higher levels of agitation than others.

"Reading therapy" is more common than most realize.

The teacher who can deliver remedial/corrective help in reading while helping students to better cope with this defining factor in their lives is practicing an art once referred to as "reading therapy"—the art of concurrently teaching reading improvement and progress in social-emotional adjustment and maturity. Unfortunately, no one ever hears about it when this is done well, but news stories flow from where we have been unable to do so. In general, teachers do this quite well, although our ability is diminished by larger class sizes and more complex demands. Attention to monitoring and tangibly assessing affective issues could be a way that educators

FIGURE **5.7**

INCOMPLETE SENTENCES

Test Item	Sample Student Response	Score
I believe that family life	(stinks)	(6)
I believe that art is for	(sissies)	(5)
I believe that reading is	(OK)	(2)
The thing I really enjoy is	(I don't know)	(5)
My best friend is	(sometimes not to be trusted)	(3)
When I get older	(I'll do better)	(1)
	TOTAL	27 (High Emotionality)

A Healthy score for 7 items would be about 14; a Mildly Disruptive score would be as high as 20.

> Our classrooms contain future social welfare volunteers, but also the population of prisons.

can provide documentation for the price being paid by overburdening teachers; we are, after all, human, and not able to respond as empathetically as we might were we less stressed ourselves. The frequently reported growth in the prison population and the spiraling costs for mental health are present in some form in the nation's classrooms.

See Figure 5.8 for an example of a traditional "Incomplete Sentence Inventory" (ICI) modified by the authors to reflect contemporary culture.

Adjective Checklists and Reporting

Direct and uncomplicated, adjective checklists are not so much scored, though they can be, but perused (carefully looked over) to get a sense of how people may see themselves in familiar terms. These can be used to reflect on their self-perception and the way they are experiencing situations and interpreting what they read and hear. The Inventory shown in Figure 5.9 has students respond to the same words in terms of the way they "think they are" and the way they "would like to be." The greater the difference between these two ratings, the poorer the individual's feelings of self-concept and self-worth. (This makes the MMA Sentence Completion and the MMA Adjective Checklist instruments good pre-post measures of possible gains in positive affect following solid reading instruction.)

Students often will give some powerful clues as to what their real agenda is by the way they respond to the "would like to be" condition. The teacher who understands these responses is likely to grasp the student's most basic emotional needs and drives, and hence be better equipped to respond empathetically to these in instructional and informal settings, and to communicate this in parent conferences, professional staffings, and case reports.

FIGURE **5.8**

MANZO-MANZO-ALBEE INCOMPLETE SENTENCE INVENTORY

1. Today I feel _____

2. When I have to read, I _____

3. I get angry when_____

4. To be grown up _____

5. My idea of a good time _____

6. I wish my parents _____

7. School is _____

8. I can't understand why _____

9. I feel bad when _____

10. I wish teachers _____

11. I wish my mother _____

12. To me, books _____

13. My friends think I _____

14. I like to read/view about _____

15. After school I _____

16. I'd rather read than _____

17. I hope I'll never _____

18. I wish people wouldn't _____

19. When I grow up _____

20. I'm afraid _____

21. Video games _____

22. When I take my report card home _____

23. I do my best when _____

24. Most brothers and sisters _____

25. I won't know how _____

26. When I read math _____

27. I feel proud when _____

28. I wish my father _____

29. I like to read when _____

30. I would like to be more like _____

31. I often worry about _____

32. I wish I could _____

33. Reading about science _____

34. I look forward to _____

35. I wish _____

36. I'd read more if _____

37. When I read out loud _____

38. I'm sorry that _____

39. If I could be any animal it would be _____

40. Reading is _____

41. I like/dislike watching "captioned" television because _____

42. My favorite character is _____, because _____

43. My favorite movie is _____, because _____

44. I like/do not like to "bully" other kids, because _____

45. Adults seem to find a lot/little reasons to scold/yell at me, because _____

46. I'm happiest when I'm _____

47. The news stories that I find the most scary are the ones about _____

48. Sometimes I do strange things, like _____

49. The thing that I'd like people most to know about me is _____

50. I tend to do _____ too much.

As a general rule, Adjectives are very helpful in reporting since they are by definition "qualifiers" and "modifiers." The authors' version of the Adjective Checklist can be complemented by the Cognitive-Affective Filter Inventory on page 178, which also yields "adjectivals," though from a less transparent form. It also is of value where students might not know a word's meaning.

Adjectives are qualifiers and modifiers.

Cognitive-Affective Filter Inventory (CAFI)

Life and experience do not merely happen around us. It all passes through us, and depending on the way we are constructed, it leaves indelible marks, no more apparent or immediately evident than the billions of subatomic *neutrinos* that pass unnoticed through the earth. The cumulative effect, though, can be significant. Actually, some scientists believe that the seemingly inconsequential neutrinos are part of the force we call gravity. For determining what effects a child's experiences are having on learning and other behaviors, it is useful to have ways to characterize an individual's

Assessment of affect amounts to identifying the filters through which culture and experience are being experienced, and hence, "comprehended."

cognitive and affective *filters*. The Cognitive-Affective Filter Inventory (CAFI), formerly named the Manzo Bestiary Inventory, is a social-psychological traits inventory (Manzo, 1975b) on which students express varying degrees of identification with relatively familiar animals (it has a built-in correction factor for animals not known). The inventory can be administered orally or silently, individually or in a group (see Figure 5.10). Animal choices give insight into how people present themselves, and how they hope others perceive them; how they cope, and what they fear they may be like. The choices reveal something of how people perceive experiences, and how they influence the situations in which they find themselves, and therefore, influence the experiences of others (like peers, teachers, and family). It helps teachers to reduce missteps by being forewarned and forearmed with knowledge about how to negotiate the potentially troubling moments of early encounters with a needy student. Krashen (1982) has identified several affective filters (many of which are identifiable with this inventory) to be of considerable importance in second-language acqui-

Affective "filters" help teachers to be forewarned and forearmed.

FIGURE **5.9**

MANZO-MANZO-ALBEE ADJECTIVE CHECKLIST

Name _____ Date_____

Directions: To achieve a greater level of self-knowledge, start at the left first and check the column under "This is the way I am." Then go back and check under "This is the way I'd like to be" in the same way.

THIS IS THE WAY I AM				THIS IS THE WAY I'D LIKE TO BE		
nearly always	about half the time	just now and then		nearly always	about half the time	just now and then
_____	_____	_____	Friendly	_____	_____	_____
_____	_____	_____	Brave	_____	_____	_____
_____	_____	_____	Honest	_____	_____	_____
_____	_____	_____	Thoughtful	_____	_____	_____
_____	_____	_____	Obedient	_____	_____	_____
_____	_____	_____	Careful	_____	_____	_____
_____	_____	_____	Fair	_____	_____	_____
_____	_____	_____	Mean	_____	_____	_____
_____	_____	_____	Lazy	_____	_____	_____
_____	_____	_____	Truthful	_____	_____	_____
_____	_____	_____	Smart	_____	_____	_____

THIS IS THE WAY I AM				THIS IS THE WAY I'D LIKE TO BE		
nearly always	about half the time	just now and then		nearly always	about half the time	just now and then
____	____	____	Polite	____	____	____
____	____	____	Clean	____	____	____
____	____	____	Kind	____	____	____
____	____	____	Selfish	____	____	____
____	____	____	Helpful	____	____	____
____	____	____	Good	____	____	____
____	____	____	Cooperative	____	____	____
____	____	____	Cheerful	____	____	____
____	____	____	Jealous	____	____	____
____	____	____	Sincere	____	____	____
____	____	____	Studious	____	____	____
____	____	____	Loyal	____	____	____
____	____	____	Likeable	____	____	____
____	____	____	A good sport	____	____	____
____	____	____	Useful	____	____	____
____	____	____	Dependable	____	____	____
____	____	____	Bashful	____	____	____
____	____	____	Happy	____	____	____
____	____	____	Popular	____	____	____
____	____	____	Simple	____	____	____
____	____	____	Flexible	____	____	____
____	____	____	Easily angered	____	____	____
____	____	____	Creative	____	____	____
____	____	____	Manipulating	____	____	____

Before you read about the interpretations and uses of the next assessment technique, you might want to turn to the Manzo CFI in Figure 5.10 (page 178), and follow the directions for making choices of animals you would "most like to be."

FIGURE **5.10**

MANZO COGNITIVE-AFFECTIVE FILTER INVENTORY (CAFI)

Name _____   Date_____

A. Which of the animals listed below would you least like to or most like to pretend to be? Use this 5-point scale to show your likes and dislikes:

1—least
2—rarely
3—sometimes
4—often
5—most

(You may use a zero [0] if you do not know what an animal is.)

____ 1. horse		____ 13. tiger		____ 25. duck	
____ 2. dog		____ 14. pheasant		____ 26. peacock	
____ 3. squirrel		____ 15. horse		____ 27. squirrel	
____ 4. pheasant		____ 16. goat		____ 28. swan	
____ 5. cow		____ 17. turtle		____ 29. falcon	
____ 6. rooster		____ 18. alligator		____ 30. dove	
____ 7. lion		____ 19. porpoise		____ 31. snake	
____ 8. chicken		____ 20. leopard		____ 32. elephant	
____ 9. moose		____ 21. hog		____ 33. eagle	
____ 10. penguin		____ 22. wolf		____ 34. hippopotamus	
____ 11. owl		____ 23. giraffe		____ 35. fox	
____ 12. badger		____ 24. mink		____ 36. coyote	

B. Look back over your strongest choices (4s and 5s). Put *six* of them into the order that you *most* prefer:

1st _____   4th _____

2nd _____   5th _____

3rd_____   6th _____

C. Write the names of the *two* animals you like *least*:

low_____

lowest _____

sition. These factors include high (appetitive, or intrinsic) motivation, self-confidence and positive self-image, and low emotionality (or, social fear and anxiety) in learning-reading situations.

Animal choices have been empirically linked to common associations, as well as to a variety of other factors such as reading, writing, and two aspects of motivation: **appetitive,** or intrinsic, motivation—the desire to achieve something and/or attain some personal goal; and **aversive,** or fear, motivation—the desire to avoid failure or other negative consequences. This list of adjective associations and related factors for each animal is provided in Appendix D, as are full instructions for administering, scoring, and interpreting findings.

Review of a person's animal choices tends to reveal the descriptive words, and therefore the thoughts and feelings through which that person filters experiences, including reading, listening, and school life, and how the person influences the experiences of others in typical social interactions. Adjectives associated with a person's first-level choices are considered to represent the way that person hopes to be seen by others—the "Ideal Self;" the second-level choices reflect the way he or she thinks, he or she actually is—the "Typical Self," or *uninfluenced steady state;* the third-level choices suggest characteristics the person may allow to surface only occasionally— the "Restrained Self;" and the least preferred animals suggest characteristics the person dislikes about him- or herself—the "Feared Self." These last two both speak to one's likely attitudes and behaviors in a pressured state. Being in school—or learning what is not yet known—is almost by definition being in a fairly constant pressured state. A look into the nature of someone's "filtration system" generally reveals something about how that person is experiencing reality, and something about why the same words or actions can have the effect of a gentle stroke to one child and a sharp poke to another.

> Cognitive-affective filters influence personal experience and the experience of others.

> There's an Ideal, Typical, Restrained, and Feared Self.

If you are in doubt, as you sometimes will be, about just which traits should be associated with a given animal chosen by a particular student, ask the student questions such as "What do you picture when you think about [the animal's name]?" Remember that the CAFI, like other affective measures presented, is another useful way to build psychological-mindedness, or orientation and insight into human needs and motivation, and the language and metaphors for thinking and talking about these otherwise murky matters.

If you wish to become more insightful in detecting deeper psychological factors, see the *Luscher Color Test* (translated by Ian Scott, 1969). This adult-oriented test asks subjects to select eight colors in the order of their choice. Color choices then are matched with interpretive statements that are quite useful and self-instructional in explaining motivation and behavior. We believe that you will find both the CFI and the LCT useful with upper-elementary students as well.

Personal Traits Records

If the use of any psychological instruments seems foreign or foreboding, consider the simple re-addition of a personal traits record report such as

FIGURE **5.11**

PERSONAL TRAITS RECORD

Teacher/Evaluators

Name: Johnston, Sara   Year: 1981–82

Name: Clark, Mark   Year: 1982–83

Name:_____   Year:_____

Coleson, Andrew   Year: 1981–82

Walker, James   Year: 1982–83

Personal Trait	Year	(high) 5	4	3	2	(low) 1
Work Habits	1981–82	☐	☐	☐	☐	☐
	1982–83	☐	☐	☐	☐	☐
	1983–84	☐	☐	☐	☐	☐
	1984–85	☐	☐	☐	☐	☐
Responsibility	1981–82	☐	☐	☐	☐	☐
	1982–83	☐	☐	☐	☐	☐
	1983–84	☐	☐	☐	☐	☐
	1984–85	☐	☐	☐	☐	☐
Self-control	1981–82	☐	☐	☐	☐	☐
	1982–83	☐	☐	☐	☐	☐
	1983–84	☐	☐	☐	☐	☐
	1984–85	☐	☐	☐	☐	☐
Getting along with others	1981–82	☐	☐	☐	☐	☐
	1982–83	☐	☐	☐	☐	☐
	1983–84	☐	☐	☐	☐	☐
	1984–85	☐	☐	☐	☐	☐

were widely used on cumulative record files for many years. See Figure 5.11 for two examples.

Subjective record systems such as these make it possible to estimate whether a student is making reasonable progress toward maturity in independence, self-control, responsibility, and social adjustment. Factors such as these often become more predictive of long-term progress in learning, lifetime reading, and productive living than IQ or grade point averages.

It is always a hard sell, due to our regard for privacy, but we would add a slot to Figure 5.11 for "normal/abnormal behaviors." This may not bear on reading progress, but it definitely would help bring attention, and possibly timely help, to students who are signaling inclination toward self-destructive or violent behaviors in the future. Suicide, murder, and other violent crimes seldom explode without early signals. A holistic philosophy of education suggests that at least this modest effort to observe and possibly counter such problems should be a reasonable priority in the schools.

Chapter 11 treats this and the next topic in the context of rather traditional reading practices. Differences, the next topic, are not always distinguishable in practical terms from disruptions, since often the effects can be much the same.

DIFFERENCES

Common Assumptions about Students

All schooling, as illustrated in the initial two chapters, is based on a set of assumptions about exposure to certain environmental opportunities and of chronological development. Predominant among these is the assumption of certain common learnings, or shared experiences, concepts, and values. In addition to these common learnings, or "Literacy-Facilitating Experiences," is the unspoken expectation that we all will learn in about the same way and in about the same period of time. A sensitive school program realizes that such assumptions may not hold true for a given individual and seeks means by which to identify and address differences that put such students "at-risk" (Beane, 1990).

Literacy-Facilitating Experiences (LFEs)

Differences or mismatches between the student's Literacy-Facilitating Experiences and the general assumptions of schools and by teachers may include language, social, cultural, learning style, and related attitudinal factors. As mentioned before, Trace Elements are as much dispositional and learned in the home-community environment, as they are potentially constititutional. Again (slightly elaborated to the point of "difference"), these include:

- inclination and skill to think abstractly, or to generalize with sensible boundaries
- ability to critique and be critiqued (or give and take constructive criticism without anger and withdrawal)
- inclination and ability to simply read, and to do so between and beyond the lines

- inclination and ability to deal with ambiguities (without confrontation or rage)
- tendency toward self-examination (metacognitive operations), self-regulation, and responsibility for self-learning
- inclination to think about and refine understandings of the world into what is more civilized and civilizing (schema-building)
- inclination, opportunity, and belief in one's ability to envision and build toward a more sensible life for self, family, and community, even while experiencing a life that may be dysfunctional by social standards
- having the resilience to pursue something better in the face of out-weighing odds

At first glance, these may seem far afield from the reading–language arts curriculum. More careful thought will suggest otherwise. The goals of quality education are not merely to support and praise cultural-social differences. Many of these reflect past impoverishment, especially of recently migrated peoples. The goals are to help children overcome a variety of "differences" and hence to change by a self-selected combination of assimilation and accommodations that permit them to claim a stake in contemporary society. More on this in Chapter 12 on Assessing and Addressing Second Language and Culture.

Assessing Difference: Heroic Today

Although the concept of "differences" receives a good deal of attention in the literature on learning styles and multicultural education, it would be a heroic effort at this time because it still is in its infancy in terms of assessment and practice. Today these common-learnings would be called "cultural literacy," or as we once called it, a "cultural compatibility index." It is difficult to design such an instrument, since it would seem to support certain stereotypes while trying to act with a deep concern and respect for diversity. The instrument that we developed for assessing these factors, frankly, is out of date, and we do not know of any that has replaced it. You will find our *Difference Inventory* online at the book Web site and/or your instructor's in a usable form. Share your findings and we will revise it for the next edition of this text, or before. For now, we will cover the equally difficult issue of addressing "learning styles."

Learning Style versus Cognitive Style

"Cognitive style"—or how a brain actually functions—probably is different from "learning style."

Learning styles issues in reading, technically known as "aptitude-treatment interactions" (Cronbach & Snow, 1977; Curry, 1990), have come to focus mainly on modality (hearing, seeing, feeling) preferences. In point of fact, "cognitive style"—how a brain actually functions—probably is different from "learning style"—how a person best learns, or fails to learn. Attention to learning-style preference has also been called a "heroic effort" (Ekwall & Shanker, 1988, 108). Robert Mills (1965) pioneered the assessment of modality preference with the development of the Learning Methods Test (Mills, 1970, revised). Today this strategy would simply be called Trial Teaching. The model for the test (now out of print) was outlined in an earlier chapter. Briefly, the teacher would identify 40 words that a student between the primary and third-grade levels does not know, and then teach and test the student on these words in sets of 10, in four different ways over five days. Each teaching session is 15 minutes long. The methods are characterized as: phonic, visual, kinesthetic, and combined visual-auditory-kinesthetic.

Robert Mills and others who have attempted to refine these tests, such as Maria Carbo (1984a,b,c), offer some interesting findings in support of the principle of matching students to style of teaching. Nonetheless, several key aspects of their findings have been hotly disputed (see, for example, Ceprano, 1981; Kampwirth & Bates, 1980; Tarver & Dawson, 1978).

Currently there is little to suggest that these methods can be easily separated by "modalities," and not enough proof of a significant interaction between modality preference and method to justify whole-scale testing and matching. Three factors, however, continue to command the attention of remedial/corrective specialists to these developments. For one thing, Public Law 94-142 requires that "a specific statement describing the child's *learning style* be included in the Individual Educational Plan (IEP) for a handicapped student." This could be written off as the mere byproduct of the social-political forces that created this legislation were it not for two other considerations. An overwhelming majority of LD specialists believe in modality testing and preference (as reported in Ekwall & Shanker, 1988), and there is, as stated previously, a certain compelling logic to the significance of issues in learning styles, especially where disabled readers and learners are concerned (Witkin et al., 1977). The argument for it is based on what could be called an "extra mile" principle: Where learning consistently lags behind apparent capacity, it is time for Special Education; that is, where "optimizing" results justifies the heroics of trying to match teaching style to individual learning styles. Others are unconvinced that such matching ever needs to be done. They argue that children may actually grow to greater independence by intentional mismatching. This paradox has led Snow and Lohman (1984) to suggest matching for the initial stages of learning, and systematic mismatching thereafter. The most current theoretical position has shifted even further. It now is being argued that the best learning style is the absence of any identified style or consistency of approach,

Newer thinking on "learning styles" is to have students and teachers become more flexible in the use of all "styles" rather than some contrived "modality" preference.

The "extra mile" principle and intentional mismatching.

with the emphasis being on teaching children and teachers to be flexible in using the style or approach that best matches the content or objective rather than the individual learner (Kirby, 1988; Pask, 1988; & Curry, 1990).

Learning Preference Inventory

The emphasis that appears best to us at this time is to build some alternative ways of teaching that permit us to meet a broader variety of human style variations, needs, and capacity levels. To this end, we began some time ago to develop and use an informally administered Learning Preference Inventory (Manzo, Lorton, & Condon, 1975; Manzo & Casale, 1983). This informal inventory, to which we have recently added a few approaches and a checklist of eleven elements, seems to help both teacher and students to grow in their sense of the options that are available for conducting lessons in a variety of interesting, though not necessarily exotic or quirky, ways.

The Learning Preference Inventory (LPI) (see Figure 5.12) is not limited to early age/grade ranges or to modality issues as are most other learning styles inventories; however, it is apparent that some methods are more suitable for some age/grade levels than others. The LPI should be scored with the expectation that a student should feel relatively comfortable (3s or higher on a 5-point scale) with each of the teaching-learning styles represented. Students should be especially comfortable with the mode most used by their teacher or the mode that is necessary due to the nature of what is being taught at a given age and grade level. The chief thing to know about learning-style preference is whether a student has a strong dislike for a commonly used mode of presentation, or that a student's most preferred mode of learning is one that is seldom if ever used, and therefore ought to be included at least some of the time. Learning-style preference generally is a problem only for a small percentage of students with very specific needs, and/or strong personal preferences. As noted previously, however, students who are at risk for other reasons, or already are failing, are likely to be the ones who need the most compatible environment. The greatest concern from the point of view of instructional planning is to be careful not to develop a remedial/corrective program around "learning-style" needs that are difficult to determine and match, at the expense of more tried-and-true methods of instruction.

Teacher Preferences Affect Student Preferences

To maximize the value of the LPI in instructional planning, administer it to students informally, and talk with them about the various ways in which teaching-learning can be conducted. The illustrations are far less essential

FIGURE **5.12**

LEARNING PREFERENCES INVENTORY

....

Directions: Choose the statement that best matches how you feel about each way of learning described. Circle the number that best matches your feeling about each.
- 1. strongly dislike
- 2. dislike
- 3. no strong feelings for or against
- 4. like
- 5. like very much

TEACHING/LEARNING METHODS

1. **Lecture Learning:** The teacher does most of the talking. Questions are permitted, but there generally is little discussion.
   How do you feel about the Lecture Learning method?
   Circle one:

   1   2   3   4   5

2. **Lecture/Discussion:** The teacher talks briefly, then answers and raises questions in class discussion.
   How do you feel about the Lecture/Discussion method?
   Circle one:

   1   2   3   4   5

3. **Inquiry Lesson:** The teacher names a topic, then the class questions the teacher to discover the important information on that topic. The teacher finally tells the class what important questions they may have failed to ask. How do you feel about the Inquiry Lesson method?
Circle one:

1   2   3   4   5

4. **Incidental Teaching:** Most skills are taught as they appear to be needed. For example, a spelling, reading, or writing lesson may be taught on the spot in a social studies class because the students seem to need it at that time.
How do you feel about the Incidental Teaching method?
Circle one:

1   2   3   4   5

5. **Casual Learning:** Games are played or activities done to improve certain skills and attitudes.
How do you feel about the Casual Learning method?
Circle one:

1   2   3   4   5

6. Individual Learning: Each student is given different work to do based on need. The work must be completed before going to a higher level. This type of learning can involve workbooks.
How do you feel about the Individual Learning method?
Circle one:

1   2   3   4   5

7. Student Reporting: Individual students are responsible for finding and presenting information to the class on assigned topics.
How do you feel about the Student Reporting method?
Circle one:

1   2   3   4   5

8. Group Work: Small groups are assigned topics to look up and discuss. Their findings are then shared with the entire class.
How do you feel about the Group Work method?
Circle one:

1   2   3   4   5

9. **Individual Tutoring:** The teacher works with one student (or a small group) while the remainder of the class does some other activity.
How do you feel about the Individual Tutoring method?
Circle one:

1   2   3   4   5

10. **Team Teaching:** Two or more teachers work together to teach a class. They discuss different points of view in front of the group. The class participates in the discussion.
How do you feel about the Team Teaching method?
Circle one:

1   2   3   4   5

11. **Role-playing (simulation):** Students are guided in actually experiencing something and then discussing what they have learned.
How do you feel about the Role-playing method?
Circle one:

1   2   3   4   5

12. Mental Picturing (imaging): Students attempt to learn by trying to see a word or an idea in their minds, or by making an actual picture of it.
How do you feel about the Mental Picturing method?
Circle one:

1   2   3   4   5

13. Movement (kinesthetic): Students try to learn something by moving their hands in a tracing movement or by acting out a certain word or idea in order to remember it.
How do you feel about the Movement method?
Circle one:

1   2   3   4   5

14. Hearing and Saying (Recitation training): Students learn by having something said while they look at it, then say it, and then repeat the whole thing until they have got it down.
How do you feel about the Hearing and Saying method?
Circle one:

1   2   3   4   5

15. Hands-on: Students are asked to do or make something that aids in learning.
How do you feel about the Hands-on method?
Circle one:

1   2   3   4   5

Check each thing that you would like to see happen more or less often in the classroom. Circle one number for each item

Circle one:

	much less	less	slightly more	more	much more
16. repeating	1	2	3	4	5
17. faster pacing	1	2	3	4	5
18. moving around	1	2	3	4	5
19. writing	1	2	3	4	5
20. drawing	1	2	3	4	5
21. reading	1	2	3	4	5
22. being read to	1	2	3	4	5
23. student talking	1	2	3	4	5
24. use of TV & recordings	1	2	3	4	5
25. field trips	1	2	3	4	5

Where teaching-learning is concerned, differences between a teacher's and a student's learning/cognitive style preferences can be significant, but ideally, negotiable.

than the students' grasp and reflection on how they have felt, or would feel under the different approaches represented. It is advisable for the teacher to take the inventory, and to do so in two ways: first as you would prefer to learn, and then as you tend to teach. A simple comparison of these perspectives will result in a valuable diagnostic conversation with yourself about how to best serve student needs; ideally, without feeling too put-upon yourself.

REVIEW

This chapter covered the fundamentals of field-based assessment of reading deficits that are traceable to collateral factors such as: physical-physiological-neurological, psychological, intellectual, lifestyle and social-cultural, or difference, factors. Some of these factors are routinely measured; others receive lip service but are not measured. Very few are as seriously factored in as they should be, to the complex equations that help to pinpoint need and guide precision teaching. You now have a solid resource to help you begin to do so.

PREVIEW

The next chapter speaks to the partnership between the reading specialist and the classroom teacher. It covers generic issues in classroom corrective and intensive remedial/instruction. Of considerable interest will be a listing of principles of corrective-remedial instruction. The list, frankly, is too lengthy to keep in mind. It is difficult, however, to eliminate any one of them. Powerful, precise diagnostic-prescriptive teaching can be "rocket science."

Powerful teaching is "rocket science."

FRAMEWORKS AND PRINCIPLES FOR CORRECTIVE AND REMEDIAL INTERVENTION

Reading taste and ability are always tethered to past experience.
But reading itself is one way of increasing this venture capital fund . . .
– PARAPHRASE FROM EDGAR DALE

CONTENT AND CONCEPT ORGANIZER

You now know a good deal about the history and practices of pre-assessment, post-assessment and use of diverse information and information sources. This chapter continues with the history of past and modern practices of intervention in the classroom and "clinic." Pay particular attention to: subtle and powerful means to amplify the value of "auto-instructional" materials; the developing value of cooperative structures; the somewhat overwhelming but valuable principles of remediation; and suggestions for organizing a corrective-remedial lesson. Note, too, the nature of the "challenge case" at the end of the chapter. It is one that is common but frequently overlooked.

CHAPTER OUTLINE

THE READING SPECIALIST AND THE CLASSROOM
TEACHER
Evolving Role of "Cambrian Reading Specialists"
No Reading Teachers Left Behind

HISTORICAL PREFACE TO CORRECTIVE
AND REMEDIAL READING
Early Research Attempts to Develop a Scientific
Approach to Reading Education
Recent Research Related to Psycholinguistic Theory
What Kind of Code Emphasis and How Much?
Where We Are Now

A FRAMEWORK FOR BALANCED READING
Systematic and Ongoing, Classroom-Based
Assessment
Whole-to-Part, Concept-Based Unit Design
Plentiful and Varied Instructional Materials
Direct, Whole-Class Instruction in Grade-
Appropriate Strategies

Frequent Opportunities for "Strategy Interactions"
with Peers

REMEDIAL READING: REQUIEM OR
RESURRECTION?
It's Back!
Scope of Remedial Reading
"Remedial Needs" Does Not Equal "Remedial
Reader," and "Remedial Reader" Does Not
Necessarily Equal "Unsuccessful Life"
University-Based Reading Clinics

WHAT IS REMEDIAL INSTRUCTION?
Supplement to Classroom Instruction
Strategically Fit to Individual Need
Improvisational, "Outside-the-Box" Solutions
Strategic Parroting and Implosive Therapy
Wrapped in "Authentic Instruction"
Does Remediation Work?
Refocus Away from Economic Disadvantage
Media Magic

THE READING SPECIALIST AND THE CLASSROOM TEACHER

Diagnosis was described in Chapter 1 as a "story with a point," and the point is effective correction or remediation of reading difficulties. Many of these difficulties can be identified and corrected by the classroom teacher. Others will call for more precise and/or intensive assessment and/or intervention than the classroom teacher can provide. Reading specialists and classroom teachers can best function as "co-authors" of children's stories when they share some common understandings about: 1) the challenges they each are facing; 2) how these have evolved; 3) a general instructional framework; and 4) specific principles of corrective and remedial instruction.

Evolving Role of "Cambrian Reading Specialists"

Remedial reading, for much of its early life, was a "pull-out" program. Students were taken from their regular classrooms for individual or small group tutoring. In 1937, Monroe and Backus found that, "Teachers of the elementary school were familiar with general techniques of teaching reading but were inadequately prepared to diagnose and deal with difficulties of individual pupils; . . ." (ix). Since the need for remedial programs often was an afterthought, schools were not designed to accommodate them. Not surprisingly, reading specialists often operated in inadequately ventilated rooms, in basements, or hallways, if not in oversized broom closets.

This "add-on" picture is changing as a number of conditions are coming together—much in the way that environmental conditions came together to produce a multitude of life forms in the prehistoric "Cambrian Period," as noted in a previous chapter. With respect to teachers, reading specialists, and remedial reading, the first such condition is the nation's coming to grips with the sheer size of the need. Alongside this realization, a movement—almost an avalanche—toward more structured and direct instruction in all areas of literacy is relieving much of the tension that has restricted progress

The field of reading has evolved past crisis and entered a Cambrian Period of constructive-creative discovery.

in recent years. At the same time, national concern for quality reading instruction remains high, and teachers are better prepared than ever to evaluate and correct problems that can be handled in the classroom, and to identify problems that require collaboration with specialists. Reading specialists also continue, with little acknowledgment from the wider educational community, to implement and develop the practical wisdom and methods known as "content area reading," the subfield of reading that pioneered the concepts and methods for teaching comprehension. This confluence of conditions should reposition reading specialists to lead the twenty-first-century endeavor to provide practical remedies for the complex challenges involved in providing for the school and lifetime literacy needs of all who attend school, including those with limited English proficiency, those who are slow to learn, and those who are, at least on the surface, resentful of learning. This will require considerable imagination, collaboration, and support.

No Reading Teachers Left Behind

The way funding is sputtering, the Federal charge should be "no reading teachers left behind!"

The classroom teacher and the reading specialist are partners whose mission needs to be well funded and supported. It is not too dramatic to say that, together, they are the people who give meaning to slogans like "no child left behind" in reading. They ensure liberty by educating citizens to be literate, the most basic privilege, responsibility, and need for the preservation of a democratic society. Yet, it is an unfortunate but well-known fact that in times of budget tightening, it is the reading specialist "budget lines" that are among the first to be slashed. No matter how current and past movements and programs are viewed, there are some who view "remedial reading" as archaic, and the reading specialist's role as a "frill." This is true not only of elementary school positions, but of middle school, high school, and central office positions that are less familiar to the general public but provide essential resources to teachers and students. Specific job descriptions for these positions vary from state to state and district to district, but some of the resources they provide include:

- presenting information in inservice and faculty meetings to help keep teachers updated on new developments in literacy education
- providing demonstration lessons in content teachers' classrooms, and helping them to develop instructional materials for reading-based lessons
- working with middle school teacher teams to incorporate strong literacy strands into interdisciplinary units
- evaluating standardized test results to identify students who may need special reading assistance, and to identify specific literacy elements that may need more direct attention in subject area classes

- evaluating, and providing individual or small group assistance for students with severe reading difficulties
- teaching one or more developmental reading classes, targeting study-reading strategies and techniques
- setting up and managing a reading laboratory, often with computer-assisted assessment and instruction

Reading specialists can be very cost effective to the school, the pupil, and the taxpayer.

The Framework and Principles for Corrective and Remedial Instruction ahead in this chapter are best understood in the context in which they have evolved, as briefly described next.

HISTORICAL PREFACE TO CORRECTIVE AND REMEDIAL READING

Until about a century ago, in the one-room schoolhouse of the American frontier, being a teacher meant providing daily instruction in all subjects to students, from beginning reading through high school levels. It was not unusual for a child to begin "schooling" at age 10, with little or no learning in reading or math, nor for an 8-year-old in her second year of school to be reading in a fourth-grade book. Like water, children's abilities found their level in the multilevel daily instruction. Teaching was an awesome challenge, yet many teachers went beyond the challenge to excel at guiding their small communities of learning, and inspiring many youngsters in their charge to be lifelong learners, or even teachers.

Of course, not all children were allowed to attend school, and many attended only for a few years—long enough to acquire the "basics" in reading and "ciphering." There was no need for "corrective" or "remedial" level instruction as such. Children were grouped for instruction according to their level, and those who continued to be unsuccessful were simply not encouraged to stay.

Early Research Attempts to Develop a Scientific Approach to Reading Education

Fast-forward fifty years, and we find the graded school, and compulsory schooling for all American children. We find vocabulary-controlled basal reading textbooks implementing the "look-say" (whole-word) approach, in which direct instruction in phonics is delayed until children have acquired a basic sight word vocabulary. We find educators struggling with the unavoidable facts that: a) the "graded" classroom still has a wide range of

A picture of our
historical past.

reader competencies, even when classes are formed homogeneously by achievement, or "tracked"; and b) some children have serious difficulty learning to read, yet legally must remain in school. A proportion of students begin first grade in the lowest track, and remain there until dropping out of school as soon as they are legally able to do so. Attempts to deal with these problems lead to a continuing increase in requirements for teacher certification and growing respect for the field of Education as a science.

In 1955, Rudolph Flesch attacked the basal reader look-say approach to teaching reading in the popular bestseller, *Why Johnny Can't Read.* The 1956 launching of the Russian satellite Sputnik I raised national concern about the quality of American education. By 1967, these concerns culminated in the landmark research project known as the "First-Grade Studies."

> Prompted by the furor that had followed Flesch's book and probably encouraged about the possibilities of funding following Sputnik and the National Defense Education Act, the National Conference on Research in English established a special committee on reading research. The committee met for the first time at Syracuse University in 1959, when, according to Chall, the controversy over methods had reached its most bitter point, and laid the seeds for the First-Grade Studies (Graves & Dykstra, 1997).

Jeannie Chall of Harvard began work on another landmark project, later published as *Learning to Read: The Great Debate* (1967). Other members of the committee undertook the coordination of twenty-seven research projects designed to discover the best way to teach children to read. The latter project, which came to be known as the First-Grade Studies, focused on comparing the look-say basal reader approach with various other beginning reading approaches. These included basal plus phonics; initial teaching alphabet; linguistic, language experience; and phonics/linguistics. The First-Grade Studies was published as the entire 1967 summer issue of *Reading Research Quarterly.*

Chall was quite clear about her findings though many people, for many years, found her conclusions unsettling. She continued to voice what she found through later research and publications, including a second edition of *The Great Debate.* Here, Chall claimed that *meaning-emphasis* approaches result in more children having more severe reading difficulty than do *code-emphasis* approaches. The First-Grade Studies were more circumspect in reporting their findings, concluding that no approach is "best," and that a combination of approaches is superior to basal-only. Pearson notes, however, that:

> You would not conclude from the 1967 RRQ report that code-emphasis approaches were superior to meaning-emphasis approaches. Even though both the phonics plus basal and the phonics first (dubbed phonic-

linguistic) approaches consistently elicited higher comprehension and word reading scores than basal approaches, Bond and Dykstra avoided the conclusion. In a later article Dykstra compared Chall's (1967) conclusions with the span of first- and second-grade results from the First-Grade Studies. Dykstra (1968) concluded, "Data from the Cooperative Research Program in First-Grade Reading Instruction tend to support Chall's conclusion that code-emphasis programs produce better overall primary grade reading and spelling achievement than meaning-emphasis programs" (21).

It is testament, perhaps, to the common wisdom that teaching is part art and part science. Despite what the science of the day was clearly revealing about the teaching of beginning reading, many teachers and educators continued to resist code-emphasis approaches. Robert Dykstra himself had taught in a one-room schoolhouse before he went to college (Walradth, 1998): No doubt, he was viewing the data through the eyes of a teacher. Educators coined the term "eclectic approach" as a practical application of the conclusions of the First-Grade Studies, and basal reader publishers scurried to implement this vague concept by producing massive "scope and sequence"–referenced skills mastery learning program materials, with a stronger emphasis on phonics. The classroom management technique of creating four to five ability groups for reading (with names like "Bluebirds") was widely endorsed for dealing with the inevitable range of student achievement within a class. Corrective-remedial reading typically amounted to rerouting children through the basal reader skills sequence.

Teachers, meanwhile, began to turn, individually and then en masse, toward the voice of Ken Goodman, and his Whole Language philosophy: "Teach them to read for meaning and the words will fall into place" (from "A Conversation with Ken Goodman"). Some of the hallmarks of a Whole Language classroom included:

- replacing basal reader materials with quality children's literature
- replacing direct instruction in phonetic elements of words with a literacy-rich environment, including environmental print and authentic experiences with print
- eliminating ability grouping
- minimizing emphasis on accuracy of children's oral reading and maximizing emphasis on meaning (oral "misreadings" should not even be thought of as "errors" or "mistakes," but as "miscues"— indicators that the child has misread the cues for making meaning from the print)
- eliminating the concept of "remedial reading" (and, implicitly, associated concepts such as "IQ" testing and "Expectancy Formulas")
- replacing formal testing with more "kidwatching"

As a group, elementary school teachers of the 1970s and '80s were well educated and socially and politically sensitive. They had grown up during America's social revolution, and an unpopular war in Vietnam. Whole Language was, in many ways, a breath of fresh air for these teachers looking for alternatives to lock-step basal programs that seemed to be part of the national disgrace associated with "failing" inner-city children and a war against an agrarian people. Whole Language gave teachers license to chuck the teacher's manual, and do what they knew they could do: Teach children to read and write about meaningful ideas found in authentic literature, and have fun doing it. Like the one-room schoolhouse teachers, many did it extraordinarily well, usually teaching phonics quite directly, though "on the sly." Those who did not do it well, however, produced, as the First-Grade Studies predicted, more children with more severe reading problems than we had ever seen in previous years.

Recent Research Related to Psycholinguistic Theory

Ken Goodman's Whole Language philosophy was based on his "psycholinguistic theory" of reading, which emphasized the point that reading is a psychological process as much as a linguistic one. This theory proposed that good readers use minimal cues to make meaning from print, with "minimal" determined by the reader's level of knowledge of the topic, vocabulary, and language structures used in a given text. The greater the reader's knowledge of these factors for a given text, the fewer letters or even words need to be physically perceived. As he often phrased it, "reading is a psycholinguistic guessing game." Recent research, using eye-movement photography, has disproved this fundamental premise of psycholinguistic theory: Even when good readers are reading text for which they have a high level of knowledge of the topic, vocabulary, and language structures, they visually perceive every letter of every word. If reading is a guessing game, it seems to be one that is more informed by accurate and fluent decoding than proposed by "psycholinguistic" theory.

Research, using eye-movement photography, proved that we read and decode one word at a time. "Psycholinguists" had this all wrong.

What Kind of Code Emphasis and How Much?

While Whole Language was at its peak, the National Center for the Study of Reading underwrote a new review of research related to the role of phonics instruction in beginning reading. The conclusions of this compilation, published by Marilyn Adams in the book *Beginning to Read . . .* (1990), were the popular beginnings of putting a finer point on research questions that were too blunt to be of much value in instructional intervention. The First-Grade Studies and Chall's The Great Debate were correct in telling us that a code-emphasis approach was essential; however, they did not tell us much about what **kind** of code emphasis, or **how much.**

The rules-based phonics approaches of the time worked better than no code emphasis, but teachers and other educators resisted, based on experience-informed intuitive convictions that *we don't learn to read by learning rules.* The research threads summarized by Adams point to a very different kind of phonics used by beginning readers. It appears that the way beginning readers use sound-symbol correspondences is to gather an increasing store of known words, and then used the letter clusters from known words as the primary means of "attacking" an unknown word. In other words, *we decode by analogy.* As translated by Pat Cunningham in a 1992 keynote address to the National Reading Conference entitled "What *Kind* of Phonics Instruction Will We Have?": "the brain is a pattern detector, not a rule applier."

Where We Are Now

Today, we are either on the brink of falling back into the pre–Whole Language basal approaches, or stepping forward onto less familiar ground. The "Balanced Reading" approach that many reading educators espouse sounds a great deal like the "Eclectic" approach that was widely endorsed in response to the findings of the First-Grade Studies. "Balanced Reading," to most educators, means a combination of quality literature and direct instruction in phonics. But there is little consensus on how to achieve this. An action paper entitled "Every Child Reading: An Action Plan," adopted by the Learning First Alliance of twelve national education associations, summarizes the situation this way:

> In recent years, most educators have come to advocate a balanced approach to early reading instruction, promising attention to basic skills and exposure to rich literature. However, classroom practices of teachers, schools, and districts using balanced approaches vary widely (http://www.learningfirst.org/readingaction.html#top).[1]

---

[1] Reprinted by permission. The forward to this paper reads, "This action paper was adopted by the Learning First Alliance, an organization of twelve leading national education associations. It has been informed by many distinguished experts in reading. We are pleased to acknowledge the assistance of Robert Slavin, Johns Hopkins University, as well as advice provided by Marilyn Adams, BBN Corporation; Isabel Beck, University of Pittsburgh; Reid Lyon, National Institutes of Health; Louisa Moats, D.C. Public Schools/NICHD Early Interventions Project; Jean Osborn, Educational Consultant; Olatokunbo S. Fashola, Johns Hopkins University; David Pearson, Michigan State University; Joseph Conaty, Office of Educational Research and Information, U.S. Department of Education; and John Pikulski, International Reading Association. Although many individuals have offered suggestions that have been incorporated herein, this paper should not necessarily be considered representative of the views of any individual who assisted in the writing or provided advice and comment.

FIGURE **6.1**

WHOLE LANGUAGE PRACTICES?

Whole Language Practices

Supported by Research

Quality literature, which may be provided in a basal reader program

A literacy-rich classroom environment

Environmental print

Authentic experiences with print

Ongoing assessment in the classroom, including "kidwatching," and in-depth diagnosis when indicated

No within-class ability grouping

Corrective instruction in the regular classroom; remedial instruction in individual or small group settings

Unsupported by Research

No direct instruction in phonics

Underemphasis on accuracy in oral reading

No direct instruction in comprehension strategies

No remedial reading

No formal assessment

Phonics Practices

Supported by Research

Direct and systematic instruction in phonemic awareness

Direct and systematic instruction in phonetic elements of words, and strategies for analogic word attack

Phonics instruction that begins and ends with meaningful reading experiences

Emphasis on the need for reading to make sense

Oral reading and rereading of predictable books to build sight word knowledge and sustained attention to words in print (sight words viewed as the tools for analogic decoding)

Encouragement of invented spelling in writing, to engage children in exploring letter-sound correspondence, and letter patterns in words

Direct instruction in spelling, based on emphasis on spelling patterns

Unsupported by Research

Within-class ability grouping for reading

Synthetic phonics approaches, that begin with phonics rules and isolated skill drills

Linguistic reading approaches in which materials with "controlled" vocabulary are devoid of meaning

Analytic phonics with early emphasis on knowledge of phonics rules

Spelling instruction based on rote memory

Overemphasis on accuracy in oral reading

A "Balanced Reading Program" cannot simply be a marriage of Whole Language and phonics. Some Whole Language practices are supported by recent research and some are not; some direct phonics instruction practices are supported and some are not, as summarized in Figure 6.1.

The Framework for Balanced Reading defined below, and further detailed throughout this textbook, includes many practices developed before they were supported by research, and excludes many practices that were based on assumptions that research has since disproved, or experience has shown to be impractical. The Framework is structured to meet the needs of today's elementary and middle-school classrooms which are heterogeneously assigned, and usually include children with learning disabilities, physical and/or mental handicaps, and/or cultural and language differences.

A FRAMEWORK FOR BALANCED READING

The most significant characteristics of an Informed Intervention Framework for Balanced Reading are listed here, and described more fully below:

1. **Systematic and ongoing classroom-based assessment** that includes structured observations and student self-evaluation.
2. **Whole-to-part, concept-based instructional unit design** and implementation with an emphasis on creating a community of learners.
3. **Plentiful and varied reading materials** at controlled difficulty levels (such as, but not limited to, basal reader selections), with teacher guidance in selecting supplementary reading materials at appropriate difficulty levels for given children for given tasks, from fiction and nonfiction reading materials of all types.
4. **Direct, whole-class instruction in grade-appropriate strategies and skills for comprehension, meaning vocabulary, sight words/fluency, and phonics** with opportunity for ongoing practice at developmental and corrective level reading (refer to the chart in Figure 1.3 in Chapter 1 for grade-level specifics). Whole-class instruction, with students of varying reading achievement levels, for the purpose of modeling and engaging students in the use of various types of reading strategies is referred to as "multilevel" instruction. The skills needed for automaticity in word recognition, vocabulary meaning recognition, sentence structure, and fluency are enhanced through the use of quality instructional materials for independent or small-group "autoinstruction," or practice.
5. **Frequent opportunities for "strategy interactions" with peers:** small-group activities that are structured in ways that engage students in use of active meaning-making strategies, many of which also have **concurrent value**—adding other valued objectives (such as a *sense of social justice*) and "trace elements" (such as *being able to take critique*) . . . that is, the *hidden curriculum* made more transparent, and seamless. Many examples of such methods are found in the chapters ahead.

Systematic and Ongoing, Classroom-Based Assessment

Previous chapters presented several principles and techniques for systematic, classroom-based, and individualized assessment. However, teaching also can be a nonlinear *conversation* in which listening and responding to multiple questions and needs from several students can get more like the overlapping ripples of several pebbles hitting a pond close to one another. This can become a bit confusing for all concerned, were it not also *ongoing*. It is the systematic continuation of this **instructional conversation** that clarifies understanding. But, let's be honest, it also leads, as all teaching and learning does, to some things that are not yet fully known and therefore cannot be fully explained. This is where concept-driven teaching and learning tends to pay off.

Whole-to-Part, Concept-Based Unit Design

Concept/theme-based teaching-learning provides handrails that help learners venture out on their own.

Concept-based unit planning gives focus and purpose to teaching and learning; it can provide handrails on the narrow bridge from point to point, and ideally encourages learners to conceptually venture out on their own. A **concept-based unit** typically begins with introductory activities to engage students' interest and curiosity, then develops the concept through daily reading, writing, and application activities, many of which are directed toward a culminating activity that showcases student work. A sample format for planning a concept-based unit is provided in Figure 6.2. The nature of the teaching and learning that flows from concept-based units is well suited to today's multilevel and often multilanguage classrooms, as second-language learner experts Hurley and Tinajero (2001) point out:

> Using thematic units for literacy instruction is highly conducive to the transfer of concepts and skills between students' L1 and L2 [first language and second language]. Organization of literacy activities around themes provides many opportunities for students to utilize new vocabulary and concepts in different contexts, thus reinforcing new learning. Thematic units also integrate listening, speaking, reading, and writing skills in such a way that students can participate and succeed at whatever level of linguistic competence they have achieved.

Plentiful and Varied Instructional Materials

Concept-based unit design requires core reading materials to be used in direct instruction, and read by all students, and a variety of supplemental reading materials for theme-based activities and independent reading. Core reading materials should be at controlled difficulty levels, such as, but not limited to, basal reader selections. Most school librarians are available

FIGURE **6.2**

ORGANIZATIONAL PLAN FOR CONCEPT-BASED UNITS

Overview

Grade Level: _____   # Weeks: _____   Theme: _____

Core Literature

Other Core Resources (as relevant)

Instructional Objectives

Reading

Writing

Spelling

Oral Language

Optional: Additional subject area objectives addressed in the unit

Overview of the Unit (briefly describe)

Introductory Activity (briefly describe)

Culminating Activity (briefly describe)

Daily Activity Summary
(1 page per day)

Day # _____

Literacy Goals

Specific Instructional Objectives

Activities

Approx. time (in minutes)	Activity

Assessment *(brief description of how goals and objectives will be evaluated)*

[handwritten margin notes: Oral instructional level 150 words per min]

to help teachers collect classroom libraries of theme-related books to borrow. Many teacher-oriented Web sites offer ideas for theme-based units, and lists of supplementary materials (print and interactive) are available via Internet links.

In addition to assigned and supplemental reading, students should have access to *and guidance in* selecting materials at their Independent level for free reading, during in-class Sustained Silent Reading, and at home. Helping children select materials for free reading that are at an appropriate difficulty level is a crucial element of the reading program at all levels. Anderson, Wilson, and Fielding (1988) found that the difference in amount of free reading between students scoring at the 90th percentile in reading and those scoring at the 2nd percentile was approximately 21 minutes per day. Clearly, good readers do not necessarily read better because they read more—they read more because reading is not especially difficult for them. However, reading more does give better readers the exposure to print at increasingly difficult levels that leads to a growing sight word vocabulary, familiarity with increasingly difficult sentence structures and vocabulary, and overall fluency. Simply having poor readers read more will not necessarily improve their reading, but allowing them to continue *not* to engage in daily free reading deprives them of this important consolidating process. (More on this ahead. See The ZPD Paradox under Principles of Remediation.)

[handwritten margin notes: good Rdrs. read well ←; 21 minutes per day—a critical difference.; thus: theory is questionable]

Direct, Whole-Class Instruction in Grade-Appropriate Strategies

Reading instruction should be designed around whole-class instruction in strategies for prereading schema activation, metacognitive monitoring, and postreading schema building, such as:

- strategies for previewing, making predictions based on prior knowledge and experience, and setting purposes for reading
- strategies for "making sense" of print, including: questioning, translating, summarizing, monitoring comprehension, switching perspectives, interpreting, noting incongruities, applying, making personal connections, responding, and schema restructuring
- strategies essential to comprehension development, including: concepts about print, letter names and letter-sound associations, phonemic awareness, sight word acquisition, analogic word attack strategies and high-frequency phonics rules, word structure and syntax, fluency, study reading—in the context of strategies
- strategies essential to development in areas that strongly influence comprehension development, such as: meaning vocabulary, sentence structure, writing, and oral language

Multilevel Strategy Instruction   Multilevel strategy instruction is direct teaching of thinking strategies that makes a given reading task more accessible to students of varying levels of reading ability. This is done through **concurrent methods,** designed to directly address content understanding, as well as modeling and guiding the use of specific and individual need strategies, such as prereading purpose setting. A variety of concurrent methods are provided in the chapters ahead.

The most defining characteristic of this Framework for Balanced Reading is the absence of the "reading groups" organizational design popularized in the immediate pre– and post–*First-Grade Studies* era. Many Whole Language classrooms eliminated this design, but it is rapidly regaining popularity. The Learning First Alliance action paper referenced in a previous chapter summarizes the research on this design:

> The main problem with this strategy is that it requires follow-up activities that children can do on their own while the teacher is working with another group. Studies of follow-up time find that, all too often, it translates to busywork. Follow-up time spent in partner reading, writing, working with a well-trained paraprofessional, or other activities closely linked to instructional objectives may be beneficial; but teachers must carefully review workbook, computer, or other activities to be sure they are productive (*http://www.learningfirst.org/readingaction.html#top*).

It has been well documented that: a) children too often are assigned to reading groups according to factors other than actual reading achievement, including social, socioeconomic, cultural, and even physical appearance factors; b) once a child is assigned to a low reading group, there is only a slight chance of ever moving to a higher group; c) children in the low reading group quickly come to think of themselves as poor readers (Allington, 1977, 1980; Hoffman & Clements, 1984).

Reading educators have long advocated "flexible grouping" as an alternative to permanent grouping. In **flexible grouping,** children are grouped for short periods of direct instruction based on individual skill needs. Theoretically, the composition of these groups would change frequently. In practice, however, this rarely happens: lower-achieving readers, by definition, tend to need different specific skills than higher-achieving readers.

For today's multilevel classroom, the most viable approach to grouping is to provide direct comprehension instruction in a whole-class setting for a portion of class time. Then with the majority of time, balance this focused, often intense interaction with structured, homogeneously-formed, small-group activities and projects related to the unit theme. For an interesting real-life electronic dialog on these issues, see Figure 6.3, based on a version of multilevel instruction implemented in Patricia Cunningham's popular "4-Block" reading program (Cunningham, Hall, & Defee, 1991, 1998; Cunningham, Hall, & Cunningham, 2000).

FIGURE **6.3**

4-BLOCKS LITERACY CHATBOARD: SIFTING AND SORTING THROUGH THE 4-BLOCKS LITERACY MODEL

Cheryl/Host I guess we're about ready to begin?

Cheryl/Host Our discussion tonight centers around the perils of ability grouping. For decades we have been using this practice. Although we have done this with the best of intentions, we have caused much harm to children. We have divided and categorized them from their first day of school. I hope we can share experiences tonight and talk about solutions. Any comments to begin?

carrottop/GA Cheryl, should the guided reading be a whole class lesson or should it be done in small groups?

sherri Cheryl, how are you really supposed to group students?

Mary This is the first time in 23 years that I haven't grouped kids by ability and I am amazed at their progress.

Kathleen Really, do we even know a child's "ability" when we group? Don't we group based upon performance, not ability?

Laura I have seen tremendous gains this year in my heterogeneous groups. I will continue this way next year.

Cheryl/Host Many of your first comments center around recognizing developmental differences of kids. They aren't all ready at the same time.

sherri I'll start. I said this a little earlier. My principal makes us group our students—high, average, low. My low students KNOW that. They are depressed and hate reading. What is the correct way?

Sue I'm so confused with grouping. I just started grouping my second graders. My principal believes in ability grouping. I use *The World of Reading* by Silver Burdett Ginn. I'm not sure how to go about grouping. What do I do with the slower readers?

Cheryl/Host I think Kathleen's got a good point about what we base current grouping on.

Barb L. We started 4-Blocks a couple of years ago in my school and I have seen so much progress in those "buzzards" that previously couldn't get out of the first pre-primer. They are not on level but are much further than they would have been in groups.

Cheryl/Host We really do have to start educating our administrators, school boards, parents, and so on, about the harm of grouping.

Katharine Our district studied New Zealand Balanced Lit methods. Fluid groups. I don't think anyone ever made them truly fluid. Once you are placed, you are placed.

Laura Yes, Cheryl. Even the youngest of students is aware of these groupings and what they mean.

Kathleen Do those of you who use grouping do much multilevel instruction?

mouse Katharine: Yes, my school had "flexible groups" that weren't flexible at all.

bluebird I agree with Katherine . . . I hear folks say they have fluid groups, but I never see that really happen.

mouse Kathleen, what do you mean?

Sadie Cheryl, I have a question. In my class, for example, I have kids who are extremely limited in their concepts about print and I have kids who are reading at a second-grade level. How could I possibly meet their ever-changing needs at the same time?

Cheryl/Host Research reflects that kids don't break out of the rut of the ability groups. Not to mention the trauma for some kids!

Kathleen mouse, I use lessons and activities (like shared reading, modeled writing) that teach to many levels at the same time.

Cheryl/Host Sadie, are you familiar with 4-Blocks? That's the way we do it with such diversity in the class.

Katharine Sadie, I questioned that problem for a full year. Now I'm finding that I can make it work.

Laura My little ones are well aware of who the "good" readers are. They really puff up when placed in a group with them.

mouse Kathleen, well, I have yet to find a skill that g/t students and low students didn't both need. I can't think of one thing I'd teach one and not the other.

Cheryl/Host Believe it or not, there isn't any research to support that ability grouping is successful. There's definitely no research saying that ability grouping is even equal in success to an approach like 4-Blocks.

Kathleen mouse, what age/grade?

Katharine I have kids who don't know all their letters yet, "reading" side by side with full-tilt readers. They learn comprehension, and learn in spite of themselves.

Laurie/AR What are some alternatives to Round Robin reading?

mouse I teach 3rd, Kathleen!

Cheryl/Host Katharine is one of the best examples of a new convert from ability grouping in reading to a new approach.

Dollie We had a group of "low" fifth graders this year and grouped them in a class together (this was the first time we had ability grouped). We found that these kids did not have the models needed to improve their reading, or thinking skills, which of course filters over to other subjects. We will not be ability grouping next year!

teach Laurie, have you tried buddy reading?

Cheryl/Host Laurie, one of the problems with Round Robin is that there's nothing magical about our "teacher ears." We really don't have to hear each child read every day to have them grow.

Katharine The fact that I don't have to listen to every child read every day was one of the hardest for me (and my district) to accept.

Laurie/AR I do buddy reading. I have even tried a game called "Stump the Teacher." After a while these get boring.

Cheryl/Host Let's clarify that 4-Blocks isn't really whole -group instruction. It's multilevel instruction. There is a big difference.

Karma Laurie, what is "Stump the Teacher?"

Laurie/AR We both read one or two pages of the story. I ask them questions. They ask me questions. They try to "stump" me.

teach That sounds fun.

Kathleen *Goodbye Round Robin, Twenty-Five Effective Oral Reading Strategies* by Michael F. Opitz, Timothy V. Rasinski, Lois Bridges Bird.

First, identify high-interest, controlled vocabulary materials.

Evaluating and Amplifying Instruction with Quality Materials Materials are the teacher's silent partner in instruction. There is a clear trend back to the value and good sense in using "autoinstructional" materials— exercises that once would have been called "inauthentic," "isolated," and "fragmented." Now these materials are being seen as a means of providing practice in skill areas that are not really isolated but intentionally separated, for purposes such as drill and repetition, to more automatic levels of response that would make reading more fluent and beneficial. The effective teacher uses a wide variety of such methods and materials.

Where practice exercises are called for, the first thing the remedial specialist looks for is high-interest, controlled-vocabulary material. This permits the teacher to control the level of difficulty that the child encounters in the early, tender stages of growth beyond reading disability.

The next things the remedial teacher often looks for are materials designated for practice in specific skills. These often vary in quality and in the relative merit of what they ask students to do in order to learn. A system for assessing tasks in materials, devised by Eanet, Condon, and Manzo (1974), is built on four concept terms: counterproductive, perfunctory, incremental, and generative, as described below.

"Incremental Learning" alone won't get you where you need to go.

The terms offered here should serve as useful guides for thinking about and appraising most any instructional plan or methodology under consideration. Of course, the value of any material or program can be enhanced or diminished by the purpose for which it is used and how it actually is presented and employed. An illustration is presented further ahead in the chapter for how mediocre material and tasks are enhanced by thoughtful usage.

Counterproductive. Some tasks and exercises found among materials and in teacher's guides are well intended, but can induce defensive reactions that result in "avoidance" and negative learning outcomes. It is difficult to give examples since it is the context, or the way that it is presented, that determines whether it will be productive or counterproductive. However, here are examples of practices that are at risk of becoming counterproductive:

- Whole-class spelling bees and other such competitive systems can breed more fear and anxiety about spelling than interest and learning.
- Materials that ask students who are poor readers to rely on standard dictionaries to learn new words can be counterproductive, since such students rarely can read and abstract appropriate meanings without further assistance.
- Textual materials that are "inconsiderate," or assume knowledge that students don't have, or are too dense, can be frustrating and therefore counterproductive (math and science materials are notorious for this, but novels with huge casts of characters can be equally inaccessible).
- Materials that make little instructional sense can be counterproductive (for example, "underline the letters of the alphabet in order as you find them on this page of print until you reach 'z'").

If diagnosis suggests a special benefit for running in place then the task is no longer perfunctory, but rather precision teaching.

Generally, few tasks and materials are counterproductive *in and of themselves*. The classroom climate, the context for learning, and student levels need to be taken into consideration when evaluating instructional tasks.

Perfunctory. These tasks and activities are superficial, though largely painless, except they may waste valuable instructional time. Many "visual-perceptual" training programs contain tasks that fit in this category. They have students draw lines connecting one thing to another, to improve "eye-hand-motor coordination," an operation that has no proven bearing on reading, thinking, or learning (Leibert & Sherk, 1970).

Perfunctory tasks are rather like running in place: much activity, lots of sweat, but no progress to speak of. But again, if diagnosis suggests a possible benefit for running in place, and the teacher realizes this, then the task is no longer perfunctory: it is a prescription mapped into a diagnosed need. Put another way, when a match can be found between a task or material and a need, go ahead and light it, no matter how inconsequential the task or material may appear without that context. This is the weighty prerogative of the specialist.

The next concept-term refers to a category that is a considerable step above this and is characteristic of most materials and school learning tasks.

Incremental. These tasks and materials tend to result in average increments of learning. That is, increments that tend to be small, but achieve competence in a fashion. Many remedial reading methods and materials fit this description. They plug along, but fail to engage students to think about and otherwise practice desired skills or objectives outside of the strictly instructional setting. They tend to lead students through repetitive exercises in a mind-numbing way. They make a one-hour trip feel like two.

Remedial students are characteristically incremental learners to begin with. This is their greatest problem. They usually learn what they are taught each period, but do not reach independence. There are several reasons why they remain "suboptimal-incremental" learners:

1. They fail to learn something deeply enough to begin with.
2. They do not think about it any further outside of class time.
3. They live in a nonreinforcing environment.
4. And/or it just isn't high on their personal agenda.

Whatever the reason, their learning, in effect, remains summative. To become secure, learning must be synergistic and generative.

Generative. In one stage theory of reading, Gray (1925) identified a "stage 3" progression (occurring between second and third grades) that he called a period, or stage of "unusually rapid development" in word recognition, rate, silent and oral reading, comprehension, and ability to read for different purposes (as cited in Chall, 1983c). Such obvious leaps in learning must be preceded by periods of knowledge seeking and consolidation.

"Generative Learning" tends to engender inner-speech that is active mental play with a target objective.

Certain tasks spur these periods of apparent growth. We have labeled these _generative tasks_. As a general rule, such tasks tend to occupy the student's mind beyond the classroom, and tend to result in inner rehearsals that build strategies for learning, more so than just new increments of knowledge. Generative learning, in the language of Rosenblatt (1969), is more transactional—or interactive and process oriented, or, knowledge-enriching than transmissional—or product oriented.

Tasks that are generative tend to be _epistemological_ in the sense that they engender inner-speech that is active mental play with the concepts and skills in a variety of contexts and cause further and deeper learning to occur. They raise a teaching episode from a merely summative, or incremental level, to a synergistic one—that is, the amount learned is greater than the mere sum of the increments, or units of instructions. This, of course, is the ideal purpose of all instruction, and is assumed to be part of schooling, whether we realize it or not. It is impossible, for example, to teach students all the possible combinations of ways letters can be pronounced in every possible word; therefore, the implicit expectation is that they must leave the classroom and in some way engage letters, words, and print on signs, in names, and on labels in some way that ultimately results in synergistic leaps that lead to mastery. Ironically, the strongest criticism that can be made of many "mastery learning" programs is that they try to accomplish all learning through these incremental units, with little reference to authenticity and inspiration.

The corrective/remedial teacher needs to actively seek methods and materials that can combine to induce generative learning. It is not enough to offer up tasks and materials that tend to produce incremental outcomes. Consider an example of how a greater level of generativeness can be achieved even with a simple autoinstructional task.

Converting an incremental activity to a generative one. Presume that fifth-grade students are doing comprehension practice work such as in an old-fashioned, and now new-fashioned, *SRA's Reading for Understanding Kit*. The instructional task is to select the best word or phrase to complete a sentence or brief paragraph.

Sample (card 08, #5)

Fixed stars actually move about in space but the ancients who first saw and named them were unable to discern their:

a. arrangement   b. size   c. motion   d. light

(Correct answer is "c. motion." The key words in the sentence are "move about.")

Certain strategic conversions can be transformative.

While students are doing such exercises, and self-correcting them, the teacher usually supervises by walking about and monitoring their work. This typically involves pausing when a student is making errors and helping the student to puzzle out the correct answer.

As described, this is a solid incremental learning activity involving close-knit analytical reading, self-pacing, self-scoring, and teacher monitoring. It is not generative, however, since feedback is shallow, there is no incentive to think deeply, and whenever the teacher stops at a desk there is the implicit suggestion that the student has erred. This causes most students to become distracted and to terminate thinking in order to solve the new social problem created by the impression that the teacher only stops to talk to those who are weak and wrong. To overcome this, students typically will quickly (and mindlessly) select another answer so that, if correct, the teacher will keep moving.

This incremental lesson can become somewhat more generative by a little fine-tuning. In this case, when stopping at a desk, the teacher should ask the student to explain answers that are correct as well as incorrect.

This slight adjustment can result in several positive and generative outcomes. First, it releases the impression that the teacher stops only when errors are being made. Second, it gives students an opportunity to demonstrate competent thinking. Third, it gives the teacher a chance to reinforce and refine solid thinking. Fourth, it develops stronger examination of one's own thinking and responding.

Frequent Opportunities for "Strategy Interactions" with Peers

Active, thoughtful speaking and listening are the foundation for active, thoughtful writing and reading. Therefore the first essential step in any reading program is to be sure students are talking and listening to one another, and be sure they are writing and reading. There is growing evidence for the belief that we can get more than a little help from our friends (Fisher et al., 2003). When students are engaged in structured small-group activities, each child spends more time on-task through speaking, listening, reading, and writing than in a teacher-directed lesson. As a rough rule of thumb, reading/language arts instruction probably should be no more than 30 percent teacher directed. The remaining 70 percent should occur via planned, guided, monitored, but open-ended small-group work that gets children talking to one another in structured ways: Before we read, while we are reading, and after we read, we use language to process our thoughts. The more students talk, the better they become at using language to process their thoughts. Examples of such cooperative structures appear as Figure 6.4, Corners and Paired Reading; Figure 6.5, Numbered Heads Together and Fishbowl; Figure 6.6, Think-Pair-Share and Write-Pair-Share; Figure 6.7, Paired Strolling and Inside-Outside Circle (Kagan, 1994).

30% theory

REMEDIAL READING: REQUIEM OR RESURRECTION?

Evidence suggests that we can get more than a 'little' help from our friends.

Under the subtitle *Requiem for Remedial Reading*, Klenk and Kibby (2000) write that "the field of remedial reading is mired in arcane terminology representing an outdated conceptualization of reading problems" (680). They go on to say that the "requiem we compose here is not a signal for the demise of intensive instructional interventions . . . [but] a turning point, a new era for the field" (680). Their strongest suggestion is that "the term *remedial reading* needs to be cast off." They would like to see it replaced with the term "mediation" to correct the impression that the field needs merely to rid itself of "the metaphor of the *remedy*"—a term meaning "to cure or to restore to natural or proper condition." Our take is similar though a bit simpler: The term remediation, as they suggest, is a metaphor. It has always had complex meanings shaped by the different ways it was interpreted into practice. Call it *remedial,* or *medial,* but let's proceed quickly to reconnect and restore the good sense and good practices of this historically significant set of principles and practices, because we are already well into a new era for the field. The rudiments of "diagnostic-prescriptive" teaching are part of the requirements for the certification of teachers in most every

FIGURE **6.4**

COOPERATIVE STRUCTURES: CORNERS AND PAIRED READING

Corners

Preparation

Identify an issue, related to the topic of the lesson, about which students might have differing opinions. Prepare labels for differing points of view on the issue. (This might be two "Corners" or more.) Create a handout listing questions related to the issue.

Steps

1. Tape labels on the classroom walls, and announce the issue to be considered. Have students take a pencil or pen, remove their books/notebooks from desktops, and go to the label that best represents their personal point of view. You may want to have them move desks into a group before they begin. (If one or more group is quite large, you might want to divide it in two so that more students will have an opportunity to interact at this point.)

2. Distribute the handout, and have students work in their "Corners" groups to respond to the questions.

3. Conduct a whole-group discussion of the questions on the handout, comparing how groups differed in their responses.

Paired Reading

Preparation

Copies of a reading selection for all students (or textbooks), and a postreading activity on a handout.

Steps

1. Form student pairs and be sure each student has a copy of the reading selection.

2. Identify Student A and Student B in each pair.

3. Divide the reading selection, noting which sections will be read aloud by Student A and which by Student B. (When first using this structure, the teacher should usually divide the reading selection in half, with Student A reading the first half aloud, and Student B the second half. After students have used the structure a few times, the teacher can instruct them to divide the reading selection themselves.)

4. Student A reads aloud softly, while Student B follows along, moving his/her finger down the side of the page to indicate the line being read. (This helps the teacher monitor that the listening student is also following the print.) Student B is instructed to be ready to ask at least two questions at the end of the section.

5. Student A summarizes what was just read, in his/her own words, and Student B asks at least two questions, which Student A answers.

6. Student B then reads aloud, while Student A follows the print. Student B summarizes what was read, and Student A asks at least two questions.

7. When each pair completes the oral reading, the teacher gives them the postreading activity handout to complete together.

Adapted from Kagan, 1994, *Cooperative Learning.*

*[handwritten margin notes: * good for opinions]*

*[handwritten margin notes: * students summary / create questions]*

FIGURE **6.5**

COOPERATIVE STRUCTURES:
NUMBERED HEADS TOGETHER AND FIND SOMEONE WHO

Numbered Heads Together

Preparation

Any set of short discussion questions, problems, or fact "recitation" questions; heterogeneous groups of four

Steps

1. When students have formed groups of four, have each group identify persons 1, 2, 3, and 4.

2. Give the first question, and have groups discuss together to agree on an answer and (if relevant) their explanation of why they think this is the answer.

3. Call any number, 1 through 4, and the person with that number in each group stands. Call on any of the standing students, or ask for volunteers from these students, to give the answer their group agreed on, and (if relevant), why. Have representatives from several groups (but not necessarily all) respond to each question.

4. Continue through the questions in the same manner.

5. Increase individual accountability by having the questions on a worksheet for individual students to complete as you work through the activity. Collect and give credit for the worksheets at the conclusion of the lesson.

Find Someone Who

Preparation

A worksheet on the topic just covered or to be covered next (questions in teachers' manuals or workbook pages are great for this)

Steps

1. Distribute the worksheets and give a time limit for students to work on them individually.

2. When time is up, ask students to "Find Someone Who" can give them an answer they did not know, or who agrees with their answer to an item, and write their initials above the item. Tell students how many such partners they should find.

3. Collect the worksheets (for individual accountability), for an actual grade or credit/no credit.

Adapted from Kagan, 1994, *Cooperative Learning.*

state in the union, and this *pre-assess and precise-teach* idea, as developed in Chapter 2, is looking more like the future of general as well as corrective-remedial education. It is more effective and more efficient. This trend is evident in the recent title cited above of a new collection of articles from the International Reading Association edited by McCormack and Paratore (2003).

FIGURE **6.6**

COOPERATIVE STRUCTURES: THINK-PAIR-SHARE AND WRITE-PAIR-SHARE

Think-Pair-Share

Preparation

A topic, situation, or question, related to the lesson topic, for students to consider and discuss; a means of pairing students for the activity

Steps

1. Present the topic, situation, or question, and give students 2 minutes to think about how they will respond.

2. Form student pairs, and have pairs identify which will be A and B.

3. As are given an exact time limit (usually 1 to 3 minutes) to tell their response to their partner. Bs are not to respond during this time limit.

4. Bs are given the same time limit to tell their response, and, if they wish, respond to A's statements.

5. At the end of B's time limit, give another specified time limit for pairs to continue and conclude their discussion.

6. Some sort of whole-group sharing of the paired discussions should follow (for individual accountability). For example, each pair might be directed to join another pair for groups of four for Numbered Heads Together.

Frank Lyman, Jr., & Arlene Mindus, Howard County, Maryland.

Write-Pair-Share

Preparation

A topic, situation, or question, related to the lesson topic, for students to consider and discuss; a means of pairing students for the activity

Steps

1. Present the topic, situation, or question, and give students a specified time limit to write their responses. Hold to the rule that everyone must be writing for the entire time—even if they are writing "I don't know what to write," over and over.

2. Form student pairs, and have pairs identify which will be A and B.

3. As are given an exact time limit (usually 1 to 3 minutes) to tell their partner what they wrote. Bs are not to respond during this time limit.

4. Bs are given the same time limit to tell what they wrote and, if they wish, respond to A's statements.

5. At the end of B's time limit, give another short time limit for the pair to continue and conclude their discussion.

6. Some sort of whole-group sharing of the paired discussions should follow (for individual accountability). For example, each pair might be directed to join another pair for groups of four for Numbered Heads Together.

Adapted from Kagan, 1994, *Cooperative Learning*.

[Handwritten margin notes: "Excellent ELL." / "get back to-gather" / "Everyone wants to speak — 'Turn to a partner + share for 2 minutes'"]

Good for discussion (where everyone wants to talk)

fishbowl → 7 chairs — 5 contributors
2 empty chairs [student rotate in + out after make point]
only people in chairs get to speak

FIGURE 6.7

COOPERATIVE STRUCTURES: PAIRED STROLLING AND INSIDE-OUTSIDE CIRCLE

Paired Strolling

Preparation

Several topics or questions, related to the lesson topic, for students to briefly discuss with partners. A "route" for strolling in two parallel lines—around the classroom or around a hallway, or on an outdoor route

Steps

1. Have students form two parallel lines for walking in pairs.
2. Tell students that you will give them a question or topic to respond to as they "stroll" along a specified route.
3. Identify one line as As, and the other as Bs.
4. Present the topic or question, and direct students that As are to respond, as they stroll in the line together, until you give a signal. Bs are not to respond, other than to show polite interest. At the signal, Bs are to respond, while As listen.

teach this skill →

5. After As and Bs have both responded, have the A line take a few steps forward, so that they are with a new partner in the B line. The front person in the A line goes to the back of the line to partner with the B student there.
6. Announce the next topic or question for Paired Strolling discussion with the new partners, continuing through several changes of partners.
7. Some sort of whole-group sharing of the paired discussions should follow (for individual accountability). For example, each final pair might be directed to join another pair for groups of four for Numbered Heads Together.

Inside-Outside Circle

Preparation

Short-answer questions on a reading assignment or lesson, with the questions & answers on 3x5 note cards. You'll need half the number of question/answer cards as you have students in the class for one round of Inside-Outside Circle.

Steps

1. Have students line up and number off by 2s. Direct 1s to form a circle facing out, and 2s to form a circle outside the 1s, facing in, so that you have two concentric circles, with partners facing each other. Be sure each student knows who his or her beginning partner is.
2. Distribute note cards with questions & answers to students in the inside circle—one card each, each card with a different question/answer.
3. Direct inside-circle students to read their question to their outside-circle partner. The outside-circle student answers the question, or makes his or her best prediction of the answer (he or she must make an attempt to answer—not just "I don't know"). The inside-circle student praises correct answers, and assists with incomplete ones.
4. At the teacher's signal, the outside circle takes a step to their right, so that new pairs are formed. The inside-circle students pass their question & answer cards to their left, so that each has a different question & answer.
5. The questioning & answering proceeds as in #3 above, shifting the outside circle to the right and cards to the left on the teacher's signal, until each outside-circle student has attempted to answer each question, and each inside-circle student has asked each question.

good w/ movement / new chapter - fact → student develop question then...

Adapted from Kagan, 1994, *Cooperative Learning.*

It's Back!

Just as corrective classroom reading has returned with some innovations, remedial reading is also making a return with the benefits of the last thirty years of reading research to support it. Much of this research, curiously, was conducted in remedial settings. In short, we seem to be looking at a reunited family of principles and practices. A brief historical-social background serves here to set the stage for several guiding principles and recent innovations. These include a greater emphasis on self-regulation (or self-teaching), acceptance of the realities of specific aptitudes as a consideration in intervention, and the simple solutions for how to select and use "autoinstructional" or practice materials described previously in this chapter.

Call it Remediation or Mediation, let's re-engage this sensible system of educational support.

Scope of Remedial Reading

The term *remedial reading*, according to Nila Banton Smith (1965), was first used in an article by Uhl in 1916. The title of that 1916 article still defines one of the most basic functions of diagnostic and remedial reading: "The Use of Results of Reading Tests as Bases for Planning Remedial Work."

One way to get a quick overview of the field of "remedial reading" is to answer the question, "Who needs remedial help?" Not many years ago, the answer was thought to be clear: *Students whose reading test scores were below a certain level, based on their IQ and grade-level expectancy.* Today, remedial readers are defined in more operational terms: ?? *processing capacity so limited*

"D & R"–the use of results of reading tests to plan remedial work.

- Remedial readers are unreflective, and do not self-monitor or self-correct (Brown, 1980; Torgesen, 1982).
- Remedial readers are less positive about reading and writing—less inclined to write independently (Anderson, Wilson, & Fielding, 1988; Juel, 1988).
- Remedial readers are less likely to actively construct meaning and see patterns in reading and writing (Johnston & Winograd, 1985; Vellutino, 1987).
- Remedial readers are less persistent when faced with frustrating text (Andrews & Debus, 1978; Chapin & Dyck, 1978).
- Remedial readers are far less strategic or flexible in the way they read (Diener & Dweck, 1978; Torgesen, 1982).
- Remedial readers have low self-esteem, reflected in a tendency to make negative statements about themselves while performing tasks (Diener & Dweck, 1978; Johnston & Allington, 1991).
- Remedial readers are individuals with language-learning disabilities (LLD), irrespective of the lack of discrepancy of their measured IQs with their reading progress (Catts & Kamhi, 1999).

As previously noted regarding "(in)flexible grouping," children *labeled* "remedial readers" have tended in the past to *remain* remedial readers. This puzzling but apparently widely documented fact was a motivating force behind recent efforts to better understand the reading process. Clearer understandings of what reading "is" have suggested the need to further revise our definitions of "remedial."

"Remedial Needs" Does Not Equal "Remedial Reader," and "Remedial Reader" Does Not Necessarily Equal "Unsuccessful Life"

When a comprehensive view of the reading process is taken, it becomes clear that *all* of us reach points at which we could benefit from some remedial assistance (or assistance from our friends), *many* of us have fairly frequent remedial needs, and a few of us have extensive remedial needs. (See the revised news on "Functional Literacy" in Chapter 13 on Adolescent-Adult Literacy.) This realization alone illustrates that where literacy needs are concerned, we are all in this together! The distant "they" of illiterates versus "we" who are literate is more illusion than fact. There really is no such thing as *a* "remedial reader"; there are only people with remedial needs. This expanded scope of remedial reading is based on four trends in the field of reading: conceptualizing reading as an interactive process that readers go through to understand the printed page; a preference for the term "literacy needs" over "reading needs"; an increased awareness of the increasing levels of literacy required to deal with the spiraling complexity of daily life; and, ironically, the realization that there are many people who live rather successful lives, irrespective of their "reading problems." And, there are about an equal proportion of seemingly proficient readers, some of whom read "floods" of books, whose intellectual and social-emotional growth does not begin to equal their "reading fluency." These newer perspectives are causing us to re-evaluate some overgeneralizations, such as the "Matthew Effect"—or "the rich get richer and the poor get poorer." This was born in an effort to win empathy for the "remedial readers'" situation but may be stirring more pathos and inaction than focused concern and assistance. This *No Pobrecito* amendment to the Matthew Effect (Manzo, 2003) has many implications for reading instruction across age-grade levels and ethno-cultural lines. For further discussion of this emerging realization see Chapter 12 on Assessing and Addressing the Needs of English Language and Culture Learners, and Chapter 13 on Adolescent-Adult Literacy.

Let us now take a brief look at the recent history of school-based *remedial* reading. This should help you to get a better perspective on the role you might wish to play in its rebirth and renewal.

Where remediation is concerned, we are all in this together.

There is no such thing as a "remedial reader;" only people with remedial needs.

University-Based Reading Clinics

The "return" of remedial reading can also be seen in the reinstitution of university-affiliated reading clinics as the staging area for a culminating course in graduate reading programs. Many universities dispensed with this course in clinical diagnosis, and their clinics, during the time when diagnosis and remediation were in disfavor, but most of these courses, like remedial reading itself, now are back. The results of a descriptive study of university-based clinics conducted by Lois A. Boder and Katherine D. Wiesendanger in 1986 provide an inside look university-based clinics, at least of that time. The 1986 study found the following:

1. Male clients outnumber female by a 3 to 1 ratio.
2. Most clients are in the 7 to 12 age range.
3. Over 90% are individually treated.
4. Clinics tend to operate in summers only.
5. Parents make over 80% of referrals to clinics.
6. More than half have insufficient space.
7. Clinics tend to have very good relationships with public schools.
8. Clinics tend to provide excellent training in diagnosis.
9. Regarding instruction in the 6 to 9 age range:
    a. writing is heavily emphasized
    b. decoding instruction is strong, with analytic phonics being emphasized three times as much as synthetic phonics
    c. readiness, sight words, and oral language receive more emphasis than explicit comprehension instruction
10. Regarding instruction in the 10 to 13 age range:
    a. comprehension and content area reading and study skills are most heavily emphasized
    b. writing also is heavily emphasized
    c. sight vocabulary, decoding, and oral language dropped a bit in emphasis, but still are held to be important
11. Regarding instruction in the 14 to 17 age range:
    a. the major emphasis is comprehension, content area reading, and reference skills
    b. oral language, writing, and reading rate receive "some" emphasis.
    c. word analysis receives only token attention
12. There is heavy emphasis at all levels on building positive attitudes.
13. Computers are used in only 19% of clinics (at the time of the study).
14. The most frequently used methods and approaches (again, at the time of the study) were: Language Experience Approach (87%); "linguistic patterns" (no other elaboration available) (52%); Fernald VAK(T) (37%); Directed Reading-Thinking Activity (31%); basal reading series (6%).

more specifically applied

Remedial reading is like all good teaching, only more so.

Remedial reading instruction is like all good teaching, only more so: more difficult to pinpoint the problem; more precise in intervention; and more focused on a single individual. Aspects of remedial reading that go beyond the scope of classroom instruction are detailed in the remainder of this chapter, including an an example of the type of Case-Based Reasoning that is the essence of this problem-solving process.

WHAT IS REMEDIAL INSTRUCTION?

Reading specialists will be the future advocates of a new blend of multiple and higher-order literacy.

Remediation is a process for achieving *precision teaching*. It is a well-thought-out, provisional—*written in pencil*—form of academic help. Remediation is monitored for effectiveness and efficiency, and aimed at whatever is *hurt or underdeveloped*. In reading, it is the *strategic use of teaching strategies*. Generally, it is provided by a well-informed professional, and delivered with care, concern, and sensitivity, to meet individual needs and differences. It often is thought of as rehabilitative—or *remedial*. In education, remediation is largely habilitative—or *mediational*. It supports and assists initial developmental processes. The basic issue of whether remediation works periodically needs to be thought through and sometimes defended, just as we asked the policy question, in a previous chapter, whether diagnosis is necessary. However, the answer to this question must be preceded by a more elaborate explanation of just what is meant by "remedial reading instruction."

Supplement to Classroom Instruction

Remediation is more "habilitative" than "rehabilitative."

In minimal terms, remedial instruction is supplemental to regular instruction, and *generally* should not supplant it *except* as a student may be non-functional, and hence, the time out of class might best be spent in being prepared to return to class. However, remedial instruction can be much more, depending on needs and resources. It can be based on a system of referral whereby a classroom teacher requests the reading specialist to take a closer look at a student and to prescribe a plan of assistance. A "referral" typically is taken to mean that the student should see the reading specialist on a pull-out basis, in addition to regular classroom reading instruction, and that remediation should be terminated when the student can better keep pace with the class. Referrals should, but seldom do, include students who are reading at grade level, but who are below their measured capacity levels. Referrals also should, but almost never do, include students with various kinds of higher-order literacy needs, such as have been alluded to in this and other chapters.

Strategically Fit to Individual Need

Actual instruction can vary from providing more of whatever the child receives in class, to any array of methods that the remedial instructor has come to master and believe in. Careful matching of student needs to appropriate methodology is ideal but seldom found. It can be a tedious task, fraught with tricky questions such as, should we have them do more of what they clearly cannot do well? or have them do more of what they can already do? The short answer, of course, is both, and *more*. However, the "more" often adds to the problem, since it can involve providing exotic, in the sense of not well known, forms of remedial therapy. Some of these methods might seldom be called for in a given school, but more than likely are needed with some regularity on a district-wide basis. For that reason, progressive school districts operate a clinic program staffed by highly-trained specialists, who may regularly confer with one another and with university-based specialists in a variety of related disciplines. Initially, this may involve some additional expense, but it is wise, and it can be very cost effective in the longer term to the school, the pupil, and the taxpayer.

> Remediation is precision teaching: the strategic use of teaching strategies.

Improvisational, "Outside-the-Box" Solutions

Once a sound degree of accuracy has been achieved, in or through the usual sequence of pre-assessment, diagnosis, and diagnostic-teaching, it swings the door wide open to more creative-constructive problem solving. These solutions in turn can become part of the clinical and pioneering ideas in a field. They also can interject a reminder to us that there are paradigms and possible practices that may be underutilized for a variety of usually social reasons that are nonetheless powerful and effective, and viable where more popular conventions have failed. Two quick examples will illustrate the several more that can be found throughout the text.

Strategic Parroting and Implosive Therapy

One idea is "strategic parroting," or Facilitative Role Play. This outside-the-box solution has been referenced by at least two sets of researchers (Palinscar & Brown, 1984; Manzo & Legenza, 1975). Essentially, it requires having a student parrot back a set of words that he or she otherwise cannot be induced into saying, so that he or she experiences the cerebral and behavioral (subcortical) sense of the potential power and personal value of those words. In both cases referenced here, the words were related to asking questions and making comments that reflected, then also ignited a healthy, inquiry-type flow of higher-order thinking. The other poignant example concerns the effects achieved using "implosive" methods, that is,

> Facilitative Role Playing can catapult literacy and learning.

Selectively used, "Implosive Methods" work.

seemingly sharp, critical address given to someone's weakness, especially when it seems to be self-induced. This approach may be recognizable in the barbs of coaches in athletics who may spur some players to extraordinary achievement, even as it sends others running for cover. Such "tough-love" approaches are well documented in psychological literature in terms of promoting achievement. They are used less so in education, possibly because it offends our sensibilities (therefore such documents are rarely accepted for publication in juried journals). The creative-constructive, diagnostic-prescriptive, reading specialist would be wise to know about these. The individuals who come before us will include cases resistant to conventional remedies; for them, the cost-benefit risk ratio has already shifted to place a higher value on correction before the problem becomes irreversible.

To self-discover other attributes and "principles" of the *strategic teacher*, try the Reflective Remedial Activity in Figure 6.8.

Wrapped in "Authentic Instruction"

Instructional intervention has been found best served on a bed of characteristics that epitomize high-quality, *authentic instruction* (D'Agostino, 1996). The elements of *authentic instruction* tend to include:

- engagement in higher-order thinking, such as is required in inference, prediction, concept formation, and evaluative reasoning (supported opinions)
- coherent instruction characterized by interrelated concepts and themes whose sequence and scope support one another
- connections drawn to students' prior and current life experiences and knowledge
- substantive dialog and conversation

FIGURE **6.8**

REFLECTIVE ACTIVITY OF THE STRATEGIC TEACHER: WHEN IN DOUBT

Hit the bat with ball, if that is what it takes.

The greatest asset in planning and providing instruction to reading and learning disabled youngsters is our personal capacity to call up an appropriately empathetic sense of what will get the job done. When you are in doubt about what you should do, picture yourself trying to help an uncoordinated child to hit a ball with a bat.

Try this right now and list some things you might try to do to help such a child. Compare your thoughts with those of others in training.*

*Move closer; tell the child to swing while you literally try to hit the bat with the ball; get a bigger ball; get a "t-ball" holder. . .

- a fair degree of social support
- systematic actions to support the internalization of skills into self-regulated strategies for independent learning

These points are repeated and extended ahead as principles of remedial intervention. But first, let's address a question that underlies, some would say *haunts,* all *remedial instruction.*

Does Remediation Work?

The most popular thing said in the last twenty years about remediation is that its effectiveness is "mixed" (Harris & Sipay, 1985; Johnston & Allington, 1991). This "faint praise" review stems from the fact that some studies have shown that a few programs and practices do not have immediate impact (Raim, 1983; Spreen, 1982). Some have suggested the effect is not long-lasting (Balow & Blomquist, 1965; Carroll, 1972), or that the outlook is not rosy for children who come from low SES families and/or whose instruction did not rely on a program of intensive treatment (Schonhaut & Satz, 1983) and quality instruction (D'Agostino, 1996).

Others are just plain sour on *remedial reading.* Peter Johnston and Richard Allington (1991) have identified several writers (for example, Bowles & Gintis, 1976; Giroux, 1981; Fraatz, 1987) who essentially believe that ". . . remedial instruction is simply a lavishly concealed way of maintaining a classed society . . ." (1006). As previously noted, Klenk and Kibby (2000) seem to feel that it needed to die in order to be reborn, with a less tainted name. Our conclusion has been that remedial efforts have tended to be soundly and predictably effective, and, more than that, represent a humane and demonstrably effective means of dismantling class-based societies (Manzo & Manzo, 1993). This conviction is strengthened when consideration is given to the odds against which remedial efforts are provided, and when the incidental findings from empirical studies are added to the few that explicitly address this issue.

Consider first the issue of odds. Remedial programs, by definition, address the needs of those who are failing or have failed. Reasons for failure, as already noted, can come from a confluence of sources: constitutional defects, emotionally disruptive thinking patterns, as well as from learning, thinking, cultural, and lifestyle differences (Cazden, 1988). Most of these causes are outside the realm of school operations, and reversing them constitutes a great challenge to our collective ingenuity and resourcefulness. Nonetheless, schools—and specifically remedial programs—have tackled many of these problems, and have been able to affect change and growth in many pupils. Consider the hard evidence.

Remedial efforts tend to be soundly and predictably effective; often at twice the rate of prior learning.

In a review of some forty earlier studies, George Spache (1981) concluded that students make about two months of progress for each month of remediation. More recent studies have also found significant improvement due to remediation (Gittelman & Feingold, 1983; Ito, 1980). In one study, 95 percent of *dyslexics* studied made significant gains as a result of remediation (Kline & Kline, 1975). To these findings can be added more recent meta-analyses of hundreds of studies in which researchers comparing specific remedial approaches report gains for disabled readers that surpass average gains for average students (Klenk & Kibby, 2000). In short, the conclusion from research, ecological evidence, and intuition must be that remediation, in general, *works* quite well.

There are, of course, circumstances and conditions that tend to increase or decrease the effectiveness of remediation. Joan Coley and Dianne Hoffman (1990), for example, identified a group of six youngsters who exhibited signs of "learned helplessness and inadequate self-esteem." The teacher-researchers modified these students' programs to include elements such as teaching them how to use question response cues, double-entry response journals, and self-evaluation. As a result, all subjects began to view themselves more positively. John Guthrie, Mary Seifert, and Lloyd W. Kline (1978) did a masterful job of identifying other factors that result in increased effectiveness. They considered fifteen studies that met fairly stringent standards for research design in field work. What they found was that:

- remedially tutored groups had greater improvements in reading than non-treatment groups
- a learning rate double that of normal children was obtained in several studies
- several studies reported gains that were discernible two years following initial remediation
- elementary and secondary students both made solid gains, although the secondary students tended to require more time
- middle-class students and students with IQs over 90 tend to do better than low SESs with IQs below 90
- remediation was most effective when it continued for fifty hours or more and was delivered by certified and experienced teachers or supervised tutors

Findings from three other studies contribute to our understanding of how to sustain gains. Long-term gains were sustained when:

- the remedial reading teacher maintained some contact with the students after terminating routine lessons (Balow & Blomquist, 1965)

- students were encouraged to read and write extensively (Rennie, Braun, & Gordon, 1986)
- the remedy was provided within one year of identification of the problem (Clay, 1985)

Refocus Away from Economic Disadvantage

It is notable that in the last decade or two, explanations of reading difficulty have been moving away from "economic disadvantage" and toward an emphasis on individual cases (Allington, 2000). This seems to strengthen the argument for a return to addressing students as individuals more than simply as part of a larger "at-risk" group, although it would be foolish not to take Socio-Economic-Status (SES) into account in individual cases. In a related vein, there now is some thought being given to better preparing students to make as well as take jobs. It is called "Entrepreneurial Literacy" (Manzo, 2003; Manzo, Manzo, & Estes, 2002). (More on this in Chapter 12.)

Media Magic

Ironically, "media," once considered the demon competing with reading time, now appears to be resurfacing as a remarkable and far-reaching influence in developing general knowledge, vocabulary, acculturation, representation of diverse cultures, and familiarity with standard English forms, such as are found in print. Let us look now at some specific precepts and practices that can be relied upon to produce high-quality remediation. Many of these would be of value to consider by anyone who teaches at any level.

> "Media" is "modern magic"; it doesn't compete with reading but builds knowledge, vocabulary, empathy, and cultural commonality.

GETTING DOWN TO BUSINESS: PRINCIPLES OF REMEDIATION

This section further answers the recently posed questions: "After Early Intervention, Then What?" and, "How do we teach struggling readers in grades 3 and beyond?" (McCormack and Paratore, 2003, title page). Ironically, more "principles of remediation" exist than most of us have capacity to easily learn and immediately draw upon. When a list becomes this extensive, it is natural to reduce it to meet our capacity levels. However, these principles represent the factors found to most positively influence learning outcomes. None can readily be deleted simply to make a more manageable list. On a more optimistic note:

- You are probably already inclined to tend to most of these, based on prior training and personal experience.
- Not all of these principles need to be employed in each and every segment of teaching.
- We must have greater capacity to learn and internalize complex rules and patterns than we realize, or how could anyone ever learn to be a "strategic reader?"

Academic courses and texts can merely set one on the path to professional competence: Becoming a *"strategic teacher"* is a lifelong developmental process. In time, veteran teachers reflect wisdom as well as academic knowledge in their instructional and management decisions. Our ability to learn from rules and patterns, after all, is the reason and justification for salary schedule raises that reflect seniority, or experience.

Veteran teachers reflect wisdom as well as knowledge.

A list such as the one here resonates with the complexity of being a professional teacher. In a parallel way, it might help to know that a veteran pilot and co-pilot have laminated copies of over 100 things that they must check and do before a 747 airplane takes off. This analog alone may justify and explain why the nation needs "reading specialists" just as we need well-trained pilots, pediatric specialists, or any specialization within any modern field. Assembling and executing a successful remedial plan is at least as complicated and challenging, if not more so, than what stock analysts and pharmacists are expected to do. To realize this is also to understand why we recommend that these interacting and overlapping principles need to be read repeatedly and recursively over your career. Start by identifying two or three that resonate most with you, then systematically add others in increments over the semester, and as student needs arise. When we are challenged we talk most intensely to ourselves. Let these constructive "principles" be part of that inner-speech, along with your natural tendency to say and think some things that can lead to *defensive*—often *reductionist*—*teaching*.

As an in-service or faculty development project, distribute one of these principles to each teacher in a school. Then invite one or two to comment on their related experiences at each faculty meeting throughout the year. To do something more encompassing and enduring, set up each "principle" on your equivalent of a www.BlackBoard.com "Discussion Board." It probably still is a good idea to assign each faculty member to be a custodian to one principle.

Veteran pilots enter the plane with a laminated checklist of over 100 items; they don't fly by the seats of their pants, and neither should we.

1. *Teach within the student's zone of proximal development (ZPD).* The "zone of proximal development" (Vygotsky, 1978) is the region of greatest sensitivity, or receptivity, to instruction. It is the level at which students, with help from some adult or peer support, are most able to engage and learn from an instructional task that otherwise might be too

Student teach
each other

Frustration
[Instructional] ZPD
Independent 98%
Not
learning

difficult. It is the student's "Instructional level." The ZPD Paradox is a box within this box: Easier texts can bar access to content, concepts, and ideas otherwise acquired by reading grade-appropriate material (McCormack & Paratore, 2003). Several of the steps addressed ahead must be taken to overcome this "cumulative deficit." They include attention to capacity-enriching vocabulary, and lessons that contribute to cognitive development. Look also at the methods described above as Multi-Level Strategy Instruction and ahead in the text under Content Area Literacy for means and methods to teach content and concepts to problem readers in an otherwise heterogeneously grouped class.

2. *Promote self-teaching. Self-teaching* is the *sine qua non,* or essential purpose, of all teaching. The goal, in a word, is to influence students' inner-speech such that they are more likely to talk to themselves about learning objectives, and therefore learn from all that the environment and daily experience has to offer. This can take many forms. In the case of vocabulary acquisition, for example, it means raising "word consciousness" so that the student "sees" and "reflects" on words that otherwise would go unnoticed. (See the Cultural Academic Trivia game in Chapter 12 on vocabulary as a case-in-point.) In the case of promoting self-analytical thinking it may mean having students talk to themselves about what they are doing "right" and "wrong" while puzzling over a specific exercise. (See the "Autoinstructional Materials Generative" learning example in this chapter as a poignant way of inducing this kind of self-talk.)

3. *Use a "diagnostic-teaching" model.* All teaching, like all diagnosis, must be provisional. It should be done with an eye toward collecting information on how students learn, what obstacles they tend to encounter, and what provisions need to be made to attempt to overcome these. To this end, Jeanne Paratore and Roselmina Indrisano (1987) recommend that the diagnostic-teacher develop a set of (improvised but not extemporaneous) methods and materials (passages, tasks, and prompts) that they *routinely* use to teach each student experiencing difficulty in learning. Using these, the teacher can note student patterns of success and difficulty with passages of various subject type and difficulty, with different types of tasks (from unaided retelling to multiple-choice recognition), and with different levels of (improvised) prompts or supports; this version is also known as "trial teaching."

4. *Establish initial rapport, mindset, and motivation to learn.* The first five minutes of every instructional hour usually determines what, if anything, of value will occur thereafter. Give considerable thought to what you will do or say, or have students do or say, to win their attention and commitment. It need not be dramatic, and it is best when it is diagnostically suited to the student's area of greatest need. For some students, it may be as simple as a self-starting, self-pacing activity to orient them to the printed page; for others, a few moments of eye contact and congenial conversation. Begin now to collect a set of starters and motivators that are suitable to you and that seem appropriate for your students. Doing so will also help to raise your own enthusiasm and readiness for your next remedial group. This bit of simple wisdom is part of most every culture's experience, as attested to by the old French proverb that says: "A good meal ought to begin with hunger." The next point continues this simple wisdom to a slightly deeper level of significance.

5. *Make sure students are engaged* during *instruction.* "Academic engaged time" is one of the best predictors of achievement in reading and learning in school (Fisher et al., 1978). Academic engaged time is another name for attention, or situational motivation (Anderson, Evertson, & Brophy, 1979; Chall & Feldman, 1966; Cobb, 1972; Luce & Hoge, 1978). Academic engaged time can be improved through direct training or through mastery learning techniques that incidentally increase attention and commitment to learn (Anderson, 1975). Dixie Lee Spiegel (1980a) stresses the importance of providing time and opportunity before reading for students to orient and familiarize themselves with the content of the new material. Studies of "advance organizers" (Ausubel, 1964) (as are used in at the beginning of each chapter in this book), and research on schema theory (Anderson et al., 1977) have shown a strong and consistent effect of prereading orientation on subsequent reading effectiveness. Prereading and purpose-setting strategies are the most prized by reading specialists (Gee & Raskow, 1987). Michael Kirby (1989) validated a related notion called the "focus of attention" hypothesis. He was able to show that engagement can be achieved by focusing student attention on a target task by intentionally minimizing other important but potentially distracting tasks at that time. Accordingly, he showed that the rate of words learned per minute of instruction was twice as great when students were trained in visual word recognition under a minimal context condition as compared with one emphasizing context, meaning, and usage. This study also tends to support the reasonableness of the traditional notion of isolating and focusing instruction on areas of diagnosed need. Of course, it should not be taken to mean that context usage and practice should not follow closely. The next point relates to a counterintuitive means of heightening attention and engagement.

6. *Quicken the pace and the amount covered.* (A recent variation is the Rapid Prompting Method, a strategy that quickens the pace by stressing high-energy persistence from the teacher working with autistic children.) Slower coverage of less material is a perceived cornerstone of remedial instruction. This is a fallacy probably based upon an incorrect inference that *rate*—or the amount of time it takes a pupil to learn is synonymous with the *pace*—or speed of presentation of information. While the precise reasons are not yet fully understood, it seems that increasing the pace of instruction increases rate of learning. In other words, it is better to cover more material faster. The principle of quick pacing with more content is supported by many studies, covering material from number of words learned to books covered (Anderson, Evertson, & Brophy, 1979; Barr, 1973–74; Beez, 1968). Contrary to common intuition, this same finding seems to hold true in mathematics and science (Comber & Keeves, 1973; Good, Grouws, & Beckerman, 1978; Walker & Schaffarzick, 1974), and irrespective of the typical learning rate of the pupils (Carroll, 1963, 1977; Chang & Raths, 1971; Paulsen & Macken, 1978). In quickening the pace, or covering more in less time, you also must be sure that other principles are met, especially the next one calling for "distributed practice."

7. *Provide frequent and spaced practice to insure deep and effective learning.* The simple strategy of providing students with "distributed," or frequent, short, and spaced practice, as opposed to "massed" or long-duration teaching and practice, has been called "one of the most remarkable phenomena to emerge from laboratory research on learning" (Dempster & Farris, 1990, 97). Despite over a hundred years of research to support this effect, remedial sessions still tend to be conducted infrequently and for more than one hour, when shorter and more frequent sessions clearly would be more beneficial. If scheduling forces an hour-plus slot, then the hour should be arranged so that the critical feature of the lesson is spaced and repeated two to four times during the hour. *Distributed practice* will incidentally quicken the pace of instruction, adding some of the benefits of the previous principle.

8. *Build self-efficacy—it will build self-concept.* Attempts to build self-concept as a means of prompting effective learning tend to rely on verbal encouragement, and other, somewhat hollow, praising comments. These have a positive, though relatively weak effect on improving learning and belief in self (Bandura, 1977a). On the other hand, self-efficacy, or actual effectiveness as a student, is a key component of self-concept based on performance accomplishments, real experiences, and personal mastery. Self-efficacy, or conscious evidence of progress, routinely leads to increased academic success and feelings of self-worth (Campbell & Hackett, 1986). Self-efficacy, according to social learning theorists, is raised or lowered by a combination of factors based on past performance, observations of others successfully modeling a task, verbal encouragement, and the level of emotional intensity (not enough or too much) that is experienced in doing a certain task (Gorrell, 1990). In other words, the cornerstone of all remedial efforts must include having students experience greater success and less anxiety in reading, before they can be brought to believe that they will be able to persist in mastering reading. Since it sounds circular to say "success breeds success," four quick reminders of how to do this are in order. One is to provide pupils with a manageable, self-correcting, and self-pacing task on which they can chart their own day-to-day progress. Another is to selectively use portfolios to collect and represent progress over longer time frames. A third is not to shy from mixing *correction* with *encouragement*—gratuitous encouragement turns kids into dependent "praise junkies," whereas the philosopher Goethe observed, "Encouragement after censure is as the sun after a shower." Finally, remember to ask questions that have more than one right answer (Spiegel, 1980a). Curiously, further complexity can decrease the likelihood that a pupil will be completely wrong when answering.

9. *Include a high proportion of directed instruction.* Direct instruction typically is recognizable by the fact that the teacher generally tells students what they are going to learn, how they are going to learn it, why they are going to learn it, when they are going to learn it (Pearson & Fielding, 1991), and even when they have learned it. It can sound rather authoritarian, but it has been consistently found that learning takes place best (at least short term) when the teacher takes charge and reduces *extraneous* choices (Rosenshine & Stevens, 1984). This has been found to be true at every socioeconomic level, in every grade, and for bright as well as for remedial students (Soar, 1973; Stallings & Kaskowitz, 1974; Solomon & Kendall, 1979). Permissiveness, "spontaneity," and lack of control have even been found to be *negatively* correlated to growth in creativity, inquiry, writing ability, and self-esteem (Rosenshine & Stevens, 1984). *Too many choices* left to students seems to reduce academic engaged time and to leave students and teacher distracted and feeling uncertain. It has sometimes been suggested that "direct instruction" is the antithesis of reflective teaching (Kameenui & Shannon, 1988). However, as Edward Kameenui (in Kameenui & Shannon) points out, "Direct instruction is not the whole of education nor should it be. Neither, I suspect, is reflective teaching" (41). See the next guideline for a means of achieving a balance between teacher and student control, or *agency*.

10. *Use heuristic, or (self-discovery) instructional strategies.* The last twenty years have produced some carefully designed and robust methods of teaching in remedial situations. Rely upon these carefully crafted and proven methods to anchor your craft as an instructor. Many of these strategies, described in the chapters ahead, have a naturally *heuristic* (evocative) value that tends to evoke appropriate responses from students, and self-explorations and discoveries in yourself for how to be a more reflective, flexible, and strategic teacher. In other words, in addition to following your subjective judgments, inform your instincts by developing expertise in the methods and practices that are the foundations of your profession. As an additional advantage, heuristic—or self-discovery—methods tend to encourage the teacher to become a co-learner with the student. Such methods tend to be built of tactical "gambits"—little tricks that alter typical responding. The next point, reciprocal, or rotation, responding, is a good example of such a *gambit*.

11. *Select methods that utilize modeling and reciprocity.* Cognitive modeling and reciprocity, or rotation (Palinscar & Brown, 1986; Manzo, 1969a,b; Rosenshine & Stevens, 1984) have been called the most important discoveries in instructional science in the 20th century. Reciprocity is the most often overlooked cornerstone of effective cognitive modeling instruction (Manzo & Manzo, 2002). It means providing opportunities for students to exert a sense of *agency,* or influence over the direction of the lesson in a way that slightly *rotates* the *instructional conversation* (Tharp & Gallimore, 1989a,b). The teacher does not relinquish responsibility or professional control over lesson objectives (Manzo & Manzo, 1990a), but rather incorporates a fixed means for students to seamlessly but gently "poke-back" and interject needed breaks, repetitions, and clarifications while the teacher hones in on students' ZPD and specific needs. Importantly, mental modeling and reciprocity are fluid, and can be misperceived by students and unsophisticated observers as appearing random. Together, they nearly define the concept of "instructional conversation."

12. *Build students' metacognitive awareness and sense of personal responsibility.* Ask students to tell what they are doing to learn. For over three generations now, students have been coached in what to expect from their teachers. A shift is long overdue to greater personal responsibility for learning, especially among college students who have the unmitigated privilege of submitting anonymous critiques of professors. One way to help this process is to have students articulate what they are learning, why they are learning it, and the extent to which they have learned it (Brown, Campione, & Day, 1981; Sanacore, 1984). They should also consider what they may need to do to learn more and better. Self-questioning and self-appraisal of the level of effort required to do a task are critical elements in achieving this goal (Good, 1987). (See the Guided Reading Procedure as a tangible example of how to impart the skill of self-appraisal of the level of effort required to achieve a *students highest self concept on 1st day of K.*

certain academic goal; in this case, effective recall of a passage.) Now add to this a growing emphasis on self-appraisal of what the student has done, or failed to do.

13. *Build students' schemata as well as their "skills."* All new learning is built, in some way, on prior and growing knowledge and experience. Building students' fund of background knowledge, vocabulary, and concepts prepares them to comprehend new information and ideas. Topical knowledge (the curriculum) and an elevated classroom vocabulary improves schema, capacity to comprehend (Vygotsky, 1962), and ability to think, speak, and write. Hold students accountable for learning (remembering and internalizing) a certain percentage of the content of what they read. This is an operational definition of what it means to be *literate*, as opposed to *nonilliterate*.

14. *Teach the whole person.* Instruction tends to be addressed chiefly to the cognitive domain, to a lesser degree to the affective domain, and rarely, if at all, to the sensory-motor, or physical, and *associative learning* domains (Ceprano, 1981; Manzo & Manzo, 1990a). (See Motor Imaging, a vocabulary-building strategy, for a particularly vivid example of this point in the sensory-motor domain, and Glass's Analysis in the associative learning domain.) The full significance of involving all domains in learning is further realized in the next point addressing the behavioral aspects of learning.

motivation is a chemical or the brain that is released by success

15. *Provide for behavioral reconditioning through extensive review and practice.* Failure has biological consequences. It changes the chemistry of human functioning so that failure becomes a "habit" of body as well as of mind. To build success where habits of failure have become embedded, it often is necessary to employ methods that neutralize negative chemistry and inappropriate coping systems. One means of aiding in this is by behavioral reconditioning; that is, where students are led to engage in review and extensive practice. Drill and practice are used far less than they should be because teachers tend to select methods based on what "expert readers" would do, more so than what "sub-par" students need. The teaching methods that best countercondition the chemistry of failure with the feel and chemistry of success (Bandura & Walters, 1963; Oldrige, 1982; Manzo, 1977a) are very likely to include a considerable amount of preview, review, *associative learning*, and occasional ability grouping. The soundness of these practices is easily demonstrated by a simulation summarized in Figure 6.9. This simulation can be replicated with most any group of adults. (Replication, or simply re-doing an experiment, is the highest level of confirmation of its veracity, or good sense.)

FIGURE **6.9**

TEACHING TO HIGH/LOW APTITUDE

Ask yourself, and then others in your group the following two *interrupting,* or *heuristic,* questions:

A. How would I like to be taught something for which I have a low specific aptitude?

B. How would I like to be taught something for which I have a high specific aptitude?

Typical responses to "how I would like to be taught in my low-aptitude areas":

- Tell me about it before I do it.
- Tell me about it while I'm doing it.
- Provide direct instruction.
- Tell me what I should have learned.
- Repeat what you first said.
- Tell me what the questions are as well as the answers.
- Write it so I can copy it.
- Slow the pace of instruction.
- Break it down into smaller parts.
- Give me some key words and meanings (a glossary).
- Let me talk about it with other students.
- Make it as hands-on as possible.
- Let's do some whole-class drill.
- Remind me what good this will do (why I'm asked to learn it).
- Let me experience it in different forms—hearing, reading, speaking about it, and maybe doing it, but with a lot of help.
- Don't give it to me for homework, nor as a long-term project.
- Give me a top-down and a bottom-up look at it.
- Tell me interesting things about it, but not too many and not for too long.
- Group me (mostly) with some people who are really good at this, and sometimes with people whom I can help.
- Connect yesterday to today.

- Don't ask me to write about it until I really know it.
- Review what was covered.
- Teach me where I have the least possible exposure, or other people watching.
- Connect me to a help line.
- Don't make me have to bring this to my parents or to get help from my parents. I don't need to have them reminded of another thing I can't do or where I'm disappointing them.
- Develop some *compensatory* systems for people who can't do this well, and tell everyone that it's not really that important.

Typical responses to "how I would like to be taught in my high-aptitude areas":

- Say it quickly.
- Give me a project.
- Surround me with people and books and activities.
- Let's talk and write and read about it.
- It doesn't matter much where you start, I'm with you.
- I can learn from indirect, even incidental, instruction.
- Tell me where there's more of this to be had/done.
- Are there jobs for people who do this? Can we meet/see them?
- Are there rules for doing this well?
- Give me a reason to do more of this at home.
- Are there clubs/Web sites/interest groups?
- Are there people I might mentor?
- Let me do this where I can be seen and heard.
- Let's talk about what it's good for, and let others know.
- Let's read biographies about people who were really good at this.
- Stand back and let me at it.
- Give me this for homework.
- Let's take tests to see how we're progressing.
- Teach me about other newer things through this.

16. *Reduce Distractions.* For many years, a standard rule of remediation was that children with reading and learning problems should be taught in a physical setting that had a greatly reduced level of "extraneous stimuli" (Strauss & Lehtinen, 1947). This rule lost favor when evidence mounted to show that reading and LD kids are not any more hyperactive than other children. However, the general rule should still be followed, not because there are more remedial readers who are hyperactive and highly distractible, but because those who *are* need more help in focusing on the reading task, and hence will be more adversely affected by a distracting environment. In practical terms, this may mean exercising reasonable controls over the remedial environment by closing the door to the hallway, turning students' seats away from distracting bulletin boards, and perhaps from one another. It does not and should not result in the creation of a sterile cell.

17. *Phase yourself out.* All learning is built on the expectation that the student is working toward independence. This is *the* most basic principle of teaching. Design instruction so as to fade out, or "gradually release responsibility" (Pearson, 1985). Encourage ever-greater self-reliance. Bruner (1978) first referred to this as the principle of "scaffolding," which implies removal of the scaffolds. It can take the form of verbal directions and support (Roehler, Duffy, & Warren, 1987), or of combined physical and verbal support (Manzo & Manzo, 1990b; Scardamalia, Bereiter, & Steinbach, 1984). (See the Note Cue method in Chapter 12 on English-Language Learners for a poignant example of this principle applied to promoting a highly-scaffolded instructional conversation.)

18. *Teach self-questioning.* Many goals and remedial principles, such as phasing the teacher out, and self-teaching, rest on the success of the teacher to teach students to ask themselves questions (Pressley, 2000). This is easily done by asking and therefore modeling thinking that utilizes why-questions about facts presented in connected text. Most every point in a story or nonfiction selection is tied to every other by a meaningful thread that can be made vivid by asking "why" these things are presented together: "Why are horses and zebras mentioned together here?" and "Why do you suppose zebras are not used as horses?" Such questions not only produce large-comprehension effects, but they tend to leave the mind open to further learning and inquiry rather than having it terminate with questions that tend to close down inquiry with the closing of the book. (See the ReQuest procedure as a cornerstone method for teaching self-questioning.)

19. *Provide for students' basic needs before attempting instruction.* Whenever possible, try to at least situationally provide for students' basic human needs. These are necessary requisites before expecting students to be responsive to cognitive development—a higher-order need. This point is a fundamental and inescapable aspect of human motivation. It was best described by Abraham Maslow (1954), and is illustrated in the triangle seen in Figure 6.10. In very practical terms, this "needs hierarchy" is meant to remind us of such things as that a child may be hot/cold, hungry, or need to go to the rest room before being ready to engage and learn. Our colleague, John George, reports a telling story of how easy it is as instructors to become preoccupied with our own needs to the detriment of the child's. He had teachers in a tutoring situation pointedly ask students questions like, "Are you too hot or cold?" "Would you like to go to the rest room first?" and similar questions. Later, he observed a lesson in which a student responded "yes" to three such questions, after which the teacher absentmindedly said, "Good, okay, now let's begin to learn" (George, personal communication).

FIGURE **6.10**

MASLOW'S HIERARCHY OF NEEDS

This theory of motivation assumes that human needs are arranged along a hierarchy of potency. Lower-level needs that have not been met take on the strongest priority, and must be satisfied before the next level of needs can emerge and press for satisfaction. Triggered by the satisfaction of more basic needs, those from the next level of the pyramid then may surface, but not before. This need structure is represented by the pyramid shown below.

AESTHETIC
NEEDS
(beauty, harmony,
proportion)

COGNITIVE NEEDS
(knowledge, information, ideas)

NEED FOR SELF-ACTUALIZATION
(developing one's capacities)

ESTEEM NEEDS
(personal and social worth)

BELONGING AND LOVE NEEDS

SAFETY NEEDS

PHYSIOLOGICAL NEEDS

20. *Avoid confounding elements.* Teachers often attempt to support and enrich instruction by introducing ideas or concepts *similar* to the one being taught. The problem with this is that students tend to learn the similar ideas together in a confused lump of interrelated details. A simple way to avoid this problem is to identify new concepts to be taught in each lesson and introduce related concepts only after the target concept has been thoroughly learned. For example, don't teach **"p," "b,"** and **"d"** at the same time, but one at a time until each is separately mastered. This is technically known as problems of "proactive inhibition," where new learnings interfere with immediately subsequent ones, and "retroactive inhibitions," where subsequent learnings undo or interfere with things previously learned (Manzo & Manzo, 1990a).

21. *Use concurrent teaching methods.* Concurrent teaching methods, as used in this text, are designed to simultaneously serve more than one objective (Manzo & Manzo, 1990a; Rubin, 1997). Typically, such methods tend to focus on one conventional objective (Rubin, 1997) such as comprehension, and one or more *collateral objectives* such as student questioning skill (Yopp, 1988), or selected aspects of personal-social adjustment.

22. *Let students read!* Reading alone, as Carver (1991) eventually discovered, will not appreciably improve reading. However, the absence of ample opportunity to read both orally and silently does impede reading progress (Allington, 1977). During silent reading, children have opportunity to control their own pace, review material, and formulate personal reactions (Richek, List, & Lerner, 1989). Nonetheless, it has been found that poor readers are given only a third as many opportunities to read as are good readers. In one study, the low-achieving group in a first grade averaged only five words of silent reading per day (Allington, 1984)! Furthermore, during oral reading, better readers tend to be encouraged to figure out a word for themselves, while low-achieving readers tend to be supplied the word too quickly by the teacher (Allington, 1980; Hoffman, et al., 1984). The need for selective and supported practice in independent reading is made clearer in the next principle.

23. *Provide environmental support.* In order for reading, writing, and thinking skills to take hold and flourish, there must be an ecologically conducive, or literate, environment (Morrow, 1989). Each school must create an environment that consciously, though largely incidentally, supports literacy. This can be done in a variety of ways, ranging from regular classroom teachers using literacy-nurturing strategies to the skillful use of support personnel and community resources. Several such support systems are described ahead in this chapter.

24. *Exercise student minds in areas often left to atrophy.* Several studies, as well as good sense, now confirm that remedial-level students genuinely benefit from engagement with activities and mental operations that they frequently are deprived of during conventional remedial and even normal school instruction. These include higher-literacy questions (Beck, 1989; Spiegel 1980a) and activities to stir inventive thinking (Haggard, 1976). The chapters ahead further explain and illustrate how each of these neglected areas can profitably be attended to within the framework of remedial reading instruction. For now, ask yourself where lessons may be inviting playful divergent thinking. The unplayful type is higher-order problem solving, and will follow.

25. *Do something joyful!* We are aware of no research that has explicitly tested this proposition, but that may be because it is so obvious that no one has set out to formally test it. We suspect, because there may be little agreement on just what may be considered "joyful." Nonetheless, all children have things that cause them to feel better, happier, and more optimistic. The good teacher should begin to collect a treasure chest of these and use them on a trial and error basis. A few examples will suffice for now; others are mentioned throughout the text:

- Read a rousing tale or sentimental piece to your students each session. This may be a continuing story or a series of short stories.
- Open your eyes wide. Engage the student in a conversation about something that he or she wishes to talk about, and listen with real and observable interest. (Several studies by social psychologists have shown that persons with the *pupils* of their eyes dilated are immediately perceived as warm and caring.)
- Help the child to read about and better understand some personally selected goal (anything from weight loss to a pressing assignment).
- Use a teaching method that the child clearly enjoys.
- Read joke books and humorous tales.

26. *Connections and carry-outs.* In order for learning to reach a generative state, it is necessary not only to conjure and bring relevant prior knowledge and experience to the classroom, but to engage in activities and discourse (Hall, 1979) that cause students to conjure and bring learning home from the classroom. This is "homework" at its best. One example: Consider the recommendation of Sigrid Renner and Joan Carter (1991), to have youngsters learn more about the folkways of their families by collecting examples of family sayings, recipes, jokes, and songs.

The laminated principles of remediation include: ZPD; engagement; self-teaching; quicker pacing; reciprocity; and lots of practice.

These twenty-six principles of teaching and learning, as well as others, are concretely represented ahead under individual teaching methods and other recommended practices. The remainder of this chapter is dedicated to describing some basic remedial lesson structures and providing examples of how to foster a literate environment.

ORGANIZING THE REMEDIAL SESSION

School-based remedial sessions tend to involve one to ten students, and typically last between 30 and 50 minutes, depending on whether they are in an elementary or secondary school. A plan to maximize utilization of that time should be a high priority.

There has been relatively little research on possible ways to organize and use remedial time. Ample research exists to indicate that the more remedial time is spent as academic "engaged time," the greater will be the gains in learning (Rosenshine & Stevens, 1984). Achieving this in real circumstances often involves attention to a variety of logistical and human needs, including the needs of teachers and remedial specialists.

One of the best means of using remedial time effectively is to have a clear grasp of the activities or components of an *ideal* remedial program. Seven components of an ideal remedial reading program are described here, primarily from the perspective of a single remedial session. These components tend to follow the master plan inherent in the Directed-Reading Thinking Activity, a lesson structure that is over 100 years old. The actual order of these, and the extent to which they may blend into one another, may vary with circumstances. Initially, it is advisable to take these in the order shown, since it will ensure that you attend to and develop expertise in each, and the child will get to experience each.

SEVEN COMPONENTS OF REMEDIAL PLANNING

Self-esteem grows from self-efficacy, or conscious evidence of progress, not the other way around.

I. *The Orientation Component.* The orientation component provides continuity and focus to the remedial session. It may be an engaging question or statement related to local or national news, or school life. Ironically, this works best when it is served on a plate that is structured and fairly routine. This should include an agenda for the day written on the chalkboard. Part of the routine can be based on a task that the student is expected to do independently, immediately on entering class. Often this is part of ongoing, autoinstructional material that also provides a reasonable level of corrective feedback. Most instructional "kits" and computer-assisted instruction (CAI) programs are suitable for this purpose. Free reading is not recommended at this time. Free reading is better done once attention is oriented and fixed. This 5- to 10-minute activity period is a good time to take roll and otherwise tend to "housekeeping" functions.

Catch 'em all

II. *Direct Instructional Component.* During this segment of the period, it is best to conduct a hard-hitting and robust type of lesson activity. This is the instructional heart of the remedial session, and should never be traded away, even for one period, without some compelling reason. There is strong evidence that learning, for most all age subjects, declines sharply after 20 minutes of instruction. Many of the methods described in the chapter ahead will help meet this requirement.

attention span

III. *Reinforcement and Extension Component.* This period of time, ideally, should build on the direct instructional period and be spent in enabled reading, writing, and discussion of what was read. Writing activities may vary from simply listing key words, to summarizing and reacting.

IV. *Schema-Enhancement Component.* This unit of time should be spent in building a knowledge base for further reading and independent thinking. It is an ideal time to teach study skills such as outlining, note-taking, and memory training. Ideally, it should flow from or precede Component III.

V. *Personal-Emotional Growth Component (in and beyond class).* Little learning of any consequence can occur without the learner being involved and anticipating personal progress. This unit can be built into any of the other components in a variety of ways, including doing reading that is akin to one's interests and emotional concerns (bibliotherapy), writing for self-exploration or toward some authentic objective (a letter to someone), and through attempting to identify and develop strategies for dealing with personal study and learning needs. (See the Problem-Solving Approach to Study Skills in Chapter 10.) Remember that students can only be guided to identifying and selecting what they will work on out of personal need. This component should serve as a reminder to the teacher to have students pause to hear, record, and then state what they learn each day (Poostay, 1982). It is also a good time to have students say what they might be doing or thinking to help themselves outside of class, and in preparation for the next remedial session. The latter function comprises a metacognitive thread that continues in the next component.

VI. *Cognitive Development Component.* Back in the late 1960s and early '70s there was great interest in a "cognitive development" approach to reading. There is much to support this proposition, but only when it is done in the context of reading instruction. Accordingly, this component should be largely addressed to a reading goal that simultaneously contains elements that enhance basic and higher-order thinking functions, such as:

- inference
- abstract verbal reasoning
- analogical reasoning
- constructive-critical/creative reading
- convergent and divergent analysis
- problem solving
- metacognition

Most of these forms of thinking can be taught concurrently as a routine part of word analysis, vocabulary, comprehension, and study skills instruction. However, they may be pursued individually for brief periods of time to draw further attention to them as viable instructional goals. Methods that meet this standard are identified in the chapters ahead. For example, look at Botel's Discovery approach to teaching phonics while developing inquiry and problem-solving skills; proverbs study for improving reading comprehension simultaneously with abstract, or two-level, thinking; and at Frayer's model for teaching vocabulary while improving concept formation.

VII. *Literate Environment Component.* The value of creating a literate environment is best illustrated with a metaphor. It is easier to heat and cool a home to 70 degrees when the ambient, or outdoor, temperature is 60 degrees than when it is 20 degrees or 90 degrees. This is also true of building literacy. It is not easy to build a conducive ambient temperature for effective reading, writing, and thinking, but it can be done, and it can be very efficient to do so. Here are some operations that can be undertaken to create a conducive environment for learning within the school. It may even be possible to transfer some of that ambient effect to home and community. Think of these as heroic environmental or ecological strategies. Most require considerable cooperation and support from others. Several of these are ideal projects for grant proposals to special sources of state or private funding designated for innovative educational programming.

CAMBRIAN SOLUTIONS: HEROIC ENVIRONMENTAL/ECOLOGICAL STRATEGIES (AND GRANT OPTIONS)

To even out the ambient temperature in a school and community is heroic, generative, and creative-constructive. Such strategies continue to promote literacy even while class is out and students are on break. And that's a good thing.

   1. *Enriched community of language.* All teachers and support staff in a school or clinic situation are given a list of 100 words that they all try to use in a variety of situations and circumstances. In this way, students come to learn new, slightly elevated vocabulary in much the same way that all other language learning occurs: naturally, and in authentic contexts.

   This plan can have effects far beyond the classroom. When students learn new words in this natural fashion, they are more likely to use them with each other and at home. Consequently, the students themselves become models of a richer language in their communities and a source of influence on the language of siblings and parents (Manzo & Manzo, 1990a).

   2. *Student advocates.* This is a simple plan to prevent students from "falling between the cracks" of whatever organizational scheme or curricula that come to dominate a school (Manzo & Manzo, 1990). In brief, each student in the school is assigned to a teacher ombudsman who should make every reasonable effort to get to know that student on personal terms, and be ready to hear him or her out and represent his or her interests on thorny issues or problems arising in school. The idea is to serve as a student's personal counselor and advocate, not merely as an agent of the school. Playing this role can raise the empathy of the teacher for the student, and the student's respect for and sense of responsibility to the teacher. Some schools have attempted to do this in a group fashion through the "homeroom" plan. Under this arrangement, pupils come to a designated room for about 20 minutes, first thing each day. Following general school announcements, the "homeroom teacher" tries to make human contact with students by expressing interest in their other classes and encouraging them to do better, or asking about their report cards. Students often are quite touched by such simple gestures. It has been wisely observed that everyone needs "someone to show their report card to" throughout life. Another practical means of accomplishing this is to have someone openly represent any child who is the subject of a "staffing," or conference, to assess a child's placement and instructional program. The act of serving as a student's advocate can be a powerful heuristic in guiding remedial specialists to better represent students in a holistic manner. School can be particularly harsh to students with artistic temperaments and "offbeat" views, a fact verified each day on talk shows as actors and comedians recount a litany of demoralizing experiences in school.

3. *ThemedSchool.* ThemedSchool is little more than a focus that a school adopts for a given year. It can range from "artistic expressions" to "inventive thinking." Ideally, the theme ought to culminate in a fair or display such as an Invention Convention. (For more information, contact Invent America! on the Internet. ThemedSchool tends to bring the community into the school and school learning out to the community. The broad, cross-disciplinary nature of the project tends to create authentic opportunities for cooperative work and learning.

4. *A Living Library.* A Living Library (Manzo, 1973; Manzo & Manzo, 1990a) encourages the active participation of users in a variety of ways. It collectively encourages constructive, reactive reading and incidentally builds, aids, and encourages students to read, write, and think in a more literate and constructive way. Four examples are presented here.

   a. WeeWriters—This is a section of the library designed to house student, faculty, and community essays, plays, poetry, books, and other literary productions. Desktop publishing systems can now have these printed, bound, and catalogued for circulation as part of the library's regular collection.

   b. Inquiry Books—These are books of interesting questions that refer the student to precisely the book and page where an answer might be found. These can be accumulated from the reading and writing of students, teachers, and community members.

> *Examples:*
>
> Which animals that grow larger than people are born smaller than a hand? (*World Book,* Vol. 2, 36) Answer: panda bears and kangaroos.
>
> In what way are humans more powerful than most animals? (*The Human Ape,* 12) Answer: We have more lung power for our size and can travel farther in a day than most animals.
>
> There are two books that we have found especially useful in teaching students how to construct questions of this type: *Can Elephants Swim?* by Robert Fores (Time Life, 1969) and *Fabulous Fallacies* by Thaddeus Tuleja (1982).

   c. Certified Independent Study—It has been noted that selective study on most any topic for just 15 minutes a day will make one a specialist in that subject within just four years. Focused study of most anything, as Vygotsky (1962) has noted, greatly enhances schema, prior knowledge (a key to successful comprehension), vocabulary, and a sense of the structure of all knowledge. The reading specialist and school librarian can aid in this goal by instigating and certifying planned independent study. Several software programs are available for printing very impressive looking certificates. Teachers, students, and even community members can be brought together monthly to share questions, knowledge, and related interests and hobbies (Manzo, Sherk, Leibert, & Mocker, 1977).

d. Exchange Reading System—Dialectical, or back and forth, discussion and thinking is the basis for all learning. It is a strong source of motivation to further read, think, and write (Manzo & Manzo, 1990a; Riegel, 1979). The Exchange Reading Program (more fully developed under the heading REAP and electronic "discussion boards" like Blackboard.com offer means for better readers and thinkers to share their thoughts and insights with each other and with less capable readers. These systems invite participation from teachers and community members alike.

5. *Cross-age and peer reading.* Under this plan, below-average readers from grades 4 to 8 serve as readers to kindergartners and first graders. This simple weekly program can help poor readers gain practice and self-esteem as well as adding to the overall sense that books and reading are prized activities. Labbo and Teale (1990) report reading gains and improvements in self-concept from just such a program. There was a further incidental benefit in that the tutors became much more open and willing to learn how to read effectively to the kindergartners. These fifth graders were taught how to improve their own fluency and to focus on comprehension through "repeated readings" and "mental modeling" (Duffy, Roehler, & Hermann, 1988). The mental modeling was limited to relating personal experiences to the stories read, a valuable strategy for active text processing, as proven by Mason and Au (1986). Susan Coleman (1990) reports similar results from a three-year, cross-age tutoring program in which middle-school Chapter I students plan and conduct reading and writing sessions with kindergarten and second-grade students. The middle schoolers developed greater self-confidence, library skills, and leadership skills, as well as their own reading and writing skills. (Coleman, 1990). In addition, by stepping into the teacher's "shoes," these youngsters developed more understanding and positive attitudes toward teachers and school in general.

EXTENDING CASE-BASED REASONING (CBR)

As suggested previously, one of the ways that the human mind is able to digest complex rules is to be exposed to case-based examples that can be grasped as patterns, something that the mind is exceedingly good at identifying. Case Study, in fact, is the basis of most Masters degree programs in Business, such as Harvard's MBA. Below is a real case on which to practice and compare your diagnostic and prescriptive thinking. See what comes to mind as you review the case. Based on the information available, decide where this child seems to be, the direction the child seems to be going, and what you would prescribe as follow-up teaching and testing to verify and/or refute your first impressions. The case below has a high frequency of occurrence, but is not of the variety that wins much attention.

Case

Third-grade boy. Comprehension relatively weak (2.9), but vocabulary solid (3.7). High social awareness. Does not seem to profit from seatwork. Oral responding unpredictably hit-and-miss. Emotionally "field-dependent"— overly influenced by peers and social outcomes. His IR-TI is erratic, with fair listening comprehension, low "congruency" ratio, though sometimes insightful "reading beyond the lines."

State your Suppositions/Prescriptions/Why. Include your Prognosis (future outlook), as relevant.

Case Critique

Suppositions. When taken together, this child's poor independent seatwork, along with a solid vocabulary (a strong predictor of capacity), and occasional peak, even insightful, answering suggest that he probably has a solid aptitude for school-type learning, but is overly tethered to the social scene. His effort and learning are regulated by his "read" of what is "in." His problem is not so much how well he reads, but in the overly self-centered meanings, or world view, that he is building out of what he reads and experiences.

Prescription: He appears to need a program that emphasizes close analytical reading and critical thinking, with considerable discussion of the value and purpose of these skills. *Increase response to text writing* (see REAP writing in index); utilize more evaluative thinking questions (see InterAct—a Valuing method of teaching comprehension—in Index); provide literature and nonfiction that build a deeper sense of empathy for social-cultural differences. Do an Improvisational review of his responses to the "beyond the lines" questions of the IR-TI to possibly identify reasons for when and where he is insightful or not. Trial-teach that which was missed, and determine whether these were the result of misunderstanding or unexamined convictions. Overall: The goal of higher academic achievement needs to be seen as a worthy life goal, irrespective of peer and other social pressures.

Prognosis: This boy is bright, socially aware, and able to extract value from the day to day. He probably will be quite successful in modern business. Having him read and discuss literature and nonfiction that reflect worthwhile civic convictions could greatly aid his identification with and deeper understanding and commitment to ideals and a code of ethics that rise above pure self-interest.

REVIEW

You now have a considered understanding of typical classroom and clinical principles and practices that guide precise intervention. The contents of this academic chapter will grow vastly richer each time you come back to read a few pages. "Rules" become most meaningful when they are informed by experience and detailed knowledge.

PREVIEW

Much of what follows is specification of the general principles of diagnostic-prescriptive teaching. Fine points will be put on some areas of assessment and capability to prescribe precise interventions.

WORD RECOGNITION: PHONEMIC AWARENESS, SIGHT WORDS, AND PHONICS

Decoding is a comprehension skill. – NANCY LEWKOWICZ, 1987

*Minds grow rich and agile by learning patterns more than rules;
this may explain why a little bit of phonics goes a long way.*

CONTENT AND CONCEPT ORGANIZER

Prior chapters acquainted you with foundational concepts and means of assessing specific reading, language arts, and study skills, and identifying stages of development in each. Here, you will be exposed to linking options for instruction. Side notes will point out where these might be used as appropriate prescriptions. Phonemics, phonics, rapid word recognition, and spelling are the focus. Look for methods that also are basic paradigms— or examples that can serve as patterns or models—and that can further build your conceptual basis for solid, prescriptive teaching.

CHAPTER OUTLINE

"LEARNING TO READ"

Cracking the Code

A teacher in one of our classes told us this about how she learned to read: "I was in kindergarten, and I desperately wanted a puppy. Finally one Saturday, my Dad said that when I learned to read, he would get me a puppy. I went into my room, and by the next Saturday I could read." She got the puppy. Another teacher recalled standing beside her mother in church, singing a hymn and watching as her mother moved her finger along the words in the hymnal as she did every Sunday, but this time, looking at the words, she suddenly realized that she was reading them. Another teacher told how she read and reread the book *Here Comes Judy!* to her younger sister, who happened to be named Judy, so many times that her sister memorized the book, and proudly "read" it to anyone who would listen. Then one day, Judy brought the book to her sister and said, "I can read this book." To which her sister replied with that patronizing older-sister voice, "You can't read it, you've just memorized the words." "No," said Judy, "I can *really* read it—I can read it *backwards*!"

Together, these stories illustrate how fundamentally simple it can be for some to "crack the code." The difficult question is why some children fail to do so. One common thread in each of these stories is the fact or implication that the novice reader has spent a great deal of time *looking at print*. All that is really needed to reach that "ah-ha!" moment of realization that one has cracked the code, are a few sight words, familiarity with the material, and enough knowledge of letter-sound associations to make accurate guesses about words that are not yet sight words. For many children, that "ah-ha!" moment, and the social reinforcement that accompanies it (another implicit common strand in the three stories above) are sufficient motivation to continue to spend a great deal of time *looking at print*. In doing so, they build their sight word vocabularies, and their familiarity with frequently occurring regular and irregular letter-sound associations.

> Why some children fail to learn to "crack the code" is more mysterious than why so many learn to do so easily.

The challenge to teachers in the early grades, and to reading specialists working with older students with decoding difficulties, is to somehow reconstruct that *wave of motivation* that propels one from initially cracking the code to mastering the code. Research and experience have a lot to tell us about how to do so. In fact, we can do so flawlessly: There is not a single documented case of *anyone* who has not been able to learn to read when properly and persistently taught to do so.

> It appears that everyone can learn to read.

Mastering the Code in the Early Grades

Children who have "caught the wave" come to kindergarten with an enormous advantage in reading: They have extensive knowledge of fundamental concepts about print; they know the alphabet, some sight words, and many letter-sound associations. They already are in transition from cracking the code to mastering the code. Many other children, however, enter kindergarten without these advantages. Research-based, diagnostic-prescriptive instruction in preschool through second grade should quickly bring these children "up to speed" so that very few children (but upward of 2 million nationally) should be entering third and fourth grade without having "mastered the code."

The fact that this corrective intervention is not occurring more consistently continues to be cause for national concern. In a recent study, Foorman (2000) reported that "88 percent of students who were poor readers in first grade were poor readers in fourth grade. Likewise, 87 percent of students who were good readers in first grade were good readers in fourth grade" (9). These findings confirmed those of an earlier longitudinal study by Juel (1988), in which students who performed in the lower portion of the class in first grade were still in the lower portion after four years of school instruction. Storch and Whitehurst made this point even more poignantly, estimating that "in many affluent school districts, less than 10 percent of fourth-grade children will be reading below grade level, whereas in inner-city systems, up to 70 percent of children will be reading below grade level" (2001, 3–4).

Another recent study looked at "impaired readers" whose reading performance improved rapidly during the course of intervention, to determine whether these students' reading difficulties were caused by cognitive Deficits or by limitations in their early literacy experiences and/or De-limitations in their initial reading instruction. For the majority of these students, reading difficulties were the result of De-Limiting experiential and instructional Deficits (system mistakes). This led researchers to conclude that, "if some attempt is made to ensure that the child's preliteracy experiences, and her or his language arts programs in kindergarten and first grade are characterized by the depth and breadth needed to effect the proper balance between learning to decode print and reading for meaning and comprehension, fewer beginning readers would require remedial reading" (Vellutino, Scanlon, & Tanzman, 1998, 392).

There are volumes of research with similar findings: Children who enter school with an advantage maintain the advantage; children who enter without the advantage remain disadvantaged. It approaches the proportions of a national tragedy that this research is so widely misinterpreted to mean that this has to be the case: The current solution, which favors the

---

Less than 10 percent of children in affluent schools will be below grade level, whereas up to 70 percent of those in inner-city systems will be below grade level.

Today, many parents supplement the education of their children; schools are under-resourced, and the least able parents are unable to help the most needy children.

affluent, is to have more parents do more to ensure that their children enter school with an advantage. The more realistic interpretation is that schools need to be better funded to make a difference, irrespective of what parents are *able* to do.

Walton, Walton, and Felton (2001) found that when first graders with weak prereading skills (the lowest 40 percent of the class) were taught individually or in a small group (two to four children) for about 25 minutes per session for 11 weeks using direct instruction in letter-sound associations emphasizing onset (beginning letter sounds) and rime (ending letter cluster sounds or "word families"), they caught up to the strongest children (top 60 percent) on letter-sound knowledge and phonemic skills. Kindergarten children in a second study had similar, but not as strong, increases. Precise diagnostic-prescriptive teaching makes a difference. It can make an even greater difference when woven into the larger picture of shared reading experiences, in a classroom community of learners.

> Diagnostic-prescriptive teaching can guide early intervention as well as later remediation.

INSTRUCTION AT EMERGENT LITERACY LEVELS

Theme-based approaches capitalize upon children's natural motivation to learn. Through direct, informed instruction the advantages that some children bring to kindergarten can easily be extended to all children. Concepts and learnings that take hours, months, and years to acquire "naturally" can be directly taught much more quickly, particularly since we know precisely what these are. It is not unreasonable to expect that by the end of kindergarten, all children will acquire all of the concepts and learnings in Figure 7.1 (which also are represented in the assessment inventory in Chapter 3).

Reflection

Before reading the next section, please write about a thematic unit that you experienced in school. What do you remember about this experience? How did your schema (cognitive framework) for the theme expand through this experience?

FIGURE **7.1**

EMERGENT LITERACY CONCEPTS AND LEARNINGS

Knowledge of the alphabet

Upper and lower case letters

Sounds made by most consonants in the initial position

Concepts about print

Directionality: front to back, left to right, return sweep, top to bottom

Print (rather than pictures) carries the meaning

Words are discrete segments of language, composed of letters that make sounds

What can be spoken can be written, and what is written can be read

Words in language are combined in sentences

In written language, pauses in and between sentences are marked with commas, periods, and question marks

Books may be fact or fiction

Fictional stories have a beginning, a middle, and an end

Many stories have characters and events similar to our own

Phonemic awareness

Hears discrete words in speech

Hears syllables in words

Hears differences in beginning sounds of words

Hears differences in ending sounds of words

Hears rhyming sounds in words

Blends discrete sounds to make words

Hears separate sounds within a single word

Knowledge of a few sight words

Frequently occurring regular and irregular words such as "the" and "run"

Theme-based learning is hands-on, interactive, authentic; it is a conceptual thread for beads of otherwise loosely connected information.

The difference between skills-based and theme-based approaches can be like the difference between trying to move a string along a tabletop by pushing it from behind, or by pulling it from the front. Theme-based approaches to instruction create language and concept-rich environments for developing readers. During a thematic unit, students participate in a variety of meaningful experiences related to a particular topic or theme. Skills and strategies are taught directly and systematically, but in a larger context of connected and in-depth learning experiences that are used to develop students' vocabulary, oral language, concepts about print, and phonemic awareness during active learning.

For instance, let's step into a kindergarten classroom and observe a theme-based unit on the farm. On the first day of the unit, children arrive in the classroom to find two bales of hay in the reading corner, and a new classroom library (selected with assistance from the school librarian) filled with books about farm life and farm animals. A large bulletin board has been cleared and covered with colored paper in the shapes of a big red barn, green grass, and blue sky. During the course of the unit, the bulletin board will be filled with a few theme-related sight words, pictures, and the children's art and writing. On each child's desk is a blank book in the shape of a barn to be used as a journal during the unit. A recording of "Old Mac-Donald Had a Farm" is playing, and across the teacher's desk is a line of stuffed animals—one for each animal named in the song (to be used to guide children in singing the song together after the morning opening activities). Some of the activities in this unit might include:

- daily teacher read-alouds of books on the theme (such as *To Market, To Market* by Miranda, 1997)
- poems ("Milk" by Prelutsky, 1996, 114), songs (like "Old MacDonald Had a Farm"), rhymes (such as "Little Bo Peep"), and chants
- a Big Book (try *Click Clack Moo, Cows That Type* by Cronin, 2000), used in shared reading
- the Big Book is used to model the one-to-one correspondence of spoken to written words through the use of a pointer as the teacher reads aloud
- the Big Book is retold and dramatized by the students throughout the week
- the Big Book is also used as the basis for repeated readings and instruction in concepts of print and alphabetic principles
- at a flannel board center, flannel cut-outs of characters in the book are placed in order while children retell the story to each other
- the children experience shared writing as they compose a letter that might be written by another animal to Farmer Brown or a letter that the children would write to their teacher, based on the pattern found in the Big Book
- a field trip to the farm, or a videotape of a day on the farm
- each day the children write using invented spelling (or draw pictures that the children or teacher labels) in their journals about the day's theme activities
- related songs, poems, and chants (printed on large posters on the wall) are introduced in the large group and repeated as the children change activities or line up for recess
- the experience of milking a cow is simulated with a sawhorse, a surgical rubber glove (filled with water or milk) with a tiny hole in each fingertip, and a bucket
- a baby pig (or other farm animal) is brought into the classroom if there is a farm nearby
- a group Language Experience Story is created by the class about their favorite farm animal or their shared farm experiences; the story, printed on chart paper, is posted in the classroom and children are invited, from time to time, to use a pointer to read the story aloud
- a recipe for milk shakes is written collaboratively by the students and the teacher, read chorally, and the (revised, if necessary) directions are followed for making a tasty treat
- during a silent reading time each day, all children and the teacher select fiction and nonfiction books about the farm and farm animals from classroom displays to "read" (children are encouraged to make up their own stories by looking at the pictures in books); teacher briefly introduces and builds interest in a few new books each day

> Ways to *pull* rather than *push* a thematic string.

- each student creates a page of a book related to his or her favorite animal on the farm using drawings and inventive (temporary) spelling, and this class book becomes a frequently read class treasure
- a class *Farm ABC* book is created during the unit as children try to come up with something on the farm for every letter of the alphabet
- nutrition (the importance of milk and calcium), science (animal care), math ("How many pigs are in the pen?"), and other subject areas are easily integrated into the farm unit
- parents are asked to write, send farm pictures, or come into the class-room to discuss their farm experiences; the children bring these items to school and share them with the class

When children have completed this unit, they have a rich schema about the farm and farm animals that will provide success for future books that they encounter on this topic. At the same time, the children have learned many basic concepts about reading, writing, and the print in books. The-matic units also make memorable experiences for children. Each time the authors ask university students to list important memories from their ele-mentary school years, thematic units head their lists (remember pioneer days; culture units where students learned about various countries and their customs; reading *Stone Soup* and making it?).

Thematic units can become as vivid as life experiences.

Theme-based learning is hands-on, interactive, and authentic. It is a practical way to recreate the motivational wave that impels natural learning. Caine and Caine (1991) suggest that it directly engages more global opera-tions of the brain "because many areas of the brain, including the senses and emotions, are brought into play. This type of learning disperses learn-ing throughout the brain, and there is much less stress on specific brain cells." As a result, children become more deeply involved and excited and remain actively engaged in this type of learning for longer periods of time (Caine & Caine, 1991).

Let's take a closer look at some of the activities in the thematic farm unit that encourage emergent literacy development. These activities in-clude: reading aloud, shared reading, guided reading, and language experi-ence story activities.

Reading Aloud to Children

Listening to stories read aloud is a critical early reading experience. This modeling of fluent reading helps children see that reading is meaningful communication. It is the single most important factor in vocabulary devel-opment, contributing about half of the roughly 3,000 words that children who progress adequately in school learn each year (Nagy & Herman, 1987). The amount of time spent listening to stories read aloud has been shown to have a strong correlation with eagerness to read and success in overall beginning reading in school (Schwarz, 1995; Sulzby, 1992; Wood, 1994).

An ounce of prevention is . . .

The benefit of reading aloud to 3- and 4-year-old children was shown in a program developed by Newman (1999) called Books Aloud. This program placed five books per child and open-faced bookshelves in 337 not-for-profit childcare centers on the basis of economic need. In addition to receiving books, the child-care workers also received 10 hours of training in effective reading-aloud techniques and thematic activities through monthly sessions at the local library. A random sample of children in the daycare centers participating in the Books Aloud program performed statistically significantly better on letter-name knowledge of uppercase and lowercase letters, rhyming, alliteration, and concepts of writing than comparable children in other daycare centers who did not receive the books and training.

The power of reading aloud as an early literacy intervention for "at-risk" kindergarten children who had limited exposure to storybooks and lacked basic understandings about print was documented by Wood and Salvetti (2001). In Project Story Boost, at-risk kindergarten students were removed from the classroom and read to individually or in pairs three times a week by trained volunteers. Participating children had longer, more accurate, and more complete retellings than students who were qualified to participate but did not. More importantly, two and three years after the intervention the children were rated by their second- and third-grade teachers in four areas: motivation/interest in reading, appropriateness of book selections, engagement during reading, and reading competency as measured by fluency and comprehension. Project Boost children were rated higher in the identified areas than all of the other students, including those who were not considered at-risk in kindergarten. Shared reading is a natural extension of reading aloud to children.

Reading aloud to children, especially from pieces that they finish silently, is simple, robust, and empowering.

Shared Reading with Children

One of our teacher-students told us of how, as a young child, her favorite read-aloud book was a large book of Mother Goose rhymes, in which each rhyme was accompanied by a picture. She asked her mother to read from it to her almost every night. It was the first thing she packed as she prepared to visit her grandmother, and she looked forward eagerly to having her grandmother read the book to her. Finally the moment arrived, and her grandmother began to read. Before long, the grandmother noticed that the little girl was in tears. "Why, what is the matter, dear?" she asked. The little girl told her that she had been waiting and waiting to see what stories her grandmother would tell from the pictures, but her grandmother's stories were *exactly* the same as her mother's stories. Shared Reading (Holdaway,

1979) is the ideal diagnostic-prescriptive approach to observing needs and providing direct instruction in basic concepts about print that children in the early grades may not yet have acquired (print carries the meaning, directionality, letter identification). It also introduces transitional instruction in phonemic awareness, sight words, and letter-sound associations.

Shared Reading provides precision instruction in basic concepts about print.

For a Shared Reading lesson, the teacher selects a "Big Book" that is interesting and contains rhyme, repetition, or predictable text. The teacher first "sells the book" to the children who make predictions about the story line from picture clues, share personal connections with the story, and set purposes for reading. Then the teacher reads the story aloud, sweeping a finger under each word as it is read. The children often join in the reading when familiar words or patterns are recognized. At the end of the first day's Shared Reading session, the teacher and children reread the book orally together. The same book is revisited for several days, as children do different activities (such as focus on concepts of print, clap to syllables in a word or line, join in rereading, act out the story, note punctuation marks, or others). The simple addition of the question, "What can you show us?" (Richgels, Poremba, & McGee, 1996) at the very beginning of the Shared Reading process can provide insight into the phonemic awareness level and literacy development of children. When the teacher asks, "What can you show us?" children take turns volunteering to come before the class to show their knowledge of the displayed Big Book. Students may identify letters or words, tell the name of a punctuation mark, or any knowledge that they have of the text. Students share their knowledge with each other in this process. The teacher gains insight into what concepts of print and phonemic awareness skills the students have learned, so scaffolding of that knowledge can take place during the shared reading process.

Guided Reading by Children

Early in first grade, most Guided Reading time is spent in shared reading with predictable books and Big Books. As the children's literacy ability progresses, the teacher selects one book on grade level and one easier book to read each week. The whole class participates in the Guided Reading lessons that include:

- a teacher-led picture walk and highlighting of difficult vocabulary
- children making predictions about the book
- children reading the book together, with partners, in a small group or alone
- the class reconvenes, discusses the book, and rereads it (chorally or in some other format)
- comprehension strategies are taught from the context of the book and practiced

- predictions made before reading are checked
- story maps and webs are completed
- might include: writing activity or acting out the selection (Cunningham, Hall, & Defee, 1991, 1998)

Cunningham, Hall, and Sigmon (1999) used Guided Reading as one component in the "4-Blocks Approach," which also included Self-Selected Reading, Writing, and Working with Words as the three additional components. The 4-Blocks Approach was implemented in first- through third-grade classrooms for eight years at a large, diversely populated suburban school in North Carolina. They found that "at the end of first grade, 58 to 64 percent of the children read above grade level (third grade or above); 22 to 28 percent read on grade level; 10 to 17 percent read below grade level (preprimer or primer). At the end of the second grade (second year of instruction in the 4-Blocks Approach), the number at grade level was 14 to 25 percent; the number above grade level (fourth-grade level or above) was 68 to 76 percent; the number reading below grade level dropped to 2 to 9 percent, half what it was in first grade" (185). The results have been *replicated*—the strongest level of scientific support—at numerous schools in other states.

> The 4-Blocks Approach has had astounding success.

Language Experience Stories from Children

The Language Experience Approach (Allen, 1976; Hall, 1981; Stauffer, 1980) is based on using children's own language as the content for reading instruction. The lesson begins with a discussion about a question, event, idea, or a story that has been read aloud, until a topic for the story is decided, at which point the discussion is guided toward "how should our story begin?" The teacher records the story on chart paper as told by the students, saying each word as it is printed. After each sentence is written, the teacher and students read the sentence together (or, the teacher and students can reread all sentences starting at the beginning of the story after each new sentence is added). After the story is written, the teacher reads the entire story, then the teacher and class read the story together. The completed story is then used in any combination of reading activities appropriate to students' levels and needs. Sample activities include:

- ask individual students to come up and point to and say three words in the story that they know
- ask individual students to come up and point to a word that starts with or ends with a given sound
- have children work in pairs to copy several words from the story on note cards, then take turns showing and saying these "flash cards" to each other

A caution in using LEAs
with older struggling
readers.

- type the story (in large font) and make copies for each student to practice reading individually or with a partner

The Language Experience Approach can be an effective strategy for older readers who have experienced years of frustration and lack of progress in literacy development, and are reading on an early emergent level. An important word of caution related to using the Language Experience Story Approach has been offered by Sandra McCormick, based on research with nonreaders at an Ohio State reading clinic. Severely disabled readers, she notes, tend to produce stories that, reflecting their oral language, have too *many* words, and too few *repetitions* of words for these nonreaders to learn and remember (1990). This can result in lessons that are more frustrating than they are empowering. With this forewarning, however, teachers can provide the needed guidance to keep the stories as simple as possible.

Numerous researchers have suggested that the single best predictor of learning to read in both children and adults is *phonological awareness* (Wagner & Torgesen, 1987; Elbro, 1996), not only for English-speaking people, but also for the French, Norwegian, and Swedish (based on research studies as cited in Walton, 1995). When discussing phonemic awareness it is easy to become confused by related terms such as auditory discrimination, phonetics, phonics, phoneme, and phonemic awareness in this area of study. Let's examine H. Yopp and R. Yopp's (2000) definitions and examples of these terms in Figure 7.2.

FIGURE **7.2**

DEFINITION OF TERMS

Term	Definition	Example
Auditory Discrimination	The ability to hear likenesses and differences in phonemes and words	Say these sounds: /t/ /p/. Are they the same or different?
Phonetics	The study of speech sounds that occur in languages, including the way these sounds are articulated	The first sound in *pie* is a bilabial—it is made with the two lips.
Phonics	A way of teaching reading and spelling that stresses symbol-sound relationships (in alphabetic orthographies)	The symbol *m* is used to represent the italicized sounds in the following words: ha*m*, ju*m*p, *m*y.
Phoneme	The smallest unit of speech sounds that makes a difference in communication	The spoken word *fly* consists of three phonemes: /f/-/l/-/i/. It differs from the word *flea* by one phoneme.
Phonemic awareness	The awareness that spoken language consists of a sequence of phonemes	How many sounds in the spoken word, *dog*? Say all the sounds you hear.

Yopp & Yopp, 2000, 131.

Edelen-Smith (1997) outlines numerous specific activities for simple and compound phonemic awareness skills, such as: rhyming, alliteration and assonance, word families/phonograms, isolated sound recognition, word/syllable counting, sound synthesis, sound to word matching, identification of sound positions, sound segmentation, word to word matching, and sound deletion. Examples of activities to encourage simple phonemic awareness (sound synthesis and sound segmentation) and complex phonemic awareness (sound deletion) are shown in Figure 7.3.

The predictive and prerequisite value of phonological awareness.

FIGURE **7.3**

PHONEMIC AWARENESS ACTIVITIES

Sound Synthesis Activities

Sound synthesis is blending an initial sound onto the remainder of a word, blending syllables of a word together, blending isolated phonemes into a word.

- Teach blending initial sound to the remainder of a word by saying, "It starts with /p/ and it ends with /at/, put it all together and it says 'pat'." Continue until children can give the final word. Use children's names for more meaning.

- Use a puppet to teach syllable blending or phoneme blending. Have the puppet segment words by saying "back" "pack" "What's my word?" or "/f/-/i/-/sh/ — What's my word?"

- Play "What's In the Bag?" The teacher gives a sound by sound or syllable by syllable clue such a /a/-/p/-/l/. The students guess what is in the bag.

- Play song games such as:

  If you think you know this word, shout it out!
  If you think you know this word, shout it out!
  If you think you know this word,
  Then tell me what you've heard,
  If you think you know this word, shout it out!

  Teacher says: /k/-/a/-/t/.

Sound Segmentation Activities

Sound segmentation is isolating the sounds of spoken words by separately pronouncing each one in order.

- Use Elkonin boxes to represent this concept. Prepare a card with a simple word picture on top such as "mitt." Prepare a row of boxes underneath, one for each phoneme in the word, not each letter (three boxes for "mitt"—/m/-/i/-/t/). Model the process of putting one phoneme in each box while slowly articulating the word. Use markers (or blank tiles or pieces of paper)

to begin this process rather than having the child write the appropriate letter in each box. Choose words from familiar text to segment. Next have students use the pictures and place the markers (one for each phoneme) without the box below.

- Gradually this process will move into a letter-sound association. Blank tiles or paper can be marked with letters representing the phonemes.

- The concept of developmental spelling can be introduced.

- Interactive writing can take place.

Sound Deletion Activities

Sound deletion is taking a phoneme or syllable away from a word.

- Teacher says: "If I say 'seesaw' without 'see,' the word is 'saw.' Now say 'hot dog' without 'hot.'"

- Play Simon Says: "Simon says, 'Say *bookmark* without *book*.'"

- Play "What's Missing": Say "eat—meat. What is missing from eat that was in meat?" or "What's missing in 'play' that you can hear in 'plane'?"

- Play Sound Takeaway: "It starts with /ch/ and it ends with /air/; take the first sound away and it says _____?"

- "Say 'ball' without the /b/."

- Use blocks to represent sounds. Yellow block is "moo," the red block is /n/. Take the red block away and you have "moo."

Edelen-Smith, P. J. (1997). "How now brown cow: Phoneme awareness activities for collaborative classrooms." *Interventions in School and Clinic*, 33, 103–111. Reprinted by permission of Pro-Ed journals.

Pretend Reading

Pretend reading can play an important role in a child's emergent literacy development. It is the accurate recitation of the words on the pages of a book that a child has "memorized" by listening to the book read aloud many times. When a child is able to pretend-read a book, she or he is on the way to becoming self-instructional in reading, since each time he or she "reads" the book, he or she is looking at the words on the page, as he or she recites what he or she has memorized. This repetition soon makes sight words of many or most of the words in that book. Pretend reading is not a "prerequisite" to reading development, and there are no ill effects to children who never do it. However, it is a worthy classroom goal, since it can build children's confidence in themselves as readers, and provide important "practice time." Children can be encouraged to pretend-read by helping them to select short books to be reread to them many times, and by praising them as they begin to pretend-read, rather than scoffing that they have "just memorized" the words.

Sulzby (1985) developed a classification scheme for children's emergent "reading" performances to aid observation of their progress. A simplified version of this classification is shown in Figure 7.4.

Reflection

Before you read the next section, write your own definition of "invented spelling." List benefits of encouraging emergent readers (and writers) to use invented spelling, and list possible criticisms or concerns of "invented spelling."

Writing: Invented Spelling

Invented spelling, as defined by Burns and Richgels (1989) is "children's ability to attend to sound units in words and associate letters with those units in a systematic though nonconventional way before being taught to spell or read" (1–2). We expect to observe the developmental process in children's spoken language, as we celebrate a child's *"ma ma"* that stands for *mother*. However, as a child grows older, we expect *"ma ma"* to be replaced

FIGURE **7.4**

SIMPLIFIED VERSION OF THE SULZBY STORYBOOK READING CLASSIFICATION SCHEME

Broad Categories	Brief Explanation of Categories
1. Attending to Pictures, Not Forming Stories	The child is "reading" by looking at the storybook's pictures in view; the child is not "weaving a story" across the pages. (Subcategories are "labeling and commenting" and "following the action.")
2. Attending to Pictures, Forming ORAL Stories	The child is "reading" by looking at the storybook's pictures. The child's speech weaves a story across the pages but the wording and the intonation are like that of someone telling a story, either like a conversation about the pictures or like a fully recited story, in which the listener can see the pictures (and often *must* see them to understand the child's story). (Subcategories are "dialogic storytelling" and "monologic storytelling.")
3. Attending to Pictures, Reading and Storytelling Mixed	This category for the simplified version was originally the first subcategory of (4). It fits between (2) and (4) and is easier to understand if it is treated separately. The child is "reading" by looking at the storybook's pictures. The child's speech fluctuates between sounding like a storyteller, with oral intonation, and sounding like a reader, with reading intonation. To fit this category, the majority of the reading attempt must show fluctuations between storytelling and reading.
4. Attending to Pictures, Forming WRITTEN Stories	The child is "reading" by looking at the storybook's pictures. The child's speech sounds as if the child is reading, both in the wording and intonation. The listener does not need to look at the pictures (or rarely does) in order to understand the story. If the listener closes his/her eyes, most of the time he or she would think the child is reading from print. (Subcategories are "reading similar-to-original story," and "reading verbatim-like story.")
5. Attending to Print	There are four subcategories of attending to print. Only the *final* one is what is typically called "real reading." In the others the child is exploring the print by such strategies as refusing to read based on print-related reasons, or using only some of the aspects of print. (Subcategories are "refusing to read based on print awareness," "reading aspectually," "reading with strategies imbalanced," and "reading independently" or "conventional reading.")

Sulzby, 1991, *The Reading Teacher,* 500.

with the conventional term of *mother* or *mom.* The spelling process is very similar. While teachers celebrate the spelling attempt of each newly written word when children are learning to express themselves in writing, we also need to actively move children toward conventional spelling. Invented spelling should be considered temporary, and it is critical that teachers actively balance their encouragement of invented spelling while applying Vygotsky's (1978, 1986) scaffolding to instruction in conventional spelling (Gentry, 2000). Invented spelling should not be synonymous with an absence of direct teacher influence in spelling, although some teachers have interpreted it that way. When learning to speak, children experience scaffolding, or interactions with someone who knows more in that area. In the same way, teachers need to provide active support for students in their spelling development.

Invented spelling enhances children's writing because it frees them from the fear of misspelled words that can inhibit their creative flow of words on paper (Brasachhio, Kuhn, & Martin, 2001; Gill, 1997; Nicholson, 1996). While encouraging invented spelling, Gentry (2000) suggests that the emergent reader's spelling program should include: a Word Wall with high-frequency words *that are practiced* (emphasis is the author's), letter tiles to teach children patterns and how to form correct spellings, wall charts of word families with high-frequency phonograms (such as, *-at*, *-ot*, *-it*, *-ap*) and spell checks on words (for example, *hen, pet, yes, bed,* and *get,* or *did, it, in, if,* and *him* by January of first grade). Personal spelling journals containing words that a child can spell correctly are also important.

To assess phonemic awareness (discussed in a previous section), in January of first grade ask the class to spell *camel* (CAML), a familiar word in spoken vocabulary but not often seen in print at this age. The words *eagle* (EGL), *bacon* (BAKN), or *magic* (MAJEK) could also be used. If a child's spelling represents all of the phonemes in the spoken word, the child has phonemic awareness. Gentry (2000) notes that "how children handle phonics patterns in invented and conventional spelling ought to be one powerful indicator of the phonics knowledge that they access when they read" (330). When children have learned to read a specific pattern in words—consonant-vowel-consonant (c-v-c) or combinations of consonant sounds—it is helpful to give a spelling test with that pattern (for example, *pup, run, bib,* and *web* or *milk, hand, stamp,* and *nest*) to see if the students are transferring the knowledge into their own reading and writing. If students are not transferring and applying the knowledge they are learning, then it is necessary to use direct intervention strategies. These strategies will be discussed later in the chapter with spelling assessment. "Beginning writing with invented spelling can be helpful for developing understanding of phoneme identification, phoneme segmentation, and sound-spelling relationships" (Snow, Burns, & Griffin, 1998, 323), skills that encourage transition from emergent to beginning literacy.

Add the security of a "word wall" to spelling and word attack.

BEGINNING READING INSTRUCTION

Word Walls anchor **sight word acquisition,** phonetic word attack strategies, and spelling development. The focus of beginning reading instruction is on "growing" children's sight word vocabularies as the information base for using elements of known words to decode unknown and longer words in order to reconstruct and respond to the meaning of written material. Sight words and decoding strategies must be taught together, since one needs a core sight word vocabulary to use in decoding, and one needs to be able to decode in order to increase one's sight word vocabulary—which, eventually, needs to include almost all words one encounters in print. One of the most effective ways to do this is the Word Wall approach. A **Word Wall** is a collection of easy words, each containing one of the most frequently occurring letter clusters in the English language. These words are taught a few at a time as sight words (usually three to six per week), and posted to the wall on the day they are introduced. Once a word is on the wall, and learned as a sight word, it becomes a tool for decoding and spelling other words containing that letter cluster, and children are taught strategies for doing so. For example, if a child encounters "frowning" as an unfamiliar word, he might say, "what are some words I know with these parts? I know *frog*, and *down*, and *king*, so this would be *fr* like in frog and *own* like in down, and *ing* like in king—*frowning*." Teaching children to use known words to decode unknown words in this way is referred to as an **analogic approach** to phonics instruction.

Researchers and teachers at the Benchmark School, a private school in Philadelphia, developed the Word Wall list in Figure 7.5, along with many techniques for using the words to teach decoding with direct instruction in strategies such as: 1) stretch out the pronunciations of words to analyze each sound in the words; 2) analyze the visual form of words; 3) talk about matches between sounds and letters and group letters into chunks; 4) note similarities to sounds and letters in other words already learned; and 5) remember how to spell the words (Gaskins et al., 1996, 319).

Word Walls are environmental anchors for sight word acquisition.

FIGURE **7.5**

BENCHMARK SCHOOL WORD LIST

Words for teaching the most frequently occurring spelling patterns in the English language:

-a		-e		-i		-o		-u		-y	
gr	ab	h	e	h	i	g	o	cl	ub	m	y
pl	ace	sp	eak	m	ice	b	oat	tr	uck	(ba)b	y
bl	ack	scr	eam	k	ick	j	ob	bl	ue	g	ym
h	ad	y	ear	d	id	cl	ock	b	ug		
m	ade	tr	eat	sl	ide	fr	og	dr	um		
fl	ag	r	ed	kn	ife	br	oke	j	ump		
sn	ail	s	ee	p	ig		old	f	un		
r	ain	bl	eed	r	ight	fr	om	sk	unk		
m	ake	qu	een	l	ike		on		up		
t	alk	sl	eep	sm	ile	ph	one		us		
	all	sw	eet	w	ill	l	ong		use		
	am	t	ell	sw	im	z	oo	b	ut		

-a		-e		-i		-o		-u	-y
n	ame	th	em	t	ime	g	ood		
ch	amp	t	en		in	f	ood		
c	an		end	f	ind	l	ook		
	and	t	ent	f	ine	sch	ool		
m	ap	h	er	k	ing	st	op		
c	ar	y	es	th	ink	f	or		
sh	ark	n	est	sh	ip	m	ore		
sm	art	l	et	squ	irt	c	ome		
sm	ash	fl	ew	th	is	n	ose		
h	as			w	ish	n	ot		
	ask				it	c	ould		
c	at			wr	ite	r	ound		
sk	ate			f	ive	y	our		
br	ave			g	ive	sc	out		
s	aw					c	ow		
d	ay					gl	ow		
						d	own		
						b	oy		

g	g = j	c = k	c = s
girl	gym	can	city
go	giraffe	corn	excitement
bug		club	princess
grab		discover	centipede
dragon			
glow			

an i mal	choc o late	thank ful	ex cite ment	ques tion	un happy
con test	dis cover	drag on	pres i dent	re port	va ca tion
crea ture					

Note: The Benchmark School found it useful to add several "glue words" to this list—words like *the, this, which, what*—selected not for phonogram representation but for their high-frequency functional nature. These words are put on cards of a different color and shape to differentiate them from the other words on the wall.

Reprinted by permission of Irene W. Gaskins, director of the Benchmark School.

Phonograms, word families, onsets and rimes, and letter clusters are all near-identical names for a powerful way to teach phonics by the groupings of letters.

The worksheet activities in Figure 7.6 also were developed to guide children to think about and work with words on their own and with their classmates.

See Figure 7.7 (page 264) for an example of how the new words for the week are introduced and taught at the Benchmark School.

Allen (1998) used the Word Wall approach to teaching word identification, selecting words from children's literature. In this approach, which he called the Integrated Strategies Approach, the words to represent high-frequency phonograms were selected for the Word Wall from children's

FIGURE **7.6**

SAMPLE WORD WALL ACTIVITIES

Talk-to-Yourself Chart

1. The word is _____.

2. Stretch the word. I hear _____ sounds.

3. I see _____ letters because _____. (Students reconcile the number of letters they see with the number of sounds they hear.)

4. The spelling pattern I know is _____.

5. This is what I know about the vowel: _____.

6. Another word on the Word Wall with the same vowel sound is _____.

Partner-Sharing Chart

Person 1:

1. My word is _____.

2. My Word Wall word is _____.

3. The words are alike because _____.

4. Do you agree?

Person 2:

Give one of these answers:

Yes/No, because _____.

Switch roles.

Making Words Chart

Person 1:

1. My word is _____.

2. My new word is _____.

3. I made this word because I know _____.

4. Do you agree?

Person 2:

Give one of these answers:

Yes/No, because _____.

Switch roles.

If you finish early, pick other Word Wall words and make them into new words.

_____

Gaskins, Ehri, Cress, O'Hara, & Donnelly, 1996/1997, *The Reading Teacher,* 320–322.

FIGURE **7.7**

TEACHING WORDS FOR THE CLASSROOM WORD WALL

Monday New Words

- *Introduce new words.* Put the six new weekly anchor words (familiar words are vocabulary words containing a high-frequency spelling pattern) at the top of chart paper.

  Example: nose, princess, round, make, stop, rain.

- *Student volunteers pronounce a word and think of one to two rhyming words.* Choose a student volunteer to pronounce one of the new key words and think of one or two words with the same spelling pattern. Write the rhyming words under the new word (if children suggest a word that rhymes but doesn't have the same spelling pattern, put that word in brackets).

- *Structured Language Experience Exercise.* Guide students in making up a story using the six new words. ("The reasons to do that are, we want to get these new words up here in isolation, or singly, into a story real fast so you see that words belong with other words to make sentences. Does anyone have an idea how we might start this?") Write the story on chart paper, making revisions as you go. Students read the finished story along with the teacher.

- *Students write each new word and a rhyming word.* Say one of the new words and use it in a sentence. The children write the word on their paper. Then say a word with the same spelling pattern, and use that word in a sentence. Children may look at the words as you write them on chart paper, but encourage them to look at the letters as clusters, rather than individual letters. Go through all the new spelling patterns in the same way. Children now have each of the new words on their paper, paired with a second word with the same spelling pattern. Give children an opportunity to check their papers.

- Oral spelling and rhyming word recitation. Point to the first word on the chart, and have children spell it aloud together. Ask one child to spell the word from his or her paper that has the same spelling pattern as the word they just spelled together. Go through all words in the same way. Walk around and double-check that everyone has a perfect paper.

- *"What's In My Head?" review.* Give five clues to help children guess the word you are thinking of. (Use *"onset," "rime,"* and syllable clues: The word begins

with the letter ____; the word is a "one-beat" word; the word rhymes with ____; and so on.) Later in the week, use words from the entire wall for the game.

Daily Word Study

- *Use Word Wall anchor words to decode long words.* Model the use of word identification strategies by putting up a sentence containing a long word that has word patterns like those already on the Word Wall.

  Example: Many trademarks on cereals are familiar.

  Then say, for example, "Many BLANKS on cereals are familiar. Well, I know *made* and I know *shark,* and in my head, I'm just taking off the ending, like we do. Because I'm not going to worry about that quite yet. And then I'm going to say, If this is *made,* this is *trade,* and if this is *shark,* this is *mark.* And then, of course, the *S* makes [*s*]. Now, am I finished? No, because reading always has to make sense and you have to read it over. Many trademarks on cereals are familiar. Do you know what a trademark is?"

  Another Example: Prepayment

  "I'm going to look at this and I'm going to say, "You must make a BLANK to get the TV.""

  "So, I know the word *he* (writes the word *he* on the board.) I know the word *day* (writes day). And I know the word *tent* (writes *tent*). So I would say to myself, "If this is *he,* this is *pre.* If this is *day,* this is *pay.* If this is *tent,* this is *ment. Prepayment.*"

  "Am I finished?—No, I have to go back and read the sentence over. Because reading always makes sense."

  "You must make a *prepayment* to get the TV." Do you know what *prepayment* means? (Ask for suggestions from the class.)

- *Tongue twisters using onsets.*

  Example: "Scrawny scribble scratched his scribbles into his scrapbook."

- *"Ready-Set-Show."*

  Example: Have children take out index cards with the words *scream, spider,* and *splash* written on them. Call out words that begin with either *s-c-r, s-p-l,* or *s-p* sounds. Because you can see all children's cards as they hold them up, you can immediately help children who are having difficulties.

• *Worksheet activities.* Have children complete a worksheet to give more guided practice with compare/contrast. As children finish, they can become checkers, using the compare/contrast scripts to help classmates:

Example: "If this is *rain*, this is *pain*. If this is *make*, this is *take*. If this is *snail*, this is *trail*.

Teaching Reading: Strategies for Successful Classrooms. Word Identification (videotape), Center for the Study of Reading. Reprinted by permission of Irene W. Gaskins, director of Benchmark School.

FIGURE **7.8**

INTEGRATED STRATEGIES APPROACH

Essential Components

1. Understanding rhyme (rhyming games and activities based on children's needs, reciting and acting out rhymes, puppet games to produce or identify rhyme pairs, reading aloud from texts that rhyme)

2. Learning key words and their spelling patterns (rimes or phonograms) to spell and decode new words by analogy (compare and contrast procedure like Benchmark Word Identification program)

3. Learning to use the cross-checking strategy (students make the first sound of the unknown word, skip the word and read on, then return to the word to look for other letter-clues that might work with what makes sense in the sentence or passage)

4. Learning to spell and read a core of high-frequency words (sight words)

Instructional Tools and Techniques

1. Teacher modeling and student application of integrated strategy

2. Using a Word Wall to support spelling and reading activities

3. Opportunities to practice strategy use in quality, developmentally appropriate children's literature

4. Writing and other response activities that are naturally developed from the literature

Compiled from Allen, 1998, 256

literature: Each word was taken from a children's book that includes repeated examples of the targeted phonogram. The -*at* phonogram, for example, might be introduced from the literature base of *The Cat in the Hat.* Frequently occurring sight words also were identified for direct instruction and practice. Essential components and instructional tools and techniques of this approach are shown in Figure 7.8. Notice in particular the "cross-checking" strategy described as item 3 under "Essential Components."

The Integrated Strategies Approach was used as a tutoring approach for primary-grade (mostly second and third graders who read at a primer level or below) urban children who were considered at-risk and participated in an after-school small-group tutoring project. Allen (1998) reports that data collected over three years shows that 70 percent of the children tutored could read grade-level materials after 1 year of tutoring. A follow-up study of the graduates of the tutoring program showed that "80 percent of the children who were part of our tutoring project in the primary grades are now reading at grade level or above as intermediate-grade students" (Allen, 1998, 266).

Integrated Strategies as Early Intervention.

Students who used the analogy approach together with cross-checking showed the greatest gains. Adding the cross-checking procedure to the analogy approach holds promise for the classroom and for remediation as it connects a focus on decoding with a focus on meaning. It is important to remember that when facing any unknown word, students should first be encouraged to pronounce any word part that they already know, since it is more direct and easier to use, before guiding them to think of an analogous word (Gunning, 1995). Word building is one way to enhance the decoding and invented spelling connection.

Word-building, or *making words*, activities (Cunningham & Cunningham, 1992) engage individual children to use given letters to make two-, three-, four-, five-letter and even longer words until the final word is made using all of the letters. It is designed to be used along with invented spelling and other writing activities, to encourage children's decoding ability. The specific steps for planning a Making Words lesson are listed in Figure 7.9. During the Making Words lesson, each student has a set of letters and the teacher has a pocket chart (or uses the chalk ledge) with large letter cards. The teacher writes the number of letters in the words on the board, and students make one word at a time as the teacher says it. After the teacher has guided the making of two-, three-, four-, and five-letter words,

FIGURE **7.9**

STEPS IN PLANNING A MAKING WORDS LESSON

1. Decide what the final word in the lesson will be. In choosing this word, consider its number of vowels, child interest, curriculum tie-ins you can make, and the letter-sound patterns you can draw children's attention to through the word sorting at the end.

2. Make a list of shorter words that can be made from the letters of the final word.

3. From all the words you listed, pick twelve to fifteen words that include: a) words that you can sort for the pattern(s) you want to emphasize; b) little words and big words so that the lesson is multilevel; c) words that can be made with the same letters in different places (for example, *barn, bran*) so children are reminded that when spelling words, the order of the letters is crucial; d) a proper name or two to remind them where we use capital letters; and e) words that most of the students have in their listening vocabularies.

4. Write all the words on index cards and order them from shortest to longest.

5. Once you have the two-letter, three-letter, and longer words together, order them further so that you can emphasize letter patterns and how changing the position of the letters or changing or adding just one letter results in a different word.

6. Store the cards in an envelope. Write on the envelope the words in order and the patterns you will sort for at the end.

Cunningham & Cunningham, 1992, *The Reading Teacher.*

the teacher asks, "Who can guess what word can be made using all of the letters?" Then the children make that word. Next, the teacher leads the children in a word sort activity. An example warm-up Making Words lesson, from Hall's book *Making Words* (1994) is in Figure 7.10.

Children view the Making Words activity as a game, and they enjoy the fast pace, every-pupil-response, hands-on activity while they are learning phonics patterns. While building words, the children construct, break apart, and reconstruct common word patterns (Clay, 1993). The teacher can choose a model word for the pattern used, that can be posted on the Word Wall for future reference. This activity is not limited to beginning

FIGURE **7.10**

WARM-UP LESSON #1

Make Words

Take two letters and make *at.*

Add a letter to make the three-letter word *art.*

Change the letters around and turn *art* into *tar.*

Now change just one first letter and *tar* can become *car.*

Now we are going to make some four-letter words. Hold up four fingers! Add one letter to *car* and you have *cart.* (The little boy pushed the cart.)

Change the last letter and you can change *cart* into *cars.* Instead of one cart you now have a number of cars.

Don't take any letters out, change the letters around, and you can make *cars* into *scar.*

Change one letter and you can change *scar* into *star.* (Maybe someday you will be a star.)

Now take all the letters out and make another four-letter word, *scat.* (The woman told the cat to scat.)

Let's make another word, *cash.*

Change just the first letter and you can change *cash* into *rash.* (When you have poison ivy, you have a rash.)

Now let's make a five-letter word. Hold up five fingers! Add a letter to *rash* and you can make *trash.*

Change the first letter and you can change your *trash* to *crash.* (Often race-car drivers end up in a crash.)

Let's make another five-letter word. Use five letters to make *chart.* (The teacher likes to make a new chart every time we study something new.)

Has anyone figured out what word we can make with all seven letters? Take all seven of your letters and make *scratch.*

Sort

When the children have made *scratch,* draw their attention to the words they made and help them sort for a variety of patterns: *at, art, tar, car, cart, cars, scar, star, scat, cash, rash, trash, crash, chart, scratch.*

Take the word *car* and have them find the other words that begin with c—*cart, cars, cash.*

Take the word *car* and have them find the other *a-r* words—*scar* and *star.*

Take the word *art* and have them find the other *a-r-t* words—*cart, chart.*

Take the word *cash* and have them find the other *a-s-h* words—*rash, crash,* and *trash.*

Take the word *at* and have them find words that have the same vowel sound as in *at*—*cash, scat, rash, trash, crash,* and *scratch.*

Take the word *car* and have the children find words that have the same vowel sound as in *car*—*art, tar, cart, cars, scar, star,* and *chart.*

Writing and Need to Spell

What if you were writing about yourself and you needed to spell *smart*? Which words would help you spell *smart*? What if you were writing about swimming and needed to spell *splash*?

Cunningham & Hall (1994) *Making Words, Good Apple,* 9.

FIGURE **7.11**

MAKING BIG WORDS LESSON

Letters:	e i i g h n p r s w
Words to make:	wish ring rise wise wipe wire hire wren
	wring gripe swipe
	perish wiping wiring hiring
	wishing griping swiping inspire whisper
	perishing whispering
Sort for:	ing wr ire ipe ise ring-wring
Writing and need to spell:	rap, wrap (wr-) rapping, wrapping (-ing)

Cunningham & Hal (1994), *Making Big Words, Good Apple,* 109.

readers, because more complex words can be built. An example Making Big Words lesson (Cunningham & Hall, 1994) is shown in Figure 7.11.

While teaching parents to use word-building activities with their children, an author used the letters *a e n p r r s t.* After leading the parents through a word-building lesson with -*at*, -*ar*, and other patterns, the parents ended by making the words *parents, are, partners.* Sending a set of letters home with students and the directions for guided word-building activities once a week is a good home-school connection.

Teachers and reading specialists who work with older students with word identification needs—individually or in small groups—can use a variety of inventive and dynamic adaptations of the Word Wall approach to anchor word attack:

- Use a large but portable foamcore board as the "wall," and have students print and post the cards themselves.
- Have each student individually make his or her Word Wall on the inside of a file folder: Using both sides, make enough lines for all of the words that will eventually be included. As words are introduced, have the student write them on the lines.
- For each student, type, 3-hole punch, and laminate a single-page list of the Word Wall words, such as the one in Figure 7.11, and cover each block of words to be introduced in a session with colored tape. As each block of words is introduced, remove the tape to uncover the words. Students' word lists can be kept in a binder with lists of books read, Language Experience stories, and other writing samples.

Next consider some very direct instructional methods that are organized and sorted to some very specific word analysis and recognition needs. The first one could be called a "legacy" method since it has a rich and continuing historical role in reading instruction.

STRATEGIC WORD ANALYSIS TECHNIQUES

Gray's Paradigm for Word Analysis

This approach tends to merge synthetic and analytic phonics. It is based on teaching students to recognize words that they already have in their speaking vocabulary, and to successfully decode words not previously known. The paradigm for teaching in this way often is attributed to William S. Gray, sometimes called the "founder of modern reading instruction." This model for analytical-synthetic phonics instruction probably represents the earliest and most complete articulation of this approach to reading instruction, and remains the basis for most subsequent forms of word analysis training (Gray, 1948). Notice as you review this slightly modified version that this four-step procedure regularly teaches visual identification of graphemes and aural (or auditory) identification of phonemes (Steps 1 and 2). It then proceeds to teach phonemic/phonetic blending—called an *analogic* approach because it uses one of the most basic principles of learning, namely, using "known" parts of words to unlock "unknown" parts: seeing *as* in *has* (Step 3). It comes together in another basic principle of teaching-learning known as *application and transfer of training*. Here, it requires a Context-Comprehension Activity (Step 4), which reinforces both word analysis and rapid word identification with relatively simple text (that is, within a child's *Zone of Proximal Development*, as we would refer to it today). This "fail-proof" paradigm is detailed and illustrated below using the "**squ**" blend.

> A professional "prescription" of phonics instruction should include some precise ways to do so.

STEP 1: VISUAL AND AURAL "FIXING"

a. Recognizing visual similarities: Words are written on the board. The student circles the part(s) that all the words have in common:

> *squirrel   squeeze   squeak   square   squint*

b. Recognizing aural similarities: Using the same list as above, the teacher reads each word from the board, giving only slight emphasis to the **squ** sound. The students try to identify the sound that each word has in common. The auditory step may precede the visual step if the student tends to have an auditory orientation.

STEP 2: VISUAL AND AURAL DISCRIMINATION

a. Visual discrimination: Presenting words in groups of three, the student first underlines **squ** in each word where it is found. Next, the student attempts to say only those words containing the **squ** sound:

queen	*retire*	*squirrel*	*shrimp*
squat	*squirt*	*squirm*	*spring*
whom	*whenever*	*sprint*	*squeaky*

b. Auditory discrimination: The teacher says three words. Without seeing the words, the student identifies the word(s) containing the **squ** sound:

squeal	*squash*	*shield*	*squelch*
spur	*squid*	*square*	*squeak*
dig	*send*	*squash*	*squat*

STEP 3: BLENDING (SUBSTITUTION)

The teacher shows the student how to blend and substitute sounds to form new words.

Example: Substitute the **squ** sound for the existing sound at the beginning of each word:

> *ball – b = all + squ = squall* *wire – w = ire + squ = squire*
>
> *what – wh = at + squ = squat* *tint – t = int = squ = squint*

STEP 4: CONTEXTUAL APPLICATION

The student underlines words containing the **squ** sound, which are embedded in sentences:

- *He led a **squad** of men into battle.*
- *He leads a **squadron** in the army.*
- *Try not to **squash** it, please.*

> Gray's Paradigm is a comprehensive model for phonics instruction; though few seem to remember it.

Word Building with Phonograms

With a growing knowledge of high-frequency phonograms, students can generate many new words that are "the basis for syllabic chunks that occur in thousands of multisyllabic words as well" (Johnston, 1999, 67). Since the vowel pronunciation in the words-within-a-word family is more stable than across families (Adams, 1990; Whylie & Durrell, 1970), it is much easier for children to read the words and generalize the pattern to syllables in other words. *Word families* are sets of words made from the same *phonogram* or *rime*. A *phonogram* or *rime* is the vowel sound plus the consonants that follow in a syllable (Fry, 1998). Onsets are the beginning consonants that are placed in front of a rime to make words (for example, when the onsets *s, h,* and *m* are added to the rime *-at,* the words formed are *sat, hat,* and *mat*). "The ability to hear, see, and use the rime as a reliable cue for reading new words and spelling words that sound alike offers students a powerful insight into how English spelling (and reading) works" (Johnston, 1999, 64). Analyzing the readings of 7-year-old children showed that no matter what approach to reading instruction was used, the most frequent strategy children used was to pronounce the beginning consonant and then the whole

FIGURE **7.12**

MOST COMMON PHONOGRAMS IN RANK ORDER BASED ON FREQUENCY
(number of uses in monosyllabic words)

Frequency	Rime	Example words	Frequency	Rime	Example words
26	-ay	jay say pay day play	16	-op	mop cop pop top hop
26	-ill	hill Bill will fill spill	16	-in	pin tin win chin thin
22	-ip	ship dip tip skip trip	16	-an	pan man ran tan Dan
19	-at	cat fat bat rat sat	16	-est	best nest pest rest test
19	-am	ham jam dam ram Sam	16	-ink	pink sink rink link drink
19	-ag	bag rag tag wag sag	16	-ow	low slow grow show snow
19	-ack	back sack Jack black track	16	-ew	new few chew grew blew
19	-ank	bank sank tank blank drank	16	-ore	more sore tore store score
19	-ick	sick Dick pick quick chick	15	-ed	bed red fed led Ted
18	-ell	bell sell fell tell yell	15	-ab	cab dab jab lab crab
18	-ot	pot not hot dot got	15	-ob	cob job rob Bob knob
18	-ing	ring sing king wing thing	15	-ock	sock rock lock dock block
18	-ap	cap map tap clap trap	15	-ake	cake lake make take brake
18	-unk	sunk junk bunk flunk skunk	15	-ine	line nine pine fine shine
17	-ail	pail jail nail sail tail	14	-ight	knight light right night fright
17	-ain	rain pain main chain plain	14	-im	swim him Kim rim brim
17	-eed	feed seed weed need freed	14	-uck	duck luck suck truck buck
17	-y	my by dry try fly	14	-um	gum bum hum drum plum
17	-out	pout trout scout shout spout			
17	-ug	rug bug hug dug tug			

Fry, 1998, *The Reading Teacher*, 621.
All 634 words are available in Fry, Kress, & Fountoukidis, 2000, *The Reading Teacher's Book of Lists*, 31–40.

word (*ruh-rip*) (Gunning, 1995), or the use of onsets and rimes and word identification by analogy.

Fry (1998) determined that 654 different one-syllable words can be made from just 38 phonograms with beginning consonants added (see Figure 7.12).

How do we know when and how to teach phonograms? Children's invented spellings reveal what the children already know and what they are ready to learn (Invernizzi, Abouzeid, & Gill, 1994). Johnston suggests four stages based on invented spelling that should guide word family instruction (see Figure 7.13).

FIGURE **7.13**

USING CHILDREN'S SPELLING TO PLAN WORD STUDY INSTRUCTION

Stage and sample spellings	What the child knows and confuses	What the child is ready to study
Emergent pan = STU, wet = SMB, pan = P, wet = T, bug = B	Words are made of letters, but letter-to-sound consonant correspondences are lacking or incomplete.	Study alphabet if needed, and beginning consonant sounds. Plan language play with rhymes.
Early Letter Name pan = PN, wet = YT, bug = BG, chin = JN	Initial and final consonants are represented consistently, but medial short vowels are missing.	Start with one word family at a time and then compare word families with the same vowel.
Letter Name pan = PAN, bug = BOG, chin = JEN, trip = CHRP	Short vowels are used but are generally inaccurate; some blends and digraphs are in place.	Compare words families with mixed vowels and include words with blends and digraphs.
Within Words Pattern PAN, BUG, CHIN, FLIP, boat = BOTE or BOATE, Steam = STEME or STEEM, float = FLOTE or FLOWT	Short vowels, blends, and digraphs are correct for the most part. Using but confusing long vowel patterns.	Compare and contrast short and long vowel patterns. Occasionally explore word families.

Johnston, 1999, 68

Glass's "No Rules" Phonetic Analysis

Two simple "scripts" guide word analysis and recognition.

Gerald G. Glass (1973) developed a simple method for teaching the decoding aspects of reading. The method, called Glass Analysis, consists of two "scripts" for analyzing the ways letters and letter clusters combine to form words. This approach tends to appeal to a common human capability called *associative learning*—it goes right to our ability to quickly learn patterns from repeated exposure and conditioned responding. (See Figure 7.14 for details on this odd fact.) The scripts are compatible with strategies used by successful decoders (Glass & Burton, 1973). One script is to ask what *sound* a given letter or letter cluster makes; the other script is to ask what *letter* or *letter cluster* makes a given sound.

Glass has identified 119 letter clusters by their frequency of occurrence in initial reading material, and their utility in helping children to decode more rapidly. These letter clusters (listed in Figure 7.15) can be used to develop word lists for Glass Analysis instruction. Glass also has marketed boxed word cards, arranged by letter cluster, to facilitate use of the Glass Analysis decoding approach. These inexpensive materials also include a quick program for teaching the alphabet.

The Glass Analysis method emphasizes the following basic ideas:

- Students should look at the target word throughout the lesson.
- Avoid undue attention to word meaning during the initial emphasis on sound decoding and word recognition.

FIGURE **7.14**

ASSOCIATIVE LEARNING: UNRECOGNIZED COMMON GROUND?

The decoding aspect of reading, which is like *training*, relies in great part on *associative learning.* Most all human beings have about an equal capacity for such conditioned response learning—at least there is far less variability on this factor than other "higher" cognitive abilities. This fact, or some part of it, may explain why explicit or synthetic phonics, which looks mentally challenging but is very drill-oriented, works a bit better with low SES children (U.S. Department of Health and Human Services, 2000). Most IQ tests, with the exception of the Digit Span subtest of the WISC-R (which only approximates it) do not even bother measuring this factor. High-level cognitive functions, such as problem solving and rule-based learning, can aid progress, but it can be argued that much of this seemingly higher cognitive learning simply provides longer exposure to letters and words, and therefore raises consciousness of letter-sound patterns. There is some inferential logic to support this. If reading were not largely an *associative learning,* or pattern-recognition, rapid-response skill, many *fewer* people would be able to learn how to read; but most all do, even those assessed as "low functioning." Of course, the 50 percent of youngsters below 100 on the bell-shaped curve will tend to learn to read at a slower rate. However, the fact that the decoding aspect of reading is more *associative* than we might think for average students is convincing, based on research on exceptional children with William's Syndrome. These youngsters, for the most part developmentally disabled with an IQ range of 50 to 70, often learn "how to read" at a rather extraordinary rate, though with very weak comprehension, and despite remarkably high levels of vocabulary. One William's Syndrome child, when asked to name all the animals he could think of, quickly reeled off over twenty, including "brontosaurus, tyranadon, whale, yak, koala, and ibex" (Finn, 1991).

- Keep a very brisk pace.
- Avoid discussion of phonic rules such as dropping the final "e" before adding a suffix.
- Avoid breaking up units that logically belong together (for example, *th, wr, ing, st*).
- Reinforce correct responses, and do not punish incorrect ones. If a student cannot answer a question, merely state the answer and return to it again before leaving that word.

STEPS IN GLASS ANALYSIS

Step 1   Check to make sure the student knows the alphabet and most of the letter sounds.

Step 2   Pick a set of word cards that teach a particular letter cluster.

example: the letter cluster "eck"

Step 3   Seat the student beside you, and show the first word card. Ask if the student can pronounce it; if not, you pronounce it and have the student repeat it.

example: What is the word? [pecking]

Step 4   Starting with the letter cluster of the packet, focus on as many letters and letter clusters as is reasonable, asking what *letters* make a given sound.

FIGURE **7.15**

LETTER CLUSTERS (BY DIFFICULTY LEVEL) FOR USE WITH GLASS ANALYSIS

Starters	Medium One	Medium Two	Harder One	Harder Two
1. at	1. ed	1. all	1. fowl	1. er
2. ing	2. ig	2. aw	2. us	2. air
3. et	3. ip	3. el	3. ll(l)	3. al
4. it	4. ud	4. eck	4. ite	4. ied
5. ot	5. id	5. ice	5. es(s)	5. ew
6. im	6. en	6. ick	6. om	6. ire
7. op	7. ug	7. if(f)	7. oke	7. ear
8. an	8. ut	8. ink	8. ore	8. eal
9. ay	9. ar	9. ob	9. *tow*	9. *tea*
10. ed	10. em	10. od	10. ast	10. ee
11. am	11. up	11. og	11. ane	11. *care*
12. un	12. ate	12. ub	12. eat	12. d*eaf*
13. in	13. ent	13. uf(f)	13. as(s)	13. oat
14. ap	14. est	14. ush	14. ev	14. ue
15. and	15. ake	15. able	15. ind	15. oo
16. act	16. ide	16. ight	16. oss	16. ou
17. um	17. ock	17. is(s)	17. oem	17. ound
18. ab	18. ade	18. on	18. ost	18. ure
19. ag	19. ame	19. or	19. r*ol(l)*	19. ture
20. old	20. ape	20. ul(l)	20. one	20. ur
21. ash	21. ace	21. ac	21. ate	21. ir
22. ish	22. any	22. af(f)	22. ave	22. ai
	23. enk	23. ook	23. ove	23. au
	24. ong	24. tion	24. *folly*	24. oi
	25. age			

example: *What letters make the* eck *sound?*
What letters make the ing *sound?*
What letters make the p *sound?*

For words that contain only the teaching cluster plus an initial letter (like *cat*), treat the initial letter as you would a cluster so that the student has been exposed to all letter sounds in the word.

Step 5   Focus on sounds next, asking what *sound* is made by a given letter cluster or letter.

example: *What sound does the letter **p** make?*

*What sound do the letters **p-e-c-k** make?*
*What sound do the letters **e-c-k** make?*
*What sound do the letters **i-n-g** make?*

Paraprofessionals and Volunteers

The ease and rapid pace of Glass Analysis offers two special advantages for combating functional illiteracy at any level. The first is that paraprofessionals and volunteer workers can be easily trained to use the method with children or adults. The second is that schools can set up "decoding stations" (just two desks facing one another in a quiet place). Here, students with word analysis and recognition problems can be scheduled to make stops for 5- to 15-minute training sessions as often as several times a day until they become proficient (Manzo & Manzo, 1990a).

Discovery (InQuiry) Phonics

The Discovery Phonics Paradigm doubles as a quick technique that can be easily woven into most any phonics lesson. It is a highly cognitive-conceptual approach most often attributed to Morton Botel (1964), but otherwise so intuitive that it is hard to imagine anyone trying to teach phonetic analysis who would not *re-discover* it in the give and take with students. This paradigmatic method is designed to help students to learn to discover for themselves some of the phonetic and structural patterns, or *generalizations*, that make many words decodable. The teacher helps students to "discover" these patterns through *inductive* questioning that develops students' powers of observation, sensitivity to language, and capacity to form concepts about how sounds and words have come to be encoded.

Phonics rules by inductive reasoning.

STEPS IN (BOTEL'S) DISCOVERY TECHNIQUE

Step 1. The teacher provides accurate sensory experiences.

Example: When teaching that some words drop the *e* before endings are added, the teacher might:

a. Put the following known words on the board:

make—making   hope—hoping   ride—riding

b. Ask students to enunciate the words accurately

c. Ask students to note how the base words are alike, and what change to the base word took place each time we added the *ing*. If response comes quickly and accurately, move to Step 2. If not, do not move on to Step 2 for a while. Even when students seem ready for Step 2, the teacher always reviews Step 1, at least briefly.

Step 2. Students examine the structural pattern with teacher guidance, but the teacher does not state the rule.

Example: In adding *ing* to words that end in a silent *e*, the teacher questions students until they arrive at the following findings:

a. The base words have a silent *e* preceded by a long vowel sound.

b. The base words drop the *e* when *ing* is added.

Step 3. Students collect words that fit the pattern.
Students practice finding other words in their word lists and in general reading that fit the pattern, such as:

chase—chasing   close—closing   skate—skating

Step 4. Students generalize the pattern.
A written or oral statement of the rule is formulated. For example, the rule on dropping the *e* before adding *ing* could be stated: *"If a base word contains a long vowel sound and ends in a silent* e, *you drop the* e *before adding* ing.*"*

Botel adds that it is important to the Discovery Technique to also teach students that rules can have many *exceptions*. As students begin to apply rules, he points out, they will find words that do not "behave" according to principles. Therefore, teach rules by pointing out that:

> "A rule tells us what sound to try first. If the word makes sense in the sentence, it is probably right. If not, try another sound. The final test is always the meaning of the word in context" (Botel, 1964, 49).

For example,

She is my <u>niece</u>.

Mother baked <u>bread</u> for us.

Assume that the underlined words in each of these sentences are unfamiliar at sight to the student. If the child has learned the rule that when two vowels appear together the first is generally long and the second silent, the child's first attempts to decode the word will use a long *i* sound in *niece* and the long *e* sound in *bread*. In each case, however, if reading is meaning-driven, the student will reject these choices and keep trying to find a context-appropriate alternative.

Instructional Conversation Paradigm for Teaching Phonics

There are meaning-centered approaches to teaching phonetic analysis. One uses a comprehension-based teaching strategy to teach *phonics* rather explicitly. It can be used as a vehicle for each of the previously-described paradigms, and has some particular attributes of its own. It can be easily customized to subtle individual needs as picked up by the teacher on-the-fly in teaching-learning interactions. It also reaches out to the most essential of all teaching goals: self-instruction.

This type of teaching is meant to become a self-guided strategy, more than just an automatic response skill. The borrowed instructional paradigm for doing so is the ReQuest Procedure (Manzo, 1969; Manzo & Manzo, 1993). ReQuest, as you will see in the next chapter, pioneered the use of *mental modeling* to teach reading comprehension. It did this through an inquiry approach that scaffolds a student's efforts to achieve an initial, self-generated purpose for reading the remainder of a selection. The ReQuest paradigm is based on a game-like situation: Create a reciprocal (rotational) interaction with students over the concepts to be learned. Have them observe, then overtly try to emulate a mental model of high competence as students and teacher ask each other a series of questions about the first few sentences of a selection until a provisional purpose for reading the remainder is identified. Students and teacher read to determine whether they evolved an appropriate purpose-setting question. Then ask what the answer might be to that question. The expectation is that the words spoken and heard in this public conversation will become part of students' internal, or covert, conversations within themselves. This generates the internal guidance, or *strategy*, necessary for ongoing self-instruction. Once the teacher and students have established this *cognitive apprenticeship* relationship, the teacher can easily shift from modeling comprehension processes to other "think alouds" (Davey, 1983) that further model decoding processes. This shift can be seamlessly achieved in regular classrooms as well as in tutorial settings.

Reciprocal Phonics teaches simple and complex scripts through "think alouds."

One way to step down into this more basic word decoding function is simply to ask any of the questions from preceding paradigms. Using either of the two "scripts" from the Glass paradigm, for example, the teacher might ask, when encountering and pronouncing the word "lakefront" in a passage: "Which letters make the 'ache' sound in lakefront? Which letters make the 'fr' sound? Which make the 'ont' sound?" Once students begin to emulate this decoding strategy, the second, inverse script can be introduced into the process: "What sound do the letters 'a-k-e' make in this word (pointing to it)? What sound do the letters 'l-a-k-e' make? What about 'f-r'? 'o-n-t'? How do you say this word?"

In using this approach, the teacher typically will engage in a great deal of *private speech,* or inner-speech, that is audible: for example, "Let's see, where should this word first be divided? What are the regular sounds? Which are irregular?" To gain the secret-sharing effect of this mental-modeling procedure, the teacher has only to mutter loudly enough to be overheard engaging in this complex mental process. Kathleen J. Brown (2003) suggests several prompts to the question: "What do I say when they get stuck on a word?" (720). These can be converted into self-prompting questions; for example, "Break the word into parts and pronounce each one. What sound does _____ make?" Brown adds one further piece of cost-benefit wisdom that every teacher of reading can empathize with: Evaluate the word's orthography against the student's abilities, and determine whether it is best to supply the word to reduce unsettling interference with comprehension (731).

Developmental Precision

Align strategies with a student's stage of development.

A good deal of the teaching of beginning reading occurs when the teacher listens to the child read aloud, providing on-the-spot assistance and (occasional) correction, and talking with the student about the content of what is read. This interaction becomes precision teaching when the teacher aligns the types of assistance, correction, and prompts to the student's developmental level.

Beginning readers who lack word recognition automaticity rely on context, memory, pictures, and blending of individual letters (Chall, 1983; Ehri, 1998; Juel, 1991). At this level, teachers should not attempt to correct all "errors." Kathleen Brown (2003) suggests that word recognition prompts that are appropriate at this level, such as, "What's the first sound? Now look at the picture," are not appropriate for more advanced beginners, with whom more appropriate prompts would include, "Do you see a chunk you know in that word?" and vice versa. As readers progress to higher developmental stages, teachers should expect and scaffold children's oral reading toward greater accuracy and fluency.

SUMMARY OF RESEARCH ON DECODING INSTRUCTION

In a thorough review of the early stages of learning to read, several conclusions were reached which are pertinent to understanding and providing instruction in the decoding process (Juel, 1991). The conclusions most relevant to remedial instruction are summarized here.

- Good decoders encounter roughly twice as many words as poor ones in the earliest stages of reading (Juel, 1988). This suggests that a key goal of beginning reading is to intentionally and systematically ensure that all children spend as much time as reasonably can be allotted in focused and engaged interaction with print.

- There is little evidence to suggest that good readers use context clues more than poor readers. On the contrary, good readers decode words using word analysis techniques that then strengthen their understanding of the context. Readers can only predict about one out of four words from context (Gough, Alford, & Holly-Wilcox, 1981).

- Reading errors of a single word tend to be made in inverse proportion to the number of times a word has been previously exposed in print (Gough, Juel, & Roper-Schneider, 1983). This highlights the importance of high-frequency and phonetically regular text for beginning readers.

- Most poor readers have a "strategy imbalance"—they tend to rely excessively on one (Default) tactic to the exclusion of others (for example, context but not sounding, or glued-to-print, laborious sounding to the exclusion of visual imprinting and context) (Sulzby, 1985; Hill, 1999).

- Several studies and theories have led to the belief that there are essentially three stages to developing decoding skill:

  1. *The selective-cue (pre-decoding) stage:* At this stage, the child initially tends to rely upon three categories of cues and in roughly this order:

     a. random cues—most any visual clue which is present is used to remember what a word might mean, even a thumbprint on a flashcard (Gough, 1981)

     b. environmental cues—such as where the word is located on the page

     c. distinctive letters (the "y" in "pony")

  2. *The spelling-sound stage:* At this stage, the child tends to recognize some words by a combination of visual recall of its spelling and a beginning sense of sounds of some of the letters. The pinnacle of this stage is sounding out and plausibly decoding most words.

  3. *The automatic response stage:* At this stage, a fair-sized vocabulary of frequently-occurring words is recognized automatically. Juel (1991, 783) notes that "We do not know exactly what it is about word recognition that becomes automatic"—recognition of whole words, due to frequent exposure to a small number of words, or letter-sound relations, due to exposure to letter-sound patterns in many different words.

On a cost/benefit basis, it is sometimes best to supply a challenging word when reading for meaning.

- A little bit of phonics can go a long way. It takes a fairly minimal amount of explicit phonics instruction to induce the learning and use of even untaught spelling-sound relationships when the text children are exposed to contains a number of regular decodable words (Juel & Roper-Schneider, 1985).

- The least time should be spent teaching specific phonic rules per se, and a greater amount should be spent in spaced, short-term practice, and actually reading.

Other practices, in combination, can successfully build strategic cue use:

- labeling of objects with printed cards (let children help make the labels and be sure to include multiple languages on the cards for English-language learners)
- language experience activities where students dictate words, sentences, or stories
- use of "Big Books" where children can see the words the teacher is reading (Holdaway, 1979)
- use of patterned, predictable chart stories (Bridge, 1986; Bridge, Winograd, & Haley, 1983)
- when a child asks the question "what's this word?" this gives the strongest evidence that he or she is thinking about reading and print decoding, and hence is on the way to becoming a generative learner (Clark, 1976; Durkin, 1966)

Poor readers generally have a "strategy imbalance"—they tend to excessively Default to one tactic to the exclusion of others.

PHONICS RULES

Teachers and reading specialists working with students at beginning reading levels need to be fairly familiar and conversant with the fundamental rules of phonics for several reasons:

- to select words for sight word, word attack, and spelling instruction
- to analyze students' spelling and oral reading to identify possible areas of need
- to understand the concepts and know the language for explaining to students some of the many seeming "irregularities" of English spelling
- to gradually introduce these rules to students, as they learn to read and spell words that exemplify the most frequently encountered rules
- to follow the professional literature, as it continues to provide insight into the complex systems that determine the way words are spelled

A Primer on Phonics will make you expert on phonics rules in about an hour.

If you are uneasy about teaching phonics rules, in all probability, you are under 40 years old, and have missed such instruction yourself. See Appendix E: Primer on Phonics. It is abridged from much larger compilations.

SIGHT WORD BUILDING

About 85 percent of the words in the English language are phonetically regular; however, the 15 to 20 percent that are *not* appear with the greatest frequency in print, or about 80 percent of the time (Hanna, Hodges, Hanna, & Rudolph, 1966). This happens neither by conspiracy nor by accident. It is in the nature of language: The more a word is used, the more its sounds tend to become relaxed, clipped, or otherwise suitable to oral use, while its print characteristics remain fairly constant. In addition to teaching Word Wall words as sight words, it is practical to teach phonetically irregular, high-frequency words as sight words. An intensive technique for focusing attention on words to be taught as sight words is described next.

About 85 percent of the words in the English language are phonetically regular . . . however, those tend to be the words with the lowest frequency of occurrence.

Intensive Sight Word Paradigm

This technique is highly inclusive and can serve as a general paradigm to guide several alternate and abridged ways to teach sight words. It can be done with one student, a small group, or a whole class. The teacher holds up a flash card or writes a word on the chalkboard:

Teacher: See this word? The word is **and**. Everyone look at this word, and say it together.

Students: And

Teacher: That's correct. Now say it five times while looking at it.

S's: And, and, and, and, and

T: Good. Now say it louder.

S's: **And**!

T: Come on, you can say it louder than that!

S's: **AND!**

T: Okay, I have three other cards here ("again," "answer," "arrange"). When I show a card that is not "and," say "No!" in a loud voice. But when you see "and," say it in a whisper.

S's: No!

S's: No!

S's: (whisper) And

T: Great. Look at it carefully, and when I remove it, close your eyes and try to picture the word under your eyelids. Do you see it? Good. Now say it in a whisper again.

S's:	And
T:	Good. Now spell it.
S's:	A . . . N . . . D
T:	Now pretend to write it in the air in front of you with your finger while saying each letter.
S's:	A . . . N . . . D
T:	Good. Now describe the word. The way you would describe a new kid to a friend who hasn't seen him yet.
S1:	It's small.
S2:	It has a witch's hat in the beginning.
S3:	It has a belly at the end.
T:	What's its name again?
S's:	AND!
T:	Let's search for "and's" throughout the day and even after you go home tonight. We'll ask you later if you found any in school and again tomorrow morning if you found any at home.

In the morning, have on the board, "***Did you find any and's last night***?" Over the next few lessons, ask if the student has seen an *and*. Up to three words a day usually can be taught in this general way. Be sure that the target words do not look at all alike. Words that are shown in context with the object word and that do look like the object word should not be overstressed. These often will be learned incidentally, as the student sets about distinguishing them.

Techniques for Reinforcing Sight Words

Sight word acquisition is a memorization process. As such, the key to reinforcing the process is repeated exposures. Some techniques for providing the necessary repetitions include:

a. Put the words on oak tag and place them around the room.
b. Have the child put the words on a ring that can be carried about for self-review.
c. Create a buddy system that has students checking and helping one another to learn the words.
d. Distribute word cards to students and have them sort them into known and unknown words. Have them say all the words they (think) they know. Next, begin to use the look-alike words by asking them to try to figure out what each of them says. Note the letters and sounds

that give trouble and teach the student how to decode these using the cluster of methods ahead under word analysis.

e. Have children practice eidetic (visual retention) imaging techniques with spelling words. Gerald Glass (personal communication), a veteran diagnostician and clinician at Adelphi University, maintains that this also is a formidable means of teaching children how to spell correctly.

f. Have students try to construct sentences from their flash cards. Tell them that you will help them to add any words they wish, but that words added then become part of their personal word card file, and they must learn to read them at sight.

> The Intensive Sight Word Technique is a "must" paradigm for Rapid Word Recognition Training; and, yes, it can be fun!

Harry	can	ride	a

scooter	and	a	bicycle

g. Use media-assisted reinforcement devices that permit the user to select an unfamiliar word and hear it pronounced. There are so many new products of this type that it is pointless to identify any particular ones by name. All are excellent for sight word practice.

h. Connect sight words to meaningful contexts by grouping new words in categories, such as words associated with activities and tools used in the classroom (chalkboard, eraser, desk, and others).

i. Connect sight words to authentic experiences with "Postcard" and other Language Experience activities—have students write brief post-card letters to friends and family. Mention the weather, what they are doing, how they are feeling, and some special salutation and closing (Dear Cousin. . . . .Your grandson). Similarly, have students tell a story or relate an experience. Write it out for them on oak tag or on the chalkboard as they tell it. Have them indicate which words they have seen before. Underline these and have them try to read them in the story context.

j. Use word games—commercial and teacher-made (word bingo, conso-nant lotto, word dominoes, crossword puzzles, word wheels). Hang-man, one of the oldest, can be used with little preparation, and can be used as a large-group, small-group, or paired activity.

Some children have extreme difficulty learning sight words, due to dif-ferences in neurological processing. The next section offers a system for categorizing severe word recognition difficulty, and a well-known remedial technique for working with these students on an individual basis.

UNDERSTANDING AND REMEDIATING
SEVERE WORD RECOGNITION DIFFICULTY

Boder's Classification System

Elena Boder's (1971a,b) system for classifying severe decoding and related spelling problems includes three conditions:

- The *dysphonetic* condition is a severe deficit in letter-sound integration with a resulting inability to learn phonetic word analysis skills. Reading, for these youngsters, is global and based almost wholly on sight recognition. Spelling, even of *known* words, seems to be based more on the look of the word than its sound units ("letter" for "little"; "wet" for "was"). According to an earlier account by Boder (1970), these students' spelling of *unknown* words tends to be totally non-phonetic ("arefl" for "story"; "alley" for "almost"; "rsty" for "guess"). The most striking errors, however, are semantic substitution errors, as in reading "funny" for "laugh," "chicken" for "duck," and "answer" for "ask" (289).
- The *dyseidetic* condition is an inability to easily recognize (really recall) words on sight, with a resulting overreliance on phonetic analysis, even for frequently-encountered words. This ability is sometimes referred to as an aspect of short-term memory.
- The *combined dysphonetic/dyseidetic* condition is characterized by poor phonetic *and* poor eidetic reading and spelling. It is the most severe form of reading disorder.

Of students with severe reading problems, about 10 percent are dyseidetic, 59 percent were dysphonetic, and about 25 percent were combined dysphonetic/dyseidetic. About 6 percent had patterns of errors that could not be classified in any of these three ways (Boder & Jarrico, 1982). These same types of disorders have been found to a lesser extent in those with less severe reading disabilities. This effectively means that there are "milder" forms of each of these conditions, and that you probably will be seeing many more of these than the more serious or acute forms.

Visual-Auditory-Kinesthetic-Tactile (VAKT) Method

The idea behind this intensive remedial method is to help children to develop automaticity in sight word recognition by helping them to form multiple sensory connections with sight words: see the word (visual), hear the word (auditory), perform a "finger spelling" of the word (kinesthetic), and touch the shape of the word (tactile). The roots of this classic method were developed by Helen Keller and her teacher, Anne Sullivan. Sullivan taught Keller to communicate by tapping letters out on her hand. Years later, Keller was able to refine the method with the help of Grace Fernald (Fernald, 1943) into its current form.

VAKT Steps (freely adapted from Fernald, 1943)

Step 1. Ask the learner to suggest a word that she or he wishes to learn.

Step 2. The teacher then writes the word in large handwriting, speaking the word in a natural way as it is written. Use a black magic marker or grease pencil.

Step 3. The learner traces the word with his or her finger while speaking the *whole* word (*not* being permitted to say the individual letters of the word) and being careful to begin and end speech and writing at the same time.

Step 4. The learner does this as often as is needed, until the child feels certain that he has learned it.

Step 5. The learner then visualizes it and traces it in the air with his finger.

Step 6. The learner then turns the word card over, takes another piece of paper, and tries to write the word from memory, writing and speaking at the same time.

Step 7. The learner compares this production with the original model.

Step 8. In extraordinary cases, a tray may be filled with moist sand, and the child may be urged to trace the word in the sand.

Step 9. The words taught in this way should be reviewed daily in a short list with other words.

Additional Notes from Fernald

- At any point that an error is noted, the incorrect word is simply crossed out and the learner again begins at Step 3. The error may be noticed during the attempted writing of the word or during the comparing of the production and the model. In any case, it is important to maintain the unity of the word being learned. *Do not erase or correct parts of the word, or else the word is no longer a unit.* Simply draw a single line through the error and return to Step 3.

- There is little relation between the sound of the word and the sound made by the names of the letters. The auditory stimulation desired is the sound of the word as near to normal speech as possible. There is a great temptation to call off the names of the letters rather than to say the word. Watch carefully at Step 3 and Step 6 for this problem. The learner needs to say the word, not the letter names.

- Connect word study to writing, using the "normal experience story approach" (Fernald, 1943, 48).

STEPS IN THE NORMAL EXPERIENCE STORY APPROACH

Step 1. Ask learners about their interests, then ask them to tell you a related experience or story. Say, "We will write a story together. If you don't know how to spell a word, we will learn it together."

Step 2. The student then begins to write the story. As each unfamiliar word appears, the teacher goes through the same procedure as outlined above.

Step 3. When the story is finished, it is typed immediately and the learner attempts to reread it from the typed copy.

Step 4. At the start of each subsequent session, the student is asked to reread the latest story.

VAKT is a powerful procedure, but it loses much of its impact when it is overdone. The "T" (tactile) step usually is only necessary with a few students who have very severe reading difficulty. A "VAK" approach can be used with most students by simply deleting the tracing steps. This modified version can be used in group settings when students are learning the same words. The teacher also should watch for signs that students are ready to go "V-A," deleting the "K" (kinesthetic) step as well, for some words.

The Normal Experience Story is an often forgotten, integral part of VAKT.

It is recommended that systematic phonics and structural analysis be taught as soon as reading skill begins to emerge (Cooper, 1947; 1964). Most clinicians have found no additional benefit in the tactile step, the place from which it all got started, and simply use a V-A-K procedure. Susan Bryant (1979) found no differences between VAK and VAKT on reading or spelling. On the other hand, Charles Hulme found the tracing step to significantly benefit *disabled* readers but not normal readers (1981a,b). Edward Dwyer and Rona Flippo (1983) have offered a similarly abbreviated form for teaching spelling as well as sight words. It has the following steps:

1. Look at the word carefully.
2. Discuss the word to further note its pronunciation and meaning.
3. Close your eyes, mentally visualize the word, and write it in the air.
4. Write the word on paper without looking at it.
5. Check its spelling, and write it again from memory.
6. Write the word in a sentence.

SPELLING INTERVENTION STRATEGIES

Direct instruction in spelling is appropriate for all children in the elementary grades, but it is especially important for students experiencing spelling difficulties. Following are five intervention strategies that can be used to scaffold spelling development: Elkonin boxes, Have-a-Go Chart, Interactive Writing, and Linking the Known to the New, or Analogic Spelling, are strategies identified by Sipe (2000) and the Directed Spelling Thinking Activity (DSTA), developed by Zutell (1996).

Elkonin boxes is a strategy that Reading Recovery borrowed from an Eastern European source (Clay, 1979). In this strategy, the child generates his or her own sentence or story on the bottom portion of a page, and the top portion is the practice page for trying to spell words the child does not know. When a child is struggling to spell a word correctly, for instance, the word *hat*, the teacher says, "Let's make a box for it." Then the teacher draws a rectangle on the top practice portion (see Figure 7.16) and puts three partitions in it so that it has a space for each sound (not necessarily each letter). The teacher puts three round markers or pennies below each space. As the child slowly stretches out each sound, he or she pushes up the markers or penny into the boxes. Then the child moves the markers back below the boxes, and pushes them up again as he or she tries to determine each specific sound. This time, the child writes the letter for each sound in the box after it is identified. The teacher gives hints of similar words until the child hears all of the sounds and is able to write the letter for the sound in each box. When the child needs help spelling another word, the process is repeated.

As spelling ability progresses, a box can be made with spaces for each letter, not just each sound. If the word has more than one syllable, the teacher will lead the student to clap each syllable to separate the segments then try to spell each segment. An Elkonin box can be made for each syllable. Applying the Elkonin box strategy to future words will help the child to segment the word and take time to hear each part. The next strategy also uses a chart format and is called "Have-a-Go Chart."

The *"Have-a-Go Chart" Intervention Strategy* developed by Bolton and Snowball (1993) is another technique that Sipe (2000) identified to

> The Elkonin box will help the child to segment a word and take time to hear each part.

FIGURE **7.16**

ELKONIN BOX EXAMPLE

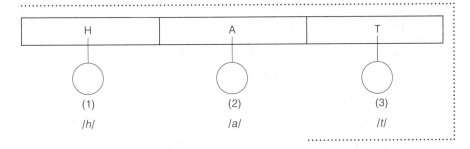

FIGURE **7.17**

HAVE-A-GO CHART

Word from Text	Have-a-Go	Correct Spelling	Copied Spelling
Birds	birds		Birds
Luch	Inch	lunch	lunch

Example from Sipe, 2000, 269

scaffold invented spelling into conventional spelling. In this procedure, the child uses a Have-a-Go Chart for words within a text that he or she realizes are not spelled correctly and desires to correct (see Figure 7.17). Here are the steps for this technique:

1. The child writes one misspelled word in the left column.

2. Next, the child tries to spell the word correctly with the help of the teacher or a peer, and records this attempt in the second column. The teacher actively supports this attempt by asking the student to clap the syllables or stretch the word, or to use other instructional techniques.

3. In the third column, the student writes a revision of the word. If the word is still incorrect, the teacher either spells the word for the student or suggests dictionary usage and the correct spelling is written.

4. In the last column, the student writes the word correctly. Some memory technique should be encouraged to help students remember the last spelling.

Interactive writing (Pinnell & McCarrier, 1993) is a third spelling intervention strategy. Interactive writing is similar to the Language Experience Approach in that a group of children and their teacher write a message (sentence or short story) using the children's own language to preserve their experiences and oral language. The message is written in large print on chart paper, with the children and the teacher *sharing the pen*. During interactive writing the children write most of the words as they come up to the chart to write letters and words that they know. The teacher scaffolds their knowledge by providing instructional strategies and by supplying spellings they do not know. In addition to spelling, many other writing conventions are modeled (such as, "How do we begin a sentence?" "What do we do when we are out of room on this line but it's not the end of our sentence?" "What do we put at the end of a question?"). The students orally

FIGURE **7.18**

DIRECTED SPELLING THINKING ACTIVITY (DSTA)

Before the session

1. The teacher assesses students' spelling to see which patterns of errors should be remediated and which students (6 to 10) are ready for help with that skill.

2. The teacher thinks through the relevant pattern (ones that students have some knowledge of but are confusing) and selects a set of words (16 to 20). Some of the words are direct examples of a pattern, others provide contrast to see how patterns complement each other, and a few words are exceptions (for example, for difficulty with the long vowel markers: *brave, came, plane, bake, trade, page, tape, space;* contrast pattern: *bag, plan, last, black, tap, mad, land, fast;* and exceptions: *have, they, eight, far*).

3. The teacher makes a list for testing and writes each individual word on an index card or piece of paper.

4. Half of the words from each category (direct example, contrast pattern, and exceptions) are listed in random order for the pretest activity.

During the DSTA strategy with children

1. *Prediction and discussion.* The teacher gives the pretest and each student in the group tries to spell each word. Next the teacher leads the children to discuss how they spelled specific words, what they were thinking when they were spelling, and why they thought that would be the spelling.

2. The teacher presents the correct spelling of the words to the group, and validates students' attempts. Difficult word parts are highlighted.

3. *Assisted word sorting.* Using the words on the pretest, the teacher helps students complete a group word sorting activity to visually clarify the pattern, contrast, and exceptions. The students will orally explain the

reason for each placement and why it belongs in that category. A second deck of word cards, those not used on the test, is presented to the students for sorting, and students add their own examples to the different groups. At the end of this activity, students orally state the orthographic principle that they have been learning.

Follow-up activities on following days

4. *Word hunting.* Students look through books, magazines, newspapers, and other sources of print to find examples of the patterns. Personalized spelling lists can be developed from the words.

5. *Cooperative and individual word sorting.* In pairs and then individually, the students sort the words from the teacher and from their "finds." The key words from the group sort are used for the patterns, then students pick up the first word, read it, and place it under the correct key word. When all words are sorted, the teacher or a master list is used for a final check.

6. *Practice activities.* Different practice strategies can be used to help students write the words and develop ways to remember the difficult parts.

7. *Measuring and recording student success.* A peer (or teacher) gives an individualized spelling review at the end of a lesson cycle. The students keep track of their own growth by keeping a list of their own "new words learned." In their personalized notebook, the students can also list key words and/or brief pattern descriptions at the top of a page or column and list the words from the word sort and personal word finds. Contrasts can be made in a list on the same page (for example, short *e* words, and short *i* words, then later long *e* words might be added to that page).

Adapted from Zutell, 1996, *The Reading Teacher*, 98–108.

think through the spelling of each word, while remembering the message. A fourth spelling method focuses on connecting the known with the unknown.

Linking the known to the new, or *analogic spelling,* is a fourth intervention technique (Sipe, 2001). Although some students seem to naturally generalize (or even overgeneralize) spelling patterns, other students need explicit instruction in this process. In this technique students are taught how to link new spellings with words they already know how to spell. If a child is trying to spell "strike," a teacher would call the child's attention to the word "bike" that the child already knows how to spell. The teacher would say, "You already know how to spell *bike*, so how do you think you would spell *strike*?" Through repeated use, hopefully the child will begin to automatically think of words with a similar pattern when a spelling challenge is encountered.

Spelling problems remain one of the most resistant to significantly alter; we don't know why.

The *Directed Spelling Thinking Activity (DSTA)* (Zutell, 1996) is directly modeled after Stauffer's Directed Reading Thinking Activity (DRTA) (1969) "but its concepts are grounded in recent work on the developmental and conceptual nature of learning to spell" (99). Several of its components are based on Invernizzi, Abouzeid, and Gill's (1994) research with word sorts. The steps in the DSTA are listed in Figure 7.18 (page 289).

The DSTA procedure can also be adapted for older students, who might compare *-tion* with *-sion* and *-ian* word endings, or more complex spelling patterns. Zutell's (1996) DSTA model can be modified and personalized by effective teachers to meet the particular needs of their students.

Teaching low-achieving spellers at their Instructional level, rather than at grade level, may also hold promise for students who are struggling. Morris, Blanton, Blanton, and Nowacek (1995) found that "low spellers who received below-grade-level instruction did not fall further behind, but actually gained ground on a comparison group who had been taught at grade level" (175).

REVIEW

This chapter covered the methods for improving the most frequently cited problems of reading deficiencies, word recognition, and analysis. Every educator should have mastery of these methods since they are fundamental to all reading and learning, at all levels. Spelling, also a bane to many students and their teachers, was addressed, but frankly, it is window dressing when compared with decoding. Furthermore, we have not been terribly successful in improving spelling. Fortunately, it does not correlate very well with reading beyond the primary grades.

PREVIEW

The next two chapters focus on accurate comprehension across time and place; the reason that humankind ever bothered to construct reading-writing systems. You will find the ideas and practices to be of extensive value in working with a wide range of reading-thinking-language needs.

PRECISION TEACHING OF COMPREHENSION

Comprehension is inherently reconstructive.
— ROBERT CALFEE AND ELFRIEDA HIEBERT

Understanding is the beginning of empathizing, solving, and evolving.
— ANDRE GIDE, 1902 (PARAPHRASE)

CONTENT AND CONCEPT ORGANIZER

This chapter addresses aspects of Corrective and Remedial reading comprehension, as defined in Chapter 1: "Reading is fluently recognizing words in print while applying strategies for schema activation, metacognition, and "fix-up" of comprehension or word identification, as needed, to make supportable reconstructions of a writer's stated and implied meanings, with sufficient reference to prior knowledge and experience to construct relevant internally or externally suggested evaluations and applications." The premise of the chapter is that, where there are no serious compounding problems, children's comprehension difficulties can be fairly easily identified, and instruction can be planned to target those difficulties with great precision. Look ahead for the ReQuest Procedure, a particularly robust, diagnostic-prescriptive teaching method developed in a "clinic" setting for improving comprehension with problem readers.

CHAPTER OUTLINE

PREFACE TO PRECISION TEACHING OF COMPREHENSION

All comprehension, if not all learning, seems to pass through four (recursive) cycles: *evocation*—or stirred engagement; *realization of meaning; reflection on implications;* and *endless cross-verification by an increasingly sensitive paradox detector.* For this reason, every new idea and piece of information presented by every teacher contributes to comprehension growth. Every proverb spoken by every grandparent at some significant life moment, every dinner table discussion, every homily, every human experience that is somehow "languaged through" in some conscious way adds to understanding. For that matter, every television program viewed makes possible a greater sense of familiarity, recognition, and hence comprehension of story, facts, and perspectives yet to be encountered in listening, observing, experiencing, and reading. Comprehension isn't leveled, in the sense that it is a painfully steep climb, or something that one can or cannot do. Rather, it is a collection of gradual spirals of many things that we have learned and understand. Sometimes learning is inhibited without the proper background but most anyone can learn to absorb with a little help. Everything we do, say, see, and experience adds to comprehension's spiraling and organic nature.

So how can a process that is so fully supported become impaired or, more correctly, remain underdeveloped? Once the decoding aspects of reading have been mastered, how can comprehension *not* follow? Answering these questions, and understanding precisely why comprehension is not occurring, requires a "detailed understanding of the reading task" (Pressley, 1994, 66).

Each friendly prompt, stubbed toe, and moment of reflection influences comprehension.

Traditionally, research has found such a high correlation between reading comprehension and measures of IQ that one was used to estimate the other. This also led some professionals to quietly conclude that reading comprehension could not be improved to any degree that exceeded the combination of one's word recognition skills and listening comprehension (or "capacity," as estimated by understanding without having to decode written speech). Today this assumption is called the "Simple View" of reading comprehension. However, two teaching methods, the ReQuest procedure (Manzo, 1969) and the Directed Reading-Thinking Activity (Stauffer, 1969), empirically demonstrated that reading comprehension could be improved, irrespective of IQ. These findings led to an era of concentrated research and development of reading comprehension improvement methods. The Simple View is discussed next (and summarized in greater detail in Figure 8.1) followed by the evolving Strategic View, which is rich in implications for precision teaching of comprehension.

> Comprehension, whether textual or otherwise, is a recursive cycle of evocation, realization of meaning, reflection, and endless cross-verification.

Simple View of Reading

Comprehension processes are so complex that many educational psychologists have reduced it, for purpose of study, to "operational definitions"—or, things measurable. This view is summarized as:

Decoding + Listening Comprehension = Reading Comprehension

This view is receiving a good deal of recent attention as researchers concentrate on the lower grades where it is more true than at any point thereafter. In fact, the Simple View does account for nearly 50 percent of the possible explanations for Reading Comprehension ability in a largely monolingual population of third graders. It accounts for up to 82 percent in a longitudinal study of English-Spanish bilingual children in first through fourth grades (Hoover & Gough, 1990). As such, this model deserves immediate respect and attention at the early grade levels, and with bilingual students, in diagnostic-prescriptive problem solving. (See Figure 8.1, page 294) for a critique of the Simple View of Reading.)

> There are aspects of comprehension that are elementary, but none that are simple.

Real-world efforts to actually improve reading comprehension cannot afford the luxury of simplification, however. Nor should recognition of the complexity of comprehension lead to the conclusion that teaching for reading comprehension improvement is too difficult to address. In order to design precise interventions, it is necessary to have precise knowledge, or at least somewhat more precise theories. Much that we know about comprehension has been deduced from the results of empirical, clinical, and logical/intuitive attempts to improve reading comprehension even while we do not yet fully understand it. The methods that "work" are themselves proofs of theorized principles. Similarly, in classroom and clinical reading instruction, comprehension needs often are most accurately determined by diagnostic-teaching approaches more than by test and teach approaches. Doing so, however, requires that we turn to more sophisticated models of reading comprehension.

FIGURE **8.1**

CRITIQUE OF THE *SIMPLE VIEW* OF READING

This operational-definition–bound model of reading says that reading comprehension is the sum of abilities to decode words and comprehend oral-aural speech (listening). This has led to some neat models that emphasize factors that fit this simplification, but that are wholly inadequate to produce comprehension gains in most school-based situations, especially beyond the third-grade level. These models also lead to an overemphasis on marginal factors such as "working memory," "speed of processing," and recognition of language patterns. Working memory involves holding semantic meanings in signs and symbols in (very) short-term memory (analogous to SD RAM on a computer) as one reads from one idea unit to the next. This factor is measured by tasks such as: short-term memory of random numbers or letters, and more recently, to short-term memory of random and phrased words. This recent step was urged by the realization that there is little relationship between speed and accuracy in remembering numbers and with thinking up antonyms.

The second factor in the Simple View, to make it a bit more complicated, is the emphasis on "speed of naming of letters" (Joshi & Aaron, 2000). The third is the ability to easily recognize syntactic, or predictable, language patterns in text (such as exactly replacing deleted words in "cloze" passages). The Simple View tends to pay little attention to such things as background knowledge, will (volition), and interest. It also pays little heed to earlier empirical research based on factor-analytic studies of comprehension that since the 1940s have yielded a Factor X; that is, a specific Reading Comprehension Ability factor with no decomposable parts to further explain it. Also, while the Simple View seems to offer some very specific measures, two of these—namely, short-term memory and "naming rate" indicators—are not yet sufficiently understood and documented for diagnostic use. However, the two major factors—decoding and listening comprehension—are norm-based and easily measurable with most any Informal Reading Inventory.

Strategic Views of Reading

Many comprehension strategies and skills can be taught; but we are all dabblers in understanding a *process* that is entangled in epistemology (reflections on how we "know" anything), psychology, semantics, culture, and the organization of individual brains.

In more complex Strategic Views of reading, comprehension is characterized as "a process of using one's own experiences and text clues to infer [reconstruct in one's own mind] the author's intended meaning" (Wilson & Gambrell, 1988, 12). Such views of reading have been termed *interactive*, in the sense that several processes are occurring simultaneously and interactively within the reader, rather than occurring sequentially and independently. For example, in the Simple View, the reader first recognizes letters, then words, then combines these into sentences, and gradually, sequentially, builds toward overall meaning. In interactive, or Strategic Views, the processes of meaning anticipation, word recognition, vocabulary meaning recognition, and others work together simultaneously, as the reader processes text. It is important to note here, that some have taken the term "interactive" to mean that the reader interacts *with the text*. There can be no interaction between reader and text—the text can't talk back. This misinterpretation of the use of the term interactive is understandable, because in current Strategic Views the reader is seen as "talking" (mentally) to and about the text—engaging in inner-conversations or "self-talk" to construct probable meanings of the text.

In Strategic Views of reading, three essential systems must work together smoothly and virtually flawlessly (and interactively) for effective comprehension to occur in both Independent level and Instructional level reading. We have categorized these as: skills, strategies, and attitudes.

Skills   The first category, *skills,* includes factors which must be present to the level of subconscious application, or automaticity:

- rapid and fluent identification of 95 to 99 percent of the words, and effective rapid decoding of the remaining words
- immediate recognition of vocabulary meanings and contextual connotations
- familiarity with the sentence and paragraph structures, and use of punctuation as a means of chunking flowing thoughts into manageable units

Strategies   Comprehension also requires selection and use, as needed, of multiple *strategies* for reconstructing the author's meaning, and constructing personal connections with and responses to the author's meaning, including:

- begin with an organizing question or purpose to guide comprehension
- generate personal motivation to read for understanding
- make continuous personal connections to background knowledge and experience—which requires knowledge and experience in a vast number of domains and topics
- maintain a metacognitive sense of one's progressive grasp of the material
- use fix-up strategies as needed to support understanding, such as: stop and reread, self-question, read ahead a bit, translate, summarize, categorize, or seek clarification through questions and sharing thoughts with others
- infer and reasonably justify (verify) such small inferential leaps as are necessary for understanding the text
- interpret and justify (verify) such larger conjectural leaps as are necessary for understanding the realities reflected in the text
- critically counter-reason with the author's "print" voice
- leave the road that print conveys to a potentially more creative insight
- identify the patterns of ideas and facts as part of some subject domain, and be able to answer questions raised by that domain; in other words, accumulate conventional knowledge for durable periods of time, otherwise known as study-type reading

In Strategic Views of reading, three essential systems must work together smoothly.

Attitudes   Finally, comprehension is supported and propelled by certain personal cognitive sets or *habits of mind.* These include:

- open-mindedness, so as not to misinterpret the author's intended message

- an impelling sense of inquiry that sustains interest, reading, and learning beyond classroom requirements
- a tendency to intentional listening, our main source of receptive communication and knowledge growth

Clearly, the Strategic View is far from simple. Ironically, however, when it is understood it suggests simple, efficient, and workable principles, approaches, and methods for comprehension improvement.

PRINCIPLES TO GUIDE PRECISION TEACHING OF COMPREHENSION°

Scaffolding: Training Wheels and Self-Mediation

Traditional schooling tends to interrupt the process of innate inquiry—at least for a while.

Find the student's Instructional level, provide "scaffolding" in the form of guidance and support as needed, and gradually "fade" supports as the student gains mastery. This is one of the most familiar principles of teaching. The metaphor of a scaffold alongside a struggling student has become synonymous with Vygotsky's concept of *assisted learning* and, implicitly, with caring teaching. To attribute anything but the *word* "scaffolding" to Vygotysky, however, would be like saying that no one in the Western world understood teaching to be anything but telling prior to the 1978 popularization of his work. Nonetheless, it is a good metaphor, though one that may benefit from two additional points of clarification. The first is that a scaffold is stationary while learning is dynamic: "on the move." Therefore, we would urge consideration of an extension of the metaphor to "training wheels." In this case, the student is urged to cycle away from the scaffold, and explicitly given preparation for doing so in the form of practice in "self-mediating." In mediated learning the teacher assists by acting as an intermediary between the objective to be learned and the learner. In supporting comprehension of a typical reading selection, the teacher might scaffold assistance with prereading questions to guide silent reading and/or by restating what the text has said in more familiar and friendly language.

This same guidance was offered in the early 1930s in the Directed Reading Activity (often attributed to Emmett Betts, but as you will learn

---

°Comprehension instruction is the upward and outward utilization of *reading to learn*, a process begun in early childhood, and in a way, interrupted by having to learn to read. The principles stated here are based on several reviews of the literature on comprehension methods: Levin & Pressley, 1981; Pearson & Fielding, 1991; Pearson & Gallagher, 1983; Santa & Hayes, 1981; Tierney & Cunningham, 1984. Additional information was drawn from chapters and critiques of methodologies: Duffy et al., 1987; Gaskins, 1981; Manzo & Manzo, 1990a; Maria, 1990; Pressley, 2000.

ahead in the chapter, merely pulled together from what teachers were doing). The additional insight that sprang up (probably not for the first time) in the late 1960s and '70s was the importance of self-mediation. That is, teaching students how to set their own purposes for reading, and ride off—on training wheels, often with the teacher running alongside—until the student self-mediates almost everything that can be called "learning." Under this bit of wisdom the critical value in teaching would occur when the student "languaged" something through in his or her own words (Manzo & Manzo, 1990; Postman & Weingartner, 1969), thereby bringing his or her own active mental participation and personal phrasing to the task. Two simple techniques illustrate student mediation: the *translation* question—or asking students to say in their own words what has been written and/or spoken by another; and the charge to write something brief and responsive following reading. One very popular teaching method is called KWL: what I *K*now about the topic, what I *W*ant to learn about the topic, and what I *L*earned about the topic. KWL proved to be less than robust until a later version added a "Plus" step that required self-written or self-reorganized textual material (see details ahead). The critical factors here, as in all learning, are the student's functions and determination as much as those of the teacher. Emphasis on how teachers might better teach sometimes drowns out the essentials of how students might better learn.

Toward Self-Scaffolding: The Brain Loves Efficiency

Capitalize on the brain's natural tendency to search for patterns and templates. It may sound a little schizophrenic, but the mind has a mind of its own, and that mind loves efficiency. The brain is a primitive instrument with a primary drive to feed and nurture itself first and foremost. It will not let the body, or itself, engage in useless consumption of energy. It needs to be convinced that greater effectiveness and efficiency will follow from expenditure of any effort, but particularly of great effort, such as is often required to master something new. Accordingly, it is always on the lookout for patterns, or *templates*, to simplify its job of making sense of the world around it; call it *self-scaffolding*. Many of the methods ahead in this book amount to precisely this: offering templates, in the form of phrases that, when added to one's self-talk while reading, result in quicker and fuller comprehension. When the mind—which never rests—apprehends the efficiency of this self-talk, it begins to find it self-gratifying to rehearse and fine-tune itself. It is in this way that its next challenge—say, to read and comprehend the next story or the next chapter in a textbook—is accomplished with greater speed, insight, and, most importantly, less work. The *sine qua non*, or ultimate reason, for all teaching is to induce this self-instruction. If the mind can be persuaded to engage a topic or

The mind never rests; harness this, and it can be induced into rehearsing and fine-tuning itself.

notion outside the regular class time, learning proceeds in spurts and leaps, rather than in slow, plodding increments.

Mental Modeling

Model self-talk phrases as templates for building meaning from print. Think-aloud strategies, or talking through the process of how something is done, may be the best type of direct instruction available (Strickland, 1996). The human inclination to seek out the most efficient and effective masters of any environment formed the basis for what is known as "social and imitation learning theory" (Bandura & Walters, 1963), and then later for mental modeling, such as first illustrated by the ReQuest procedure (1969). The ReQuest method was designed to efficiently result in mastery of the complex mental process of reading comprehension by employing socially and psychologically structured "reciprocal interactions," or back-and-forth questioning, between teacher and students. Within this structure, the teacher models the use of self-talk phrases and protocols for building meaning from text. These reciprocal interactions serve as the means by which to accelerate, intensify, and convert the *internalization* of the interactions with others into efficient *intra-actions,* or self-talk within oneself (Manzo & Manzo, 2002). The ReQuest procedure is described ahead in this chapter.

Active Listening

Teach engaged active listening as a foundation for reading comprehension. Too little thought and attention tends to be given to the importance of speaking-listening interactions between teacher and student(s) during actual teaching. Catts and Kamhi (1999) put it simply: "If students [and we would add, *teachers*] do not monitor their comprehension during [instructional] conversation and repair conversational breakdowns, they are unlikely to monitor their comprehension during reading and engage in strategic reading practices to ensure that they comprehend text" (205). However, the brain is not fond of careful listening. Intensive listening is terribly energy consuming. The brain needs to be convinced of its benefits before serious learning will occur. It is for this reason, you will recall, that the IR-TI includes a "congruency ratio" (or, "are we communicating?") measure.

Enticing the brain into engaged listening is accomplished through methods built on authentic interactions between teacher and students, and students with one another. Such interactions have been referred to as "reciprocal interactions," as described above, and as "instructional conversations" by Tharp and Gallimore (1989a). They characterize them as tending to "rouse minds to life," as "responsive teaching," and as "cognitive apprenticeships."

Active listening includes asking questions to clarify, and contributing relevant additions to the speaker's message: This may be done mentally, as when listening to a video or audiotape, or aloud, where appropriate, when listening in person. Teaching listening through structured reciprocal interactions intensifies this process of clarifying on-the-fly. It works with a certain ease when there is a wiser, more competent model available and alertly interacting with the learner.

Frontloading

Help students activate or build appropriate schema before they read. Frontloading is instruction that empowers students before they read. It may include:

- preteaching vocabulary that might present obstacles to comprehension—usually by writing words on the board, giving the meanings, and offering some additional form of assistance in remembering the word meaning, and/or
- helping students call to mind relevant prior knowledge and experiences—as in giving students the general topic and brainstorming all the related information and details they can think of, and/or
- providing or enriching background knowledge and experiences (as in viewing clips from a videotape), and/or
- providing a "heads-up" on how the text is organized—as in providing an incomplete outline or graphic organizer to be filled in while reading, and/or
- providing actual facts covered in the text.

Frontloading enables students to engage a selection as if they have elevated IQs, reading skills, and prior knowledge.

Frontloading methods of these types enable students to engage a reading selection as if they had heightened IQ, skill, and knowledge. This principle has been found to be the most powerful means of improving reading comprehension.

Translation

Teach students to reconstruct the author's meanings by translating the author's words into their own. Translation is the bridge from literal to higher levels of understanding. Accurate, complete, deep, connected, and personal comprehension is best achieved by reprocessing the information. Readers are made more alert, active, and engaged by a requirement to reconstruct text in their own terms through tasks such as:

- retelling—with and without the option to look back at the text
- summarizing—with and without the option to look back at the text

- outlining—usually with text available
- representing the text in a student-constructed graphic organizer—usually with text available
- creating some form of nontextual representation of the text, as an illustration or a model

Additional types of constructive translations for remedial readers are discussed in Chapter 10, on Content Area Literacy. These include compressing and categorizing information for long-term memory (study skills), and various means of writing, reflecting, and connecting.

Authentic Texts and Tasks

Design authentic tasks, and select instructional reading materials that will help in completing these tasks. Humans are innate inquirers. From earliest childhood we derive a certain *epistemological gratification* from learning. Traditional schooling tends to interrupt that process in order to provide us with the tools to do so more efficiently and independently through focused listening and reading. Unfortunately, many children never find their way back to that kind of self-initiated, focused, engaged inquiry—or do so only in nonacademic areas such as sports or hobbies. There are many possible ways to achieve greater authenticity. The concept-based theme unit approach described in Chapter 6, for example, is a fairly simple and practical way to organize instruction. It does so in a way that directs energies toward a larger goal—such as the unit-culminating activity—and works better than correctly completing a worksheet that is unconnected to anything else that is going on during the day. When books, articles, and stories used for reading instruction are related to the theme unit, it has more authentic purpose and uses, and comes closer to the way that real interests are built, and the way language is really used and learned.

COMMON SOURCES OF COMPREHENSION DYSFUNCTION, AND SUGGESTED REMEDIES

Even a cursory listing of some of the sources of comprehension dysfunction serves to illustrate why the remedial specialist and classroom teacher need to be high-level problem solvers. This list also supports the need for differential diagnosis and precision teaching. The chief factors and functions related to comprehension dysfunction are listed below, in roughly the order of their frequency of occurrence. Alongside each is a method or technique that would likely constitute an appropriate prescription. Most of these pre-scriptions can be found in this chapter; others are found in the chapters ahead.

1. Need: Orientation and motivation to read (Mason, Herman, & Au, 1991). Remedies: Guided Reading Procedure; several methods in Chapter 11 on Remedies for Reading-Related Difficulties
2. Need: Word recognition and phonetic analysis (Chall, 1983a; Holmes & Singer, 1961; LaBerge & Samuels, 1974; Lewkowicz, 1987). Reme-dies: methods in Chapter 7 on Decoding
3. Need: Knowledge of word meanings and ability to infer meanings from context (Graves, 1986). Remedies: methods and approaches in Chapter 9, cloze-type activities
4. Need: Prior knowledge and experience (schema) (Bartlett, 1932; Gray, 1948; Langer, 1981; Rumelhart, 1980; Meeks, 1991). Remedies: listen to books read aloud, hands-on direct experiences, field trips, video-tapes of experiences, realia
5. Need: Adequate mental aptitude and basic thinking skills such as identifying a main idea, seeing details, and being able to make logical inferences (Marzano, 1991). Remedies: summarizing, paraphrasing, Possible Sentences
6. Need: Fundamental curiosity and the ability to ask appropriate ques-tions (Baker, 1979a,b; Maw & Maw, 1967; Manzo, 1969a). Remedies: ReQuest Procedure, Collins' Clarifying Questions, Question Only
7. Need: Familiarity with the language patterns in prose, and hence with the syntactic and semantic clues used to anticipate meaning and read with fluency at Independent level (Mason, Herman, & Au, 1991). Remedies: Cloze Inferencing Technique; Story Frame
8. Need: Adequate social-psychological maturity to respond empatheti-cally and objectively to information and story narratives (Mason, Herman, & Au, 1991; Rumelhart, 1980); Remedies: proverbs study
9. Need: Continuously developing metacognitive skills that permit the self-monitoring and self-fixing of comprehension problems as they arise (Paris, 1986). Remedies: Guided Reading Procedure; Collabora-tive Strategic Teaching
10. Need: Ability and willingness to see and find *larger* structures and organizational patterns in print (Meyer, 1975). Remedies: Story Maps; Graphic Organizers
11. Need: Ongoing development of higher mental processes, such as the ability to reason analytically and to think metaphorically, evaluatively, and constructively (Gaskins & Elliot, 1991; Manzo & Manzo, 1990a). Remedies: QARs; analogies

12. Need: Ability and skill in taking notes, summarizing, and critiquing (Bromley & McKeveny, 1986). Remedies: summarizing, paraphrasing, Two-Column Notes, KWL+

13. Need: Ability and skill to write reflectively in response to what one has read and thought (D. Anderson & Hidi, 1988–89; Graves, 1983; Eanet & Manzo, 1976). Remedies: REAP annotation writing

14. Need: Continuing evolution of a "world view" (Chall, 1983b), or of appropriate values (Hoffman, 1977; Schell, 1980), interests, and understandings of how things are and ought to be (Knafle, Legenza-Wescott, Passcarella, 1988). Remedies: proverbs study

Item number 6 above—"*Fundamental curiosity and the ability to ask appropriate questions*"—suggests just two of the several values in the ReQuest Procedure. Aspects of this teaching method align with most all of the other target areas of comprehension need due to its malleability; it pretty much can be directed wherever a teacher finds need.

Reciprocal Questioning (ReQuest) Procedure

The Reciprocal Questioning (ReQuest) procedure was designed to teach students how to set their own purpose for reading through self-directed inquiry (Manzo, 1969a,b; 1985). Originally developed in a clinical setting, ReQuest represents a form of apprenticeship training that also pioneered the ideas of *mental modeling* and diagnostic-prescriptive teaching. Prior to ReQuest, "modeling" was used exclusively for teaching external or visible behaviors. However, the modeling process, as structured by the ReQuest procedure, proved to be an effective means of externalizing and teaching the internal mental processes, as well as related attitudes and behaviors, involved in reading, discussing, and strategic thinking. In the ReQuest procedure, the teacher engages in "reciprocal interactions" that create a procedurally-enforced *rotation* in "instructional conversations" that can otherwise tend to be quite one-sided. This interactive sharing of "cognitive secrets" (Pearson & Fielding, 1991) tends to sharpen the student's attention to the teacher as a model of effective thinking and related conduct. The teacher also gains a great deal of diagnostic information about the student's thinking as this is externalized in the questions the student chooses to *ask*, as well as in responses to the teacher's questions.

ReQuest is a psycho-educational procedure that concurrently attends to several reading, language, thinking, and personal-social adjustment needs. Meeting these "collateral" objectives has been found to be a key feature of effective cognitive and affective education (Rubin, 1997). This is significant in dealing with remedial readers since much of their inability to make progress in reading can be traced to a variety of social and emotional inhibitions, such as fearing further failure and other social consequences for appearing incompetent.

STEPS IN THE REQUEST PROCEDURE:

Step 1 Both teacher and students read the *title and first sentence only* of the first paragraph of a selection, and look at any pictures or graphics that are part of the introduction.

Step 2 The teacher tells students to ask as many questions as they wish about the first sentence, the title, and/or pictures or graphics. The teacher turns his or her copy of the selection face down, but students may continue to look at their copies. Students are told that they should ask the kinds of questions that they think a teacher might ask. (This permits students to ask "ego-protective" questions since they need not reveal whether *they* know the answers to the questions they ask.)

Step 3 When all student questions have been fully and politely answered, the teacher turns the book face *up* while students are instructed to turn theirs face *down*. The teacher then asks as many additional questions (about the title, first sentence, and illustrations) as seems appropriate to bring about a sense of focus and purpose for reading the selection. The last of these questions (regarding the first sentence, and then in subsequent question sets on following sentences) should simply be, "What do you suppose the remainder of this selection will be about?"

Step 4 The next sentences are handled in the same way, with the students again leading the questioning, followed by teacher questioning, and concluding with the question, "What do you suppose the remainder of this selection will be about?" The number of sentences covered should be based on teacher judgment: The ReQuest activity should conclude as soon as a plausible purpose for reading has been evolved, but should not last *more* than about 10 minutes. Write the purpose question on the chalkboard.

Step 5 At the conclusion of the ReQuest activity, the students are encouraged to continue reading the selection silently for the purpose that has been developed.

Step 6 Following silent reading, the teacher should *first ask the evaluative question*: "Did we read for the right purpose?" ? *Can you confirm your prediction?*

This final question is asked before the purpose-setting question for three reasons. First, it helps to overcome what has been called "confirmation bias" (Garrison & Hoskisson, 1989), or the tendency to conclude only what has been predicted. Second, it helps to keep the focus of instruction on the development of effective strategies for independent reading and learning, more so than merely comprehending a given selection. Third, it further develops the important metacognitive habit of monitoring one's own comprehension and use of strategies while reading.

ReQuest has a strong body of research and clinical trials to support it. It has been shown to be successful in individual and group settings in the improvement of comprehension and student questioning behaviors (Larking, 1984), and in incidentally improving the questioning of teachers (Manzo, 1969a; Helfeldt & Lalike, 1979). It also has been used effectively with juvenile delinquents (Kay, Young, & Mottley, 1986); in accommodating learning-disabled youngsters who have been "mainstreamed" (Alley & Deshler, 1980; Hori, 1977); with second-language students (McKenzie, Ericson, & Hunter, 1988); in content area reading (Gaskins, 1981) and to teach general purpose-setting to elementary school students (Spiegel, 1980b). Additionally, ReQuest provided the basis for a more encompassing and well-validated strategy of Reciprocal Teaching (Palinscar & Brown, 1984), covered in Chapter 10 on Content-Area Reading and Study Skills.

The ReQuest Procedure addresses the micro elements of comprehension. Several approaches to building reading fluency address macro elements. Fluency is an important bridge from word recognition to comprehension. Methods for building fluency are provided in the next section, followed by methods for teaching a variety of strategies for prereading, silent reading, and postreading.

Building Fluency

The smooth flow of words with expression in reading text, or *fluency*, has a direct effect on comprehension (Reutzel & Hollingsworth, 1993). In the Strategic View of reading, fluency is seen as a prerequisite "skill" for successful comprehension; that is, it must be practiced to the point of automaticity. This is not a process that *ever* is fully accomplished—it needs to be re-accomplished with increasingly difficult materials, and in different genres and content areas. Note that the aim of fluency instruction is neither rate nor accuracy. The primary aim is to develop children's ability to read in a natural way that resembles speaking: at a natural pace, with natural and appropriate phrasing, stress, pauses, and facial and vocal expression.

The National Assessment of Educational Progress (NAEP FACTS, 1998, 1) found that higher levels of fluency were associated with higher average reading proficiency for the representative sample of 1,136 fourth-grade students in the study. It has also been found that lack of fluency is a frequent characteristic of struggling readers (Adams, 1990; Mathes, Simmons, & Davis, 1992).

The primary means of building fluency is repeated readings. S. Jay Samuels (1979, 1997) is credited with the first use of the term "repeated readings" as a method, though a number of earlier methods employed the technique: Chomsky (1978) used an audiotape-assisted version; Koskinen and Blum (1986) developed shared oral repeated readings; and Dowhower (1987) conducted research on various combinations of these approaches. One of the earliest methods for improving fluency is the Neurological Impress Method (Heckelman, 1966), designed for use in severe cases of fluency difficulties in individual remedial settings. The Neurological Impress Method is described following several versions of repeated readings for classroom and small-group settings.

The *trick* to repeated reading is making this requirement engaging and even fun by creating interesting contexts and audiences as the purpose for rereading. Many children respond well to seeing concrete evidence of their progress on a simple chart.

Charted Repeated Reading

The version of charted repeated reading described here has been fashioned from several accounts of this approach (Allington, 1983; Samuels, 1979; Ballard, 1978; Topping, 1987; Koskinen & Blum, 1986; and Dowhower, 1989).

STEPS IN CHARTED REPEATED READING:

1. Help a child select an interesting portion of a selection (50 to 300 words) at his or her own Instructional level, and set a goal for an appropriate oral reading rate, in words-per-minute.
2. Time the student's initial, unrehearsed oral reading of the passage.
3. Instruct the student to practice in pairs and at home.
4. Time and graph reading rate again.
5. Continue oral rereadings, timing, and graphing of times, at intervals of several days.
6. When the pre-set goal is reached, begin a new passage or continue using the remainder of the passage.

Mark Aulls and Michael Graves provide a handy chart (see Figure 8.2, page 306) for practicing and visualizing progress from repeated readings.

In order to make repeated readings a successful technique in your classroom, consider these specific research-based procedural tips from Dowhower (1989).

- Sources of passages: basals, literature books, language experience texts, newspaper articles, and student writing. Rasinski (2000) suggests that poems make excellent repeated reading material.

FIGURE **8.2**

REPEATED READING CHART

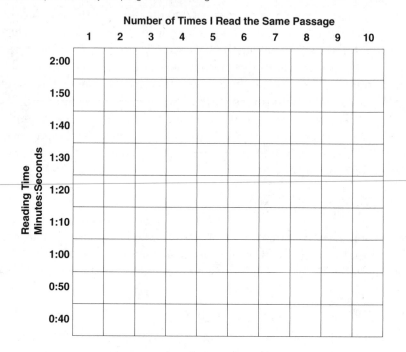

If you repeatedly read the same passage, you will soon read it smoothly and easily. This sheet will help to record your progress in reading.

Number of Times I Read the Same Passage

Number of Miscues Each Time

1st Time ___   3rd Time ___   5th Time ___   7th Time ___   9th Time ___

2nd Time ___   4th Time ___   6th Time ___   8th Time ___   10th Time ___

Aulls & Graves, 1985

- Closely monitor the word recognition level of the passages. If the child's accuracy is less than 85 percent on the first reading (before starting to practice), that passage is too hard and an easier passage should be selected.
- Keep the practice passage at the same level of difficulty until an acceptable rate of speed and accuracy is reached on the first or second reading.
- It is not necessary to provide stories with a high degree of shared words. There is a cumulative vocabulary effect with repeated readings.

- When children are reading with few errors but below 45 words per minute (WPM), use the assisted read-along approach (read with a model or tape). These children need the model of proper phrasing and speed of fluent reading.
- When children reach a rate of over 60 WPM on their first reading of a practice passage, use the independent repeated readings procedure (unassisted).
- Predetermine the mastery level of speed for very slow word-by-word readers and remedial students. Make this a reasonable level so the students experience success. For regular second-grade students who were reading below 50 WPM, 100 WPM criterion was effective (Dowhower, 1987). Older remedial readers' criterion level was 85 WPM (Samuels, 1979; Herman, 1985).
- When children are reading at relatively high rates of speed and accuracy, consider setting a specific number of rereadings rather than a criterion. Three to five rereadings for each passage is a good goal for mastery. Eighty-three percent of the fluency increase (speed) takes place by the fourth reading (O'Shea, Sindelar, & O'Shea, 1985). Students' optimal fluency is reached between three and five rereadings (Spring, Blunden, & Gatheral, 1981).

Partner-Evaluated Repeated Reading

In this technique, students work with partners—a peer, a tutor, an older "buddy," or even a parent. Peer partner pairs can take turns reading, rereading, and evaluating one another's reading. The partner gives the student evaluative feedback on his or her oral reading fluency. The partner can serve as a "talking dictionary," providing any word the student calls for with the phrase, "word, please" (Ballard, 1978; Topping, 1987). The partner also can have the reader self-evaluate progress (see Figure 8.3, page 308, for guidelines from Koskinen and Blum, 1986).

Partners as "Talking Dictionaries"

A meta-analysis of the research on partner repeated reading concluded that this approach results in significant gains in oral reading fluency (Mastropieri, Leinart, & Scruggs, 1999, 280). The effect on comprehension is not as clear. New research is being reported that suggests that while most children profit by peer interactions and support, for others it may be a source of stress (Matthews & Kesner, 2003). Monitoring this new line of investigation should help us to discover whether and how such interactions may be tweaked to adjust for possible downside effects. Jay Simmons (2003) has already begun to raise the bar on peer responding in a longitudinal study of differences in the ways peers respond to each other's writing. His early conclusion is that "Responders are taught, not born" (684).

FIGURE **8.3**

SELF-EVALUATION AND PEER-EVALUATION OF READING 1, READING 2, AND READING 3

Reading 1 *(Self-Evaluation)*
How well did you read? (Circle one.)

| terrible | not so good | fair | good | fantastic |

Reading 2 *(Peer Evaluation)*
How did your partner's reading get better? (Check *all* that apply.)

_____ He or she read more smoothly.

_____ He or she knew more words.

_____ He or she read with more expression.

** Tell your partner one thing that was better about his or her reading.

Reading 3 *(Peer Evaluation)*
How did your partner's reading get better? (Check *all* that apply.)

_____ He or she read more smoothly.

_____ He or she knew more words.

_____ He or she read with more expression.

** Tell your partner one thing that was better about his or her reading.

Drawings from Campbell, 1966
Inventory from Koskinen & Blum, 1986, *The Reading Teacher,* 72.

Repeated Reading as Homework

A form similar to the one above can be used as a short and simple homework assignment that many parents appreciate and actually enjoy. Using time outside class to practice repeated readings avoids use of instructional time for what essentially is a "drill" activity, and the assignment can be given only to those students who need it.

In one study, the addition of an audiotaped reading of a take-home book was conducted with 162 first-grade students, 57 native English speakers, and 105 English-as-second-language (ESL) students. The study explored "the impact of book-rich classroom environments that support repeated readings at home, both with and without an audio model, on fluent oral reading, comprehension, and reading motivation (Koskinen et al., 1999). The students in two experimental groups reread books at home, one group with an audiotape and one group without. A third experimental group did not include rereading at home. The first-grade students who reread books with audiotapes at home showed more interest in reading, talked more about books, took more books home to read and chose to read books in their free time significantly more than the students in the other experimental and control groups. Using books with audiotapes was beneficial for all students, but it was particularly motivating for the students who were least proficient in speaking and reading English. One parent mentioned, "The family is very happy that it's not only Lu [who] can benefit from the program, but the whole family can benefit from listening and learning to speak English" (Koskinen et al., 1999, 32). Repeated readings for the parents of ESL students is an added benefit of this procedure.

Repeated Reading for Performance

Techniques for implementing repeated readings are limited only by the teacher's imagination. One technique, called "Radio Reading," has students placed in small groups, each given a different reading selection to practice reading aloud to the class over a microphone. It is a good idea to have the reader seated behind a large box or screen, removing some part of the "performance anxiety" of reading in front of the class. This technique might be adapted today to "Video Reading." Students might practice reading a play or other selection to another class, the principal, or visitors to the school.

Neurological Impress Method (NIM) for Severe Fluency Difficulties

The Neurological Impress Method (Heckleman, 1966, 1969) is a technique in which the teacher and student read aloud simultaneously from the same material. R. G. Heckleman, a learning psychologist, hypothesized that individuals with severe fluency difficulties have actually established "neurological traces" for the *nonfluent* style in which they read, and that the problem could only be corrected by re-establishing new, fluent neurological traces. The simultaneous oral reading of student and teacher is structured in the following way.

STEPS IN THE NEUROLOGICAL IMPRESS METHOD:

Step 1. The teacher sits slightly behind the student.

Step 2. The teacher reads into the student's preferred ear. (This is usually the right: It has stronger connections to the left hemisphere, and does not have to cross the sometimes fragile corpus callosum as does sound to the left ear. However, sound to either ear should give the sensation of the sound to the other ear. If it does not, this can be taken as an indication of a possible neurophysiological problem requiring a referral.)

Step 3. The teacher slides a finger under each word being read.

Step 4. The teacher first reads in a slightly louder and slightly faster voice than the student, and then with time, lower and slower, and with the student's finger setting the pace.

Step 5. The teacher does not attempt to teach word analysis skills at this time.

Step 6. The teacher attempts to provide words in advance of the student's need when it is believed that it will slow the student down, even after the shift to student control of pacing and louder oral reading.

Echo reading (Anderson, 1981), a variation on NIM, also for remedial settings, has the teacher first read segments of the material to establish cadence and comprehension. On rereading, the student reads in a lower voice, echoing the material.

Reflection

Think about the comprehension strategies you typically use when reading. While reading the last section of this chapter, list the ways that you monitored your own comprehension. List what you did before reading the section, while reading silently (that is, what did you do when you came to an unfamiliar word? or when something did not make sense? how did you remember important information? how did you decide what was important?) and after reading a passage. Try to become aware of your thinking and the strategies you use in the reading process.

INCLUSION METHODS FOR COMPREHENSION DEVELOPMENT

Duffy (1993) has noted, " . . . if low-achievers are to be strategic (that is, if they are to be flexible adapters of strategies as needed to construct meanings), their teachers must themselves be strategic (flexible adapters of professional knowledge in response to students' developing concepts), and the teachers of teachers must also be strategic (adapting innovations and research findings to teachers' situations and involving them as co-constructors of knowledge rather than telling them what to do)" (245). Knowing a comprehension strategy framework is a beginning point for the reading specialist, and encouraging staff development on strategic reading strategies is also important. See Figure 8.4 for an example of a comprehension strategy framework from Dowhower (1999).

Strategic readers, also known as competent comprehenders, exhibit a pattern of characteristics that are different from ineffective readers (or comprehenders) (Flood & Lapp, 1990). The following sections of this chapter will focus on comprehension methods that facilitate development in three areas where strategic readers and ineffective readers differ: 1) prereading schema activation; 2) metacognitive monitoring and fix-up strategies; and 3) reflection and schema-building after reading.

FIGURE **8.4**

COMPREHENSION STRATEGY FRAMEWORK

I. **Prereading:** Enabling Activities

A. Assess/elicit prior knowledge

Teacher determines with students what they already know about the topic, ideas, structure, or contents of the text to be read. Also, the teacher checks students' knowledge of what a "strategy" is and if they have ever used the particular strategy targeted or others to increase their understanding of what they have read.

B. Build background/relate to prior knowledge

Teacher and students build bridges from known to unknown through use of questions, statements, and activities. What do the students know that will help them understand the text and the new strategies introduced here?

C. Focus attention on strategy

Teacher establishes *what* comprehension strategy students are going to learn and *why* it will help the students. The teacher gives a model or brief description of *how* the strategy works.

II. **Active Reading:** Interaction between Students, Teacher, and Text

A. Cycle 1:

Establish purpose for reading. Reasons for reading the selection are set by either the students or teacher, or jointly.

Read silently designated pages. Students should be encouraged to self-monitor, think about, and react to what they are reading, and to use the strategy, as well as other known strategies to understand what they are reading.

Discuss/work the story. Together, students and teacher negotiate the meaning of the section. The teacher includes one to two open-ended questions for discussion, starting first with the purpose(s) for reading. Utmost in the teacher's mind is working toward meaningful themes. The teacher also supports strategy construction by naming the strategy and showing how she or he uses it personally.

B. Cycle 2 and beyond:

Establish purpose for reading.

Read silently designated pages.

Discuss/work the story.

Repeat cycle as needed.

C. *Final discussion:* Theme and comprehension strategy

Teacher includes one to two open-ended questions that get at the heart of the story (theme) and tie the discussion of the sections together. It is important for the students to explicitly discuss *what* strategy they learned, *why* it helped comprehension, and *when* they could use the strategy again in other texts, particularly in their independent reading. Encourage students to identify other comprehension and decoding strategies that they used as they read.

III. **Postreading:** Independent Activities

These activities are done after reading and working the text. They are done alone or in small groups without the teacher.

A. *Recall of content*

This may include the traditional activities of answering comprehension questions, sequencing text parts, drawing a picture of an important episode, and so on.

B. *Reader response*

Students respond in some fashion to the text. This may include both efferent and aesthetic responses.

C. *Extension of text*

Students go beyond text doing other reading, writing, listening, or speaking activities that are related, such as repeated reading, partner reading, taping the story, Readers' Theatre, or writing a new ending.

D. *Strategy use and transfer*

Students practice the strategy with the specific text or a new text.

E. *Informal or self-assessment*

Students may retell the story or demonstrate comprehension of the text and strategy use in some way. Also, students might explain and evaluate how effectively they were using certain strategies "in flight" by recording and rating them as they read.

IV. **Evaluation of Teaching:** Reflection

How clear were your explanations of the strategy? How well did you use "what, why, how, and when?" How well did you reinforce the strategy throughout the lesson? How well do you think the students understand the strategy and how to apply it to help their comprehension? In what ways did you support the coordination and use of other strategies? How well did the students appreciate and develop understanding of the text on their own terms? Why was the theme(s) constructed appropriate?

Dowhower, 1999, *The Reading Teacher*, 684–685.

Strategic readers have a consistent yet flexible before-reading plan that includes: 1) previewing the text visually with the purpose of calling up relevant thoughts and memories; 2) building background knowledge by activating prior knowledge about the story (or topic), the vocabulary, and the way the topic is presented (textbook, story, diary entry, or other); and 3) setting purposes for reading by predicting questions to answer during the reading section (Flood & Lapp, 1990). Because ineffective readers habitually participate in these characteristics, it is necessary to directly teach struggling readers these processes, then gradually release responsibility to students. The goal is for these activities to become an internalized and automatic part of students' reading characteristics. The following strategies focus on direct instruction in the first area: prereading schema activation.

DIRECT INSTRUCTION IN PREREADING SCHEMA ACTIVATION

Reconciled Reading Lesson

Reutzel (1985) noticed that basal reading lessons placed an emphasis on building background knowledge at the end of the lesson, instead of at the beginning. His solution was to *reverse* the basal reading sequence. This reversed basal lesson, called Reconciled Reading Lesson (RRL) (Reutzel, 1985), includes activation of schema and background knowledge building by using post-reading activities selected from the basal manual at the beginning of the lesson, and extending these activities after the lesson (Thames & Readence, 1988). In a study of second-grade students, Thames and Readence (1988) found that students who used RRL understood the stories to a greater extent than students who used List-Group-Label, a semantic mapping activity, or traditional basal lessons (Thames & Readence, 1988). An additional bonus of the RRL is that vocabulary knowledge accounted for a substantial part (46 percent of the variance) in the scores on the comprehension posttest measure. The next method also focuses on front-loading information to aid comprehension.

Listening-Reading Transfer Lesson

Patricia Cunningham (1975-76) designed this "frontloading" method to teach students to first find the main idea by listening to a passage, then to transfer the same task to a different passage.

STEPS IN THE LISTENING-READING TRANSFER LESSON:

Step 1   Prepare three sentences related to a passage that the students will listen to, with one of the three being the best representation of the main idea.

Step 2   Tell pupils that the main idea of the selection that they will listen to is stated in one of three sentences that you will present to them (either as a handout, on the board, or on an overhead).

Step 3   Following listening, have youngsters indicate which sentence best captures the chief ideas.

Step 4   Repeat the same process with a passage that is read.

The next two methods are especially effective for improving the reconstructive, or "get-the-facts," level of comprehension. They rely heavily on listening, and the third can be converted into a listening activity. Several other excellent means support relying on the listening ability of remedial-level students to compensate for, or otherwise enhance, comprehension. J. S. Choate and Thomas A. Rakes (1987), for example, offer the Structured Listening Activity, which essentially is a Directed Reading-Thinking Activity with the focus on listening instead of reading.

As children are read to, they construct mental images that aid the comprehension process. Consider now those techniques that make use of the mind's eye to image and follow analogies. Imaging is something that proficient readers do naturally, but poor readers do not.

Guided Imagery (Dual Coding Theory)

Ann Hibbing and Joan Rankin-Erickson (2003) claim that visual material can enhance the reading experience for reluctant and low-ability readers. One strategy that they have used relies on an analogy of a *television in the mind*. They use think-alouds to encourage children to talk about a television screen that they are "watching" as they read. This technique has some obvious diagnostic value since the teacher then can determine whether the images described are compatible with the text. The power of imagery in making sense of texts is based on "dual-coding theory"—that is, strengthened mental perception due to a combination of verbal and nonverbal representations (Sadoski, Pavio, & Goetz, 1991).

It has been shown that the act of attempting to construct mental images can help remedial readers to better integrate new learning (Pressley, 1976, 1977) and detect inconsistencies (Gambrell & Bales, 1986; Gambrell & Jawitz, 1993) in textual material. Mark Sadoski (1983; 1985) found that those pupils who were able to image the climax of the story also were those who comprehended it best. This is not conclusive proof that imaging improves comprehension, but it does require a personalized transformation of textual material, and hence is a good bet to activate appropriate prior knowledge and comprehension strategies.

Following is a model for guided imagery instruction, liberally borrowed from a volume called *200 Ways of Using Imagery in the Classroom* (Bagley & Hess, 1982), and from specific recommendations (steps 2 and 6) by Mark Aulls (1978) and Katherine Maria (1990).

STEPS IN GUIDED IMAGERY:

1. Have children relax and attempt to concentrate.
2. Demonstrate (model) for them what you mean by imaging, using a very brief piece.
3. Have them try to form images of the concrete objects mentioned in a second piece.
4. Have them attempt to broaden the pictures of the objects into pictures of large settings.
5. Ask students to think and say what else they see, smell, hear, and feel.
6. Have students record or represent by stick figure drawings what they are imaging before it is spoken aloud by anyone. (This is done in order to permit them to first find their own images before being influenced, and perhaps distracted, by those of others.)

Guided imagery has several uses in the literacy classroom (Anarella, 2000). According to Anarella (2000), it can be used as a prereading experience that sets the mood and time of a story and helps students understand story elements. Guided Imagery can also be used as a prewriting or brainstorming experience to help students "connect to the inside world of character, plot, theme, and imagination" (Anarella, 2000, 5). Listening and speaking skills are encouraged as students listen to the teacher for directions and to other students as they describe their visualizations. As a motivation for creative writing, students can be encouraged to make a graphic organizer of their own to share their five senses, feelings, and any visualization related to the senses (Anarella, 2000). The information on the graphic organizer can be turned into a rough draft, then worked through the writing process.

When a child sees a movie based on a book before reading the book, we know that the power of imagery sometimes can be weakened because the child only pictures in his or her mind what was shown on the screen. The child's identification with that image holds so strongly that a teacher often hears, "That's not right. That's not the way it happened." The power of guided imagery fixes the content of the text in the child's mind as "the way it really happened." Maria (1990) notes that visual images can be so powerful as to be emotionally disquieting to some children. The authors have even witnessed that effect on graduate students who were reading *The Devil's Arithmetic* (Yolen, 1990) and could not erase the book's vivid images from their minds. Missed meals and restless nights were the result. We concur that this is a possibility, but also feel that the quality of the information received from the students on what they may be experiencing tends to outweigh the risks. Further, teachers and reading specialists are professionals who must be trusted to use certain disquieting techniques judiciously: Most things that are powerful also are potentially upsetting when used inappropriately or in excess (think: *controlled substances!*).

Professionals have the authority to use potentially disquieting techniques.

DIRECT INSTRUCTION IN METACOGNITIVE MONITORING AND FIX-UP STRATEGIES

After the strategic reader has activated schema to prepare for reading a text, the reader must continuously self-question while reading by asking questions such as: "Does this make sense?" "What is the author trying to say here?" "What can I do to figure out that word?" "When have I felt like that?" and "What could that word mean?" *Active reading* cycles are repeated for each section of the text as students read and self-monitor (interact with text). Then they should hold discussions with the teacher and other students to work toward understanding of the content, strategy, and theme (Dowhower, 1999). Metacognition refers to introspective awareness

Self-regulation is one of the highest orders of human functioning.

of the factors that influence our ability to monitor and fix internal problems that arise in effective reading, language use, and thinking. It represents one of the highest orders of human functioning. "The goal of metacognitive instruction is to make students aware of the mental processes involved in reading and to equip them with processing strategies that will help them become more active readers" (Loxterman, Beck, & McKeown, 1994, 354).

In practical terms, Annemaire Palinscar and Kathryn Ransom (1988) observe that such training is important for struggling readers since they especially need to be made aware of and participate in efforts to take control of their lives and learning environments. They can and should be taught to be agents, advocates, and teachers, since it is impossible for any other individual or agency to do so for them completely. Students who do not actively think while reading can be taught this process through metacognitive monitoring and fix-up strategies such as the Oral Reading Strategy.

Oral Reading Strategy

The Oral Reading Strategy (Manzo, 1980b), briefly described in an earlier chapter, is a simple way to model the complex "inside the head" processes that enable the reader to comprehend and think about text. The teacher reads content-rich material aloud to students, pausing at logical points to comment or pose simple translation questions. In effect, the teacher models the active reading process of an effective reader, and urges student readers to come along. In addition, the strategy builds student familiarity with the cadence and patterns of language and thought that are characteristic of different subject areas, and introduces correct pronunciations of new words in a straightforward, informal manner.

STEPS IN THE ORAL READING STRATEGY:

Step 1 In preparation, the teacher should always preread the selection that will be used. This makes oral reading more fluent and poignant. At the most basic level, the teacher should be sure about how to pronounce all the words.

Step 2 The teacher reads the first few pages of a selection to the class while they follow along in their texts. The teacher pauses periodically and comments or asks a few simple translation questions: "What do you suppose this word means here?" or "Tell in your own words what point was just made here." At first, the teacher may have to answer the questions, because students are unaccustomed to translating what they read and could have difficulty understanding what they are being asked to do. It also is helpful, especially the first few times the teacher uses this strategy, to jot down some comments or questions to use during this step.

Teacher reading from text:	*The Jura (joo'-ruh) is a mountain range that lies between two rivers, the Rhine and the Rhone.*
Teacher question to class:	What do you picture when you hear that the Jura lies between two rivers?
Teacher comment:	This reminds me of a row of tall office buildings between two streets.
Teacher reading from text:	*The Jura forms part of a natural boundary between Switzerland and France. The Jura extends from the northeast to the southwest in parallel ridges.*
Teacher question to class:	What other kinds of "natural boundaries" do you know of? Can someone define "parallel ridges?"

Step 3 The teacher reads the next page or so with fewer questions and comments. Students are told to listen for the main ideas presented, to pronunciation of unfamiliar words, and for questions they might want to ask before they are asked to continue reading silently.

Step 4 The teacher tells the class to read the next portion of the selection silently. It is important that time be provided for students to continue reading *immediately*, to apply the active reading strategies the teacher has been modeling.

Cloze Techniques for Improving Linguistic Awareness

Patricia Cousin (1991) reminds us of the challenge to help remedial readers, who almost by definition do not have adequate experience with written language, to learn to deal with the "complex linguistic structures used in both literature and expository text" (9).

Using a factor-analysis technique, Wendell Weaver and Albert Kingston (1963) established that cloze procedure, or the fixed deletion of every fifth to ninth word, is a measure of a student's familiarity with the "language redundancy" patterns of prose. James Bowman (1991) notes that "redundancy helps readers predict, thereby increasing their odds in favor of suitable comprehension" (66). Its value as a testing and teaching method in reading comprehension has been called into question by Victor Culver and associates (1972), and more recently by Timothy Shanahan and Michael Kamil (1983). The reason that these researchers have questioned the value of cloze *training* as a means of improving reading comprehension is primarily because of its minimal relationship to key comprehension factors such as background knowledge, connections between sentences,

Cloze training must be used correctly and judiciously.

rate of reading, and reading vocabulary. There also is the fact that insignificant gains were shown in several early studies relying on cloze training (Jongsma, 1980).

Several researchers have found rather inventive ways to use cloze-passage exercises that take advantage of their value in improving familiarity with linguistic patterns in prose, while overcoming their dubious value to the meaning side of comprehension (Schell, 1972; Jongsma, 1980; Guthrie, Barnham, Caplan, & Seifert 1974; Guice 1969; Cunningham and Tierney, 1977; Meeks, 1980; Blachowicz & Zabroske, 1990).

The Inferential (Cloze) Training Technique described below was developed from earlier works by Peter Dewitz, Eileen Carr, and Judith P. Patberg (1987). The technique has been shown to improve general inferring ability, reading comprehension, self-monitoring, and, implicitly, "linguistic awareness"—the area to which cloze is the most significantly related (Weaver & Kingston, 1963). The "active ingredient" in the Inferential (Cloze) Training Technique seems to be the instructional conversation it generates, more so than any inherent value in cloze exercises.

Step 1 Begin with a cloze passage of 5 to 25 words deleted following every fifth to ninth word, depending on the level of difficulty you wish for the pupil to encounter.

Step 2 Pre-teach students essential vocabulary from the passage.

Step 3 Beginning first with one sentence and increasing progressively to paragraphs, demonstrate to students, by sample talk-throughs, how to infer a correct word replacement by using semantic (context) clues, syntactic (grammatical structure) clues, and background knowledge. This can be done with the teacher and then the students alternately talking through each deletion or sentence unit containing more than one deletion.

Step 4 During the talk-through, try to use these self-monitoring guidelines (Cambourne, 1977):

   a. Does the replacement make sense?

   b. Does the replacement cause the sentence to make sense?

   c. Does the replacement combine prior knowledge with clues in the passage?

   d. Is there a forward clue in the same sentence, paragraph, or passage?

   e. Is there a backward clue in the same sentence, paragraph or passage?

   f. Did the clue cause you to change your replacement?

Step 5 The teacher explains why a certain replacement seems correct, then helps the student to do the same thing by asking questions that aid in inferring why certain replacements are more correct than others.

Step 6   The teacher asks students to read a second intact (usually continuing) sentence, paragraph, or passage.

Step 7   The teacher checks overall comprehension with typical main idea, detail, and inferential questions.

Struggling readers often find the cloze task frustrating, especially if they think a grade will be given on this activity. A word bank of options helps ease the frustration level, but still assesses their ability to predict meaning from passage clues. Reassure students that they will not be graded, but that their answers will support the discussion. Just one or two sentences with one, two, or three key words omitted (modified cloze) can provide a prereading, during reading, and/or postreading activity. The cloze task can be made more accessible by offering choices for the words that are deleted. The "Maze" format (Gutherie et al., 1974) provides three choices for each omitted word: the correct word, an incorrect but syntactically correct word, and a syntactically and semantically incorrect choice.

In general, the absence of choices tends to put the emphasis on language pattern training, and the presence of choices tends to shift the task to comprehension, or meaning seeking. Select the emphasis that best meets the students' language and comprehension needs.

An adaptation of the cloze task is to delete only one or two words, but delete the words every time they appear in several paragraphs of text (Blachowicz & Zabroske, 1990). Using this text, directly teach students why and when to use context clues. Some types of text are more explicit about word meaning, while other texts provide hints concerning attributes or relationships but do not clarify meaning. Next, students must be taught the types of clues provided by context and *how* to look for and *use* context clues (Blachowicz & Zabroske, 1990). Some clues include: look before, at, and after the word, connect what you know with what the author tells you, predict a possible meaning; then teacher should resolve or re-do to decide if students know enough, should try again, or consult an expert or reference (Blachowicz & Zabroske, 1990, 506). To model this task, a key word is blacked out of a few paragraphs from a content-area text, and students are guided to determine the missing word.

Once students become familiar with the procedure, student teams are asked to bring in text (photocopied pages from books, news articles, magazine articles, and so on) to post on the chalkboard daily with one or two words blacked out and designated as the "mystery words." Note cards are available so students can write the specific text clues they discovered about the "mystery words" and their hypothesis of the word and its meaning. At

Most English language learners need close training.

There are reasoning strategies for predicting deleted words.

the end of the day the student team that posted the text reviews all the cards with the class and leads a discussion about the word. A point system may be created, if desired (Blachowicz & Zabroske, 1990). This activity helps students to understand how to use context and language patterns to determine word meanings.

Lane Roy Gauthier (1990) devised Inverse Cloze: Delete all but every fifth word of a passage and ask students to try to write a connected story of their own making. Have students share their creations. Students seem to really enjoy this unlikely-looking task. The next section discusses "text structure," another form of pattern recognition.

Text Structure

K. Denise Muth offers a means of teaching text structure incidentally. She suggests that the teacher merely construct "Connection Questions" that follow the format of the text. To ensure that the point of the lesson is not missed, Muth advises that the teacher comment on how a certain question parallels the compare-contrast, or cause-and-effect nature of the expository task (see Figure 8.5).

FIGURE **8.5**

TEXT CONNECTION QUESTIONS

Compare-Contrast

People who want to buy a horse for pleasure riding usually choose between the Quarter horse and the Saddle horse. The Quarter horse has a thick mane and tail. It is strong and able to carry heavy riders over rough trails for several miles. It is also very healthy and does not catch diseases easily. However, the Quarter horse is not comfortable to ride. It has a jerky walk which bumps its rider up and down. Also, it is nervous and hard to control when something unexpected happens.

The Saddle horse is usually brown with dark eyes. It has a steady walk, which is comfortable for riding. It is also easy to control, responds instantly to commands, and is always ready for unexpected things that might lie in its path. The Saddle horse is not very healthy, though, and tends to catch diseases easily from other horses. Also, it is not strong enough to carry heavy loads.

The teacher's questions should focus on helping students understand the author's purpose for using the compare-contrast structure and on the relationships among the ideas in the passages. Here are some questions (and possible student answers) which could help students build "internal connections" among the ideas in the passage.

1. What is the author comparing and contrasting? (the Saddle horse and the Quarter horse)
2. Why is the author comparing and contrasting these two types of horses? (so we can decide which horse is best for pleasure riding)
3. Why did the author use the compare-contrast structure in this particular passage? (to show us that each type of horse has advantages and disadvantages for pleasure riding)
4. What are the advantages of the Quarter horse for pleasure riding? (strong and healthy)
5. What are the advantages of the Saddle horse? (comfortable and easy to control)
6. What are the disadvantages of the Quarter horse for pleasure riding? (uncomfortable and hard to control)
7. What are the disadvantages of the Saddle horse? (not healthy or strong)
8. What other characteristic of the two horses does the author include in the passage? (physical appearance)

9. Is the appearance of the horses important in determining which horse is best for pleasure riding? (no)

10. According to the passage, which of the two types of horses is best for pleasure riding? (there is no clear-cut answer)

11. How would someone decide which of the horses to buy based on what he or she read in this passage? (he or she would have to decide which horse is best for his or her particular needs)

Here are some questions that could help students build "external connections":

1. Which of the two horses would you pick, and why? (I'd pick the Saddle horse because I'm light and wouldn't be carrying heavy loads; also, I don't have any other horses, so it would be hard for my Saddle horse to catch a disease if there aren't any other horses around.)

2. Do you know anyone who might be concerned with the appearance of the horses? (My aunt would. She participates in horse shows, and appearance is very important for show horses.)

Cause-Effect

Why do some things become rusty? Perhaps you found out if you left a shovel or rake outside overnight. When you picked it up a few days later, you might have seen rough, brown spots of rust on it. Air is composed partly of oxygen. Oxygen combines with iron to make rust. Moisture or water helps to bring about the change. Tools like rakes and shovels are made of iron, and they rust quickly if they are left out in wet or damp air. If you left them out long enough, they would rust completely and crumble away.

Again, teacher's questions should focus on helping students understand why the author used the cause-effect structure and how the ideas in the passage are related to each other.

Here are some questions that could help students build "internal connections" among the ideas:

1. Why did the author use the cause-effect structure for this passage? (to describe a process; to give an example of one thing causing something else to happen)

2. What is the cause-effect process that the author is describing? (how things rust)

3. Describe the process of how some things rust. (oxygen and moisture in the air combine with the iron in the objects to cause rust)

4. What causes the process? (the oxygen and the moisture combining with the iron)

5. What is the effect of this combination? (rust)

6. What are the three necessary "ingredients" for rusting? (oxygen, moisture, iron)

These questions could help students build "external connections":

1. Why don't most things usually rust inside your house? (there's not enough moisture)

2. When do you think things might rust in your house? (when the humidity is very high)

3. Can you think of some things that might rust in your house? (the scale in the bathroom, the pipes in the basement)

4. Can you think of some things that you own that might rust if you left them outdoors long enough? (bicycle, wheelbarrow, car)

5. Can you think of some things that you own that won't rust if you leave them outdoors? (basketball, book, sweatshirt)

Muth, 1987, *Journal of Reading*, 254–259.

DIRECT INSTRUCTION IN REFLECTION AND SCHEMA-BUILDING AFTER READING

Strategic readers find ways to respond to the material that they read. Struggling readers need to be guided in responding to text in a variety of ways. The next cluster of techniques tends to rely on deducing or following text structure to build comprehension.

Graphic Organizers: Grammars/Maps/Guides

The mind looks for, and organizes around, categories.

The theory underlying grammars, maps, and guides is that students will be better able to follow a story or line of exposition if they have a set of categories to help them anticipate and recognize information or story parts when they see them. From these, an outline can be constructed. The most common story grammar categories are: setting, problem, goal, action, and outcome. Results of studies on story grammar instruction have been mixed. However, two studies are especially worth noting. In one study, learning-disabled and low-achieving readers were better able to participate in and follow materials up to a year or more above their level, in a heterogeneously grouped class, when story grammar information was provided to guide reading (Idol, 1987). In a second study, it was shown that story grammar instruction of very low-achieving fourth graders resulted in their producing much more complex and fully-formed stories than did a control group (Spiegel & Fitzgerald, 1986). This finding is consistent with many anecdotal reports of the value of various means and methods of structuring, mapping, and charting, which are described next.

Story Mapping is one means of teaching story grammar. It is identified as an effective instructional intervention for students with mild disabilities (Keel, Dangel, & Owens, 1999). Story Mapping helps students build prior knowledge and schema, and interpret and comprehend new information (Sorrell, 1990; Idol, 1987; Idol & Croll, 1987). In this technique the teacher explains and demonstrates how a story can be reduced to a series of frames, detailing factors such as setting, characters, time, place, problem, action, and resolution or outcome. Students then are led through several stories as the teacher gradually fades support and urges students to complete these for themselves, and to begin to make maps that others might use to follow or complete. For additional story maps see the teacher resource *Responses to Literature* by Macon, Bewell, and Vogt (1991). It contains a variety of both standard (Venn Diagram and Story Frames) and unique (Story Pyramid and Story Chart) response formats. See Figure 8.6 for a teacher-generated example.

Joan E. Heimlich and Susan D. Pittelman (1986) compiled an entire monograph that details several classroom applications of a related technique called Semantic Mapping (see Figure 8.7, page 324, for an example). Brenda Spencer (2003) offers a recent and interesting variation on these techniques called *text maps*. These tend to be based on the recurring organizational features in content material. These include features such as: chapter titles, headings, boldface print, illustrations, glossaries, and previews/reviews—essentially the same features assessed with an Informal Textbook Inventory, detailed in Chapter 4. Spencer further suggests that

FIGURE **8.6**

STORY GRAMMAR

My Story Map

Name _____ Date _____

Characters:	Time:	Place:
Bessie and friends	*now*	*Antarctica*

The Problem:
The other penguins made fun of her because she was always so messy.

Action:
She ran away to find a skin that would not get messy. She met a monkey, a porcupine, a bear, a deer, and a wise old owl that told Bessie that she had just the right skin for a penguin. So Bessie went home.

Resolution/Outcome:
Bessie went back home and her friends had made her a bib to keep her clean.

Courtesy of Debbie Fidler and Maryann Spears,
Kansas City Public School District, 1989

such *text maps* can be customized to different subject areas and themes, and to specific texts and sources.

A variety of graphic organizers are also helpful in the comprehension of expository text. Venn diagrams (interlocking circles with common features in the middle section) and H-maps (Hadaway & Young, 1994) are two of many structures that visually depict text organization. Figure 8.8 (page 325) contains an example of an H-map.

These graphic methods and approaches appear to have begun with the pioneering research of Richard Barron (1969) on Structured Overviews and M. B. Hanf (1971) on student mapping. The general objective of

FIGURE **8.7**

A CLASSROOM MAP (FOR *KATE AND THE ZOO*)

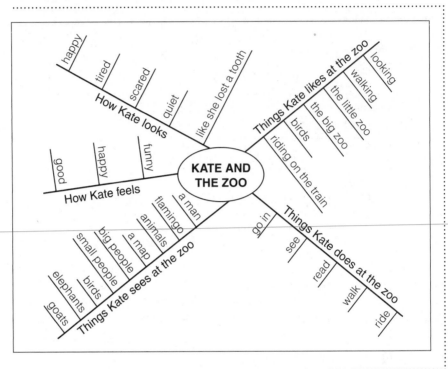

structuring is to help students to become more sensitive and active in forming a conceptual overview of a piece. This is also the role of reading guides that are textual rather than graphic organizations of a piece (Clewell & Heidemenos, 1983). All Write is another technique that actively involves all students at the same time.

All Write

Writing following reading is basic diagnostic-teaching.

After students have read a passage, a quick and easy way to assess their comprehension and to motivate discussion is to have every student write a response for a specified period of time. One-, two-, three-, five-, and ten-minute All Write sessions can be used, depending on the age of the students and the complexity of the material. During the session, the students write quickly and spontaneously to get down on paper everything they remember about the text. Students must spend all of their time writing,

FIGURE **8.8**

H-MAP (COMPARE-CONTRAST MAP)

Cold Front		Warm Front
cold air warm air sudden changes moves fast very windy air rises thunderstorms rain storms air cool	**Both** warm, cold air weather changes some precipitation some wind	warm air cold air slow changes moves slowly light wind air showers air warm

Hadaway & Young, 1994, 524

even if they must repeatedly write a word while they are thinking of the next sentence. This process is similar to brainstorming on paper, and the teacher simply says, "Write everything that you learned from this passage."

After the students have written their responses, Think-Pair-Share (Kagan, 1997) can be used. The "Think" portion is completed in the writing, so students quickly get with a partner to read what they have written. Next, students can volunteer to share their response or their partner's response to motivate class discussion of the passage. An adaptation of All Write that the authors have found to be successful with middle school and high school students, is to require students to write an on-your-own All Write in the form of a filled note card response over an assigned reading passage. As the students walk in the classroom door, the teacher collects their "classroom passes" that activate their schema for the topic of discussion and hold them accountable for the assigned reading. Collecting these note card responses for credit increased the amount of out-of-class textbook reading at several schools. By reading the All Write responses, the teacher can tell how well students comprehend the material and what strategies need to be taught. The next technique allows students to put down their pencils and become actively involved with their bodies and minds.

InQuest

Mary Shoop's (1985, 1986) "interview" technique called Investigative Questioning, or "InQuest," involves the reader or listener with narrative text through student questioning and spontaneous drama techniques. As a

Dramatization can be a form of Facilitative Pretending.

precondition, students are led through a discussion and practice of the techniques involved in journalistic interviewing. The following points are made to students in the discussion:

1. Ask questions that get longer responses.
2. Follow *yes/no* questions with "*Why?*"
3. Try to elicit *reflections and evaluations* as well as simple information.
4. Use a variety of question *types*.

Students may also have had experience using the ReQuest procedure to develop further incidental knowledge about questioning types and strategies.

Subsequent steps in InQuest include:

1. The teacher selects an interesting story that is read by the teacher or students up to a critical point or incident.
2. The teacher suggests to students that they try to think of questions that they would like to ask a character as the story unfolds.
3. Students role-play a news conference in which someone plays the character, and everyone else assumes the roles of investigative reporters. (The teacher may model role-playing of either of these parts.)
4. Students are directed to read on to a next point, and repeat the interview process with a different or the same character.
5. Have students evaluate which questions proved most interesting, in the sense of bringing characters to life.

InQuest tends to engage students in a level of *Facilitative Pretending* that is discussed more fully in a chapter ahead. This kind of teaching can powerfully affect students' sense of the *experience* of learning, as well as the fact of it.

REVIEW

This chapter covered many of the fundamental concepts and practices most often associated with learning to read to comprehend in the elementary and intermediate grades. The process could be said to begin at the preschool level, and gains momentum at the secondary and even college and adult levels. The most powerful principles and robust methods are those that begin at the prereading or frontloading stage.

PREVIEW

The next two chapters continue the development of comprehension processes, at a spiraling more than a different level. Chapter 9 speaks to "meaning" as it is captured and codified in words, also known as vocabulary acquisition. In some ways, word knowledge sets the stage for comprehension, and also "locks it up" in a few portable terms. Chapter 10 continues discussion of comprehension development into content areas, and through study-type reading.

VOCABULARY: PRESCRIPTION FOR CONCEPT, CONTENT, AND COGNITIVE DEVELOPMENT

*The most powerful thing that can be done
for a phenomenon is to name it.* – ALBERT EINSTEIN

CONTENT AND CONCEPT ORGANIZER

The words we use influence as well as reflect our knowledge, feelings, sentiments, and mental occupations. The opportunity to teach someone new words is like being given access to a computer's "source code." This chapter will guide you to responsibly make the most of this privilege and trust. Perhaps not so surprisingly, one of the most powerful methods for teaching new terms connects word meanings to sensorimotor expression, one of the earliest means by which we learn, since it is channeled into one of the most primitive parts of the human brain.

CHAPTER OUTLINE

VOCABULARY CONCEPTS
  AND COGNITIVE DEVELOPMENT
  Benefits of Vocabulary Instruction
  How Is Vocabulary Naturally Acquired?

CONSIDERATIONS IN VOCABULARY INSTRUCTION
  Align Instruction with the Process
  Impart a Facilitative Disposition
  The Paradox of Incidental versus Direct Teaching

METHODS TO HEIGHTEN
  WORD CONSCIOUSNESS
  Community of Language Approach
  Vocabulary Self-Collection Strategy (VSS)

INTRODUCING NEW VOCABULARY
  Subjective Approach to Vocabulary (SAV)
  Motor Imaging (MI)
  Incidental Morpheme Analysis (IMA)
  The Keyword Method

METHODS FOR IN-DEPTH WORD STUDY
  Concept-Based Approach to Vocabulary Building
  Semantic Feature Analysis (SFA) and SAVOR
  Possible Sentences
  Themed Vocabulary Study (TVS)
  Vocabulary Classmates
  Wear-A-Word
  Dictionary Use

GAMES TO REINFORCE WORD LEARNING
  Wordy Gurdy Puzzles
  Oxymorons

WORDS CAN BRING US TOGETHER

ELL VOCABULARY INSTRUCTION

HOW THE LITERACY SPECIALIST CAN HELP

REVIEW

PREVIEW

VOCABULARY CONCEPTS AND COGNITIVE DEVELOPMENT

Words are food for the brain. In principle, most people agree that students with literacy needs should be taught new words. Too often, however, programs for struggling readers neglect this source of academic nourishment (Nagy & Scott, 2000). In fact, in an annual survey of areas of interest, vocabulary acquisition was rated as a low priority by most practitioners for two years running (Cassidy & Wenrich, 1997, 1998). There seems to be a sense that there is no rush to teach vocabulary since corrective/remedial students have a more pressing need to learn how to read *known* words. There also is a reductionist sense that *words* are the smallest units of meaning, and that they are learned by memorizing short definitions used in contrived sentences (Nagy & Scott, 2000). It doesn't take much examination to see that this sentiment tends to add to the deprivation of students with literacy deficits, who are already cut off from reading, one of the main sources of normal concept and vocabulary growth. Ironically, if you could do just one thing to help someone to become more literate, it probably would be to teach him or her a new word.

> Struggling readers rarely are given instruction in New Words, the WD-40 of smooth and effective thinking and cognitive enrichment.

Just as "automaticity" in word recognition makes smooth and fluent decoding possible, a quick and thorough recognition of the *meanings* of each word read, and the sentence structures in which words are set, makes smooth and accurate comprehension possible. Let us now consider further possible benefits, and reasons, for promoting vocabulary development in students at the corrective/remedial levels. Many of the same arguments could be made for giving greater attention to vocabulary in working with average and above-average students.

Benefits of Vocabulary Instruction

A rich vocabulary enhances "inner-speech," or the mediating system by which we process information, reflect, think, feel, and formulate responses (Manzo & Sherk, 1971–72; Graves & Hammond, 1980; Vygotsky, 1962). Words are labels for concepts: from simple to extraordinarily complex. Word labels make concepts more memorable, portable, manipulatable, and malleable. Set into the syntax of language, they are the vehicle for the inner-speech of thinking as well as for communicating. Enlarging the range of words available for improving inner-speech tends to improve:

- comprehension of what is read and heard (Davis, 1944; Anderson & Freebody, 1981)
- accuracy and clarity of thinking
- school and real-life problem solving

- access to new concepts, allusions, and other new words
- access to, and comprehension of, one's own feelings and experiences
- one's sense of self-efficacy and self-worth (Gauthier, 1992; Stahl & Kapinus,1991; O'Brien, 1986)

Level of vocabulary is the best single predictor of IQ, GPA, and most cognitive factors.

In a word, *words* are *empowering*, and promote cognitive development. Vocabulary size is the best single predictor of IQ and intellectual ability (Manzo & Sherk, 1971–72). Curiously, words are more easily learned than is commonly recognized: Students learn about 2,000 to 5,000 words per year, accumulating to nearly 25,000 words by the eighth grade and more than 50,000 words by the end of high school (Nagy & Scott, 2000; Graves, 2000).

How Is Vocabulary Normally Acquired?

New vocabulary words are initially acquired in four ways:

- incidentally, through reading and conversation
- through direct instruction, as when a teacher or autoinstructional material is used to intentionally build vocabulary power
- through self-instruction, as when words are looked up in a dictionary, or their meanings are sought from others in a conscious manner
- through mental manipulation of words and the concepts they represent while thinking, speaking, and writing

Words are labels for concepts, and where the culture of school is concerned, both words and concepts are the "coin of the realm."

Each of these sources of knowledge, as shown in the following illustration, is impelled and amplified by an appropriate social/cultural climate and conducive community of language (Manzo & Manzo, 1990a; Whorf, 1956; Vygotsky, 1962). Importantly too, vocabulary enrichment has been found to have the greatest effect on reading comprehension when it was offered in a wrap-around way, as in one classic study that used radio broadcasts and an assortment of follow-up activities (Draper & Moeller, 1971).

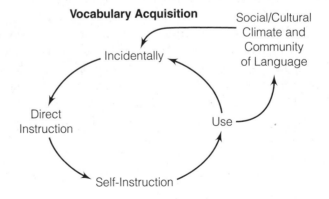

Learning a word is not a "know it" or "do not know it" process. Students sometimes can even give a definition for a word, yet not understand the word when it is used in context. Word knowledge is best represented as a continuum. Beck, McKeown, and Omanson (1987) suggest these labels for such a system:

1. no knowledge
2. general informational level
3. narrow recognition (usually context-bound)
4. need to hesitate to remember a meaning
5. easy recognition and full knowledge

Paribakht and Wesche (1997) refer to the fifth level as the ability to use the word in a sentence, although this might be better thought of as a sixth level: We are able to easily recognize many words when reading that do not come readily to mind for use when speaking or writing. Thinking of word knowledge on this continuum also sheds light on the perplexing fact that many students can read a passage quite fluently and, when asked, tell the meanings of the more difficult words in it but are unable to answer the simplest question about the meaning of the passage itself. To read with comprehension, virtually all the words in the passage must be known at level 5.

> Vocabulary growth includes making "known" words more useable.

Vocabulary acquisition is a process of moving words through each of these stages. It involves both learning "new" words, and making "known" words increasingly usable.

CONSIDERATIONS IN VOCABULARY INSTRUCTION

Several comprehensive reviews of the literature on vocabulary acquisition, including those by Baumann and Kameenui (1991), Blachowicz and Fisher (2000), and Nagy and Scott (2000), make it possible to summarize research-supported findings related to readers with corrective/remedial needs. Three considerations emerge: the need to connect instruction of the *process* of vocabulary learning; the need to impart a positive *disposition* to acquire words; and overcoming a paradox between incidental and direct teaching-learning. Each of these is discussed below, followed by teaching methods that translate these considerations into practice.

Align Instruction with the Process

It has been estimated that only about 20 percent of the words in the average adult's vocabulary were learned through direct instruction. The other

80 percent were learned incidentally in the course of reading, listening, and learning something new. Rather than attempting to teach *more* words directly—there simply is not enough time in the day or the year—vocabulary instruction can be made much more powerful when words are taught in ways that teach students to more easily learn words on their own, even if this means actually teaching *fewer* words. Some students acquire word-learning habits easily and others encounter obstacles, but all can be helped to improve their word learning through instruction that is designed to instill the fundamental elements of word learning:

- *Word consciousness*—recognizing when an unknown (or shallowly known) word or a new meaning for a known word is encountered
- *Personal connections*—establishing ties between the meaning of a new word and the student's existing experience, knowledge, attitudes, and even motor (gestural) associations
- *Automaticity*—automatic recognition of full and contextually appropriate word meanings requires practice distributed over time, as well as opportunities for frequent encounters with the word in similar and differing contexts—in natural word learning, this is accomplished through wide reading, but it can be even more efficiently accomplished through game-like activities
- *Meaningful use*—words are learned to the extent that there is a felt need for them, in order to communicate important information or ideas in a way that conforms to one's self- and social-image

> Vocabulary acquisition requires multiple exposures, and many attempts at usage.

Impart a Facilitative Disposition

Since a positive disposition, or attitude, is an essential prerequisite for effective word learning, teachers need to do at least three things in teaching vocabulary. First and foremost, *model an interest in words*; that is, view *every* instructional episode as an opportunity to show that words are fascinating, and that knowing words and how to use them is a desirable goal. Second, it is important for vocabulary lessons to be varied and engaging. Vocabulary instruction should be more than dictionary worksheets. Use methods that exploit *all domains* of language learning—cognitive, affective, and sensorimotor. Third, increase student involvement by asking *students* to select some methods that they feel to be most profitable and using these more frequently. It is *not* a good idea, however, to surrender the right and responsibility to use less preferred methods. Occasionally, a less popular method may be related to considerations that the student may not understand, such as the paradox described next.

The Paradox of Incidental versus Direct Teaching

No matter which methods are chosen to provide instruction in vocabulary, there is a paradox in the research literature that needs to be considered and addressed. The paradox is as follows: Direct instructional approaches are almost always more effective than wide reading and other incidental means of promoting word learning (Nagy & Herman, 1984; Nelson-Herber, 1986). Nonetheless, most knowledge of word meanings, as noted above, seems to be acquired incidentally and through wide reading and listening (Harris & Sipay, 1990). The reason, Nagy (1988) speculates, is the "sheer volume" of new words encountered in reading. An additional possibility is that we may not acquire many "new" words through wide reading but move many words that are slightly known into the full and "usable" realm. In point of fact, research indicates that learning a new word from print takes about six to ten exposures (Beck & McKeown, 1991). A solid vocabulary development program needs to involve both direct instruction—which, like thunder, gets everyone's attention—and indirect and incidental methods—which, like rain, grow new words on old branches, and new branches on old trees.

> Vocabulary Paradox Resolved: Direct instruction is like thunder; incidental acquisition is like the rain . . . one gets your attention; the other grows conceptual crops.

The remainder of this chapter provides specific methodologies for implementing these considerations.

The methods in the next section are categorized in three groups:

- methods and approaches for heightening word consciousness
- methods for introducing new vocabulary
- methods for in-depth word study

Reflection

Think about your reading and speaking vocabulary. Would you rate it as excellent, moderate, or limited? Take a few minutes to list the ways that you were taught vocabulary terms. Do you think these were effective methods of instruction? As you read about the following vocabulary strategies, think of ways that you might apply them in your classroom and personal growth.

Many of the methods accomplish multiple objectives: They are categorized here according to their primary emphasis or "salient feature" in terms of instructional planning objectives.

METHODS TO HEIGHTEN WORD CONSCIOUSNESS

The first three vocabulary methods address the matter of student disposition toward words and word learning. They are extensions of the idea of "organic words," a means used by Sylvia Ashton-Warner (1959) to describe her chief method of encouraging the Maori children of New Zealand to become literate. They would tell her a word they wished to know, she would show them how to spell it out and give it to them on a card, and they then would *own* the word. However, they were expected to read it any time she asked. If they missed their own word three times, they would lose it. The methods presented next extend this organic, or words-as-an-extension-of-self-and-environment approach from word recognition to word meaning level.

Community of Language Approach

School is life; create a richer *community of language,* and students will absorb it.

Cultural studies have revealed what has come to be known as the *Sapir-Whorf Hypothesis* (Whorf, 1956). Or, a culture's interests and occupations, and therefore the words and concepts known by the "tribe," will be reflected in the number of words and fine distinctions they make in certain areas of human experience. As an example, in Inuit languages (formerly referred to as Eskimo) it is said that there are fourteen words for snow. The distinctions include fallen snow on ice, fallen snow on water, fresh snow, clinging particles of snow, soft deep snow, and snow formations about to collapse. Most everyone, including those who are relatively low functioning, grasp these terms from their use in that cultural setting. School also is a cultural setting with a community of language and occupations.

Words can keep us apart, and bring us together.

The Community of Language Approach to vocabulary/concept development logically is one of the most effective ways to build word consciousness, concepts, and knowledge. It begins with identifying a list of key concept vocabulary words from a theme unit to be implemented in a classroom or clinic setting (the number of words on the list will vary according to grade level and student achievement level). Ideally, in a school setting, the list would be developed and used by all teachers of a grade level. Then teachers, and possibly even the principal, and support staff simply are asked to *use* the words on the list as often as they can in their everyday interactions with students throughout the school day. Teachers tape the word list to their desks or outside frequently used notebooks as a constant reminder to use the words whenever possible. Children begin to *notice* the frequent occurrence of the words, and the fact that the words are being used in different places by different people in the school: word consciousness. In this way, words as esoteric as *bucolic* are learned as naturally as we learn more frequently-used synonyms like *rural, rustic, countryside,* and *pastoral.* If students ask about the word lists, as they almost always do, and whether they have to "look them up for a test or something," they are told that these are the important words from the unit they are beginning—so important that the teacher(s) will try as hard as they can to use them often enough that the students will learn them without ever *having* to look them up. The fact that the adults in the building are making this cooperative effort sends a clear message to children: words are important, and we are committed to helping you learn them.

The Community of Language Approach builds word consciousness by implanting words into students' experience. The next method does so by having students "find" one word a week, in their reading or listening inside and outside of school, to nominate for the weekly word list.

Vocabulary Self-Collection Strategy (VSS)

The Vocabulary Self-Collection Strategy, or VSS (Haggard, now Ruddell, 1982, 1986), is a fundamental way of opening students' minds to the wealth of words they encounter in print and the oral language that surrounds them each day: raising word consciousness. As described by Ruddell and Shearer (2002), the method is implemented as follows.

> Self-collection approaches raise word consciousness.

Step 1   Students are asked to search their viewing, reading, and home environments for a word to nominate for the weekly class vocabulary list. The nomination process involves telling: a) where they found the word; b) what they think it means; and c) why they think it should be on the class list. The teacher also nominates a word each week, giving the same information.

Step 2   In discussing each word, definitions are refined, and dictionaries or other sources are consulted as needed.

Step 3   When the final list of words has been selected, students record the words and definitions in their vocabulary journals.

Step 4   The words are further studied through the week, using discussion, semantic mapping, semantic feature analysis, and other interactive activities.

Step 5   At the end of each week, students are tested on their ability to spell each word, explain its meaning, and use it in a sentence.

Step 6   Every three weeks, past word lists are reviewed, and students are tested on five randomly selected words from past weekly lists.

The VSS procedure implemented in this way was evaluated in a recent study involving seventh- and eighth-grade students reading from two to four years below grade level and performing at an average of C level on traditional vocabulary/spelling lists (Ruddell & Shearer, 2002). The lists that students nominated and selected over the nine weeks were judged to "meet the criterion of 'significant difficulty' for seventh- and eighth-grade students" (Ruddell & Shearer, 2002, 357). The combined word meaning scores on the VSS weekly tests and three-week review tests yielded a mean of 94%: an A– average. The combined spelling scores yielded a mean of 76%, which was found to be statistically significantly higher than on spelling lists from the curriculum. Blachowicz and Fisher (2000) cite several studies showing that when students at various grade levels select their own words for literature circles, vocabulary, and/or spelling instruction, they consistently choose more difficult words and learn the words more effectively.

VSS could be criticized for the fact that a good deal of class time is spent on words that are not likely to be in the required curriculum. However, it builds important strategies for word learning. It sends students on a real-world "word search"—for words their classmates will find interesting and valuable. It builds in practice and in-depth word study as well, but its salient feature is that it heightens their attention to words around them at school and at home, building the habit of word consciousness. A related method, the Cultural Academic Trivia "game," has the same premise but it is based on a slightly broader definition of vocabulary building. It is detailed in the last chapter of this textbook, on secondary and adult learners.

Introducing New Vocabulary

Definitions often seem to be written in a secret code.

An important objective in vocabulary instruction is to introduce students to new words. "Definitions almost seem to be written in a secret code, accessible only to those with the inside knowledge" (Nagy & Herman, 1987, 29). A strategic game plan for vocabulary acquisition must include training in how to transform this *definition code* into something that a novice can get his or her arms around. The first two methods in this section each contribute to doing so by providing the dictionary definition for openers, and then simultaneously teaching a strategy for grasping and *remembering* new word meanings.

Subjective Approach to Vocabulary (SAV)

The SAV procedure (Manzo, 1983) builds on students' personal views and associations with a new word meaning. It uses these "knowns" to anchor fleeting word meanings, keeping them from drifting off and being forgotten. The method imparts a self-instructional strategy as well, since students learn how to use their own prior knowledge and experiences to connect the new word with personal experiences, knowledge, and attitudes, much like good word learners do naturally as they encounter new words. The connective value of *human experience* in word learning is supported by both anecdotal and experimental scholarship (Nilsen & Nilsen, 2003).

> SAV anchors words that otherwise would drift off in a sea of language.

The teacher, using a "talk-through" technique, simply helps students to tie their lives and experiences to new words. Thus, the biographies of individual lives become part of the ongoing biography of a word, much as in Vocabulary Classmates (described ahead). When used in a group situation, the method offers keen diagnostic opportunities for discovering how students think and what they might be saying to themselves. It also gives students a chance to hear the views of others. In this way, multicultural knowledge and insights can occur in a very natural and authentic manner.

SAV has another important characteristic. It tends to speed up transfer of learning and application because the associations used to understand the word arise from the context of the students' lives, and are easily applicable to school and life outside of school (see Figures 9.1 and 9.2).

STEPS IN THE SAV GROUP REMEDIAL FORM

Step 1   The teacher identifies two to four words to be taught, or "pretaught" if SAV is used as a prereading activity. If a word list is used, be sure to include as many words as possible which impart concepts and feelings that you wish students to learn.

Step 2   The teacher tells the student the full meaning of a word, much as it might be found in a dictionary. It is recorded in a Word Study Journal as the "objective," or dictionary meaning.

Step 3   The teacher asks the student(s), "What does this word remind you of?" or "What do you picture or think of when you hear this word?" (Explain that discussion of a personal association with a word can be very helpful in remembering and clarifying its meaning.)

Step 4   The teacher talks the students through this personal search for meaning by asking further clarifying questions. Do this in group situations by pointing out suggested images that seem most vivid. The teacher may also suggest images, especially when student images appear vague. Students are then directed to write some "subjective," or personal, associations for the new word under the previously written dictionary definition in their Journals. Drawings can be added (see Figures 9.1 and 9.2).

Step 5   Silent reading follows next when SAV is used for prereading vocabulary development. When it is being used for general vocabulary development, students are given 5 to 10 minutes to study and rehearse the new and previously recorded words.

Step 6   The teacher has students close their Word Study Journals and asks them the meanings of the words studied that day and a few others from previous days. This step can be tied to seat exercises in conventional workbooks such as crossword puzzles, category games, and so on. This manipulation and reinforcement step can be made easier by selecting the words to be taught from the exercise material.

The Subjective (Connection) Approach to Vocabulary plays into our innate interest in our own story.

The next strategy makes further and deeper use of personal associations. It taps into a seldom-used domain of school teaching-learning, though one fundamental to most all human experience.

FIGURE **9.1**

SUBJECTIVE APPROACH TO VOCABULARY

The Word Is "Magnetic"

Teacher: Do you know what a **magnet** is?

Student: Yeah, you have one on your desk with paper-clips stuck to it.

Teacher: Well, the word **magnetic** comes from **magnet**, and, according to the dictionary, it means two things: 1) having the properties of a magnet—that is, doing what magnets do; 2) being attractive and charming, therefore drawing people to you, such as having a "magnetic personality." Let's write these meanings down in your Word Study Journal. [Pause to record meanings.]

Teacher: What comes to mind when you hear the word **magnetic**?

Student: My brother, Billy. Mr. Ablomp, our neighbor, is a grump. But he gave Billy some of his old golf clubs. Everyone likes Billy, and they give him things.

Teacher: I guess you'd say that he has a "magnetic personality?"

Student: He has a lot of "magnetic personality."

Teacher: Another way to say that is, "He has a great deal of **personal magnetism**."

Student: He's got it, whatever you call it.

Teacher: Do you think that you'll mention Billy's magnetic personality to anyone at home? It's good to use new words.

Student: Yeah, I guess I'll tell my dad. He says that being pleasant is important in selling stuff.

Teacher: Being **magnetic**?

Student: Right.

Teacher: Let's write out your personal association with **magnetic** to help you to remember it. See if you can illustrate the word with a drawing.

Student: Okay.

FIGURE **9.2**

THE SAV MATRIX

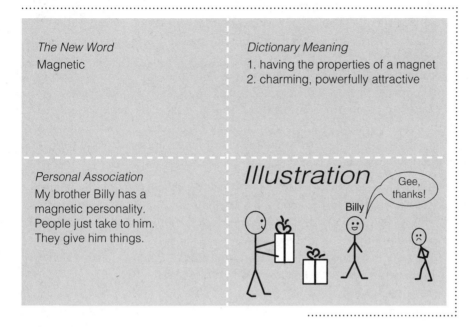

Motor Imaging (MI)

Motor Imaging (Casale [Manzo] & Manzo, 1985) involves the physical-sensory, as well as affective and cognitive domains. There has been little recognition even of the existence of this domain; it was not acknowledged by Bloom (1956) nor by Krathwohl, et al. (1964), the chief architects of the handbooks of the cognitive, affective, and attitudinal domains. MI relies on a form of learning that incorporates meaningful gestures to supplement verbal word learning. It is known technically as *proprioceptive learning*—learning that comes to reside within the nervous system.

The basic idea is very old, though generally overlooked in the design of instruction for all but seriously disabled readers with basic word recognition problems (see the Visual-Auditory-Kinesthetic-Tactile technique in Chapter 7). Developmental psychologists, such as Jean Piaget, have observed that young children first respond to a stimulus with meaningful motor movements. Over time, these motor responses are "abbreviated" into more subtle motor responses, and eventually are "interiorized" as verbal language is acquired (Piaget, 1963). To test the effect of linking new word meanings to "interiorized" motor meanings, a study was conducted that compared three approaches to vocabulary learning: one relying heavily on cognitive training—a dictionary-based technique; one based on the affective domain—a subjective association method similar to SAV; and a

Motor Imaging suggests the need for an addition to Bloom's Taxonomy.

motor-based method—Motor Imaging, described ahead. Fifth- and sixth-grade students were rotated through each of these three treatments in different orders. The words they were exposed to had been shown to be equally difficult. The study showed that the motor and subjective approaches were superior to the dictionary method, and that the motor was superior to both on four of five possible measures. This was true across ability levels (Casale [Manzo] & Manzo, 1983).

It appears that even the highest forms of vocabulary and concept learning have psychomotor connections. Hence, motor movements associated with certain stimuli can become interiorized as "symbolic meaning" (Piaget, 1963). There are four considerable advantages to knowing this where remediation is concerned:

- First, since physical-sensory, or proprioceptive, learnings can be interiorized, they also can be self-stimulating, therefore easier to rehearse and recall with the slightest mental reminder, or from external stimulation.
- Second, proprioceptive learning is so basic to human learning that it is common to all learners, fast and slow, hence, ideal for heterogeneously grouped classes.
- Third, the act of identifying and acting out a word becomes a life experience in itself —a value that Frederick Duffelmeyer (1980a) demonstrated when he successfully taught words using an "experiential" approach.
- Fourth, there is a "dual-coding" (Sadoski, Paivio, & Goetz, 1991) of words and meanings that, by this theory, should enhance perception and therefore depth of learning and recall.

STEPS IN MOTOR IMAGING

Step 1   The teacher writes the target word on the chalkboard, pronounces it, and tells what it means.

Step 2   The teacher asks students to imagine a simple pantomime or gesture for the word meaning ("How could you 'show' someone what this word means with just your hands or a gesture?").

Step 3   When the teacher gives a signal, students do their gesture pantomimes simultaneously.

Step 4   The teacher selects the most common pantomime observed. The teacher then demonstrates it to all the students, who then say the *word* while doing the pantomime.

Step 5   The teacher repeats each new word, this time directing the class to do the pantomime while saying a brief *meaning* or *simple synonym*.

FIGURE **9.3**

MOTOR IMAGING EXAMPLES

New Word	Language Meaning	Motor Meaning
appropriate	right or fit for a certain purpose	both palms together matching perfectly
convey	take or carry from one place to another	both hands together, moving from one side to the other
woe	great sadness or trouble	one or both hands over the eyes, head slanted forward
dazzle	shine or reflect brightly	palms close together, facing outward, fingers spread
utmost	the very highest or most	one or both hands reaching up as far as possible
abode	place where you live	hands meeting above the head in a triangular "roof" shape

Step 6   The students' next encounter with the word is in the assigned reading material.

Step 7   The teacher should try to casually use the pantomime whenever the new word is used for a short time thereafter.

Figure 9.3 presents some examples from a Motor Imaging lesson.

Several teachers and specialists have reported that they have successfully used this same basic approach in teaching students letter sounds: a hand gesture or expression is selected for a troublesome sound; the same gesture then is used each time the sound occurs, no matter what grapheme is present (for example, a finger pointing to the eye, for the long sound of "i," whether in **sigh, lie,** or b**y**; a hand compressing for any vowel forming a *schwa*—the neutral vowel sound of most unstressed syllables in English, as of "*a*" in *ago* or in *cobra*.

Forming teams to play "Vocabulary Charades" is a related physical-sensory activity. Students are divided into several teams, and each team is given a portion of the words on a list of vocabulary words that they have had some opportunity to study (*not* entirely new words). Taking turns, the first student on a team acts out a word and the other teams try to guess the word. The first team to correctly identify the word earns 1 point. The winning team is the one with the most points at the end of the game (Foil & Alber, 2002).

The next method makes use of structural analysis of words to teach their meanings more so than to promote effective word decoding and spelling—although the latter two benefit as well.

Sensorimotor connection to words is rooted in our primordial brain . . . it may be the most counter-intuitive and yet best way to teach new words.

Incidental Morpheme Analysis (IMA)

A *morpheme* is the smallest meaningful part of a word. Sometimes it is the entire word, as in: *the, spider,* and *claw.* IMA (Manzo & Manzo, 1990a) was developed to teach students how to "unlock" the meanings of many words by using the morphemes within words that they know, and without excessive memorizing of lists of morpheme meanings or reference to rules and issues in syllabication. It is described as "incidental" because it is done on an opportunistic basis, and it cannot be used with all words—only those with two or more meaningful word parts. In fact, it can require preparation, as does most successful "incidental" teaching.

Morphemes provide the most basic means for making sense of new words.

Most expert readers and language users use morphemes to make sense out of and remember new words. The Incidental Morpheme Analysis strategy teaches students to apply knowledge of morphemes to "doping-out" plausible meanings of new words encountered in reading. It is further aided by using context effectively. It also is orderly, lesson plan friendly, and frequently used by expert readers. Remember, however, that both morpheme analysis and context clues are "in-flight" maneuvers that can be misleading; they influence the meanings we make as well as the meanings we might take.

STEPS IN INCIDENTAL MORPHEME ANALYSIS

The teacher first identifies words in a reading selection that probably are unfamiliar to students but have familiar word parts, or morphemes. Use the following steps to pre-teach and/or reinforce these terms.

Step 1 Write the term on the chalkboard and underline the meaningful word parts, or morphemic elements, that might help students understand the word's concept base.

   Example: *seis* mo *graph*

Step 2 Ask students if they can use the underlined parts to grasp the word meaning, and why. If the word meaning is predicted correctly, write it under the word and proceed with steps 3 and 4 as reinforcement.

Step 3 Tell students you will give them additional clues for predicting (or remembering) the word meaning. Beneath the underlined word parts, write "level one" clues which are other, easier words using those morphemes. If students have not yet correctly predicted the word meaning, continue to ask for predictions.

Step 4 Beneath the "level one" clues, write "level two" clues, which are the word part meanings, and continue to ask for predictions until the correct definition is reached and written below the clues.

Example:	*seis*	mo	*graph*
Level one clues: familiar word containing the underlined morphemes	seizure		telegraph graphic
Level two clues: word part meanings	to shake		written
Definition:		an instrument that records the direction, time, and intensity of earthquakes	

Minor Caution: Morpheme analysis influences the meanings we make and therefore the meanings we (speculatively) take about a word's meaning.

A list of frequently used Latin and Greek morphemes can be useful in developing this strategy.

The next method relies on teacher-focused analytical reasoning as a form of cognitive enrichment. The method is based on an ancient technique for improving memory—best implemented with an imaginative and lighthearted air.

The Keyword Method

The Keyword method links a new word meaning to a "rememberable" mental image by hooking the *sound* of the word to the *sound* of a known word that is then connected in some way to the meaning of the new word. For example, to remember the meaning of the word "plateau," it could be connected, from its sound, with "plate," pictured or drawn as being raised up—and connecting that image to the meaning of plateau—"a raised flatland."

This method has been reported as effective with LD students (Gutherie, 1984; Condus, Marshall, & Miller, 1986), and in learning content material (Levin et al., 1986; Konopak & William, 1988). Students in grades 3, 4, 7, and 8 who used the Keyword method performed higher on recall of definitions and sentence and story comprehension usage than students who used a sentence context method (Levin, Levin, Glasman, & Nordwall, 1992). Pressley and associates, who have studied Keyword the most extensively, maintain that it helps students learn how to form connections and to develop elaborations on concepts (Pressley, Levin, & Miller, 1981; Pressley, Johnson, & Symons, 1987; Pressley, Levin, & McDaniel, 1987). They do note, however, that it can be demanding for children under 11 years old. Young children tend to require several explicit examples (Pressley, Levin, & Miller, 1981).

Keyword is best used with older children.

Some critics have maintained that the Keyword method is cumbersome and artificial (Moore, 1987). However, when vocabulary learning is thought of as a several-stage continuum, this method is seen to do a good job of moving word knowledge from zero or minimal into the mid-range of having to pause a moment to recall the word meaning, though it does not accomplish the final stage of full and automatic word knowledge.

Keyword does create an interesting instructional conversation in which the teacher and students come to the workbench together, and it inculcates a potentially useful memory training device (see Chapter 10 for additional memory devices). The Keyword method also tends to incidentally reveal students' thought processes, always a plus in diagnosis.

METHODS FOR IN-DEPTH WORD STUDY

To review, word meanings are moved from a superficial knowledge level to full concept understanding when they have been connected to personal and vicarious experiences, familiar examples, and compared and contrasted with similar words. It is this interconnected conceptual level of understanding that enables automaticity in recognizing word meanings in oral and written language, and in using words accurately and artfully when speaking, writing, and thinking. There is one method that is a "paradigm" for concept development that lends itself to various modifications and adaptations. Two simpler adaptations are provided.

Concept-Based Approach to Vocabulary Building

The concept-based approach as described here is based on the work of Frayer, Fredrick, and Klausmeir (1969). It involves considering a word in terms of inclusion, exclusion, subordination, and superordination, a process that can be guided with the graphic organizer found in Figure 9.4 (page 346). The model, or paradigm, for the concept-based approach is as follows:

There is a foolproof model for teaching new words; it's the Concept-based approach . . . it isn't much fun, but inventive teachers can fix that.

STEPS IN THE CONCEPT-BASED APPROACH

Step 1 Identify relevant and irrelevant features of the concept in question (see Semantic Feature Analysis ahead as another technique that does this well). For example, a relevant feature of the concept of "globe" is that it is round, or spherical, and three-dimensional. Irrelevant features include size, substance, or whether it is solid or hollow.

Step 2 Provide examples of the concept. For example, a classroom globe—pointing out that it is more rounded than the actual earth.

Step 3 Provide non-examples—based on possible misunderstandings of the concept, such as a two-dimensional drawing of a circle.

Step 4   Relate the concept by some smaller, or subordinating, concepts, such as ball, egg, or moon.

Step 5   Relate or categorize the concept by some larger, or superordinating concepts, such as "spherical objects" and stars (which are not really star-shaped but only appear that way due to the effect of viewing them through the atmosphere which causes their light to disperse and appear to twinkle).

Step 6   Relate or categorize the concept alongside equal, or coordinating, terms, such as other planets.

This approach leaves little to chance. It covers most of the possible areas in which a student's grasp of a word's meaning might go astray; hence it tends to be a bit arduous. This method cannot be used for all words, not without becoming overwhelmingly abstract. See Figure 9.4 (page 346) for a graphic organizer that can be used with this method, and a simpler graphic organizer for somewhat less intensive word study.

Based on the Frayer Model (Frayer, Frederick, & Klausmeier, 1969) and the Basic Concept of Definition Map by Schwartz and Raphael (1985), Catherine Rosenbaum developed a word map that she found to be successful with struggling readers in the sixth, seventh, and eighth grades (2001). Rosenbaum's map (see Figure 9.5 on page 347) contains many of the same elements of the previous maps, but is intended to be used for words from specific reading selections.

The next method is particularly useful in reviewing vocabulary from a unit of study. It is based on teacher-focused analytical reasoning as a means of vocabulary concept development.

Semantic Feature Analysis (SFA) and SAVOR

SFA (Johnson & Pearson, 1984) is a method designed to teach students how to systematically think about words in terms of their relevant and irrelevant features, similar to a portion of the previously described paradigm by which concepts are learned. The method has been shown to be especially effective in improving content area reading vocabulary and comprehension (Anders & Bos, 1986). The version described and illustrated below was refined by Stieglitz and Stieglitz (1981) for use with content material, and thus to enhance information and schema. They call it SAVOR, for Subject Area Vocabulary Reinforcement.

Steps in SAVOR

Step 1   The teacher identifies a category of words highly familiar to students. For a fun example, try "monsters," a category within the

FIGURE **9.4**

GRAPHIC ORGANIZERS FOR WORD STUDY

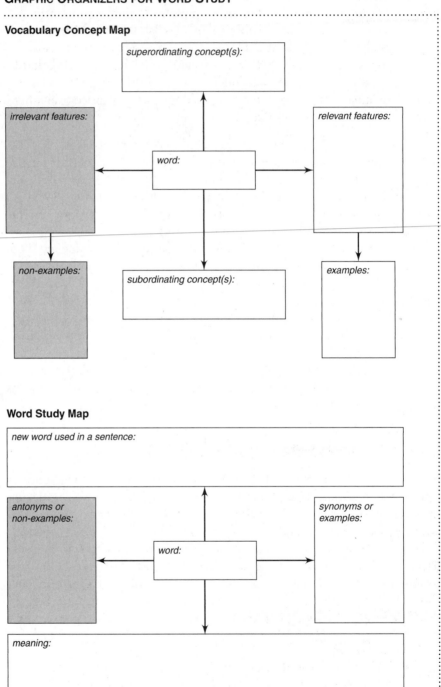

FIGURE **9.5**

WORD STUDY MAP FOR TEXT-BASED VOCABULARY

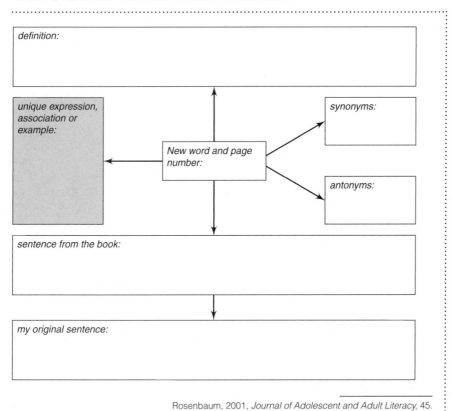

Rosenbaum, 2001, *Journal of Adolescent and Adult Literacy,* 45.

interest range of many students (see Figure 9.6). The teacher first elicits words from the pupils that fit in this category (King Kong, Dracula, Cookie Monster, Godzilla) and has the students list these examples in a column on their own papers.

Step 2   The students list some features of these monsters (hairy, huge, strong, mean, transforming) across the top of the page. Following this, they fill in the matrix by using plus (+) or minus (−) signs to indicate whether a monster has a particular feature.

Step 3   After the matrix is filled in, the teacher leads students to study the different patterns of pluses and minuses and to discover the uniqueness of each word (or, in this case, monster).

Johnson and Pearson (1984) state that as students gain more experience with Semantic Feature Analysis, the teacher may wish to switch from a plus/minus system to a graduated numerical system (0 = none, 1 = some,

FIGURE **9.6**

SAMPLE SAVOR WORKSHEET: MONSTERS

Monsters	Hairy	Huge	Strong	Mean	Transforming
King Kong	+	+	+	+	−
Dracula	−	−	−	+	+
Cookie Monster	+	−	−	−	−
Godzilla	−	+	+	+	−

FIGURE **9.7**

SAVOR WORKSHEET WITH MATHEMATICS: SHAPES

Shapes	Four-Sided	Curved or Rounded Lines	Line Segment	All Sides Equal in Length	Right Angles
Triangle	−	−	+	+	+
Rectangle	+	−	+	−	+
Parallelogram	+	−	+	+	+
Circle	−	+	−	−	−
Trapezoid	+	−	+	−	−
Semicircle	−	+	+	−	−
Square	+	−	+	+	+

2 = much, 3 = all). The method is particularly suitable for helping remedial students to clarify frequently confused terms (see Figure 9.7 on Semantic Feature Analysis in Mathematics).

The next method has students create sentences based on anticipating word meanings that will be developed in text. It also contributes to writing, comprehension, concept formation, and acquisition of a greater fund of information.

Possible Sentences

Possible Sentences challenges students to think about how to work together.

Possible Sentences (Moore & Moore, 1986) provides the kind of word study that moves word knowledge from partial to automatic. Although it is designed as a prereading activity, it requires some knowledge of the words identified for instruction. Its most distinctive feature is the way in which it calls attention to the subtle shades of meaning words take on when used in differing contexts.

STEPS IN POSSIBLE SENTENCES

Step 1 The teacher selects five to eight key concept words from a selection that might cause difficulty for students, and four to six words that are more familiar to the students.

Step 2 These ten to twelve words are listed on the overhead or chalkboard. The teacher pronounces them, and elicits and/or gives meanings for them.

Step 3 Students are encouraged to predict sentences that could possibly appear in the textual material containing at least two of these words. Students' sentences are recorded on the overhead or chalkboard, without regard for accuracy of content.

Step 4 Students read the textual material to check the relative accuracy of their sentences, in the sense that their sentences seem to be compatible with, though not identical to, those in the text.

Step 5 The students then analyze, evaluate, and correct the sentences, as needed.

Step 6 New sentences are called for that reflect the sum of information gained from the prediction, reading, and sentence analysis steps.

When used in this way, Possible Sentences significantly improved vocabulary acquisition and recall of text (Stahl & Kapinus, 1991; Bismonte, Foley, & Petty, 1994). Again, as Stahl and associates have pointed out, it appears to be the discussion—or pointed instructional conversation—that makes Possible Sentences really work (Stahl, 1986; Stahl & Vancil, 1986; Stahl & Kapinus, 1991). See Figure 9.8 (page 350) for an example of Possible Sentences used in a science unit on the water cycle.

Learning outcomes can be amplified by tying concept-based learning to subjective and motor-based equivalents. The next method offers another means of noting the distinctive features of words from an even broader concept base.

Themed Vocabulary Study (TVS)

One of the best and oldest means of vocabulary enrichment is based on theme studies, also called Semantic Clusters, by Marzano and Marzano (1988). Themed Vocabulary Study (TVS) permits students to take well-known, partially-known, and barely-recognized words, and link them together into a semantic web able to catch and hold entirely new words and unusual nuances of meaning for familiar words. It also builds precision in thinking and writing and causes knowledge of words to continually accumulate. Ironically, continued word study is necessary because many words do not always have precise, distinct, and unchanging meanings—a point

FIGURE **9.8**

POSSIBLE SENTENCES

Potentially Difficult Vocabulary Words	Easier Words Related to Topic
evaporation	rain
condensation	snow
water cycle	clouds
precipitation	ocean
surface water	water
ground water	

Students' Possible Sentences

Rain is one kind of **precipitation.**

Surface water and **ground water** are two different types of water.

Water that collects in **clouds** is **condensation.**

Water is in the **ocean.**

Evaporation happens when the **ocean water** gets hot.

When **snow** melts, it is part of the **water cycle.**

Next, students read the text and then discuss, clarify, and correct the sentences.

well developed by Anderson and Nagy (1991) in a review of the literature on word meanings.

STEPS IN THEMED VOCABULARY STUDY

Step 1   Identify a theme.

Step 2   Ask students to state those words they think to be related to the designated theme, and to say what they think those words mean.

Step 3   Use dictionaries to check word meanings and to find synonyms, antonyms, and nuances of meaning.

Step 4   Link the relevant words to one another (with brief definitions) in the form of a semantic map (see illustration on next page).

Step 5   Reinforce and evaluate by testing students' recall and by having them write sentences or descriptive pieces designed to use the new words. [Note: The once-traditional practice of having students write a sentence or two containing a new word still makes sense. It has the diagnostic advantage of revealing whether the students' knowledge of the word includes the often context-specific way in which a given word is used. Anderson and Nagy (1991) give the example of the word *"correlate."* The dictionary definition says, *"to be related one to the other."* This led a student to write "Me and my parents *correlate*, because without them I wouldn't be here" (719).] In a diagnostic-teaching situation, this would immediately reveal that the term *"correlate"* is not yet within the student's grasp.

EXAMPLE OF THEMED VOCABULARY STUDY

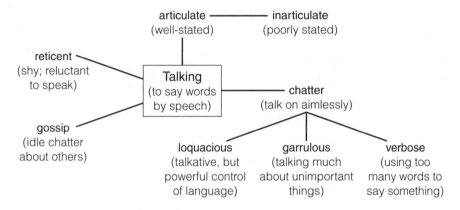

Other themes to consider in word study:

- noncomplimentary but non-vulgar terms (pesky, brusk, prissy, antsy, bawdy, addlebrained)
- behavior-related terms (manners, comportment, deportment, inappropriate, maladaptive, poised, irascible)
- character traits (endurance, restraint, perseverance, reflection, tolerance)
- thinking terms (abstract, concrete, rational, irrational, creative, critical, cognition, diffusive, coherent)
- temperament labels (sanguine, industrious, hyper, choleric, mercurial, pensive)
- attitudes (positive, negative, hostile, aggressive, assertive, constructive)

Vocabulary learning from themed study can be greatly amplified when combined with Semantic Feature Analysis, Subjective/Objective Vocabulary recording, and/or Motor Imaging. Coupling student reactions to the words in themes such as those described above also provides excellent opportunities for diagnosing aspects of personal-social adjustment and getting a fix on a student's "world view"—or the way in which he or she is *experiencing* reality.

All vocabulary learning is a form of categorization and theme study.

Children can learn to understand the many facets of word meanings much as they do the personalities of classmates.

Vocabulary Classmates

This child-centered approach to vocabulary seats a child in a classroom, imaginary or real, made up of "classmates" named from a list of new words (Manzo & Manzo, 1995). The teacher aids students in getting to know their new "vocabulary classmates" by asking questions and encouraging activities that build increasingly greater empathy and understanding with their new-found word friends. Giving words "personalities" contributes to general awareness of words in the environment. Sample questions and activities include the following:

- How does this person say his or her name (pointing to a seat and word)?
- Let's check the dictionary to find out what this person's name means. (A good lead-up to this is to illustrate that many popular names, first and last, have meanings—the library will have a book of these.)
- Let's check the dictionary to learn this person's country of origin. (Check the derivation of the word.)
- Let's check the dictionary to learn about this person's family heritage. (Check the dictionary for the word's "parentage"—meaningful affixes and morphemes brought together to form the word.)
- To whom is this person related? (synonyms)
- Who is most different from this person? (antonyms)
- What is this person's usual job? (noun, verb, and so on)
- Tell a story about these three classmates on the playground (for example, *glorious, pageant,* and *pale*): What are they doing? What are they saying?
- Who would you like to have sit near you? (The teacher should find a reason to move a "classmate" near the child he or she is having trouble learning about—proximity, in this case, breeds familiarity.)
- Which classmates do you think are likely to be friends? Why?
- Draw or describe the clothing each would wear and what he or she might look like physically (see Figure 9.9).
- Have classmates say something they might have on their minds. The teacher can provide some statements that may stimulate deeper understandings, associations, and further word study (see Figure 9.10, page 354).

"Classmates" is designed to stimulate deeper learning than typically occurs with vocabulary instruction. To evaluate progress in word learning:

- Look for compatibility between word meanings and story lines developed.
- Ask leading questions that can best be answered with word names: Do you have classmates who you think could be film star material? (*glorious* and *radiant*) Why?

FIGURE **9.9**

**ILLUSTRATIONS FROM VOCABULARY CLASSMATES
AS ASSEMBLED WITH "MANDY" (AGE 10)**

Glorious
(worthy of praise)
"I wish I could always look glorious."

Bustle
(move about quickly)
"My great-grandmother was a
dress designer."

Hustle
(hurry about; do too quickly)
"There's a dance named after me."

Me
(Mandy—or an assigned or
selected word)

Bovine
(ox- or cow-like)
"I do not have many stomachs."

Radiant
(shining; splendid)
"You know, I'm related to radio."

Quantity
(number or amount)
"We come in large and small quantities."

Pale
(having little color)
"No, I feel fine!"

Gaga
(silly)
"Better to be gaga than goofy."

Pagaent
(show)
"Pomp is good too!"

Glorious' story*
Glorious is English and French.
She wears wonderful clothes.
Her best friend is Radiant, and
she also likes Pale, even though
Pale has poor color. Maybe that's
why Glorious is so worthy of praise.

* Mandy looked up the word "glorious" in the dictionary

- Select the original words to be learned from a book of crossword puzzles and other vocabulary exercises, then give the puzzles as tests of knowledge.
- Administer conventional matching, recall, and multiple-choice tests on the new words.

Other activities and considerations:

- Have youngsters fill about a third of the seats in the room with their own self-selected words. Also, have them fill other rooms at upper- and lower-grade levels with words they think to be easier and more difficult.
- When using an actual classroom, be careful not to select names for the children that may have derisive meanings or connotations. Have

FIGURE **9.10**

AUTOBIOGRAPHY OF PALE HUSTLE

Pale
Hustle

Gaga
Hustle

My name is Pale Hustle. This is my little brother Gaga Hustle.
Dad is called Bovine, 'cause he's as strong as an ox.
Mother is Radiant, because she has happy eyes.

I heard a man on TV say that he made a movie with my name
in it called "He Rode a Pale Horse." I think that he meant the
horse was light gray and ghostlike.

Bovine
Hustle

Radiant
Hustle

students select their own middle and last names and nicknames from
word lists.

- Have students create "autobiographical notes" for new words,
  complete with illustrations. Have them add places where they
  subsequently find the word in context (see Figure 9.10).

Wear-A-Word

Wear-A-Word is a quick and active variation on Vocabulary Classmates.
Start with sheets of colored paper, string, and tape. Either assign or have
children select a word or two from the dictionary. Write that word(s) in
capital letters as a Name Tag worn about the neck. Have the children write
a meaning for each word on an index card (so that they can remember the
word's precise meaning). Hold a social event of most any kind and have students introduce themselves (and what they do, mean, stand for) to one
another. Here are two examples from a fourth-grade scenario: " Hi, I'm
Mayhem. People say that I bring confusion and mess wherever I go." "Hi,
I'm *Serenity*. Folks say that I bring peace and quiet wherever I go." For
added reinforcement, have youngsters make up and/or write short stories
about the characters they have met.

Dictionary Use

Emerson once wrote: *Neither is the dictionary a bad book to just read . . . it
has neither cant nor excesses, and is full of suggestions—the raw material of
poems and history.* It may be due to its raw power that the dictionary has

become another skill that struggling readers desperately need, but seldom receive in remedial programs. The impression seems to be that remedial students have more pressing needs. Vocabulary studies also frequently find that direct teaching methods are better than dictionary methods that amount to "looking up words" (Gipe, 1978–79; Casale & Manzo, 1983). Such results must be interpreted with caution, however, since they rarely involved explicit and extensive teaching of the use of the dictionary, and often did not account for possible long-term effects. Further, and most importantly, the dictionary is a vital piece of a total literacy program. It is not so much an approach to vocabulary instruction, as it is an essential component of it.

A review of the parts and functions of the dictionary reveals its intrinsic worth. It can be a passkey that can open most every lock on the entry door to full literacy.

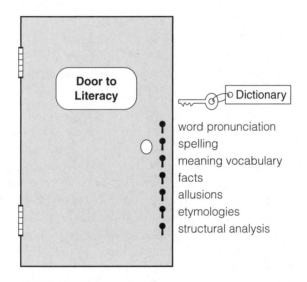

Much of what is described ahead on how to promote dictionary study is derived from two classical sources: William S. Gray's text, *On Their Own in Reading* (1948, 1960), and Clyde Roberts' *Teacher's Guide to Word Attack* (1956). These exercises can be done independently or in cooperative learning pairs.

There are legacy methods to support our word heritage.

1. A good place to begin dictionary study is to show that it can be a fun book to browse through. One way to do this is to use it to learn what certain unusual things are, or what some very usual things are called, or are also called. Gray (1960) recommends uncommon animals for the first category, for example, rhea, marten, pelican. The second category would be covered by words such as: hinge (as on a door), and mucilage (another name for common sticky glue).

2. Write adjectives such as "agile," "smug," and "arrogant" with appropriate page numbers after each and ask students to decide whether they would like to have these words used to describe them.

3. Make a point of showing how words in the dictionary are arranged in alphabetical order, and how this can be used to help spell words correctly as well as to look up their meanings. Illustrate how to look up the spelling of a word by considering several possible ways it might be spelled other than the way it immediately sounds (for example, the word *mucilage* sounds like musilage, but is spelled mucilage). Take this point a bit further and show how the dictionary can be used to discover, more or less, how to pronounce words encountered in print.

rhea = rē´·ä

Give students a great deal of practice in doing this with known words and then less known and finally unknown words. Have them study and create pictorial representations of key sounds. In this way, a student could conceivably learn how to decode most any word in the language. The effort spent doing this also increases time on-task in acquiring basic word analysis and recognition skills.

> The dictionary is the final arbiter on words; it is 80,000 lessons waiting to be learned.

4. The dictionary contains a wealth of etymological information on the origins of words. This activity, which often is considered an additional burden for the remedial student, can be a helpful way to remember meanings and spellings. When combined with Vocabulary Classmates, it can be like learning about the background of a new acquaintance. Teach students to look at the information between the brackets—[ ]— when these are available, to find out about the origins and special features of a word (for example, horology [<Gr. hora, hour + logy]—the science or art of measuring time; bonfire [literally, bone fire, fire for burning corpses]—a fire built out-of-doors).

5. Familiarize students with any additional informational values that the particular dictionary may have; for example, geographical and biographical information. Older dictionaries—which often can be acquired inexpensively at garage sales, can be expected to contain any number of other bits of fascinating information; for example, flags of nations, military uniforms, the dress of various countries.

If dictionary study, and for that matter all word study, is combined at every opportunity with authentic experiences in reading, writing, and further understanding of a student's environment, it will be engaging, satisfying, and empowering. At an anecdotal level, we are always surprised at how enthusiastic students are about writing a letter to a grandparent, or other relative, requesting that he or she consider giving them a dictionary, even an old one, for a birthday or holiday present.

Children without skill or natural aptitude for language need vocabulary training, conducive language environments, and dictionary study more, not less, than other achieving students. Metaphorically speaking, if children lived on boats and didn't take to the water immediately, we would put "floogies" on their arms to keep them afloat and build confidence until they learned how to swim. It seems wise to do the same with children who don't take to the sea of printed and spoken language we are immersed in each day. The dictionary can be a life raft until they get their literacy "sea-legs."

GAMES TO REINFORCE WORD LEARNING

Word games help to build motivation for and playful practice in self-directed vocabulary study. James Bowman (1991) suggests that two classes of games based on word pairs, "Wordy Gurdy Puzzles" and "Oxymorons," are especially useful because they are based on cues within words and word relationships. By providing practice in attending to these types of cues, these games reinforce comprehension processes as well as contextual vocabulary processes.

Wordy Gurdy Puzzles

Develop a list of definitions that could be associated with two rhyming words—each of the rhyming words having the same number of syllables. Give the definitions to students, indicating the number of syllables in each word of the "answer":

principal plumbing outlet [1]   (main drain)
Henry's practical jokes [1]   (Hank's pranks)
comical rabbit [2]   (funny bunny)

Once students have provided the "answers" to several Wordy Gurdy Puzzles, challenge them to make up their own "definitions" and trade puzzles.

Oxymorons

An oxymoron is a word pair in which one word contradicts the other, such as *jumbo shrimp, cruel kindness,* and *eternal moment.* Introduce several such oxymorons to students, pointing out their contradictory nature. Have students compose definitions for oxymorons. Then furnish definitions and have students create an oxymoron for each.

WORDS CAN BRING US TOGETHER

A currently developing technique that will have broad appeal to all children is the IMPS project. This project is an incidental learning activity that is best described as Pokemon with more meaningful vocabulary. It is discussed more fully in Chapter 12 on English-Language Learners. It seems to create a new, hybrid culture, common frame of experience, and a self-teaching, playful atmosphere that is more inclusive of children of diverse backgrounds. For now, the most important thing to note about this developing project is that kids create their own Vocabulary Imps from word lists provided by the teacher and from words they discover themselves in the dictionary. They enthusiastically seek out and learn words that teachers would never think to teach them. See Photosynthesis, for example.

Vocabulary development is a frequently overlooked part of informed prescriptive reading instruction. If you have not previously been concerned about students' vocabulary development, consider it now with an open mind since it is an important part of overall literacy development. The next section will highlight vocabulary strategies that are especially beneficial to English Language Learners.

Photosynthesis
Michael Trombatore, 10 years old

ELL Vocabulary Instruction

Several factors impact the vocabulary development of English as a Second Language or English Language Learning. It appears that ELL students need to learn a core vocabulary before they can successfully use context to aid learning. Researchers differ considerably in the number of words that should be in the core vocabulary, varying from 2,000 words (Coady, Magoto, Hubbard, Graney, & Mokhtari, 1993) to 10,000 words for university students (Hazenburg & Hulstijn, 1996). The function of these high-frequency words is the same as the sight word vocabulary that all students need to build. A second factor involves the impact that proficiency in the first language has upon the second language. A certain level of oral language proficiency in the second language may need to be reached before students can transfer skills from the first language to the second language (Brisbois, 1995).

Dictionaries often provide weak differentiation between words in definitions, wording that is not clear, and many pieces of information that can be confusing to English Language Learners (McKeown, 1993). Yet they are the vocabulary tool used most often by these students. "Dictionary consultation is the initial step in learning a new word. It provides fast and reliable support for learners who have vocabulary and language limitations" (Gonzalez, 1999). Teachers need to teach ELL students how to effectively use the dual-language dictionary and provide practice in class that will facilitate more efficient use (Gonzalez, 1999, 269). Beginning language learners benefit from a specialized, simplified dictionary format to lessen misinterpretations (McKeown, 1993). The authors have helped ELL students develop personal dictionaries with brief definitions and photos taken in the classroom and community. Linking these photos and definitions with the words in the purchased dictionary provides a meaningful connection that increases students' vocabulary development. The use of a dictionary in the students' first language also reinforces the importance of that language and when "minority students' first-language skills are strongly reinforced, the students tend to be more successful" (Cummins, 1989, 111). See chapter 12 for more on the topic of English Language Learning.

How the Literacy Specialist Can Help

The literacy specialist may assist in developing a theme for the school year and work with faculty members to compile a list of vocabulary terms to be emphasized in all classrooms. A "word of the day" for the school, sponsored each morning by a different class, might also stimulate vocabulary development on a school-wide level.

In the clinic or remedial session, struggling readers may benefit from facilitated dialogues between the teacher and two peers that focus on intensive help with independent word-learning strategies (Harmon, 2002). The purpose of facilitated peer dialogues is to explore, use, and analyze independent word-learning strategies during a reading assignment. As soon as the reading assignment is given, the group convenes. When one student meets a confusing or unfamiliar word, the reading is interrupted and the discussion begins. Harmon (2002) found that taping the discussion can be both motivational and instructive because participants are allowed to later replay the discussion to analyze the word-learning strategies that they used. During the discussions, the teacher can analyze the word-learning strategies used by the students and identify strategies that need to be taught. Word-learning strategies typically used by students include skipping unfamiliar words and reading on or asking others for help (Harmon, 2002). To expand the students' repertoire, several additional independent word-learning strategies may need to be taught (see Figure 9.11).

To encourage a facilitated peer dialogue, Harmon (2002, 614) suggests fourteen prompts that the teachers can use:

1. What do you think the word means?
2. What makes you say that?
3. Are there other clues that made you think of that?

FIGURE **9.11**

INDEPENDENT WORD LEARNING STRATEGIES

What can I do to help myself figure out the meaning of an unfamiliar word? (not necessarily in this order)

1. Figure out the purpose of the word. Does it describe something? Show action? Name something?

2. Find out what clues are in the sentence. Does the author use a definition, synonym, description, listing, contrast, or a common expression?

3. Look before and after the sentence containing the word. Are there any clues like in #2?

4. What kind of connections can I make? Think of things in my life, the whole story, immediate events, how the author uses the word, or why the author would use the word.

5. Study the word itself. If the pronunciation does not help, look at word parts or the appearance of the word. Does this tell me anything?

6. Consider using a dictionary if this word is important to the story or text. (Does the word appear several times in the text?) Does the dictionary definition make sense to me?

7. Think of the meaning of the word. State the meaning. Does it seem to fit the context?

Harmon, 2002, *Journal of Adolescent & Adult Literacy*, 613.

4. What is happening right here in the story?
5. What events are we reading about right here?
6. Why would the author use this word?
7. What does the word make you think of?
8. What do you notice about this word?
9. How did you figure that out?
10. What did you notice about what your partner said?
11. What strategies did you use?
12. What strategies did your partner use?
13. Were these strategies helpful?
14. Does the word meaning make sense?

The literacy specialist needs to bring the need for vocabulary instruction out of the basement and into light so that students can grow in this important literacy area.

REVIEW

This chapter covered the topic and methods for improving one of the core elements of reading, learning, and thinking: the words we think and speak in, and the unappreciated fact that vocabulary improvement can actually increase intellectual capacity. Students with the smallest vocabularies tend to be taught the fewest new words. Become committed to changing that and schooling can be made somewhat easier for our struggling pupils.

PREVIEW

Several more methods for improving reading comprehension are covered in the next chapter. It could be called Comprehension II. It takes all that you have learned thus far about decoding, vocabulary enrichment, and comprehension, and adds the most important ingredient of all, improving content and concept acquisition. The next chapter also addresses study skills, among the most frequently overlooked areas of need for corrective and remedial readers. You have learned how to assess study needs in an earlier chapter; now learn how to set them into an action—prescriptive—plan for needy students. Look especially for the Problem-Solving Approach to Study Skills, since it emphasizes one of the basic themes of powerful diagnostic-prescriptive teaching: self-diagnostic and prescriptive teaching.

IMPROVING CONTENT AREA READING AND STUDY STRATEGIES

Every teacher, a teacher of reading. – WILLIAM S. GRAY

CONTENT AND CONCEPT ORGANIZER

The term *Content Area Reading* (CAR) refers to means and methods for increasing knowledge acquisition from reading, writing, reasoning, and studying. In the last 50 years, Content Area Reading has grown from a small subset of reading education into a large body of knowledge in response to growing recognition that there is a great deal that teachers can do to help students make the important transition from learning to read to reading to learn. CAR methods offer ways to provide "sheltered" and compensatory assistance in heterogeneously grouped classrooms to English Language Learners and underprepared students. Note especially those methods that stress interactive speaking, mental modeling, and active involvement of students in problem solving their own particular (prescriptive) needs.

CHAPTER OUTLINE

TECHNIQUES AND METHODS FOR CONTENT
    AREA READING

FRAMEWORKS AND METHODS FOR GUIDING THE
    THREE-PHASE READING PROCESS
    Directed Reading–Thinking Activity (DR-TA)
    Specially Designed Academic Instruction In
        English (SDAIE)
    Listen-Read-Discuss (L-R-D)
    Anticipation-Reaction Guide
    Graphic Organizers
    Know–Want to Know–Learned Plus (KWL+)
    Guided Reading Procedure

PRECISION INSTRUCTION FOR SCHEMA
    ACTIVATION
    Question-Only
    Reciprocal Teaching

PRECISION INSTRUCTION FOR METACOGNITIVE
    MONITORING AND SELF-HELP STRATEGIES
    About-Point
    Coding the Text
    Monitoring Cards
    Language Chunking Cues
    Lookbacks
    Paraphrasing/Translating
    Summarizing

PRECISION INSTRUCTION FOR POSTREADING
    SCHEMA BUILDING: REAP
    Read-Encode-Annotate-Ponder (REAP)
    Guided Reading, Writing, and Thinking

GUIDING INDEPENDENT STUDY
    Primary Grades' Foundations for Study Strategies
    Following Directions

Techniques and Methods for Content Area Reading

Children who have learned to read in classrooms with a strong focus on comprehension and *strategies* for making meaning from print will more easily make the transition to more challenging reading contexts. Many methods from the previous chapter on comprehension can be used with nonfiction content area reading selections and textbooks. This chapter provides additional methods and techniques specifically designed for content area reading instruction, and for guiding students' acquisition of independent study strategies. In general, content area reading is best understood as methods designed to improve content instruction and learning. In a manner of speaking, every course is a course in reading, the primary access to independent and continuing knowledge acquisition in a field of study.

"Prior Knowledge" is the best predictor of reading comprehension. Content Area Reading improves knowledge acquisition.

Frameworks and Methods for Guiding the Three-Phase Reading Process

By way of elaboration on a point from Chapter 8, where learning is concerned, comprehension processes, whether text- or lecture-driven, must pass through four (recursive) cycles: *evocation*—or stirred engagement; *realization of meaning*—a conscious sense that something new has been learned; *reflection on implications*—what it connects to, enhances, or might modify; and *ongoing cross-verification*—a raised awareness of possible supporting or refuting facts and perspectives. The methods in this section are designed to provide such assistance with the active reading-thinking strategies needed at each stage of the content area comprehension process: prereading, silent reading, postreading, and continuing independent study-type learning thereafter. These methods are designed to make fact-based content area reading selections "accessible" to students across a wide range of ability levels. Additional methods ahead in the chapter target more specific aspects of comprehension, from question asking and answering, to critical and creative response to a wide array of texts.

Directed Reading–Thinking Activity (DR-TA)

The DR-TA has been called a "master plan," or basic paradigm, for teaching reading for meaning (Stauffer, 1975). It can be used profitably with narrative or content area materials of most any length.

STEPS IN THE DR-TA

Step 1 *Prereading: Relate, Reduce, Anticipate*
    a. Discuss and expand students' background experience and knowledge related to the selection.
    b. Reduce obstacles to comprehension by pre-teaching difficult words and concepts.
    c. Preview the reading material (look at title, pictures, summaries, and so on).
    d. Help students to anticipate what the remainder of the selection is likely to be about.

Step 2 *Active Reading: Predict-Read-Prove*
    a. Guide thinking by interrupting reading to ask for predictions of what the selection will say next.
    b. Have pupils read silently to test their hypothesis (which may differ from student to student).
    c. Ask for proof or verification from the material that they predicted correctly, or if incorrectly, find out why.

Step 3 *Postreading: Check, Refine, Relate, Re-anticipate*
    a. Check comprehension by discussing answers to general purpose-setting questions, and by additional recognition, recall, inferential, explanatory, and evaluative questions.
    b. Refine understanding by seeking verifications for comprehension questions that require silent and oral re-reading and citing of the material.
    c. Relate the story or information covered to other materials read, or to common experience or mass media events.
    d. Build fresh anticipation of something to be read at a later time by connecting it to some relevant aspect of the postreading discussion.

When properly orchestrated, the DR-TA has an attractive symmetry that begins and ends with anticipation, or *evocation,* hence creating an im-

[handwritten annotations: DR-TA / ① comprehension / ② improve classroom interaction]

pelling reason to read immediately, and again recursively on the same topic thereafter. Classroom, as opposed to remedial, versions tend to put addi-tional emphasis on a follow-up phase that may involve any number of things, from writing activities to dramatization of the story line.

The DR-TA has been shown to be quite effective for teaching reading comprehension, and improving classroom interactions (Bear & Invernizzi, 1984; Davidson, 1970; Grobler, 1971; Petre, 1970). Kern (1992) suggests that the DR-TA is especially useful during the first two years of second-language instruction, when students need the support of what is properly called *sheltered instruction*. A set of questions and prompts has evolved to guide sheltered instruction for second-language learners.

> DR-TA is a "master plan," and an inherently *sheltered* way to teach content through reading comprehension.

[handwritten annotations: ESL ed.]

Specially Designed Academic Instruction In English (SDAIE)

The influence of the DR-TA can be seen in many of the SDAIE frameworks. These typically are built around the several points that support second-language learners in content learning situations. SDAIE (pronounced *sa-dié*) is a dynamic series of guiding questions that often are used in teacher certification classes and workshops as a framework for raising consciousness about the level of scaffolding necessary to construct a lesson plan to accommodate the needs of English Language Learners.

CONSIDERATIONS IN SPECIALLY DESIGNED ACADEMIC INSTRUCTION IN ENGLISH

1. Lesson Rationale—Why are you teaching this particular lesson? Who are the students you will be teaching and how does this lesson fit into their experiences and knowledge? What are their special needs? How does this lesson fit within the larger unit or curriculum? Upon what previous learning is it dependent? What learning follows this concept? How does this lesson fit within the previous and future lessons in a sequence?

2. Standards—What State Content Standards are being addressed with this lesson? What should students know and be able to do as a result of this learning experience? What State English Language Development Standards are you taking into account? How will you promote growth in Listening, Speaking, Reading, and Writing? What Grade Span are you working in? What Skill Level will you address?

3. Assessment—What evidence will you use to find out whether or not the students have met your target Standards (journals, questioning, authentic assessment, performance-based assessment, writing activities, solving problems, restating ideas, applying skills to life situations, and so on)? If you are using a traditional form of assessment, how will

SDAIE calls for highly scaffolded instruction for English Language Learners.

you modify to allow for English-language learners' needs (extra time, alternate answer forms, foreshadowing of test contents, or others)?

4. Materials—What materials will you need in order to teach the lesson? What realia, manipulatives, teaching media (text, computers, video, and so on) will students use? What handouts, readings, overheads, audiovisual materials, graphs, or charts will you need to prepare?

5. Instructional strategies—What activity or activities will lead students into the lesson? How will you "open the door" to the new concept being introduced?

6. Language considerations—What can the students do in English? How would you characterize their English proficiency? What linguistic and cultural idioms might be unclear to students? Have you identified key vocabulary terms necessary for understanding the concept being addressed? How will you introduce the vocabulary (Word Bank, anecdotal definitions, pictograms, and so on)?

7. Tapping prior knowledge—What prior knowledge are you assuming from the students? Are there any culturally-based assumptions that your ELLs may not have experienced that are important to the understanding of the concept to be taught? What strategies will you use to activate (or create) that knowledge (free recall, KWL, journal entries, cooperative interviews, graphic organizers, warm-ups, homework check, review, or others)?

8. Focusing tactics—What sensory (music, colored visuals, touch, smell), emotional (laughter, fear, excitement, wonder, security), and/or intellectual (novelty, surprise, ambiguity, uniqueness, incongruity, puzzlement) stimulation will you provide?

9. Instructional strategies ("Instruct/Interact")—What specific strategies and tactics will form the core of your lesson? How have you contextualized your instructions? What modeling will you provide? How will you know if all your instructions are understood? If you are teaching in an expository mode, what contextual clues will you provide (graphic organizers, modeling, gesturing, props, or others)? If you are using discussion, how will you provide an environment to encourage this for English-language learners? What questions and/or prompts will you use? If you are using collaboration, what structure will you provide to ensure positive interdependence? How will you provide for individual accountability? Group accountability? If there is a group product, do you have a sample finished product to model? What social skill will you stress? How will you process the skills (academic and social) at the end of the activity? What listening, speaking, reading, and writing opportunities will you provide? What scaffolding will you provide to assist students in negotiating their way through written text? What strategies will you use to ensure students are actively learning (any physical movement?)? What formative assessments will you use to check for student understanding? When in the lesson sequence will you do that (confirmation checks, comprehension checks, clarification, repetition, expansion, open-ended questions, two-way interactions, teacher observations, and so on)?

10. Instructional strategies ("Extend"): Writing to Learn—What activity can you provide that allows students to assimilate the new concept into their prior learnings (discussion, writing, group products/performance)? If process writing is being taught, how will you provide structure to encourage prewriting, revision, and publication? What type of closure activities will you incorporate? How will you tie this lesson into future lessons? How will you encourage students to reflect on their learning (metacognition): journal entries, learning log, quick write, or others?

11. Homework—Will homework be meaningful? If so, how? Will it focus on practicing what has been learned or extending the learning? Will the homework segue into future lessons?

12. Follow-up activities—What additional activities will you provide for those students who don't meet the target Standards based on your assessment? What further assessments might you use in addition to the measures mentioned above?

The next method, and several others ahead, will assist with the instructional questions raised by SDAIE. Chapter 12 addresses many of these same points in a more intensive diagnostic-prescriptive, and tutorial context.

Listen-Read-Discuss (L-R-D)

A common school practice is to have students read a section of text, often for homework, then listen to the teacher's explanation of the information, then participate in question-answer recitation and discussion. The problem with this read-listen-discuss approach is that students receive little, if any, help with silent reading. Struggling readers also are ill prepared to participate and potentially profit in the postreading recitation and discussion. L-R-D (Manzo & Casale, 1985) offers an alternative to this approach. Simply by inverting the *sequence* of conventional instruction, all students are better prepared for reading. Notice, in the steps below, how this approach also quickens the pace of instruction, and provides for several repetitions of the information: two key principles of effective remedial instruction.

The LRD is an "inversion" technique that is "front-loaded" with support for reading and discussion.

STEPS IN THE LISTEN-READ-DISCUSS HEURISTIC

Step 1   Select a portion of text to be read.

Step 2   Present the information from that portion of text in a short but well-organized "lecture" format, following the sequence of main topics presented in the text, and pointing out important types of details to look for when reading.

Step 3   Have students read the book's version of the same material. Students now will be reading in an "empowered" way, since they have just listened to an overview of the information.

Step 4   Discuss the material students now have heard and then read. Three questions, adapted from Smith (1978), are useful in guiding this postreading discussion:

- What did you understand *most* from what you heard and read?
- What did you understand *least* from what you heard and read?
- What *questions or thoughts* did this lesson raise in your mind about the content and/or about effective reading and learning?

The L-R-D has "heuristic," or learn-by-doing, effects for both teachers and students. Following the empowering lecture/listen presentation, teachers observe even reluctant readers approaching the text with more confidence. Teachers also find that following empowered reading, all students bring more information and enthusiasm to the postreading discussion. Students learn that they are capable of reading with greater understanding than they may have imagined, and that, having read, they have more to contribute to class discussion.

Several variations on the L-R-D have been designed to teach other components of strategic teaching and strategic reading. These variations also serve to keep the learning process fresh and ongoing for both teacher and students. The variations are listed in Figure 10.1, in order of increasing difficulty. This "ladder" of variations can be thought of as a suggested sequence for further exploring and developing one's knowledge and skill base as a reflective, strategic teacher of reading. The L-R-D has been found to be a powerful means of improving reading comprehension and content learning in both weak and proficient readers (Watkins, McKenna, Manzo, & Manzo, 1993).

If all the teachers in a school employed L-R-D on a regular basis, it would have the effect of increasing:

- *Attention during "lecture-presentation."* This is the primary means by which all teaching-learning occurs. L-R-D lectures are crisper and more focused than traditional ones. They are prepared not as explanation of or elaboration on what students are presumed to have read, but to introduce the material. In addition, as students listen, they are not anxiously struggling to recall what they read, but are listening for help with what they are about to read.

Inversion methods may be the Silver Bullet.

- *Time spent in engaged, empowered reading.* There is a strong human tendency to avoid the unknown, and any new reading assignment is an unknown. The L-R-D lecture brings the reading assignment into the realm of the known, increasing the likelihood that students will *do* the reading, with greater chance of success.
- *Participation in class discussion.* More students reading the assignment and all reading with greater comprehension mean more students able to participate knowledgeably in discussion.
- *Meeting the needs of ESL and underprepared students.* The L-R-D lecture provides precisely the type of scaffolding needed by these students: assistance with identifying key vocabulary and concepts, basic organization of the material, and guidance in what to look for as they read.

This amounts to creating a near-total reading-listening-speaking program, across all content areas with essentially one core method. This method also includes a ladder of variations that can be used to guide ongoing, in-service teacher education (see Figure 10.1 on page 370).

Instead of beginning the lesson with a short lecture, the following strategy uses agree/disagree type statements to stimulate prior knowledge and to activate students' schema.

Anticipation-Reaction Guide

An Anticipation-Reaction Guide (Herber, 1978) is a prereading method that helps connect readers with the text by activating their schema and giving them purposes for reading. Responding to agree/disagree statements before they read causes students to pay closer attention to the related information when they encounter it in reading. Careful preparation of the statements can help the teacher assess and correct students' misconceptions about a topic.

STEPS IN PREPARING AND USING THE ANTICIPATION-REACTION GUIDE

Step 1   Identify the main ideas and details to be learned in the text, and what *misunderstandings* or unexamined *attitudes or beliefs* students may have about these.

Step 2   Create three to ten statements (depending on the age of the students) that support or challenge students' knowledge, beliefs, and/ or experiences related to the topic. The statements may be based

FIGURE **10.1**

L-R-D LADDER OF VARIATIONS

1. Have students reread the information covered in the L-R-D format *rapidly* to increase their speed of reading and thought processing. Reading speed tends to increase as a result of increases in prior knowledge.

2. Inform the class that as you tell them about the content material, you will intentionally leave out a few important details that they will need to read their texts to discover. This provides practice in recognizing what is not yet known and experience in careful reading. This can be supplemented with an incomplete graphic organizer.

3. Inform the class that your presentation will cover all the details of the material, but that they will need to read to discover what *questions* these details answer. This is one way to teach students to actively seek an understanding of the concept, or main idea around which an area of study is focused.

4. Inform the class that a quiz will follow the L-R-D sequence. Allow a short study period. This is recommended to activate a high level of focused attention, give practice in test-taking, and set the stage for questions and discussion about how to study effectively.

5. Invert the core process *occasionally* by having the class R-L-D: read (for about 15 minutes), then listen, then discuss. This variation tends to focus and improve independent reading as well as the ability to learn from subsequent lecture—a frequent format in all further schooling. This can be even more effective when combined with the other listening activities and note-taking techniques covered in the study strategies section of this chapter.

6. Watch an informative videotape on a text topic before reading. This format is compatible with the habits of contemporary students and can help them build new bridges to print.

7. Ask students which parts of the text seemed most difficult. Ask if it was poorly written, or poorly organized, or just poorly explained. This can help students learn when to ask for help with reading. It also helps the teacher become more alert to student learning needs. Analysis of the writing in texts is also a good way to informally teach some of the basics of effective writing.

8. Give students a clear purpose for reading and discussing that will require critical and/or creative expression or application. State that purpose clearly on the chalkboard for easy reference: "As you read this section on the steam engine, try to figure out why it was sure to be replaced by the gasoline engine."

9. Have a postreading discussion on teaching and learning strategies. Make the discussion positive by asking students what they or you may have done that helped them learn. Such discussion gives credit to student intuition and develops "metacognitive" processing, or thinking about thinking. It also builds rapport with and regard for the teacher as a source of personal help and comfort, along with challenges and fair criticism.

10. Create research teams, and provide time for students to delve into a topic in greater depth. One group could simply see what other textbooks say on the topic. Another could check with other authoritative references—persons and books. Another could write their best estimate of which real-life problems the information they learn might help solve or answer. Still another group, where appropriate, could try to identify and discuss theme-related stories, poetry, music, or art. Activities such as these provide links between text topics and non-print resources and among school learning, artistic expression, and the real world.

on factual information in the text or opinion-type statements, but they must be statements for which students will have sufficient background knowledge to have some basis for agreeing or disagreeing. Arrange the statements on the worksheet in the order in which concepts are presented in the text, with blanks for *agree* and *disagree* (or yes and no) before reading, and another set of blanks for after reading (see examples in Figure 10.2).

FIGURE **10.2**

SAMPLE ANTICIPATION-REACTION GUIDES

Anticipation-Reaction Guide based on the short story "Caged" by Lloyd E. Reeve

Directions: Read each statement below. Put a check in the "Before Reading" blank, under "Agree" or "Disagree." If you do not agree, do *not* put a check in the blank. After reading, reread each statement and put a check in the After Reading "Agree" or "Disagree" blank.

BEFORE READING			AFTER READING	
Agree	Disagree		Agree	Disagree
_____	_____	The creatures in pet stores are happy and contented.	_____	_____
_____	_____	People sometimes commit cruel acts without realizing that they are cruel.	_____	_____
_____	_____	Freedom is more valuable than money.	_____	_____
_____	_____	Unusual behavior sometimes frightens people.	_____	_____
_____	_____	Two people can be a part of the same event yet have totally different understandings of it.	_____	_____

**Anticipation-Reaction Guide based on *Ranchers and Cowboys*
by Charles L. and Mary A. Convis (Carson, Nevada: Pioneer Press, 1997).**

Directions: Read each item and decide if you agree with it or disagree. Put a "yes" on the line next to the item labeled "Before Reading" if you agree, a "no" if you disagree. Think about how you would defend your point of view.

Before Reading	After Reading	
_____	_____	Cattle-raising techniques were developed by American ranchers (513).
_____	_____	You would enjoy life as a cowboy (514).
_____	_____	You would not mind a cattle drive going through your land (515–516).
_____	_____	You would have a comfortable life as the wife of a cowboy (520–521).
_____	_____	Overstocking cattle and overgrazing resulted in the end of open-range ranching (523).

Ericson, Hubler, Bean, Smith, & McKenzie, 1987, *Journal of Reading,* 434 and 437.

Step 3   Present the Anticipation-Reaction Guide worksheet to students and ask them to record their answers (Agree or Disagree) to each statement in the prereading column, and be prepared to defend their responses.

Step 4   Discuss each statement briefly, encouraging response from each side of an issue.

Step 5   Direct students to read the selection with the purpose of finding evidence to determine if their positions were correct.

Anticipation-Reaction Guides are as much a life strategy as a reading strategy.

Step 6 After students have read, have them answer each statement again (Agree or Disagree or Yes or No) in the postreading column. Begin postreading discussion by asking students to confirm their original predictions, revise them, discard them, or decide if additional information is needed. Students may rewrite each false statement in a way that makes it true.

Anticipation-Reaction Guides provide prereading, silent reading, and postreading guidance, but the main benefit is the self-monitoring that happens while a student reads to support or refute the statements related to the main concepts.

Duffelmeyer, Baum, and Merkley (1987) developed what they called the Extended Anticipation-Reaction Guide. When students review the statements after reading, they are directed to rewrite any statements that are not accurate according to the information in the passage. This is a high level of challenge, but an excellent one for diagnostic-prescriptive teaching. The next strategy moves from a written to a visual emphasis.

Graphic Organizers

A Graphic Organizer is a visual representation of the organization of information and ideas (see Figure 10.3 for sample Graphic Organizer formats). A Graphic Organizer that represents the organization of a reading selection can provide an excellent vehicle for guiding the three phases of comprehension.

When the Graphic Organizer is used as the instructional focus of the lesson, it is called a Three-Phase Graphic Organizer.

STEPS IN THE THREE-PHASE GRAPHIC ORGANIZER

Preparation: Analyze the reading selection to determine a graphic organizer format that illustrates its organization. Prepare a graphic organizer that includes all important information in the selection.

Step 1 *Prereading Schema Activation.* Without showing the prepared graphic to the class, announce the topic, and ask students what they think they will read about in the selection. As students make suggestions, begin a rough construction of the graphic organizer on the board or overhead, while students copy it on their papers. Typically, the first suggestions will be details, rather than major subtopics. For example, in a selection about spiders, one of the students' first suggestions would likely be that "they have eight legs," rather than the subtopic, "body parts." For some selections, students will be able to generate the needed subtopics or anchor information; for other selections, the teacher will need to supply

FIGURE **10.3**

SAMPLE GRAPHIC ORGANIZER FORMATS

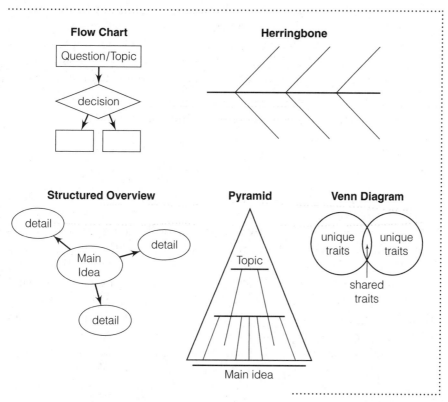

some if not most of these. During this interaction, the teacher should be open to modifying the planned structure of the graphic organizer if students make reasonable alternative suggestions. For maximum support, the teacher may show students where to draw blank lines for information to find in their reading. By the end of the prereading session, students will have an incomplete graphic organizer that they have helped to develop.

Step 2 *Metacognitive Monitoring.* Students read silently to complete the graphic organizer. While they read silently, students add information to their graphic organizers as they find it in the selection. The incomplete graphic organizer produced in Step 1 provides a ready-made "reading guide," reminding students to read actively, question their understanding, and note important points, details, and relationships.

Step 3 *Schema Building.* Once students have read, the teacher guides a discussion based on students' additions to the prereading graphic organizer, or students are directed to compare their work in cooperative groups. Optionally, the graphic organizer (GO) may be used as a writing prompt. For example, the GO may be divided into sections, with each section assigned to a small group of students. Each group then works together on their portion of the organizer to "retranslate" it from pictorial form into a connected paragraph or to add some deeper level of understanding and research on the topic.

The next strategy is a familiar one to many students and teachers.

Know–Want to Know–Learned Plus (KWL+)

KWL is traceable to Emmet Betts' (1957) cornerstone text, *Foundations of Reading Instruction* (654), and closely parallels the effective reading-learning process. More recently researched by Eileen Carr and Donna Ogle (1987), it can be used as a total lesson plan since it has prereading, guided silent reading, and postreading components. Its most significant contribution, however, is in activating prior knowledge in such a way that it stirs students to be able to say what they **Know (K),** realize what it is they **Want (W)** to know from the textual material, and what they have **Learned (L)** following reading. The **Plus** refers to the mapping or summarizing step that seemed to provide the additional active ingredient that an earlier version of this method needed to bring about more predictable benefits.

STEPS IN KWL+

Before Reading

Step 1   The teacher helps students "brainstorm" what they know about a topic. The information is noted in the "K" (Know) column of a three-column chart.

Step 2   Students categorize information they have generated and anticipate categories of information that they may find in the selection.

Step 3   The teacher models categorizing by "thinking aloud" while combining and classifying information.

Step 4   Students generate a list of questions they want answered as they read. Questions are written in the "W" column of the KWL chart.

Silent Reading

Step 5   During reading, students pause to answer the questions raised in the "want to know" list. (New questions can be added as they read.)

Step 6   Students list things they have learned while reading.

Postreading

Step 7   Discussion of what was learned takes place, and questions raised before reading are reviewed to determine whether they were resolved.

Follow-up

Step 8   Students are guided in developing a graphic organizer for the information from their "learned" list.

A KWL lesson offers several opportunities for having students work collaboratively in pairs or small groups. The next method also is a good way to get kids talking—constructively and creatively.

KWL+ is a near description of the reading-learning process.

Guided Reading Procedure

This method addresses the most frequent problem identified in weak comprehension. Poor readers tend to view reading as something that one should be able to do effortlessly: When they attempt to read, they do not actively engage in constructing meaning (Paris & Oka, 1989). They do not make plans or vary their strategies as they read (Walker, 2000), nor do they dig in and intensify their effort as needed, probably so as not to signal that they are struggling where others may appear to be cruising. This becomes a social-psychological and metacognitive paradox that is difficult to readjust. The Guided Reading Procedure (GRP) was developed to demonstrate to such "trapped" low-achieving students that they could greatly increase their reading comprehension by fortifying themselves with confidence-building self-determination (Manzo, 1975a). It does this by having students experience a reading-learning activity in which, by self-monitoring their level of attention, concentration, and commitment, they actually do comprehend and remember more information than they typically seem able to handle. This effect is further insured as a result of the repetitive nature of the GRP lesson, in which the facts and ideas in the selection are stated, repeated, and reviewed in various forms. Students, even those who were not willing or able to read the selection initially, acquire a firm grounding in the reconstructive-level information in the selection. Ideally, then, a new facilitating inner-script—that says, "you can do this, if you really try"—replaces the prior ones that tend toward variations on "don't let anyone see how hard you need to try."

The Guided Reading Procedure is a metacognitive strategy for teaching students how to draw upon their intrinsic ability to increase comprehension by a simple act of will.

In analyzing the steps of the GRP, notice that it guides students toward greater independence by stressing some of the most frequent but least taught requirements of school: factual reading, note-taking, organizing, and test preparation. Notice, too, how steps 4 and 8 reinforce metacognitive development. When used in a remedial situation to help students prepare for conventional content area tests, the method tends to validate the remedial sessions by building real self-image, sometimes known as self-efficacy, in students who might never have faced a test better prepared. In short, the GRP teaches an aspect of metacognition that has been called "executive control" (Paris, Cross, & Lipson, 1984). Here, the reader takes conscious control of the learning process. The GRP empowers poor readers to master reconstructive-level comprehension, an important step on the road to constructive concept-formation and analysis (Dempster, 1991).

The method is presented here as it would be used with a group or class. It can be similarly done with individuals, by using shorter passages and having the teacher provide slightly more help with the initial recall portion of the lesson.

STEPS IN THE GUIDED READING PROCEDURE

Step 1 *Teacher Preparation.* Identify a selection, to be read or listened to, of moderate to high difficulty and not exceeding 2,000 words for a senior-high class, 900 words for a junior-high class, 600 words for an intermediate class, and 100 to 250 words for a remedial or LD class. Prepare a 10- to 20-item test on the material to be given at the end of the class period. A recognition type test such as a multiple-choice test tends to insure early success.

The GRP stresses factual learning and knowledge acquistion.

Step 2 *Student Preparation.* Solicit background knowledge on the topic, then explain to students that they are to "Read to remember *all that you can*, because after you have read, I will record what you remember on the chalkboard just as you restate it to me."

Step 3 *Reading and Recalling.* Following silent reading, begin asking for free recalls. Record all information on the chalkboard until students have retold all that they can remember. Difficulties in remembering and differences in what students do remember form the implicit questions that set up the next steps.

Step 4 *Self-Monitoring/Self-Correcting.* Instruct students to review the material read, self-correct inconsistencies, and check for information overlooked in their initial attempts to retell. Note changes and additions on the chalkboard.

Step 5 *Restructuring.* Encourage students to organize their retellings into outline form. It gives a sense of authenticity and purpose to this effort if pupils are encouraged to record this information in their notebooks. The outline can be as simple or elaborate as ability level permits. You may ask nonspecific questions at this time, such as "What was discussed first?"; "What details followed?"; "What was brought up next?"; and "What seems to be the main idea?"

Avoid questions that are too specific or leading if you wish to keep them focused on the text cues rather than the teacher's clues.

Step 6   *Teacher Monitoring and Correction.* If it appears that students have overlooked any important ideas, raise focusing questions about these points, such as "What do you suppose is the most important of the five points made by the author?"; "How do you suppose this information relates to what we talked about last week in the selection 'Man and the Moon?'"

Step 7   *Evaluation.* Give the test prepared in step 1. A score of 70% to 80% should be required for a "pass." Students see this as a fair "pass" level due to the extraordinary level of empowerment they have received. They also tend to look forward to the test as an opportunity to show what they have learned.

Step 8   *Introspection.* Discuss any insights students may have reached about their own learning processes as a result of the GRP experience. The chief point to be made is that accuracy in comprehension and recall can be improved to a great degree by an act of will to do so.

Step 9   *Optional but Important Study Step.* Several days later, give a second test on the same material. Allow students about 15 minutes prior to the test to review material from their notes. The exam can be half the items from the original multiple-choice test or another "unaided recall" test. This step also can serve to establish the "teachable moment" for further study skills training of the type presented in the chapter on study, writing, and higher-order thinking.

The GRP has been supported by several experimental and field studies testing its use from fourth-grade through high-school levels (Ankney & McClurg, 1981; Bean & Pardi, 1979; Culver, 1975) as well as by anecdotal accounts at the elementary level (Gaskins, 1981) and at the secondary level (Maring & Furman, 1985; Tierney, Readence, & Dishner, 1990).

The next method described has been evolving for decades. It relies on combining "off-the-shelf" methods in an inventive way.

PRECISION INSTRUCTION FOR SCHEMA ACTIVATION

As noted previously, effective readers activate their schemas before reading a selection by recalling information and experiences related to the topic. Struggling readers need to be guided in this process, and benefit from modeling, until the action becomes automatic. Question Only, along with Reciprocal Teaching and ReQuest—discussed in Chapter 8 on Comprehension—are three particularly effective strategies to use in the prereading, continue-reading component.

Question-Only

Question-Only is an inversion technique that rotates students into a role in which they ask the questions for which teaching and texts provide answers.

The Question-Only Procedure (Manzo, 1980), is a content-based strategy similar to "20 Questions." Students of all ages can be taught to ask more and better questions—an important component of higher-order thinking and active comprehension. The basic Question-Only strategy can be used in any subject area, at any grade level. Prior to the Question-Only session, the teacher has thoroughly read the material and is ready to answer questions without referring to the text.

STEPS IN QUESTION-ONLY

Step 1 The teacher announces a topic to the class and explains that they must learn about it solely through their questions, and they will be tested on the topic. The test should include all the information the teacher considers important, whether or not the students actually extract the information with their questions.

Step 2 Students ask all the questions they think are relevant about the topic, and the teacher answers. The teacher should answer fully, but avoid providing more information than is specifically called for in the question (that is the hard part for most teachers). The purpose is to challenge students to form relevant questions that elicit the important information. Of course, the teacher should also be ready to take advantage of "teachable moments" that may occur. The discussion will continue for approximately 10 minutes, with the students deducing information about the topic.

Step 3 Finally, a "test" of the important concepts is given. Test questions should be given orally, rather than in written form—selecting questions that students have elicited answers for, with only one or two that they have not thought to ask.

Step 4 In a whole-group discussion, the teacher and students note which questions were raised and which *should* have been raised but were not.

Step 5 Students are directed to read their texts carefully or listen to a short lecture to discover what they failed to learn through their initial questions.

On their first experience with Question-Only, students may ask very detailed questions to see if they can "stump the teacher," but the thinking soon turns to "What kinds of questions does the teacher ask?" This helps students to begin asking themselves those same types of questions as they read. The strategy that follows uses cooperative learning groups and role cards to aid the comprehension process.

Reciprocal Teaching

Based on a review of the research on comprehension and content learning instruction, seven practices have been identified as "proven to be successful in helping at-risk (middle- and secondary-level) students develop their comprehension abilities" (Haller, Child, & Walberg, 1988, as cited by Flood & Lapp, 1990, 492). Reciprocal Teaching is one strategy on this list. "A technique born of Manzo's original ReQuest Procedure, reciprocal teaching, proceeds in a paragraph-by-paragraph manner" (Gipe, 1998, 254). Developed into its most widely known form by Annemarie Sullivan Palinscar and Ann Brown (1985), Reciprocal Teaching—which *Time* magazine (circa, 1988) called the most important breakthrough in pedagogy in the 20th century—actively engages students in constructing meaning through summarizing, questioning, clarifying, and predicting. Using a paragraph from a content area textbook, the teacher models each of the four distinct comprehension strategies and then students practice these strategies.

STEPS IN RECIPROCAL TEACHING

Preparation:

1. Place students into cooperative groups of four.
2. Determine four stopping points in the passage.
3. Give each person in the group a different card (see Figure 10.4, page 380).

During reading time:

4. Request that students read silently to the first stopping point. When all students have finished reading, begin the group discussion with each student fulfilling the task on the card.
5. After students have completed their roles and the group has discussed the paragraph, the students switch cards.
6. Each student reads to the next stopping point and performs the role on the new role card.
7. This procedure continues until all four sections have been read and each student has fulfilled all four roles.

After the groups have finished this sequence, a teacher or student leads a discussion of what has been read during the lesson. Groups compare

FIGURE **10.4**

ROLE CARDS FOR RECIPROCAL TEACHING

1. Summarize	**2. Question**
Summarize in a simple sentence the paragraph that was read. (What is the main idea?)	Think of a question about the paragraph that was read to ask another student.

3. Clarify	**4. Predict**
Clarify anything in the text that was unclear. You may ask group members to help you clarify the confusing parts.	Make a prediction about what will happen next in the text.

Reciprocal Teaching has been called the pedagogical breakthrough of the 20th century.

and contrast the information they shared about the sections. Reciprocal Teaching involves student-to-student and teacher-to-student discussions, critical components of effective comprehension and content instruction. "It is through discussion that the teacher learns what is in the students' minds, and thereby can restructure the situation to aid the student in understanding" (Flood & Lapp, 1990, 493). This is close to a definition of sound diagnostic-prescriptive teaching.

PRECISION INSTRUCTION FOR METACOGNITIVE MONITORING AND SELF-HELP STRATEGIES

Reading is thinking, and thinking is an active, self-regulating process. Students must monitor their own comprehension by frequently asking themselves, "Does what I'm reading make sense?" and then be prepared to fix the problem when the answer is "No." Methods and techniques that help students to acquire these strategies represent an important new direction in contemporary education. This new direction teaches students to be self-teaching, rather than trying to build self-esteem (a *product* of real growth). Following are several techniques that help students become more active readers.

About-Point

About-Point (Martin, Lorton, Blanc, & Evans, 1977) is a simple guide for silent reading. Students are instructed to stop at logical points, such as at the end of paragraphs or text subsections, and complete the following two phrases:

This section is about _____; and the point is _____.

Reflection

Stop and write an About-Point Statement on the Reciprocal Teaching approach described and discussed above. Compare your About Point statement with a classmate's.

First, teachers must model the use of About-Point Statements and then guide students to write them for selected passages. Next, when giving reading assignments, guide students to place pencil checks or post-it notes beside selected paragraphs for which they are responsible to write About-Point Statements. Students may work individually, in pairs, or in cooperative learning groups to write the statements. Allow students to share their statements orally and discuss similarities and differences. Finally, students can select on their own a certain number of About-Point Statements on paragraphs of their choice. The goal is that this process will become internalized and that students will stop periodically during silent reading to make sure that they understand what the section is about and try to determine the main point. About-Point is an easy-to-use content area learning technique, and the next technique, Coding the Text, is also easy for students to learn.

Coding the Text

Another metacognitive technique that helps students monitor their comprehension while reading content area materials is Coding the Text (Smith & Dauer, 1984). It is easy for students' minds to "stray" while reading content text materials, so this strategy was designed to help students stay focused while monitoring their own comprehension during reading.

STEPS IN CODING THE TEXT (adapted from Hagerty, 1999)

Here are some concrete methods for minds that tend to stray.

1. The teacher creates a code for students to use, based on the information desired and the characteristics of the material. It is helpful to begin with two codes and add others as the students become comfortable with the procedure.

Possible Codes

Grades 2–3	*Grades 4–12*
M = Main Idea	A = Agree
D = Difficult	C = Confused
I = Important	D = Disagree
√ = Understand	I = Interesting
? = What does this mean?	
! = Interesting	

2. Using the codes, the teacher models the process.

3. The students read the material and code by using post-it notes, highlighter tape, or by writing lightly in the text.

4. The discussion of the material starts with the codes; for example, the teacher may begin the discussion with a question like "What were you confused about?" or "What did you think was interesting in this passage?"

Students enjoy using this strategy, and a rich instructional conversation follows as students share what they have marked. The next technique encourages students to revisit the text to clarify confusion.

Monitoring Cards

Patricia Babbs' (1983) method directly teaches students about the reading process over several initial sessions. The discussion, she says, should center around five questions related to a reader's strategic planning:

1. What is reading?
2. What is my goal?
3. How difficult is the text?
4. How can I accomplish my goal?
5. How can I check on whether I have achieved my goal?

Once students reach reasonable proficiency in handling these questions, they are trained in the use of nine prompt cards that can be employed in silent reading in class or at home. The cards are used in the following manner:

After silently reading the first sentence, students should consider the first two cards

1. *clink* = "I understand."
2. *clunk* = "I don't understand."

If a *clunk* is raised, the student first attempts to classify it as a *word* or a *sentence* problem. Then the student reviews the cards in order until the problem is resolved with the help of one of the other cards that say:

3. Read on.
4. Re-read the sentence.
5. Go back and re-read the paragraph.
6. Look in the glossary.
7. Ask someone (such as the tutor in a remedial session).
8. What did it say at the paragraph level?
9. What do I remember at the end of the page?

Using this method, Babbs found that fourth graders in an experimental group spent more time on the reading task and had more than twice as many recalls of important ideas (Babbs, 1983). However, strategy use did not transfer as well as was hoped when the cards were not used with these fourth graders. You will need to think about how you might help achieve effective transfer of these strategies to new material. Of course, one way is merely to extend the period of using the cue cards.

Struggling readers sometimes need assistance in grouping words into chunks that yield more meaning. The next technique provides practice in *chunking* text.

Language Chunking Cues

This notion, also sometimes known as *phrase training,* attempts to focus students' attention on meaningful units of language by breaking sentences up into phrases, or ideational chunks. This is especially appropriate for second-language learners, and those with most any form of lower aptitude for language learning. (See Chapter 12 on the assessment of Language Arts functions for guidance in making identifications of specific need.) For example, the sentence below would be "chunked" as indicated by the slash marks:

> Watch out, Henry, / the cabinet door is opened above you, / and the floor is slippery, too.

Training in reading pre-chunked material, and in chunking material with slashes (/) can draw attention to wording, ideas, and sequencing, but it also needs to be accompanied by a good deal of discussion about meaning, which really is the chief dictate of phrasing. Asking students to indicate where they would place phrase markers evokes discussion about meaning in a close-knit, analytical way.

Kathleen Stevens (1981) found chunking procedures to be of considerable value to tenth-grade boys. Similarly, William Brozo and associates concluded that while such training helps poor readers, few studies have been able to show similar effects for competent readers (Brozo, Schmlzer, & Spires, 1983). This suggests that phrase training and related activities are best saved for remedial classes and tutoring sessions. Most competent readers have already learned all that they need to know about phrasing.

At an anecdotal level, several specialists have noted that phrase training can be effectively used to teach the use and connection between punctuation and communication. They have done this by stressing the role of clause markers such as "but," "and," "if," and so on. Subtleties of language such as these can also be taught incidentally in a ReQuest conversation with questions like: "What does the word 'but' signal to you about what will come next?" and "Why do you suppose it is preceded by a comma?"

The next technique encourages students to revisit the text to clarify possible confusions. Pupils need to be taught this seemingly simple self-governing task.

Lookbacks

The idea of "lookbacks" is to get students to *re*-read certain material in an effort to independently clarify comprehension by self-fixing misapprehensions or by figuring out word meanings from context. Several successful "lookback" procedures have been described (August, Flavell, & Clift 1984; Garner, Hare, Alexander, Haynes, & Winograd, 1984). Good readers tend to do it, and poor readers do not.

It has been suggested that questions be interspersed during reading, either orally or in written form, to require lookbacks. Sanacore recommends questions that also reveal text structure, for example, "Who is the leading character? What is the leading character trying to accomplish in the story? What stands in the way?" (Sanacore, 1984, 710).

Lookbacks get corrective/remedial students to reread—something everyone needs to do.

For related methodology that emphasizes the decoding aspects of reading comprehension, see Repeated Reading Approaches in the previous chapter. The next method also urges lookbacks, while adding a further step.

Paraphrasing/Translating

Several leading authorities in the field believe strongly in the value of oral paraphrasing as one reads, starting at the sentence level, and building up to paragraphs and passages (Haynes & Fillmer, 1984; Kalmbach, 1986; Shugarman & Hurst, 1986). Paraphrasing also is known as "translating," "transforming," and encoding, or recoding in another form. This technique can be used comfortably in the ReQuest procedure as a question type ("Can you tell me in your own words what this sentence says?"), and in the verification step of the DR-TA ("Explain how the text supports your prediction").

One example of a simple yet successful paraphrasing technique is RAP (as cited by Katims & Harris, 1997, from Schumaker, Denton, & Deshler, 1984). The three steps in this procedure are listed below:

R—Read a paragraph
A—Ask yourself questions about the main idea and details
P—Put the main ideas and details into your own words using complete sentences.

This strategy was used in a research study involving 207 seventh-grade students of mixed ability. All students participated in Reading Workshop (Atwell, 1987), the district-mandated reading program. The experimental group also received training in RAP during reading time for 20 minutes every other school day for 6 weeks (15 sessions), with the remainder of class time devoted to Reading Workshop. Students were encouraged "to keep 'rapping,' or talking to themselves as a way to improve their reading comprehension" (Katims & Harris, 1997, 117). The experimental group increased their reading comprehension performance from pre- to posttest (after adjusting for initial differences in groups) statistically significantly more than the control group who participated in Reading Workshop only.

Paraphrasing, as suggested above, tends to externalize misapprehension in reading, and naturally encourages lookbacks. In so doing, it builds the routine comprehension of main idea and supporting details, and metacognition. These are requisites to, and supportive of, summarizing, a highly respected and newly appreciated mark of a literate person.

Summarizing

When the practice of paraphrasing is extended to a complete story or passage, it is known as "retelling," or free recall. When the text may be referred to, it generally is known as summary or precis writing. Summarizing has been studied and recommended by several authorities for its positive influence on building knowledge and writing as well as reading (Bromley, 1985; Cunningham, 1982; Eanet & Manzo, 1976; Hayes, 1988; Simpson & Nist, 1990).

Summary writing is part of a rich tradition in England and most of Europe. Only in the United States is it not taught routinely from the earliest grades. The absence of such an emphasis would seem, in itself, to explain much of the difficulty experienced by students in reconstructive reading and specifically in unaided recall. Summarizing, also known as encoding, tends to increase demand for active, reconstructive reading of the type that results in effective and organized retelling.

The fact that many remedial-level and at-risk readers cannot do it should not discourage teachers from teaching it. Rather, the teacher should make it more manageable by slicing the task into manageable parts and drawing pupil attention to the "Rules for Summarizing," one rule at a time:

a. Delete trivial or irrelevant information.
b. Delete redundant information.
c. Provide a *super*ordinate term for classes of things (for example, "flowers" for roses, petunias, daisies).
d. Identify and express any main idea expressed in the selection.
e. Create your own main idea statement when the author has not provided one (Brown & Day, 1983; Simpson & Nist, 1990).

Summary writing has been part of a rich European tradition for over 400 years.

The deletion rules usually can be taught successfully to fourth- or fifth-grade students; the other rules take longer to acquire. The rules can be given to students on a "cue card" (McNeil & Donant, 1982).

In contrast to these rule-guided approaches to summarizing, James Cunningham (1982) advocates a self-discovery approach that urges students to simply get the "GIST"—*G*enerating *I*nteractions between *S*chemata and *T*ext—by writing 15-word summaries. A comparison of McNeil's and Donant's rule-governed approach with Cunningham's more intuitive approach, found them to be equally effective (Bean & Steenwyck, 1984).

Other studies on summarizing provide these additional pointers for promoting effective summarizing:

1. Focus on main-idea searching (Baumann, 1984).
2. Teach summarizing initially from familiar patterns such as those following a chronology rather than a logical order (Hill, 1991).
3. Provide frequent and extensive feedback about the general effectiveness of strategy use, especially to remedial students (Schunk & Rice, 1987).
4. Combine and integrate summarizing with questioning, clarifying, and predicting (Palinscar, Brown, & Martin, 1987).
5. Provide a lead-in sentence (Cassidy, as cited in Gaskins, 1981) or key words for constructing one.
6. Provide a simple grammar to follow, such as: First this happened . . . Then . . . Then . . . and Finally . . . (Pincus, Geller, & Stover, 1986).

7. Give students an outline of a story that has been read, or elicit one from them, and then have them reconnect it into a summary (Eanet, 1983; Hayes, 1988).

The next technique provides another way for students to summarize and otherwise respond to sections of text.

Precision Instruction for Postreading Schema Building: REAP

Students must assimilate the information read into their own schemata to facilitate long-term memory. Isolated and unconnected pieces of information easily fade from memory, but postreading activities provide the glue to make a cohesive picture of what is read. Read-Encode-Annotate-Ponder, REAP, is one of the most basic ways to facilitate higher-order thinking through reading, writing, and thinking.

Read-Encode-Annotate-Ponder (REAP)

REAP is designed to improve *thinking*, the underlying musculature for active reading and meaningful writing. The idea for this reader-writer exchange system was proposed some time ago (Manzo, 1975) as a means of improving and supporting a national content area reading and writing project essentially for urban schools. Shortly afterwards it was collected into a teaching-learning approach called REAP—Read-Encode-Annotate-Ponder (Eanet & Manzo, 1976; Eanet, 1978, 1983). The REAP system for responding to text has been in use in elementary through college classrooms for two decades. It is based on a scaffold form of writing that invites creativity, much as does *haiku*, or any other disciplined form of art (Manzo, Manzo, & Albee, 2002).

REAP primarily is a cognitive-enrichment approach that teaches students to think more precisely and deeply about what they read, by following the four-step strategy symbolized by its title:

READ	to get the writer's basic message;
ENCODE	the message into your own words while reading;
ANNOTATE	your analysis of the message by writing responses from several perspectives, and;
PONDER	what you have read and written—first by reviewing it yourself, then by sharing and discussing it with others, and finally by reading and discussing the responses of others.

REAP is a precise means of teaching several aspects of higher-order thinking, reading, and writing.

At the heart of the approach is a set of annotation types that range roughly in hierarchical order from a simple summary of the author's basic message to various perspectives for higher-order critical and creative analysis. The first few REAP annotation types require "reconstructive" thinking—understanding and perceiving the essence of the author's meaning. The remaining ones require "constructive" thinking—going beyond the author's intended meaning to form the personal schema connections, applications, and variations that permit the learner to transfer information and ideas from one context to another. This hierarchy aids assessment and gives guidance to students in reaching "up" to higher levels or "down" to more basic ones that may not yet have been mastered. Descriptions and examples of some of the basic annotation types are provided in Figure 10.5. Other types can be customized and created. For example, several teachers have had rewarding results using a "Humorous" annotation (also in Figure 10.5).

Guided Reading, Writing, and Thinking

REAP is designed to improve complex thinking.

For classroom use, the annotation types are introduced either singly or a few at a time, with the nature and pace of instruction geared to the grade level, but *without* aiming at "mastery" before moving to another annotation type. Children tend to learn to write best by struggling to express their own thoughts about rich literature selections, guided by mindfully-written models that scaffold reading and entice emulation. As soon as the class has the basic idea of a few annotation types, they begin to write annotations of things they have read, and to read annotations—perspectives—that others bring to response writing. They are reminded to write several annotations on a reading selection, as a means to cross-check their initial understandings and reach for higher-order insights and questions. Exemplary annotations are stored for other individuals and classes to read *before* reading (*frontloading*), *during* reading (as discussion points), or *after* reading (as a review). These also serve as models of well-composed written responses.

After students have had some practice writing various types of annotations, these can be used and reinforced in a variety of ways. A few are listed below:

1. When giving a reading assignment, specify three annotation types for students to write and turn in.

2. As students become more skilled at annotation writing, they can be given the option of selecting from three annotation types the one that they would like to write in response to a reading assignment.

3. Assign each cooperative group member to write a different annotation type in response to a reading assignment. When students have finished reading and writing, they move to their assigned groups to

FIGURE **10.5**

SAMPLE READING SELECTION WITH EXAMPLES OF **REAP** ANNOTATION TYPES

"Travelers and the Plane-Tree"

Two travelers were walking along a bare and dusty road in the heat of a midsummer's day. Coming upon a large shade tree, they happily stopped to shelter themselves from the burning sun in the shade of its spreading branches. While they rested, looking up into the tree, one of them said to his companion, "What a useless tree this is! It makes no flowers and bears no fruit. Of what use is it to anyone?" The tree itself replied indignantly, "You ungrateful people! You take shelter under me from the scorching sun, and then, in the very act of enjoying the cool shade of my leaves, you abuse me and call me good for nothing!"

Reconstructive Annotations

SUMMARY: states the basic message in brief form
Travelers take shelter from the sun under a large tree. They criticize the tree for not making flowers or fruit. The tree speaks, and tells them that they are ungrateful people for taking shelter under her leaves and then criticizing her.

TELEGRAM: briefly states the author's basic theme with all unnecessary words removed—a crisp, telegram-like message
Travelers stop for rest and shade under big tree. Travelers say tree is useless. Tree tells them off.

HEURISTIC: restates an attention-getting portion of the selection that makes the reader want to respond
In this story, a tree talks back to people. The tree says, "You ungrateful people! You come and take shelter under me…and then…abuse me and call me good for nothing!"

QUESTION: turns the main point into an organization question that the selection answers
What if the things we use could talk back?

Constructive Annotations

PERSONAL VIEW: answers the question, "How do your views and feelings compare with what the author says?"
We use resources like coal without thinking. Then we criticize it for damaging our lungs and dirtying our air. I guess kids sometimes use their parents the way the travelers used the tree, and then criticize them without thinking about their feelings.

HUMOROUS: can vary from bringing a slight smile, usually by flirting with a naughty suggestion, to using jest to bring enlightenment

I can just see that poor tree thinking, "I hope they're about to stop here to seek shelter and not relief."

CRITICAL: begins by stating the author's main point, then states whether the reader agrees, disagrees, or agrees in part with the author, and then briefly explains why
Not every word spoken in criticism is meant that way. The travelers were just grumpy from the trip. The tree is too sensitive.

CONTRARY: states a logical alternative position, even though it may not be the one the student supports
The travelers could be right, a better tree could produce something and also give shade.

INTENTION: states and briefly explains what the reader thinks was the author's intention, plan, and purpose for writing the selection
The author wants us to be more sensitive to the people and things we depend on—especially those we see and use often.

MOTIVATION: states what may have caused the author to have written the selection—the author's personal agenda
It sounds like the author may have felt used, after having a bad experience with friends or family.

DISCOVERY: states one or more practical questions that need to be answered before the selection can be judged for accuracy or worth
I wonder how many of us know when we are being "users." We could take an anonymous poll to see how many class members secretly feel that they have been used and how many see themselves as users.

CREATIVE: suggests different and perhaps better solutions or views and/or connections and applications to prior learning and experiences

_____ *This fable made me think that teachers are sometimes used unfairly. They give us so much, and then we put them down if they make a little mistake. They're only human.*

_____ *We should put this fable on the bulletin board where it will remind us not to be ungrateful "users."*

_____ *[How would you re-title this fable if you were writing it?] I'd call it "Travelers in the Dark," to show that we go through life without knowing how many small "gifts" come to us along our way.*

share the annotations they have written and to offer constructive suggestions to one another on ways to clarify the response. Extra-credit points can be offered to the group with the best annotation of each type as judged by the teacher or the class as a whole.

4. Introduce a new reading assignment by having students read annotations written by students in previous years' classes or from a different section at the same grade level.

5. Provide incentive to read and write reflectively by posting exemplary annotations, signed by the author, on a bulletin board or Web page, including some from different age-grade levels; in other words, raise some higher targets.

6. Use REAP annotation types as a guide for phrasing postreading discussion questions. Encourage students to do the same.

7. From time to time, use the REAP annotations to guide students' responses to nontext learning experiences: a video, a laboratory procedure, a piece of music or art, or others.

GUIDING INDEPENDENT STUDY

Undoing poor habits and forming new ones can be daunting, but life altering.

Study strategies might be best thought of as the "practical" side of reading. **Study strategies** are all the activities one employs to make time spent in independent learning as efficient and effective as possible. "Study" is the self-initiated application of habits of mind that are the goal of teacher-guided content area reading. As such, they are strongly grounded in individual attitudes and habits formed over time. Acquiring a "new" study strategy often means changing an "old" study habit. It means reflecting on what one typically does, and why, then trying to do it better. The development of study strategies is an extension of metacognition. It is a personal, introspective process that can be quite difficult, given the fact that study habits and attitudes—good ones or bad ones—are formed in the earliest years of school. In general, habits are hard to form and very hard to break. The payoff, however, for undoing poor habits and forming new ones can be life altering. The next sections describe approaches and strategies that help students form good study habits early, and build on them as they grow.

Primary Grades' Foundations for Study Strategies

In the primary grades, children begin to develop their personal response patterns to the requirements of school. The teacher has much of the responsibility for children's learning, but even in these early years children are expected to begin to assume increasing responsibilities. The primary school teacher can help to lay positive study strategies foundations in the following ways:

- Reward questioning and critical-creative thinking.
- Impart the understanding that the purpose of writing is to express one's ideas and feelings.
- Teach reading lessons using methods that permit the teacher to model effective behaviors for the three stages of the reading process: prereading, silent reading, and postreading.
- Teach vocabulary in ways that also teach children to take conscious notice of unfamiliar words that they hear and see in print, and strategies for learning and remembering new word meanings.
- Teach children to organize their school materials so that they can find the proper supplies when they are needed.
- Teach children to record important information and assignments.
- Use approaches and methods that encourage effective listening.

Independent study strategies are important enough to be taught from the primary school level onward.

Following Directions

The ability to follow written directions is an important key to independent learning and functioning. It has been aptly said that "At various points in almost every school day, students are expected to follow some form of written directions," and that life outside school is full of "basic life demands that require them to follow written instructions" (Henk & King, 1984, 62).

Maring and Ritson (1980) suggest preparing "Read and Do" sheets that can be used in physical education class, at recess, or to break up the sedentary nature of schools and tutorials. Using "Read and Do" sheets, students learn required content while improving their ability to follow written directions. For example:

Following directions can be a highly disciplined, but fun, activity.

Read and Do!

Motor Development: Jump into the air, click your heels together once, and land with your feet apart.

This can be turned into an amusing exercise in which students try to write out totally unambiguous expository directions for their peers to follow. Other popular "Read and Do" activities for the classroom include:

1. having students write out explicit directions for others to follow on how to get from one place in the school to another
2. having students read and follow directions for drawing a certain graphic, or folding paper
3. having students work to assemble something from directions, such as inexpensive model cars or planes or a peanut butter and jelly sandwich

Such "real-life" directions often pose too great a challenge for poor readers. Henk and King (1984) offer these suggestions for rewriting directions to provide practice activities for these students:

1. Use one sentence per direction.
2. Substitute simple synonyms for difficult words.
3. Avoid taking background information for granted.
4. Ensure that essential intermediate steps have not been omitted or just implied.
5. Avoid using lengthy or complex sentence structures.
6. Avoid ambiguous statements.
7. Omit irrelevant information.
8. Use numbers to mark the steps to follow (1984, 63).

To add another bit of mental manipulation to this task, have students try to anticipate and write an explanation of where they think *another* student will have trouble understanding or following the directions given. In the following section we will look at study strategies that are especially appropriate for students in the intermediate grades.

Reflection

Before reading the next section, take a few minutes to describe the study strategies you use while reading this and other textbooks. Do you think your study strategies are efficient and effective? Why or why not? As you read, think of ways you might improve your study strategies.

INTERMEDIATE AND HIGHER-GRADE STUDY STRATEGIES

Instant Study Strategy Post-Its!

To win student commitment to becoming effective at reading and study, it is best to begin in an upbeat and optimistic way. The school-based reading specialist should urge the classroom teacher to post the instant study skills list for students to read and re-read at their leisure. The teacher should periodically allude to the list and invite discussion of the relative merit of each skill in different situations.

1. *Come early to class and leave late.* Important guides to the material and tips on exams frequently are given in the first and last minutes of a class.

2. *Sit close to the front of the room.* Studies have shown that students who sit in the front of class make better grades. Perhaps this is true because those who choose to sit closer to the front are the more "motivated" students—but why not assume that a positive feedback loop is at work here: that is, proximity to the instructor increases concentration, which enhances motivation.

3. *Make class notes as complete as possible.* The most effective study time may be the actual hour of the class. Take extensive notes and concentrate during class, and you will have a good record for thought and home study.

4. *Review class notes as soon as possible.* Immediate review is probably the most powerful learning strategy known. Go over the material mentally as you walk to your next class. Make it a habit to briefly review class notes each school night, preferably at the same time and in the same place.

5. *Survey a reading assignment before beginning to read.* This simple practice gives focus and purpose to reading. It creates a "frame" for the information and ideas you will be reading about.

6. *Underline after you have read a paragraph.* This focuses attention and concentration and avoids "automatic" reading or, worse, mindless reading.

7. *On tests, read slowly and answer quickly.* Focus on the question stem instead of the choices. This prevents the frequent and irritating problem of "misreading the question" due to the attractive wording of one of the foils.

8. *On tests, do the easy questions first.* Go through the test quickly. Skip and mark hard questions, and pick those up later. Attempting to do the difficult questions first can be emotionally disruptive, causing you to forget answers that you do know.

9. *Overlearn for tests.* Memorize as many things as you can. Research shows that over 90 percent of test anxiety can be reduced with better preparation.

10. *Set high goals.* There is a relatively easy formula for making an A in any class. Ask yourself, "What is the very most the teacher would expect someone to do to get an A on this paper/test/project?" Then do more!

11. *Train yourself to read faster.* Most people can read—with under-standing—much faster than they do. To train yourself to read faster, use one hand as a "pacer." Move it down the page as you read. Gradually increase the speed of movement, and try to read along. "Hand pacing" has been proven to be an effective means of increasing reading rate.

12. *Think from other perspectives.* Periodically, try to predict the com-plete opposite position of a view you now hold or have read about. Giv-ing consideration to the opposite viewpoint often stimulates thought about reasonable compromise positions that might not otherwise have occurred to you. This back-and-forth inner conversation is called "dialectical thinking." It is the foundation of all logical and critical thinking.

13. *Learn the "right words."* According to some psychologists, if you are anxious and unhappy, there is a good chance that you're saying the wrong *words* to yourself. In your conversations with yourself, try using more understated words. Think of your arch-enemy as a "scoundrel" rather than a "&S##°®®%." You will be less emotional, more stable, and have greater constructive energy.

14. *Build your knowledge base.* It has been wisely observed that "We find little in a book but what we put there." That's because the knowl-edge one *has* is the best predictor of how well one will read and learn. Build your *fund of information* by reading an encyclopedia, almanac, or other nonfiction work for at least 15 minutes every day. You will be sur-prised at how quickly facts and ideas will begin to repeat themselves.

PASS: A Guiding Principle

The selection and use of effective study strategies essentially is a problem-solving process. It requires thoughtful analysis of one's habits, an honest evaluation of one's strengths and weaknesses, and then an exploration of other possible ways of approaching reading and study tasks. The *Problem-Solving Approach to Study Skills* (Manzo & Casale, 1980), abbreviated as *PASS*, is one way to help students to develop a life-long, personal problem-solving orientation while introducing them to a variety of study strategy options. PASS is a form of intensive and extensive metacognitive examina-tion and self-regulation.

STEPS IN PASS

Step 1   *Count.* The teacher presents students with a list of common study skills problems and asks them to check those that apply to them (see Figure 10.6).

FIGURE **10.6**

COMMON STUDY PROBLEMS

Note: This sample list should be adjusted to your students' grade level and class requirements.

Directions: Check *all* that are problem areas.

_____ 1. Taking good class notes

_____ 2. Basic reading comprehension

_____ 3. Identifying the main idea

_____ 4. Noting important details

_____ 5. Drawing inferences from facts

_____ 6. Memory

_____ 7. Test anxiety

_____ 8. Concept formation

_____ 9. Paying attention in class

_____ 10. Concentration while reading

_____ 11. Concentration while studying

_____ 12. Vocabulary knowledge and strategies

_____ 13. General background of information

_____ 14. Keeping up with homework

_____ 15. Writing

_____ 16. Test-taking techniques

_____ 17. Outlining/taking notes from textbooks

_____ 18. Finding materials in the library

_____ 19. Participating in class discussions

_____ 20. Critical/creative thinking

Step 2   *Characterize.* The teacher guides students in defining selected study and learning problems in specific terms. With older students, this can be done with inventories of learning style, temperament, skills, abilities, and attitudes.

Step 3   *Consider.* Students consider how they typically have dealt with their particular needs and problems and the possible advantages of these intuitive ways of dealing with school requirements.

Step 4   *Collect.* Students discuss and judge the value of standard techniques for dealing with reading/study problems. Where these seem to be inadequate, they are set aside for reconsideration in the next step.

Step 5   *Create.* Students seek inventive modifications and alternatives that match their personal strengths and needs. This step can be handled initially in individual and small-group settings, and then in larger group discussions from which all may benefit.

Casale (Manzo) and Kelly (1980) found this technique of introducing study strategies to be an effective way to involve students in an examination of their own study habits, and exploration of fresh possibilities. Their research used medical school students as subjects. However, approaches have been used successfully with intermediate-grade children, who seem to greet the self-creation aspect of the process with a certain amount of glee. (See Dana's innovation just ahead.)

PASS Variation for Intermediate Grades

A closely related way to help students to build metacognitive awareness of their reading and study behaviors and needs was suggested by Dana (1989). Dana suggests introducing students to four major cueing strategies, or "families" as she calls them. These cueing families are labeled with acronyms to help students remember effective strategies to apply before, during, and after reading:

Before Reading: as preparation for reading	**RAM** **R**elax **A**ctivate your purpose **M**otivate yourself
During Reading: to focus on the content	**SIP** **S**ummarize natural sections **I**mage—visualize the contents **P**redict what's coming *OR* **RIPS** (to make repairs) **R**ead further/read again **P**araphrase the troublesome section **S**peed up/slow down/seek help
After Reading: to set your memory	**EEEZ** **E**xplain what it all means to you **E**xplore other versions **E**xpand with related material

Once students have become familiar with these, you can even encourage students to make up their own strategy families, as one group of boys did:

BURP
Breathe
Understand
Re-read
Predict

A field-based study of the effectiveness of strategy families showed that remedial reading students (aged 7 to 15) using their own PASS-like strategy families with both fiction and nonfiction materials made significant gains on standardized reading tests (Dana, 1989). Children can make posters of strategy families for display. To amplify their value and use, leave space for testimonials: "When I began to use BURP, I realized that I was holding my breath whenever I had to do something I was afraid of. Just remembering to breathe normally really can help" (Jackie M., fifth grade).

SQ3R: Senior Study Strategy

Robinson's (1946) "SQ3R" study technique is the classical means of introducing students to this metacognitive side of reading to learn. The acronym SQ3R is a way to remember to apply active reading strategies when reading independently: Survey, Question, Read, Recite, Review.

SQ3R is a legacy of World War II.

SQ3R was developed by Francis Robinson (1946), in response to a need expressed by the U.S. Department of Defense during World War II (Stahl & Henk, 1986). American troops had much to learn and little time in which to learn it. They needed a rigorous, *self-guided* Directed Reading Activity that they could use with minimal instruction in field-training situations. SQ3R stresses meticulous, self-guided, step-by-step analysis of text, followed by repeated efforts to "overlearn" the material to the point where key information can be recalled and recited with minimal cuing under stressful circumstances, such as tests and classroom recitations.

STEPS IN SQ3R

Survey Look over the material before you begin to read:
   a. Read the title and think about what it says or implies.
   b. Read the headings and subheadings.
   c. Read the summary if there is one.
   d. Read the captions under pictures, charts, graphs, or other illustrations.

Question Ask yourself questions about what you are going to read:
   a. What does the title of the chapter mean?
   b. What do I already know about the subject?
   c. What did my instructor say about this chapter when it was assigned?
   d. What questions do the headings and subheadings suggest?

Read Read actively:
   a. Read to answer the questions you raised when doing the survey/question routine.
   b. Read all the added attractions in the chapter (maps, graphs, tables, and other illustrations).
   c. Read all the underlined, italicized, or boldface words or phrases carefully.

Recite Go over what you read by either orally summarizing it or by making notes.

Review   Periodically survey what you read and learned:
   a. Use your notes or markings to refresh your memory.
   b. Review immediately after reading.

Review again before taking an exam on the subject.

Research on the effectiveness of SQ3R has shown that the "Recite" step of SQ3R is highly effective (McIntyre, 1991). Research on the general effectiveness of SQ3R as a whole, however, has not yielded clear support (McIntyre, 1991; Stahl & Henk, 1986; Wark, 1964). This probably is because, as Robinson himself observed, the strategy cannot be effective until it becomes "automatic" and "subordinate to the task of reading" (1946, 21). Intermediate-grade students need a great deal of teacher guidance in the use of SQ3R. For many students, SQ3R requires substantial changes in habitual study reading behaviors. Elementary school teachers can help students develop effective study reading habits by providing guided practice in the use of SQ3R as a simple extension of any basic reading lesson. The next strategy shifts the focus from print to listening.

Listening: The Guided Lecture Procedure

Listening is a skill that can be rather easily improved. Kelly and Holmes (1979) developed a variation on the Guided Reading Procedure, called the Guided Lecture Procedure to teach students to improve their ability to learn from listening during classroom presentations. A major part of school learning takes place through talking and listening. Teach children early on how to learn from this widely used mode of instruction.

Listening is easily improved.

STEPS IN THE GUIDED LECTURE PROCEDURE

Step 1   Students are directed to *take no notes* as they listen carefully to the lecture. (The idea here is to have students focus, initially, on listening for concepts rather than details.)

Step 2   The teacher writes the objectives of the lecture on the chalkboard along with key technical terms.

Step 3   The teacher presents for about half the class period, then stops.

Step 4   Students attempt to write down everything they can recall from the presentation.

Step 5   Students form small cooperative learning groups to review and discuss their notes. This discussion component involves important manipulations of ideas and facts as well as involving the related language arts of speaking, writing, and listening.

Sharp listening skills are an important part of Memory Training techniques that are examined next. Memory, pardon the pun, often is the forgotten study skill.

Memory Training as Cognitive and Affective Enrichment

Much of the basic information we expect students to acquire in school requires simple rote memorization—at least until enough information and experience has been acquired to link the information into larger concept structures. Memory training can serve as an excellent means of developing self-efficacy and self-esteem. Teaching students to use memory strategies can help them to tolerate times when school learning seems quite arbitrary, and can give them a self-empowering strategy for future school learning and success in business. Business and industry often pay huge sums of money to have these very methods taught to their employees. Long ago, Harvard psychologist George Miller determined that two-thirds of the population can only remember between 5 and 9 unrelated pieces of information (the rule of 7 ± 2). Almost everyone, however, can easily increase this capacity by making items more meaningful and manageable.

Memory training is an often forgotten study skill.

For fun and painless practice, flexibly group students into teams and have them compete periodically to see who can best "learn and recall" the most on topics from geography to parts of the body. "Quiz bowl" competitions, even once a week, are of proven value for all students, but particularly for slower learners, especially when better students serve as incidental tutors by describing the memory techniques they use. One of the incidental benefits of Bible study has been memory improvement and knowledge of common referents, or allusions.

Key Word Study Strategy   The most frequent problem with "forgetting" occurs as a result of inadequate initial learning: The reason we don't remember names is most often because we didn't hear them initially. Accordingly, Al-Hilawani (2003) recommends a variation on reciprocal teaching to get things learned deeply the first time. In the Key Word Study Strategy, students and teacher first discuss the topic of the lesson in general terms, to help retrieve prior learning of specific related ideas and vocabulary. They then try to identify key words in a paragraph as they read silently. Students and teacher take turns asking what happens before and after each word without rereading the paragraph. Next, students write questions for each paragraph in the selection, and take turns asking these. Finally, they summarize what they have learned. The teacher models this step before having students try it.

Al-Hilawani credits Mann and Sabatino (1985) with the idea of writing down important words that can serve as memory tags for retrieving stored information. The further steps of questioning one another and summarizing the passage clearly add strong memory traces and rich associations. It also is consistent with basic research that shows that remembering incoming information depends, as suggested above, on the initial levels of processing of that information (Craik & Lockart, 1972). (Note that the Key Word *Study* Strategy is different from the strategy with a similar name: the Keyword *Vocabulary* Method described in Chapter 9.)

Imaging   Teach children to take the time to form clear visual images of material studied. Have them close their eyes, while you describe the object or event in minute detail. In one study, Meier (1963 workshop) taught the elements of a brain neuron by telling students to imagine that they were floating around in the cytoplasm of a neuron. Students were told to picture the cell, to touch it and feel a mild electrical charge, and to carefully picture and even feel various parts of the neuron. They were told that they were inventing a vivid, memorable experience. These students' comprehension was compared with another group of students who were taught the same information via lecture accompanied by attractive props and illustrations. The group taught through imaging performed 12 percent better on a test of immediate recall, and 26 percent better on a test on long-term retention.

Loci Imaging   This is a specific type of Imaging that has been used since the time of the ancient Persians. Have students pick a familiar location, such as the classroom, and identify specific locations, or "loci points" within it. The items to be remembered are then mentally placed and pictured in the different loci points. When the items are to be recalled, students need only retrace their steps and retrieve the images from where they were placed.

Spatial Arrangements   Spatial Arrangement is similar to Loci Imaging, but simply uses a familiar shape, such as an X or a K, or a 2 to organize and picture the information to be recalled (see Figure 10.7).

Clustering   When there is much information of a certain type to be learned and remembered, help students break it into parts, or "clusters." For example, in trying to learn the names and discoveries of early explorers

FIGURE **10.7**

SPATIAL ARRANGEMENT MEMORY TECHNIQUE

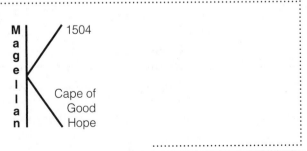

of North and South America, it helps considerably to group them by threes, or better, by the continent or parts of continents they explored.

Acronyms   This is probably the most commonly known memory strategy. It involves the creation of "memory words" from the first letter of each word in a list of words to be memorized. How many of us, for example, use the acronym ROY G. BIV to remember the colors of the spectrum (red, orange, yellow, green, blue, indigo, and violet)? Similarly, students of geography are always pleased to learn HOMES—an acronym for the names of the Great Lakes: *Huron, Ontario, Michigan, Erie,* and *Superior* (Uttero, 1988). Many of the previously discussed strategies can be adapted for upper-grade students, and the following strategies are especially effective.

STRATEGIES FOR UPPER-GRADE STUDENTS

Research Notes on Note-taking

By the upper grades, much content instruction is presented through a combination of lecture/discussion and related reading. Several study strategies have been developed and well-researched, though most at the college level. These basic models can be easily adapted for use at high school, middle, and even elementary levels. They also will be of value to the many elementary school teachers who often find themselves needing to teach study strategies to older remedial students, and to those who teach in high school equivalency and vocational education programs.

> Note-taking is done most and taught least . . . strange.

One of the best ways to teach note-taking is to begin by providing several pages of *partially completed* notes for students to follow and complete as they listen to short lecture presentations. Teaching note-taking does take some preparation on the teacher's part. However, the benefits to students will more than justify the effort.

When helping students to learn to take notes, be sure they know it's "OK"—even smart—to abbreviate! Intermediate-grade students are usually intrigued by coded messages: They enjoy learning and even creating their own abbreviations. Many are doing so in email communications that are changing spelling and speeding up writing at a rate not seen in a thousand years. See Figure 10.8 (page 402) for some examples of Speedwriting for note-taking (or, more appropriately, "spdwrtg").

> Email is spdg up the change of spelling patterns at a rate not seen in a thousand years.

Very few curricula even include attention to this easy way to help kids to help themselves. The absence of this topic from school programs is the strongest evidence that our schools are not yet "whole-child" centered. If they were, the needs of children for these easily-acquired strategies would be a top priority.

FIGURE **10.8**

"SPDWRTG" FOR NOTE-TAKING

Use symbols for words:		Shorten words by eliminating final letters:	
&	and	max	maximum
c	around, about, approximately	subj	subject
@	at	info	information
#	number		

Shorten words by omitting vowels, but keeping enough consonants to make the word recognizable:

w/	with		
w/o	without	rdg	reading
?	questionable	bkgd	background
!	surprising	gvt	government
vs	versus, against, as compared with	clsrm	classroom
=	equals, the same as	lrng	learning
≠	does not equal, different from		

Shorten frequently used words and phrases by using first letters or acronyms

<	less than, less important than		
>	greater than, more important than	GNP	gross national product
∴	therefore	NDP	National Democratic Party
→	causes, results in, produces, yields	S/L	standard of living
e.g. or ex.	for example	CW	Civil War
cf	compare, look this up		
i.e.	that is		

Manzo & Manzo, 1990a.

Note-Taking from Text and in Class: PUNS

Robert Palmatier (1971) developed a note-taking method that integrates both class and text presentation forms, and provides a built-in study system. Palmatier's Unified Note-Taking System (PUNS) has been fully validated through empirical research (Palmatier, 1971, 1973; Palmatier & Bennett, 1974).

STEPS IN PUNS

Step 1 *Record.* Use only one side of regular-sized notebook paper, with a *3-inch margin* line drawn on the left side. (Many school-supply stores now stock this type of paper for this purpose.) Record lecture-presentation notes to the right of the margin. Use a modified outline form to isolate main topics. Leave space where information seems to be missing. Use the front side of the paper only, and number each page as you record the notes.

Step 2   *Organize.* As soon after the lecture as possible, add two sections to the notes. First, place *labels* in the left margin. These should briefly describe the information in the recorded notes. Second, insert *important text information* directly into the recorded notes. If you need more space, use the back of the notebook paper.

Step 3   *Study.* Remove the notes from the looseleaf binder, and lay them out so that only the left margin of each page is visible (see Figure 10.9, page 404). Use the labels as memory cues to recite as much of the information on the right as you can recall. The labels can be turned into questions: "What do I need to know about [*insert label*]?" Check your recall immediately by lifting the page to read the information recorded to the right of the label. As you learn the material on each page of notes, set that page aside in an "I already know" stack.

Research by Victoria Risko and Alice Patterson (1989) suggests the need to add three important features to improve note-taking. They found that inner-city, remedial readers produced the best notes when they were given a fixed time to read, a strategy for personal reflection, and, most importantly, an opportunity for 10 minutes of group rehearsal. The next strategy adds a questioning component to PUNS.

With a slight format change, class notes can be transformed into a powerful study system.

Poostay's Underlining/Highlighting and Note-Taking

Edward T. Poostay (1984) combines training in underlining (or highlighting) with the ReQuest strategy. He has teachers read and underline five to seven concepts within the first 150 words of a larger selection. He then photocopies that page and distributes it to students. Next, they study the page with underlines and are encouraged to ask as many questions as they care to about how one or two of these are connected to the story and to one another. The teacher then does the same. This reciprocal interaction continues until all underlines are suitably discussed. Silent reading follows as students attempt to determine whether they have adequately inferred what the selection is about from the underlines. Poostay urges that the teacher *not* force students into a common set of predictions, but rather let them read to discover which actually turn out to be the most accurate, and which portions probably should have been underlined and were not.

The culmination of school learning is generally testing—classroom tests and/or standardized tests. Teaching test-taking skills is one way to ensure that students do their best.

FIGURE **10.9**

SAMPLE PUNS STUDY LAYOUT

Step 1. Record. Use the right-hand side of a specially divided page, leaving space to add text notes.

Step 2. Fill in labels. Write key word labels in the left-hand margin and text notes in the space used for lecture notes. Use the back of the page if more space is needed.

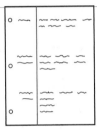

Step 3. Study key words. Lay out pages so that only key words show, and try to recite the information from the notes. Remove each page as you master the contents.

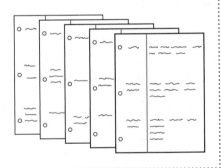

Test-Taking

One purpose of test-taking instruction is to familiarize students with the testing formats they will encounter so that they can use these easily and comfortably. When children are not able to do this, their test scores reflect what they know about *tests*, rather than what they know about the subject the test is presumed to be measuring. Here are some ideas to share with your students for taking typical standardized tests, summarized largely from Pauk (1974). These are best presented in combination with practice tests in standardized test format that can be purchased (from the test publisher itself or from teacher-supply sources) or teacher-made.

GUIDELINES FOR TAKING MULTIPLE-CHOICE TESTS

1. *Read the directions* for the whole test and for each subsection.
    a. Note the number of items, and set a rough schedule for the amount of time you have to work. Leave time to check your work.
    b. Ask about guessing penalties—whether points will be subtracted for incorrect answers or items left blank. If not, you should guess when you don't know the answer.

2. Answer the easy items first.
    a. Spending time on difficult questions will make you tense, and could cause you to forget information you knew when the test began.
    b. As you go through the test, you often will come across information that will help you remember answers to earlier items.

3. Read each question carefully.
    a. Cover the choices and read the question; try to state it in your own words. If the question is long and complex, underline the subject and the verb.
    b. With the choices still covered, make a guess at the answer. Predicting your own answer first puts you more in control. You are not as easily led astray by an incorrect answer, or as confused by two similar answers.
    c. Uncover the choices one at a time, noting each as "probable" or "not probable" before deciding. (Test makers often put a correct but not best choice at the top of the list.)

4. Try to think simply and clearly: try not to read too much into the question.
    a. If a question is in the negative form—for example, "One of the following is *not* a cause"—it is helpful to look for three "true" answers; then the remaining false answer will be the correct one.
    b. Make sure that the grammatical structure of your choice matches that of the question stem.
    c. General statements are more likely to be correct than very detailed statements, especially if you think of even *one* exception.

5. Keep a positive attitude.
    a. Don't assume that the test is loaded with trick questions. If you look for tricks, you will read too much into the questions and trick yourself.
    b. As an overall approach, read each question carefully but concentrate on the main point rather than the details.

6. Watch yourself for signs of worry.

    a. During the test, pause briefly two or three times to consider whether you are overly tense: Neck muscles contracted? Palms clammy? Weak stomach? Holding your breath?

    b. Avoid stress-related behaviors that break concentration: glancing frequently at the clock or the teacher, examining fingernails, gazing at the wall or ceiling, excessive yawning or stretching.

7. Check your work.

    a. Make sure you answered all questions you had skipped to come back to later.

    b. Check your answer sheet against your question sheet to make sure the numbers match (check about every fifth question or so).

    c. Don't waste time reviewing answers if there are still questions unanswered.

    d. Change your answers if you have reason to. Research shows that contrary to common belief, three out of four times your *changes* will be correct. This may be because during a final check, the tension begins to lessen and thought processes are clearer.

> Schooling is a sea of testing; a few swimming lessons are in order.

The best guidelines for test-taking will not be beneficial if a study plan prior to testing is not used. PLAE provides steps in preparing for tests.

PLAE to Prepare for Tests Michele Simpson and Sherrie Nist (1984) developed the PLAE model as a means of involving students in planning, monitoring, and controlling their own study. The acronym reminds students to follow these basic steps:

P *Preplanning:* Find out about the test, and answer a series of questions to set performance goals.

L *Listing:* Make a list of the most appropriate study strategies to use, and set time limits and goals for each study session.

A *Activating:* Put the study plan into action, making adjustments where necessary.

E *Evaluation:* After test scores have been received, have students engage in a self-guided form of "dynamic assessment" (Carney & Cioffi, 1990), by diagnosing errors, looking for patterns of strengths and weaknesses, and incorporating these findings into future study plans.

Three studies of the effectiveness of PLAE led to the following conclusions: planning is significantly related to test performance (Nist, Simpson, Olejnik, & Mealey, 1989); use of PLAE has a measurable effect on both test performance and metacognitive abilities (Nist & Simpson, 1989); and, students trained to use PLAE outperformed students trained in traditional time management on four different content area examinations (Nist & Simpson, 1990).

REVIEW

This chapter spoke to several fundamental remedial/corrective practices in comprehension, content reading, study, memory training, and test-taking. Several of these methods are the conceptual and practical bases for assisting ESL students, and those with ongoing content acquisition needs as a result of not yet having mastered the full range of skills necessary for learning from reading. Several of theses methods can easily be converted into school-wide programs, especially Question-Only, DR-TA, Listen-Read-Discuss, and REAP.

PREVIEW

The next chapter offers specialized guidance as well. It addresses means and methods by which teachers and reading/learning specialists and teachers can assist in a variety of collateral, and admittedly "murky" but important matters influencing the whole person, progress in reading, as well as social-emotional growth and adjustment.

REMEDIES FOR READING-RELATED MOTIVATIONAL, PSYCHOLOGICAL, GENDER, AND MEDICAL ISSUES

Let no one imagine that they are without influence.

CONTENT AND CONCEPT ORGANIZER

The ability to engage in complex thinking is marked by recognition of subtleties, ambiguities, and making decisions from available choices. This chapter addresses possible remedies and recommendations in the murky realms of Defects (physical issues such as sight, hearing, and neurological disorders), Disruptions (emotional, attitudinal, and motivational matters), De-Limitations (factors extrinsic to the student), and Defaults (the tendency of the student to overrely, or fall back on whatever worked before). Emotional and cultural factors are given the greatest attention, since these are the ones most frequently observed in the social atmosphere called School.

CHAPTER OUTLINE

PRESCRIPTIONS FOR SOME COMMON
  MEDICAL DISORDERS
  Allergies
  Hyperkinesis
  Of Different Minds: Hyperlexia, Williams Syndrome,
    and Ungeared Minds

REVIEW
PREVIEW

REMEDIES FOR DEFECTS, DIFFERENCES, AND DISRUPTIONS

School Is Life!

Children come to school representing a great variety of possibilities, and also problems and challenges. Perhaps the most important realization is that school *is* life, not merely preparation for it. School is a central, life-shaping, enduring experience, as well as a place for academic learning. The individual classroom is a mini society that draws strength but sometimes warping influences from the larger school culture, and from many helpful but some indifferent and troubled parents. Effective schools and class-rooms and influential teachers attempt to organize and conduct themselves to leverage the human experience of schooling so that it fully supports the academic aspects of learning, while nurturing the physical well-being, and social-emotional growth and adjustment of students. Long after children have forgotten the significance of a diphthong, they will be telling about their bitter and sweet experiences in school. If not one single reading prob-lem were attributable to physical or social-emotional health (although sev-eral are), these *intangibles* still should be considered important collateral objectives of the reading and language arts program.

Literature, both nonfiction and fiction, is the story of human efforts to understand, achieve, and overcome. Reading inherently is a plunge into human experience, and the various ways people have negotiated their per-sonal pilgrimages. This chapter presents reasons why, and means by which, reading teachers and specialists can present this treasure trove of wisdom to best serve struggling readers. We also strive to reach those who may appear to be *proficient*, according to the popular standard of *how many* books they can read rather than *how* they read a book.

> If not one single reading problem were attributable to physical or social-emotional health, these *intangibles* still would be important humanizing objectives of the reading/language arts program.

Influential Teachers

The broad nature and causes of "reading failure" have influenced the emphasis you will find in this text on methods that address developmental

School *is* life, not merely preparation for it.

and human problems, as well as reading problems. Not surprisingly, teachers ranked most "influential" by students later in life were those who were so inclined. They tended to raise student internal motivation by appealing to their aesthetic sense, to raise their intellectual curiosity, and to demonstrate success by modeling and teaching problem-solving approaches that reached up, through, and beyond the subject at hand (Ruddell, 1990). With this goal of the "influential teacher" in mind, we begin this chapter with one of the most frequently referenced factors in corrective and remedial reading education—*motivation.*

MOTIVATION

Generic Motivation Approaches

Common experience suggests that if a student has a keen interest in cars, he or she will be more inclined to read and learn about cars. This is called *intrinsic motivation.* To this student an otherwise wonderful but "car-less" article or story may appear irrelevant; it is not on that student's radar screen. That is not to say that the student will not, or cannot be induced to, read the piece. But a reading selection generally needs to be "sold" to reluctant readers—that is, introduced in such a way as to move it onto their agendas and up their priority list—before it will command the student's will and life energies. In other words, students need to be *extrinsically* motivated to read and engage the notion as well as the text. One seemingly more efficient way to approach this requirement is to sell students on the idea that it is in their best interest to *learn how to read* effectively, rather than entice them to read a specific book or story. This is the *generic motivation* approach. When done convincingly, it has students saying to themselves, "I want to be a competent, independent reader; therefore I will attempt to read just about anything put in front of me to strengthen my skills and knowledge." This approach attempts to build personal power or, *agency.*

Intuitively, every parent and teacher tries to promote "generic motivation" because it then becomes part of the student's *intrinsic motivation* and *inner-speech.* In this way, it unburdens us from having to deduce the best way to "sell" each and every reading and learning task we would have students undertake. When generic motivation to read takes hold, the effect tends to be synergistic—greater than the sum of the parts. That is, what is learned carries over into out-of-class activities such as trying to read signs and just plain thinking about and imagining letters and words, and possible meanings. This is almost a definition of what is meant by the *sine qua non* of all teaching, "self-teaching." We inspire students to engage in a continuing stream of inner-speech that naturally extends learning beyond the finite boundaries of classroom instruction. Sensing this, parents and teachers find themselves "preaching" the "scripts" that they hope will become inner-guidance and wisdom: "Pay attention," "Read," "Study harder," "Your life is in your hands" and the like. These may be clichés, but kids who don't hear

Trying to read (environmentally encountered) signs and . . . thinking about possible meanings . . . is almost an operational definition of self-teaching.

them often tend not to be as internally motivated. Of course, having someone who cares enough to keep saying such things also must convey a sense of self-worth.

The remedial/corrective teacher can take this approach, but with less preaching and more teaching and illustrating. The teacher realizes that reading can be used both to *inform* and to *transform* children into individuals with the will and skill necessary to think and to read as part of that internal quest to learn and to know. The basic tool of the remedial/corrective reading teacher is *reading* itself, since print contains the sum of human knowledge, stories, and wisdom. The simple act of reading and discussing text unhurriedly from different perspectives is both a means and an end in itself.

> Things change; former "adversaries"—movies, television, computer games, and the Internet— have become allies.

However, special problems emerge from following the simple dictate to have youngsters read. First, there is competition for raising their *will to read,* and second, they must be led to read in ways that are *active and engaging.* Remarkably, the former "adversaries" in this competition for children's interest and attention—movies, television, computer games, and the Internet (in a category of its own)—are becoming allies. College students can major in "Communications." Recognition is growing that multiple media contribute to our acculturation and information sources. Media expose us to various genres, everything from "travel" to "history" to "biography." To bemoan the products of media as "enemies" of civilized life and thought is to miss the opportunity to engage them as "allies."

We can induce students to read in any number of ways. Methods are most effective when grounded in the context of motivating any uninterested learners. Stephanie Hewett (1991) offers guidelines for four such generic approaches, with a fifth suggestion from Marlow Ediger (1991). The following may apply at all age-grade levels:

- Know the students' interests, hobbies, leisure-time activities, and so on.
- When possible, relate assignments and learning tasks to meaningful events and interests in the students' lives.
- Write positive comments on papers. Try to *catch them being good!*
- Let students know that you care about them by talking to them as people as well as pupils.
- Indicate when an activity or assignment might offer help with the puzzling questions that occupy children (if not all of us): What are my strengths and weaknesses? Which beliefs are vital to possess in school and society? Which life purpose should I pursue? What is ultimately good in life? Who am I? (On this last item, it is good to point out that we are not just a one and final thing, but rather in a state of becoming and changing. This provides much of the justifi-

cation for reflective reading, and reading and writing from different perspectives.)

Specific Motivators to Read

Consider these reading motivators that teachers and researchers rely upon most. Some cautions also are noted.

A reading selection generally needs to be "sold" to reluctant readers.

1. Identify and match students to materials based on compelling interests. Caution: The things students claim interest in may be difficult or too technical to read about (for example, auto mechanics). But let them try and, if possible, be there to help.

2. Cultivate their specific interests through discussion. Lead students into reading and writing in that subject area.

3. Use newspapers, magazines, Internet, movies, and television to explore interests and to stimulate reading and discussion. Several commercial publications, such as *Reader's Digest, Scholastic,* and *Weekly Reader* are especially well designed and appropriately written for this purpose. Cable TV offers programming on virtually every topic and area of literature. "WebQuests"—knowledge inquiries—on virtually any topic of interest can be as stimulating, and much more rapid and engaging, than a week in a conventional library.

4. Share interests that you may have. Show them that we are all lifelong learners and participants and your enthusiasm will be contagious.

5. Appeal to students' innate desire to be powerful and effective. These are basic human drives, well served by academic pursuits such as a broad vocabulary or the ability to remember information.

6. Ask students to tell you about their special knowledge areas and build out from these.

7. Hook them on a story by telling a portion of it and having them learn the rest through reading. This process empowers students to read more effectively by giving them a sense of story, plot, characters, and selection-specific words.

8. Tell what *question* a reading selection will answer; for example, "Is there really a 'Big Foot' in the northern U.S. forests?" Tell students, "This selection answers this question pretty convincingly." Work with students to make books of interesting questions and answers. (For fun, do a parody of the *Enquirer:* "Inquiring Minds Want to Know.")

9. Appeal to students' desire to overcome poor reading by using methods that greatly reduce the risk of failure. See especially the Repeated Readings technique in Chapter 8.

10. Use methods that permit students to actively analyze and experientially participate in what they read. See especially the InQuest method in Chapter 8.

11. Use materials and methods that are relevant to students' lives and concerns. See especially proverbs study and "valuing," dialogue journals, and bibliotherapy, ahead in this chapter.

12. Frequently ask students how they feel and think about what they read. "Constructive" questions, asked regularly, impart a sense of worth to students and can profoundly impel their will and effort to read "reconstructively"—accurately and effectively.

13. Read material that can provide solace through life's "personal pilgrimage." See the sections on humor and homilies ahead in this chapter.

14. Organize school so that "recess" and "after-care" encourage and support learning through living. See games and *intentional incidental* learning ahead.

Few things organize meaning as well as being told what *question* a piece answers.

Having discussed generic and specific motivation to read, the remainder of the chapter is an account of practical teaching methods and related recommendations. The reading teacher, and to a degree the classroom teacher, can depend upon these to inculcate motivation to read and to reduce, if not totally alleviate, internal (emotional) disruptions and lifestyle differences that may inhibit academic learning. Most of these methods rely upon *instructional conversations* that stir a natural therapeutic dialogue.

Psycho-Educational Issues

Related/Not Related to Reading Progress?

Appeal to students' desire to be powerful and effective; academic learning can fill this basic human drive.

Media stories and government-supported research reports estimate that several million people in the United States suffer from anxiety disorders. This number probably is conservative when compared with those who are just plain overstressed and overwhelmed with the frenetic pace of their lives. Record numbers of school-age kids are reflecting their conflicted feelings in ways ranging from eating disorders to sleeplessness to rage and sexual excesses. There is good evidence that emotional problems can seriously complicate reading and learning deficiencies, and appear to be causative in some situations. One explanation for seemingly miraculous "cures" (such as wearing colored lenses and sundry other "solutions") is a specific psychological problem called Conversion Reaction Syndrome. This is the most frequently occurring emotional condition found in the general public, yet is seldom referenced in literature on reading and learning disabilities. (See Appendix F: Summary of Conversion Reaction Syndrome and Dyslexia.) Oddly, there is a tendency to dismiss psychological assessment as irrelevant to reading process and progress, preferring to focus on linguistic issues. This is odd, considering the fact that we collectively support the constructivist view that meaning-making is the result of a *personal*—that is, subjective—interaction of the reader with the text. From this point of view, human psychology must at least be treated as collaterally related to reading education. These elements speak strongly to the understanding and shaping of students, who are the "meaning makers," and of the reasonability and sense of the meanings that they make. It was for this reason, and the belief that some emotional problems may cause reading-learning difficulties, that the field of remedial/corrective reading was launched by an admixture of psychologists, educators, and guidance counselors. More recently, it was insightfully written that "Meta-awareness of cognition and *emotionality* is essential for the interpretation of the landscape of consciousness in narratives" (Catts & Kamhi, 1999).

In point of fact, classrooms and teachers are not equipped to deal with serious emotional problems. However, teachers should be enabled to identify them, and to consider them in their reflections on prescriptive teaching. Most all teaching and learning challenge our emotional balance by virtue of entering our minds through the door of our delicate egos. In fact, a certain degree of discomfort, called "cognitive dissonance," requires recognition of an imbalance of what is comfortably known and the level of dissatisfaction that one must feel in order to be roused to learn yet more. This "necessary level of discomfort" is further intensified when learning needs to take place in a social situation, or in a realm of personal weakness or challenge. This means that affect is inextricably involved in most all teaching and learning. Teaching and learning essentially is about being critiqued—always an irksome issue for the ego.

> "Strengths" inflexibly applied are "weaknesses."

Luckily, the ego has multiple mechanisms for defending itself. Most of these are healthy, normal, and just a bit over-the-top during peak periods of challenge. Students at every level of education begin with, or fall into, characteristic *(Default)* ways of responding. These can become weaknesses, and defensive "reaction-formations." That is, characteristic ways of responding that cripple the delicate social balance that every teacher works hard to achieve, between challenging thinking and maintaining a healthy social climate, and achieving transitions from one task level to another without setting off hyperemotional and displaced reactions. It helps to talk to "offending" students, and in making referrals, to know how to characterize these class-disruptive expressions. Figure 11.1 describes the more common Defense Mechanisms of the Ego. These constitute the most frequent excessive, or over-the-top, means employed to protect an ego that feels under assault from any of the challenges that face us. Such challenges might be

> The most frequently occurring emotional problem (Conversion Reaction Syndrome—CRS) is almost never reported for students with reading and learning disabilities; either they are immune, or we are in Denial.

FIGURE **11.1**

DEFENSE MECHANISMS OF THE EGO

1. **SUBLIMATION:** A socially unacceptable form of gratification of an instinctive drive is given up for a somewhat more socially accepted type of satisfaction.

   Example: Thumb-sucking finds substitution in placing other objects, such as pencils, in the mouth, by smoking, or other forms of oral satisfaction such as excessive talking.

2. **DENIAL:** Refusal to acknowledge disturbing facts.

   Example: Never "knowing" what one's homework is.

3. **REPRESSION:** Subconscious denial of inner impulses or external realities that pose possible punishments or temptations.

   Example: Denial of inner drives and interests, such as of sexual awakenings and the conflicts and anxieties that often accompany these.

4. **REACTION-FORMATION:** Unconsciously repressed feelings and wishes are converted into a more socially acceptable form.

   Example: Lack of willingness to think about something personally troublesome is converted into socially acceptable means of avoiding thinking. This might take the form of excessive reading or even the inability to read, as in dyslexic syndrome.

5. **PROJECTION:** Avoiding blame or responsibility by attributing unacceptable motives, feelings, or attitudes to someone or something else.

   Example: Accusing an envied classmate of acting envious of you or others.

6. **RATIONALIZATION:** An overintellectualized explanation for actions or behaviors that are not acceptable to ourselves or others.

   Example: A student maintains that there is no sense in studying and trying, since school is a racist/impractical/boring place.

7. **DISPLACEMENT:** A transfer of feelings from one person or situation to another.

   Example: A child who misdirects excessive feelings of love or hate for a parent onto a teacher or other authority figure.

8. **COMPENSATION:** Seeking gratification that cannot be achieved in one phase of life from another phase.

   Example: A child who spends an excessive amount of energy and time on sports to make up for shortcomings in school, or one who buries him- or herself in schoolwork to compensate for a failed social life.

9. **REGRESSION:** Tendency to fall back on earlier, usually more infantile, modes of behavior.

   Example: Most conduct disorders, such as tantrums, acting out, stealing, and lying fit into this category.

10. **OBSESSIVE-COMPULSIVE ACTIVITY:** An inner drive to perform certain acts, such as hand-washing, usually as a way of coping with internal and external demands and conflicts.

    Example: Perfectly kept notebooks, to the point of recopying merely so they appear totally neat and orderly.

Note: Several of these behaviors, especially obsessive-compulsive activities, may have biochemical or constitutional components.

pressure to read when we cannot, or fear that we have done something socially unacceptable, or have a hidden desire to do so. These behaviors, which are often overly rationalized to feel justified, can have a subtly distorting effect on comprehension, writing, effective thinking, inquiry, sensible classroom participation, and on one's personal social adjustment.

Figure 11.2 describes more serious types of maladjustments that may be observed in children, and that also have been found to correlate with literacy and learning disorders, but also are found—with lesser personal consequences—among average and above-average students.

These two Figures are a summary list of nearly 100 years of psychological research, and thousands of years of human experience. Ironically, it is because they are the sum of human frailty that most of us will be able to

FIGURE **11.2**

CLASSIFICATION OF MALADJUSTMENT IN CHILDREN*

1. **Primary Behavior Disorders** (chiefly made up of sublimations, displacements, compensations, and regression):

    a. *Habit Disorders:* feeding disorders, sucking, biting, vomiting, scratching, masturbation, enuresis (involuntary urine secretion), rocking, and head banging. Forms of autoerotic activity.

    b. *Conduct Disorders:* tantrums, defiance, destructiveness, cruelty, lying, stealing, and deviant sex behavior. Various types of deviant behavior.

    c. *Mild Neurotic Traits:* inhibition of play and aggression, sleep disorders, night terrors, sleep walking, enuresis, excessive fear of animals, darkness, thunder, height, or others.

2. **Psychoneurotic Disorders** (above-average reliance on ego defense mechanisms such as: denial, reaction-formations, compensations, and obsessive-compulsive behaviors). The conflict is largely internalized, and the child is in conflict with him- or herself. Mild neuroses are converted into phobias. Fixations and regressions, considerable anxiety marked by difficulty in functioning at capacity level, rigid and repetitive behavior, hypersensitivity, egocentricity, immaturity, varied physical complaints and fatigue, dissatisfaction and unhappiness, limited insight into one's behavior, and inability to effectively test reality.

3. **Psychosomatic Disorders** (chiefly made up of reaction-formations, and repressions). In children: colic, vomiting, constipation, diarrhea, breath holding, asthma. Any of the organ systems may be affected.

4. **Psychosis** (chiefly induced by psychological trauma or chemical imbalances). Extreme personality disorganization, defensive compensation and loss of contact with reality. Marked disturbances in memory, attention, and imagination; bizarre thought processes; extreme inappropriateness of affect; hallucinations. Significant regression and poor orientation.

*Several of these disturbances may have biochemical or constitutional components.

constructively make meaning of them without 30 credit hours of course-work in psychology. This is not a case of a "little bit of knowledge is a dangerous thing." Rather, it merely is a case of becoming more conversant with the language of the human condition, and permitting it to enrich and better articulate a teacher's already rich personal and professional experiences.

Excessive and Frequent

It has been said with Mark Twain–like humor (but also some truth) that "the only people that are not 'screwy' are the ones you don't know yet." Two truths are nested in this bit of witty cynicism. One is that most of us have quirks, or "peccadilloes," and some inborn temperamental issues, like high worry and/or plain old crankiness. The other is the fact that we have all done things that we were not proud of—that may have been downright unwise or emotionally unhealthy. Such is the nature of youthful exploring, experimenting, living, and maturing.

The earmarks of maladjustment are not whether someone ever or occasionally does things like those described in Figures 11.1 and 11.2 as defensive and maladaptive behaviors, but whether these actions become excessive and frequent; that is, part of one's characteristic way of coping and behaving. In such cases, the personal problem can quickly become a classroom, family, social, and civic problem. The rate of suicide and murder of kids by kids in the United States is among the highest in the world. Don't be afraid to enter the fray. School is a relatively constant state of "cognitive dissonance." Humans are not at their best when under constant stress, no matter how we try to parcel it out in manageable quantities. Nonetheless, teachers probably effect more prevention and cure each day than the sum of all the professional counselors and psychologists combined. Several studies done in the early 1970s showed that inner-city youngsters, contrary to popular thinking, found school and teachers to be places and points of solace, not cultural and academic punishment. Ahead you will see several viable ways to assist with personal emotional and social adjustment and development while teaching reading, language proficiency, and clear thinking. You will note, too, that one of those means is to hold children to high standards of personal achievement, with virtually no more explicit attention to a perceived or diagnosed "psychological" problem than an occasionally softer and more caring look, or an extra bit of academic help.

Let's turn now to the other aspects of affect, or the assessment and advancement of a student's personal-emotional schema. Here can be found, deep within the child, the chief factors responsible for convoluting comprehension, classroom learning, and understanding one's own experiences, as well as the negative effects that one is having on the lives of others—as in the case of hyperemotional and disruptive students.

The earmarks of maladjustment simply are whether certain actions become excessive (acute) and frequent (chronic).

ADDRESSING DISRUPTIVE THINKING PATTERNS

To the keen eye, a person's *every* choice and expression can be interpreted into a clearer understanding of the person's psychological organization, drives, and dilemmas. Such "kid watching," as it has been called in school settings, assumes that teachers have the schemata to see and interpret, or read significance into what they are observing. In point of fact, some people can do this rather easily and others cannot. Everyone, however, can get better at "seeing" and dealing with the complex nature of children and their ways of being, feeling, and acting. The affective tests and inventories presented in Chapter 5 are intended as "eye-openers," or heuristics, to help one to develop better insights into the psycho-educational aspects of reading, learning, and living. Next we will give further consideration to what these instruments might be interpreted to mean.

Possible sources of emotional problems that may be reflected in the act of reading include: cultural and linguistic isolation; unsettling family relationships; gender confusion; frequent moving; divorce; peer pressure; onset of physical handicaps; racial prejudice; death of loved ones; and/or sexual/emotional abuse.

It should be clearly understood that not everyone who has a reading problem or even is entangled in an emotionally difficult situation also has either a causative or even secondary emotional problem. Many people can withstand fairly serious physical and emotional trauma without any apparent emotional side effects to life or learning. Nonetheless, it is natural to suspect that the incidence of emotional complications would be higher among remedial/corrective readers since they operate daily in a school climate that puts a heavy emphasis on their area of weakness. This is a level of "cognitive dissonance" that in itself can be stressful. We now shall consider some of these in terms of possible remedies and recommendations.

"Sometimes a cigar is just a cigar." (Freud to a news reporter)

REMEDIES AND RECOMMENDATIONS: GENERAL APPROACHES

When observation and individual diagnosis reveal strong emotional need, the professional reading or learning disability specialist should consider several things:

1. Refer the child to a school counselor or psychologist for complementary assistance.

2. Suggest to the parents that the child might need psychological services beyond that which is available in the schools. Remind the parent that many communities provide such services at reduced costs.

3. Once counseling or psychological assistance has been sought, consider either of two approaches to reading instruction (or some combination of the two):

   a. Do not address it specifically during reading instruction, but rather work to build self-efficacy in reading and learning (as described in the next section), hoping that this will also reduce the impact and complications from emotional distress. Do not overlook this seemingly "hands-off" solution. Sometimes, being held to task by a more stern hand can bring about great symptom relief and progress toward personal empowerment, and hence, self-reliance and resilience.

   b. Take some of the responsibility on yourself to work with the counselor and/or to provide psycho-educational assistance ("reading therapy") incidentally through the remedial/corrective methods you employ and the materials you select for the student to read and ponder. Many of the founders of the field of reading were psychologists who realized that the reading achievement levels of many of their clients were influenced by psychological disorders. They chose to use reading as a vehicle for indirectly addressing the primary problem. Several techniques for implementing this approach are described ahead in the chapter.

The first general approach, building self-efficacy, is discussed next, followed by a number of techniques and methods for reading therapy.

Self-Efficacy and Self-Esteem

Efforts to build self-*esteem*, or positive feelings about self, have had relatively little positive effects on learning, and tend to leave students arrested at a level of external motivation; sometimes referred to as "praise junkies." The reason for this seems to be the mismatch between the frequent praise, and actual accomplishments, which students acquire from other reality-based experiences. Efforts to build self-*efficacy*, or actual achievement, on the other hand, tend to help students develop a greater sense of intrinsic motivation *and* as a result, raise self-esteem.

The first rule for effectively remediating disruptive emotionality is to teach well; that is, to provide instruction that is so effective that it builds self-efficacy, self-worth, and willingness to continue to try to overcome reading difficulties (Cecil, 1990a). Teaching reading well involves providing careful schema activation before reading to energize and focus reading, providing guidance during reading to keep the process going, and checking and following up on students' comprehension after reading to show them what they have learned and what they might do with it. Another dimension, in classroom settings, is to intersperse instruction with cooperative structure activities, such as those detailed in Chapter 6, on a daily basis. Troubled children tend to either withdraw into themselves, or to act out inappropriately. In either case, they are starved for healthy interactions with peers. (For a window into one such world, listen to Carly Simon's lyrics in "At Seventeen," whose copyright costs prohibit us from reproducing them here.) Cooperative structures have students interacting with peers in very lowthreat situations in very specific ways, and on specific topics. Frequent opportunities to do this in the classroom can go a long way toward alleviating the "separateness" that these students feel—and toward keeping emotionally healthy children on the right track.

Some additional and more specific aspects of teaching toward selfefficacy to remediate emotionality include:

- Give "specific encouragement rather than generalized praise" (Werner & Strother, 1987, 542). For example, "Wonderful, you know seven more vocabulary terms than you did last week." *Encouragement* is realistic feedback, whereas *praise* can be patronizing and misleading.
- Identify some area of learning in which the student responds easily to training and chart his or her progress. Good candidates are rate of reading, vocabulary, and memory for facts.
- When possible, begin each lesson with areas of strength (as above), and while the student is still feeling positive, move to areas of need.
- "Exhibit respect for the child" (Werner & Strother, 1987, 543). Ask about his or her interests at and outside of school. Acknowledge mistakes while assuring him or her that they will improve.
- "Maintain a complex level of interaction with students when asking questions" (Guzzetti & Marzano, 1984, 757). Look for and respond to unspoken messages, in words or in kind, that signal states of mind, such as confusion, fear, confidence, interest, and the like.

> Efforts to focus on building self-esteem, rather than self-efficacy, have had relatively little positive effect on learning.

Also consider some "don'ts," as suggested for classroom and remedial/corrective teachers by Barbara Guzzetti and Robert Marzano (1984):

- Don't seat slower students far from yourself or in a group, as this makes it harder to monitor them.
- Don't pay less attention to "lows" in academic situations (smiling less often or maintaining less eye contact).
- Don't call on "lows" less often to answer classroom questions or make public demonstrations.
- Don't wait less time for "lows" to answer questions.

- Don't abandon "lows" in failure situations; instead ask follow-up questions.
- Don't criticize "lows" more frequently than highs for incorrect public responses.
- Don't praise "lows" less frequently than highs after successful public responses.
- Don't praise "lows" more frequently than highs for marginal or inadequate public responses.
- Don't give low-achieving students less-accurate and less-detailed feedback than highs.
- Don't give "lows" less-frequent feedback than highs.
- Don't demand less work and effort from "lows" than from highs.
- Don't interrupt the performance of low achievers more frequently than that of high achievers.

Now let's consider some actual reading practices that contain a considerable element of support in the realms of personal-social adjustment. These techniques and methods for (concurrent and incidental) reading therapy include:

1. bibliotherapy
2. valuing process
3. homilies, proverbs, and fables

READING THERAPY

Bibliotherapy

Many a life path can be traced back to a favorite book.

The basic ingredient in bibliotherapy is a teacher who loves to read, knows books, and cares deeply about children, including those in their rebellious teens. It is a means of emotionally and intellectually "empowering" students to deal with personal-social adjustment problems in a largely incidental way. Many a life path can be traced back to a favorite book. The simple act of matching a student with a book or selection that deals with the situation he or she is facing can trigger three fundamental therapeutic processes: empathy, catharsis, and insight.

1. *Empathy* is the act of associating some real or fictional character in literature with oneself.
2. *Catharsis* occurs when the reader identifies with a character and observes that character working through a problem to a successful solution, or "release of emotional tension." Through empathy and catharsis, comes further *insight*.

3. *Insight* is the sense of enlightenment that comes with recognizing aspects of oneself and one's situation in a written tale.

Insight can be uplifting, and often lends a sense of dignity to one's woes. This shift in perspective on one's personal situation is referred to by literary critics as distinction between tragedy (the failing of great people) and pathos (the problems of the weak and pathetic).

When described in these terms, this process may sound too complex for reading specialists, let alone children. However, it is a natural progression with which children generally are at ease. To activate the process, the teacher, librarian, or reading specialist who recommends a book to a student should invite the student to retell the story, highlighting incidents and feelings that are relevant to the situations portrayed. Changes in behavior, feelings, and relationships should be looked at closely to permit vivid identification and empathy with the characters. Most important, the reader should have an opportunity to form a conclusion about the consequences of certain behaviors or feelings to determine whether or not these behaviors or feelings improve human relationships and happiness (Heaton & Lewis, 1955).

Bibliotherapy may be viewed and used in a few different ways. It can be used prescriptively to help a student to solve an *existing* emotional problem or anxiety by recommending a book that recounts an experience or situation similar to the student's own. By recognizing the problem and its solution in literature, students often can gain insights about their own problems and begin to take steps to solve them. Literature tends to convert even troubled lives and times from pathos (tough times that befall the pathetic) to tragedy (tough times that befall the enviable). Bibliotherapy also may be used as a *preventative* and curative measure. A student who has experienced a situation through literature can be said to have vicariously experienced it, and should be better able to deal with similar situations encountered in real life. This technique can be compared to the process of inoculation against contagious diseases.

The basic ingredient in bibliotherapy is a teacher who loves to read, knows books, and cares deeply about kids.

Even simple reading and retelling can have a salutary effect on social-emotional growth and development. While there are direct studies of this proposition with remedial-level readers, most are very old, and hard to interpret into an action plan. However, there is a recent and possibly relevant study done with Attention Deficit Hyperactivity Disorder children. The ADHD kids were asked to tell how they would deal with complex social situations that they had read about. Their responses were characteristically ill-informed. But when they were asked first to retell the story that they had read, their responses became much more adaptive and positive. The researchers concluded that this simple formula of read and retell seemed to teach kids to stop, think, and make more acceptable outcomes reactions (Schroeder, 2002). In a more familiar situation, say that a teacher was working with a young child who consistently procrastinated, and blamed his lack of achievement on most everyone and everything but himself. This might be a good time to have him read and examine a parallel tale like *Yabbit the Rabbit*, a kind of secular parable.

Prescription: *Yabbit the Rabbit*.   In this children's book (by Paul Kinan and Mark Nassief, Yorba Linda, CA: Susie Mark Productions, 2000), an irresponsible rabbit displays a most unbearable habit. "Yeah but" was clearly his favorite phrase. This was an excuse, and everyone knew it. "Yeah but," he'd say. "She made me do it." Yabbit the Rabbit accepted no blame; in his terms, he merely had a lack of good luck. Then the teacher asked something that hit like a brick. "How about a rabbit's foot? Would that do the trick?" "Oh nothing is luckier, he answered with glee." "A rabbit's foot is luckiest, even I would agree." The teacher, answering his jabber, says, "Well now, Yabbit, your legs look complete. You have not one, but two, rabbit's feet. So tell me again why you're acting so troubled, because with two rabbit's feet, your luck should be doubled!"

> Yeah but, he stammered.
> Yeah but, he yammered.
> Yeah but, he mumbled.
> Yeah but, he clammered.
> Yabbit was stumped.
> He had nothing to say.
> That was the moment that
> Changed Yabbit's way.

> Moral: The attribution of "luck" or lack of it, is an essentially immature and superstitious attitude that has the (apparent) benefit of freeing one from responsibility for one's fate, though, ironically, sealing it!

Well-Chosen Stories Are Therapeutic.   The fact that stories, in general, have been used in this way by the wise for thousands of years would seem to suggest that they have an impact on attitudes and behavior. Whether they are called parables, fables, or tales, the effect seems to be the same: The right story at the right time crosses the line from vicarious to actual experience. Stories well prescribed seem to remain with the child as a ready "teacher" for a very long time. One of our favorite is a "circle story," also starring a rabbit.

Circle Stories.   Circle stories capitalize on visual diagrams to guide students' comprehension, discussion, and then writing of their own stories (Jett-Simpson, 1981). This strategy follows a predictable pattern that can teach students to identify story structures, and when properly selected, provide solace and self-renewal through life's warp and woof. Typically, the main character starts at one location and, after a series of adventures, returns to the starting point. To teach this story structure, while aiding personal-emotional renewal, draw a large circle on the board or butcher paper and divide it into as many pie-shaped parts as there are adventures in the chosen story. At the top of the circle, a house is drawn to represent the beginning and ending of the character's journey, whether that place is "home," the cabin of the journey cake, or Mother Rabbit's lap.

Read the story aloud and have the class recall the story to decide what events should be pictured in the circle diagram. For example, Figure 11.3 (page 426) shows the sequence of imaginary adventures in *The Runaway Bunny*.

The circle story strategy can be extended for small-group work. Each group is given a story to diagram on large paper. Each student in every group is given a portion to illustrate in order to complete the whole diagram. Using large paper for this process allows students in each group to draw pictures simultaneously, an activity that motivates a great deal of oral language. Some students will want to label pictures while others may write descriptive sentences or even include written quotations for their character as the activity progresses. Sharing the finished products increases opportunities for language, reinforces the story pattern, and above all adds to the fun of reading and discussing.

Teachers will recognize the success of this strategy when students are offered the opportunity to use this pattern independently or in small groups to write their own original stories. Equally satisfying is the spontaneous recognition of the circle story pattern weeks later when a new book or story is read, or an emotionally needy situation encountered. Other circle stories include Sawyer's *Journey Cake Ho* and Gag's *Millions of Cats*.

"Bullying" is a topic receiving considerable attention in the United States at this time. Here, as with other issues and topical matters, the librarian is the best resource for appropriate books and materials.

Stir in Dialogue Journals and Personal Exchange Email. Bibliotherapy can be enhanced by the addition of a writing component. The easiest way to do this is to have students keep personal journals in which they write brief reactions—at least one sentence—to whatever they read. These can be stored and, with the student's prior approval, the teacher may read through them on occasion, and write back personal notes and thoughts. Email, both within a school's LAN, or Intranet system, or over the Internet into the teacher's and child's home, is a growing option with tremendous "carry-out" value.

The idea of *dialogue journals* (Staton, 1980) is as old as conversation between caring friends. Teachers who use this approach regularly report touching insights were revealed and warm relationships formed with students who at first appeared apathetic, hostile, or just plain reluctant to learn (Kirby & Liner, 1981). These professionally-guided interactions are the heart of a therapeutic dialogue. It is the place where the teacher can

The idea of "dialogue journals" is as old as conversation between caring friends.

FIGURE **11.3**

CIRCLE STORY DIAGRAM

In *The Runaway Bunny*, the baby rabbit playfully tests the limits of his mother's love by threatening to run away to all kinds of adventures, while his mother resourcefully assures him of how she would always be there to protect him. When he says he will run away and become a flower in a field, she says she will become a farmer, to water and care for him; when he would become a sailboat, she would become the wind to blow him safely home; when he would be an acrobat swinging through the air, she would be a tight-rope walker to catch him if he falls; and when he would be a little boy and run into the house, she would be the mother, there to welcome him home.

Based on Brown's The Runaway Bunny *(1942, rev. 1972) Harper & Row. Figure based on a design from the Wisconsin Department of Public Instruction, 1986*

suggest ideas that transform as well as inform. In the case of *The Runaway Bunny*, for example, the teacher can facilitate emotional maturity by asking the child to speak to how he or she is, or would, or could provide the same kind of unconditional love and support to someone else rather than merely seeking it for ourselves. This small interaction teaches the big lesson that more can sometimes be gained through seeking to give, more than pleading to receive—a common childhood quest, which most every parent would appreciate help with reducing.

Peer Teaching. The concept embodied in the phrase, "When I Teach, I Learn," has been a part of sensible education since the time one insightful cave-dweller tried to communicate to a struggling other how to actually make fire. Research is telling us that learning from teaching applies to weaker readers and even learning-disabled children as well as to children with average and above-average rates of learning (Coleman, 1990; Labbo & Teale, 1990). Hence, it seems wise to have programs that allow students who are either "at-risk" or have fallen behind, for any reason, to teach as well as to be taught. Teaching is uplifting to morale and to commitment to learn to deeper and more fluent levels.

"Learning from teaching" applies to weaker readers as well as better.

To Summarize. Bibliotherapy is more than literature-based teaching. Together with dialogue journals, and now email and journaling, bibliotherapy offers students help in reading, language, thinking, and personal-social adjustment. It does this by:

1. teaching students to think deeply and positively;
2. encouraging students to talk freely to appropriate adults about their problems;
3. helping students analyze their own and others' attitudes and modes of behavior;
4. pointing out that there are alternative and constructive ways to solve most adjustment problems;
5. helping students to compare their problems with those of others as a means of lessening internal tension and conflicts in a society that sometimes can appear quite uncaring (Rongione, 1972, as cited in Edwards & Simpson, 1986);
6. providing students with vicarious experiences, to anticipate and handle the inevitable difficulties served up in living and growing; and,
7. just plain help with personal-social adjustment and the lifelong process of maturation.

In a related vein, there is the valuing process, an especially sound, reading-based means of building other "intangibles," such as character and moral courage. And, at a purely cognitive level: evaluative thinking and verifying.

THE VALUING PROCESS

Some very viable methods have been developed for integrating the "valuing process" (Raths, Harmon, & Simon, 1978) into reading and learning. At a cognitive level, this would be known as Evaluative thinking, sometimes referred to as the *highest* level of thought. Actually, while it can be the most *integrative*, it can also be the lowest level of thought. Ironically, it took a 9-year-old girl to clarify this sticky point for us. She said "We always did this 'what do we think' stuff in first and second grade; I thought that we would have to do more in third grade." And so one must. We must explain ourselves, and not with simple "I don't like it emotions," but with rational reasons. The idea of "valuing" is to create several statements relevant to a piece of textual material. These should represent the inferential and interpretative levels of reading. Then ask students to Agree or Disagree with those statements, and to justify their personal decisions with reference to the text and/or their personal beliefs, cultural customs, or other such points of reference.

In this way, the "valuing process" helps children come to grips with the forces, or values, that are subconsciously driving their behavior and responses. Though it shouldn't stop there. It is an ideal prescription for three critical deficiencies in remedial/corrective readers, as well as more than a few proficient readers. These deficiencies are:

- poor evaluative thinking—where outward expressions of feelings-based responses are required;
- emotional dependency ("I don't know syndrome")—where a student quickly answers "I don't know" to most any question as a quick relief from thinking and personal responsibility; and
- "personal agenda syndrome"—where someone cannot seem to engage any subject or topic that is not immediately current in his or her life.

The "valuing process" is an especially sound means of building "intangibles."

"Valuing" is an example of a higher-order literacy approach to improving basic literacy from the top down. In this vein, James Hoffman (1977) offers Intra-Act, described in Figure 11.4.

Leo Schell (1980) developed several other variations on the valuing process which can be used in conjunction with Intra-Act. Two of these are illustrated here: "Values Voting" (Figure 11.5, page 430), and the "Valuing Sheet" (Figure 11.6, page 430).

Beyond direct instruction, when working with children who are struggling, there is the need to touch them with the worth of learning, as much as the fact of it. The next ideas and methods are cast in this more affective and attitudinal direction.

FIGURE **11.4**

INTRA-ACT POST-READING EXERCISE SHEET

Directions: Now that you have discussed the reading selection with the members of your group, read each statement and circle "A" if *you* agree, or "D" if *you* disagree. *Do not discuss your answers* yet with your group members. Then, write the names of the other members of your group in the blanks at the top of each column, and, for each group member, circle "A" if you think *he or she* would agree, or "D" if you think *he or she* would disagree with each statement.

Your Name: _____

Group Members: (write the names of your group members in the spaces below)

	___	___	___	___
1. Men probably make better legislators than women.	A / D	A / D	A / D	A / D
2. A person should vote according to the wishes of the people he or she represents, not according to his or her own personal feelings.	A / D	A / D	A / D	A / D
3. I would have voted the same as Rankin both times.	A / D	A / D	A / D	A / D
4. The writer seems to approve of what Rankin did.	A / D	A / D	A / D	A / D

TELETHERAPY

In a slight but important extension of bibliotherapy called "teletherapy," O'Brube, Camplese, and Sanford (1987) suggest having children share the stories that have touched their lives. This, they say, can be done with creative dramatics, finger plays, a puppet show, or a movie or tape.

Puppets can also be used to engage children in conversation. With no attempt at ventriloquism, a teacher can get children to talk to a puppet with great candor. The teacher also can have the puppet answer with more candor than could ever be attempted in one's own persona. We once watched a foreign-language teacher make very pointed criticism of children's pronunciations in Spanish without offending them in the least. He simply held a large scruffy puppet on his lap and had it say things that were almost outrageously frank. The children laughed, talked back, and tried again!

You may have to try this to believe how effective it can be for broaching subjects that otherwise would be very difficult to handle. For example, the puppet turns to one child and says about another, who is characteristically loud and boisterous: "Does this kid need to chill-out, or what?" The entire

FIGURE **11.5**

VALUES VOTING

[Based on "The Black Stallion and the Red Mark" in *Moments*, grade 5(3)]

A stallion heads a band of wild horses which "steals" horses from surrounding farms. The farmers band together and capture the herd. The stallion stays with his blind mare rather than running to freedom.

After reading the story, students are told: "Listen to the following statements. If you agree, raise your hand; if you disagree, turn thumbs down, and if you are undecided, fold your arms."

1. Donald was wrong to tell his father where the wild horses were.
2. The stallion was dumb to stay with the mare and be caught.
3. Donald's father showed good judgment in letting the stallion and the mare stay together in captivity.

From "Value Clarification via Basal Readers" by L. M. Schell, 1980, *Reading Horizons 20,* 218

FIGURE **11.6**

VALUE SHEET

[Based on "The Endless Steppe," *Racing Stripes,* grade 6(5)]

A ten-year-old girl and her family live in exile in a labor camp in Siberia in the 1940s. She and her grandmother take a few of the family's belongings to a village market to trade for food.

The teacher has students write responses to the following questions. Then the teacher instructs them to discuss their responses in small groups, or reads selected student responses without revealing who wrote them and without comment.

1. If exiled to a labor camp, what five personal belongings (other than clothes) would you take with you?
2. Which would you be willing to trade for food as Esther did?
3. After being on a restricted diet for several weeks like Esther was, what are two or three kinds of food you would trade your belongings for?
4. Is it right for a whole family to be sent to a labor camp when only the father was "guilty"? Why or why not?

From "Value Clarification via Basal Readers" by L. M. Schell, 1980, *Reading Horizons 20,* 218

class chimed in with some form of "Yeah!" and "No kidding!" This may not have permanently quieted the bouncing lad down, but it did mellow him for a while, and it gave the teacher a way to express some of his frustration without injury to anyone. The teacher said that "Lenny" came to look forward to talking with the "Dummy" as he called him. "Dummies" can be more easily forgiven for being too direct, or tactless.

There is a variation on this use of puppet play, called "role-play therapy." In one form of this admittedly more sophisticated reading therapy (called Antithetical or Facilitative Role-Play), students are led to play roles of highly competent readers with rather remarkable positive impact on their learning (Manzo & Manzo, 1993).

> Play is a means of teaching without appearing to teach.

FACILITATIVE ROLE-PLAY—ACTING SO CAN MAKE IT SO

Children's play was a focus of study in the early part of the 20th century. It is only recently that it again is coming into consideration as a means of promoting literacy and academic learning (Korat, Bahar, & Snapir, 2002; Saraho & Spodek, 1998). However easy and inviting play is as a means of teaching without appearing to teach, it is not easily done. It requires considerable thought and planning on the part of the teacher.

Facilitative Role-Play (FRP) is based on just such an appearance of being a simple idea. The goal is to get kids to engage in a form of facilitative pretending that has them cue in on, and attempt to emulate, models of higher competence. Ideally, the students doing the pretending are able to interact with these mental models, and perhaps form a cognitive apprenticeship relationship with them. Additionally, the mere fact of acting-out a more-competent model of a designated behavior, also has students— according to the "social and imitation learning theory"—incidentally emulating, practicing, and acquiring collateral social and language skills. Together, these methods can remarkably raise students' levels of performance and learning, since they are not merely enacting, but functioning as more academically competent individuals.

FRP is related to a rich history of play therapy as outlined by Virginia Axeline in 1946, and psychodrama therapy, as discussed by J. L. Moreno in 1947. This technique survives today in some unrecognized forms in several reading/language arts methods and practices. It has been said that the best thing one can do to advance a particular phenomenon is to name it. This alone converts an amorphous idea into a concrete factor. It also makes the idea/factor portable and transferable to multiple other situations and possible applications. Most importantly, it isolates it as a visible, concrete entity in its many current forms. This becomes real-world validation of its existence and worthiness. Consider some of the current places that Facilitative Pretending already exists. These include:

1. Peer teaching, as when a relatively poor-reading fifth grader is asked to teach a kindergartner or first grader to read, and in the process considerably improves his own reading.

2. In the ReQuest procedure where a student is urged to ask questions the way a pretend teacher might, and does so with great ease as a result of paying closer attention to how teachers ask questions, and therefore to the material from which the questions are drawn.

3. In Radio Reading where children are asked to do repeated readings of a section of text with a partner and/or at home until they feel comfortable enough to stand behind the class and read it as if they were a radio announcer.

4. With InQuest (Schmitt, 1988) where students play the role of reporters and must question their way to successful understanding of a story or nonfiction piece.

5. With Talk-Through (Brozo & Simpson, 1999), where students are asked to read and reread something and to practice talking it through until they feel prepared to do so before a class or group.

6. With Sociodramatic play (Korat, Bahar, & Snapir, 2002) where teachers and adult voices step into the middle of child-created plays to direct attention to literacy artifacts.

7. With invented spellings and pretend reading as part of emergent literacy.

"Role-playing" converts what students do naturally into enactments of more competent models of themselves.

The essential power such "role-playing" methods exert seems to be in converting what students do most naturally into an enactment of more competent models than they feel themselves capable of outside of the dramatization. This, Vygotsky (1976) has suggested, seems instrumental in having children internalize the external coaching of teachers and models of more-competent peers. Facilitative Role Play tends, further, to add an element of practice to tasks that students tend to try without rehearsal, hence adding the simple power of "practice effects." For an illustrative example of FRP, see Figure 11.7, which tells of a specific form and case.

CIVILIZING STORY-RICH MEDIA

We all know that the world is a difficult and challenging place. This is especially so for underachievers, but also for overachievers and most everyone else in between. We know too that relief from the endless, mostly mindless, competition of daily life is therapeutic. This is where television programs for children, like *SpongeBob SquarePants*, come in. A Nickelodeon cartoon show of a sponge who lives under the sea has captured the imaginations of young and old alike. It has a nifty, uplifting ditty that it is hard not

FIGURE **11.7**

FACILITATIVE (ANTITHETICAL) ROLE-PLAY

Antithetical Role-Play is a clinical device that predates and is a more intensive therapeutic form of Facilitative Role-Play. Its elements and power are illustrated in the case called "David."

Case: A twelve-year-old boy, "David," was said to be brain damaged, mildly retarded, and unable to read a lick. After several frustrating weeks of remedial/corrective reading instruction, it was decided that the least of David's problems was the fact that he could not read. Manifesting a full array of odd behaviors, including strange, worm-like movements said to be involuntary and related to this brain damage, David was a picture of distress. The role-play treatment had David assume the role of a West Point cadet, his tutor that of a lieutenant-instructor, and other clinicians who were willing to play along enacted roles of military personnel. David became immersed in a military atmosphere. He marched to his tutoring room accompanied by cadence calls from the instructor. He stood inspection and suffered the type of "tough-love" verbal abuse that is typical of military shaping. All communication was directed to David in the form of commands, and all commands had to be carried out in accordance with military precision and form. Within 1 hour David brought many of his "involuntary" motor movements under control and began to learn and to think according to military regimen. David was prepared to accept this role using a combination of open discussion of his disheveled appearance along with expression of the fact that he looked mightily like an archetypical cadet in his basic physical features: crewcut hair, square jaw, sharp blue eyes. Before initiating the role-play, David and the first author studied cadet behavior.

Several factors combine as a possible explanation for the potency of this therapy. First, antithetical role-play forces the breaking up of inappropriate behaviors in the habituated, subcortical areas in which they reside, apparently much more quickly than by traditional behavior modification. Second, since the instructor and all other clinic personnel also assumed similar roles, the student had before him several models of more appropriate behavior, and a conducive and supportive environment. Third, teaching and learning were conducted when David was in his "empowered" role. Fourth, David could try new behaviors as the "Empowered David," that would have been too far a stretch for "Disabled David" (Manzo, 1977a).

The roles assumed by both reading therapist and child are deliberately chosen to be diametrically opposite to the child's typical patterns of behavior. This is based on the belief that we have greater awareness of our *opposite* condition than of shades in between.

to sing along with, and complex story lines that are resolved by goodness and hard work—virtues that refresh us. Each show is a little morality play with a rich story structure, and lots to comprehend and apprehend. Each contains things to talk about, write about, further read about, and from which to draw a sense of solace and renewed belief in civility. In a more sensible world, watching and reflecting and responding would be fair homework for grades K–6, and often for grades 7–12. Children's books are now available that parallel this and other such TV shows, like *The Wild Thornberrys* and *Hey, Arnold!*

HOMILIES, FABLES, PROVERBS, HUMOR, AND JOKES!

We all know that homilies, proverbs, and fables can help reduce emotionally disruptive thought patterns and heighten common sense. It is widely understood that they are brief forms of the universal truths sometimes found in great literature. However, we often forget to add jokes to this collection of elixirs. Collectively, homilies, proverbs, fables, and jokes provide a powerful way to communicate basic values and life management skills, especially when spoken at a needed "teachable moment." These compressed bits of wisdom can reset our "emotional clocks" when they become erratic from the effects of stress, conflict, or depressing times. They are to mental health what vitamin supplements are to diet: great when you need them and harmless otherwise. Proverbs, fables, and homilies tend to home in on areas of social-emotional need and find their mark like heat-seeking missiles, with almost no collateral damage. They speak to us as if they could hear our needs. The reason that they appear able to do so is because they are the codification of the "universal truths" that are in world literature, and because they speak to our common misgivings and sometimes overly emotive nature. Consider the good sense and conflict-avoidance value of the following fable/parable.

Hercules and Minerva

Slightly offended by what appeared to be an apple in his path, Hercules stomped on it with his heel. To his astonishment, instead of being crushed it doubled in size; on his attacking it again and smiting it with his club, it swelled up to an enormous size and blocked the road going forward.

Upon this he dropped his club, and stood dazed. Just then Minerva appeared and said to him: "Leave it alone, my friend: that which you see before you is the *fruit of discord*: if you do not meddle with it, it remains small as it was at first, but if you resort to angry response it swells into the thing you see."

As further evidence of the value of homilies to mental hygiene consider the value to courage, persistence, and perseverance of this anecdote. See if you can identify this man from his life story at the ages shown:

Failed in business	*22*
Ran for Legislature—defeated	*23*
Again failed in business	*24*
Elected to Legislature	*25*
Sweetheart died	*26*
Had a nervous breakdown	*27*
Defeated for Speaker	*29*
Defeated for Elector	*31*
Defeated for Congress	*34*
Elected to Congress	*37*
Defeated for Congress	*39*
Defeated for Senate	*46*
Defeated for Vice President	*47*
Defeated for Senate	*49*
Elected President of the United States	*51*

This is the record of Abraham Lincoln.

Today there are many Web sites dedicated to helping us all with our personal pilgrimages. Use search words like Personal Counseling and Spiritual Guidance to identify free sources of information and assistance with this heroic task, and come away with some free textual material, especially for upper elementary, intermediate, and secondary school students.

Proverbs and Homilies

To simultaneously teach and monitor progress in clear thinking, introduce proverbs in a variety of ways. Write a "proverb of the week" on the board, for example. Tell students to collect situations relevant to the proverb throughout the week, to share and discuss on Friday. Remember that proverbs are an essential part of most every culture's oral-language tradition, and a traditional means of teaching some of the most complex aspects of life's daily challenges. It would be neglectful of our accumulated wisdom to leave proverbs out of classroom education. Importantly, they are included

FIGURE **11.8**

PROVERB WORKSHEET

Directions: Choose the answer that is the best and most *general* way of saying what the proverb means. Be sure to read all choices *before* selecting one. Place an (**X**) in front of the letter of your choice.

1. The grass is always greener on the other side of the fence.

   (C) ____ A. A neighbor's grass often looks better than yours, because you cannot see its flaws.

   (E) ____ B. Your efforts will make your neighbor richer.

   (M) ____ C. There are two sides to everything.

   (A) ____ D. The things we see often look better than the things we have.

2. He who laughs last, laughs longest.

   (C) ____ A. If you are the last person to begin to laugh, you will be the last one to finish laughing.

   (M) ____ B. If you want to laugh best, always laugh loud.

   (A) ____ C. Be careful not to celebrate a victory until you are sure you have won.

   (E) ____ D. Laughing is important; always have a sense of humor.

Teach proverbs: They appear in many individual IQ tests as a measure of "abstract verbal functioning."

in many individual IQ tests as a measure of "abstract verbal functioning." The form shown above can be used either in a class discussion format or as an independent worksheet activity.

Proverb worksheets like the example in Figure 11.8 can be reproduced from our Web site or teacher-constructed. By studying response patterns, teachers can get a sense of students' comprehension (literal understandings) and apprehension (understanding of the larger meanings and significance) of multiple ideas. Of the four choices offered, for example, one could be considered a simple Miscue, or misinterpretation of the literal meaning of the proverb (labeled "M" in the examples here); another choice could be considered an Emotional level response (labeled "E"); another should be an accurate but a Concrete, or literal, translation ("C"); and the best translation should be an Abstract interpretation of the proverb's meaning ("A").

Proverbs study is especially useful with remedial/corrective–level readers, since each proverb is like a miniature book. For each proverb spoken, it is possible to construct a prologue, or situation, which preceded it, an event or events that make it timely, and an epilogue telling what can be learned from it. For this reason, proverbs can easily be connected to discussion, writing, and to various children's stories and books. We have found that merely putting a few proverbs around a room causes connections to form naturally as life and reading unfold.

Humor and Jokes

If jokes and joking could be sold, doctors and pharmaceutical companies would have them declared a "controlled substance," and we would all pay dearly for their medicinal effects. As it is, they are widely available, and an underprescribed homeopathic curative. They are a natural product found in some gifted people who can make light and bring light. Curiously, comedic minds are not necessarily synonymous with exceedingly bright or scientific minds. Therefore, appreciation for and ability to be humorous could be a strength in an otherwise weak reader. As such, it could be used to advantage in shoring-up a faltering ego, as well as in teaching word recognition, analysis, and comprehension.

> Jokes . . . can reset our "emotional clocks."

People who are funny are treasures. They often manage to be adroitly humorous without being injurious. All of us can participate in humor's magical effects on resetting our internal clocks by reading, learning, and sharing jokes. For some reason, boys are especially responsive to jokes. Women, especially those who are teachers, seem to fear their possible cruelty. They are not entirely harmless. Sometimes jokes not only poke good fun at stereotypes, but reinforce them. Nonetheless, they are great "take-outs" that kids can bring home and read and share with family and friends, and great "bring-ins" that kids can report and write on from TV viewing as well as reading. One 8-year-old in a clinic practicum could not wait to tell us, and write down this line from the TV program "The Proud Family": Dad says to Mom: "All these kids know about is gimmy, gimmy, gimmy. Hey, Honey, while you're in the kitchen, can you gimmy a sandwich, on rye, with some light mustard?" Jokes capture life in the raw, yet somehow soften our eyes, even while we shake our heads. Somehow, they have us saying things to ourselves like "Heck, this is life. Relax and enjoy it." This is no minor matter since it seems to build resilience as we back off from the intensity that can gather from "not being appreciated," and other such universal feelings that slide most all of us into occasional gloom, and the more susceptible into despair.

Jokes usually are built on two levels of understanding, and therefore have some of the same ability to exercise metaphoric thinking as proverbs and fables. From a strictly reading-instructional point of view, jokes tend to be self-motivating and encourage repeated reading and saying. There are many books of jokes at all levels and for all tastes, from puns to parodies. *The Wizard's Jokebook* (by Chris Tait, New York: KidsBooks, 2001) is an especially popular series with children. It offers jokes that tend to be plays on words that make a child feel smart, even when he or she needs an explanation; probably because he or she gets to repeat it to someone else:

> *What does a wizard's cat like just before going to bed? "A sorcerer of milk."*
>
> *What do math majors wizards say when they lift a curse? "Hex-a-gone!"*
>
> *What did the wizard get when he combined a necklace with an alarm clock? "A diamond ring!"*

There are many joke sites online. Pre-scan these for humor that is fitting and appropriate to age/grade levels. Just go to Google or Dogpile, or your favorite search engine and type in "jokes kids." Of course, there also are books of jokes that are art unto themselves, like Shel Silverstein's comedic poems in *A Light in the Attic* (1981) and *Where the Sidewalk Ends* (1974), among others. Kids seem to relate most to the things kids have been giggling about for generations: mostly "bathroom humor" and blatant irony, as in Silverstein's "Crowded Tub":

> I just washed a behind
> That I'm sure wasn't mine
> There's too many kids in this tub. (1981, 820)

> Peckin'
> The saddest thing I ever did see
> Was a woodpecker peckin' at a plastic tree.
> He looks at me, and "Friend," says he,
> "Things ain't as sweet as they should be."

Thank-U-Grams

Another way to help children, especially those who are not succeeding in school, to see the brighter side was suggested first by Edward L. Kramer, a St. Louis native, back in 1948 (Lenahan, 1992). He devised what today would be called a *social entrepreneurial* project—that captures the entrepreneurial spirit of doing more than one's resources would seem to allow.

Each evening after dinner, Kramer would sit down with his children and ask them for an accounting of the good they had observed that day. Then postcards expressing their appreciation were mailed to those individuals. At first the children found this difficult to do. They really hadn't thought before in terms of the many acts of kindness and generosity that were expended each day by parents, friends, teachers, relatives, and various service people (for example, postal, sanitation, and security personnel). After a time, their thoughtfulness was returned tenfold in warmth and thankfulness by the many people who felt appreciated. More interestingly, people who experienced kindness wished to share it.

It all grew so quickly that Mr. Kramer came to design a card patterned after the once-popular yellow telegram. He called it a Thank-U-Gram. He offered a two-week supply, free, to anyone who requested them. He received requests from President Eisenhower, Robert Frost, Leonard Bernstein, Bob Hope, Walt Disney, and thousands of others.

Many years have passed since that time, but the idea is still viable. Create Thank-U-Grams with your computer software, or have (remedial-level) children make up their own to do good and spread good will. It will cause them to think about their lives more positively, to write and to read with purpose, and give them an additional way in which to constructively influence their environments that so influence them (imagine this catching on as a global attitude!). To add to the fun, be sure a return address is included, and leave Thank-U-Grams in obvious places to be picked up when it is not realistic to mail them. Keep a teacher-made book of some of their Thank-U-Grams, and of responses that are received. Call it "Good Things Are Happening!" (See Figure 11.9.)

1,000 Things to Be Happy About

Another wonderfully uplifting practice that can act as a counter to squinty, defensive eyes, and replace them with the "soft eyes" that often appear

FIGURE **11.9**

GOOD THINGS ARE HAPPENING!

Maria, Sophi, and Juanada were so pleased with how school-support people who are not teachers were touched by their Thank-U-Grams that they decided to start a Christmas-presents drive for often-forgotten cafeteria and janitorial workers. They were able to buy them each a gift worth $20.

Thank-U-Gram	Sanitation Department, Texarkana, Tx

TO: Our Sanitation Workers
FROM: Katie Prine, 5th Grade
c/o Miss Debra Eubanks
Carter Elementary School,
15 Waits Ave., Texarkana, TX
 	
I saw your crew picking up the mess left by the dogs that tore the garbage bags open. Thank you for the extra effort in keeping my neighborhood clean. Have a good day.
	Dear Katie,
	   You helped settle an argument about whether we should clean up the messes dogs make, or leave them for the home owners.
	   Now that we know that someone cares, we will do our best to pick up the mess.
	   Thank you.
	
	Bud, Willie, Don, & Anthony

Thank-U-Grams were also sent out to all the parents who served as class aides. The parents were very grateful to have been recognized by the students. Many brought cookies and snacks for their classes the next week.

from seeing things we care about, is to begin a list of little things that individuals, for no big cerebral reason, find joyful. The smaller the item, the richer the impact. Here are some examples from *14,000 Things to Be Happy About* by Barbara Ann Kipfer (New York: Workman, 1990).

1. cozy jackets
2. fried chicken
3. butterflies
4. "Hi, there"
5. near-perfect weather
6. a refund
7. swing sets

Then There's the Funnies!

The Funnies. . . or, how to send a child home with homework that he or she will enthusiastically engage and share with family.

How would you like to send a child home with homework that he or she will enthusiastically engage with, interest parents in, complete, and come to school anxious to talk about? To do so, the teacher need only assign a topic or section of the funny pages in the daily paper to read and share the next day. Funnies can also be found online, for those who do not receive a paper at home. The *Los Angeles Times,* for example, offers three pages of funnies daily, along with a Kid's Reading Room section that contains children's poetry, jokes, and riddles, a continuing story (at about fourth-grade reader level), a feature story, and directions for submissions by email or regular mail. Many of the cartoons speak to life and family issues in that special way that can turn a child's moments of near-despair of his family's peculiar ways, into a slow grin of recognition of our common problems in meeting the challenges of spilled milk, running late, and not being able to find a shoe. The single-scene cartoon is especially powerful for offering a slice of life complete with opportunity to connect to what is sensed, clarify what is fuzzy, and read between and beyond the lines. The funnies are a good place to begin and end each day. A scrapbook of favorites with a written sentence or two about their particular poignancy also can be a wonderfully casual way to teach response writing, one of the most central functions in the academic tradition of summarizing and practicing critical-creative-constructive reading-writing-thinking.

The funnies are a good way to teach "response writing."

Look for students who can generate their own cartoons. There is one in almost every class. It is worth noting that two subtests of the Weschler IQ tests use comic strip pictures to assess aspects of alertness and social intelligence. Disenfranchised and second-language children especially seem to profit from such activities. They can be used in a variety of other ways as well, such as in writing Language Experience Stories.

GENDER ISSUES

Toward Androgyny

Occasionally the nation, and education in particular, tends to obsess over gender issues. Other times we tend to ignore them entirely, usually in over-reaction to a period of hypersensitivity. There is no way to pretend that this is not a "hot button" issue for some people most all of the time, therefore one that can become muted by our sense of social consequences. Nonetheless, it is like an elephant in the room that everyone knows is there, whether we dare address it or not. So let's address it with the understanding that we cannot fully do it justice in brief. But we can identify some reading-relevant points as this "story" continues to unfold.

Gender issues. Let's address them.

A number of feminist scholars now concede that gender is a very strong predictor of learning style (Belenky, Clinchy, Goldberger, & Tarule, 1986; Gilligan, 1982). However, even this simple conclusion is difficult to rely upon since biology and culture interact in ways that cause shifts to occur even as they are being identified. For example, it once was "clear" that men took to information technologies more so than women. Now, however, we see women utilizing technologies as much as, if not more than, men. Therefore what we say in Figure 11.10, about what we "know"—or what is being said and/or contested—about gender differences must be taken as neither true nor untrue, but as provisional—that is, subject to social evolutionary patterns, scientific discovery, and obviously not to be generalized to a given person without concrete evidence and reasonable qualifications. As further evidence of this transitional nature, consider business programming on television. In one generation women have gone from non-entities, to interviewers, to the business leaders and analysts being interviewed. Our (male and female) capacities to be many different things seems to trump whatever cultural limitations we create for ourselves.

Diagnostic-Prescriptive Implications

In short, boys and girls are different in brain organization, chemistry, and physique. Is it any wonder that there would be differences in reading and learning patterns? Accordingly, at least a few conclusions stand out in terms of diagnostic-prescriptive teaching. One is that girls need to be encouraged to read more nonfiction and to read more actively from the earliest grade levels. The second is that boys need to be encouraged to realize that reading, writing, and verbal exchanges on fiction are part of a long-standing tradition in most of the world, particularly for males in

FIGURE **11.10**

WHAT WE *KNOW* ABOUT GENDER ISSUES AND READING/LEARNING

- In American schools girls tend to do better, at least in the early grades, than boys on most measures of reading, spelling, and language development. This is not true in other cultures. Boys in Germany (Preston, 1962) do better, and boys and girls do equally well, with the same percentage in remedial-reading classes in Israel (Gross, as cited by Rubin, 1997).

- In American schools, boys outnumber girls by a margin of about 8 to 1 in remedial classes, and have for nearly 75 years.

- Boys have tended to do better on mathematics and spatial-perceptual tasks than girls. However, the gap is closing to nonsignificance in mathematics. Female superiority is also vanishing on verbal tests, especially beyond the fifth grade.

- Girls tend to read and prefer more storybooks than do boys. This pattern persists well into adulthood (Manzo, Manzo, Barnhill, & Thomas, 1999).

- Men tend to read more actively, often with a pencil in hand, than do women (Manzo, Manzo, Barnhill, & Thomas, 1999).

- In general, there seems to be more variability (heterogeneity) among males than females on all factors at all stages of development.

- Certain physical differences between most boys and girls seem relatively clear, irrespective of sexual preferences. For example, males have higher metabolic levels, higher levels of several hormones associated with muscular development, greater sexual urge, and a much larger area of the brain (the amygdala) identified as the seat of aggressive behavior. Conversely, the female brain produces much more serotonin, an enzyme that pacifies and calms its host (Gurian, 1999). As a probable byproduct, males take in more food and oxygen and expel more carbon dioxide and energy than do females (which may also explain the reason for earlier male demise).

- Males take longer to process feelings through the brain system than females; the male brain—specifically, the corpus callosum, the limbic system, and the frontal lobes—is not set up as well for internalizing responses, but rather for externalizing them (Gurian, 1999).

- The male brain is less neurologically "flexible" and "adapatable" than the female (there is more blood flow to more areas in the female brain during most all operations than there is in males).

- While there are no clear differences in overall intelligence, there continue (at least in American culture) to be differences in specific aptitudes (as noted above: boys appear better in math; girls in language, particularly in speech sounds—a critical element in phonemic awareness, and hence in successful early reading and spelling).

- Females at every stage and level tend to be more "field-dependent"—influenced by the situation or context—than males, who tend to be somewhat more "field-independent"— proportionately more apt to disregard social pressures and consequences.

- Stress generally causes females to call for help, to bond, and internalize angst, whereas, males tend to isolate themselves and/or to respond with acts of aggression, including to themselves, explaining the fact that females frequently attempt suicide, whereas males much more frequently succeed in commiting suicide.

- The male brain tends more toward diseases and neurological conditions that affect self-control (for example, Tourette's syndrome, autism, schizophrenia, psychopathology). The "dopamine receptor," called D2, often found in violent criminals, also occurs at much higher levels in males than in females (Gurian, 1999).

Middle Eastern, Asian, and western European traditions. Specifically, however, educators must become more skillful in using literature to explicitly teach "male brains" to be more adaptive and less aggressive. In general, our goal should not be to make girls more like boys and boys more like girls, but to produce children who are more *androgynous*, that is, less stereotypically male or female.

Recent research suggests that we are making in-roads in this regard. (Manzo, Manzo, Barnhill, & Thomas, 1999). Using the database from the previously mentioned study, we have devised an informal inventory to assess progress toward becoming androgynous, in the sense of being a more mature, gender-balanced reader-learner. It can be administered as a silent reading exercise, orally, and even as part of an interview procedure.

The Reading Sub-Style Inventory in Figure 11.11 can be used to identify the following sub-styles:

Sub-style 1 reflects an androgynous and mature type of reading.
Sub-style 2 is a stereotypic male type of reading.
Sub-style 3 is a stereotypic female type of reading.
Sub-style 4 is a self-acknowledged below-optimal reader.

In view of the many physical factors brought to bear on the issues and questions surrounding gender, the next section might better be called "More on Physical Issues." However, the next category takes up physical matters that are better categorized under "Defects" in the convenient-to-remember, though sometimes-blunt-sounding Weiner-Cromer model.

Boys and girls are different in brain organization, chemistry, and physique. Is it any wonder that there are differences in reading and learning patterns?

PRESCRIPTIONS FOR SOME COMMON MEDICAL DISORDERS

Many physical factors (evaluated under the Defect category) can impede literacy development. The most directly reading-related constitutional factors are discussed in Chapter 5: vision, hearing, neurological considerations, and intellectual capacities and aptitudes. Several additional physical conditions can influence school performance, such as allergies, hyperkinesis, and minimum brain damage. The explicit *treatment* of these constitutional problems is beyond the scope of this text. However, you probably will be expected to be conversant with and to make recommendations to help alleviate or circumvent several of these problems. So here is a running start on some common and uncommon physical issues that you should be able to address.

FIGURE **11.11**

READING SUB-STYLE INVENTORY (RS-SI)

Directions: This is a three-step process.

1. Read all the characteristics of readers' styles listed in the Boxes marked 1 to 4 below. Then, rank them in the manner that best reflects you as a reader on a five-point scale, where 1 = most represents me, and 5 = least represents me.

	Box 1	Box 2	Box 3	Box 4
Rank:	_____	_____	_____	_____

2. Next, using the rankings from above, please assign a percentage to each Box, or Sub-Style type that represents you as a reader. For example, if you ranked Box 2 as *most* representing you, what percent out of 100% would you assign to that subtype? The total of all five boxes should equal 100%.

	Box 1	Box 2	Box 3	Box 4
Percentage:	_____%	_____%	_____%	_____%

3. Draw lines through those statements in the Boxes that *do not* seem to apply to you but for which you expressed some percentage above.

Box 1

Subtype 1

1. good concentration
2. good critical analysis
3. broad reading interests—fiction/nonfiction
4. form concepts easily
5. get the facts well from print
6. read well between and beyond the lines
7. think creatively without prompts
8. write well
9. can read comfortably for long periods
10. solid vocabulary
11. take tests well
12. finish most academic tasks in a timely way

Box 2

Subtype 2

1. prefer doing repetitive, predictable tasks
2. have interests in: sports, outdoor life, business, gambling, social studies, and the mechanics of how things work
3. reading tends to be a workout
4. often mark-up what I read
5. tend to forget quickly what I've just read
6. ask myself questions while reading
7. good at applying what I've read/learned
8. do not really enjoy reading for pleasure

```
┌─────────────────────────────────────────────────────────────┐
│                          Box 3                                │
│  Subtype 3                                                    │
│    1. read mostly for pleasure                                │
│    2. find writing exhausting                                 │
│    3. have interests in fashion and children                  │
│    4. have solid literal comprehension                        │
│    5. rarely use new information toward a practical end        │
│    6. rarely think too deeply about what I've read            │
│    7. read directions well                                    │
└─────────────────────────────────────────────────────────────┘
```

```
┌─────────────────────────────────────────────────────────────┐
│                          Box 4                                │
│  Subtype 4                                                    │
│    1. good at reading material on grammar and such            │
│    2. tend to get lost in details                             │
│    3. tend to listen more than talk during discussions        │
│    4. like reading about magic                                │
│    5. good speller                                            │
│    6. like reading directions                                 │
└─────────────────────────────────────────────────────────────┘
```

Allergies

Allergic reactions can cause enormous disruption to normal functioning. In fact, they probably are responsible for more erratic brain activity than all other causes combined. Nonetheless, schools do a poor job of helping the many children who suffer from common "hay fever," and other airborne allergies. Most school buildings are not air-conditioned, nor air-filtered, despite blazing temperatures in many parts of the country from late April to June and from August to early October. It is not at all uncommon to find windows opened wide and school lawns being mowed or nearby fields being cut in many suburban and rural settings. In most city schools, noise pollution and smut are equally common.

Remedy/Recommendation: Urge parents to have the child see a physician. There are now several reasonably effective "non-drowsy" antihistamines that can be taken once a day to relieve most symptoms. The other thing we can do is to remind school boards and communities that teachers and children are the only ones in this affluent country who are still being packed 30-plus to a room in un-air-conditioned buildings. Those buildings that are air-conditioned often use large individualized systems that generate considerable sound interference and harsh bellows of blown air. Central air cooling and air cleaning could easily add thirty to sixty more *productive*

Common allergic reactions are responsible for more erratic brain activity than all other causes combined.

days to the school year without changing the school calendar or adding to labor costs. Over a student's thirteen years of schooling this can conservatively add as much as two full years of reading and instruction.

Hyperkinesis

There is a counterintuitive remedy for lack of attention; it is to increase the pace of instruction.

When a child is constantly fidgety, it is commonly referred to as Attention Deficit Disorder (ADD). When hyperkinesis is accompanied by Attention Deficit, it usually is referred to as ADH, or Attention Deficit with Hyperkinesis. Both of these conditions are largely treated by physicians with stimulant drugs such as Ritalin and Dexedrine. These stimulants, which also include caffeine, make the mind more alert, reducing the need for the body to try to stay alert through directionless activity that resembles the behavior of a tired, cranky child. Problems of this type have been shown to be relatively unrelated to severe reading disorders, but clearly compound any learning disorders.

Remedy/Recommendations: Increase the pace of instruction. Switch tasks frequently. Require a 2-second latency—wait time—between questions and answers.

Of Different Minds: Hyperlexia, Williams Syndrome, and Ungeared Minds

Two reading-related oddities, or anomalies, that clearly are medical problems stand out because they also seem to characterize some socially accepted, though lesser conditions that may deserve note and attention as psycho-educational problems. These medical conditions are (acute) hyperlexia and Williams Syndrome. Each is characterized by an exceptional ability in a sea of disability. This set of conditions has obvious social deficits, but the lesser forms (examples ahead) often draw praise where there should be some concern. First consider the obvious medical/social deficit problems.

"Hyperlexia" is the name given to a rare condition wherein a child with diminished mental capacity will learn to read, in the sense of decode, at a precocious level, but with little comprehension. Peter and Janellen Huttenlocher (1973) report one case of a boy who had been previously diagnosed as having "infantile autism." He scored below the 3-year-old level on the Peabody Picture Vocabulary (IQ) Test when he was 7 years old, yet he could sound out words that were upside down and backwards (even saying them backwards). He also was an excellent speller. While he greatly enjoyed this skill, and wanted to read everything in sight, he could hardly follow simple oral or written directions, and in a way characteristic of some autistic children, was socially withdrawn, living largely within himself.

The other clear medical problem is *Williams Syndrome*. These children tend to be very sociable. In fact, because of the friendliness and characteristic appearance of people with this rare genetic disorder, they are sometimes called "pixie people." They have narrow faces, broad foreheads with widely spaced eyes, and narrow, pointed chins. They seem to be always smiling. Their intellectual development, however, is a maze of incongruities. They typically begin speaking at a much later age than other children, but often begin speaking in sentences rather than words and phrases. Subsequent language development tends to be accelerated, and their vocabularies are peculiarly rich. One Williams Syndrome child, when asked to name all the animals he could think of, reeled off the names of about twenty animals, including "brontosaurus, tyranadon, whale, yak, koala, and ibex" (Finn, 1991). Yet the IQ range of Williams Syndrome people tends to be between 50 and 70. They have difficulty following simple directions, and have poor motor control. Despite their extensive vocabulary and language facility, they often miss the underlying meaning of simple conversation. There seems to be a disconnect between their linguistic ability and their understanding. They comprehend parts, but not the whole; they see each tree, but not the forest. As with Down Syndrome, a group marked by a facial similarity, Williams Syndrome also is accompanied by characteristic medical problems, particularly heart and gastrointestinal disorders (Finn, 1991).

In general, "idiot-savants," as this class of retarded yet specific-area geniuses is called, prove in dramatic fashion just how discrete certain brain functions are. They also help us to understand the many individuals who are gradients away but on the same continuum, such as those children found in most every class who are good at word analysis and recognition, quite good at literal comprehension, read narrative material voraciously, but who cannot seem to see the relevance and connections of what they read to anything else. This group of "lesser hyperlexics," as they might be called, is composed of socially approved sorts who simply read too much. They live in books but do not tend to profit much from reading them. Books pass through them with little digestion and growth of thought or capability to problem-solve, and most particularly an inability, or nondisposition to connect reading to the very world they read so much about. This is a case of taking occasional escapist reading, or withdrawal, to gird oneself for life, to the point where reading becomes one with life. This group tends to have little interest in social studies, history, and world

Yes, it is possible to *read* too much!

affairs. They also struggle to tend to day-to-day challenges, and overly romanticize or demonize most anything and everything. These sometimes "voracious" readers appear to use reading as a way to avoid thinking rather than to elevate thinking. Their personality profiles, as estimated on the Manzo Cognitive-Affective Filter Inventory, include a high identification with animals that symbolically are emotionally distant, like "eagle," and run easily and quickly from anything disconcerting, or socially challenging, as symbolized by their high identification with the head-in-the-sky "giraffe." They do very well on cloze passage tests that tend to measure great familiarity with language patterns in prose (Manzo & Manzo, 1993).

In general, such students need to read more nonfiction, and become more self-instructive in the subject areas that they otherwise give no thought to, such as mechanics (there are wonderful books on "how things work"), economics, and the "hard" sciences. The absence of knowledge of such subject areas leaves these otherwise proficient readers schema-deficient. As such, they are not able to benefit from conversations and print material that refer to basic concepts in these domains and ease understanding of other new ideas. Nor are they able to use these domains themselves as analogies and allusions in their communications with others, and within themselves. John Locke (circa 1706) put it succinctly, "Reading furnishes the mind only with materials of knowledge; it is thinking that makes what we read ours." Functional knowledge in the various domains and disciplines is now referred to as Multiple Literacies, and has been called one of the most important developments in the conceptualization of modern reading instruction (Manzo, 2003; Morrel, 2002). In another, less socially–politically sensitive time, Chase (1926) referred to these sometimes prolific, though narrow, readers, as "Ungeared Minds" and as "higher illiterates."

These facts and related implications to education are another example of the need and benefits for case-based study as well as large-group standardized testing. The conditions noted here would never have been discovered through group testing alone.

REVIEW

You now have a grasp of how to sensibly address issues that are part of every curriculum, but otherwise rarely addressed in the particular. Ideally, schooling will become sufficiently resourced in the future so that teachers will have specialists to fully consult and assist on these "murky" but important matters. You could be one of those specialists.

PREVIEW

The two chapters ahead offer specialized guidance as well. In the first case, guidance is offered to those who will work with children and adults from second-language and alternate-cultural backgrounds, which today is most all of us. The last chapter speaks more fully to the needs of secondary and adult students, an area of professional work that few tend to prepare for explicitly, but increasingly find themselves engaged in, since this is where the need is great and job funding has been growing for decades.

ASSESSING AND ADDRESSING READING-LANGUAGE-THINKING PROGRESS IN ENGLISH LANGUAGE AND CULTURE LEARNERS

Children grow into the intellectual life that surrounds them. – L. S. VYGOTSKY

CONTENT AND CONCEPT ORGANIZER

Second-language learners are struggling with one of the most difficult of all learning obstacles, and yet this cannot and should not be considered a *defect nor a deficit*. American education has very respectable ways and means to help them to succeed in our predominantly English-speaking classrooms. Nonetheless, progress is governed largely by social and political complexities. This chapter partially addresses these, and fully addresses several collections of pragmatic methods and means by which to diagnostically assess and precisely teach to those in need. The chapter also speaks to the evolving, and possibly positive, influence of pop and hybrid cultures.

CHAPTER OUTLINE

ENGLISH LANGUAGE LEARNING: NOT A DEFECT NOR DEFICIT

If learning a new language while having to learn *in* a new language were not so common, it probably would be considered a serious form of learning disability since its impact on schooling can be considerable. As such, it would be covered under many of the provisions and resources mandated by the Americans with Disabilities Act. Nonetheless, it is not a Defect nor a Deficit, but a Difference factor in the 6D model of assessment and diagnosis. That is to say, it can mimic the effects of a Defect—a physical or constitutional problem—and/or of a Deficit—a skill deficiency. Many teachers have difficulty differentiating the normal phases of learning a new language from "defects." This mimicking effect has teachers overidentifying English Language Learners (ELL) for Special Education (Ordonez-Jasis, 2002; Cummins, 2001). Logically, glitches of any kind in the oral-aural transmissions of typical threads of listening and instructional conversation can have distorting effects on most all aspects of communication and learning. To merely say that a Limited English Proficiency or second-language and culture learning student presents problems in assessment and learning is to minimize the import of the need. Lives often hang in the balance. Clearly, a more desirable goal would be to simultaneously support the development of the primary, or heritage, language, as well as the second language. The reasons are simple and supportable (Krashen, 2002):

- Speaking more than one language is a traditional goal of education.
- Fluency in one's heritage language supports learning in subsequent languages.
- The continuation of learning in the heritage language would ensure that valuable educational time would not have been lost during this transition.
- Everyone benefits by exposure to a more diverse language and cultural set of books and perspectives.

> Learning a new language while having to learn in a new language can mimic a form of learning disability; yet it is not a Defect nor a Deficit.

In other words, one way to overcome the view that having a different primary language is a *defect or a deficit,* would be to convert the heritage language to an asset. Having said this, it is equally important to state other truths that can be overlooked in assessment and intervention. One such truth arises from our clinical-field experience with teachers and schools whose occasional oversensitivities—or seeing with the heart—can sometimes interfere with the sensible application of the diagnostic rule of *parsimony*: Consider the simplest explanations for serious and continuous underperformance before ramping up to the next most complex one.

There are many reasons to be very cautious in judging how many ESL students are lower-functioning, and very generous in saying how many probably are average and above.

In this case, it can be worthwhile to remind ourselves that half of foreign and foreign-speaking children, like every other sampling of pupils, will have learning aptitudes that are fairly normally distributed, no matter how these are measured. That is, some will be immediately competitive academically with the best native-born students, and some will not. There are many reasons to be very cautious in judging how many are lower-functioning, and very generous in saying how many probably are average and above. A 1999 broadcast of an interview with George Brett and Orlando Cepeda, who were both being inducted into the Baseball Hall of Fame, brought this home on an anecdotal and image level. Most of the questions and answers in this interview were addressed to Brett, with just a polite few to Cepeda, who was born in Ponce, Puerto Rico. Cepeda's answers seemed brief and halting (not that Brett's were much better). Then a reporter from Peru asked if he might ask his questions in Spanish for the many who were watching from other parts of the world. Cepeda's answers were rich, colorful, and touching in his native language. His expressions and expressiveness were sensed even by those who did not speak his language. There was a palpable feeling that all watching and listening had just had a striking lesson in the care that must be taken in estimating abilities of most any type when language and cultural background are different. This has led some to conclude that it is necessary to have ELL students' abilities estimated by "co-equal analysis"—a multidimensional assessment plan (Ordonez-Jasis, 2003). Nonetheless, it is not reckless or shameful to conclude that some youngsters *appear* slower, no matter their language background. This is not a life sentence, it is just another provisional statement requiring a much fuller context and cross-verification under the guidelines of diagnostic-prescriptive teaching, and civilizing ways of thinking. Further, it should guide identification of a student's initial Zone of Proximal Development (Vygotsky, 1978) and should suggest the level of scaffolding that will be required to safely ensure progress to the next zone. Again, the purpose of assessment is to start with what *seems* obvious, then establish "peak" (or prompted and supported) performance. Remember that *peak* performance, or the highest level that students can be guided to, is the best indication of what they are capable of, and what it will take to help them get there.

Assessment and Diagnosis

It can be helpful in building the mental, diagnostic, and intervention equation that guides judgment, to assess a student's personal progress toward social-cultural-language adjustment to a new environment. A ***stage theory*** of language and cultural acquisition, and a follow-up checklist of the more specific factors that might be found at each stage are presented next.

STAGE THEORY AND CASE TYPING OF SECOND-LANGUAGE/CULTURE ACQUISITION

Stage theories are based on the belief that development progresses through a fairly fixed set of sequential phases. As such, stages tend to represent *relatively* predictable points in a developmental sequence. Of course, how quickly or slowly one passes through these stages is influenced by age, personality, familial background, instruction, and even birth order (Ordonez-Jasis, 2003): there are no impressions in life and learning without corresponding expressions. Stage theories of language development also can extend to culture. This makes it possible to *estimate* placement on both factors and to serve as a rough method of "Case Typing"—a means (discussed in the initial chapters) of quickly communicating a good deal of assessment information, assuming that reasonable qualifiers and modifiers follow in short order. A popular four-stage model is presented in Figure 12.1. It was adapted by Ernst-Slavit, Moore, and Maloney (2002), with slight modifications by the authors for this text and context. Ernst-Slavit, Moore, and Maloney (2002) rightly refer to these as *Stages of Language and Cultural Adaptation*.

> There are no impressions in life and learning without corresponding expressions.

ASSESSING *SPECIFIC* READING/LANGUAGE NEEDS OF ENGLISH LANGUAGE LEARNERS

A much more comprehensive assessment instrument is discussed next. This tool can be of considerable assistance in establishing the Zone of Proximal Development. It is biased toward bi- or dual-literacy development, which is the ideal. But it is also a worthy checklist and overview of the elements associated with progress toward English Language Learning, and from a school-based point of view, the more challenging development of the complex abilities necessary for *Learning in English*. Some of the items on this checklist require the teacher, or a school-appointed representative, to be bilingual. Some states, such as California, require evaluation in the student's primary and secondary language.

> "Stages" are relatively predictable points in a developmental sequence.

Checklist of Biliteracy Development

Mora (2001), writing in a book edited by Hurley and Tinajero (2001), offers a revised Checklist of Biliteracy (or dual literacy) Development that simultaneously provides a means of assessing student needs while implicitly

FIGURE **12.1**

STAGES OF LANGUAGE AND CULTURAL ADAPTATION

Stage I: Pre-production

Linguistic Considerations: Students listen and watch others carefully, and communicate largely with gestures and simple formula responses *("Thank You." "I do not understand.")*

Cultural Considerations: This period often is characterized as a *silent period*. It is marked by a great deal of cognitive activity, but relatively little in the way of external behaviors. It is a period of listening and observing.

Stage II: Early Production

Linguistic Considerations: This stage is characterized by the assimilation of basic vocabulary, and a sense of rule differences between the native and adaptive languages. Speaking is limited to one or two words and short, often muffled, utterances. There is a tendency later in this stage to rely heavily on high-frequency, usually pop-culture expressions, that can create humorous to overly sensitive incongruities with the actual situation at hand. (It is best here to model a correct response than to attempt a lengthy explanation of why the response seems odd. Of course, if the response could be a continuing source of embarrassment to the student, a more corrective explanation may be in order.)

Cultural Considerations: We would call this stage *joining the tribe*. It is marked by more frequent attempts at speaking and fitting in, and more trial and error learning. For some students this can be a time of *adaptation fatigue* and withdrawal as it becomes taxing to one's emotional, social, and cognitive resources to continue to produce language and affiliational responses in a high-risk, foreign mode.

Stage III: Speech Emergence

Linguistic Considerations: We see this stage as roughly equal to fourth- to sixth-grade level functioning in language and discussion. Students can participate in small-group activities, and use language purposefully to clarify, request, refuse, and even to apologetically interrupt with questions and counterstatements. It is an ideal stage to have students begin to read and write from personal perspectives, and to tell their stories with a better understanding of the social outcomes that might be associated with candor.

Cultural Considerations: This is a period of great relief. Feelings of isolation begin to recede, and a sense of personal control re-enters daily life. However, this is also a personal decision stage as to whether to try to be *assimilated*—surrendering prior language and culture—or merely *acculturated*—adding a second language and culture. (This stage can last for many years for first- and second-generation Americans. Obviously, acculturation is preferred since it is enriching to have dual-language ability and multicultural exposure and perspective.)

Stage IV: Intermediate Fluency

Linguistic Considerations: This Personal Control stage is characterized by greater levels of participation in activities that require higher levels of language usage, such as the ability to answer evaluative questions from a multiple and/or personal perspective that is not necessarily from either the original or the adoptive language/culture.

Cultural Considerations: This stage finds students functioning well in school and on a social level, though obviously relative to where they likely would be if they had not had to make this arduous journey. Fulfillment can take several years. This is evident in the fact that students' opinions of their level of proficiency in the new language are reported to be lower than that of their teachers by about two and one half to one (Strang et al., 1993).

Adapted from Ernst-Slavit, Moore, & Maloney, 2002, *Journal of Adolescent and Adult Literacy,* 121–123.

addressing principles of biliteracy and literacy instruction. It is, in effect, a summary of issues, needs, and methods to scaffold and teach English Language Learners (ELL). They suggest that a portfolio and anecdotal records be used as supplemental evidence, or cross-verification, of an individual student's level of biliteracy needs and development. Ideally, cross-verification should utilize untapped resources, such as the wisdom and knowledge of the family (Ordonez-Jasis, 2002). This checklist is, itself, considered a near-ideal way in which each English-Language Learner might be educated. It also serves as a structure for grounding and organizing much that is relevant to this topic in the text and chapter ahead. Although the checklist is set into a figure, it should be viewed as an integral part of the conceptual basis for this area of diagnostic-prescriptive teaching.

L1 and L2: Assessing Primary- and Secondary-Language Skills

The terms L1 and L2 refer to primary, or heritage, and secondary language respectively. Figure 12.2 contains a checklist of L1 Reading Knowledge and Skills. Figure 12.3 shows Notes from Anecdotal Records, or Portfolio Evaluation, related to L2 (English) skills (Hurley & Tinajero, 2001) with a few questions related to the child's L1 and L2 language-instruction history. A teacher would need to be bilingual, or supported by a bilingual team, in order to fully support second-language learning and biliteracy. Some states require assessment in both the primary and the second language.

Monitoring Linguistic Needs of Students with Limited English Language Proficiency

In general, the term Limited English Proficiency (LEP) includes English Language Learners and dialect speakers. Here we largely will be addressing the needs of ELL students, and ahead that of LEP (dialect) students as well. Linguistic needs for ELL students can include any combination of factors, listed here, in approximately their order of impact. These points can be used as a checklist for a given student and a tally for an entire class. You may need to ask for help from someone who knows both languages, but a little help is offered here.

1. The student cannot yet read in the native language, or L1.
2. There is no sound equivalent in L1 for the "morphology"—sound system—in the language to be acquired, L2.
3. There is no word form in L1 for one in L2.
4. Lack of familiarity with the grammatical and syntactical structures ("language redundancy patterns") in L2.
5. Inadequate vocabulary and concept development in L1.

FIGURE **12.2**

L1 READING KNOWLEDGE AND SKILLS

	Attempted	Mastered

I. Phonemic Awareness

1. Identifies same or different phonemes when presented minimal pairs with different initial vowel sounds.
2. Identifies differences in vowels following same initial consonant.
3. Identifies as same or different when presented minimal pairs with different initial consonant sounds.
4. Names words that begin with initial consonant sounds: b, d, f, k, l, m, n, p, r, s, t.
5. Creates rhyming words by substituting initial consonants or initial blends: bl, cl, fl, gl, pl, br, cr, fr, gr, pr, tr.
6. Identifies the number of syllables in words by tapping out the syllables as they are pronounced.

II. Word Recognition

1. Recognizes one- and two-syllable rhyming words based on patterns in a poem or story.
2. Has a sight word vocabulary for names, colors, numbers, days of the week, months of the year, and high-frequency words.
3. Uses letter-sound associations together with meaning and context clues to figure out unfamiliar words.
4. Uses syllabication when encountering new words, with subsequent recognition of the word in context.
5. Has fluent oral reading, making meaningful substitutions and omissions.

III. Comprehension

1. Reads following punctuation, using appropriate voice inflection and expression when reading orally.
2. Recalls main facts of a story.
3. Recalls the sequence of events in a story.
4. Predicts the outcome of a story or makes logical inferences about the story.
5. Retells a story in his/her own words, stating the main idea and giving some relevant detail.
6. Distinguishes between fact and non-fact or fantasy in a story.

IV. Composition

1. Writes his/her own story and reads it orally with teacher's assistance, expressing ideas clearly.
2. Attempts other forms of written communication such as letters or notes, for a variety of purposes and audiences.
3. Attempts to use various conventions of writing grammar, punctuation, spelling, and so on.
4. Uses the writing process of gathering ideas, drafting, and revision.

	Attempted	Mastered

V. Overall L1 Reading Skills and Practices

1. Is an independent reader as determined by an informal reading inventory and/or completion of basal reader at or above grade level.
2. Reads regularly to gain knowledge and for enjoyment.
3. Talks about what he/she has read and shows reflection on the content and meaning of text.
4. Is at ease during reading activities.

From Hurley & Tinajero, *Literacy Assessment of Second Language Learners.* Published by Allyn and Bacon, Boston, MA. Copyright © 2001 by Pearson Education. Reprinted/adapted by permission of the publisher.

FIGURE **12.3**

NOTES FROM ANECDOTAL RECORDS/PORTFOLIO EVALUATION: L2 (ENGLISH)-LANGUAGE SKILLS

	Attempted	Mastered

I. Language Usage

1. Asks and answers simple questions in English to acquire information.
2. Follows simple directions in English.
3. Initiates conversations with classmates and adults in English.
4. Tells a story or relates an event in English using intelligible vocabulary and grammar.

II. Phonemic Awareness

1. Identifies differences in minimal pairs of English words with short vowel sound of *a* as in *bat; i* as in *bit; u* as in *but,* and *u* as in *full.*
2. Names rhyming words with English long-vowel sounds.
3. Names English words beginning with initial consonants that are the same in L1 and English: b, d, f, k, l, m, n, p, r, s, t.
4. Names English words beginning with consonant blends: bl, cl, fl, gl, pl, br, cr, fr, gr, pr, tr.
5. Produces rhyming words by changing initial consonants and blends.

III. Vocabulary and Grammar

1. Knows the English labels for concepts from English reading readiness, such as numbers, colors, shapes, and position words.
2. Understands and uses common idiomatic and formulaic expressions for greetings, daily routines, and basic needs.
3. Understands concepts of synonym, antonym, and multiple meanings of common words (such as car, automobile; up, down).

	Attempted	Mastered

4. Understands and uses orally the vocabulary and idiomatic expressions encountered in basal readers or other texts at instructional level.

5. Understands the terminology used by the teacher in English reading instruction to give directions or assign tasks.

IV. English Reading Potential

1. Can comprehend a passage from a graded text or informal reading inventory at grade level (usually third-grade equivalent), read orally at a normal pace with comprehension.

2. Scores at fluency level on the required language-assessment instrument (BVAT, LAS, BSM, IDEA, or other standardized test) or teacher judgment indicates the equivalent of intermediate English.

BVAT = Bilingual Verbal Abilities Test
LAS = Language Assessment
BSM = Bilingual Syntax Measure
IDEA = Idea Oral Language Proficiency Test

L1 and L2 Language Instruction History

To what extent has this student received primary language instruction in previous grades in reading and writing? In the content areas?

To what extent has this student received English-language development instruction (English as a second language) in previous grades? What methods or strategies were used for this instruction?

From Hurley & Tinajero, *Literacy Assessment of Second Language Learners*. Published by Allyn and Bacon, Boston, MA. Copyright © 2001 by Pearson Education. Reprinted/adapted by permission of the publisher.

> **Native-born dialect speakers tend to think that there is no urgency to master a language that they understand and can be understood in; nonetheless, they face difficulty in the more formal language of print.**

6. Confusions arising from seeming parallels in L1 and L2 from similarities in letter clusters and idioms that are, in fact, not parallel, and therefore, are misleading.

7. Lack of, and/or incongruous, background schemata—values, customs, attitudes.

8. Lack of skills and knowledge in interpreting the communicative intent of a speaker/writer.

9. Inadequate and incongruous experience and knowledge of the acceptability of various forms of oral and written discourse.

Teaching Alternate-Dialect Students

For students with Limited English Proficiency (LEP), like those from inner-city and rural communities, the goal is to help them remain respectful of the community of language in which they live, while helping them to master a more widely used language option that will not leave them linguistically isolated, or identifiably different. Many of the language and cultural differences that distinguish us are becoming less pronounced as inner-city and rural areas that once were isolated become connected to standard English options through television, radio, magnet school programs, work-related contacts, and the stores and bureaucracies where we all do business. It is somewhat different for speakers of other languages, such as Spanish, and foreign-born children. Their first language is not a dialect of English, nor has their culture intermixed with core Anglo-American culture to a great degree. Their language may have entirely different grammatical and sound systems. Ironically, accommodating an entirely new language and cultural milieu can be somewhat less difficult than shifting to one that has a shared base.

Many foreign-born children are required to take English in school; however, the native-born tend to think that there is no urgency to master a language that they largely understand and can negotiate when needed. For both groups, there is a learning barrier, technically known as "proactive-retroactive" inhibition. This means that things previously learned that are close to what one wishes to learn can interfere with and inhibit new learnings. For native-dialect speakers, such as some African-American speakers, this might mean overcoming an ingrained pattern, such as saying "I wants" instead of "I want." For more particulars on this dialect, see Figure 12.4: African-American Vernacular English (AAVE), sometimes referred to as Ebonics. Some children's literature selections, such as *Flossie and the Fox* by Patricia McKissack (1986), use Ebonics in the text. When AAVE is printed, it is easier to recognize the differences between the dialect and standard English. Similarly, a German-born youngster learning English needs to learn the English sound of "w," while overcoming the tendency to make the German "v" sound for "w." Dialect issues are vivid across the land, from the Appalachian mountain range to Boston, New Orleans, and Brooklyn. In general, all language speakers tend to adjust their speech patterns to the social situation, using more of their dialect in informal situations and more standard English in more formal situations. Such rapid code switching takes a high level of metalinguistic awareness (Ordonez-Jasis, 1995). This obvious fact is restated to remind the teacher/examiner that a student is likely to be offering up his or her best interpretation of standard English in most testing situations, but it also is his or her most strained since the testing is inherently challenging and socially disquieting. Therefore, it is best to note deviations, irrespective of their implications to reading, and to offer standard forms as needed (though not during testing). People tend to form (overly) quick judgements of others by their language.

FIGURE **12.4**

AFRICAN-AMERICAN VERNACULAR ENGLISH (AAVE)
(formerly called Black English Vernacular, or BEV)

AAVE is governed by established rules of phonology and syntax that have considerable implications in the miscue portion of an oral reading inventory. Some of those rules and patterns include the following:

- Plural Deletion: five cent
- Past tense deletion: The boy jump high.
- *It* for *there:* It were a bunch of cars in the accident.
- Deletion of third-person singular on the corresponding verb: The cow *walk* slow.
- Invariant *be:* She be spittin' mad.
- Consonant cluster simplification: des' (desk)
- *l* deletion: seepin (sleeping)
- *d for* th: din (thin)
- Irregular third person: He do my lawn every week.

GUIDING PRINCIPLES FOR BILITERACY AND SECOND-LANGUAGE LEARNING

The larger field of reading is a wellspring of methods that are immediately useful and easily adaptable. Many methods have been celebrated and directed to ESL needs. One is Experience-Text-Relationship (E-T-R) (Au, 1979). It, like several others, essentially is an adaptation of traditional reading methods. In this case, E-T-R encourages students to talk about their experiences as they relate to a story or nonfiction piece to be read *(the experience step),* then to read natural segments of the text *(the text step),* then to relate the content of the story with prior experiences and discuss the story *(the relationship step).* These steps are not merely similar, they are nearly identical, though fewer and less comprehensive than the steps of the nearly 100-year-old Directed Reading Activity. This is not meant in any way to diminish the sense and values of the E-T-R, but to establish the point that most every textbook on reading methods at least incidentally has addressed the educational needs of the student operating with Limited English Proficiency (LEP), such as minority American-dialect speakers, and ELLs—English Language Learners—for generations of earlier immigrants and culturally-isolated peoples as well as current learners.

A recent review of the content of second-language research, as reported in two popular practitioner journals between 1990 and 2001, concludes: ". . . we still don't know enough about this field to make broad conclusions:

There is much more to be learned from and about second-language students" (Eakle, 2003, 835). If concentration of intellectual resources is an indication of coming progress, there is much to be optimistic about: The Eakle study found 879 relevant articles as compared to 49 for the prior, and format-setting analysis, done by Garcia et al. (1993).

Socially Responsive Diagnosis and Intervention would advance assimilation with accommodations.

Beginning Biliteracy Instruction

Nine guiding principles for biliteracy (or dual literacy) development are presented here; however, the individual abilities of each student will provide direction in determining the amount of time allocated to each biliteracy area. These have been gathered from over 50 years of writing on this topic, with particular support from more recent reviews by Krashen (2002) and DiCerbo, Mahoney, & MacSwan (2002). Again, several of these methods presume that the teacher is fairly fluent in the second language, and/or may consult someone who is.

GUIDING PRINCIPLES FOR BILITERACY DEVELOPMENT

1. Extend phonemic awareness in the primary language and in English.
2. Teach syllabification and word derivations such as prefixes and suffixes. Teach cognates in the first and second language. (Second-language learners, especially those who speak Romance languages, often know the affixes and roots of difficult English words and have greater capacity to acquire such terms than do some native English speakers.) Reinforce attention to spelling patterns through holistic word recognition and analysis strategies.
3. Teach sentence structure and word order patterns to increase predictability of words in context. Provide opportunities for students to practice rapid recognition of high-frequency words.
4. Link oral and written language by determining the relationship between oral language proficiency and biliteracy development. When possible, use texts with high levels of redundancy and multicultural literature.
5. Explain unfamiliar idiomatic expressions and vocabulary in context, in prereading activities so as not to impede fluent reading and comprehension.
6. Establish an experiential and cultural context through schematic mapping. Focus on the specific cultural attributes of the text.
7. Using thematic units for literacy instruction is highly conducive to the transfer of concepts and skills between students' L1 and L2. Organization of literacy activities around themes provides many opportunities for students to utilize new vocabulary and concepts in

different contexts, thus reinforcing new learning. Thematic units also integrate listening, speaking, reading, and writing skills in such a way that students can participate and succeed at whatever level of linguistic competence they have achieved.

8. Overcome the biggest problem in advancing biliteracy, which is the absence of books in the heritage language, especially for recreational, or voluntary, reading.

9. Guide students in examining the purpose and logical structure of expository and narrative text. Select universal and meaningful messages in literature.

Let's see what else can be done to accommodate children from different language and cultural milieus. The guidelines and methods presented ahead are drawn largely from prior summations by Maggart and Zintz (1992), Early et al. (1987), and Freeman and Freeman (1993).

METHODS FOR WORKING WITH ENGLISH LANGUAGE LEARNERS AND LIMITED ENGLISH PROFICIENCY (LEP) STUDENTS

Basically, children whose first language is not standard English need to be taught to *hear* the segments of sound that are used in English but not in their native language. Before tackling this requirement head-on, however, we shall describe some materials and methods for helping these students in a conventional reading program. The guiding concept in selecting these materials and methods is that both English Language Learners and Limited English Proficiency (LEP) students need to be in positive language-learning environments where risk-taking is encouraged, teacher expectations remain high, their native or dialect language *is* valued, and language is viewed as a cooperative venture between teacher and students. One way to help achieve this is to set up a permanent space in the classroom, and time of day, where students can have access to an abundance of materials that directly and incidentally aid vocabulary and concept development.

> Methods for Limited English Proficiency (LEP) and English Language Learners need to be set in positive language-learning environments and encourage risk taking, where expectations remain high and where the native language and cultural dialect are valued.

ELL and LEP Supporting Materials

The options for materials that could aid vocabulary and concept development are endless; materials to use with ELL students might include:

1. picture files illustrating vocabulary that is developed in reading selections

2. a picture dictionary of items and areas in the classroom and school, including the students and teacher

3. read-along tapes for stories

4. tapes of vocabulary words with definitions and sentences to provide opportunities for word practice

5. displays of language-experience charts to be used for matching words, phrases, and phonetic elements

6. displays of idioms and their meanings to help with concept development and story comprehension

7. library books for application of what is being learned to other materials

8. tape recorders and blank tapes, for recording students as they read aloud

9. materials for journal writing

10. areas to display student group compositions as well as individual compositions

11. synonym and antonym charts to help with student writing and vocabulary development

12. a group-developed dictionary for all new words learned during the year (a computer with a self-alphabetizing program is very useful in this ongoing activity)

13. newspapers and magazines to further familiarize students with American idioms, and to be used for finding pictures, names, numbers, and phrases

14. incidental learning/gaming activities that students will carry out of class, and that will treat school more like life and experience, than like readiness for life and experience

ELL and LEP Teaching Tips

Most methods in this text contribute to English Language Learning and provide assistance to those with Limited English Proficiency. These methods have largely emerged in America's eastern ports of entry, but continue to evolve in the far western, southwestern, and Pacific Islands of the United States. Education seems to work, and bilingual education is not in critical need of new options, although innovation and resources are always welcomed.

The following methods can be used to further aid language development in most any reading/language arts program, and with most any content or material:

- Encourage students to watch captioned TV, and to play with other children, especially to "play school." This is fun, inexpensive, and essential life-learning experience. This can be done in *bonus time slots* that otherwise would not be used for schooling.

- Encourage students to comment on materials to be read, by trying to predict what the selections in each unit of study might be about. Record students' predictions on a chart. At the end of a unit, encourage students to discuss whether or not their predictions were correct and why.

- Have as many books as possible available for students. Read the descriptions of books to them, encouraging them to select books from this list. In addition, select one book from each unit and read it to students.

- Have a variety of multiethnic literature available, such as *Jack and the Beanstalk: Juan y Los Frijoles Magicos* by Bofill (1998), including materials from your students' cultures and some in their native languages. Help them to build on their strengths, from a strong base of confidence and self-esteem.

- Exercise materials in any lesson should be read to students and discussed, not merely assigned.

- Read poetry aloud to students and discuss. If possible record the poetry on a tape so students can hear the poet's language again and again.

- Read plays to students before they are asked to take character parts. If possible, provide audio or video recorders so students can practice their parts and hear (and see) themselves before they are asked to read aloud.

- Read postreading questions to students and discuss answers with them before having them write out their own answers.

- Have bilingual students read and write with aides, parents, and former ELL children who speak a student's first language.

- Second-language students are likely to have a developmental gap between their ability to read and their ability to write in the second language. These students will benefit by working through stages of the Writing Process as a group activity. After a suitable prewriting activity and/or discussion, students should be asked to talk through the "drafting" stage, while someone records what they say on chart paper. Students then should be asked to reread the composition and make any needed revisions. The recorder should make these revisions, while students observe and suggest any editing corrections that need to be made (spelling, usage, punctuation, and so on). Each student should then copy the finished work from the chart, so that he or she has a sense of ownership. As students gain a sense of confidence in their ability to write, pair students and have them write their compositions together. Move from this to having students write independently.

- Seek advice and counsel from available specialists and veteran teachers.
- Let the inevitably humorous miscommunications that arise carry you and the children through the edginess that also is likely to arise in an active classroom.
- Remind yourself that these children enjoy a certain advantage in speaking more than one language, and in knowing another culture.
- These children can be a valuable resource as representatives from an alternate cultural perspective, and as potential teachers of a second language.
- Use songs and poems related to themes of books (Ordonez-Jasis, 1995).
- If you are proficient in the child's native language, use it to "remediate" misunderstandings that might be best clarified with a reference to something in the child's native language or culture.

In a more general sense, it is a good idea to partner with parents. Comprehension can be developed from a balanced and fun literacy component that draws on family resources. Such efforts aid ELL students in making connections in and to families that may feel isolated from school's sometimes-austere image. Some states require that any material sent home be translated into the heritage language. This may not always be practical, but it is genuine, and often richly appreciated and generative of good will.

Now let's look more carefully into one of the root problems of learning another language: unfamiliar phonemic sounds. If you will recall from an earlier chapter, learning to read aids phonemic awareness as much, if not more than, phonemic awareness aids learning to read. For this reason, teach children to read and discuss in English as soon as, and as often as, possible.

Learning to read aids phonemic awareness.

Decoding Strategies

Certain English grapheme/phoneme correspondences are particularly difficult for Limited English Proficiency students because they are not part of the student's first language. The most common missing sounds are presented in chart form in Figure 12.5.

Some words have difficult phoneme/grapheme correspondences (see Figure 12.6, page 467). As a general approach to teaching these "difficult sounds," use the teaching strategies (such as Gray's Paradigm and various phonemic awareness training methods) found in the decoding chapter,

FIGURE **12.5**

ENGLISH SOUNDS NOT USED IN OTHER LANGUAGES

Language	Sounds Not Used
Spanish	dg j sh th z
Chinese	b ch d dg g oa sh *s* th *th* v z
French	ch ee j ng oo th *th*
Greek	aw ee i oo schwa
Italian	a ar dg h i ng th *th* schwa
Japanese	dg f l th *th* oo v schwa

th—voiced sound "*th*ank"

th—unvoiced sound "wi*th*"

Fry, Kress, & Fountoukidis, 2000, *The Reading Teacher's Book of Lists,* 358.

always beginning with auditory discrimination before moving to auditory/visual association. Use concrete materials (pictures and objects) when dealing with phoneme/grapheme correspondences. This practice will not only help "fix" the elements so that they can be heard and visualized, but will increase second-language vocabulary acquisition.

Incidental Reinforcement

Incidental reinforcement appears casual and coincidental to the student, but in fact is assistance provided at watchful "teachable moments." It is based on modern research, but also the ancient wisdom found in the proverb: "When the mind is ready, the right teacher will appear."

Students need a great deal of practice with "difficult sounds," to overcome proactive interference—the often-unrecognized disruptive effect of certain prior learnings on new learning. The following is an effective way to provide needed reinforcement: Gather a picture file representative of the "difficult sounds." Make a library pocket chart and write a phonetic element in the context of a word on the outside of each pocket. Underline the phonetic element. Have students choose a picture from the box, say the picture name, and place the picture in the appropriate pocket chart. Encourage students to use the words in sentences. If students can only name the object, then model sentences for them: "Yes, Sammy, that is a ball. You can play games with the ball." In activities of this kind, it is important to remember that proper pronunciation does not take precedence over clear understanding. If a child mispronounces a word (*base* for *vase*), then repeat the correct pronunciation: "Yes, that is a *vase*."

FIGURE **12.6**

DIFFICULT GRAPHEME/PHONEME CORRESPONDENCES

The authors are especially grateful to the following foreign-speaking teachers for their advice in the adaptation of this chart: Janice Thang, Harry Tong, Oanh Tran, Arh Tren, Jennifer Castillo, and Rosobelda Landa.

Difficult Sound	Affected Group	Suggestions for Teaching
/b/ as in *bat* (as distinct from /p/ as in *pat* and /d/ as in *dad*)	Samoan, Korean	Have student listen to and repeat these words: bat-pat-dad-big-pig-day-bee-pea-deer. Have pictures available to illustrate the words. Mirrors are also useful for helping students differentiate the way these sounds are made by the mouth
/d/ as in *dog* (as distinct from /b/ as in *bed*)	Cantonese	Use pictures and related practice using the words: dog-door-donkey-dollar-duck-doctor-doll
/f/ as in *fat* (as distinct from /p/ as in *pat*)	Tagalog	Use pictures and related practice using the words: fin-fail-fig-fat-feel-fit-fool-four-fast-fan-few-fault-ferry-fine-pin-pail-pig-pat-peel-pit-pool-pour-pan-past-van-vat-veal-view-vast-veil-very-vine
/g/ as in *goat* (as distinct from /k/ as in *coat*)	Spanish	Check students' ability to distinguish these sounds auditorily and to pronounce them correctly: Say a word beginning with one of these sounds, and have the student repeat it. Say word pairs, and ask if the beginning sounds are the same or different. Use word pairs such as: goat/coat; gap/cap; gill/kill; gate/Kate; game/came/; goal/coal; good/could
/h/ as in *hot*	Spanish	In Spanish, the letter h is silent; hence, students may forget to pronounce this sound. Because the /h/ sound is represented by the letter j in Spanish, this letter may be used to spell English words that begin with h (*jat* for *hat; jot* for *hot*). Have students repeat words beginning with *h*. Have them repeat the sound they hear at the beginning of words beginning with *h*. Write *h* words on the board, repeating and underlining the h sound. Have students copy the words and illustrate them. The teacher may write a *j* in parentheses in dictated stories as a transition step: "(J)He put on (j)his (j)hat"
/j/ as in *jar* (as distinct from /ch/ as in *chest*, and /y/ as in *yam*)	Spanish	In Spanish, the /y/ sound as in *yellow* is often substituted for the /j/ sound. Say words beginning with *j*, and ask students to repeat the words. Provide practice in listening to the sounds, hearing the difference, and using the words in context. Use word pairs such as: Jane/chain; jeep/cheep or cheap; Jerry/cherry; jest/chest; jacks/yellow; jet/yet; jam/yell; job/yes
/k/ as in *cat* and *king* (as distinct from /g/ as in *go*)	Korean, Samoan, Vietnamese, Thai, Tongan, Indonesian	This sound is especially difficult for speakers of Vietnamese and Thai when it comes at the end of a word. Tell students the /k/ sound can be represented by the letters *k* or *c*. Make 3×5 note cards with a *g, k,* or *c* word on one side and a picture on the other side. Have students look at the picture and say the word. Then ask if the word begins with the same or a different sound than another *g, k,* or *c* word. Students can also be asked to write the correct word for the picture on a piece of paper. Use words such as: back-crack-brick-duck-snack-tack-wick-buck-bag-rag-wig-big
/l/ as in *lamp* (as distinct from /n/ and /r/ sounds)	Asian languages	Provide practice through simple repetition, picture cards, and words in context, using words such as: lemon-letter-lion-lamp

Difficult Sound	Affected Group	Suggestions for Teaching
/n/ as in *net* (as distinct from /l/ as in *lot*)	Chinese	Provide repetition with words such as: net-night-nest-needle; and word pairs such as not/lot; knee/Lee; knack/lack; knife/life; know/low; knock/lock
/kw/ as in *queen* (as distinct from /w/ as in *wet*)	general	Provide repetition with words such as: queen-quick-quiet-quack-question; and word pairs such as: wit/quit; wick/quick; wake/quake; well/quell; wilt/quilt; will/quill; whack/quack
/p/ as in *pet* (as distinct from /f/ as in *far*)	Tagalog and Vietnamese	Use picture cards of words beginning with *f* and *p*. Have students sort words by beginning sound, using words such as: four-five-fort-fire-frog-pail-pig-pen-pear-people
/r/ as in *ran* (as distinct from /l/ as in *lip*)	Chinese, Japanese, Korean, Vietnamese, Thai	Provide repetition with /l/ words such as: lip-lock-lace-leaf-low-lamp; and word pairs such as: list/wrist; long/wrong; lake/rake; lead/read
/v/ as in *vent* (as distinct from /b/ as in *boy*)	Spanish	Have students listen to and repeat word pairs such as: van/ban; veil/bail; very/berry; vet/bet; vat/bat
/v/ as in *vent* (as distinct from /f/ as in *far*)	Tagalog, Vietnamese	Have students listen to and repeat word pairs such as: van/fan; veil/fail; vat/fat; veal/feel
/w/ as in *wet* (as distinct from /v/ as in *van*)	Chinese, Arabic, German, Samoan, Thai	Have students listen to and repeat word pairs such as: wet/vet; wail/veil; west/vest; went/vent
/y/ as in *yam* (as distinct from /j/ as in *jet*)	Spanish, Portuguese, Indonesian, Thai	Provide repetition with /y/ words such as: yam-yoyo-yolk-yak-yard-yellow-yawn
/z/ as in *zoo* (as distinct from /s/ as in *soap*)	general	Provide repetition with /z/ words such as: zoo-zebra-zoom-zip-zipper-zero-zone; and word pairs such as: Sue/zoo; sing/zing; sip/zip; see/zee; sink/zinc
final consonants and consonant clusters	Spanish	In Spanish, there are only a few consonants that appear at the ends of words (n,s,z,r,d,l,j), and many Spanish speaking people tend to drop the final consonant in conversation. Use picture word cards and varied activities to provide practice with words pairs such as rope/robe; ape/ate; add/at; sad/sat; bag/back; wipe/wife; lad/lab; bead/bees; cried/cries. Provide practice with final consonant cluster sounds of /ld/, as in old-gold-cold-sold; /nt/, as in bent-tent-went-spent; /nd/ as in band-wind-pond-spend-find; /ngk/ as in sink-drink-chunk-pink; and /st/ as in west-first-toast-fast-test
initial /s/ and consonant clusters beginning with /s/ as in *school, sleep, star, street*	Spanish	In Spanish, letter clusters beginning with *s* never appear at the beginning of the word. Spanish speaking students often add /e/ before the /s/ sound; thus, *spot,* for example, is pronounced /espot/. Provide practice with initial "s" and "s" cluster words such as: sleep-spoon-smile-star-skirt-street-screen
/sh/ as in *ship* (as distinct from /ch/ as in *chin*)	Spanish	There is no /sh/ sound in Spanish, and Spanish speaking students find this sound difficult to distinguish from the /ch/ sound. Provide repetition and practice with word pairs such as: sheet/cheat; Sherry/cherry; ship/chip; shop/chop; shows/chose; sheer/cheer; shoe/chew; shoes/choose; shore/chore
/fr/ as in *frog* (as distinct from /fl/ as in *flat*)	Spanish, Chinese, other Oriental languages	Provide repetition of /fr/ words such as: frog-fruit-friend-front-frozen-fresh. Provide practice distinguishing /fr/ words from /fl/ words such as: float-flower-flag-flat

Difficult Sound	Affected Group	Suggestions for Teaching
/tr/ as in *train*	general	Provide repetition with /tr/ words such as: tree-trip-trick-truck-true-treat
/kr/ as in *cream*, /kl/ as in *clown*, /gl/ as in *glue*	Chinese, Vietnamese	Provide repetition with /kr/ words such as: cry-crab-crack; /kl/ words such as: class-closer-cloth; and /gl/ words such as: glad-glass-glove
Short sound of /a/ as in *bat*	general	Short vowel sounds are among the most difficult for ELL students to master. Provide repetition with short /a/ such as: bat-cat-hat-pat
Short sound of /e/ as in *pen*	general	Provide practice with short /e/ words such as: pen-ten-then-men-hen
Short sound of /i/ as in *did*	Spanish, Chinese, Vietnamese, Tagalog	ELL students often confuse the short /i/ sound with the long /e/ sound as in *feed*. Provide practice with word pairs such as: seat/sit; heat/hit; green/grin; feet/fit
Short sound of /o/ as in *cot*	Spanish, Chinese, Vietnamese, Tagalog, Thai	ELL students often confuse this sound with the long /o/ sound in *coat*. Provide practice with word pairs such as: hop/hope; rod/road; tot/tote; not/note; cot/coat
Short sound of /u/ as in *umbrella*	general	This is another difficult sound for ELL students because it does not exist in many languages, yet is one of the most common sounds in English. ELL students often confuse this sound with the /a/ as in *bat* and the /e/ as in *bet*. Provide practice with word pairs such as: cup/cap; fun/fan; bug/bag/bet; nut/net/gnat; run/ran
Long sound of /a/ as in *race*	Vietnamese, Spanish, Tagalog	These students find it difficult to differentiate the long /a/ sound from the /e/ sound in *pet*. Provide practice with word pairs such as: jail/jell; bail/bell; fail/fell; nail/Nell; sail/sell; tail/tell
Long sound of /i/ as in *five*	general	ELL students find it difficult to differentiate the long sound of /i/ from the /a/ sound in *bat*. Provide practice with word pairs such as: pine/pan; bite/bat; like/lack; bike/back; kite/cat; side/sad
Long sound of /o/ as in *rope*	general	ELL students find it difficult to differentiate the long sound of /o/ from the /o/ sound in *pot*. Provide practice with word pairs such as: rote/rot; note/not; coat/cot; hope/hop; mope/mop

Adapted from Early et al., 1987, Harcourt, Brace, Jovanovich, T2–T12.

Auditory Discrimination in Depth (now LiPS)

Charles and Pat Lindamood (1975) founded a program called Auditory Discrimination in Depth (ADD) that uses nonsense words to train students to feel and label the various mouth and vocal forms associated with the major sounds of the English language. Since the acronym ADD is now strongly identified with Attention Deficit Disorder, this program has recently been renamed the Lindamood Phoneme Sequencing (LiPS) Program. It is, in effect, a form of direct training in the area of phonemic awareness and hence phonemic sound differences from one language to another. Providing a way for the teacher and students to identify and discuss unfamiliar sounds is a considerable step toward teaching difficult phoneme/grapheme correspondence. Bs and Ps, for example are "lip poppers"; Ts are "tip toppers"; Ms and Ns are "nose sounds"; Ss are "skinny sounds", Gs are "scrapers"; and Fs are "lip coolers." A mouth picture represents each type of sound and it is associated with the corresponding letter symbols. Students and teacher then talk about, or engage themselves in, phonics, or how words sound. The teacher might ask a student: "How does the sound of ZAB differ from ZAF?" And the student, by thinking and feeling while he or she speaks the two, would answer, "the lip popper, B, has been replaced by the lip cooler, F."

This program requires extensive teacher training. Although it has been said to be a bit rigid in its orthodoxy, it does produce *sound* results (Vickery, Reynolds, & Cochran, 1987; Calfee, 1976; Howard, 1986). Teachers with backgrounds in speech and theatre are likely to have the best prior training and native skill to easily adopt and adapt this approach to phonemic-phonetic training.

Students with learning difficulties are the primary target audience for the Lindamood-Bell programs. Functional Magnetic Resonance Imaging (MRI) brain mapping has been used to monitor changes in the brain, especially in the right inferior parietal, for dyslexic children in a five-year longitudinal research study at Georgetown University, funded by the National Institutes of Health (NIH), and in adult dyslexics at Wake Forest University who experienced portions of the program. More recently, Lindamood-Bell has expanded into other literacy areas, beyond phonemic awareness and symbol imagery. Their Visualizing and Verbalizing for Language Comprehension and Thinking (V/V) Program helps students develop clear mental pictures, or concept imagery, with the goal of improving language comprehension and expression, as well as higher-order thinking skills. More information on the Lindamood-Bell Learning Processes can be found at *http://www.lblp.com/*.

Note Cue and Reciprocal Questioning (ReQuest)

School is part of human experience as well as preparation for it. The two methods described next were designed to generate positive experiences and appropriate mental images of group and classroom discussion, the most fundamental means of teaching and learning. As you read about Note Cue, notice its particular suitability for use with ELL students, and others who may have had limited exposure to the social and language conventions of U.S. classrooms. Notice, too, how as it progresses it also offers valuable diagnostic insights into students' language and cognitive development, and how it is designed to release responsibility and privilege to students until they have mastered certain strategies, more than just reactive skills. It is almost like having students enact a skit, to experience the nature and flows of class discussion.

Note Cue   Note Cue (Manzo & Manzo, 1987, 1990b) is a highly-structured method to scaffold students' participation in a focused class discussion. It helps to *get* discussion going, *keep* it going, and keep it *from becoming random*. It builds the behavioral and social learnings that come from actually doing something. More specifically, it teaches students to *ask* questions and, more importantly, to *comment* on the text, as well as simply *answering* questions. It does this by relieving students of the complex burden of having to think about what to say and how to say it, leaving them only to think about *when* to say it.

Note Cue, as its name suggests, provides *cues* to students, in the form of written *notes*, that guide them through participation in a "model" discussion—"model" because it is pre-scripted by the teacher. Initially, almost the entire discussion is pre-scripted. Enactment of these *early* Note Cue discussions is a form of "strategic parroting" in which students are expected to participate with relatively little thinking. The potential value of "strategic parroting" was discovered separately by two sets of researchers working with reluctant learners (Manzo & Legenza, 1975a; Palinscar & Brown, 1984). You will be pleasantly surprised to see how this opportunity for class participation through simple "parroting" can provide a form of instructional scaffolding that can gradually be removed as students begin to internalize the many complex aspects of effective classroom discussion. Note Cue is outlined in Figure 12.7.

The Note Cue system can be used to structure prereading as well as postreading discussion. For a prereading discussion, Questions should be written that will elicit students' background of information about the topic of the reading selection or that urge predictions that could be made from a quick preview of the selection. Similarly, write Comment cards that contain relevant thoughts that might be sparked by previewing the reading selection.

The second author (U. Manzo) piloted Note Cue in an inner-city middle school with low-achieving minority youngsters who had an established pattern of low participation, poor oral reading, and ineffective participation in pre- and postreading discussions. Although these early trials of the strategy were not objectively measured, when students' participation was prompted with Note Cue lessons, their behavior seemed to be more "on task" for longer periods of time, and their written responses on short tests showed higher levels of comprehension than they typically demonstrated.

Note Cue is a method that provides cue cards to students.

FIGURE **12.7**

STEPS IN NOTE CUE POSTREADING DISCUSSION

Question	Answer	Comment
How did the lead from the Roman mine get to Greenland?	The lead from the Roman mine got to Greenland by getting into the air, as pollution.	I wonder what kind of brain damage lead poisoning causes.

Preparation: Prepare a set of "cue cards" for discussion of the material. These should be prepared as follows:

   a. Write several **Questions** on 3×5 index cards (one Question per card), based on information from the reading selection. Include questions that go beyond the fact, such as translation, interpretation, inference, evaluation, and application questions.

   b. Write complete but brief **Answers** to each Question on separate cards (one Answer per card). When writing **Answer** cards, use complete sentences that include enough context to make it clear what **Question** it answers (see sample above).

   c. Write several **Comment** cards (one per card)—relevant thoughts that might be sparked by the reading selection.

   d. Label each card at the top as appropriate: Question, Answer, or Comment.

Step 1: After students have read, the teacher places one or more of the prepared *prereading* cards on each student's desk. *A few students may be given blank cards.*

Step 2: Students are instructed to read the card(s) they have been given, and think about when they should read it (them) during the discussion; *students with blank cards are instructed to try to think of their own **Question** or **Comment** related to the material they are surveying, and write it on the blank card.*

Step 3: The teacher begins the discussion by asking who has a **Question** or **Comment** card to read that seems to be a good place to begin the discussion. If a **Question** is read, the teacher asks who has an **Answer** that seems to fit. This process continues until most or all students have had a chance to participate. At this point, the teacher should ask, "Who has other personal reactions or comments?" This last question is intended to encourage personal-evaluative thinking and responding apart from the statements on the cards, but modeled after them in terms of relevance to the topic.

Step 4: (OPTIONAL) Within the same or the next class period, give a test of 5 to 10 questions that require brief written responses. Questions should be taken directly from the note cue cards and relevant comments made during the discussion. This builds appreciation of the value of reading one's card so that all might hear and learn, and respect for independent commenting.

Fading: As a group of students becomes familiar with Note Cue (as they quickly do), subsequent lessons should include *fewer teacher-prepared cards* and *more blank cards* for students to generate their own Questions, Answers, and Comments. In this way, responsibility is gradually turned over to students as they become increasingly more equal to the expectation.

In a set of field-based studies that *did* include objective measures, three of four teachers obtained similar results (Educational Specialist Degree projects, University of Missouri–Kansas City, 1986–87).

There are some other incidental diagnostic benefits in using Note Cue. The cards students write offer insight into their thinking. Collections of student cards, and their placement in students' individual portfolios, can offer an overview of student progress in written and oral communication. Now let's look at a comprehension strategy that has specific benefits for ELL students.

Reciprocal Questioning (ReQuest)   The Reciprocal Questioning procedure is outlined in Chapter 8, and its effectiveness as a comprehension strategy has strong experimental support (Manzo, 1969; Croll, 1990; Dao, 1993; Feldman, 1986; Gilroy & Moore, 1988; Helfeldt & Lulik, 1976; Lysynchuk, Pressley, & Vye, 1990; Lijerion, 1993). Its specific benefit for English as a Foreign Language (EFL) students was documented by El-Koumy (1996) through a research study involving 86 first-year EFL students at Suez Canal University in Egypt who were randomly assigned to three treatment groups. The group who used ReQuest scored significantly higher on comprehension measures than either the group with teacher-questioning or the student-generated questions group. Consideration of the following factors contributed to the effectiveness of the slightly adapted ReQuest strategy in this study:

1. asking questions that trigger and probe thinking
2. distributing the questions in terms of students' abilities
3. presenting questions to class before calling upon someone to answer
4. accepting correct answers sincerely and correcting wrong ones only
5. displaying the correct answer when students fail to provide it
6. giving students the opportunity to raise their own questions
7. handling students' questions with appropriate consideration, no matter how silly they may be
8. asking students to rephrase wrong questions due to poor syntax and/or incorrect logic (El-Koumy, 1996, 11)

As students use ReQuest, they begin to monitor the questions they bring to a text and expand their thinking as they hear the questions posed by the teacher and other students. This increases the variety of questions available to students for future use. Questions are empowering. The questioner sets the agenda. The key element in building this option into instruction from our perspective is the built-in *rotation* of teacher and student talk. This seems to be crucial in raising student consciousness of effective models of language and thinking, while providing the protected condition

Questions are "agency." They set the agenda; answers merely flesh it out.

under which they might explore the social-academic language of classroom empowerment. Its required rotation of roles allows students to near-copy then emulate sophisticated questioning and answering, and practice complex thinking and use of social conventions. Modern writers refer to this as *agency*—or power to constructively influence their circumstances. The reciprocal interaction seems to be the *active ingredient* that makes this rotation form of cognitive apprenticeship/mental modeling work (Manzo & Manzo, 2002).

Learning from Limited English Proficiency and ESL Students

Agency often begins with self-change.

Consider our recurring theme of empowering children to be agents of self-change, and therefore being influential of their environments as well as influenced by them. This is almost a definition of *agency*. Change within any aspect of a closely operating system will cause changes to all other parts.

Picture, for example, a school that has youngsters from Thailand. These children could be asked if they would like to teach about their language and culture during an occasional activity period. If enough of the other children are interested, this could be done on a more scheduled basis. Within one term, children would undoubtedly learn and go home with understandings of aspects of Thai geography, language, religion, political structures, and culture. There also are wonderful books available for children that reflect life and thinking all over the globe. All we need is a reason to seek them out. Such learnings might not be in the elementary curriculum guide, but they are enlightening, educational, and enriching in every sense of these words.

For a list of books and magazines of a multiethnic and multilingual nature, see your resource librarian and local bookstores, yearly, since this list is too dynamic to be served in conventional text.

Cultural Academic Treasures (CAT) for ELL Students

American culture may need to be taught.

Throughout the text we have addressed a range of social-economic, cultural, and linguistic issues affecting and effecting reading-writing-thinking. In the language of "critical literacy," this is sometimes known as issues in *equity, plurality, diversity, and linguistic parity*. Here we will speak more directly to a point that sometimes may get lost in our efforts to be fair and equitable and respectful of other cultures. It is spoken plainly by Maria Estela Brisk in her text on Bilingual Education. It reads as follows: "Bilingual students may or may not be familiar with American culture, depending on how much contact with the culture they have had. Thus teachers cannot assume knowledge or understanding: American culture needs to be taught" (1998, 113).

Cultural Academic Trivia game quickly infuses knowledge of the academic side of American culture. The CAT game (Manzo, 1970, 1985) is designed to build *background knowledge*, schemata, and vocabulary. It says to the student: Be attentive to your environment for anything that you don't know, make a note of it on a 3×5 card (given to students once a week), and bring it as your admission ticket to class. The card is intended to serve as a constant reminder to be thinking about words, facts, and ideas in American society as these unfold outside of the school and classroom environment.

When students bring their CAT cards to class, the teacher is obliged to tell whatever he or she knows about the word, fact, or idea. This information is written on the back of the card, which can then be used to play the "trivia" game. If the teacher is uncertain about an item, the teacher and student together try to clear it up by checking appropriate sources—dictionary, almanac, encyclopedia, Internet, and other teachers.

The CAT game can be played noncompetitively and individually by simply keeping count of the number correct out of 10 each time the game is played, or it can be played competitively for points. It also can be tied to a random factor to make it more game-like; for example, each time a correct answer is given, the student gets to roll a die and the number shown is recorded and added until a winner is declared (25 points or more to a game).

CAT is an especially good means of helping children learn the many allusions or referents that are used by others in speaking and writing. To that extent, it helps with schema building and comprehension. For example, to teach students who "Freud" is, is to help them understand what ideas people are referencing when they use his name. The same could be said for Gandhi, Jesus Christ, and Gallileo. Students quickly learn that there is no such thing as trivia, only minds that lack sufficient knowledge to give meaning to the referents that surround us. The students who first played the game came eventually to suggest that it should be called "Cultural Academic Treasures" (Manzo, 1970) because they realized that "trivia" is in the eye of the beholder.

A variation on CAT, called a Friday "Quiz Bowl Competition" is a major component in the most successful program in the country at preparing black minority youngsters for medical school. The other major components of this Xavier University of New Orleans program are practice in analytical reasoning and "think-alouds" (Whimbey & Lochhead, 1980), both of which were developed in earlier chapters. Consider now some other customizations, or specialized uses of the CAT model.

CAT cards also can be customized to include short-answer questions keyed to reading/learning living strategies. The simple premise is that the words and coaching we hear progress from external speech, to internalized

The CAT game is designed to raise consciousness of words and allusions.

language and principles that we then apply strategically as inner-speech—the "sources code" or software that guides much of what and how we feel and hence what we do. Cards could say: "What should you say to yourself when you encounter a word that you cannot easily decipher/read?" Answer Card: "Look at the first sound, then see if there are any familiar words or letter clusters within it that you may recognize. Next look at the final letters, then any context in which it is used. If it still doesn't make sense, ask someone what it says, and if necessary, what it means." This is a complicated set of rules; learning them "by heart" can have the same value as being able to recall how many days are in October by saying the internalized script: "Thirty days hath September, April, June, and November…" This same "inner-speech/sources code" notion can be extended to motivational and life guidance: "What might you say to yourself when you have encountered failure or poor performance?" Answer: "We all pass 'failure' on the way to success. I'm capable of more." "Did I prepare as I should have?" Or, as we have heard one teacher say to her students frequently: "What should be one of your life goals?" Answer: "To become a person who helps others." The reason that this sounds like programming is because that's precisely what it is. However, it is enlightened, filtered-through-the-ages programming, which when freely selected by the student, is converted from overt coaching to empowerment and *agency,* and can result in self-regulating wisdom. Ideally, it also counters and overcomes some of the more negative codes that each of us seems to learn too easily.

Using Pop Culture

It may be time to capitalize on children's interests in popular-culture topics as a way to enhance literacy.

There is a somewhat newer, stronger influence in the march toward "modernity" and potentially greater tolerance among diverse peoples for one another. The new century is evolving media-amplified hybrid cultures, much as did the 20th century that produced "swing" then "rock and roll," James Dean movies, the Beatles, and Rap. This entertainment sidebar to education probably has done more to help diverse, often-feuding cultures engage and mix freely with one another than all other efforts to teach "tolerance" and fraternity, perhaps combined. Researchers are reporting rather sophisticated levels of language and thought being expressed in response "fanfictions" on the Internet—email and story enhancements (Chandler-Olcott & Mahar, 2001, 2003; Williams, 2003). Admittedly some of this new mix of modern myth and faux cultures, has no agenda other than the "free market" interest in selling artifacts. It is, nonetheless, in this unenlightened commercial marketplace that children today meet, and in minutes move beyond recognition of their cultural and ethnic differences, and begin to find common ground in neo-mythological stories and heroes, from Harry Potter to Pokemon, SpongeBob, Yu-Gi-Oh, and the remarkably entertaining "Amanda Show."

The value inherent in these commonly shared shows, games, stories, and collectibles amounts to a new world that belongs to the young, and that is relatively untainted by traditional competing cultures. What is most amazing about these new media kids is that they seem comfortable within themselves, and happy to be the age they are. This not only defines "agency"—or peoples' felt capacity to act upon their world (Heron, 2003), but it also defines *contentment*—the ability to live in the present (of course, without disregard for the future). Fully realizing this can lead to capitalizing on children's interests in popular culture topics as a way to enhance literacy (Owens & Powers, 2003).

At the moment we are working to develop one such tool, called the Imps Project at *www.LiteracyLeaders.com.* It essentially is Pokemon and Yu-Gi-Oh with real vocabulary terms strung together with a common myth. Ideally, children will engage these characters and collectibles with the same enthusiasm that they have Pokemon and Digimon. In the process they incidentally acquire a rich "background knowledge"—their greatest need—and learn some academically challenging terms and concepts, from "Charlemagne" to "Pi" to "Hexagonal," that would be mastered in advance of their academic place in the curriculum. Importantly, these games and activities claim the minds and interests of children in ways that promote incidental self- and peer-teaching, in otherwise nonacademic periods such as recess and after-care (where paraprofessionals could support the related activities). This spills over to Saturday den meetings, and at home, with peers, siblings, and interested parents. As if this were not enough of a direct benefit, these engaging levels of play could produce a genuine peace dividend as children around the globe begin to have more shared experiences and a vicarious level of contact and empathy with one another. The project, as now being designed, would include a rich number of cross-cultural referents and heroic characters, and some fairly "dark and threatening" characters, since boys seem to gravitate toward these on initial contact, while they also build courage and empathy for the heroes who dare to face the dark side. Projects such as these nearly define the 21st century's growing emphasis on creative-constructive solutions, more so than those arising from "critical thinking" alone. This project also makes possible a belief in a more socially responsive form of diagnosis and prescription with greater leveraging of incidental resources and untapped times for learning, and with fewer unwanted side effects from solutions that can drain other resources.

The mix of modern myth and pop culture is becoming a common hybrid culture for most all of us.

This inquiry and discovery approach to building common ground is very compatible with what unfolds each day within each of us who go to school and strive to teach and learn with open minds. Walter Lippman, a popular journalist of the prior century, put it more or less this way: *There is but one bond of peace that is both permanent and enriching: the increasing knowledge of the world in which brave thoughts are welcomed, and experiment continues to occur.*

Other Methods for ELL Students

Early in this chapter it stated that many of the methods designed for literacy education also are suitable for ELL circumstances. The most valuable include: REAP, KWL+, Cloze Inferential Training, Phonemic Awareness methods, and the Listen-Read-Discuss method. For an overview of ELL student needs in content area subjects, see SDAIE in Chapter 10.

REVIEW

Learning a new language while having to learn in a new language can be a serious form of learning disability, yet it is neither a "Deficit" nor a "Defect." Further, aiding students to fully develop biliteracy, or dual-language capacity, is to everyone's benefit. The methods and means designed to teach, scaffold, and shelter reading and thinking through the grades fully support second-language learning goals and objectives.

PREVIEW

The next chapter contains a methodology called the Language-Shaping Paradigm. It is addressed in terms of its value to adults and secondary students, but it is equally applicable for helping young children to tell their own stories so that they can be shared with others in the special ways that literature can touch hearts and minds.

ADOLESCENT AND ADULT STUDENTS WITH FUNCTIONAL LITERACY PROBLEMS

A helping word to one in trouble is often like a switch on a railroad track—
an inch between wreck and smooth-rolling prosperity. – HENRY WARD BEECHER

CONTENT AND CONCEPT ORGANIZER

The career paths of elementary and secondary teachers often wend their way toward working in various forms of secondary school remedial and adult education programs. A primer on these sub-fields (specifically their assessment practices) will help prepare you for such possibilities. In general, functional illiteracy is overestimated, though it is a great need nonetheless. Calling it a crisis gives the misimpression that education is uniformly not working. This can be counterproductive at every level, from funding to discouragement of efforts by teachers and students. Methods for assessment and instruction are equal to the job, but must be considered against heroic efforts it can take to educate secondary school students to sustain their reading skills post-graduation, and to reach out to those in adult life who did not graduate, but must attain the literacy standards necessary for modern life.

CHAPTER OUTLINE

INTERMIXING OF ISSUES IN FUNCTIONAL LITERACY: EDUCATIONAL OR SOCIOLOGICAL DILEMMA?

Does America have a wide-spread illiteracy problem? If so, is there one primary cause, or many? The failure of schools (De-Limitations in our 6D Assessment model) has been an easy out, while acknowledgment of the increasing level of literacy required to survive in our advancing technological society is not forthcoming.

Alarms: Parsing Functional Literacy from Sociological Issues

Over fifty percent of each fall's ABE class is gone by Halloween.

Functional literacy refers to the level of learning at which one is able to read well enough to negotiate life's everyday activities and demands. The first alarm that the United States was a nation of near-illiterates percolated up from a series of sociological studies, books like *Why Johnny Can't Read,* and Sputnik-driven fears that America was in great peril. These fears led to massive federal and state-funded programs designed to *fix* the problem in the high schools and in the streets. It was assumed that about every fourth person was illiterate because he or she had not been taught properly. This precipitated several large-scale ABEs—Adult *Basic* Education (ABE) programs. However, most such programs, no matter how they were packaged, were unable to maintain regular attendance; in most cases up to 50 percent of each fall class was gone by Halloween. Of the nearly four million adults participating in such programs, over half do not complete more than thirty hours (Smith, 2002). Nonetheless, the programs continued to be funded, to the tune of $1.2 billion annually, but with fewer news stories and generally less attention.

The story that did persist, and has been converted into a sociological rule, is the overstated fact that most of the population of prisons was virtually illiterate, and that if we could only teach them to read (and presumably access righteous texts), they would become straight and productive citizens. As a result, prison education programs grew, but the prison population grew even faster. Unnerving to some, was a new condition whereby many prisoners who took advantage of these programs, and others involving physical fitness, did become "literate" and spent their time clogging up the courts with technical challenges to their convictions. And when released, they emerged as better-educated and physically more powerful people with only a slightly reduced level of recidivism. For about the next twenty years little more was said or done about the problem of American "illiteracy," and less yet about our failure to transform convicts into self-regulating citizens. To solve the latter problem we have built more prisons per capita than exist anywhere else in the civilized world. The initial problem of a high rate of illiteracy continued to perplex most everyone, since we also were spending more on education than anywhere else in the Western world. Less and less was said about this, until the second alarm.

Based on results of the 1992 National Adult Literacy Survey (NALS), it was widely broadcast that nearly half (47 percent) of Americans had scored in the lower two levels of a five-category rubric assessing *functional literacy.* More chillingly, 21 percent, more than one in five, were *functionally illiterate*. The 26,000 participants were asked to do a variety of "real-world" tasks, such as locating specific information on a pay stub, estimating the price per pound of peanut butter, and completing a Social Security card. The primary test used was the Test of Basic Education (TABE), developed by the commercial giant, Educational Testing Service (ETS). A "PDQ" analysis presumed to provide diagnostic as well as large-scale assessment in three aspects of reading: Prose (fiction, editorials, poems), Document (locating and using information in job applications and manuals), and Quantitative literacy (balancing checkbooks, summing purchases on a catalog order form and, as mentioned above, estimating per-pound costs from information on product labels). A high correlation among the subtests suggests that these "separate" measures all seem to be assessing the same general ability (Reder, 1998): namely, the *Deficit* aspects of the 6D diagnostic models. However, extensive interview data also were collected on educational background, language, and literacy practices (more on the findings and implications ahead).

Some states, most notably California, have developed their own instruments as well. The CASAS—Comprehensive Adult Student Assessment— goes well beyond traditional literacy skills and includes measures of basic communication (writing a letter), filling out medical-history forms, interpreting a ballot, demonstrating domestic care knowledge and ability to read and interpret related documents. This instrument is more diagnostic, though all states adopting it also must use the TABE for national reporting of adult progress, and program evaluation for federal renewal of funding. There are several other commercially available standardized tests, such as the Adult Basic Examination (ABLE), Basic English Skills Test (BEST), English as a Second Language Oral Assessment (ESLOA), and the Reading Evaluation of Adult Diagnosis (READ). There also is the high school equivalency exam, or GED (General Educational Development), that allows school dropouts to receive a high school diploma by "testing out" on five formal categories of academic study: Interpreting Literature and the Arts, Mathematics, Science, Social Studies, and Writing Skills. Oddly, this test does not directly measure reading skills. A passing score is based on norms showing that 70 percent of graduating high school seniors would have passed this test.

Triage Mentality Affects Public Policy

The impression that the United States was a nation of near-illiterates percolated up from misguided sociological studies.

Assessment of the levels of literacy in the adult population are used to gauge the soundness of the entire educational enterprise. Again, the 1992 NALS study sounded the second alarm throughout the U.S. It resulted in a good deal of new angst and public policy (re)actions to fix something that, as it turns out, was not really broken. The "quick, do something" attitude has created a triage/ER mentality that has contributed to the reduction of "nonessentials." Subjects such as art, music, and physical education in the public schools have been eliminated, and many state and federal agencies have come up with their own criterion-referenced, "high-stakes" tests, where public funding and jobs are determined by "measured progress." But what if there was no crisis? Could we live with that, and what would it mean? A recent re-assessment of some very bad news, and re-release of some pretty good news, suggests that we may need to rethink several aspects of what has become a sorry picture of teachers as hapless quasi-professionals.

No Crisis, but Considerable Need

Re-Assessment Says: There Is NO Literacy Crisis

Crisis thinking and planning created a triage mentality that has cost education, not supported it.

It now appears that the NALS government survey was harshly, even wrongly, interpreted. The statisticians set the "criterion" for who is literate and illiterate at a quite high 80% accuracy level. Andrew Kolstad, author of the first and revised report, concedes that this was much too high (Baron, 2002). It could further be argued that "literacy" is not a black or white matter, but rather a sliding scale. Using a more realistic cutoff of 65%, which is the same used by the National Assessment of Educational Progress (NAEP) that monitors school learning, the same data yield a quite different picture. When the data points are connected in this way, only 13 percent are in the lowest two categories. Using this lower percentage still amounts to over 20 million people, so it is hardly a non-problem. However, this figure may be an overestimate skewed by disproportionate facts that also need to be factored in to estimates of post-tenth-grade adolescents who are failing:

- About a fifth to a half (depending on which report is consulted) of those scoring very poorly included immigrants with limited English-language proficiency.
- Others have physical and linguistic challenges.
- Still others have mental impairments.
- Many are high-school dropouts.

- Many, in this nonstratified sample, had IQs below 80, which by the definition of the bell-shaped curve could have included between 7 and 13 percent.

While it remains a matter of statistical correlation that those in the lower categories do not earn nearly as much money as those in the top two categories, and that the racial divide remains an area for deep concern, the scales are tipped to a different balance by these findings. So let's address the issue of racial divide. It clearly remains a pocket of crisis.

Pockets of Continuing Crisis: Minority Student Gap

The problem that is commanding the most concern in American schools is the gap in standardized test scores between Caucasians and Asians on one hand and African Americans and Latinos on the other. The differences are considerable and despite many experimental programs and large-scale efforts to narrow margins have remained fairly constant over time. For example, Iowa Tests of Basic Skills (ITBS) reading scores reported for the Kansas City, Missouri, Public Schools for grades 3, 8, and 11, show White kids in the same (relatively poor) district scoring in about the 55th per-centile, while Black kids score in the 34th percentile, and Latino kids in about the 35th percentile. Math scores are similarly disconcerting: Whites about 53rd, Blacks about 36th, and Latinos about 37th percentiles (*Kansas City Star,* August 16, 1999). In general, the Black-White gap is about 12 percentile points in the early grades, and grows to 18 percentile points in the upper grades. More recently, the *Los Angeles Times* (July 21, 2002) reported similar data for the Los Angeles School District. While not men-tioning race, per se, they report the magnitude of illiteracy in the city's sec-ondary schools that have a population of about 125,000, to be between 35,000 and 67, 000, depending on the criterion used. *This is a national cri-sis* with implications for how society is, and likely will continue to be, strat-ified. It requires unrestricted dialog, and re-evaluation of most everyone's pat answers and especially of certain socially-driven educational experi-ments that may be complicating the problem.

This is not to say that the solutions that have been tried to date are of no value. Each prior effort has taught us much about what to question and possibly eliminate as a solution. One thing that the experiments of the last 30 years seem to be saying clearly is that programs, consultants, and strate-gies should not be put to social litmus tests (or whose "side" are you on?), but determined by substantive changes on instruments like the Stanford 9 and the ITBS, and other more enlightened tests as well. The past may even be telling us to think more deeply about social issues and answers, but not to overburden an educational system that already is challenged beyond its limits. Good intentions, such as jobs programs in the schools for minorities, have led to "mission creep"—or trying to do more than the school situation and resources will allow. This tends to nullify even that which could have been achieved with a clearer mission focus. Several leading Black educators, such as Thaddeus Lott, speaking to the Kansas City, Missouri, school board, are saying things like: "[Educators] are hooked onto the latest classroom fad at the expense of methods already proven successful. They may even avoid things that they are opposed to philosophically even though they work" (*Kansas City Star,* November 6, 1998).

The critical element is Reading!

The problems are massive and complicated. One thing, however, is clear: Efforts to end segregation are not the same as making provisions for quality education. Let us see now what seems to work, philosophically and practically. After nearly 30 years of backsliding, it appears that board members, school administrators, community groups, and courts may finally be ready to seriously address this core school issue. Los Angeles is doing so in much the manner that 2,000 other schools nationwide have turned to. That is, by directly addressing the critical element, reading—a durable skill, unlike "self-esteem," which is a fragile, fleeting feeling. Relying largely on a less-than-inspired but highly-focused program called "Language!" teachers of English are teaching basic word recognition and analysis in lesson units such as might be found in elementary school. Early reports indicate that the secondary-school students feel deeply offended, but are rapidly making progress toward a third- to fourth-grade level of "proficiency."

This is hardly worth celebration. But it is one way to address the primary, individual student problem rather than the "deeper social issues." While it may be a problem with complex social implications, it is a fundamental school problem that must be considered in terms of "net" effects. For the last 20 to 30 years, the net effects seem to be characterized by at least three negative outcomes: 1) very little educational progress; 2) expressed concerns for conditions such as "learned helplessness" that seem to only intensify "learned helplessness"; and 3) a good deal of animosity toward a society that presumably is intentionally responsible for underachievement, and a growing resentment for that society, which seems to be complicating the problem. It is in the spirit of reducing these growing negatives that the next concept is suggested as a point of renewal.

Learned Helplessness

Learned helplessness may be taught by overly dwelling on it.

Johnson and Winograd (1985) referred to students who were failing, as suffering from a *passive failure* syndrome. They ascribed this to *learned helplessness.* To their credit, they did not say that anyone had done this to the students, but rather that these failing students did not understand the relationship between effort and success. Importantly, some do. This is somewhat observable even in the before-mentioned interviews of the 1992 Literacy Report that in passing suggested that *some* low-scoring though apparently *resilient* respondents held management jobs, earned good wages, and were living otherwise fulfilling lives. These points deserve much more weight than they have been given. Acknowledgment of these points may lessen the "helplessness" syndrome that has become associated with failure, which became represented in educational thought as the "Matthew Effect." It had been known earlier (in the 1960s) as a "cumulative deficit" hypothesis—the cumulative effect of learning less each year in school than the next year required. The Matthew Effect was intended to motivate teachers and society to try harder to save those who were failing; however, it is based on misassumptions that have led to a sense that these "poor souls" are not only helpless, but hopeless. Neither the 1992 Literacy report, nor the biblical basis for the "Matthew Effect," support this misdirected conclusion.

No Pobrecito *Amendment to the Matthew Effect*

First introduced by Merton (1968, then Walberg and Tsai, 1983), and popularized in reading education by Keith Stanovich (1986), the Matthew Effect says that in education, as in capitalist societies, the "rich get richer and the poor get poorer." The frequent interpretation of "Matthew" needs to be challenged on several grounds. In Education, the "poor do *not* get poorer," they merely do not achieve as well and therefore as rapidly as those who start out more able and enabled. It also is politically tainted to say the "rich get richer" since this leaves the populist impression that their progress is at the expense of the "poor." Not so. This coupling of economics and educational progress was based on a sociological study done in the early 1950s with a narrow population base, and when financial need kept many people from completing high school.

This strained metaphor, originally from Matthew (25:29), probably needs to be amended, beginning perhaps with consideration of another biblical reference. We reluctantly make this reference, because it never seems to be a good idea to complicate a complicated matter with faith issues. Nonetheless, since this is the prevailing metaphor, one must also consider Matthew (20:1–16), also known as the "eleventh-hour parable" (where workers arriving at the eleventh hour—when the land owner was desperate to get his crop gathered—received as much in pay as did those who worked for an otherwise fair wage all day). The point of this parable is that everything that is not *equal* is not necessarily *inequitable*. It also is interpreted to speak more directly to self-reliance and less to the bathos, or *Pobrecito Syndrome* (Garcia,1997; Manzo, 2003). This "Poor Child" view implicit in the Matthew Effect can have a de-energizing influence on

> Where schooling is concerned, the poor do not get poorer at the expense of the rich.

To be less critical and more constructive, the "Matthew Effect" needs a *No Pobrecito* amendment.

teachers and students alike. It not only lowers expectations (which may reasonably need to be adjusted to ability level), it says don't even try: the way you read is the way you are, and what you are (Manzo, 2003).

Clearly, many professors use this version of Matthew to motivate teachers to work harder to help kids overcome "helplessness." However, the net effect on the job may be quite different. Applying the educational maxim that "more is caught than is taught," it seems evident that carrying this "hopelessness" impression is likely to be underscored and subtly communicated in ways that are more negative than positive. The simple fact that other, equally weak readers, and others with physical disabilities have become successful and live fruitful lives is often as much as most of us need to sustain ourselves through our personal pilgrimage. This "common sense" wisdom has not gone totally unappreciated. Two book titles sum-up the growing belief in resilient kids: *Kids with Courage—True Stories About Young People Making a Difference* (Lewis, 1992) and *Kid Stories—Biographies of 20 Young People You'd Like to Know* (Delisle, 1991).

Open-Admissions Policies to Two- and Four-Year Colleges

Today very few quit high school for economic reasons and nearly half continue on to some level of postsecondary education. Most states have open-admissions policies such that anyone graduating from high school is guaranteed a place in a community college, and those finishing in the top half are guaranteed a seat in a state college, and those in the top 10 to 15 percent are similarly guaranteed a spot in their state's research universities. As a result, "The explanation for reading difficulties has moved away from a focus on economic disadvantage" (Allington, 2002, 263). Of course, this does not mean that it is no longer a factor. It merely says that there are at least minimal to near-optimal levels of opportunity for most everyone to succeed in American schools and society, though clearly wealth and family privilege provide special opportunities. We must be especially vigilant that economic growth be addressed nationally and globally, if for no other reason than to reduce the number of people who live desperate and eventually resentful (and terrorist-leaning) lives.

Two-year colleges have fully responded to the needs of underprepared adults . . . a heroic objective, supported by a diligent, caring faculty.

Clearly, the two-year colleges have been most responsive to this more broadly defined level of equal opportunity. It is not unusual for community college classes to include students whose range of abilities can span 10 years on most reading and academic achievement tests. Many of the methodologies described in this text, and ahead in this chapter, apply to the two- and four-year colleges with open-admissions policies. This should not be taken to mean that it is easily done. It is a heroic objective, supported by a highly diligent faculty who are as unsung as were firemen before 9/11.

Resources Are the Greatest Need

After all is said and done, the greatest need is for resources. Just a quarter century ago, almost every intermediate and high school had one reading specialist for every 400 students. Today few have any. After a 20-year increase in the number of Developmental Learning Specialists at the college level, and even into the professional schools of Medicine, Law, and Pharmacy, these positions are drying up under budget crunches and competing demands.

DIAGNOSTIC-PRESCRIPTIVE PRACTICES FOR ADOLESCENTS AND ADULTS

Categories of Adolescent Readers

Norman Unrau (2004) has created a wonderfully encompassing set of categories of adolescent readers. Using the multiple assessment tools covered in previous chapters, those ahead, and the five-point universal system (1–emergent; 2–below average; 3–average; 4–above average; 5–superior/advanced), you should have all that you need to identify and sort students by the ten categories of need and development that Unrau suggests. (Actually, he suggests an eleventh category that is implicit: *Advanced Highly Proficient Readers.*)

1. *Non-Decoders or Weak Decoders:* Nonalphabetic readers who have not grasped the alphabetic principle that each sound has a graphic representation; very impaired reading comprehension and word recognition; little letter-sound or phonological knowledge; profound spelling difficulty.

2. *Compensatory Readers:* Grasp alphabetic principle, but have impaired word recognition and reading comprehension; limited orthographic and phonological knowledge; use sight words and sentence context to compensate for lack of phonological knowledge; significant spelling difficulty.

3. *Slow Comprehenders or Non-Automatic Readers:* Accurate but non-automatic, effortful word recognition; naming-speed correlated with slowness in word recognition; lack of practice reading also contributes; use sentence context to help with word recognition; impaired reading comprehension; significant spelling difficulty.

4. *Delayed Readers:* Slow acquisition of automatic word recognition skills; few comprehension strategies, lack awareness of text organization;

impaired reading comprehension; lag behind others of similar age; some difficulty with spelling; attribute problems with reading to ability ("stupid") rather than to lack of effort; thus, use fewer strategies; questions arise about cause of strategy deficits.

5. *Readers with Monitoring Difficulties:* Fail to monitor comprehension; experience "illusions of knowing"; root of monitoring difficulty may lie in one or more of the following areas (Hacker, 1998):
- lack linguistic or topic knowledge to detect dissonance
- have linguistic and topic knowledge but lack monitoring strategies
- have knowledge and strategies but lack conditional knowledge about when and where to apply them
- comprehension and/or monitoring demand too much of reader's memory and other resources
- lack motivation to engage in monitoring

6. *Readers with Control Difficulties:* Fail to execute control over perceived breakdowns in reading process; root of control difficulty may lie in one or more of the following areas (Hacker, 1998):
- lack knowledge needed to control problems monitored
- have knowledge needed to control problems but lack strategies to apply their knowledge
- have strategies for application but lack conditional knowledge about when and where to apply them
- comprehension and/or control demand too much of reader's memory and other resources
- lack motivation to engage in monitoring

7. *Readers Lacking Specific Topic Knowledge:* Able to decode but trouble making meaning because of weak topic knowledge in particular domain, including vocabulary, specifically in relation to subject of current reading; these readers may attain proficiency in some topic domains.

8. *Sub-Optimal Readers:* No problems with word recognition; limited repertoire of basic comprehension strategies; few higher-level language skills/strategies, such as knowledge of different genres, syntax sophistication, grammar mastery; adequate spelling skills.

9. *Disengaged or Inactive Readers:* Have adequate to advanced knowledge bases, skills, and strategies but lack motivation or sufficient degree of connection with schooling to read; don't make time in their schedules for reading; may also be seen as disaffiliated or disidentified readers.

10. *English Learners:* Includes students in "immersion" programs, English as a Second Language programs; bilingual programs; programs using specially designed academic instruction in English techniques (Unrau, N. [2004]. *Content area reading and writing: Fostering literacies in middle and high school cultures.* Upper Saddle River, NJ: Pearson Education, Inc., 119).

Intake Interview

Adolescents and adults have a keen insight into their literacy strengths and weaknesses from years of personal experience. Instruments like intake interviews are important when gathering preliminary diagnostic information. An interview is a conversation with a clear purpose (Opitz, 2002). There is a diagnostic, though admittedly regrettable, benefit to be achieved in the history of failure in adolescents and adults: They are mature enough to know a great deal about their own histories, and probably have given it considerable thought. This makes the intake interview a most valuable step toward an instructional plan. Interviews often can reveal information that cannot be obtained from most any other type assessment (Opitz, 2002). See Figure 13.1: Adolescent and Adult Literacy Intake Inventory (AALII). Select questions that seem appropriate to the age-grade and life experience of the subject being interviewed. Notice that some questions are quite open-ended, while others are narrowly specific. Interviews do not need to take place in one intensive period, nor is it necessary to maintain a standard structure (Cole, 2002).

> Do a careful Intake Interview . . . adults know a great deal about themselves.

Diagnostic Inventories and Tests

A number of tests and inventories covered in earlier chapters can be useful in diagnosis of adolescent and adult literacy needs if used skillfully. The following are most basic:

1. Informal Reading Inventory—Even though most of these go up only to the 8th reader level, they can serve as good sources of quick assessment of adult/adolescent basic skills in: word recognition and analysis; oral and silent reading comprehension; and listening comprehension.
2. Vocabulary—Some IRIs also contain a survey inventory of vocabulary knowledge; however, a more extensive test of vocabulary knowledge, such as can be found in Appendix A, is recommended for a sampling of vocabulary power to the 16th grade level (college graduates).
3. Capacity Estimates—Where IQ and/or standardized aptitude and achievement tests are not available, the Listening Comprehension subtest of an IRI and the vocabulary test will provide a solid estimate of intellectual/academic exposure and potential. If language background

FIGURE **13.1**

ADOLESCENT AND ADULT LITERACY INTAKE INVENTORY (AALII)

Rapport Setting

1. Tell me about your work history.
2. Tell me about your family. (Who have you/do you live with; siblings; background; primary language?)
3. Are you aware of anyone else in your family with reading problems?
4. Tell me about some typical, or particularly embarrassing problems that have arisen as a result of your reading needs.

Reading History

5. Do you recall any unusual or severe childhood illnesses or injuries? (Hearing; vision: allergies; handicapping conditions?)
6. Have you ever taken IQ and achievement tests? Do you recall your scores? May I request them?
7. Tell me about subjects and teachers that you particularly liked or did not like. (Why?)
8. Do you remember being taught to read? How did that go? What may have gone wrong?
9. Have you been to a reading specialist before? How did that work out?
10. What is your goal in learning to read better now? (Auto license? career advancement? read to kids? overcome embarrassment?)

Specifics of Reading Problems

11. Tell me the things that you *can do* that are reading or reading related. (Alphabet? many sight words? phonics? read newspaper? spelling?)
12. Tell me about the things that you can *not* do that are reading or reading related. (Above, plus: job applications? license examinations? use job manuals?)
13. What have you done/will you do to improve your reading? (Read signs? do homework? ask for help? attend special classes?)
14. Talk about what you are ready to do now to improve your reading and educational status.

Summing Up

Using one (lowest) to seven (highest), estimate student characteristics on each of the following factors:

15. Past motivation
16. Current motivation
17. Resilience
18. Mental abilities
19. Emotional maturity (especially personal responsibility for self and current state)
20. Physical condition

is a consideration, it may be necessary to add a nonverbal "Perceptual Quotient" test, such as the Raven's Progressive Matrices, and/or test in the heritage language.

4. Informal Textbook Inventory (ITI)—The Informal Textbook Inventory, also known as the Content Reading Inventory, is an open book test. It is group-administered and involves assessment and implicit

teaching of basic study skills. Essentially, it asks students to answer an array of questions that help in determining whether they know how to use their course textbooks and related resources effectively. Any question answered incorrectly is indicative of a specific need. This format is an ideal form of diagnostic-teaching since needs are identified and filled in near-simultaneous fashion. See Chapter 4 for further details.

5. Cloze Testing—To get an estimate of a student's ability to read and learn from a particular book, use the Standard Cloze procedure recommended in Chapter 4. This same instrument can be used to determine a student's level of proficiency in recognizing and being able to ride the wave of the redundancy patterns, or frequent phrases, that are inherent to the English language. One way to get an index of second-language students' real potential is to have them silently read and then, either silently or orally, respond to routine comprehension questions on a passage that then is administered as a cloze passage test. The difference between the conventional comprehension test—say, 80%—and the cloze test—say, 40%, or about Frustrational level by the Bormouth criteria, would in this scenario be interpreted to mean that this student has good comprehension, except for the problems associated with trying to learn in a second language. Ask students to identify patterns they may encounter in content texts. This external searching tends to raise consciousness and receptivity to English language patterns, structures, and vocabulary.

PRESCRIPTIONS: DIRECT AND COMPENSATORY

Many of the methods covered in earlier chapters apply to the literacy needs of adolescents and adults. A list follows of methods and means that are particularly suitable for these students. These are based on the proposition that such students tend to need both strategy instruction—independent means of *learning how to learn,* and ongoing scaffolding—*help in learning from text.* This used to be called Compensatory, though now the term has lost favor since some believe it to be an attempt to serve up a watered-down curriculum. Lately, this form of help in learning from a given text is being called Sheltered (Brisk, 1998) and Scaffolded Reading Experience (Fourier & Graves, 2002). Pearson (1996) refers to such scaffolding as most anything that allows the teacher and institution to provide cueing, questioning, coaching, corroboration, and plain old prompts and information when needed to allow a student to complete a task *before* he or she achieves independence. There are many such means and methods. Most can be found in Chapter 10, and in most any good Content Area Reading/Literacy text. Methods and techniques range from cueing systems, to reading/writing/study guides, to text-specific glossaries, to aids built into the page (Embedded Aids and Marginal Gloss). Most of these options are costly and require considerable training and support by the institution, but they also are essential assistance for students who are in the process of acquiring higher-functioning skills at the same time as they are needed to complete immediate course and vocational demands.

Contracts

Since the most difficult obstacle to overcome with adolescents and adults is attendance, it is advisable to draw up a contract with these students that specifies that they will be in attendance, and that further specifies what they will do to aid their own learning. Much of their "inability" to learn can be traced back to a mistaken sense that others are learning easily and incidentally. They do not, as noted above, seem to grasp the significance of their own role in self-teaching, self-regulating, and self-learning. A Contract example is included in Figure 13.2.

Materials

Most anything in print is fair to use as material for teaching reading, since students in this age group are encountering a variety of print in any case. Assistance in learning more about what print addresses, or says, is of considerable compensatory value. Materials may include print sources that

FIGURE 13.2

SAMPLE CONTRACT

I (_____) will attend class every Tuesday and Thursday, be on time, and complete all homework as assigned. I also will make every effort to learn to read on my own by:

1. Reading signs that I come across.
2. Trying to read at least one news story daily and talking with someone about what I have read.
3. Watching and trying to read along with Captioned Television.
4. Identifying at least three new words whose pronunciation or meaning I don't know, and bringing them to class each week.

Signature: _____   Date: _____

strictly speaking are above their Zone of Proximal Development. These might include drivers' manuals, service contracts, prescription warnings, and the like. This said, older students and adults still need practice and instruction at their level of functioning. The primary source for appropriate materials is local librarians. They will have materials on hand that have been designated specifically for such purposes by various grants and local programs. For a one-stop book that is suitable for many of the purposes of teaching adolescents and adults, try *The Reading Teacher's Book of Lists* (Fry, Kress, & Fountkidis, 2000). This handy aid for all reading/language teachers contains lists that are especially suitable to those who need to operate as adults. For example, one called "Near Misses" includes words that often are confused in daily use, and can make one appear foolish: cease and seize; click and clique; confidant and confident. It also contains lists of Proverbs, which are an excellent way of teaching basic reading with higher-level materials.

Specific Methods Described Elsewhere in Text

Several methods discussed elsewhere in this text are suitable to adolescent and adult students. These include:

- Proverbs Mastery Paradigm
- REAP
- About-Point
- KWL+
- Content Reading methods: especially Listen-Read-Discuss; Guided Reading Procedure; Note Cue
- Question-Only
- PASS—Problem Solving Approach to Study Skills
- Self-Discovery Phonics
- Glass Analysis
- Sight Word Paradigm
- Captioned TV
- The Guided Reading Procedure (This procedure, you will recall, teaches students to benefit by a voluntary act of the will, an important lesson for those for whom failing and dropping out is a major cause of continuing personal crisis.)
- Cultural Academic Trivia (Treasures)

Cultural Academic Trivia originally was developed to help adults with GEDs transition to college.

The following method was created in an ABE and Community College environment. Suitable to the secondary level as well, it is a modified form of the Language Experience Approach, or Dictated Story, called the Language-Shaping Paradigm.

Language Experience Approach (LEA) for Adults

The Language Experience Approach (LEA, Ashton-Warner, 1965; Stauffer, 1970), or Dictated Stories, are typically used with children to convert their thoughts, interests, and language into textual material appropriate to their age-grade level. They are, in effect, a means of customizing material to a student's Zone of Proximal Development and interests. The Language-Shaping Paradigm method described below is an adaptation of the LEA that is best used with a small group; however, it also can be used to create, accumulate, and store life episodes for use with students from similar backgrounds and interests. This particular method is oriented toward teaching writing, comprehension, and various aspects of language use. It is inherently diagnostic since it is based on the students' own life experiences and how they have perceived and interpreted experience.

Language-Shaping Paradigm

Two fundamental problems may be encountered in improving adolescent and adult language and writing. The first is to get students to write sufficiently to generate an adequate sample for editing, or shaping. The second is to win students' cooperation in a critical review of the personal patterns of language and thought that their writing reveals.

The basic idea of the *Language-Shaping Paradigm* (Manzo, 1981) is to connect students to the printed page through their own writing, and to create an audience for a piece. This is one of the more important actions to engender focused effort and receptivity to revision and editing: two essential elements of the *writing process*. As collateral values, the method helps students to value and profit from personal thoughts and experiences and to lead more valued and examined lives. It also provides a diagnostic look into a student's interests, life story, and reading-writing needs. It is based on a method called Read and Meet the Author, or RAMA (Santeusanio, 1967). In RAMA, one student's composition is selected, reproduced for the class, and used for a full pre-, during, and post-reading lesson.

The efficacy of the Language-Shaping Paradigm is inferred from a study of the parent, RAMA, and from experience and anecdotal accounts. Santeusanio (1967) found RAMA to be significantly more effective than a control treatment in improving the reading comprehension and writing of adult college students. Our own experience with the Language-Shaping Paradigm has tended to support and extend the generalizability of this approach to other levels, including adult basic education students.

The basic teaching strategy entails having students read an essay that was written (or dictated) by a classmate. Each time the method is used, someone's essay is treated as an important work. The essay is co-edited (by both the teacher and the student-author), and to a lesser extent by class-mates. The edited essay then is reproduced with accompanying exercises designed (largely by the teacher) to improve reading comprehension, language usage, and attention to the craft of creative writing. The steps in this method are shown in Figure 13.3.

The theme shown in Figure 13.4 is the product of a nearly illiterate adult named "Frank" who had enrolled in a night school equivalency program. The story was stimulated by a discussion of dreams and their interpretation: a universal interest. The instructor worked individually with Frank, writing his story for him as Frank dictated it. The other class members wrote their own stories. Frank and the instructor edited the theme together until it was to Frank's liking. Frank took the editorial suggestions in good spirit. The forthcoming "publication" of the written piece seemed to offer its own justification for such straightforward editing and correcting of the more glaring grammatical and logical inconsistencies.

Frank's essay was reproduced for the other students. After an oral comprehension check, using a set of who, what, where, when, how, and why questions, the students did the Language Improvement Exercises (arranged in order of increasing difficulty) illustrated in Figure 13.4.

As a rule, students find the experience of having their stories treated in this respectful and attentive way is transformative on at least two levels that ideally suit the academically unsuccessful student. They learn that they have something worthwhile to say, but also that a good deal of hard work and

> The Language-Shaping Paradigm is an upper-grade version of the Language Experience Story.

> Simple life stories well told can become elevated and enviable.

FIGURE 13.3

STEPS IN THE LANGUAGE-SHAPING PARADIGM

1. The teacher begins with a provocative discussion to establish a purpose for writing.
2. Students write themes in a conventional way (or the teacher writes as the student dictates his or her essay).
3. The teacher selects a student story or essay and edits it jointly with the student-author, informing the student that his or her work will be used for class study.
4. The teacher prepares relatively conventional comprehension questions and language improvement exercises for the material, being sure, however, to add one or two questions that require conjecture and inference to take advantage of the fact that the author will be present to clarify.
5. The teacher duplicates the theme and exercises for the class to read and discuss. The student-author is urged to maintain a "low profile" during this initial discussion.
6. The teacher invites the student-author to participate more openly as the discussion moves to the language improvement exercises. This is the student-author's greatest learning opportunity in terms of writing, speaking, and learning to benefit from constructive criticism (an area of great need in most underachieving students at all levels).

FIGURE **13.4**

LANGUAGE-SHAPING PARADIGM:
STUDENT THEME AND LANGUAGE IMPROVEMENT EXERCISES

"I Dreamed I Was Green"

by Frank X, age 31

1   I fell asleep late last night on the couch in front of my TV. I was watching
an old movie called the "Boy with the green Hair." My Body ached from
another long day. My stomach was now working on the corn beef and
cabbage. Dynamite! The combination made me dream a strange dream.

5   I dreamed that I woke up and had turned green. God, it was so real! At first
I thought it was the light. Then I thought someone was playing a practical
joke on me. But none of those things made sense. The kids were fast asleep
and my wife had not yet come home from her part-time job. She is a ticket
girl at the Waldo. I Called the doctor. The answering service wanted to know

10   what was wrong. I told them. He never called back. I went next door to my
neighbor. Bud. He was shocked. He brought me to the hospital. His wife
watched our kids.

The doctors said there is nothing wrong with you that we can tell, except
that you are definitely green!

15   Now the dream gets all crazy. All I know is that I find myself planted in
the backyard and beginning to look more and more like a tree. Then a lot of
time passes. And the house is old and my wife and kids are gone, but I'm still
in the backyard. No one seems to notice me. I'm not unhappy. I'm not
happy. I'm nothing. I'm just there.

20   Well, that's not really true, about me just being there, I mean. There are
moments when I'm very happy, like when squirrels and birds are playing on
my branches. And I really feel good when I turn beautiful colors in the fall.
And even though I don't like the winter, it's kind of nice to be covered with
blue-white snow.

25   February is the worst. Dark and sad. But then in March I begin to swell
on the inside. I feel life stirring inside me, like a woman does long before anyone even knows she is pregnant. Then April showers and then in May I bust-
out of myself and turn beautiful green.

I woke up at about that time. This may sound crazy, but I was a little dis-

30   appointed that I was not green.

Comprehension and Language Development

Level I: Choosing More Appropriate Words

Sometimes replacing or modifying a few words in a paragraph can greatly enhance the
clarity and sharpness of an essay. Carefully study the paragraph below. Decide which of
the underlined words you would replace from the list of words in the left column.

1   2
I called the doctor. The answering service wanted to know what
was wrong.

3
I told them. He never called back. I went next door to my neighbor,
Bud.

4   5   6
He was shocked. He brought me to the hospital. His wife watched
our kids.

Replacement Words

spoke to	I ___(1)___ the doctor. The answering service ___(2)___ what was
phoned	wrong.
asked	
the doctor	I told them. ___(3)___ never called back. I went next door to my neigh-
Bud	bor, Bud.
drove	
looked after	___(4)___ was shocked. He ___(5)___ me to the hospital. His wife
told	___(6)___ our kids.

Level 2: Improving Style/Mood

"I Dreamed I was Green" is written in a half-humorous, half-serious vein; that is to say, the language is quite casual. Decide which of the sentences below best matches the mood of "I Dreamed I was Green." Underline the words, phrases, and/or punctuation that seem to contribute to, or take away from, that mood. Write "I" for improved, "N" for not improved. (Number 1 is done as an example.)

___N___ 1. I asked the doctor's answering service if they might have an opinion on why I was green.

_____ 2. I called the doctor. Naturally, I got some corny answering service.

_____ 3. You got it! The doc never called back.

_____ 4. I went next door to consult with my neighbor, Bud. He was shocked.

_____ 5. Bud's wife, Martha, volunteered to look after the children while I was at the hospital.

Level 3: Rewriting or Reorganizing

Do *either* A or B:

A. Pretend that you are the author of the article, and rewrite the paragraph between lines 16 and 21 in a way that you believe would improve it.

_____

_____

_____

_____

_____

B. Reorganize: Can you see any means by which this piece can be reordered so that the basic story remains the same but the effect is more imaginative or stylish? (You may rewrite small sections, if necessary, to show what you mean.)

_____

_____

_____

_____

_____

energy goes into effective thinking and expression. There also is something cathartic and ennobling about revisiting life through artistic representation.

Complementary/Supplementary Programs

Many volunteer and federally funded programs exist to aid, assist, and support adolescents and adults seeking tutoring with reading/writing and life management. These include:

- The U.S. Department of Education's Division of Adult Education and Literacy (DAEL), which administers Title II block grants to the States
- National Institute for Literacy, which promotes improved services and research
- The National Center for the Study of Adult Learning, which pursues broad-based research on adult teaching and learning
- National Coalition for Literacy, a consortium of institutions involved in, and advocating for, continuous funding
- The National Center for Family Literacy, which provides technical assistance to family-based projects
- Laubach Literacy Volunteers of America, which operates on the same principle of "each-one-teach-one" that Frank Laubach first used in Africa in the early 20th century

Using the call word "Literacy" on an Internet search engine, many of these programs can be found, with specifications for particular geographic areas and details as to who qualifies and what type of assistance may be available. Many urban school districts have their own programs, as do many local libraries. American corporations also contribute generously to secondary and adult education programs.

Teach-Up

Basic skills programs such as Language! can be an important part of addressing a critical problem. However, such approaches cannot be permitted to totally dominate postelementary education. There is a real affective and cognitive dilemma in fixing functional illiteracy, and "learned helplessness" (minus excessive pity and blaming society) is a term that fairly describes it. The content area teacher cannot be reduced to being a mere teacher of basic skills. This is something that even fleas can tell us.

Try this: Put some fleas in a glass jar with a lid, and observe. At first the fleas will try eagerly to get out, jumping all around and up and down in the jar. After just a few minutes, however, they will no longer hit the lid. Now take the lid off. The fleas will still jump now and then, but they not will jump out of the jar.

The lesson in this mini-experiment is obvious, but bears underscoring. School systems and community colleges must be especially careful about inadvertently creating a glass ceiling of literal level expectations for students by redesignating content teachers as "basic skills" teachers. There is a wealth of ways that they can scaffold learning and incidentally teach basic skills. However, it is just as important to "teach-up" for remedial-level learners as for those who are average and above. Several studies have definitively shown that teaching weaker students to read between and beyond the lines actually boosts their ability to read the lines, or at the literal level (Collins, 1991; Cooter & Flynt, 1986; Haggard, 1976). However, this is not the same thing as saying that those found to be low-functioning are not low-functioning, or that they can do anything if teachers would only challenge or teach them properly. Everyone does better when they are treated as if they are whole and unique, rather than defined by a deficiency. For that matter, judge not by high proficiency either, as in the case of those who are academically gifted but may have areas of need. This may mean that a "diluted curriculum" is a practical necessity. It may well mean reading *A Midsummer Night's Dream* in abridged and language-modified form and having the instructor orally read some parallel passages in Shakespearean and contemporary language. A good deal of word attack, vocabulary, and reading comprehension can be incidentally taught in this way.

Embracing Edutainment

Most everyone now watches a lot of television. Further help for secondary and adult students can be garnered from cable television and Public Broadcasting Systems (PBS) that regularly offer classical plays and novels as part of regular programming. "Edutainment" through mass media is a modern-day curriculum and library containing engaging versions of history, science, literature, and public policy along with lively attention to life-enhancing topics from cooking to travel to decorating small home spaces inexpensively. Today's television can be a subject teacher's great ally beyond the classroom.

Captioned Television

In a related vein, it is notable that most television sets are equipped to provide live "captions"—written transcripts on the screen. While this remarkable technology originally was created to assist the deaf, it also may be used for practice in reading along while listening. This option has been used by some specialists, such as Patricia Koskinen of the University of Maryland, though the details remain fuzzy regarding implementation and measurable

Captioned television can be an older student's untiring tutor.

outcomes. When reading is very weak, so is rate of reading, which makes it difficult to keep up with the dialog in print form. It may be best to encourage limited use, to keep this option fresh and positive.

REVIEW

Secondary and postsecondary education is provided for increasingly more people, from more backgrounds, and with more legally covered handicaps each year. This is the way a democratic society conducts itself. Let's concentrate on innovative ways to meet this challenge, and in so doing, write the next episode of this historical, and unfinished, journey.

(Manzo/Manzo)
Informal Vocabulary Estimator

Percentages identify the proportion of youngsters who know a word and the meaning shown at the grade level indicated. (Adapted from the Dale-O'Rourke lists.) Revised word list from a much broader base with frequency counts will be available online at *www.LiteracyLeaders.com* by Spring 2004.

Grade 3 Word Lists

Score		Word	Word Meaning
1.	74%	accuse	to blame
2.	80%	acrobatic	skilled in gym
3.	89%	adventure	exciting happening
4.	83%	balloon	kind of aircraft
5.	72%	bargain	to discuss prices
6.	94%	camel	humped desert animal
7.	87%	camera	takes pictures
8.	80%	check	an order for money
9.	70%	discuss	talk over
10.	79%	snap	to break suddenly
11.	80%	tender	loving and gentle
12.	85%	election	selection by vote
13.	93%	Eskimo	lives in Arctic north
14.	82%	ferry	a river-crossing boat
15.	84%	fool	to play a trick on
16.	90%	harbor	where ships unload
17.	92%	hobby	favorite fun
18.	83%	hurricane	bad storm
19.	84%	inventor	the one who thought it up
20.	89%	joyful	happy
21.	93%	lazy	won't work
22.	86%	lifeless	dead

23. 89%	lonely	not visited much
24. 86%	loudmouth	talks too much
25. 86%	messy	not neat

Grade 4 Word Lists

SCORE	WORD	WORD MEANING
1. 75%	ball	big dance
2. 77%	band	musical group
3. 75%	banquet	big, formal meal
4. 70%	charcoal	fuel
5. 77%	coffin	case for dead person
6. 86%	collection	things brought together
7. 73%	concert	musical program
8. 67%	continent	land mass, like Asia
9. 74%	desert	very dry land
10. 72%	diamond	expensive jewel
11. 71%	dike	dam
12. 68%	treat	to entertain
13. 67%	temple	place of worship
14. 92%	eagle	large, strong bird
15. 78%	equator	map line dividing earth
16. 68%	forbid	do not allow
17. 67%	foreigner	from another country
18. 68%	forgive	pardon
19. 68%	grassland	pasture land
20. 69%	industrious	hard-working
21. 68%	innocent	free from wrong
22. 69%	manufacture	makes things
23. 70%	mask	to disguise
24. 84%	mightier	more powerful
25. 79%	nasty	not pleasant

Grade 5 Word Lists

SCORE	WORD	WORD MEANING
1. 85%	abolish	get rid of
2. 82%	abuse	treat badly
3. 91%	blackmail	threat of harm
4. 84%	darkroom	photo workshop
5. 83%	daydream	unreal fancies
6. 95%	debate	to discuss
7. 68%	hostage	person held as pledge

8.	93%	empire	countries under one ruler
9.	76%	enthusiastic	very eager
10.	81%	flexible	adapts easily
11.	82%	flutist	a flute player
12.	90%	sculpture	a three-dimensional work of art
13.	85%	fragile	easily broken
14.	85%	furious	very angry
15.	79%	generous	unselfish
16.	80%	heiress	woman inheriting money
17.	76%	horrify	make afraid
18.	80%	hourglass	measures time
19.	82%	icebreaker	kind of ship
20.	87%	ignore	pay no attention to
21.	84%	initial	to mark with first letters of name
22.	76%	inventive	creative
23.	84%	juror	member of a jury
24.	87%	kayak	Eskimo canoe
25.	78%	kerosene	colorless oil

Grade 6 Word Lists

SCORE		WORD	WORD MEANING
1.	71%	acquaint	make familiar
2.	96%	biographer	a writer of life stories
3.	75%	boastful	bragging
4.	77%	Caesar	a dictator
5.	69%	camouflage	disguise
6.	78%	cancel	to destroy the force or effect
7.	68%	canvas	oil painting
8.	68%	caravan	traveling group
9.	73%	dainty	fine and pretty
10.	71%	dazzle	make very bright
11.	71%	editor	corrects writing
12.	67%	eliminate	get rid of
13.	68%	embarrass	make uncomfortable
14.	78%	emigrate	leave own country
15.	75%	fragrant	sweet-smelling
16.	78%	gambler	a person who takes chances
17.	72%	generation	people about the same age
18.	77%	headstone	marker for grave
19.	68%	hilarious	very funny
20.	74%	holy day	a religious holiday
21.	70%	hospitable	friendly to guests
22.	68%	hostage	person held as pledge

23.	70%	hysterical	out of control
24.	74%	luxurious	rich and comfortable
25.	73%	society	group of people

Grade 7 Word Lists

Score		Word	Word Meaning
1.	79%	attack	start work on
2.	78%	catch	get the disease
3.	77%	laborious	requiring hard work
4.	81%	majestic	impressive
5.	83%	manual	book of instruction
6.	78%	mariner	sailor
7.	86%	memorandum	a reminder
8.	87%	mint	money-coining agency
9.	78%	misquote	use another's words incorrectly
10.	83%	mission	church building
11.	92%	mockery	ridicule; scorn
12.	97%	nightmare	a horrid experience
13.	79%	nuclear	atomic
14.	85%	parson	minister
15.	84%	reformatory	prison for youth
16.	84%	regretfully	sadly
17.	77%	scripture	sacred writing
18.	82%	seafaring	traveling on the sea
19.	79%	semicivilized	part savage
20.	73%	sociology	study of society
21.	79%	solar	of the sun
22.	81%	stanza	verse of poem
23.	79%	tender	young and immature
24.	85%	treat	try to cure
25.	89%	snap	to move quickly and smartly

Grade 8 Word Lists

Score		Word	Word Meaning
1.	68%	astound	surprise greatly
2.	69%	befuddle	to confuse
3.	75%	benumb	take away feeling
4.	70%	flourish	thrive
5.	70%	knighthood	rank of knight
6.	76%	legislator	a lawmaker

7.	72%	lyric	poem expressing feeling
8.	74%	microfilm	very small photograph
9.	76%	mischievous	harmful
10.	72%	navigation	steering a boat
11.	73%	notable	worthy of recognition, as in a famous person
12.	72%	notorious	of bad reputation
13.	68%	obituary	death notice
14.	78%	pallbearer	carries coffin
15.	72%	palmist	sees future in hands
16.	79%	password	a pre-arranged sign
17.	68%	pavilion	shelter for short time
18.	75%	peeper	spies on people
19.	67%	Pentagon	Army headquarters
20.	69%	persuasive	convincing
21.	68%	pessimistic	gloomy
22.	70%	racist	believes own race is superior
23.	75%	radiate	shine brightly
24.	72%	reverent	worshipful
25.	76%	Satan	the Devil

Grade 9 Word Lists

Score		Word	Word Meaning
1.	78%	academician	scholar
2.	84%	adolescence	youth
3.	83%	bar	group of lawyers
4.	77%	battery	unlawful attack
5.	78%	campaign	war operation
6.	79%	candlepower	measure of light
7.	79%	cardinal	church officer
8.	81%	deduction	process of reasoning
9.	80%	defame	slander
10.	71%	depressed	lowered
11.	79%	descendants	children
12.	78%	elaborate	give more details
13.	86%	electrometer	measures electric potential
14.	75%	emissary	sent as an agent
15.	83%	formally	in customary manner
16.	77%	fortification	a defense building
17.	80%	forum	an arena, usually for debate or sports; the Roman market
18.	75%	fossil	an artifact so old that it has turned to stone figuratively, an old-fashioned person

19.	89%	genetics	science of heredity
20.	81%	gorge	eat greedily
21.	75%	habitual	regular
22.	77%	hideous	very ugly
23.	79%	identify	to class in a group
24.	79%	illuminate	to explain, make clear
25.	75%	mandatory	compulsory

Grade 10 Word Lists

	SCORE	WORD	WORD MEANING
1.	69%	admirably	excellently
2.	77%	adorn	decorate
3.	72%	Advent	a holy period
4.	70%	backslapper	an overly sociable person
5.	74%	baroness	noblewoman
6.	73%	capitalist	wealthy investor
7.	67%	carnivorous	meat-eating
8.	65%	desegregate	to open to all races
9.	73%	devout	religious
10.	67%	empress	woman ruler of an empire
11.	63%	fiery	easily excited
12.	67%	fiscal	about money
13.	70%	flagship	commander's ship
14.	68%	flowery	full of fancy words
15.	68%	heartfelt	sincere
16.	68%	heroine	main actress
17.	76%	idolatry	worship of images
18.	73%	leak	tell secret information
19.	76%	limerick	nonsense verse
20.	73%	linguist	has language skill
21.	74%	lore	traditions and legends
22.	70%	lynch	to hang unlawfully
23.	74%	Magi	three wise men
24.	67%	malcontent	dissatisfied
25.	70%	matchmaker	helps people get married

Grade 11 Word Lists

	SCORE	WORD	WORD MEANING
1.	85%	abdicate	give up rights
2.	73%	balance	harmony
3.	75%	blaze	brilliant display

4.	78%	bleed	take money by force
5.	77%	cahoots	in partnership
6.	74%	cakewalk	kind of dance
7.	73%	calendar	things to do
8.	80%	cantankerous	never agreeable
9.	93%	debutante	girl entering society
10.	75%	defamation	harming reputation
11.	80%	effigy	image
12.	78%	ego	the conscious self
13.	84%	elaboration	to give more details about
14.	95%	elite	upper class
15.	84%	embark	begin a voyage
16.	74%	fieldpiece	wheeled cannon
17.	78%	flophouse	cheap hotel
18.	83%	gaudy	showy
19.	79%	highwayman	robber
20.	77%	hosanna	a religious cry
21.	77%	humble	not rich
22.	81%	indifferent	not caring
23.	79%	ironical	means opposite of what it says
24.	77%	irrelevant	having no relation
25.	87%	jam	to spoil radio reception

Grade 12 Word Lists

SCORE		WORD	WORD MEANING
1.	72%	abandon	reckless enthusiasm
2.	65%	abbey	group of monks
3.	74%	antagonistic	enemies to each other
4.	68%	bar	legal profession
5.	67%	blight	to frustrate
6.	68%	cadence	rhythmical movement
7.	71%	callous	not sensitive
8.	61%	canticle	a hymn or chant
9.	69%	cantilever	type of bridge
10.	61%	dastard	a mean coward
11.	73%	dauntless	brave
12.	66%	egghead	a professor
13.	75%	electric	exciting
14.	75%	emancipate	set free
15.	64%	fine	the end in music
16.	70%	fishwife	a rough-talking woman
17.	70%	focus	central point

18.	69%	following	supporters
19.	74%	gate	ticket money
20.	68%	gawky	awkward
21.	73%	high-hat	a snob
22.	74%	hit	to criticize sharply
23.	76%	homogenize	to make all parts the same
24.	71%	intelligence	information
25.	71%	invocation	an opening prayer

Grade 13 Word Lists

Score		Word	Word Meaning
1.	84%	loquacious	talkative
2.	76%	manna	food from heaven
3.	75%	matricide	murder of the mother
4.	78%	medium	a means for doing
5.	83%	mercurial	very changeable
6.	83%	nihilist	believes in nothing
7.	73%	nullify	make useless
8.	85%	objective	led by facts
9.	80%	oppressive	very severe
10.	73%	outrage	a shocking offense
11.	88%	predestination	fate
12.	79%	railroad	to force through
13.	75%	recant	withdraw statement
14.	81%	refraction	deflection of light
15.	80%	sector	military area
16.	81%	seditious	stirs rebellion
17.	78%	seismograph	earthquake recorder
18.	74%	tit for tat	return in kind
19.	78%	topflight	the best
20.	79%	tribunal	court of justice
21.	80%	tropic	circle 23.5 degrees from equator
22.	84%	ultra	extreme
23.	76%	undercurrent	hidden tendency
24.	80%	undermine	weaken gradually
25.	88%	unfathomable	can't be understood

Grade 14 Word Lists

Score		Word	Word Meaning
1.	70%	kernel	the essential part
2.	66%	knave	tricky person
3.	72%	larder	food storage place

4.	66%	lethargy	lack of interest
5.	72%	libretto	words of opera
6.	65%	licentiate	holder of permit
7.	69%	magnitude	star's brightness
8.	62%	messianic	believing in future savior
9.	73%	naturalism	represents everyday life
10.	69%	omnivore	eats everything
11.	72%	papacy	Pope's term of office
12.	78%	passe	out of date
13.	65%	perpetuate	to continue
14.	69%	polyglot	has many languages
15.	67%	precursor	forerunner
16.	60%	recapitulation	a review by summary
17.	76%	saucy	disrespectful
18.	73%	schizophrenia	a personality disorder
19.	77%	sectarian	narrow-minded
20.	74%	Teleprompter	shows speech to speaker, usually on TV
21.	66%	tender	to offer
22.	68%	theocracy	government by priests
23.	60%	transcendental	beyond experience
24.	66%	trauma	a damaging shock
25.	73%	underground	secret activity

Grade 15 Word Lists

SCORE		WORD	WORD MEANING
1.	89%	aboriginal	native
2.	84%	absent	not present
3.	92%	adage	proverb
4.	88%	basilica	early form of cathedral
5.	83%	bereavement	feelings associated with loss by death
6.	71%	bestial	very brutal
7.	76%	charge	responsibility
8.	85%	chastisement	punishment
9.	75%	cockle	animal with shell
10.	89%	codify	systematize laws
11.	79%	desecrate	spoil sacred things
12.	94%	differential	distinguishing factors
13.	84%	disseminate	spread far and wide
14.	96%	dissertation	formal discourse
15.	78%	enclave	a surrounded section
16.	79%	euphemism	flowery expression
17.	90%	exploit	take advantage of
18.	75%	Gestalt	structural form or pattern

19.	83%	heliotherapy	sun treatment
20.	81%	hexameter	line in poetry (with 6 metrical feet)
21.	78%	induction	way of reasoning
22.	85%	inflection	variation in word form
23.	73%	lacteal	milky
24.	75%	licentious	not moral
25.	71%	lithe	flexible

Grade 16 Word Lists

SCORE		WORD	WORD MEANING
1.	71%	absolution	forgiveness
2.	67%	abstractionism	modern art style
3.	74%	adulation	excessive praise
4.	71%	bile	ill humor
5.	66%	bully	pushy; overbearing person
6.	68%	chaise	lightweight carriage or lounge chair
7.	72%	cherubim	child angels
8.	71%	clairvoyant	fortune teller
9.	78%	colloid	suspended matter
10.	66%	degenerate	grow worse
11.	60%	disrepute	bad reputation
12.	73%	eureka	triumphant discovery
13.	61%	exponent	believes strongly
14.	65%	fire-eater	bold person
15.	72%	French leave	depart without notice
16.	73%	gladiator	slave fighter
17.	60%	heady	exciting
18.	74%	hydrotherapy	water treatment
19.	71%	imagery	figurative language
20.	67%	immemorial	very old
21.	64%	infirm	weak
22.	61%	lama	a Buddhist monk
23.	79%	litigation	a lawsuit
24.	74%	liturgy	the church service
25.	70%	mandarin	Chinese official

WISC-R Subtest Descriptions and Interpretations

There are separate WISC tests available for very young children and for adults; respectively they are called the Wechsler Preschool and Primary Scale of Intelligence (WPPSI) and the Wechsler Adult Intelligence Scale (WAIS). A brief description follows of the more widely used Subtests of the Wechsler Intelligence Scale for Children-Revised (WISC-R). The WISC-R has 12 subtests, six verbal and six performance

Six Verbal Subtests of the WISC-R

1. Information (30 items). This subtest is composed of a wide spectrum of general information–type questions. It effectively measures "prior knowledge" and aspects of schema, and therefore has a high correlation with reading and academic achievement. It has been found to be significantly influenced by experiential background, memory, auditory deficits, and certain emotional and cultural orientation factors such as intellectual ambition.

2. Similarities (17 items). This subtest is made up of pairs of words. The student is asked to tell how the two things are the same. ("How are an eagle and a pig alike?") This task is very nearly a "pure" measure of abstract verbal reasoning, and is recognized as the best measure of verbal aptitude. Oddly, analogical thinking is a factor that is highly influenced by training, yet few reading programs provide this type of instruction.

3. Arithmetic (18 items). This subtest consists of word problems that are presented orally and must be solved without the use of pencil and paper. Each item is timed and may be repeated only once. Performance on this subtest is affected by attention deficits, intrusive

A careful look at the tasks used on the WISC to assess multiple factors increases realization that teachers have daily access to such data in the form of classroom interactions and assignments; teachers' impressions need to be heeded.

thoughts, computational weaknesses, as well as math and general anxiety. Related training in arithmetic computation often will strengthen test performance and, in fact, provide a more accurate indicator of potential rather than achievement. The Arithmetic subtest is a solid, though often overlooked, predictor of reading and academic success.

4. Vocabulary (32 words). This subtest calls for definitions. Words are arranged in ascending order of difficulty, beginning with concrete and familiar terms and rising to words of greater abstractness and lower frequency of occurrence. Variable credit is given based upon the accuracy and extensiveness of the definitions given. Of all subtests on the WISC-R, Vocabulary has the highest correlation with the Full-Scale IQ score, and is the best predictor of reading and academic success.

5. Comprehension (17 items). This subtest measures social intelligence, and "world view"—the highest stage of literacy, by some accounts (Chall, 1983c). It is not a measure of reading or listening comprehension. It measures common sense reasoning and problem-solving skills ("What would you do if you saw a child alone in a car with the engine running?"). In a manner of speaking, this subtest assesses the primary purpose of going to school: to learn how to learn from experience as well as instruction, to be able to transfer and apply all learnings in a wide variety of circumstances. Scores are affected by cultural opportunity, socialization, inclination to think practically, self-reliance, and overall personal-social maturity. Impulsive students sometimes will do poorly because they are inattentive to the question. Highly compulsive students also tend to do poorly as a result of inability to tolerate ambiguous tasks. This subtest seems similar to reading tasks that require critical and evaluative thinking; however, the writers have looked for this relationship in data from several studies, and have not found strong correlation between the two factors (Manzo & Casale, 1981).

6. Digit Span (14 number series). This subtest is optional, but is almost always included in reading and learning evaluations. It requires the subject to simply repeat, in order, a series of numbers given at 1-per-second intervals. It also requires repeating number series backwards. Forward repetition seems to be a measure of "associative" intelligence and results in even performance among youngsters of all social and ethnic groups, whereas repeating numbers backwards requires a higher level of attention, cognitive operation, and task orientation and shows up in larger differences among various socioeconomic and ethnic/racial groups (Jensen, 1980). It has also been called a measure of stress tolerance and control over intrusive thoughts. This subtest does not have a high correlation with the Full-Scale IQ score, but as suggested above, appears to participate as a sequencing task in early reading development.

Six Performance Subtests of the WISC-R

1. Picture Completion (26 incomplete pictures). The child must study a picture and find some subtle missing element, such as eyelashes on a human face or a hand on a clock. It presumably measures visual discrimination, visual memory, and attention to details. It does not, however, have a high correlation with the Full-Scale IQ score. It seems to be a distinct mental ability that is said to tap into "spatial awareness" (Goldberg, Schiffman, & Bender, 1983). Impulsive children generally tend to do poorly, though some seem to be especially alert and do quite well. Moderately perfectionist students tend to do especially well on this task, as do children with high artistic aptitudes.

2. Picture Arrangement (12 series of comic strip–like pictures). The child, in this subtest, is asked to uncover the story behind a group of pictures and then to arrange the pictures in sequence. There are time limits and credit given for rapid completion. The task requires attention to visual details to reconstruct the plot structure of the story. Generally this task is easily mastered with age, so scoring has been tied to speed of response for children over 8 years old. This subtest is not correlated in any significant way with Full-Scale IQ or school success. Clinicians use the subtest as an opportunity to observe a child doing a comprehension and sequencing task.

3. Block Design (11 two-color designs are constructed from 4, 6, or 9 blocks). The child is shown a geometric design and asked to reproduce it using three-dimensional blocks. This subtest provides the purest measure of abstract, nonverbal intelligence and correlates most highly with the total Performance IQ score. Youngsters with known neurological and severe emotional disorders tend to have their lowest scores on this subtest. Block Design scores are strongly influenced by time limitations, since, given enough time, most youngsters can make most designs. Clinicians tend to use this task to observe whether a child works essentially on a trial-and-error (or bottom-up) basis, or takes a more conceptual (or top-down) approach. (Another excellent test using block design, the Goldstein-Scheerer, 1964, is constructed to further offer opportunity to learn how much support, or cuing, a youngster may need to complete such tasks.)

4. Object Assembly (4 puzzles of familiar objects). The subject is asked to assemble puzzles of familiar objects. Each puzzle assembly is timed, with bonus points for rapid assembly, or partial credit given for incomplete assembly at the end of the time limit. The emphasis on timed performance makes this subtest a measure of rate of learning, more so than power or depth of learning. The task also is said to be a measure of visual-spatial closure skills, and attention to details. As with Block Design, the task is considered most useful for the opportunity it provides to observe trial-and-error versus reflective problem-solving. The subtest also is considered diagnostically useful in identifying organic damage, particularly to the right hemisphere, as well as in detecting serious psychiatric disorders. It does not correlate well with general intelligence, nor with reading, except to a slight degree in young children.

5. Coding (2 different forms, one of 45 symbols for children below 8 years old, another of 95 items for youngsters above 8 years old). Children are asked to use a key to copy the correct symbol into a series of boxes. The task requires rapid copying in a limited time and is another measure of rate of learning, but also of willingness to do a relatively meaningless task. It presumably measures speed of movement, accuracy, visual sequential memory, visual-motor integration, discrimination, and shifting. Depressed scores, relative to other subtests, can be taken as a diagnostic indicator of poor motor coordination, tendency to perseverate (uncontrolled motor persistence), high impulsivity, or inadequate orientation and preparation for doing paper-and-pencil tasks. Coding does not correlate well with Full-Scale IQ, or associative intelligence, but has been called a good predictor of clerical skills.

6. Mazes (an optional test of 9 mazes of increasing difficulty that must be completed without raising the pencil off the paper). This subtest, first developed by Porteus (1956), was intended to be a culturally fair test of IQ. It presumably measures problem-solving ability, and ability to plan ahead before moving. It has relatively weak correlations with Full-Scale IQ and with other subtests. It is useful, however, in getting a more accurate fix on the mental abilities of youngsters with IQs below 95. Observations of children taking the Mazes subtest reveal their ability to understand and follow directions and to learn from one trial to the next. Mazes scores typically will improve purely as a function of having done the task before.

Re-Shuffling WISC Subtests   A. Bannatyne (1974) has suggested that the Wechsler Scales make more sense in educational diagnosis when they are grouped into four categories rather than two. The categories suggested are as follows:

Acquired Knowledge	Information, Vocabulary, Arithmetic
Verbal Conceptualization	Similarities, Vocabulary, Comprehension
Spatial	Picture Completion, Block Design, Object Assembly
Sequential	Arithmetic (again), Digit Span, Coding

Despite the wide use of the WISC, there is no agreed-upon pattern of weakness that has been clearly tied to reading deficiencies. However, a pattern is frequently cited for learning disabilities, and reading deficiencies associated with learning disabilities. Not surprisingly, it also is tied to organicity, or neurological factors. This pattern is referred to as the ACID test. It refers to lower scores in *A*rithmetic, *C*oding, *I*nformation, and *D*igit Span (Kaufman, 1976).

PROVERBS INVENTORY OF ABSTRACT VERBAL REASONING AND COMPREHENSION

Note: This appendix may also be used as exercises for discussion and in diagnostic-teaching. Wherever possible, students should be permitted to silently read and consider options. The words are relatively simple and aural processing can overcomplicate and invalidate the task and therefore neutralize the diagnostic goal of assessing inclination to think abstractly, concretely, emotionally, or just incorrectly.

PART I

Directions: Choose the one that best represents the idea stated. Be sure to read all choices before selecting one. Place an (X) in front of the letter of your choice.

Example:

Look before you leap.

X A. Do not act in haste.

___ B. Watch about you before you jump forward.

___ C. Do not leap, just look.

___ D. We see further in Leap Year due to the extra day.

Answer Key for Questions Below

A = Abstract

C = Concrete

E = Emotional

M = Miscue (simple error)

1. Clothes make the man.

___ (A) A. A proper look brings out proper behavior.

___ (E) B. Don't judge a book by its cover.

___ (C) C. People who dress right tend to be successful.

___ (M) D. A man is what he is no matter how he dresses.

2. Many hands make light work.

___ (C) A. Six hands can often lift what four could not.

___ (M) B. Many helpers lead to much confusion.

___ (E) C. Light work requires many hands.

___ (A) D. Cooperation brings relief.

3. When the cat's away, the mice will play.

___ (C) A. When cats are not around, mice can have a good time.

___ (E) B. Don't trust people who stare at you.

___ (A) C. Some people can only be good when they are afraid to be bad.

___ (M) D. Mice can play when cats are around.

4. You can't have your cake and eat it too.

___ (C) A. You can't save money and spend it too.

___ (M) B. It is better to eat cake than to save it.

___ (A) C. Most every choice has its cost.

___ (E) D. Don't risk the price—make no choice.

5. If you can't stand the heat, get out of the kitchen.

___ (C) A. If the heat in a room bothers you, go to another.

___ (E) B. The kitchen is often the hottest room in a house.

___ (M) C. Heat can make you sick, so get going.

___ (A) D. If you want the best of something, expect to pay the price.

6. It is no use crying over spilt milk.

___ (C) A. Do not cry when you spill your milk.

___ (E) B. Avoid getting upset over little things.

___ (A) C. Do not get upset over things you cannot fix.

___ (M) D. Crying is not good, but being careful is.

7. Too many cooks can spoil the broth.

___ (M) A. Do not permit too many people into the kitchen.

___ (C) B. Many things are done better by one person.

___ (A) C. Work can be ruined by too many people and too many opinions.

___ (E) D. Many hands make light work.

8. When angry, count to ten.

___ (A) A. Delay is one remedy for anger.

___ (C) B. If you are upset, then you should count to ten to calm down.

___ (M) C. It is harmful to hold in your feelings.

___ (E) D. Haste makes waste.

9. East, West, home is best.

___ (A) A. There is no place like home.

___ (M) B. There are many hurricanes on the east and the west coasts.

___ (C) C. Once you have been east and west, then you know that home is best.

___ (E) D. When you cannot go east or west, then home is best.

10. The restless sleeper blames the couch.

___ (M) A. There is fault in every person.

___ (A) B. Where fault is concerned, look first within.

___ (C) C. The person who sleeps poorly says the couch was bad.

___ (E) D. Couches make for restless sleep.

11. Out of sight, out of mind.

___ (A) A. Immediate needs tend to get attention.

___ (M) B. Old friends are soon forgotten.

___ (C) C. The mind depends on sight for all it does.

___ (E) D. Things not seen are things not thought of.

12. You grow up the day you have the first real laugh—at yourself.

___ (C) A. Don't take yourself too seriously.

___ (A) B. Maturity comes from recognizing acts of immaturity.

___ (E) C. Laughing is emotional release.

___ (M) D. Stop laughing and you will start crying.

13. Don't bite off more than you can chew.

____ (C) A. It is difficult to chew when your mouth is stuffed.

____ (M) B. Don't swallow without chewing.

____ (E) C. Take risks, it is worth the price.

____ (A) D. Stretch your feet as far as your sheet will cover.

14. Give a boy a fish and feed him for a day. Teach him how to fish and feed him for life.

____ (C) A. Someone chopping wood can be better off than someone receiving it.

____ (A) B. Giving spoils, helping strengthens.

____ (E) C. The hungry are better left unfed.

____ (M) D. Children must be taught how to eat fish.

15. Barking dogs seldom bite.

____ (E) A. Don't do all the talking.

____ (M) B. See someone who looks very angry.

____ (C) C. Those who yell, seldom hit.

____ (A) D. Those who brag usually can't live up to it.

16. Once bitten, twice shy.

____ (C) A. Once a child has learned that something might cause pain, he will avoid things like it in the future.

____ (A) B. A person who has been tricked is more careful.

____ (M) C. The child who likes to bite is always very shy.

____ (E) D. People do not like to be faced with their problems.

17. You do not teach the paths of the forest to an old gorilla.

____ (A) A. Experience can teach what words can hardly describe.

____ (C) B. Animals know things by instinct, and instincts are best.

____ (E) C. You can't teach an old dog new tricks.

____ (M) D. The older animal certainly knows the forest.

18. A prosperous fool is a great burden.

____ (C) A. Good fortune sometimes goes to fools and wrong-doers.

____ (E) B. It is difficult to argue with those who have the look of success.

____ (M) C. A prosperous person carries a fool's burden.

____ (A) D. A fool with money can get away with a lot.

19. All cruelty springs from weakness.

___ (E) A. Weakness makes for kindness.

___ (A) B. He struck first because his fear was greater.

___ (C) C. Beware of weakness.

___ (M) D. Cruelty can be found in everyone.

20. No author is a man of genius to his publisher.

___ (E) A. Publishers see errors and therefore weaknesses in the best of writers.

___ (M) B. Those who cannot are quick to find the flaws in those who can.

___ (C) C. Mothers know weaknesses in children better than anyone else ever could.

___ (A) D. Writing is a plunge into the unknown; no one can do it perfectly.

21. You can't lead anyone farther than you have gone yourself.

___ (C) A. You can't take others where you have not been.

___ (E) B. Good leaders go farther.

___ (A) C. Improve yourself first, and then others.

___ (M) D. If you haven't been bad, you can't be good.

22. Birds of a feather flock together.

___ (A) A. We tend to be friends with those who think as we do.

___ (C) B. Birds of the same color stay together.

___ (E) C. Beware of the bird that stands alone.

___ (M) D. Birds that stay together are flocking.

23. When life hands you a lemon, make lemonade.

___ (C) A. In life, lemons can be used to make lemonade.

___ (A) B. There's often a brighter side, if you look for it.

___ (E) C. Life is more like a lemon than like lemonade.

___ (M) D. In life you can make lemons or lemonade.

24. There is nothing either good or bad, but thinking makes it so.

___ (A) A. Nature happens, mankind appraises.

___ (M) B. It is written, what is good or bad.

___ (C) C. Behavior cannot be judged without examination of motives.

___ (E) D. What is good is what we value.

25. Brevity is the soul of wit.

___ (M) A. Be brief and have wit.

___ (C) B. Witty sayings use few words.

___ (A) C. Where cleverness is concerned, less is more.

___ (E) D. The heart of wit is cunning.

26. Cast pearls before swine.

___ (E) A. Every form of life is worth something.

___ (M) B. Offer something valuable to someone who is poor.

___ (C) C. To throw pearls to a pig is foolish.

___ (A) D. It is useless to say wise things to those who are not ready to hear.

27. Rome was not built in a day.

___ (M) A. Some jobs are just too big.

___ (C) B. Great cities like Rome took workers years to build.

___ (A) C. Keep your goal in sight.

___ (E) D. You cannot do anything all at once.

28. When in Rome, do as the Romans do.

___ (E) A. Romans are warlike people. If you do not do things their way, you will be in trouble.

___ (C) B. When you go to Rome, eat, sleep, and play like Romans.

___ (M) C. If you go to Rome, try to blend in.

___ (A) D. Adapt your conduct to the situation.

29. You can take a horse to water but you can't make him drink.

___ (M) A. You can show someone something but it doesn't mean he or she understands.

___ (C) B. A horse does not have to drink just because you offer him water.

___ (A) C. Giving someone an opportunity is no guarantee he or she will choose to try it.

___ (E) D. There are many times when people will not do what you want, and then you must force them to do so.

30. The squeaking wheel gets the grease.

___ (E) A. Silence can be like a scream.

___ (C) B. Loud children get the love and attention.

___ (A) C. Non-complaint gets non-results.

___ (M) D. Wheels need grease to roll smoothly.

31. All that glitters is not gold.

___ (E) A. Glitter is the downfall of mankind.

___ (M) B. Not all gold glitters.

___ (C) C. Things other than gold can glitter.

___ (A) D. Looks can deceive.

32. Where there's smoke there's fire.

___ (E) A. It's hard to cover up mistakes.

___ (C) B. With fire often is smoke.

___ (A) C. Signs of trouble usually mean that there is trouble.

___ (M) D. Let sleeping dogs lie.

33. Still waters run deep.

___ (C) A. When water is deep it does not move quickly.

___ (A) B. Lack of speech doesn't mean lack of thought.

___ (E) C. Some people think more than they say.

___ (M) D. Still waters are used in alcohol making.

34. Mediocre men often have the most acquired knowledge.

___ (E) A. "C" students are more practical than "A" students.

___ (M) B. Facts change minds—not words.

___ (A) C. Lesser minds can store but cannot create new knowledge.

___ (C) D. Knowledge of many facts does not make a person wise.

35. Better to die on your feet than live on your knees.

___ (C) A. It is better to die standing than live kneeling.

___ (M) B. If forced to fight, you should give your all.

___ (E) C. Feet or knees, we all must die.

___ (A) D. Freedom can cost a lot.

36. Happy is the man who can enjoy the scenery when he has to take a detour.

___ (M) A. Detours sometimes have enjoyable scenery.

___ (E) B. Be smart: Avoid detours.

___ (A) C. Difficulty must be expected: Make the best of it.

___ (C) D. Sometimes a detour can be more pleasant than the original route.

37. He who will not where he may, when he will shall have nay.

___ (A) A. Be open to opportunity.

___ (E) B. The chance to say no is a chance to grow.

___ (C) C. If you do not do a thing when there is opportunity, you may not get to do it at all.

___ (M) D. Act in haste, pay in leisure.

38. Temper the wind to the shorn lamb.

___ (C) A. Give shelter to shaved lambs.

___ (E) B. Bad temper scares the meek.

___ (M) C. Control sheep in a storm.

___ (A) D. Adopt gentle methods to get things done.

39. One should not wash one's dirty linen in public.

___ (A) A. Personal matters are best kept personal.

___ (C) B. It is not right to wash in front of others.

___ (E) C. Secrets should be exposed in public.

___ (M) D. Linen rarely needs to be washed after one use.

40. The grass is always greener on the other side of the fence.

___ (C) A. A neighbor's grass often looks better than yours, because you cannot see its flaws.

___ (E) B. Your efforts will make your neighbor richer.

___ (M) C. There are two sides to everything.

___ (A) D. The things we see often look better than the things we have.

41. He who laughs last, laughs longest.

___ (C) A. If you are the last person to begin to laugh, you will be the last one to finish laughing.

___ (M) B. If you want to laugh best, always laugh loud.

___ (A) C. Be careful not to celebrate a victory until you are sure you have won.

___ (E) D. Laughing is important, always have a sense of humor.

42. You can catch more flies with honey than you can with vinegar.

___ (C) A. Flies are attracted to honey, not to vinegar.

___ (E) B. To get what you want, you sometimes have to be tricky.

___ (M) C. To get a job done right, use the right tools.

___ (A) D. You can get further by being thoughtful than by being demanding.

43. Out of the frying pan and into the fire.

___ (C) A. You no sooner solve one problem and another one comes up. That's life!

___ (M) B. Sometimes mistakes cannot be corrected.

___ (E) C. Trying to hide your mistakes can be dangerous.

___ (A) D. Some solutions are worse than the problem.

44. The used key is always brightest.

___ (C) A. Metal gets shiny from being touched.

___ (M) B. Something old is better than something new.

___ (A) C. One who is always making himself useful usually amounts to something.

___ (E) D. To be bright, you need the key.

45. Improve yourself today, your friends tomorrow.

___ (C) A. Improve yourself before trying to improve your friends.

___ (M) B. Pointing out the faults of your friends will strengthen them and you.

___ (A) C. If something is wrong, look within yourself first for a reason.

___ (E) D. Friends don't always appreciate advice.

PART II

Directions: Select the statement which is most nearly the **opposite** of the first stated idea. Place an (X) in front of the letter of your choice.

Example:

Clothes make the man.

___ A. Great bodies move slowly.

X B. Don't judge a book by its cover.

___ C. The more cost, the more honor.

___ D. New things are fine to look at.

46. Like to like.

___ (E) A. One must draw a line somewhere.

___ (A) B. Opposites attract.

___ (M) C. Live and let live.

___ (M) D. Money makes money.

47. Revenge is sweet.

___ (A) A. Two wrongs don't make a right.

___ (E) B. One man's meat is another man's poison.

___ (M) C. Don't cry over spilled milk.

___ (M) D. There is no easy road to learning.

48. Out of sight, out of mind.

___ (M) A. There is time to speak and time to be silent.

___ (M) B. Silence gives consent.

___ (M) C. A friend to all is a friend to none.

___ (A) D. Absence makes the heart grow fonder.

49. Spare the rod and spoil the child.

___ (A) A. Boys will be boys.

___ (E) B. A stick is quickly found to beat a dog with.

___ (E) C. Laugh before breakfast, and you'll cry before supper.

___ (M) D. Better to be safe than sorry.

50. Never trouble trouble till trouble troubles you.

___ (M) A. Do not cross the bridge till you come to it.

___ (M) B. Truth is stranger than fiction.

___ (A) C. Forewarned is forearmed.

___ (M) D. Don't let the sun go down on your anger.

COGNITIVE-AFFECTIVE FILTER INVENTORY*

SCORING AND INTERPRETATION

Overview   The CAFI uses a highly structured metaphor, based on levels of identification with selected animals to infer possible psychological trait characteristics. It is a projective test based on the assumption that most common associations have high face validity of (symbolic) characteristics that can be safely interpreted into provisional impressions of the inner sentiments of the person expressing different levels of identification, in this case with selected animals. The psychological associations were established by counting the most frequent "free" associations made by about 400 experimental subjects (ages 7 to 32). Further information on some of these same subjects permitted the creation of a matrix indicating degrees of correlation of animal choices with certain academic performance indicators.

Validity and Reliability   The likely reliability of each test administration can be estimated by comparing the responses made on the three animals that are repeated: horse, squirrel, and pheasant. Ideally, responses should not differ by more than 1 point. If responses are found to vary more greatly, exercise even greater caution in drawing firm conclusions.

Several studies of the CAFI have provided a rich database for interpretation of test protocols for classroom and school use. A good deal is known, for example, about the relationship of animal choices to several aspects of academic skills, interests, and abilities. These are listed ahead. First, however, consider the different levels of interpretation of the CAFI. These parallel the Luscher Color Test,[†] from which it derives its structure and construct and concurrent validity.

---

*Formerly the Manzo Bestiary Inventory.

[†]Max Luscher. (1948). Test-Verlag, Basel, Switzerland. Translated from German by Ian A. Scott. (1969). New York: Random House.

Levels of Interpretation

A CAFI protocol can be interpreted on several levels. In general, the order of preference of choices offers the most stable and predictive meanings. Here is a guideline for interpreting order of preference.

> **First-Level Choices:** Describes the "Ideal Self," or what the student most wants to be or tries to be
>
> **Second-Level Choices:** Describes the "Typical Self," or the way the student usually behaves and expresses feelings
>
> **Third-Level Choices:** Describes the "Restrained Self," or behavior and feelings reserved for triggering occasions (such as stress, anger, or high ambition)
>
> **Rejections:** Describes the "Feared Self," or the way the student does not want to be, or fears to be (but may occasionally lapse into)

Generally, choice "levels" may simply be: first level = first and second choice; second level = third and fourth choice; and third level = fifth and sixth choice. However, in some cases, it may be more appropriate to determine levels according to clear patterns: for example, if the top two or three choices are similar animals (such as eagle and falcon), these should be grouped together.

The chart that follows provides adjective descriptors for each animal, and key associations and information on school-related and other factors also found to be associated with each animal identification. For example, youngsters who have strong identification with "dog" have been found to profit more readily from attention and remediation, but tend to lack self-initiative. Students who identify with "eagle" tend to have strong verbal comprehension and vocabulary but also tend to be aloof, impractical, fragile, and somewhat cunning.

A good deal is also known about the type and level of motivation associated with most of the animals on the inventory. *"Aversive"* motivation is an externally directed desire to avoid negative consequences. Some forms of "aversive motivation," or intense fear of consequences, such as fear of failure, may lead to superficial levels of success, usually in the form of good grades but poor abstract and evaluative thinking. Strong identification with "chicken" is correlated to a high level of aversive motivation. Conversely, *"Appetitive"* motivation is an internally directed desire to achieve personal goals, irrespective of externally controlled reward systems. Identification with "lion" is strongly correlated to high-appetitive and low-aversive motivation. Some identifications indicate high levels of both types of motivation ("eagle") or low levels of both ("moose"). Two animal identifications tend to be most indicative of hyperemotionality and poor personal-social adjustment: "snake" and "alligator."

   A word of caution: Should you decide to talk to youngsters or their parents or other teachers about your findings, be sure to stress that the CAFI was used as an initial, or "eye-opening" tool, to help in understanding the reader as well as his or her reading. Ultimately, you will need to further verify, refute, or add to the findings from the inventory with specific examples of observed behavior and/or with information derived from other tests and other persons.

SELECTED WORD ASSOCIATIONS AND KEY FACTORS SIGNIFICANTLY CORRELATED TO CAFI ANIMAL IDENTIFICATIONS

ANIMAL	ADJECTIVALS		OTHER FINDINGS	
1. alligator	powerful ruthless cunning	dangerous mean	male defensive	hostile unstable
2. badger	aggressive unfriendly stubborn	sneaky offensive	male strong vocabulary high aversive motivation	
3. chicken	cackling follower coward	dumb flighty	high cloze performance high aversive motivation	
4. cow	slow lazy big	serene dumb	emotionally dependent weak comprehension low appetitive and aversive motivation	
5. coyote	howling scavenger cunning	loner sneaky		
6. dog	loyal affectionate	lovable frisky	benefit from remediation high vocational aspirations	

7. dove	peaceful graceful free	gentle quiet	strong cloze performance female
8. duck	noisy follower foolish	playful cute	weak writing skills
9. eagle	soaring proud alone	bold courageous	strong comprehension strong vocabulary emotionally distant high aversive and appetitive motivation
10. elephant	big powerful gentle	strong awkward	helpful well-behaved low aversive motivation
11. falcon	soaring fierce majestic	predatory aggressive	male high appetitive motivation high aversive motivation
12. fox	sly smart fast	clever sneaky	strong vocabulary high aversive motivation moderate appetitive
13. giraffe	tall quiet friendly	gentle passive	strong cloze performance weak comprehension female no benefit from remediation high aversive motivation moderate appetitive motivation
14. goat	smelly destructive	stubborn dumb	emotionally unstable high aversive motivation moderate appetitive motivation
15. hippopotamus	enormous homely dull	lazy dumb	no benefit from remediation high aversive motivation
16. hog	dirty gross unimaginative	fat dumb	emotionally unstable weak comprehension
17. horse	strong thoroughbred noble	spirited proud	female good comprehension high appetitive motivation

18. leopard	stalking sleek fearless	cunning silent	weak writing skills strong cloze performance high appetitive and aversive motivation
19. lion	majestic leader dominant	proud powerful	weak writing skills emotionally strong high appetitive motivation low aversive motivation
20. mink	furry scurrying elegant	small beautiful	female weak comprehension high aversive motivation
21. moose	big towering	powerful awkward	male low aversive motivation low appetitive motivation
22. owl	wise self-assured haughty	watchful silent	high aversive motivation
23. peacock	beautiful arrogant vain	proud regal	female high aversive motivation moderate appetitive motivation
24. penguin	amusing friendly gregarious	cute distinguished	strong cloze performance female
25. pheasant	colorful proud alert	wild graceful	weak writing skills
26. porpoise	smart friendly helpful	playful gentle	strong comprehension strong cloze performance emotionally stable low aversive motivation
27. rooster	cocky aggressive leader	arrogant chauvinistic	high aversive motivation moderate appetitive
28. snake	slithering ugly	deadly evil	weak comprehension no benefit from remediation male emotionally unstable high aversive motivation

29. squirrel	frisky hoarder cute	industrious nervous	weak cloze performance no benefit from remediation high aversive motivation
30. swan	graceful dignified lovely	beautiful quiet	female high aversive motivation moderate appetitive motivation
31. tiger	fierce free dominant	proud brave	strong comprehension high aversive motivation high appetitive motivation
32. turtle	slow cautious quiet	steady patient	high aversive motivation
33. wolf	sly savage resourceful	wild fast	male weak cloze performance weak writing skills high aversive motivation moderate appetitive motivation

A Primer on Phonics*

Definitions

Phonics	the sound-symbol associations and generalizations that facilitate decoding
Phoneme	the smallest unit of sound in a language; each of these words contains 3 morphemes: hat, hate, freight, sly
Grapheme	a written symbol for a phoneme; a grapheme may be composed of 1 or more letters, and the same grapheme may represent more than 1 phoneme. The 26 letters of the alphabet in their various combinations form 251 graphemes that represent from 44 to 46 phonemes.
Morpheme	the smallest *meaningful* part of a word; *ed* in jumped, *s* in flowers, *ing* in running, as well as single words such as cup, hat, cabinet
Vowel	the letters *a, e, i, o,* and *u;* the letters *w* and *y* take on the characteristics of vowels when they appear in the final position in a word or syllable; the letter *y* also has the characteristics of a vowel in the medial (middle) position in a word or syllable
Consonant	the letters other than *a, e, i, o,* and *u* generally represent consonant sounds. The letters *w* and *y* have the characteristics of consonants when they appear in the initial position in a word or syllable.
Consonant digraph	two adjacent consonants that represent a single sound; *sh* in shore

---

*Assembled and adapted from previous works by: Anna Cordts (1965), Marion Hull (1976), Manzo & Manzo (1993), and Burns, Roe, & Smith (2002).

Consonant blend	(or cluster) two or more adjacent consonants that produce a blended sound, with each individual sound retaining its identity; *str* in strike, *fr* in frame, *cl* in click
Vowel digraph	two adjacent vowel letters that represent a single speech sound; in the word foot, *oo* is a vowel digraph
Diphthong	two adjacent vowels that produce a blended sound, with each vowel retaining part of its own identity (a diphthong is a vowel blend); *ou* in out
Syllable	the basic unit of pronunciation. There are as many syllables in a word as there are separate vowel sounds; there is only one vowel phoneme in a syllable.
Accented syllable	the syllable that receives the greatest emphasis in the pronunciation of a word (di'-gest; char'-ac-ter)
Closed syllables	syllables that end with a consonant phoneme (*sup* in sup-pose'); the vowel in a closed syllable usually has its short sound
Open syllable	a syllable that ends with a vowel phoneme (*fe* in fe'-ver); the vowel in an open syllable usually has its long sound.
Diacritical mark	a mark used to indicate how to pronounce a word or group of letters
Macron	a diacritical mark (*as in iron*) used to indicate the long sound of a vowel. The long sound of each vowel is its alphabet name.
Breve	a diacritical mark (ˇ)used to indicate the short sound of a vowel, as *a* in hat, and *e* in red
Schwa	the sound "uh," as taken by the vowel in the unaccented syllable(s) in most words, as in the first and last "a" in America. An "upside-down e" (ə) is the diacritical mark used to represent the schwa sound.
Onset	the part of a one-syllable word that comes before the vowel
Rime	the part of a one-syllable word that comes after the onset (vowel plus word ending sound). Nearly 500 words can be made from the following 37 rimes:

ack	ank	aw	ick	ing	op
ain	ap	ay	ide	ink	ore
ake	ap	eat	ight	ip	uck
ale	ash	ell	ill	ir	ug
all	at	est	in	ock	ump
ame	ate	ice	ine	oke	unk
an					

SOUNDS

Consonant sounds

b	ball	*l*	lake	*t*	teacher
c	cat	*m*	monkey	*v*	vase
d	dog	*n*	nice	*w*	wagon
g	go	*p*	pear	*x*	box
h	hat	*q*	queen	*y*	yellow
j	jug	*r*	race	*z*	zebra
k	king	*s*	seven		

Vowels—short sounds

a apple   *e* elephant   *i* Indian   *o* orange   *u* umbrella

Vowels—long sounds

a take   *e* eat   *i* ice   *o* open   *u* use

Vowels—r-controlled

far   her   dirt   more   fur

Consonants with two or more sounds

c	consonant	*g*	got	*s*	six	*x*	xylophone
c	city	*g*	gyrate	*s*	is	*x*	exist
				s	sure	*x*	box

Consonant blends—initial position

bl	blue	*gr*	grow	*sw*	swim
br	bring	*pl*	play	*tr*	tree
cl	clap	*pr*	pretty	*tw*	twenty
cr	cry	*sc*	score	*wr*	wreck
dr	drink	*sk*	sky	*sch*	school
dw	dwell	*sl*	slip	*scr*	scream
fl	fly	*sm*	smell	*shr*	shrimp
fr	fry	*sn*	snow	*spl*	splash
gl	glass	*sp*	spot	*spr*	spring
gr	grass	*st*	stop	*thr*	through

Consonant blends—final position

ld child   *mp* camp   *nd* send   *nt* sent   *sk* risk

Consonant digraphs—regular

ch church   *sh* ship   *th* that   *wh* when

Consonant digraphs—variant

ch character   *gh* enough   *ph* phone

Diphthongs

oi boil   *ou* out   *ow* cow   *oy* toy

Phonics generalization, with percent utility based on Clymer's study of number of conforming words and number of exceptions

1. When *ck* are the last two letters in a word, the sound of *k* is given (check, brick) (100%)
2. When *kn* are the first two letters in a word, the *k* is not sounded (know, knight) (100%)
3. When *wr* are the first two letters in a word, the *w* is not sounded (write, wrong) (100%)
4. When *ght* is seen in a word, *gh* is silent (fight) (100%)
5. The double *e* grapheme usually takes its long sound (seem) (98%)
6. When two like consonants are next to each other, only one is sounded (hall, glass) (99%)
7. When *c* and *h* are next to each other they make only one sound (100%); usually the sound in church (95%), although it sometimes sounds like *sh* (machine) or *k* (chemistry; chord)
8. When *a* is followed by *r* and a final *e*, we can expect to hear the sound heard in care (90%)
9. When the letters *c* and *g* are followed by *e, i,* or *y,* they generally have soft sounds: the *s* sound for the letter *c* and the *j* sound for the letter *g* (cent, city, cycle, gem, ginger, gypsy). When *c* and *g* are followed by *o, a,* or *u,* they generally have hard sounds: *g* has its own special sound, and *c* has the sound of *k* (cat, cake, go, game, gum) (100% for hard sound of *c* rule; 96% for soft *c* rule; 64% for soft *g* rule)
10. When *y* is the final letter in a word, it usually has a vowel sound (dry) (84%)

11. In the vowel combinations *oa, ea, ai, ay,* the first vowel is generally long and the second one is not sounded. This may also apply to other double-vowel combinations (boat, feet, rain, play); *"When two vowels go walking, the first does the talking"* (*oa*—97%, *ea*—66%, *ai*—64%, *ay*—78%)

12. The sound of a vowel preceding *r* is usually neither long nor short (car, fir, her); this is referred to as an *"r-controlled vowel"* (78%)

13. The vowel in an open syllable usually takes its long sound (74%)

14. The vowel in a closed syllable usually takes its short sound (62%)

15. When *i* is followed by *gh,* or when *i* or *o* is followed by *ld,* the vowel usually represents its long sound (71%)

16. If a word has two vowels and one is a final *e,* the first vowel is usually long and the final *e* is not sounded (cape, cute, cove, kite); this is referred to as the *"silent e"* or *"magic e"* rule (63%)

Masquerading Symptoms: Severe Reading Disability as Conversion Reaction Syndrome (CRS)

Conversion Reaction Syndrome (CRS)

CRS is said to be a subconscious process by which deep emotional conflicts or fears which otherwise would give rise to considerable anxiety are disowned or reduced in intensity by converting them into an external expression of some type. This results in a feeling of detachment, which may appear as relaxed indifference toward the (symbolic) problem—or *la belle indifference.* This condition has been found in some dyslexics and in some persons with specific neurological damage. Denckla (1972), for example, identified a subtype of dyslexics that she called a "dyscontrol" group because they were "sweet, sloppy, and silly." Satz and Morris (1981), and Lyon and Watson (1981) also have identified subgroups of dyslexics who have related "motivational and emotional" problems. Curiously, a similar form of indifference has been found in patients with right-hemisphere damage: They seem indifferent to the point of denial of other severe symptoms of physical illness (Segalowitz, 1983, 215).

Similarly, the CRS condition seems to arise when a deep conflict is converted to a form which symbolically represents the repressed ideas or repressing forces, whatever these might be. Examples of some typical child-centered fears and conflicts would include:

- fear of the parents' learning of the child's "intellectual inadequacy" relative to excessive parental expectations;
- fears related to revelations about premature sexual interests, activity, abuse, or gender confusion; and
- fear that a family might break up without some crisis to hold it together.

Consider now the symbolic meaning of reading. Reading generally symbolizes growing up and being responsible. The knowledge, insights, and universal truths it brings are supposed to help one face complex issues. But sometimes a child is faced with an issue that appears bigger than life, one so insurmountable that it seems best to deny it. In order for denial—a fundamental defense mechanism—to be complete, and for life to go on, the problem must be converted or restructured into something less intrusive in the child's life and more acceptable to public attention.

This syndrome tends to take either of two forms: One called Somatic Conversions typically results in the apparent loss of control over fundamental voluntary muscles (Laughlin, 1967); an example there is the conflict experienced by the soldier who wishes to be brave and yet fears dying. Repression of the fear leads to a heightened anxiety level. Sensing that he or she might be near hysteria or likely to faint, the soldier subconsciously converts the repressed desire to run away into a psychologically saving illness or incapacitation, such as loss of control of the muscles in the legs which carry one to battle.

A similar condition can occur physiologically to involuntary muscles and functions. In these cases, so-called organ (or vegetative) difficulties occur. These tend to incapacitate or delimit sensory awareness, resulting in apparent losses or distortions of vision, hearing, speech, and the like. These incapacities sound and look remarkably like the word reversals, semantic paralexics (word distortions), auditory discrimination problems, speech impediments, and (odd and indeterminate) visual problems, that have been found to be associated with some reading and learning disabilities. The possible connection between these two sets of conditions is made clearer when the next two ideas are considered.

Substitution and Net Gain

Both somatic and physiologic conversion conditions become an alternate, or surrogate, expression of the deeper repressed conflict or nagging problem. This substitution can serve several useful purposes for the person who is disabled.

The student who is diagnosed as dyslexic, particularly the preteen whose life is largely influenced by parental rather than peer dynamics, can win considerable attention from his parents while reducing his or her preoccupation with the true emotional conflict (whatever it might be), and do so at the relatively small inconvenience of simply not being able to read. This is known as an "endogain." That is, a *net* gain arising from what seems, on the surface, to be a negative condition or liability.

In the case of dyslexia, the parents also are inconvenienced and made to feel guilty. In this way, the child's problem is passed on to the parents, who not only bear the student's pain but must wonder what in them may have created the disorder—even to the point of feeling guilt about whether they have transmitted damaging genes (and that is not to say that some have not).

Further, the child not only (net) gains the attention of his parents but the outside assistance and empathy of teachers, doctors, and other specialists in resolving the symbolic, or surrogate problem. More importantly, hope of resolving the real problem is kept alive by those pressed into service to work on its symbolic representation.

In brief, a learning disability such as dyslexia can provide several possible "endogains" for a troubled child:

- It can sharply reduce anxiety and pressure to resolve a difficult personal problem.
- It can win the assistance and empathy of many adults.
- It offers the hope of resolving the real, or repressed, problem through extensive examination and consideration given to the surrogate problem.

Diagnostic Indicators of CRS

There are six diagnostic indicators of psychologically induced dyslexia or learning disability. Three or more would provide fairly telling evidence of this condition.

1. Considerable emotional gain from an apparent negative condition, or liability
2. Evidence of generative learning in most areas other than reading, or whatever the specific disability might happen to be
3. A logically inconsistent or unreliable pattern of errors on an IRI, miscue analysis, or reading test battery; for example, strong comprehension/weak vocabulary; or the inverse
4. Reversal of subtest scores on standardized tests, from one testing to the next (for example, high Verbal/low Performance one time, low Performance/high Verbal another)
5. A look of relaxed, resigned indifference to the disability (*la belle indifference* condition)
6. If learning can be greatly accelerated with an essentially placebo ("No Treatment") treatment

Clinical Evidence

Working from the premise that a reading dysfunction could be a symbolic representation of a deeper conflict, Manzo (1977) developed a simple test of this proposition. With four graduate students, he set out to try to teach two dyslexic students to read using a system which was identical to conventional reading but which they were told was recently invented for children who had special problems like theirs. They also were told that no one could really be sure that they ever would be able to read regular print, even if they learned the alternate system.

If they could be taught to read by this surrogate, but even more difficult, system it was reasoned, then it would *not* be logical to attribute their disability to a neurological impairment, but to some psychological explanation. They employed an alternate alphabet (Paul McKee's funny squiggles [1948] that he used to show parents how difficult it is to learn how to read). Both youngsters had been in clinic programs for several continuous semesters and tested at primer levels. They were by all indications "severe dyslexics."

Findings: Exceeding every expectation, the two children learned the new code more rapidly than their tutors, who had to work as a team to keep abreast of their rate of learning. In about 15 hours they were reading at about third to fourth reader level in McKee's orthography. This effect gave strong reason to believe that the children could learn to read, and rather easily, once their minds permitted them to do so.

REFERENCES

Adams, M. J. (1990). *Beginning to read: Thinking and learning about print*. Cambridge, MA: MIT Press.

Adams, M. J., & Collins, A. (1977). *A schema-theoretic view of reading comprehension*. Champaign: Center for the Study of Reading, University of Illinois.

Afflerbach, P. P., & Johnston, P. H. (1986). What do expert readers do when the main idea is not explicit? In J. Baumann (Ed.), *Teaching main idea comprehension*. Newark, DE: International Reading Association.

Aiken, E. G., Thomas, G. S., & Shennum, W. A. (1975). Memory for a lecture: Effects of notes, lecture rate, and information density. *Journal of Educational Psychology, 67*, 439–444.

Al-Hilawani, Y. (2003). Clinical examination of three methods of teaching reading comprehension to deaf and hard-of-hearing students: From research to classroom applications. *Journal of Deaf Studies and Deaf Education, 8*(2).

Allen, L. (1998). An integrated strategies approach: Making word identification work for beginning readers. *The Reading Teacher. 52*, 254–268.

Allen, R. V. (1976). *Language experiences in communication*. Boston: Houghton Mifflin.

Alley, G., & Deshler, D. (1980). *Teaching the learning disabled adolescent: Strategies and methods*. Denver, CO: Love.

Allington, R. L. (1977). If they don't read much how they ever gonna get good? *Journal of Reading, 21*, 57–61.

Allington, R. L. (1980). Teacher interruption behaviors during primary grade oral reading. *Journal of Educational Psychology, 72*, 371–377.

Allington, R. L. (1983). Fluency: The neglected reading goal. *The Reading Teacher, 36*, 556–561.

Allington, R. L. (1984). Oral reading. In P. D. Pearson (Ed.), *Handbook of reading research* (pp. 829–864). New York: Longman.

Allington, R. L. (2000). *What really matters for struggling readers: Designing research-based programs*. Cambridge, MA: Perseus Publishing.

Allington, R. L. (2002). *Big brother and the national reading curriculum: How ideology trumped evidence*. Portsmouth, NH: Heinemann.

Anders, P. L., & Bos, C. S. (1986). Semantic feature analysis: An interactive strategy for vocabulary and text comprehension. *Journal of Reading, 29*, 610–616.

Anderson, B. (1981). The missing ingredient: Fluent oral reading. *Elementary School Journal, 81*, 173–177.

Anderson, K. (1985). Spelling errors and strategies of college students who are good readers/good spellers and poor readers/poor spellers on four complex word patterns. Doctoral dissertation, Georgia State University, 1982. Dissertation Abstracts International.

542

Anderson, L. M., Evertson, C. M., & Brophy, J. E. (1979). An experimental study of effective teaching in first-grade reading groups. *Elementary School Journal, 79,* 193–222.

Anderson, R. C., & Freebody, P. (1981). Vocabulary knowledge. In J.Guthrie (Ed.), *Comprehension and teaching: Research reviews* (pp. 77–117). Newark, DE: International Reading Association.

Anderson, R. C., & Nagy, W. E. (1991). Word meaning. In R. Barr, M. Kamil, P. Mosenthal, & P. D. Pearson (Eds.), *Handbook of reading research,* vol. 2, (pp. 690–724). New York: Longman.

Anderson, R. C., Reynolds, R. E., Schallert, D. L., & Goetz, E. T. (1977). Frameworks for comprehending discourse. *American Educational Research Journal, 14,* 367–381.

Anderson, R. C., Wilson, P., & Fielding, L. (1988). Growth in reading and how children spend their time outside of school. *Reading Research Quarterly, 23,* 285–303.

Anderson, V., & Hidi, S. (1988–89). Teaching students to summarize. *Educational Leadership, 46,* 26–28.

Anderson, W. W. (1975). Evaluation of college reading and study skills programs, problems and approaches. *Reading World, 14,* 191–197.

Andrews, G. R., & Debus, R. L. (1978). Persistence and the causal perception of failure: Modifying cognitive attributions. *Journal of Educational Psychology, 70,* 154–166.

Ankney, P., & McClurg, P. (1981). Testing Manzo's Guided Reading Procedure. *The Reading Teacher, 34,* 681–685.

Annarella, L. A. (2000). Using creative drama in the writing and reading process. Washington, DC: National Institute of Education (ERIC Document Reproduction Service No. ED445358).

Applebee, A., Langer, J., Mullis, I., Lathan, A., & Gentile, C. (1994). *NAEP 1992 Writing Report Card.* Washington, DC: US Department of Education, Office of Educational Research and Improvement.

Ashton-Warner, S. (1959). *Spinster.* New York: Simon & Schuster.

Athey, I. (1985). Reading research in the affective domain. In H. Singer & R. B. Ruddell (Eds.), *Theoretical models and processes of reading,* (3rd ed., pp. 527–557). Newark, DE: International Reading Association.

Atwell, N. (1987). *In the middle.* Portsmouth, NH: Boynton/Cook.

Au, K. H. (1979). Using the experience-text-relationship method with minority children. *The Reading Teacher, 32,* 677–679.

August, D. L., Flavell, J. H., & Clift, R. (1984). Comparison of comprehension monitoring of skilled and less-skilled readers. *Reading Research Quarterly, 20,* 39–53.

Aulls, M. W. (1978). *Developmental and remedial reading in the middle grades* (abridged ed.). Boston: Allyn & Bacon.

Aulls, M. W., & Graves, M. F. (1985) Repeated reading chart. In *Quest, Desert Magic, Unit 1, Electric Butterfly and other Stories.* New York: Scholastic.

Ausubel, D. P. (1964). Some psychological aspects of the structure of knowledge. In S. Elam (Ed.), *Annual Phi Delta Kappa Symposium on Educational Research.* Chicago: Rand McNally.

Babbs, P. (1983). The effects of instruction in the use of a metacognitive monitoring strategy upon fourth graders' reading comprehension and recall performance. Doctoral dissertation, Perdue University, West Lafayette, IN. *Dissertation Abstract International, 5,* 44/06A.

Bagley, M. T., & Hess, K. (1982). *200 ways of using imagery in the classroom.* Woodcliff Lake, NJ: New Dimensions of the 80's.

Baker, L. (1979a). Comprehension monitoring: Identifying and coping with text confusion. *Journal of Reading Behavior, 11,* 365–374.

Baker, L. (1979b). Do I understand or do I not understand: That is the question. (Reading Education Report No. 10). Washington, DC: National Institute of Education (ERIC Document Reproduction Service No. EC174 948.)

Bakhtin, M. M. (1986). The problem of speech genres. Speech genres and other late essays, (translated from the Russian by Vern W. McGee and edited by Caryl Emerson & Michael Holquist). Austin, TX: University of Texas Press.

Ballard, R. (1978). *Talking dictionary.* Ann Arbor, MI: Ulrich's books.

Balow, B., & Blomquist, M. (1965). Young adults ten to fifteen years after severe reading disability. *Elementary School Journal, 66,* 44–48.

Bandura, A. (1977). *Social learning theory.* Englewood Cliffs, NJ: Prentice-Hall.

Bandura, A., & Walters, R. (1963). *Social learning and personality development.* New York: Holt, Rinehart & Winston.

Bannatyne, A. D. (1974). Diagnosis: A note on recategorization of the WISC scaled scores. *Journal of Learning Disabilities, 7,* 272–273.

Baron, D. (2002, February 1). Anyone accept the good news on literacy? *Chronicle of Higher Education,* B10.

Barr, R. C. (1973–74). Instructional pace differences and their effect on reading acquisition. *Reading Research Quarterly, 9,* 526–554.

Barr, R., Sadow, M. W., & Blachowizc, C. L. Z. (1990). *Reading diagnosis for teachers: An instructional approach* (2nd ed.). White Plains, New York: Longman.

Barron, R. (1969). The use of vocabulary as an advance organizer. In H. L. Herber & P. L. Sanders (Eds)., *Research in reading in the content area: First report* (pp. 29–39).

Bartlett, F. C. (1932). *Remembering: A study in experimental and social psychology.* Cambridge, England: Cambridge University Press.

Baumann, J. F. (1984). Implication for reading instruction from the research on teacher and school effectiveness. *Journal of Reading, 28,* 109–115.

Baumann, J. F. (1988a). Direct instruction reconsidered. *Journal of Reading, 31,* 712–718.

Baumann, J. F. (1988b). *Reading assessment.* Columbus, OH: Merrill.

Baumann, J. F., & Kameenui, E. J. (1991). Research on vocabulary instruction: Ode to Voltaire. In J. Flood, J. M. Jensen, D. Lapp, & J. R. Squire (Eds.), *Handbook of research on teaching the English language arts* (pp. 604–632). New York: Macmillan.

Baurgimeister, B. B., Blum, H., & Lorge, I. (1972). *Columbia Mental Maturity Scale.* New York: Harcourt, Brace & World.

Bean, R. M., Lazar, M. K., & Zigmond, N. (1987). *System for observing reading instruction (SORIN).* Unpublished observation instrument, University of Pittsburgh, Institute for Practice and Research in Education, Pittsburgh, PA.

Bean, R.M., Swan, A.I., & Knaub, R. (2003) Reading specialists in schools with exemplary reading programs: Functional, versatile, and prepared, *The Reading Teacher 56*(5), 446–454.

Bean, T. W. (1979). The miscue mini-form: Refining the informal reading inventory. *Reading World, 18*(4), 400–405.

Bean, T. W., & Pardi, R. (1979). A field test of a guided reading strategy. *Journal of Reading, 23,* 144–147.

Bean, T. W., & Steenwyck, F. C. (1984). The effect of three forms of summarization instruction on sixth grades' summary writing and comprehension. *Journal of Reading Behavior, 16,* 297–306.

Beane, J. A. (1990). *Affect in the curriculum: Toward democracy, dignity, and diversity.* New York: Teachers College Press.

Bear, D. R., & Invernizzi, M. (1984). Student directed reading groups. *Journal of Reading, 28,* 248–252.

Beaven, M. H. (1977). Individualized goal setting, self-evaluation, and peer evaluation. In C. Cooper &, L. Odell (Eds), *Evaluating writing: Describing, measuring, judging.* Urbana, IL: National Council of Teachers of English.

Beck, I. L. (1989). Reading and reasoning. *The Reading Teacher, 42,* 676–682.

Beck, I. L., McKeown, M. G., & Omanson, R.C. (1987). The effects and uses of diverse instructional techniques. In M. G. McKeown, & M. E. Curtis (Eds.), *The nature of vocabulary acquisition.* Hillsdale, NJ: Erlbaum, 147–163.

Beez, W. V. (1968). Influence of biased psychological reports on teacher behavior and pupil performance. In *Proceedings of the 76th Annual Convention of the American Psychological Association.* Washington, DC: American Psychological Association.

Belenky, M. F., Clinchy, B. M., Goldberger, N. R., & Tarule, J. M. (1986). Women's ways of knowing: The development of self, voice, and mind. New York: Basic Books.

Bender, L. (1946). *Instructions for the use of the Visual Motor Gestalt Test.* New York: American Orthopsychiatric Association.

Betts, E. A. (l936). *The prevention and correction of reading difficulties.* Evanston, IL: Row Peterson.

Betts, E.A. (1957). *Foundations of reading instruction.* New York: American Book.

Bismonte, A.R., Foley, C.L., & Petty, J.A. (1994). Effectiveness of the possible sentences vocabulary strategy with middle school students in Guam, *Reading Improvement,* 31(4), 194–199.

Blachowicz, C. L. Z. (1986). Guidelines for evaluating vocabulary instruction. *The Reading Teacher, 41,* 132–137.

Blachowicz, C. L. Z., & Fisher, P. (2000). Vocabulary instruction. In M.L. Kamil, P.B. Mosenthal, P.D. Pearson, & R. Barr (Eds.), *Handbook of Reading Research Volume 3.* (pp. 503–523). Mahwah, NJ: Erlbaum.

Blachowicz, C. L. Z., & Fisher, P. (2000). *Teaching vocabulary in all classrooms.* Boston: Prentice Hall.

Blachowicz, C. L. Z., & Zabroske, B. (1990). Context instruction: A metacognitive approach for at-risk readers. *Journal of Reading, 33,* 504–508.

Bloom, B. S. (Ed.). (1956). *Taxonomy of educational objectives, Handbook I: Cognitive domain.* New York: David McKay.

Boder, E. (1970). Developmental dyslexia: A new diagnostic approach based on identification of three subtypes. *Journal of School Health, 40,* 289–290.

Boder, E. (1971a). Developmental dyslexia: A diagnostic screening procedure based on three characteristic patterns of reading and spelling. In B. D. Bateman (Ed.), *Learning disorders,* vol. 4 (pp. 298–342). Seattle, WA: Special Child Publications.

Boder, E. (1971b). Developmental dyslexia: Prevailing diagnostic concepts and a new diagnostic approach. In H. Myklebust (Ed.), *Progress in learning disabilities,* vol. II (pp. 293–321). New York: Grune & Stratton.

Boder, E., & Jarrico, S. (1982). *The Boder test of reading-spelling patterns.* New York: Grune & Stratton.

Bofill, F. (1998). *Jack and the beanstalk: Juan y los frijoles magicos.* Vancouver, British Columbia, Chronicle Books.

Bolton, F., & Snowball, D. (1993) *Ideas for Spelling.* Sidney, Australia: Heinemann.

Bond, G. L., & Tinker, M. A. (1973). *Reading difficulties: Their diagnosis and correction* (3rd ed.). New York: Appleton-Century-Crofts.

Bormuth, J. R. (1965). Validities of grammatical and semantic classifications of cloze test scores. In J. A. Figurel (Ed.), *Reading and inquiry.* International Reading Association Conference Proceedings, 10, *(pp. 283–286). Newark, DE: International Reading Association.*

Bowles, S., & Gintis, H. (1976). *Schooling in capitalist America.* New York: Basic Books.

Bowman, J. D. (1991). Vocabulary development by "twosies." *Arizona Reading Journal, 19*(2), 66.

Bradley, J. M., & Ames, W. S. (1977). Readability parameters of basal readers. *Journal of Reading Behavior, 9,* 175–183.

Brasacchio, T., Kuhn, B., & Martin, S. (2001). *How does encouragement of invented spelling influence conventional spelling development?* New York (ERIC Document Reproduction Service No. ED 452546).

Bridge, C. A. (1986). Predictable books for beginning readers and writers. In M. R. Sampson (Ed.), *The pursuit of literacy.* Dubuque, IA: Kendall/Hunt Publishing Company.

Bridge, C. A., Winograd, P. N., & Haley, D. (1983). Using predictable materials vs. preprimers to teach beginning sight words. *The Reading Teacher, 36,* 884–891.

Brisbois, J. I. (1995). Relations between First and Second Language Reading, Journal of Reading Behavior, 27 (4) 565–584.

Brisk, M. E. (1998). Bilingual Education: From Compensatory to Quality Schooling Mawah, NJ: Erlbaum.

Bromley, K. D. (1985). Precis writing and outlining enhance content learning. *The Reading Teacher, 38,* 406–411.

Bromley, K. D., & McKeveny, L. (1986). Precis writing: Suggestion for instruction in summarizing. *Journal of Reading, 29*(5), 392–395.

Brown, A. L. (1980). Metacognitive development and reading. In R. Spiro, B. Bruce & W. F. Brewer, (Eds.), *Theoretical issues in reading comprehension* (pp. 453–481). Hillsdale, NJ: Erlbaum.

Brown, A. L., & Day, J. D. (1983). Macrorules for summarizing texts: The development of expertise. *Journal of Verbal Learning and Verbal Behavior, 22*(1), 1–14.

Brown, A. L., Campione, J. C., & Day, J. D. (1981). Learning to learn: on training students to learn from texts. *Educational Researcher, 10*(2), 14–21.

Brown, W. T., & Holtzman, W. H. (1967). *Survey of study habits and attitudes.* New York: The Psychological Corporation.

Brozo, W. G., & Simpson, M. L. (1999). *Readers, teachers, learners: Expanding literacy across the content areas,* (pp. 65–66). Englewood Cliffs: Prentice Hall.

Brozo, W. G., Schmlzer, R. V., & Spires, H. A. (1983). The beneficial effect of chunking on good readers' comprehension of expository prose. *Journal of Reading, 26,* 442–445.

Bruner, J. S. (1978). The role of dialogue in language acquisition. In A. Sinclair, R.J. Jarvelle, & W. J. M. Leveet (Eds.), *The child's conception of language.* New York: Springer.

Bryant, S. (1979). Relative effectiveness of visual-auditory versus-auditory-kinesthetic-tactile procedures for teaching sight words and letter sounds to young disables readers. Doctoral dissertation, Teachers College, New York.

Buck, J. N., & Hammer, E. F. (1969). Advances in the House-Tree-Person Technique: Variations and applications. Los Angles, CA: Western Psychological Services.

Buck, J. N., & Jolles, I. (1966). *H-T-P: House-Tree-Person projective technique.* Beverly Hills, CA: Western Psychological Services.

Burke, H. R. (1958). Raven's Progressive Matrices: A review and critical evaluation. *Journal of Genetic Psychology, 93,* 199–228.

Burns P.C., Roe, B.D., & Smith, S. H. (2002). *Teaching reading in today's elementary schools* (8th ed.). Boston: Houghton Mifflin.

Burns, J. M., & Richgels, D. J. (1988). A critical evaluation of listening tests. *Academic Therapy, 24,* 153–162.

Burns, P. C., & Roe, B. D. (1985). *Informal reading inventory* (2nd ed.). Boston: Houghton Mifflin.

Caine, R.N., & Caine, G. (1991). *Making connections: Teaching and the human brain.* Alexandria, VA: Association for Supervision and Curriculum Development.

Calfee, R. (1976). Letter addressed to Mr. and Mrs. Lindamood. Reported in D. B. Clark (1988). *Dyslexia: Theory practice of remedial instruction* (p. 136). Parkton, MD: York.

Cambourne, B. (1977, August). *Some psycholinguistic dimensions of the silent reading process: A pilot study.* Paper presented at the annual meeting of the Australian Reading Conference, Melbourne.

Campbell, J., Donahue, P., Reese, C., & Phillips, G. (1996). NAEP 1994 reading report card for the nation and the states. Washington, DC: US Department of Education, OERI.

Campbell, N. K., & Hackett, G. (1986). The effects of mathematics task performance on math self-efficacy and task interest. *Journal of vocational behavior, 28*(2), 149–162.

Campbell, P. (1966). *Reading attitude inventory.* Livonia Public Schools, Livonia, Michigan.

Camperell, K. (1984). Equal educational opportunities and a core curriculum. In G. H. McNich (Ed.), *Comprehension computers communication. Fifth yearbook of the American Reading Forum* (pp. 15–19). Athens, GA: University of Georgia.

Carbo, M. L. (1984a). Research in learning style and reading implications. *Theory Into Practice, 23,* 72–76.

Carbo, M. L. (1984b). Reading styles: How principals can make a difference. *Principal, 64,* 20–26.

Carbo, M. L. (1984c). You can identify reading styles and then design a super reading program. *Early Years, 14,* 80–83.

Carlson, R. K. (1965). *Sparkling words: Two hundred practical and creative writing ideas.* Berkeley, CA: Wagner Printing Co.

Carney J. J., & Cioffi, G. (1990). Extending traditional diagnosis: The dynamic assessment of reading abilities. *Reading Psychology, 11,* 177–192.

Carr, E., & Ogle, D. (1987). K-W-L Plus: A strategy for comprehension and summarization. *Journal of Reading, 30,* 628–629.

Carroll, H. C. M. (1972). The remedial teaching of reading: An evaluation. *Remedial Education, 7,* 10–15.

Carroll, J. B. (1963). A model of school learning. *Teachers College Record, 64,* 723–732.

Carroll, J. B. (1977). Developmental parameters of reading comprehension. In J. Guthrie (Ed.), *Cognition, curriculum, and comprehension.* Newark, DE.: International Reading Association.

Carver, R. P. (1982). Optimal rate of reading prose. *Reading Research Quarterly, 18*(1), 56–88.

Carver, R. P. (1991). Using letter-naming speed to diagnose reading disability. *Remedial and Special Education, 12*(5), 33–43.

Carver, R. P., & Hoffman, J. V. (1981). The effect of practice through repeated reading in gains in reading ability using a computer-based instructional system. *Reading Research Quarterly, 16*(3), 374–390.

Casale (Manzo), U. C. (1985). Motor imaging: A reading-vocabulary strategy. *Journal of Reading, 28,* 619–621.

Casale (Manzo), U. C., & Kelly, B. W. (1980). Problem-solving approach to study skills (PASS) for students in professional schools. *Journal of Reading, 24,* 232–238.

Casale (Manzo), U. C., & Manzo, A. V. (1983). Differential effects of cognitive affective, and proprioceptive approaches on vocabulary acquisition. In G. H. McNinch (Ed.), *Reading research to reading practice. Third yearbook of the American Reading Forum* (pp.71–73). Athens, GA: American Reading Forum.

Cassidy, J. (1981, January). Lecture at Benchmark School, Media, PA.

Cassidy, J., & Wenrich, J.K. (1997). What's hot, what's not for 1997: A look at key topics in reading research and practice. *Reading Today, 14*(4), 34.

Catts, H. W., & Kamhi, A. G. (1999) Language and Reading Disabilities. Boston: Allyn & Bacon.

Catts, H. W., Frey, M., & Tomblin (1997) Language basis for reading disability. Papers, Society for the Study of Reading, Chicago.

Cazden, C. B. (1988). *Classroom discourse: The language of teaching and learning.* Portsmouth, NH: Heinemann.

Cecil, N. L. (1990a). Diffusing the trauma: An exit interview for remediated readers. *Journal for Affective Reading Education, 10,* 27–32.

Cecil, N. L. (1990b). Where have all the good questions gone? Encouraging creative expression in children. *Contemporary Issues in Reading, 5*(2), 49–53.

Ceprano, M. A. (1981). A review of selected research on methods of teaching sight words. *The Reading Teacher, 35,* 314–322.

Chall, J. S. (1967). *Learning to read: The great debate.* New York: McGraw-Hill.

Chall, J. S. (1983a). *Learning to read: the great debate* (updated edition). New York: McGraw-Hill.

Chall, J. S. (1983b). Literacy: Trends and explanations. *Educational Researcher, 12*(9), 3–8.

Chall, J. S. (1983c). *Stages of reading development.* New York: McGraw-Hill.

Chall, J. S., & Feldman, S. (1966). First-grade reading: An analysis of the interactions of professed methods, teacher implementation, and child background. *The Reading Teacher, 19,* 569–575.

Chamot, A.U., & O'Malley, J.M. (1986). *A cognitive academic language approach: an ESL content-based curriculum.* Washington , DC: National Clearinghouse for Bilingual Education.

Chandler-Olcott, K., & Mahar, D. (2003). Adolescents' anime-inspired fanfictions: An exploration of multiliteracies. *Journal of Adolescent and Adult Literacy, 46*(7), 556–568.

Chandler-Olcott, K., & Mahar, D. (2001, November). Considering genre in the digital literacy classroom. *Reading Online, 5*(4).

Chang, S. S., & Raths, J. (1971). The school's contribution to the cumulating deficit. *Journal of Educational Research, 64,* 272–276.

Chapin, M., & Dyck, D. (1976). Persistence in children's reading behavior as a function of N length and attribution retraining. *Journal of Abnormal Psychology, 85,* 511–515.

Choate, J. S., & Rakes, T. A. (1987). The structured listening activity: A model for improving listening comprehension. *The Reading Teacher, 41,* 194–200.

Chomsky, N. (1978). *Intellectuals and the state.* Baarn, Netherlands: Wereldvenster.

Christie, J. F. (1979). The qualitative analysis system: Updating the IRI. *Reading World, 18,* 393–399.

Cioffi, G., & Carney, J. J. (1983). Dynamic assessment of reading disabilities. *The Reading Teacher, 36,* 764–768.

Cioffi, G., & Carney, J. J. (1990). Extending traditional diagnosis: The dynamic assessment of reading abilities. *Reading Psychology,, 11,* 177–192.

Clark, C. H. (1982). Assessing free recall. *The Reading Teacher, 35,* 764–768.

Clark, D. (1988). *Dyslexia: Theory and practice of remedial instruction.* Parkton, MD: York Press.

Clark, M. (1976). *Young fluent readers.* London: Heinemann Educational Books.

Clay, M. M. (1985). *The early detection of reading difficulties* (3rd ed.). Auckland, New Zealand: Heinemann.

Clay, M. M. (1979). *Reading: Patterning of complex behavior* (2nd ed.). Auckland, New Zealand: Heinemann.

Clay, M. M. (1993). *Reading recovery: A guidebook for teachers in training.* Auckland, NZ: Heinemann.

Clewell, S. F., & Haidemenos, J. (1983). Organizational strategies to increase comprehension. *Reading World, 22,* 314–312.

Coady, J., Magoto, J., Hubbard, P., Graney, J., & Mokhtari, K. (1993). High frequency vocabulary and reading proficiency in ESL readers. In T. Huckin, M. Haynes, & J. Coady (Eds.), *Second language reading and vocabulary* (pp. 217–228). Norwood, NJ: Ablex.

Cobb, J. A. (1972). Relationship of discrete classroom behavior to fourth grade academic achievement. *Journal of Educational Psychology, 63,* 74–80.

Cole, J. E. (2002). Assessment interviews. In B. J. Guzzetti (Ed.), *Literacy in America: An encyclopedia of history, theory, and practice,* vol. 1 (pp. 30–31). Santa Barbara, CA: ABC-CLIO, Inc.

Coleman, S. (1990). Middle school remedial readers serve as cross-grade tutors. *The Reading Teacher, 43,* 524–525.

Coley, J. D., & Hoffman, D. M. (1990). Overcoming learned helplessness in at-risk readers. *Journal of Reading, 33*(7), 497–502.

Collins, C. (1991). Reading instruction that increases thinking abilities. *Journal of Reading, 34*(7), 510–516.

Comber, L., & Keeves, J. P. (1973). *Science education in nineteen countries.* New York: Wiley.

Condus, M. M., Marshall, K. J., & Miller, S. R. (1986). Effect of the key-word mnemonic strategy on vocabulary acquisition and maintenance by learning disabled children. *Journal of Learning Disabilities, 19,* 609–613.

Cooper, C. R., & Odell, L. (1977). *Evaluating writing.* Urbana, IL: National Council of Teachers of English.

Cooper, J. L. (1947). A procedure for teaching non-readers. *Education, 67,* 494–499.

Cooper, J. L. (1964). An adaptation of the Fernald-Keller approach to teach an initial reading vocabulary to children with severe reading disabilities. *The Australian Journal on the Education of Backward Children, 10,* 131–145.

Cooter, R. B., & Flynt, E. S. (1986). *Reading comprehension: Out of the ivory tower and into the classroom.* Unpublished paper, Northwestern State University, Natchitoches, LA.

Cordts, A. D. (1965). *Analysis and classification of the sounds of English words in the primary reading vocabulary.* Unpublished dissertation, University of Iowa.

Cousin, P. T. (1991, April/May). Helping learners with special needs become strategic readers. *Reading Today, 8*(5), p. 9.

Craik, F. M., & Lockart, R. S. (1972). Levels of Processing: A Framework for memory Research. *Journal of Verbal Learning 11,* 671–684.

Croll, V. J. (1990). Reading comprehension improvement when readers use pictures and

Cronbach, L. J., & Snow, R. E. (1977). *Aptitudes and instructional methods.* New York: Irvington.

Cronin, D. (2000). *Click Clack Moo, Cows That Type.* New York: Simon & Schuster.

Culver, V. I. (1975). The guided reading procedure: An experimental analysis of its effectiveness as a technique for improving reading comprehension skills. Doctoral dissertation, University of Missouri-Kansas City. *Dissertation Abstracts International, 36,* 7062A.

Culver, V. I., Godfrey, H. C., & Manzo, A. V. (1972). A partial reanalysis of the validity of the cloze procedure as an appropriate measure of reading comprehension (research report summary). *Journal of Reading, 16,* 256–257.

Cummins, J. (1989). A theoretical framework for bilingual special education. *Exceptional Children, 56*(2), 111–120.

Cummins, J. (2001). *Language, power, and pedagogy: Bilingual children in the crossfire.* Clevedon, England: Multilingual Matters.

Cunningham, J. W. (1982). Generating interactions between schemata and text. In J. A. Niles & L. A. Harris (Eds.), *New inquiries in reading research and instruction. The 31st yearbook of the National Reading Conference* (pp.42–47). Washington, DC: National Reading Conference.

Cunningham, J. W., & Tierney, R. J. (1977). *Comparative analysis of cloze and modified cloze procedures.* Paper presented at the National Reading Conference, New Orleans.

Cunningham, P. M. (1975–1976). Investigating a synthesized theory of mediated word identification. *Reading Research Quarterly, 11,* 127–143.

Cunningham, P. M. (1984). Curriculum trends in reading. *Educational Leadership, 41,* 83–84.

Cunningham, P. M., Hall, D. P., & Sigmon, C. M. (1999). *The teacher's guide to the four blocks: A multimethod, multilevel framework for grades 1–3.* Greensboro, NC: Carson-Dellosa.

Cunningham, P. M.,& Hall, D. (1994). *Making big words.* Carthage, IL: Good Apple, Inc.

Cunningham, P.M., & Cunningham, J. W. (1992). Making words: Enhancing the invented spelling-decoding connection. *The Reading Teacher, 46* (2), 106–116.

Cunningham, P.M., Hall, D. P., & Cunningham, J.W. (2000). *Guided reading: The four-blocks way.* Greensboro, NC: Carson-Dellosa.

Cunningham, P.M., Hall, D. P., & Defee, M. (1998, May). Non-ability-grouped, multilevel instruction: Eight years later. *The Reading Teacher, 51*(8), 556–571.

Cunningham, P.M., Hall, D. P., & Defee, M. April, (1991). Non-ability-grouped, multilevel instruction: A year in a first-grade classroom. *The Reading Teacher, 44*(8), 556–571.

Curry, L. (1990). A critique of the research on learning styles. *Educational Leadership, 48*(2), 50–56.

D'Agostino, J. (1996) Authentic instruction and academic achievement in compensatory education classrooms. *Studies in Educational Evaluation, 22* (20), 139–155.

Dale, E., & O'Rourke, J. (1976). *The living word vocabulary.* Elgin, IL: Dome.

Dale, E., & O'Rourke, J. (1981). *The living word vocabulary* (3rd ed). Chicago: World Book-Childcraft International.

Dana, C. (1989). Strategy families for disabled readers. *Journal of Reading, 33*(1), 30–35.

Dao, M. N. (1993). An investigation into the application of the reciprocal teaching procedures to enhance reading comprehension with educationally at-risk Vietnamese American pupils. Unpublished doctoral dissertation, California University.

Davey, B. (1983). Think aloud—modeling the cognitive processes of reading comprehension. *Journal of Reading, 27,* 44–47.

Davey, B. (1987). Postpassage questions: Task and reader effects on comprehension and metacomprehension processes. *Journal of Reading Behavior, 19*(3), 261–283.

Davey, B. (1988a). Factor affecting the difficulty of reading comprehension items for successful and unsuccessful readers. *Journal of Experimental Education, 56*(2), 67–76.

Davey, B. (1988b). The nature of response errors for good and poor readers when permitted to reinspect text during question-answering. *American Educational Research Journal, 25*(3), 399–414.

Davey, B. (1989). Assessing comprehension: Selected interactions of task and reader. *The Reading Teacher, 42*(9), 694–697.

Davey, B., & LaSasso, C. J. (1984). The interaction of reader and task factors in the assessment of reading comprehension. *Journal of Experimental Education, 52*(4), 199–206.

Davidson, J. L. (1970). The relationship between teacher's questions and pupils' responses during a directed reading activity and a directed reading thinking activity. Doctoral dissertation, The University of Michigan, Ann Arbor. *Dissertation Abstracts International, 31,* G273A.

Davis, F. B. (1944). Fundamental factors of comprehension in reading. *Psychometrika, 31,* 185–187.

Davis, H., & Silverman, S. (Eds.). (1970). *Hearing and deafness.* New York: Holt, Rinehart & Winston.

Dechant, E. (1968). *Diagnosis and remediation of reading disability.* West Nyack, NY: Parker.

Delisle, J. (1991). *Kid stories.* Minneapolis, MN: Free Spirit.

DeMaster, V., Crossland, C., & Hasselbring, T. (1986). Consistency of learning disabled students' spelling performance. *Learning Disability Quarterly, 9,* 89–96.

Dempster, F. K. (1991). Synthesis of research on review and tests. *Educational Leadership, 48*(7), 71–76.

Dempster, F. N., & Farris, R. (1990). The spacing effect: research and practice. *Journal of Research and Development in Education, 23*(2), 97–101.

Dewitz, P. B., & Dewitz, P. K. (2003). They can read the words, but they can't understand: Refining comprehension assessment. *The Reading Teacher, 56*(5), 422–435.

Dewitz, P. B., Carr, E. M., & Patsberg, J. P. (1987). Effects of inference training on comprehension and comprehension monitoring. *Reading Research Quarterly, 22,* 99–121.

Diederich, P. B. (1974). *Measuring growth in English.* Urbana, IL: National Council of Teachers of English.

Diener, C. I., & Dweck, C. (1978). An analysis of learned helplessness: II. The processing of success. *Journal of Personality and Social Psychology, 39,* 940–952.

Dolch, E. W. (1951). *Psychology and teaching of reading.* Champaign, IL: The Gerrard Press.

Dolch, E. W. (1936). A basic sight vocabulary. *Elementary School Journal, 36,* 456–460.

Dowhower, S. L. (1987). Effects of repeated reading on second-grade transitional readers' fluency and comprehension. *Reading Research Quarterly, 22,* 389–405.

Dowhower, S. L. (1989). Repeated reading: Research into practice. *The Reading Teacher, 42*(7), 502–507.

Dowhower, S. L. (1999). Supporting a strategic stance in the classroom: A comprehension framework for helping teachers help students to be strategic. *The Reading Teacher, 52*(7): 672–683.

Draper, A. G., & Moeller, G. H. (1971). I/we think with words. *Phi Delta Kappan 52*(8), 482–484.

Duffelmeyer, F. (1980a). The influence of experience-based vocabulary instruction on learning word meanings. *Journal of Reading, 24,* 35–40.

Duffelmeyer, F. (1980b). The passage independence of factual and inferential questions. *Journal of Reading, 24,* 131–134.

Duffelmeyer, F. A., & Duffelmeyer, B. B. (1989). Are IRI passages suitable for assessing main idea comprehension? *The Reading Teacher, 42,* 358–363.

Duffelmeyer, F., Baum, D., & Merkley, D. (1987). Maximizing reader-text confrontation with an extended anticipation guide. *Journal of Reading, 31,* 146–151.

Duffelmeyer, F., Long, J., & Kruse, A. (1987). The passage independence of comprehension question categories: Evidence of non-uniformity. *Reading Improvement, 24,* 101–106.

Duffelmeyer, F., Robinson, S., & Squier, S. (1989). Vocabulary questions on informal reading inventories. *The Reading Teacher, 43,* 142–148.

Duffy, G. G., Roehler, L. R., & Hermann, B. A. (1988). Modeling mental processes helps poor readers become strategic readers. *The Reading Teacher, 41,* 762–767.

Duffy, G. G., Roehler, L. R., Sivan, E., Rackliffe, G., Book, C., Meloth, M. S., Vavrus, L. G., Wesselman, R., Putnam, J., & Bassiri, D. (1987). The effects of explaining the reasoning associated with using reading strategies. *Reading Research Quarterly, 22,* 347–368.

Duffy, G.G. (1993). Rethinking strategy instruction: Four teachers' development and their low achievers' understandings. *The Elementary School Journal, 93*(3), 231–247.

Dunn, L. M. (l965, 1970). *Peabody Picture Vocabulary Test expanded manual.* Circle Pines, MN: American Guidance Service.

Durkin, D. (1966). *Children who read early.* New York: Teacher's College Press.

Durrell, D. D. (1955). *Durrell analysis of reading difficulty.* New York: Harcourt, Brace & World.

Durrell, D. D. (1969). Listening comprehension versus reading comprehension. *Journal of Reading, 12,* 455–460.

Dwyer, E. G., & Flippo, R. F. (1983). Multisensory approaches to teaching spelling. *Journal of Reading, 27*(2), 171–172.

Dykstra, R. (1966). Auditory discrimination abilities and beginning reading achievement. *Reading Research Quarterly, 1,* 5–34.

Dykstra, R. (1968). Summary of the second grade phase of the cooperative beginning reading research program in primary instruction. *Reading Research Quarterly, 4* (1), 21, 49–70.

Eakle, J. A. (2003). A content analysis of second-language research. In *The reading teacher and lnguage arts, 1990–2002. The Reading Teacher, 56*(8), 828–836.

Eanet, M. G. (1978). An investigation of the REAP reading/study procedure: Its rationale and efficacy. In P. D. Pearson, & J. Hansen (Eds.), *Reading: Disciplined inquiry in process and practice. The 27th yearbook of the National Reading Conference* (pp. 229–232). Clemson, SC: National Reading Conference.

Eanet, M. G. (1983). Reading/writing: Finding and using the connection. *The Missouri Reader, 8,* 8–9.

Eanet, M. G., & Manzo, A. V. (1976). REAP—A strategy for improving reading/writing/study skills. *Journal of Reading, 19,* 647–652.

Eanet, M. G., Condon, M. W. F., & Manzo, A. V. (1974). Subjective assessment of auto-instructional learning tasks in secondary and college reading materials. In G. H. McNinch & W. D. Miller (Eds.), *Reading convention and inquiry. The 24th yearbook of National Reading Conference* (pp.94–99). Clemson, SC: National Reading Conference.

Early, M., Cullinan, B. E., Farr, R. C., Hammond, W.D., Santeusanio, N., & Strickland, D. S. (1987). *Wishes: Teacher's Edition, Part II, Level 4,* HBJ Reading Program. Orlando, FL: Harcourt Brace Jovanovich.

Edelen-Smith, P.J. (1997). How now brown cow: Phoneme awareness activities for collaborative classrooms. *Intervention in School and Clinic, 33,* 103–111.

Ediger, M. (1991). The affective dimension in middle school reading. *Journal for Affective Education, 11*(fall), 35–40.

Edwards, P. A., & Simpson, L. (1986). Bibliotheraphy: A strategy for communication between parents and their children. *Journal of Reading, 30,* 110–118.

Eeds, M. (1985). Bookwords: Using a beginning word list of high frequency words from children's literature K-3. *The Reading Teacher, 38,* 418–423.

Ekwall, E. E., & Shanker, J. L. (1988). *Diagnosis and remediation of the disabled reader* (3rd ed.). Boston: Allyn & Bacon.

Elbro, C. (1996). Early linguistic abilities and reading development: A review and a hypothesis about underlying differences in distinctness of phonological representations of lexical items. *Reading and Writing: An Interdisciplinary Journal, 8*, 453–85.

El-Koumy, A.S.A. (1996). Effects of three questioning strategies on EFL reading. Paper presented at the Annual Meeting of the Teachers of English to Speakers of Other Languages, Chicago, IL (ERIC Reproduction Information Services No. ED411696).

Elliott, J., & Dupuis, M.M., Eds. (2002). *Young Adult Literature in the Classroom.* Newark, DE: International Reading Association.

Erickson, L. G., & Krajenta, M. A. (1991). How fast should young readers read? *Illinois Reading Council Journal, 19*(2), 10–14.

Ericson, B., Hubler, M., Bean, T. W., Smith, C. C., & McKenzie, J. V. (1987). Increasing critical reading in junior high classrooms. *Journal of Reading, 30*, 430–439.

Ericsson, K. A., & Simon, H. A. (l980). Verbal reports as data. *Psychological Review, 87*, 215–251.

Ernst-Slavit, G., Moore, M., & Maloney, C. (2002).Teaching English and literature to ESL students. *Journal of Adolescent and Adult Literacy, 45*, 4, 386–394.

Faltis, C. J., & Hudelson, S. J. (1998). *Bilingual education in elementary and secondary school communities: Toward understanding and caring.* Needham Heights, MA: Allyn & Bacon.

Feldman, J. A. (1986). Connectionist models and their properties. *Cognitive Science, 6*, 205–254.

Fernald, G. M. (1943). *Remedial techniques in basic school subjects.* New York: McGraw Hill.

Feuerstein, R. (1979). *Instrumental enrichment.* Baltimore: University Park Press.

Finn, R. (1991). Different minds. *Discover, 12*(6), 52–58.

Fisher, C. W., Filby, N. W., Marliave, R. Cahen, L. S., Dishaw, M. M., Moore, J. E., & Berliner, D. C. (1978a). *Teaching and learning in the elementary school: A summary of the beginning teacher evaluation study* (BTES Rep. VII-I). San Francisco: Far West Laboratory for Educational Research and Development.

Flesch, R. (1955). *Why Johnny Can't Read.* New York: Harper & Row.

Flood, J., & Lapp, D.. (1990). Reading comprehension instruction for at-risk students: Research-based practices that can make a difference. In D. Moore, D. Alvermann & K. Hinchman (Eds.), *Struggling Adolescent Readers: A Collection of Teaching Strategies* (pp. 138–147). Newark, DE: International Reading Association.

Foil, C. R., & Alber, S. R. (2002). Fun and effective ways to build your students vocabulary. *Intervention in School and Clinic, 37* (3), 131–139.

Foorman, B. R. (2000). Brain activation profiles in dyslexic children during non-word reading: A magnetic source imaging study. *Neuroscience Letters, 290*, 61–65.

Ford, M. P., & Opitz (2002). Using centers to engage children during guided reading time: Intensifying learning experiences away from the teacher. *The Reading Teacher, 55*(8), 710–717.

Fores, R. (1969). *Can elephants swim?* New York: Time Life Books.

Fournier, D. N. E., & Graves, M. F. (2003). Scaffolding adolescents' comprehension of short stories. *Journal of Adolescent and Adult Literacy, 46*(1), 30–39.

Fraatz, J. M. (1987). *The politics of reading: Power, opportunity, and prospects for change in America's public schools.* New York: Teachers College Press.

Frayer, D. A., Fredrick, W. C., & Klausmeir, H. J. (1969). *A schema for testing the level of concept mastery* (Working Paper No. 16). Madison: University of Wisconsin Research and Development Center for Cognitive Learning.

Freeman, D., & Freeman, Y. (1993). *Teaching reading and writing in the Spanish bilingual classroom.* Portsmouth, NH: Heinemann.

Fry, E. B. (1980). The new instant word list. *The Reading Teacher, 34,* 284–289.

Fry, E. Kress, J. E., & Fountoukidis, D E. (2000). *The Reading Teacher's Book of Lists* (4th ed). Englewood Cliffs, NJ: Prentice Hall.

Fry, E., Kress, J. E., & Fountoukidis, D E. (1998). *The Reading Teacher's Book of Lists* (3rd ed). Englewood Cliffs, NJ: Prentice Hall.

Fuller, F. F. (1969). Concerns of teachers: Developmental conception. *American Education Research Journal, 6,* 207–226.

Gable, R. A., Hendrickson J. M., & Meeks, J. W. (1988). Assessing spelling errors of special needs students. *The Reading Teacher, 42*(2), 112–117.

Gambrell, L. B., & Bales, R. J. (1986). Mental image and the comprehension monitoring performance of fourth- and fifth-grade poor readers. *Reading Research Quarterly, 21,* 454–464.

Gambrell, L. B., & Jawitz, P. B. (1993). Mental imagery, text illustrations, and children's story comprehension and recall. *Reading Research Quarterly, 28* (3), 265–273

Garcia, E. E. (1992). Educating teachers for language minority students. In W. R. Houston (Ed.), *Handbook of research on teacher education* (pp. 717–729). New York: Macmillan.

Garcia, G. E., Montes, J., Janisch, C., Bouchereau, E., & Consalvi, J. (1993). Literacy needs of limited-English proficient students: What information is available to mainstream teachers? In D. J. Leu & C. K. Kinzer (Eds.), *Examining central issues in literacy research, theory, and practice. Forty-second yearbook of the National Reading Conference* (pp. 171–177). Chicago: National Reading Conference.

Garcia, G.E. (1998). Bilingual children's reading. In M. Kamil, P. Mosenthal, P.D. Pearson, & R. Barr (Eds.), *Handbook of reading reseach,* vol. 3. Mahwah, NJ: Erlbaum.

Garner, R., Hare, V. C., Alexander, P., Haynes, J., & Winograd, P. (1984). Inducing use of a text lookback strategy among unsuccessful readers. *American Educational Research Journal, 21,* 789–798.

Garrison, J. W., & Hoskisson, K. (1989). Confirmation bias in predictive reading. *The Reading Teacher, 42*(7), 482–486.

Gaskins, I. W. (1981). Reading for learning: Going beyond basals in the elementary grades. *The Reading Teacher, 35,* 323–328.

Gaskins, I. W., Ehri, L. C., Cress, C., O'Hara, C., & Donnelly, K. (1996). Procedures for word leaning: Making discoveries about words. *The Reading Teacher, 50,* 312–327.

Gaskins, I., & Elliot, T. (1991). *Implementing cognitive strategy training across the school.* Media, PA: Brookline Books.

Gauthier, L. R. (1988). A study of listening comprehension as a predictor of reading gains. *Reading Improvement, 25,* 276–281.

Gauthier, L. R. (1990). Five informal ways to assess students' reading comprehension. *Reading: Exploration and Discovery, 12,* 31–38.

Gauthier, L. R. (1991). The effects of vocabulary gain upon instructional reading level. *Reading Improvement, 28*(3), 195–202.

Gee, T. C., & Raskow, S. J. (1987). Content reading specialists evaluate teaching practices. *Journal of Reading, 31,* 234–237.

Geissal, M. A., & Knafle, J. D. (1977). A linguistic view of auditory tests and exercises. *The Reading Teacher, 31*(2), 134–41.

Gentry, J. R. (1982). An analysis of developmental spelling in GYNS at WRK. *The Reading Teacher, 36*(2), 192–200.

Gentry, J. R. (2000) *The literary map: Guiding children to where they need to be (K–3).* New York: Mondo.

Gentry, J. R., & Gillet, J. (1993). *Teaching kids to spell.* Portsmouth, NH: Heinemann.

Gill, D.A. (1997). *The effectiveness of encouraging invented spelling: A research study.* M.Ed. research project, Pennsylvania: Shippensburg University (ERIC Document Reproduction Service No. ED406645).

Gilligan, C. (1982). *In a different voice: Psychological theory and women's development.* Cambridge, MA: Harvard University Press.

Gilmore, J. V., & Gilmore, E. C. (1968). *Gilmore oral reading test.* New York: The Psychological Corporation.

Gilroy, A., & Moore, D. (1988). Reciprocal teaching of comprehension-fostering and

Gipe, J. (1978–1979). Investigating techniques for teaching word meaning. *Reading Research Quarterly, 14,* 624–644.

Giroux, H. (1981). *Ideology, cultural, and the process of schooling.* Philadelphia, PA: Temple University Press.

Gittelman, R., & Feingold, I. (1983). Children with reading disorders: Efficacy of reading remediation. *Journal of Child Psychology & Psychiatry & Allied Disciplines, 24,* 167–191.

Glass, G. G., & Burton, E. H. (1973). How do they decode? Verbalization and observed behaviors of successful decoders. *Education, 94,* 58–64.

Goldberg, H. K., Schiffman, G. B., & Bender, M. (1983). *Dyslexia: Interdisciplinary approaches to reading disabilities.* New York: Grune & Stratton.

Goldstein, K., & Scheerer, M. (1964). Abstract and concrete behavior: An experimental study with special tests. In J.F. Dashiell (Ed.), *Psychological Monographs.* Evanston, IL: American Psychological Association.

Gonzalez, O. (1999). Building vocabulary: Dictionary consultation and the ESL. *Journal of Adolescent and Adult Literacy, 43*(3), 264–270.

Good, T. L. (1987). Teacher expectations. In D. C. Berliner & B. V. Roseshine (Eds.), *Talk to teachers* (pp. 67–79). New York: Random House.

Good, T. L., Grouws, D. A., & Beckerman, T. M. (1978). Curriculum pacing: Some empirical data in mathematics. *Journal of Curriculum Studies, 10,* 75–82.

Goodman, K. S. (1973). Miscues: Windows on the reading process. In K. S. Goodman (Ed.), *Miscue analysis: Applications to reading instruction* (pp. 3–14). Urbana, IL.: National Council of Teachers of English.

Goodman, Y. A., & Burke, C. L. (1972). *Reading miscue inventory manual: Procedure for diagnosis and evaluation.* New York: Macmillan.

Gorrell, J. (1990). Some contributions of self-efficacy research to self-concept. *Journal of Research and Development in Education, 23*(2), 73–81.

Gough, H. G. (1975). *California Psychological Inventory.* Palo Alto, CA: Consulting Psychologist Press.

Gough, P. B. (1981). A comment on Kenneth Goodman. In M. Kamil (Ed.), *Directions in Reading: Research and instruction* (pp. 92–95). Washington, DC: National Reading Conference.

Gough, P. B., Alford, J. A., Jr., & Holley-Wilcox, P. (1981). Words and contexts. In O. J. L. Tzeng & H. Singer (Eds.), *Perception of print* (pp. 85–102). Hillsdale, NJ: Erlbaum.

Gough, P. B., Juel, C., & Roper-Schneider, D. (1983). A two-stage model of initial reading acquisition. In J. A. Niles, & L.A. Harris (Eds.), *Searches for meaning in reading/language processing and instruction* (pp. 207–211). Rochester, NY: National Reading Conference.

Graham, J. R., & Lilly, R. S. (1984). *Psychological Testing.* Englewood Cliffs, NJ: Prentice Hall.

Graves, D. H. (1983). *Writing: Teachers and children at work.* Portsmouth, NH: Heinemann.

Graves, M. F. (1986). Vocabulary learning and instruction. In E. Z. Rothkopf, & L. C. Ehri (Eds.), *Review of research in education,* vol. 13 (pp.49–89). Washington, DC: American Educational Research Association.

Graves, M., & Dykstra, R. (1997). Contextualizing the first grade studies: What is the best way to teach children? *Reading Research Quarterly, 32*(4), 342–347.

Graves, M., & Hammond, H. (1980). A validated procedure for teaching prefixes and its effect on student's ability to assign meaning to novel words. In M. Kamil & A. Moe (Eds.), *Perspectives on reading research and instruction. 29th yearbook of the National Reading Conference* (pp. 184–188). Washington, DC: National Reading Conference.

Graves, M.F. (2000). A vocabulary program to complement and bolster a middle-grade comprehension program. In B.M. Taylor, M.F. Graves, & P. van den Broek (Eds.), *Reading for meaning: Fostering comprehension in the middle grades.* New York: Teachers College Press.

Gray, W. S. (1925). *24th yearbook of the NSSE, Part I—Report of the National Committee on Reading.* Bloomington, IL: Public School Publishing Co.

Gray, W. S. (1948). *On their own in reading.* Glenview, IL: Scott, Foresman.

Gray, W. S. (1960). Reading. In C. W. Harris (Ed.), *Encyclopedia of educational research* (end. ed.) (p. 1106). New York: Macmillan.

Grobler, C. Van E. (1971). Methodology in reading instruction as a controlling variable in the constructive or destructive channeling of aggression. Doctoral dissertation, University of Delaware, Newark, 1970. *Dissertation Abstracts International, 32,* 6197A.

Groff, P. (1980). A critique of an oral reading miscues analysis. *Reading World, 19*(3), 254–264.

Guice, B. M. (1969). The use of the cloze procedure for improving reading comprehension of college student. *Journal of Reading Behavior, 1,* 81–92.

Guilford, J. P. (1967). *The nature of human intelligence.* New York: McGraw-Hill.

Gunning, T.G. (1995, March). Word building: A strategic approach to the teaching of phonics. *The Reading Teacher, 48*(6). 484–488.

Gurian, M. (1999). *Fine young man.* Seattle: Putnam Publishing Group.

Guthrie, J. T. (1984). Lexical learning. *The Reading Teacher, 37,* 660–662.

Guthrie, J. T., Barnham, N. A., Caplan, R. I., & Seifert, M. (1974). The maze technique to assess, monitor reading comprehension. *The Reading Teacher, 28*(2), 161–168.

Guthrie, J. T., Seifert, M., & Kline, L. W. (1978). Clues from research on programs for poor readers. In S. J. Samuels (Ed.), *What research has to say about reading instruction* (pp.1–12). Newark, DE: International Reading Association.

Guzzetti, B.J., & Marzano, R. J. (1984). Correlates of effective reading instruction. *The Reading Teacher, 37*(8), 754–758.

Hadaway, N., & Young, T. (1994). *Transactive Writing Journal of Adolescent and Adult Literacy, 44,* 234–239.

Hagerty, P. (1999). Making a difference: Designing the "ideal" literacy classroom at the intermediate level. 44th Annual International Reading Association Convention, San Diego, CA.

Haggard, M. (Ruddell). (1976). *Creative Thinking-Reading Activities (CT-RA) as a means for improving comprehension.* Unpublished doctoral dissertation, University of Missouri-Kansas City, Kansas City, MO.

Haggard, M. R. (1982). The vocabulary self-collection strategy: An active approach to word learning. *Journal of Reading, 27,* 203–207.

Hall, M. A. (1981). *Teacher reading as a language experience* (3rd ed.). Columbus, OH: Charles C. Merrill.

Hall, M. A. (1979). Language-centered reading: Premises and recommendations. *Language Arts, 56,* 664–670.

Halliday, M. A. K. (1975). *Learning how to mean: Explorations in the development of language.* London: Edward Arnold.

Hamilton, J. L. (1983). Measuring response to instruction as an assessment paradigm. *Advances in Learning and Behavioral Disabilities, 2,* 111–133.

Hammill, D. D., & Larsen, S. C. (1983). *Test of written language (TOWL).* Austin, TX: Pro-Ed.

Hanf, M. B. (1971). Mapping: A technique for translating reading into thinking. *Journal of Reading, 14,* 225–230, 270.

Hanna, P. R., Hodges, R. E., Hanna, J. L., & Rudolph, E. H. (1966). *Phoneme-Grapheme Correspondence as Cues to Spelling Improvement.* Washington, DC: Department of Health, Education, and Welfare, Office of Education.

Harmon, J. M. (1998). Constructing word meanings: Strategies and perceptions of four middle school learners. Journal of Literacy Research, *30, 561–599.*

Harmon, J. M. (2002). Teaching independent word learning strategies to struggling readers. *Journal of Adolescent and Adult Literacy, 45*(7), 606–615.

Harris, A. J. (1961). Perceptual difficulties in reading disability. In J. A. Figurel (Ed.), *Changing concepts in reading instruction (pp.* 281–290). Newark, DE: International Reading Association.

Harris, A. J., & Sipay, E. R. (1975). *How to increase reading ability.* (6th ed.). New York: David McKay.

Harris, A. J., & Sipay, E. R. (1980). *How to increase reading ability.* (7th ed.) New York: Longman.

Harris, A. J., & Sipay, E. R. (1985). *How to increase reading ability* (8th ed.). New York: Longman.

Harris, A. J., & Sipay, E. R. (1990). *How to increase reading ability: A guide to developmental and remedial methods* (9th ed.). New York: Longman.

Hasselbring, T., & Owens, S. (1982). *A microcomputer-based system for the analysis of student spelling errors.* Unpublished manuscript, George Peabody College of Vanderbilt University, Nashville, TN.

Hathaway, S. R., & McKinley, J. C. (1967). *Minnesota multiphasic personality inventory.* New York: Psychological Corporation.

Hayes, D. A. (1988). *Guided reading and summarizing procedure.* Manuscript, University of Georgia, Athens.

Haynes & Fillmer, 1984; 10

Haynes, J. E., & Fillmer, H. T. (1984). Paraphrasing and reading comprehension. *Reading World, 24,* 76–79.

Hazenburg, S., & Hulstijn, J. H. (1996). Defining a minimal receptive second language vocabulary for non-native university students: An empirical investigation. *Applied Linguistics, 17,* 145–163.

Heaton, M. M., & Lewis, H. B. (1955). *Reading ladders for human relations* (3rd ed.). Washington, DC: American Council on Education.

Hebb, D. O. (1949). *The organization of behavior.* New York: John Wiley & Sons.

Heckelman, R. G. (1966). Using the neurological impress remedial technique. *Academic Therapy Quarterly, 1,* 235–239

Heimlich, J. E., & Pittelman, S. D. (1986). *Semantic mapping: Classroom applications.* Newark, DE: International Reading Association.

Helfeldt, J. P., & Henk, W.A. (1990). Reciprocal questioning: Answer relationship, an instructional technique for at-risk readers. *Journal of Reading, 33,* 509–514.

Helfeldt, J. P., & Lalik, R. (1979). Reciprocal student-teacher questioning. In C. Pennock (Ed.), *Reading comprehension at four linguistic levels* (pp. 74–99). Newark, DE: International Reading Association.

Helfeldt, J. P., & Lalik, R. (1976). Reciprocal student-teacher questioning. *The Reading Teacher, 30*(3), 283–287.

Heller, M. F. (1986). How do you know what you know? Metacognitive modeling in the content areas. *Journal of Reading, 29*(5), 415–422.

Henderson, E. (1985). *Teaching Spelling.* Boston: Houghton Mifflin.

Hendrickson, J. M., Gable, R. A., & Hasselbring, T. (1988). Pleez lit me pas spellin: Diagnosing and remediating errors in spelling. *Education and Treatment of Children, 11*(2), 166–178.

Henk, W. A., & King, G. T. (1984). Helping students follow written directions. In G. H. McNinch (Ed.), *Reading teacher education. Fourth yearbook of the American Reading Forum* (pp. 62–64). Athens, GA: American Reading Forum.

Henk, W. A., & Selders, M. L. (1984). A test of synonymic scoring of cloze passage. *The Reading Teacher, 38*(3), 282–287.

Herman, P. A. (1985). The effects of repeated readings on reading rate, speech pauses, and word recognition accuracy. *Reading Research Quarterly, 20,* 553–565.

Heron, A. H. (2003). A study of agency: multiple constructions of choice and decision making in an inquiry-based summer school program for struggling readers. *Journal of Adolescent and Adult Literacy. 46*(7), 568–580.

Herrmann, B. A. (1992). Teaching and assessing strategic reasoning: Dealing with the dilemmas. *The Reading Teacher, 45,* 428–433.

Hewett, S. (1991). Motivating a noninterested learner. *Journal for Affective Reading Education, 11*(fall), 21–22.

Hibbing, A. N., & Rankin-Erickson, J. L. (2003). A picture is worth a thousand words:Using visual images to improve comprehension for middle school struggling readers. *Journal of Reading, 56*(8), 758–770.

Hieronymus, A. N., Hoover, H. D., & Lindquist, E. E. (1986). *Iowa test of basic skills.* Chicago: Riverside.

Hill, M. (1991). Writing summaries promotes thinking and learning across the curriculum—but why are they so difficult to write? *Journal of Reading, 34*(7), 536–539.

Hill, S. (1999, November). A study of the knowledge of phonics, phonemic awareness, and developmental spelling ability in primary non-readers. Paper presented at the Annual Meeting of the Mid-South Educational Research Association, Point Clear, AL 1999.

Hittleman, D. R. (1978). *Developmental reading: A psycholinguistic perspective.* Chicago: Rand McNally.

Hoffman, J. V. (1977). Intra-Act: A language in the content areas teaching procedure. Doctoral dissertation, University of Missouri-Kansas City. *Dissertation Abstracts International, 38,* 3248A.

Hoffman, J. V., & Clements, R. (1984). Reading miscues and teacher verbal feedback. *The Elementary School Journal, 84,* 423–439.

Hoffman, J. V., O'Neal, S. V., Kastler, L. A., Clements, R. D., Segal, K. W., & Nash, M. F. (l984). Guided oral reading and miscue focused feedback in second-grade classrooms. *Reading Research Quarterly, 14,* 367–384.

Holdaway, D. (1979). *The foundations of literacy.* New York: Ashton Scholastic.

Holmes, J. A., & Singer, H. (1961). *The substrata-factor theory: Substrata-factor differences underlying reading ability in known groups.* (Final Report No. 538, SAE 8176.) US Office of Education.

Hood, J. (l975–1976). Qualitative analysis of oral reading errors: The inter-judge reliability of scores. *Reading Research Quarterly, 11*(4), 577–98.

Hoover, W. A., & Gough, P. B. (1990). The simple view of reading. Reading and Writing: An Interdisciplinary Journal, 2(2), 127–160.

Hori, A. K. O. (1977). *An investigation of the efficacy of a questioning training procedure on increasing the reading comprehension performance of junior high school learning disabled students.* Unpublished master's thesis, University of Kansas, Lawrence, Kansas.

Howard, M. (1986). Effects of pre-reading training in auditory conceptualization on subsequent reading achievement. Doctoral dissertation, Brigham Young University, UT.

Hull, M. A. (1976). *Phonics for the teacher of reading* (2nd ed.). Columbus, OH: Charles C. Merrill.

Hulme, C. (1981a). The effects of manual tracing on memory in normal and retarded readers: Some implications for multi-sensory teaching. *Psychological Research* (Developmental Dyslexia Issue), *43*, 179–191.

Hulme, C. (1981b). *Reading retardation and multi-sensory teaching.* Boston: Routledge & Kegan Paul.

Hunt, K. (1965). *Grammatical structures written at three grade levels.* Urbana, IL: National Council of Teachers of English

Hurley, S. R., & Ryan, L. (2000). Collaboration to save struggling readers. *Affective Reading Education Journal, 18,* 17–23.

Hurley, S. R., & Tinajero, J. V. (2001). *Literacy assessment of second language learners.* Boston: Allyn & Bacon.

Huttenlocher, R. R., & Huttenlocher, J. (l973). A study of children with hyperlexia. *Neurology, 23,* 1107–1116.

Idol, L. (1987). Group story mapping: A comprehension for both skilled and unskilled readers. *Journal of Learning Disabilities, 20,* 196–205.

Idol, L., & Croll, V. J. (1987). Story-mapping training as a means of improving reading comprehension. *Learning Disability Quarterly, 10*(3), 214–229.

Indrisano, R. (1982, January). An ecological approach to learning. *Topics in Learning and Learning Disabilities, 1,* 11–15.

Invernizzi, M., Abouzeid, M., & Gill, T. (1994). Using students' invented spelling as a guide for spelling instruction that emphasizes word study. *The Elementary School Journal, 95,* (2), 155–167.

Ito, H. R. (1980). Long-term effects of resource room programs on learning disable children's reading. *Journal of Learning Disabilities, 13,* 322–326.

Jaggar, A. (1985). An observing the language learner: Introduction and overview. In A. Jaggar & M. T. Smith-Burke (Eds.), *Observing the language learner* (pp. 1–7). Newark, DE: International Reading Association.

Jensen, A. R. (1980). *Bias in mental testing.* New York: The Free Press.

Jett-Simpson, M. (1981). Writing stories using model structures: The circle story. *Language Arts, 58*(3), 293–300.

Johnson, D. D., & Pearson, P. D. (1984). *Teaching reading vocabulary* (2nd ed.). New York: Holt, Rinehart & Winston.

Johnston, F. R. (1999). The timing and teaching of word families. *The Reading Teacher, 53*(1), 64–75.

Johnston, P. H. (1987). Teachers as evaluation experts. *The Reading Teacher, 40,* 744–748.

Johnston, P. H., & Allington, R. (1991). Remediation. In R. Barr, R., M. L. Kamil, P. B. Mosenthal, & P. D. Pearson (Eds.), *Handbook of reading research,* vol. II (pp. 984–1012). New York: Longman.

Johnston, P. H., & Allington, R. (1991). Remediation. In R. Barr, M.L. Kamil, P.B. Mosenthal, & P.D. Pearson (Eds.), *Handbook of reading research,* vol. 2 (pp. 984–1012). New York: Longman.

Johnston, P. H., & Winograd, P. N. (1985). Passive failure in reading. *Journal of Reading Behavior, 17,* 279–301

Jongsma, E. (1980). *Cloze instruction research: A second look.* Newark, DE: International Reading Association.

Joshi, R. M., & Aaron, P. G. (2000). The component model of reading: Simple view of reading made a little more complex. *Reading Psychology, 21,* 85–97

Juel, C. (1988). Learning to read and write: A longitudinal study of fifty-four children from first through fourth grades. *Journal of Educational Psychology, 80,* 437–447.

Juel, C. (1991). Beginning reading. In R. Barr, M. L. Kamil, P. Mosenthal, & P. D. Pearson (Eds.), *Handbook of reading research,* vol. II. New York: Longman.

Juel, C., & Roper-Schneider, D. (1985). The influence of basal readers on first-grade reading. *Reading Research Quarterly, 20,* 134–152.

Kagan, S. (1994). Co-op lesson designs. San Clemente, CA: Kagan Cooperative.

Kagan, S. (1997). Cooperative learning. San Clemente, CA: Kagan Cooperative.

Kalmbach, J. R. (1986). Getting at the point of retellings. *Journal of Reading, 29,* 326–333.

Kameenui, E. J., & Shanon, P. (1988). Point/counterpoint: Direct instruction reconsidered. In J. E. Readence, R. S. Baldwin, J. P. Konopak, & P. R. O'Keefe (Eds.), *Dialogues in literacy research. 37th yearbook of the National Reading Conference* (pp. 35–43). Chicago: National Reading Conference.

Kampwirth, T. J., & Bates, M. (1980). Modality preference and teaching method: A review of the research. *Academic Therapy, 5,* 597–605.

Katims, D., & Harris, S. (1997). Improving reading comprehension of middle school students in inclusive classrooms. *Journal of Adolescent and Adult Literacy, 41*(2), 116–123.

Kaufman, M. (1976). Comparison of achievement for Distar and conventional instruction with primary pupils. *Reading Improvement, 13,* 169–173.

Kay, L., Young, J. L., Mottley, R. R. (1986). Using Manzo's ReQuest model with delinquent adolescents. *Journal of Reading, 29,* 506–510.

Keel, M., Dangel, H., Owens, S. (1999). Selecting instructional interventions for students with mild disabilities in inclusive classrooms. *Focus on Exceptional Children 31,* 1–16.

Kelly, B. W., & Holmes, J. (1979). The Guided Lecture Procedure. *Journal of Reading, 22,* 602–604.

Kern, R. G. (1992). Teaching second language texts: Schematic interaction, affective response and the directed reading-thinking activity. *The Canadian Modern Language Review, 48* (2), 307–325.

Kinan, P., & Nassief, M. (2000). *Yabbit the Rabbit.* Yorba Linda, CA: Susie Mark Productions.

Kirby, D., & Liner, T. (1981). *Inside out: Developmental strategies for teaching.* Montclair, NJ: Boynton/Cook.

Kirby, J. R. (1988). Style, strategy, and skill in reading. In R. R. Schmeck (Ed.), *Learning strategies and learning styles* (pp. 229–274). New York: Plenum.

Kirby, M. W. (1989). Teaching sight vocabulary with and without context before silent reading: A field test of the "focus of attention" hypothesis. *Journal of Reading Behavior, 21*(3), 261–278.

Klasen, E. (1972). *The syndrome of specific dyslexia: With special consideration of its physiological, psychological, test psychological and social correlates.* Baltimore: University Park Press

Klenk, L., & Kibby, M. W. (2000). Re-mediating reading difficulties: Appraising the past, reconciling the present, constructing the future. In Michael Kamil, Peter Mosenthal,

P. David Pearson, & Rebecca Barr (Eds.), *Handbook of reading research,* vol. III (pp. 667–690). New York: Longman.

Kline, C. L., & Kline, C. L. (1975). Follow-up study of 216 dyslexic Children. *Bulletin of the Orton Society, 25,* 127–144.

Knafle, J. D., Legenza-Wescott, A., & Passcarella, E. T. (1988). Assessing values in children's books. *Reading Improvement, 25*(1), 71–81.

Koenke, K. (1978). A comparison of three auditory discrimination-perception tests. *Academic Therapy, 13,* 463–468.

Konopak, B. C., & Williams, N. L. (1988). Using the key word method to help young readers learn content material. *The Reading Teacher, 41,* 682–687.

Korat, O., Bahar, E., Snapir, M. (2002). Sociodramatic play as opportunity for literacy development: The teacher's role. *The Reading Teacher, 56*(4), 386–393.

Koskinen, P. S., & Blum, I. H. (1986). Paired repeated reading: A classroom strategy for developing fluent reading. *The Reading Teacher, 40*(1), 70–75.

Koskinen, P. S., Blum, I. H., Bisson, S. A., Phillips, S. M., Creamer, T. S., & Baker, T. K. (1999). Shared reading, books, and audiotapes: Supporting diverse students in school and at home. *The Reading Teacher. 52*(5), 430–444.

Krashen, S. D. (2002). The NRP comparison of whole language and phonics: Ignoring the crucial variable in reading. *Talking Points, 13*(3): 22–28.

Krashen, S. D. (1982). *Principles and practices in second language acquisition.* New York: Pergamon Press.

Krathwohl, D. R., Bloom, B. S., & Masia, B. B. (1964). *Taxonomy of educational objectives; the classification of educational goals; handbook 2: Affective domain.* New York: David McKay.

Labbo, L. D., & Teale, W. H. (1990). Cross-age reading: A strategy for helping poor readers. *The Reading Teacher, 43*(6), 362–369.

LaBerge, D., & Samuels, S. J. (1974). Toward a theory of automatic information processing in reading. *Cognitive Psychology, 6*(2), 293–323.

Langer, J. A. (1981). From theory to practice: A prereading plan. *Journal of Reading, 25,* 152–156.

Larking, L. (1984). ReQuest helps children comprehend: A study. *Australian Journal of Reading, 7,* 135–139.

Leibert, R. E. (1981). The IRI: Relating test performance to instruction—A concept. *Reading Horizons, 22*(2), 110–115.

Leibert, R. E., & Sherk, J. K., Jr. (1970). Three Frostig visual perception sub-tests and specific reading tasks for kindergarten, first, and second grade children. *The Reading Teacher, 24*(2), 130–137.

Lenahan, A. V. (1992). *Bits and Pieces.* Fairfield, NJ: The Economical Press.

Leslie, L., & Osol, P. (1978). Changes in oral reading strategies as a function of quantities of miscues. *Journal of Reading Behavior, 10*(4), 442–45.

Levin, J. R., & Pressley, M. (1981). Improving children's prose comprehension: Selected strategies that seem to succeed. In C. M. Santa & B. L. Hayes (Eds.), *Children's prose comprehension* (pp. 49–60). Newark, DE: International Reading Association.

Levin, J. R., Levin, M. E., Glasman, L. D., & Nordwall, M. B. (1992). Mnemonic vocabulary instruction: Additional effectiveness evidence. *Contemporary Educational Psychology, 17,* 156–174.

Levin, J. R., Morrison, C. R., McGivern, J. E., Mastropieri, M. A., & Scruggs, T. E. (1986). Mnemomic facilitation of text-embedded science facts. *American Educational Research Journal, 23*(3), 489–506.

Lewis, B. A. (1992). *Kids with courage.* Minneapolis, MN: Free Spirit.

Lewkowicz, N. K. (1987). On the question of teaching decoding skills to older students. *Journal of Reading, 31,* 50–57.

Liddell, H. G., & Scott, R. (1940). *A Greek-English lexicon.* (Revised by H. S. Jones, & R. McKenize.) Oxford, England: Clarendon Press.

Lijeron, J.T. (1993). Reciprocal teaching of metacognitive strategies to strengthen reading comprehension of high school students in Spanish: A descriptive case study. Unpublished doctoral dissertation, Akron University, Akron, OH.

Lindamood, C. H., & Lindamood, P. C. (1975). *The A.D.D. program, auditory discrimination in depth,* Books 1 and 2. Hingham, MA: Teaching Resources.

Lipson, M. Y. (1982). Learning new information from text: The role of prior knowledge and reading ability. *Journal of Reading Behavior, 14,* 243–262.

Lipson, M. Y. (1983). The influence of religious affiliations on children's memory for text information. *Reading Research Quarterly, 18,* 448–457.

Lipson, M. Y., & Wixson, K. K. (1991). *Assessment and instruction of reading disability.* New York: HarperCollins.

Lonberger, R. (1988). Effects of training in a self-generated learning strategy on the prose processing abilities of 4th and 6th graders. Paper presented at the annual meeting of the Eastern Education Association, Savannah, GA.

Loxterman, J., Beck, I., & McKeown, M. G. (1994). The effects of thinking aloud on student comprehension. *Reading Research Quarterly, 29*(4), 358–368.

Luce, S., & Hoge, R. (1978). Relations among teacher rankings, pupil-teacher interactions, and academic achievement. *American Educational Research Journal, 15,* 498–500.

Lundsteen, S. W. (1979). *Listening: Its impact at all levels on reading and other language arts* (rev. ed.). Urbana, IL: National Council of Teachers of English.

Luscher, M. (1969). *The Luscher color test* (I.A. Scott, Ed. and Trans.). New York: Random House. (Original work published as *Psychologie der Farben,* first published as *Psychologie der Farben: Textband zum Luscher-Test,* 1949).

Lysynchuk, L. M., Pressley, M., & Vye, N. J. (1990). Reciprocal teaching improves standardized reading-comprehension performance in poor comprehenders. *Elementary School Journal, 90*(5), 469–484.

MacGinitie, W. H., & MacGinitie, R. K. (1989). *Gates-MacGinitie Reading Tests: Manual for scoring and interpretation—level 4* (3rd ed.). Chicago: Riverside.

Maggart, Z. D., & Zintz, M. V. (1992). *The reading process: The teacher and the learner* (6th ed.), Dubuque, IA: WC Brown & Benchmark.

Maier, N. R. F. (1963). *Problem-solving discussions and conferences: Leadership methods and skills.* New York: McGraw-Hill.

Malicky, G. V., & Norman, C. A. (1988). Reading processes subgroups in a clinical population. *The Alberta Journal of Educational Research, 34*(4), 344–354.

Mann, L., & Sabatino, D. A. (1985). *Foundations of cognitive process in remedial and special education.* Rockville, MD: Aspen Publishers.

Manzo, A. V. (1969a). Improving reading comprehension through reciprocal questioning. Doctoral dissertation, Syracuse University, Syracuse, NY, 1968. *Dissertation Abstracts International, 30,* 5344A.

Manzo, A. V. (1969b). The ReQuest procedure. *Journal of Reading, 13,* 123–126.

Manzo, A. V. (1970). CAT—A game for extending vocabulary and knowledge allusions. *Journal of Reading, 13,* 367–369.

Manzo, A. V. (1973). CONPASS English: A demonstration project. *Journal of Reading, 16,* 539–545.

Manzo, A. V. (1975a). Guided Reading Procedure. *Journal of Reading, 18,* 287–291.

Manzo, A. V. (1975b). *Manzo's bestiary inventory.* Monograph of the Center for Resources Development in ABE, University of Missouri-Kansas City.

Manzo, A. V. (1977a). Dyslexia as specific psychoneurosis. *Journal of Reading Behavior, 19*(3), 305–308.

Manzo, A. V. (1977b). *Recent developments in content area reading.* Keynote address, Missouri Council of Teachers of English, Springfield, MO.

Manzo, A. V. (1980). Three "universal" strategies in content area reading and languaging. *Journal of Reading, 24,* 146–149.

Manzo, A. V. (1981a). The Language Shaping Paradigm (LSP) for improving language, comprehension, and thought. In P.L. Anders (Ed.), *Research on reading in secondary schools: A semi-annual report* (Monograph No. 7, pp. 54–68). Tucson: University of Arizona, College of Education, Reading Department.

Manzo, A. V. (1981b). Using proverbs to teach reading and thinking; or, Com faceva mia nonna (the way my grandmother did it). *The Reading Teacher, 34,* 411–416.

Manzo, A. V. (1983). "Subjective approach to vocabulary" acquisition (Or ". . . I think my brother is arboreal!"). *Reading Psychology, 3,* 155–160.

Manzo, A. V. (1985). Expansion modules for the ReQuest, CAT, GRP, and REAP reading/study procedures. *Journal of Reading, 28,* 498–502.

Manzo, A. V. (1987). Psychologically induced dyslexia and learning disabilities. *The Reading Teacher, 40*(4), 408–413.

Manzo, A. V. (2003). Literacy crisis or Cambrian period: Implications to theory, public policy and practice. *Journal of Adolescent and Adult Literacy.*

Manzo, A. V. (2003). *Literacy crisis or Cambrian Period? Theory, practice and public policy implications.* Journal of Adolescent and Adult Literacy, *46*(8), *654–661.*

Manzo, A. V., & Casale (Manzo), U. C. (1980). The five c's: A problem-solving approach to study skills. *Reading Horizons, 20,* 281–284.

Manzo, A. V., & Casale (Manzo), U. C. (1981). A multivariate analysis of principle and trace elements in mature reading comprehension. In G. H. McNinch (Ed.), *Comprehension: Process and product. First yearbook of the American Reading Forum* (pp. 76–81). Athens, GA: American Reading Forum.

Manzo, A. V., & Casale (Manzo), U. C. (1983). A preliminary description and factor analysis of a broad spectrum battery for assessing "progress toward reading maturity." *Reading Psychology, 4,* 181–191.

Manzo, A. V., & Casale (Manzo), U. C. (1985). Listen-read-discuss: A content reading heuristic. *Journal of Reading, 28*(8), 732–734.

Manzo, A. V., & Legenza, A. (1975). Inquiry training for kindergarten children. *Journal of Educational Leadership, 32,* 479–483.

Manzo, A. V., & Manzo U. C. (1990a). *Content area reading: A heuristic approach.* Columbus, OH: Merrill.

Manzo, A. V., & Manzo, U. C. (1985). Listen-read-discuss: A content reading heuristic. *Journal of Reading, 28,* 732–734.

Manzo, A. V., & Manzo, U. C. (1987a). *Asking, answering, commenting: A participation training strategy.* Paper presented at the annual meeting of the international Reading association, Anaheim, CA.

Manzo, A. V., & Manzo, U. C. (1987b). Using proverbs to diagnose and treat comprehension dysfunctions. *Rhode Island Reading Review, 3*(2), 37–42.

Manzo, A. V., & Manzo, U. C. (1990b). Note cue: A comprehension and participation training strategy. *Journal of Reading, 33*(8), 608–611.

Manzo, A. V., & Manzo, U. C. (1993). *Literacy disorders: Holistic diagnosis and remediation.* Fort Worth, TX: Harcourt, Brace.

Manzo, A. V., & Manzo, U. C. (1995). *Teaching children to be literate: A reflective approach.* Fort Worth, TX: Harcourt, Brace.

Manzo, A. V., & Sherk, J. K., Jr. (1971–1972). Reading and "languaging in the content areas": A vocabulary acquisition. *Journal of Reading Behavior, 4,* 78–89.

Manzo, A. V., Lorton, M., & Condon, M. (1975). *Personality characteristics and learning style preferences of adult basic education students.* Research monograph of Center for Resource Development in Adult Education University of Missouri-Kansas City.

Manzo, A. V., Manzo, U. C., & Albee, J. J. (2002). iREAP: Improving reading, writing, and thinking in the wired classroom. *Journal of Adolescent and Adult Literacy, 46*(1), 42–47.

Manzo, A. V., Manzo, U. C., & Estes, T. H. (2001). *Content area literacy: Interactive teaching for active learning* (3rd ed). New York: John Wiley.

Manzo, A. V., Manzo, U. C., & McKenna, M. C. (1995). *Informal reading-thinking inventory.* Fort Worth, TX: Harcourt Brace.

Manzo, A. V., Manzo, U. C., Barnhill, A., & Thomas, M. (2000). Proficient reader subtypes: Implications for literacy theory, assessment, and practice. *Reading Psychology, 21*(3), 217–232.

Manzo, A. V., Sherk, J. K., Jr., Leibert, R. E., & Mocker, D. W. (1977). *Re: Reading and the library (Improvement of learning monograph series no.1).* Kansas City: University of Missouri-Kansas City, Reading Center.

Maria, K. (1990). *Reading comprehension instruction: Issues and strategies.* Parkton, MD: York Press.

Maring, G. H., & Furman, G. (1985). Seven "whole class" strategies to help mainstreamed young people read and listen better in content area classes. *Journal of Reading, 28,* 694–700.

Maring, G. H., & Ritson, R. (1980). Reading improvement in the gymnasium. *Journal of Reading, 24,* 27–31.

Marshall, N. (1983). Using story grammar to assess reading comprehension. *The Reading Teacher, 36,* 616–621.

Martin, D. C., Lorton, M., Blanc, R. A., & Evans, C. (1977). The learning center: A comprehensive model for colleges and universities. Grand Rapids, MI: Central Trade Plant.

Marzano, R. J. (1991). Language, the language arts, and thinking. In J. Flood, J. M. Jensen, D. Lapp, & J. R. Squire (Eds.), *Handbook of research on teaching the English language arts* (pp. 559–586). New York: Macmillan.

Marzano, R. J., & Marzano, J. S. (1988). *A cluster approach to elementary vocabulary instruction.* Newark, DE: International Reading Association.

Maslow, A. H. (1954). *Motivation and personality.* New York: Harper Brothers.

Mason, J. M., & Au, K. H. (1986). *Reading instruction for today.* Glenview, IL: Scott, Foresman.

Mason, J., Herman, P., & Au, K. (1991). Children's developing knowledge of words. In J. Flood, J. M. Jensen, D. Lapp, & J. R. Squire (Eds.), *Handbook of research on teaching the English language arts* (pp. 721–731). New York: Macmillan.

Mastropieri, M. A. (1988). Using the keyboard [SIC] method. *Teaching Exceptional Children, 20,* 4–8.

Mathes, P. G., Simmons, D. C., & Davis, B. I.. (1992). Assisted reading techniques for developing reading fluency. *Reading Research and Instruction, 31,* 70–77.

Matthews, M. W., & Kesner, J. E. (2000). The silencing of Sammy: One struggling reader learning with his peers. *The Reading Teacher, 53*(5), 382–390.

Maw, W., & Maw, E. (1967). Children's curiosity as an aspect of reading comprehension. *The Reading Teacher, 15*(2), 236–240.

McClelland, D. C., Atkinson, J. W., Clark, R. A., & Lowell, E. L. (1976). *The achievement motive.* New York: Irvington.

McCormick, S. (1987). *Remedial and clinical reading instruction.* Columbus, OH: Merrill.

McCormick, S. (1990, December). *Multiple-exposure/multiple-context longitudinal study of Peter Parsons.* Paper presented at the National Reading Conference, Austin, TX.

McInstosh, M. E., & Draper, R. (1995). Applying the question-answer relationship to mathematics. *Journal of Adolescent and Adult Literacy, 39,* 120–131.

McIntyre, J. (1991, June). *The developmental difference: "Skill and will": An investigation into the reported feelings of personal control and competency of community college developmental students.* Presentation to "ABD Club," University of Missouri-Kansas City.

McKenna, M. C. (1976). Synonymic versus verbatim scoring the cloze procedure. *Journal of Reading, 20,* 141–143.

McKenna, M. C., & Robinson, R. D. (1980). *An introduction to the cloze procedure: An annotated bibliography.* Newark, DE: International Reading Association.

McKenzie, J. V., Ericson, B., & Hunter, L. (1988). *Questions may be an answer.* Manuscript, California State University at Northridge.

McKeown, M. G. (1993).Creating effective definitions for young word learners. *Reading Research Quarterly 28*(1), 17–31F.

McKissack, P. C. (1986). *Flossie & the fox.* New York: Dial Books for Young Readers.

McNeil, J., & Donant, L. (1982). Summarization strategy for improving reading comprehension. In J. A. Niles & L. A. Harris (Eds.), *New inquiries in reading research and instruction* (pp. 215–219). Rochester, NY: National Reading Conference.

McWilliams, L., & Rakes, T. A. (1979). *Content inventories: English, social studies, science.* Dubuque, IA: Kendall/Hunt.

Meeks, J. W. (1980). Effects of imbedded aids on prose-related textual material. *Reading World, 19,* 345–351.

Meeks, J. W. (1991). Prior knowledge and metacognitive processes of reading comprehension: Applications to mildly retarded readers. In *Advances in mental retardation and developmental disabilities,* vol. 4 (pp.123–144). Lanhen, MD: Jessica Kingley.

Mellon, J. C. (1969). *Transformational sentence-combining.* Urbana, IL: National Council of Teachers of English.

Merton, R. K. (1968). The Matthew effect in science. *Science, 159,* 56–63.

Meyer, B. J. F. (1975). *The organization of prose and its effect on memory.* Amsterdam: North-Holland.

Miller, S. D., & Smith, D. E. (1990). Relationships among oral reading, silent reading, and listening comprehension of students at different competency levels. *Reading Research and Instruction, 29*(Winter), 73–84.

Mills, R. E. (1965). An evaluation of techniques for teaching word recognition. *Elementary School Journal, 56,* 221–225.

Mills, R. E. (1970). *Learning methods test* (rev. ed.). Fort Lauderdale, FL: The Mills School.

Moe, I. L., & Nania, F. (1959). Reading deficiencies among abled pupils. *Developmental Reading.* Newark, DE: International Reading Association. Reprinted in Lawrence E. Hafner (Ed.). (1974). *Improving reading in middle and secondary* (2nd ed.) (pp. 172–185). New York: Macmillan.

Moore, D. W. (1987). Vocabulary. In D. E. Alvermann, D. W. Moore, & M. W. Conley (Eds.), *Research within reach: Secondary school reading* (pp.64–79). Newark, DE: International Reading Association.

Moore, D. W., & Moore, S. A. (1986). Possible sentences. In E. K. Dishner, T. W. Bean, J. E. Readence, & D. W. Moore (Eds.), *Reading in the content areas* (pp. 174–178). Dubuque, IA: Kendall-Hunt.

Moore, R. A., & Brantingham, K. (2003). Nathan: A case study in retrospective miscue analysis. *The Reading Teacher, 56*(5), 466–474.

Morgan, C., & Murray, H. A. (1935). A method for investigating fantasies: The Thematic Apperception Test. *Archives of Neurology and Psychiatry, 34,* 289–306.

Morris, D., Blanton, L., Blanton, W., & Nowacek, J. (1995) Teaching achieving spellers at their "instructional" level. *The Elementary School Journal, 92,* 145–162.

Morrow, L. M. (1989). Creating a bridge to children's literature. In P. Winograd, K. Wixson, & M. Lipson (Eds.), *Improving basal reading instruction* (pp.210–230). New York: Teachers College Press.

Muth, K. D. (1987). Teachers' connection questions: Prompting students to organize text ideas. *Journal of Reading, 31,* 254–259.

Myklebust, H. R. (1965). *Development and disorders of written language,* vol 1: *Picture story language test.* New York: Grune & Stratton.

NAEP facts: Long-term trends in student reading performance. National Center for Education Statistics. (1998). Publication # NCES 98464. Jessup, MD: Education Publications Center. Available at: http://nces.ed.gov/pubsearch/pubsinfo.asp?pubid=98464.

Nagy, W. E. (1988). *Teaching vocabulary to improve reading comprehension.* Urbana, IL: National Council of Teachers of English.

Nagy, W. E., & Herman, P. A. (1987). Breadth and depth of vocabulary knowledge: Implications for acquisition and instruction. In M.G. McKeown & M.E. Curtis (Eds.), *The nature of vocabulary acquisition* (pp. 19–35). Hillsdale, NJ: Erlbaum.

Nagy, W. E., & Scott, J. A. (2000). Vocabulary processes. In M. L. Kamil, P. B. Mosenthal, P. D. Pearson, & R. Barr (Eds.), *Handbook of reading research,* vol. III (pp. 269–284).

Nagy, W. E., Anderson, R. C., & Herman, R. (1987). Learning word meanings from context during normal reading. *American Educational Research Journal, 84,* 237–70.

Nagy, W. E., & Herman, P. A. (1984, October). *Limitations of vocabulary instruction.* Technical Report No. 326. Champaign, IL: Center for the Study of Reading, University of Illinois.

Nelson-Herber, J. (1986). Expanding and refining vocabulary in content areas. *Journal of Reading, 29,* 626–633.

Newman, S. (1999). *The child with special needs: Encouraging intellectual and emotional growth.* Reading, MA: Addison-Wesley.

Nicholson, M. J. (1996). The effect of invented spelling on running word counts in creative writing. M.A. research project, Kean College, Union, NJ (ERIC Document Reproduction Service No. ED 393108).

Nilsen, A. P., & Nilsen, D. L. F. (2003). A new spin on teaching vocabulary: A source-based approach. *The Reading Teacher, 56*(5), 436–444.

Nist, S. L. (1984). *Developing textbook thinking.* Lexington, MA: DC Heath.

Nist, S. L., & Simpson, M. L. (1989). PLAE, a validated study strategy. *Journal of Reading, 33,* 182–186.

Nist, S. L., & Simpson, M. L. (1990). The effects of PLAE upon students' test performance and metacognitive awareness. In J. Zutell & S. McCormick (Eds.), *Literacy theory and research: Analyses from multiple paradigms. The 39th yearbook of the National Reading Conference* (pp. 321–327). Chicago: National Reading Conference.

Nist, S. L., Simpson, M. L., Olejnik, S., & Mealey, D. L. (1989). *The relation between self-selected text learning variables and test performance.* Manuscript submitted for publication.

O'Brube, W., Camplese, D., & Sanford, M. (1987). The use of teletherapy in the mainstream era. In K. VanderMeulen (Ed.), *Reading Horizons: Selected Readings* (pp. 163–165). Kalamazoo, MI: Western Michigan University.

O'Brien, D. (1986). A test of three positions posed to explain the relation between word knowledge and comprehension. In J. A. Niles & R. V. Lalik (Eds.), *Solving problems in literacy: Learners, teachers, and researchers. 35th yearbook of the National Reading Conference* (pp. 81–91). Rochester, NY: National Reading Conference.

Ogle, D. M. (1989). The know, what to know, learn strategy. In K. D. Muth (Ed.), *Children's comprehension of text* (pp. 205–223). Newark, DE: International Reading Association.

Oldridge, O. A. (1982). Positive suggestion: It helps LD students learn. *Academic Therapy, 17*(3), 279–287.

Opitz, M. F. (2002). Assessment interviews for parents and teachers. In B. J. Guzzetti (Ed.), *Literacy in America: An encyclopedia of history, theory, and practice,* vol. 1 (pp. 30–31). Santa Barbara, CA: ABC-CLIO, Inc.

Ordonez-Jasis, R. (1995). Language, culture, self-identity and the school: Calo as a learning tool. Unpublished MA Thesis, University of California, Berkeley.

Ordonez-Jasis, R. (2002). Latino families and schools: Tensions, transitions and transformations. Unpublished doctoral dissertation, University of California, Berkeley.

Ordonez-Jasis, R. (2003, May). Chicano families and special education: Reconstructing the "reluctant" reader. Presentation given at annual conference the Linguistic Minority Research Institute.

Ordonez-Jasis, R., & Jasis, P. (2004, January). Rising with De Colores: Tapping into the resources of la comunidad to assist under-performing Chicano/Latino students. *Journal of Latinos and Education, 3*(1).

O'Shea, L. J., Sindelar, P. T., & O'Shea, D. J. (1985). The effects of repeated readings and attentional cues on reading fluency and comprehension. *Journal of Reading Behavior, 17*(2), 129–142

Owens, P., & Campiranonta, K. (1988). *Thai proverbs.* Bangkok: Darnsutha Press Co.

Palinscar, A. S., & Brown, A. L. (1984). Reciprocal teaching of comprehension-fostering and comprehension-monitoring activities. *Cognition and Instruction, 2,* 117–175.

Palinscar, A. S., & Brown, A. L. (1986). Interactive teaching to promote independent learning from text. *The Reading Teacher, 39,* 771–777.

Palinscar, A. S., & Ransom, K. (1988). From the mystery spot to the thoughtful spot: The instruction of metacognition strategies. *The Reading Teacher, 41*(8), 784–789.

Palinscar, A. S., Brown, A. L., & Martin, S. M. (1987). Peer interaction in reading comprehension instruction. *Educational Psychologist, 22,* 231–253.

Palmatier, R. A. (1971). Comparison of four note-taking procedures. *Journal of Reading, 14,* 235–40, 258.

Palmatier, R. A. (1973). A notetaking system for learning. *Journal of Reading, 17,* 36–39.

Palmatier, R. A., & Bennett, J. M. (1974). Notetaking habits of college students. *Journal of Reading, 18,* 215–218.

Paratore, J. R., & Indrisano, R. (1987). Intervention assessment of reading comprehension. *The Reading Teacher, 40,* 778–783.

Paribakht, T. S., & Wesche, M., (1997). Vocabulary Enhancement Activities and Reading for Meaning in Second Language Vocabulary Development. In J. Coady & T. Huckin (Eds.), *Second language vocabulary acquisition: A rational for pedagogy.* Cambridge: Cambridge University Press, 174–200.

Paris, S. G. (1986). Teaching children to guide their reading and learning. In T. E. Raphael (Ed.), *The contexts of school-based literacy* (pp.115–130). New York: Random House.

Paris, S. G., & Myers, M., II. (1981). Comprehension monitoring, memory and study strategies of good and poor readers. *Journal of Reading Behavior, 13*(1) 5–22.

Paris, S. G., & Oka, E. R. (1989). Strategies for comprehending text and coping with reading difficulties. *Learning Disability Quarterly, 12*(1), 32–42.

Paris, S. G., Cross, D. R., & Lipson, M. Y. (1984). Informed strategies for learning: A program to improve children's reading awareness and comprehension. *Journal of Educational Psychology, 76,* 1239–1252.

Parry, K. (1991). Building vocabulary through academic reading. *TESOL Quarterly, 25* (4), 629–653.

Pask, G. (1988). Learning strategies, teaching strategies, and conceptual or learning style. In R. R. Schmeck (Ed.), *Learning strategies and learning styles* (pp. 83–100). New York: Plenum.

Pauk, W. (1974, 1989). *How to study in college.* Boston: Houghton Mifflin.

Paulsen, J., & Macken, M. (1978). *Report on the level of achievement in CAI reading programs.* Palo Alto, CA: Computer Curriculum Corporation.

Peabody picture vocabulary test. (1970). Circle Pines, MN: American Guidance Service.

Pearson, P. D. (1985). Changing the face of reading comprehension instruction. *The Reading Teacher, 38,* 724–738.

Pearson, P. D. (1996). Reclaiming the center. In M. F. Graves, P. van den Broek, & B. M. Taylor (Eds.), *The first R: A right of all children* (pp. 259–274). New York: Teachers College Press.

Pearson, P. D., & Fielding, L. (1991). Comprehension instruction. In R. Barr, M. L. Kamil, P. Mosenthal, & P. D. Pearson (Eds.), *Handbook of reading research,* vol. 2 (pp. 815–860). New York: Longman.

Pearson, P. D., & Gallagher, M. C. (1983). The instruction of reading comprehension. *Contemporary Educational Psychology, 8,* 317–345.

Petre, R. M. (1970). Quantity, quality and variety of pupil responses during an open-communication structured group directed-thinking activity and a closed-communication structured group directed reading activity. Doctoral dissertation, University of Delaware, Newark. *Dissertation Abstract International, 31,* 4630A.

Pflaum, S. W. (1979). Diagnosis of oral reading. *The Reading Teacher, 33,* 278–284.

Piaget, J. (1963). *The child's conception of the world.* Paterson, NJ: Littlefield Adams.

Pichert, J. W., & Anderson, R. C. (1977). Taking different perspectives on a story. *Journal of Educational Psychology, 69,* 309–315.

Pincus, A., Geller, E. B., & Stover, E. M. (1986). A technique for using the story schema as a transition to understanding and summarizing event based magazine articles. *Journal of Reading, 30,* 152–158.

Pinnell, G. S., & McCarrier, A.(1993). Comparing instructional models for the literacy education of high risk first graders. *Reading Research Quarterly, 29,* 8–39.

Poostay, E. J. (1982). Reading problems of children: The perspectives of reading specialists. *School Psychology Review, 11*(3), 251–256.

Poostay, E. J. (1984). Show me your underlines: A strategy to teach comprehension. *The Reading Teacher, 37*(9), 828–830.

Poostay, E. J., & Aaron, I.E. (1982). Reading problems of children: the perspectives of reading specialists. *School Psychology Review, 11*(3), 251–256.

Porter, D. (1978). Cloze procedure and equivalence. *Language Learning, 28,* 333–341.

Porteus, S. D. (1956). *The maze test and clinical psychology.* Palo Alto, CA: Pacific Books.

Postman, N., & Weingartner, C. (1969). *Teaching as a Subversive Activity.* New York: Dell.

Powell, W. R. (l978). *Measuring reading performance informally.* Paper presented at annual meeting of International Reading Association, Houston, TX (ERIC No. ED 155–589).

Powell, W. R., & Dunkeld, C. G. (1971). Validity of informal reading inventory reading levels. *Elementary English, 48*(6), 637–642.

Prelutsky, J. (1996). *A pizza the size of the sun.* New York: Greenwillow Books, a division of William Morrow.

Pressley, G. M. (1976). Mental imagery helps eight-year-olds remember what they read. *Journal of Educational Psychology, 68,* 355–359.

Pressley, G. M. (1977). Imagery and children's learning: Putting the picture in developmental perspective. *Review of Educational Research, 47,* 585–622.

Pressley, G. M. (1994). Elaborative interrogation: using "why" questions to enhance the learning from text. *Journal of Reading, 37* (8), 642–645..

Pressley, G. M. (2000). What should comprehension instruction be the instruction of? In M. Kamil et al. (Eds.), *Handbook of reading research,* vol III. Mahwah, NJ: Erlbaum.

Pressley, G. M., Johnson, C. J., & Symons, S. (1987). Elaborating to learn and learning to elaborate. *Journal of Learning Disabilities, 20,* 76–91.

Pressley, G. M., Levin, J. R., & MacDaniel, M. A. (1987). Remembering versus inferring what a word means: Mnemonic and contextual approaches. In M. C. McKeown, & M. E. Curtis (Eds.), *The nature of vocabulary acquisition* (pp. 107–129). Hillsdale, NJ: Erlbaum.

Pressley, G. M., Levin, J. R., & Miller, G. E. (1981). How does the keyword method affect vocabulary comprehension and usage? *Reading Research Quarterly, 16*(2), 213–225.

Preston, R. C. (1962, October). Reading Achievement of German and American Children. *School and Society, 90,* 352–357.

Raim, J. (1983). Influence of the teacher-pupil interaction on disabled readers. *The Reader Teacher, 36,* 810–813.

Raphael, T. E. (1982). Question-answering strategies for children. *The Reading Teacher, 36,* 186–190.

Raphael, T. E. (1986). Teaching questions-answers relationships, revisited. *The Reading Teacher, 39,* 516–522.

Rasinski, T. V. (2000). Speed does matter in reading. *The Reading Teacher, 54*(2), 150.

Raths, L. E., Harmon, M., & Simon, S. B. (1978). *Values and teaching* (2nd ed.). Columbus, OH: Merrill.

Raven, J. C. (1938). *Progressive Matrices: A perceptual test of intelligence, 1938, Individual Form.* London: H.K. Lewis.

Reder, S. (1998). *The state of illiteracy in America: Estimates at the local, state, and national levels.* Washington, DC: National Institute for Literacy.

Renner, S. M., & Carter, J. M. (1991). Comprehending text-appreciating diversity through folklore. *Journal of Reading, 34*(8), 602–604.

Rennie, B. J., Braun, C., & Gordon, C. J. (1986). Long-term effects of clinical intervention: An in-depth study. *Reading Horizon, 27,* 12–18.

Reutzel, D. R. (1985). Reconciling schema theory and the basal reading lesson. *The Reading Teacher, 39,* 194–197.

Reutzel, D. R., & Hollingsworth, R. M.(1993). Reading fluency. *The Reading Teacher, 52*(4), 370–378.

Reynolds, M., Wang, M., & Walberg, H. (1987). The necessary restructuring of special and regular education. *Exceptional Children, 53,* 391–398.

Richards, J. C., & Anderson, N. A. (2003). What do I See? What do I Think? What do I Wonder? (STW): A visual literacy strategy to help emergent readers focus on storybook illustrations. *The Reading Teacher, 56*(5) 442–444.

Richek, M. A., List, L. K., & Lerner, J. W. (1989). *Reading problems: Assessment and teaching strategies.* Englewood Cliffs, NJ: Prentice Hall.

Richgels, D., Proemba, K., & McGee, L. (1996). Kindergarteners talk about print: Phonemic awareness in meaningful contexts. *The Reading Teacher, 49*(8): 632–642.

Riegel, K. (1979). *The relational basis of language: Foundations of dialectical psychology.* New York: Academic.

Ringler, L. H., & Weber, C. K. (1984). *A language-thinking approach to reading.* San Diego: Harcourt Brace Jovanovich.

Risko, V., & Patterson, A. (1989). Enhancing students' independent learning and text comprehension with a verbally rehearsed composing strategy. In B. L. Hayes & K. Camperell (Eds.), *Reading researchers policymakers and practitioners. The yearbook of the American Reading Forum,* vol. IX (pp. 61–71). Logan, UT: Utah State University.

Roberts, C. (1956). *Teachers' guide to word attack: A way to better reading.* New York: Harcourt, Brace, & World.

Robinson, F. (1946). *Effective study.* New York: Harper Brothers.

Robinson, H. M. (1946). *Why children fail in reading.* Chicago: University of Chicago Press.

Roehler, L. R., Duffy, G. G., & Warren, S. (1987). Adaptive explanatory actions associated with effective teaching of reading strategies. In J. Readence & S. Baldwin (Eds.), *Dialogues in literacy research. Thirty-Seventh yearbook of National Reading Conference* (pp. 339–346). Chicago: National Reading Conference.

Rogers, D. B. (1984). Assessing study skills. *Journal of Reading, 27*(4), 346–354.

Rongione, L. A. (1972). Bibliotherapy: Its nature and uses. *Catholic Library World, 43,* 495–500.

Rosenbaum, C. (2001). A word way for middle school: A tool for effective vocabulary instruction. *Journal of Adolescent and Adult Literacy, 45* (1), 44–49.

Rosenblatt, L. M. (1969). Towards a transactional theory of reading. *Journal of Reading Behavior, 1*(1), 31–49.

Rosenshine, B., & Stevens, R. (1984). Classroom instruction in reading. In P. D. Pearson (Ed.), *Handbook of Reading Research* (pp. 745–798). New York: Longman.

Rubin, D. (1997). Diagnosis and correction in reading instruction. Boston: Allyn & Bacon.

Rubin, L. J. (1984). *Artistry in teaching.* New York: Random House.

Ruddell, M. R., & Shearer, B.A. (2002). Avid word learners with the Vocabulary Self-collection Strategy (VSS). *Journal of Adolescent and Adult Literacy, 45*(6), 352–356.

Ruddell, R. B. (1990). A study of the effect of reader motivation and comprehension development on students' reading comprehension achievement in influential and non-influential teachers' classrooms. Paper presented at the annual meeting of the National Reading Conference, Miami, Florida.

Rude, R. T., & Oehlkers, W. J. (1984). *Helping students with reading problems.* Englewood Cliffs, NJ: Prentice-Hall.

Rumelhart, D. (1980). Schemata: The building blocks of cognition. In R. J. Spiro, B. C. Bruce, & W. F. Brewer (Eds.), *Theoretical issues in reading comprehension.* Hillsdale, NJ: Erlbaum.

Sadoski, M. (1983). An exploratory study of the relationships between reported imagery and the comprehension and recall of a story. *Reading Research Quarterly, 19,* 110–123.

Sadoski, M. (1985). The natural use of imagery in story comprehension and recall: Replication and extension. *Reading Research Quarterly, 20,* 658–667.

Sadoski, M., Paivio, A., & Goetz, E. T. (1991). A critique of schema theory in reading and a dual coding alternative. *Reading Research Quarterly, 26,* 463–484.

Samuels, S. J. (1979). The method of repeated readings. *The Reading Teacher, 32,* 403–408.

Sanacore, J. (1984). Metacognition and the improvement of reading: Some important links. *Journal of Reading, 27,* 706–712.

Santa, C. M., & Hayes, B. L. (Eds.). (1981). *Children's prose comprehension*. Newark, DE: International Reading Association.

Santeusanio, R. (1967). RAMA: A supplement to the traditional college reading program. *Journal of Reading, 11*, 133–136.

Saracho, O. N., & Spodek, B. (1998). Preschool children's cognitive play: A factor analysis. *International Journal of Early Childhood Education, 3*, 67–76.

Scardamalia, M., Bereiter, C., & Steinbach, R. (1984). Teachability of reflective processes in written composition. *Cognitive Science, 8*, 173–190.

Schell, L. M. (1972). Promising possibilities for improving comprehension. *Journal of Reading, 5*, 415–424.

Schell, L. M. (1980). Value Clarification via Basal Readers. *Reading Horizons, 20*, 215–220.

Schell, L. M. (1991). In E. Fry (Ed.), *Ten best ideas for reading teachers* (pp. 115–116). Menlo Park, CA: Addison-Wesley.

Schmitt, M. C. (1988). The effects of an elaborated directed activity on the meta-comprehension skills of third graders. In J. E. Readence & R. S. Baldwin (Eds.), *Dialogues in literacy research. The 37th yearbook of the National Reading Conference* (pp. 167–181). Chicago: National Reading Conference.

Schmitt, M. C. (1990). A questionnaire to measure children's awareness of strategic reading processes. *The Reading Teacher, 43*(7), 454–461.

Schoelles, I. (1971). *Cloze as a predictor of reading group placement*. Paper presented at the International Reading Association annual convention, Atlantic City, NJ.

Schonhaut, S., & Satz, P. (1983). Prognosis for children with learning disabilities: A review of the follow-up studies. In M. Rutter (Ed.), *Developmental neuropsychiatry* (pp. 542–563). New York: Guilford Press.

Schroeder, K. (2002) Education news. *Education Digest, 67*, 8, 73–74.

Schumm, J. S., Vaughn, S., & Leavell, A. G. (1994). Planning pyramid: A framework for planning for diverse student needs during content instruction. *The Reading Teacher, 47*(8), 608–615.

Schunk, D. H., & Rice, J. M. (1987). Enhancing comprehension skill and self-efficacy with strategy value information. *Journal of Reading Behavior, 19*, 285–302.

Schwartz, R. M., & Raphael, T. E. (1985). Concept of definition: A key to improving students' vocabulary. *The Reading Teacher, 39*, 198–205.

Schwarz, D. M. (1995). Parent participation: READ-aloud handbook. *Smithsonian, 25*(1), 82–90.

Shanahan, T., & Kamil, M. L. (1983). A further investigation of sensitivity of cloze and recall to organization. In J. Niles, & L. A. Harris (Eds.), *Search for meaning in reading/language processing instruction. The 32nd yearbook of the National Reading Conference* (pp. 123–128). Rochester, NY: National Reading Conference.

Shipe, D., Cromwell, R. L., & Dunn, L. M. (1964). Responses of emotionally disturbed and non-disturbed retardates to PPVT items of human vs. non-human content. *Journal of Consulting Psychology*. Unpublished paper cited in Dunn, 1965.

Shoop, M. E. (1985). Oral language in the classroom: A foundation for literacy. *Kansas Journal of Reading, 1*, 7–12.

Shoop, M. E. (1986). InQuest: A listening and reading comprehension strategy. *The Reading Teacher, 39*(7), 670–674.

Shu, H., Anderson, R. C., & Zhang, H. (1995). Incidental learning of word meanings. *Reading Research Quarterly, 30*(1), 76–95.

Shugarman, S. L., & Hurst, J. B. (1986). Purposeful paraphrasing: Promoting non-trivial pursuit for meaning. *Journal of Reading, 29*, 396–399.

Siegel, F. (1979). Adapted miscue analysis. *Reading World, 19*, 36–43.

Simmons, J. (2003). Responders are taught, not born. *Journal of Adolescent and Adult Literacy,4*(8), 684–693.

Simpson, M. L., & Nist, S. L. (1990). Textbook annotation: An effective and efficient study strategy for college students. *Journal of Reading, 34*(2), 122–129.

Sinatra, G. M. (1990). Convergence of listening and reading processing. *Reading Research Quarterly, 25*(2), 115–130.

Sipe, L. R. (2000). The construction of literary understanding by first and second graders in oral response to picture storybook readalouds. *Reading Research Quarterly, 35*, 252–275.

Sipe, L. R. (2001). A palimpsest of stories: Young children's intertextual links during readalouds of fairytale variants. *Reading Research and Instruction, 40*(4), 333–352.

Slosson, R. L. (1982). *Slosson intelligence test* (2nd ed.). East Aurora, NY: Slosson Educational Publications.

Slosson, R. L. (1974). *Slosson intelligence test.* New York: Slosson Educational Publications.

Smith, F. (1978). *Reading and nonsense.* New York: Teachers College Press.

Smith, M. C. (2002). Adult literacy testing. In B. J. Guzzetti (Ed.), *Literacy in America: An encyclopedia of history, theory, and practice*, vol. 1 (pp. 25–28). Santa Barbara, CA: ABC-CLIO, Inc.

Smith, N. B. (1965). *American reading instruction.* Newark, DE: International Reading Association.

Snow, C. E., Burns, M. S., & Griffin, P., Eds. (1998). *The process of learning to read: Preventing reading difficulties in young children.* Washington, DC: National Academy Press.

Snow, R. E., & Lohman, D. F. (1984). Towards a theory of cognitive aptitude for learning from instruction. *Journal of Educational Psychology, 76*, 347–376.

Soar, R. S. (1973). *Follow-through classroom process measurement and pupil growth (1970–71): Final report.* Gainesville, FL: College of Education, University of Florida.

Solomon, D., & Kendall, A. J. (1979). *Children in classrooms.* New York: Praeger.

Sorrell, A. L. (1990). Three reading comprehension strategies: TELLS, story mapping, and QARS. *Learning Disability Quarterly, 12*(1), 87–96.

Spache, G. D. (1981). *Diagnostic reading scales.* Monterey, CA: CTB/McGraw-Hill.

Spencer, B. H. (2003). Text maps: Helping students navigate informational texts. *The Reading Teacher, 56*(8), 752–756.

Spiegel, D. L. (1980a). Desirable teaching behaviors for effective instruction in reading. *The Reading Teacher, 34*(3), 324–330.

Spiegel, D. L. (1980b). Adaptations of Manzo's Guided Reading Procedure. *Reading Horizons, 20*, 188–192.

Spiegel, D. L., & Fitzgerald, J. (1986). Improving reading comprehension through instruction about story parts. *The Reading Teacher, 39*(7), 676–682.

Spreen, O. (1982). Adults outcomes of reading disorders. In R. Malatesha & P. Aaron (Eds.), *Reading disorders: Varieties and treatments* (pp. 473–498). New York: Academic Press.

Spring, C., Blunden, D., & Gatheral, M. (1981). Effect on reading comprehension of training to automaticity in word-reading. *Perceptual and Motor Skills, 53* (3), 779–786.

Stahl, N. A., & Henk, W.A. (1986). Tracing the roots of textbook study systems: An extended historical perspective. In J. A. Niles & R. V. Lalik (Eds.), *Solving problems in literacy: Learners, teachers, and researchers. The 35th yearbook of the National Reading Conference* (pp. 366–374). Rochester, NY: National Reading Conference.

Stahl, S. A. (1986). Three principles of effective vocabulary instruction. *Journal of Reading, 29*, 662–671.

Stahl, S., & Kapinus, B. (1991). Possible sentences: Predicting word meanings to teach content area vocabulary. *The Reading Teacher, 45*(1), 36–43.

Stallings, J. A., & Kaskowitz, D. (1974). *Follow-through classroom observation evaluation, 1972–73.* Menlo Park, CA: Stanford Research Institute.

Stanford-Binet Intelligence Scales. (1973). Boston: Houghton Mifflin.

Stanovich, K. (1986). Matthew effects in reading: Some consequences of individual differences in the acquisition of literacy. *Reading Research Quarterly, 21,* 360–407.

Staton, J. (1980). Writing and counseling: Using a dialogue journal. *Language Arts, 57,* 514–518.

Stauffer, R. G. (1975). *Directing the reading-thinking process.* New York: Harper & Row.

Stauffer, R. G. (1980). *The language-experience approach to the teaching of reading* (2nd ed). New York: Harper & Row.

Stauffer, R. G. (1969). *Directing reading maturity as a cognitive process.* New York: Harper & Row.

Stevens, K. C. (1981). Chunking material as an aid to reading comprehension. *Journal of Reading, 25,* 126–129.

Stieglitz, E. L., & Stieglitz, V. S. (1981). SAVOR the word to reinforce vocabulary in the content areas. *Journal of Reading, 25,* 46–51.

Storch, S. A., & Whitehurst, G. J. (2001). The role of family and home in the literacy development of children from low-income backgrounds. *New Directions for Child and Adolescent Development, 92,* 53–71.

Strang, W., Winglee, M., & Stunkard, J. (1993). *Characteristics of secondary school-age language minority and limited English proficient students* (final analytic report, contract no. T292001001). Arlington, VA: Development Associates.

Strauss, A., & Lehtinen, L. (1947). *Psychopathology and education of the brain-injured children.* New York: Grune & Stratton.

Strickland, D. (1996). In search of balance: Restructuring our literacy programs. *Reading Today, 14,* (2), 320.

Sulzby, E. (1985). Children's emergent reading of favorite storybooks: A developmental study. *Reading Research Quarterly, 20*(4), 458–481.

Sulzby, E. (1991). The development of the young child and the emergence of literacy. In J. Flood, J. M. Jensen, D. Lapp, & J.R. Squire (Eds.), *Handbook of research on teaching the English language arts* (pp. 273– 285). New York: Macmillan.

Sulzby, E. (1992). Transitions from emergent to conventional writing: Research directions. *The Reading Teacher, 44*(7), 498–500.

Tarver, S. G., & Dawson, M. M. (1978). Modality preference and the teaching of reading: A review. *Journal of Learning Disabilities, 11,* 5–17.

Taylor, W. (l953). "Cloze procedure": A new tool for measuring readability. *Journalism Quarterly, 30,* 415–433.

Thames, D. G., & Readence, J. E. (1988). Effects of differential vocabulary instruction and lesson frameworks on the reading comprehension of primary children. *Reading Research and Instruction, 27*(2), 1–12.

Tharp, R. G., & Gallimore, R. (1989a). *Rousing minds to life: Teaching, learning, and schooling in social context.* New York: Cambridge University Press.

Tharp, R. G., & Gallimore, R. (1989b). Rousing schools to life. *American Educator, 13*(2), 20–25, 46–52.

Thompson, M., DiCerbo, K., Mahoney, K., and MacSwan, J. (2002). Exito in California? A validity critique of language program evaluations and analysis of English learner test scores. *Education Policy Analysis Archives, 10*(7).

Tierney, R. J., & Cunningham, J. W. (1984). Research on teaching reading comprehension. In P. D. Pearson, R. Barr, M. L. Kamil, & P. Mosenthal (Eds.), *Handbook of reading research* (pp. 609–655). New York: Longman.

Tierney, R. J., Readence, J. E., & Dishner, E. K. (1990). *Reading strategies and practices* (3rd ed.). Needham Heights, MA: Allyn & Bacon.

Topping, K. (1987). Paired reading: A powerful technique for parent use. *The Reading Teacher, 40,* 608–614.

Torgesen, J. K. (1982). The learning-disabled child as an inactive learner. *Topics in Learning and Learning Disabilities, 2,* 45–52.

Tortelli, J. P. (1976). Simplified psycholinguistic diagnosis. *The Reading Teacher, 29*(7), 637–39.

Tuleja, T. (1982). *Fabulous fallacies.* New York: Crown.

Uttero, D. A. (1988). Activating comprehension through cooperative learning. *The Reading Teacher, 41,* 390–395.

Vacca, R. T., & Alvermann, D. E. (1998). The crisis in adolescent literacy: Is it real or imagined? *NASSP Bulletin, 82*:600, 4–9.

Valencia, S. (1990). A portfolio approach to classroom reading assessment: The ways, whats, and hows. *The Reading Teacher, 43*(4), p 338–380.

Vaughn, S., Moody, S. W., & Schumm, J. S. (1998). Broken promises: Reading instruction in the resource room. *Exceptional Children, 64,* 211–225.

Vellutino, F. R. (1987). Dyslexia. *Scientific American, 256,* 34–41.

Vellutino, F. R., Scanlon, D. M., & Tanzman, M. S. (1998). The case for early intervention in diagnosing specific reading disability. *Journal of School Psychology, 36,* 367–397.

Vickery, K. S., Reynolds, V. A., & Cochran, S. W. (1987). Multisensory teaching for reading, spelling, and handwriting, Orton-Gillingham based, in a public school setting. *Annals of Dyslexia, 37,* 189–202.

Vogt, M. E. (1991). An observation guide for supervisors and administrators: Moving toward integrated reading/language arts instruction. *The Reading Teacher, 45,* 206–211.

Vygotsky, L. S. (1978). *Mind in society: The development of higher psychological process.* (M. Cole, V. John-Steiner, S. Seribner, & E. Souberman, Eds.). Cambridge: Harvard University Press.

Vygotsky, L. S. (1962). *Thought and language.* Cambridge: MIT Press.

Vygotsky, L. S. (1976). Play and its role in the mental development of the child, In J. Bruner, A. Jolly, & K. Sylva (Eds.) *Play—its role in development and evolution* (pp.537–554). New York: Basic Books.

Vygotsky, L. S. (1986). *Thought and language.* Cambridge, MA: MIT Press.

Wade, S. (1990). Using think aloud to assess comprehension. *The Reading Teacher, 42,* 442–451.

Waern, Y. (1977a). Comprehension and belief structure. *Scandinavian Journal of Psychology, 18,* 266–274.

Waern, Y. (1977b). On the relationship between knowledge of the world and comprehension of texts. *Scandinavian Journal of Psychology, 18,* 130–139.

Wagner, R., Torgesen, J. K., & Rashotte, C. A. (1994). "Development of reading-related phonological processing abilities: New evidence of bidirectional causality from a latent variable longitudinal study. *Developmental Psychology, 30,* 73–87

Wagoner, S. A. (1983). Comprehension monitoring: What it is and what we know about it. *Reading Research Quarterly, 18,* 328–346.

Walberg, H. (1988). Synthesis of research on time and learning. *Educational Leadership, 45,*(6),76–85.

Walberg, H., & Tsai, S.(1983). Matthew effects in education. *American Educational Research Journal, 20,* 359–373.

Walker, B. N. (2000). Diagnostic teaching of reading (4th ed.). Upper Saddle River, NJ: Merrill, Imprint of Prentice Hall.

Walker, D. F., & Schaffarzick, J. (1974). Comparing curricula. *Review of Educational Research, 44,* 83–112.

Walradth, E. (1998). Reading educator named distinguished alumnus. *River Falls Journal.* Available at http://www.rivertowns.net/PUBLIC/RFJRIVAL/week18/ frontpage/np/LOCAA10.HTM.

Walter, R. B. (l974). *History and development of the informal reading inventory.* Unpublished study prepared at Kean College of New Jersey (ERIC No. ED 098–539).

Walton, P. D. (1995). Rhyming ability, phoneme identity, letter-sound knowledge, and the use of orthographic analogy by prereaders. *Journal of Educational Psychology, 4,* 587–597.

Walton, P. D., Walton, L. D., & Felton, K. (2001). Teaching rime analogy or letter recoding reading strategies to prereaders: Effects on prereading skills and word reading. *Journal of Educational Psychology, 93,* 160–180.

Wark, D. M. (1964). Survey Q3R: System or superstition? In D. M. Wark (Ed.), *College and adult reading. Third and fourth annual yearbooks of the North Central Reading Association* (pp. 161–170). St. Paul: University of Minnesota, Student Counseling Bureau.

Watkins, J., McKenna, M., Manzo, A., & Manzo, U. (1995). The effects of the listen-read-discuss procedure on the content learning of high school students. Unpublished manuscript.

Weaver, C. (1988). *Reading, process and practice: From socio-psycholinguistics to whole language.* Portsmouth, NH: Heinemann.

Weaver, W. W., & Kingston, A. J. (1963). A factor analysis of cloze procedure and other measures of reading and language ability. *Journal of Communication, 13,* 252–261.

Wechsler, D. (l974). *Manual for the Wechsler Intelligence Scale for Children-Revised.* New York: Psychological Corporation.

Weiner, E. (1980). The diagnostic evaluation of writing skills (DEWS): Application of DEWS criteria to writing samples. *Learning Disability Quarterly, 3*(2), 54–59.

Weiner, M., & Cromer, W. (l967). Reading and reading difficulty: A conceptual analysis. *Harvard Educational Review, 37,* 620–643.

Weiss, S. C. (1980). Culture Fair Intelligence Test and Draw-a-Person scores from a rural Peruvian sample. *Journal of Social Psychology, 111,* 147–148.

Werner, P. H., & Strother, J. (1987). Early readers: Important emotional considerations. *The Reading Teacher, 40*(6), 538–543.

Whimbey, A., & Lochhead, J. (1980). *Problem-solving and comprehension: A short course in analytic reasoning* (2nd. ed.). Philadelphia: The Franklin Institute Press.

Whorf, B. L. (1956). *Language, thought, and reality: Selected writings of Benjamin Lee Whorf* (J. B. Carroll, Ed.). Cambridge, MA: MIT Press.

Williams, B. T. (2003). What they see is what we get: Television and middle school writers. *Journal of Adolescent and Adult Literacy, 46*(7), 548–554.

Williamson, K. E., & Young, F. (l974). The IRI and RMI diagnostic concepts should be synthesized. *Journal of Reading Behavior, 6*(2), 183–194.

Wilson, R. M., &, Gambrell, L. B. (1988). *Reading comprehension in the elementary school.* Boston: Allyn & Bacon.

Witkin, H. A., et al. (1977). Field dependent and field independent cognitive styles and their educational implications. *Review of Educational Research, 47,* 1–64.

Wixson, K. L. (1979). Miscue analysis: a critical review. *Journal of Reading Behavior, 11*(2), 163–175.

Wood, K. D. (1994). Hearing voices, telling tales: Finding the power of reading aloud. *Language Arts, 71*(5), 346–349.

Wood, M., & Salvetti, E. P. (2001). Project story boost: Read-alouds for students at risk. *The Reading Teacher, 55,*(1), 76–83.

Wylie, R. E., & Durrell, D. D. (1970). Teaching vowels through phonograms. *Elementary English, 47,* 787–791.

Yolen, J. (1990). *The devil's arithmetic.* New York: Penguin/Puffin.

Yopp, H. K. (1988). The validity and reliability of phonemic awareness tests. *Reading Research Quarterly, 23,* 159–177.

Yopp, H. K., & Yopp, R. (2000, August). *Literature-Based Reading Activities.* Newark, DE: Prentice Hall.

Zaslow, R. W. (1966). Reversals in children as a function of midline body orientation. *Journal of Educational Psychology, 57*(3), 133–139.

Zutell, J.(1996). The Directed Spelling Thinking Activity (DSTA): Providing an effective balance in word study instruction. *The Reading Teacher, 50,* 2, 2–12.

INDEX